1968

This book may

CALVIN GRIEDER, Ph.D., State University of Iowa, is Professor of Education at the University of Colorado. His former positions include: Professor of Education, University of Buffalo; Research Fellow, State University of Iowa; Fulbright Lecturer in South Africa; Member Board of Trustees, University Council for Educational Administration; and member, American Association of School Administrators Committee for Advancement of School Administration. Professor Grieder has co-authored several textbooks, including *Public School Administration*, Second Edition, with Truman M. Pierce and William Everett Rosenstengel, published by The Ronald Press Company.

STEPHEN ROMINE, Ph.D., University of Colorado, is Dean of the School of Education at that institution. He was formerly a Director of the Bureau of Educational Research and Service at the University and has served on the Association for Supervision and Curriculum Development, The National Association of Secondary School Principals, and various other educational committees. Dean Romine is the author of *Building the High School Curriculum*, and co-author with Calvin Grieder of *American Public Education: An Introduction*, Second Edition, both published by The Ronald Press Company.

# AMERICAN EDUCATION

## An Introduction to the
## Teaching Profession

**CALVIN GRIEDER**
UNIVERSITY OF COLORADO

**STEPHEN ROMINE**
UNIVERSITY OF COLORADO

*Third Edition*

THE RONALD PRESS COMPANY • NEW YORK

# PREFACE

An outgrowth of *American Public Education* by Harl R. Douglass and Calvin Grieder, and of *American Public Education: An Introduction,* Second Edition, by Calvin Grieder and Stephen Romine, the present book represents a reworking, updating, and expansion of the materials previously developed.

Written with two kinds of readers in mind, upper-level education majors preparing for the teaching profession and in-service teachers who wish to expand their knowledge of American education, this text-book presents a view of teaching and other educational services consonant with truly professional concepts and ideas.

An *introduction and orientation* to the major problems, policies, practices, and achievements is provided to help prospective teachers intelligently attack the work of succeeding courses and stimulate discussion, observation, and further reading and study.

It is the hope of the authors that the unified presentation of topics of first importance in today's education programs will help lay the foundation for full participation as professional teachers in the conduct and improvement of schools and schooling. Reference to the various aspects of educational systems in other lands will counteract, perhaps, some tendency for Americans to be a bit provincial about educational affairs.

The authors bring to bear on the study of education a wide and varied experience. They have worked at every level of education, in public and private institutions, in the United States and abroad, and are closely connected with major teacher education programs.

It is hoped that both students and laymen will find the bringing together of many research findings as well as the data on prevailing practices and expert opinion especially useful. The authors do not rely solely on their own preferences and predilections, although they do not equivocate in taking a position on important issues.

In sum, *American Education: An Introduction to the Teaching Profession* is a forward-looking and optimistic work. At the same time, it includes full recognition of the problems and difficulties still

iii

to be surmounted in achieving the historic philosophy of American education.

A debt of gratitude is acknowledged to many authors and publishers for permitting us to quote from their works as recorded in the footnotes, and for the inspiration drawn from other works not cited. To the Research Division of the National Education Association and to the United States Office of Education special thanks are tendered for data and other assistance. The authors are grateful to students and colleagues for the innumerable opportunities to discuss the subject matter of this book, and for the challenging and stimulating clashes of opinion and differences of interpretation as well as support and agreement.

Special thanks are tendered to Dr. Harl R. Douglass, Director Emeritus of the College of Education at the University of Colorado and a longtime colleague of the authors, who made substantial contributions to the contents of this book and rendered invaluable assistance by his constructive and penetrating counsel.

CALVIN GRIEDER
STEPHEN ROMINE

Boulder, Colorado
January, 1965

# CONTENTS

v

## Part III

## INSTRUCTIONAL AND RELATED SCHOOL SERVICES

## Part IV

## ORGANIZATION AND MANAGEMENT OF THE AMERICAN EDUCATIONAL SYSTEM

# I

# CAREER OPPORTUNITIES

# Prologue

# CHALLENGE AND CRITICISM

Education today is the most dynamic of man's many enterprises. Nations in which it is systematized and supported constantly seek to make it more effective and more economical. Peoples lacking it strive to secure it, believing that through education a better future may be theirs. Many terms are used to describe education. Some of the words suggest approbation and hope; others clearly indicate derision and despair. For a succinct summarization, the terms "challenge" and "criticism" are particularly descriptive of American education today.

Seemingly contradictory at first, these terms are complementary in their reference to education in the United States of America. They may connote dissatisfaction and mistrust, but they also imply hopeful confidence. As the challenge to education increases at home and abroad, it is inevitable that the demands made upon the schools increase and that impatience with imperfection grows. These conditions make conflict and criticism inescapable.

Learning was once commonly regarded as an essential activity of childhood and youth, at least for some. But it was less often viewed as fitting for mature adults. Now learning is said to be a lifelong necessity. The goals and scope of formal education have expanded as dependency upon the schools has increased. The number of persons involved, both as educational workers and learners, has multiplied tremendously. The time consumed has lengthened, and the total cost of the educational operation almost defies understanding.

These conditions attest to the vigor and promise of American education. They also indicate the presence of some confusion, if not in ultimate purpose, at least in enabling objectives and in procedures. The schools seemingly are, simultaneously, a source of salvation and a convenient scapegoat. One who would seek to understand the nature of education and of schooling in the United States of America should not be surprised at these and other inconsistencies as they appear in studying the topic.

Few social endeavors of equal significance are as controversial as education. Praised in yesterday's sunshine, the same schools are damned in today's storm. Among those whose voices are raised, pro and con, are many knowing and sincere individuals. There are also those whose only qualification is a ready pen or tongue. It is wise to listen carefully to all. Unfortunately audience reaction does not always distinguish between the two groups; frequently it exhibits a discouraging ignorance of the schools and their problems. The sincerity of many who err in the process of communication minimizes in no way the ill effects of their unsound views.

This book is written as an introduction to education in the United States of America. Understanding and support of this vast and vital enterprise are imperative. No highly organized social endeavor touches the lives of so many in a manner more fundamental to individual and societal well-being. Few activities cost the taxpayers more. None yields a higher return on the investment.

The controversial nature of education offers an approach in studying the topic that is both interesting and revealing. This chapter, consequently, is intended to deal briefly with some major selected issues, questions, and related attributes indicative of challenge and criticism. The intent is to whet the reader's appetite, not to satisfy the resultant hunger. It is to present confusion from which understanding may later emerge. Subsequent chapters deal in greater detail with the substance of education and schooling.

## CHALLENGING AND CRITICAL QUESTIONS

The pursuit of knowledge is hastened by proper questions. The reader should, therefore, consider carefully the following as illustrative of related, fundamental, and enduring queries about education in modern times.

Upon what bases shall education be founded?
What ends shall education serve?
How much education shall be provided and for whom?
What knowledge shall be considered of most worth?
How shall learning be encouraged?
What non-educational services shall our schools provide?
How shall our schools be organized?

How shall our schools be financed?
How shall our schools be governed?
How shall our schools be housed?
How shall we select and educate our teachers and other educational workers?
How shall we encourage the high-level professional performance of educators?

These are vital questions. Voiced in many different ways, they are asked repeatedly in this and other countries. Sometimes they are disguised intentionally or by accident, but they are there nonetheless.

Time and circumstance influence the answers to these questions and their acceptability. So also does the fact that we do not really have a single, centralized system of education in our nation. Basically, however, the answers that promote the American way of life are generally quite similar, in spite of small differences in particular. This book deals with these and associated questions and answers. Examination is also made of the development of education in the United States. A brief comparative study of education in other countries is also provided. These considerations enable us to understand better than is otherwise possible our own schools, their challenges, and their criticism. That we may learn from others is a possibility, too.

Initially it is helpful to view challenge and criticism briefly in broad scope as apparent in the views of a few persons who speak and write of education and the schools. This will serve to introduce the reader to the nature of the controversy. A more complete discussion is presented in subsequent chapters. The reader is encouraged to peruse books and articles to which reference is made. Only in this manner, and through reflection upon what is read, may one begin to obtain a sound grasp of education and a realization of its full significance.

## EDUCATION FOR WHOM AND FOR WHAT?

Whom shall we educate and for what ends? This is a timeless question raised again and again by those who are charged with responsibility for the education of each generation. Actually, two questions are merged into one as worded here. For purposes of discussion, it is well to separate them slightly and temporarily and then to merge them again in considering their larger and essential unity.

## Education for All?

The schools must provide for all the children of all the people. The schools are obligated to care only for those capable of high-quality intellectual achievement. Both of these statements cannot be true, but both are said. Perhaps neither answers adequately the question being raised with increasing frequency as population mounts and school enrollments soar ever higher. As an introduction to the issue, consider the words of Hutchins:

Perhaps the greatest idea that America has given the world is the idea of education for all. The world is entitled to know whether this idea means that everybody can be educated, or only that everybody must go to school. If education is to be nothing but a housing project, then we can understand why the hopes the nineteenth century had of it have not been fulfilled: the nineteenth century was afflicted with a delusion; it was off in pursuit of an impractical ideal. If the education of the whole population is impossible, the sooner we abandon the ideal the better.[1]

Something of the faith that many have in our schools, although it is not always obvious today and is seldom or never shared by all, was voiced by Warner, Havighurst, and Loeb:

The American public schools are, in the opinion of the people of the United States, basic and necessary parts of our democracy. We are convinced that they must, and we hope that they do, provide equal opportunity for every child. This means that those at the bottom can compete through education for life's prizes with those at the top. All that is needed are brains, a will to do, hard work, and plenty of ambition. In our faith every aspiring student may not have a marshal's baton in his knapsack, but in his public schooling he does have an equal chance with everyone else for the White House.[2]

Although written prior to World War I, a statement made by John Dewey bears repeating:

It is the very nature of life to strive to continue in being. Since this continuance can be secured only by constant renewals, life is a self-renewing process. What nutrition and reproduction are to physiological life, education is to social life. This education consists primarily in transmission through communication. Communication is a process of sharing experience till it becomes a common possession. It modifies the disposition of both the parties who partake in it. That the ulterior significance of every mode of human association lies in the contribution which it makes to the

[1] Robert M. Hutchins, *The Conflict in Education* (New York: Harper & Row, 1953), p. 42.

[2] W. Lloyd Warner, Robert J. Havighurst, and Martin B. Loeb, *Who Shall Be Educated?* (New York: Harper & Row, 1944), p. 11.

improvement of the quality of experience is a fact most easily recognized in dealing with the immature. That is to say, while every social arrangement is educative in effect, the educative effect first becomes an important part of the purpose of the association in connection with the association of the older with the younger. As societies become more complex in structure and resources, the need of formal or intentional teaching and learning increases. As formal teaching and training grow in extent, there is the danger of creating an undesirable split between the experience gained in more direct associations and what is acquired in school. This danger was never greater than at the present time, on account of the rapid growth in the last few centuries of knowledge and technical modes of skill.[3]

These words were written in support of the notion that education is a necessity of life for all. It is difficult to argue otherwise.

## The Impact of the Learner

The inseparableness of the two aspects of our major question and a note of complexity were provided by Keats:

No matter what we think our school might offer, our decision can't be made without reference to those on the receiving end. As the late John Dewey remarked, it is the learner, and not the subject matter, that determines both quantity and quality of learning. While this statement might sound simple enough, it by no means meant, or means, the same thing to all our educators. Some translated it to mean that each child should make up his own curriculum, and they built the experimental "child-centered schools" of the 1930's accordingly. Others reworked the statement into the teachers-college phrase, "We teach children, not subjects," construing this to mean there are more differences in educational needs than needs in common and tremendously magnifying their teaching problems in the process. Others concluded Mr. Dewey meant how much any child profits from his studies is up to that child. At one point there is general agreement, however; there are differences in learning abilities, desires and needs.

Meanwhile, the fact that the schools are asked to try to educate every child creates a complication in itself wholly apart from the problems presented by differences in the abilities of those who can, and do, learn. There are always some children among us who are not so mentally deficient that we have to shut them up in mental institutions, but who are not sufficiently intelligent to master the rudiments of the three R's. They are simply ineducable. By every sign and portent it is obvious they will occupy humble stations in their adult lives, and, meantime, they find school an incomprehensible chaos. By law, however, they must remain in public school until age sixteen, even though it may seem to make far better sense to permit them to seek their job status at a much earlier age. This, child labor laws do not permit.

There are also some children, who, while intelligent enough to master schoolwork, just plain won't. No amount of cajolery will budge them off

[3] John Dewey, *Democracy and Education* (New York: The Macmillan Co., 1916), p. 11.

their mental rumps. Others use their brains for antisocial purposes; they are disruptive in class, commit acts of vandalism, are proof against any kind of behavior-conditioning, no matter whether psychological or attempted with the aid of baseball bats. These incorrigibles also stay in school the full twelve years unless or until they run afoul of the law and are carted off to the juvenile pokey—or until their behavior, if not criminal, becomes so vile that the school at last obtains permission to boot them out.[4]

At this point it appears feasible to shift emphasis toward the purposes of education, keeping in mind the influence of the nature of the school population.

## Education of the Intellect

Children and youth attend school for a reason, indeed, for many reasons. It is commonly said that schools exist to educate students. Educate them for what? To be intelligent citizens? To be humane and reasonable men? To be adjusted to their environment? To meet their immediate needs? To develop the intellectual powers? To train them for a vocation? To prepare them for the wise use of leisure time? Many other suggestions might be proposed and often are. Disagreement soon becomes apparent in attempting to determine what education is for.

The development of the intellectual power is frequently stressed as an important, if not the single, end of education. This outcome currently receives much emphasis, and schools are criticized for failing to promote it as some would have them do. Hutchins derided certain other ends of education in his staunch advocacy of the intellectual:

Every man has a function as a man. The function of a citizen or a subject may vary from society to society, and the system of training, or adaptation, or instruction, or meeting immediate needs may vary with it. But the function of a man as a man is the same in every age and in every society, since it results from his nature as a man. The aim of an educational system is the same in every age and in every society where such a system can exist; it is to improve man as man. . . .

Education deals with the development of the intellectual powers of men. Their moral and spiritual powers are the sphere of the family and the church. All three agencies must work in harmony; for, though a man has three aspects, he is still one man. But the schools cannot take over the role of the family and the church without promoting the atrophy of those institutions and failing in the task that is proper to the schools. . . .

The prime object of education is to know what is good for man. It is to know the good in their order. There is a hierarchy of values. The task

[4] John Keats, *Schools Without Scholars* (Boston: Houghton Mifflin Co., 1958), pp. 95–96.

of education is to help us understand it, establish it, and live by it. This Aristotle had in mind when he said: "It is not the possessions but the desires of men that must be equalized, and this is impossible unless they have a sufficient education according to the nature of things."

Such an education is far removed from the triviality of that produced by the doctrines of adaptation, of immediate needs, of social reform, or of the doctrine of no doctrine at all. Such an education will not adapt the young to a bad environment, but it will encourage them to make it good. It will not overlook immediate needs, but it will place these needs in their proper relationship to more distant, less tangible, and more important goals. It will be the only effective means of reforming society.

This is the education appropriate to free men. It is liberal education. If all men are to be free, all men must have this education. It makes no difference how they are to earn their living or what their special interests or aptitudes may be. They can learn to make a living, and they can develop their special interests and aptitudes, after they have laid the foundation of free and responsible manhood through liberal education. It will not do to say that they are incapable of such education. This claim is made by those who are too indolent or unconvinced to make the effort to give such education to the masses.

Nor will it do to say that there is not enough time to give everybody a liberal education before he becomes a specialist. In America, at least, the waste and the frivolity of the educational system are so great that it would be possible through getting rid of them to give every citizen a liberal education and make him a qualified specialist, too, in less time than is now consumed in turning out uneducated specialists.

A liberal education aims to develop the powers of understanding and judgment. It is impossible that too many people can be educated in this sense, because there cannot be too many people with understanding and judgment. We hear a great deal today about the dangers that will come upon us through the frustration of educated people who have got educated in the expectation that education will get them a better job, and who then fail to get it. But surely this depends on the representations that are made to the young about what education is. If we allow them to believe that education will get them better jobs and encourage them to get educated with this end in view, they are entitled to a sense of frustration if, when they have got the education, they do not get the jobs. But, if we say that they should be educated in order to be men, and that everybody, whether he is a ditch-digger or a bank president, should have this education because he is a man, then the ditch-digger may still feel frustrated, but not because of his education.

Nor is it possible for a person to have too much liberal education, because it is impossible to have too much understanding and judgment. But it is possible to undertake too much in the name of liberal education in youth. The object of liberal education in youth is not to teach the young all they will ever need to know. It is to give them the habits, ideas, and techniques that they need to continue to educate themselves. Thus the object of formal institutional liberal education in youth is to prepare the young to educate themselves throughout their lives.[5]

[5] Hutchins, *op. cit.*, pp. 68, 70–71, 72–74.

## The Vocational Objective

By contrast, consider two related statements made recently by Conant, who does not disclaim the importance of either the intellectual powers or a liberal education in his support of vocational education:

I do not have to remind the reader that the fate of freedom in the world hangs very much in balance. Our success against the spread of communism in no small measure depends upon the successful operation of our own free society. To my mind, there is no question that a healthy society requires a sound economy and high employment. Communism feeds upon discontented, frustrated, unemployed people. As I write in June, 1961, the unemployment rate nationwide is something over seven per cent for all age brackets, but unemployment among youth under twenty-one years of age is about seventeen per cent, or more than twice the nationwide rate for all workers. These young people are my chief concern, especially when they are pocketed together in large numbers within the confines of the big city slums. What can words like "freedom," "liberty," and "equality of opportunity" mean to these young people? With what kind of zeal and dedication can we expect them to withstand the relentless pressures of communism? How well prepared are they to face the struggle that shows no signs of abating? I am deeply disturbed by the implications that widespread unemployment among the youth of our big cities has for the future of our society. . . .

At the outset I must record an educational heresy, or rather support a proposition that many will accept as self-evident but that some professors of the liberal arts will denounce as dangerously heretical. *I submit that in a heavily urbanized and industrialized free society the educational experiences of youth should fit their subsequent employment.* There should be a smooth transition from full-time schooling to full-time job, whether that transition be after grade 10 or after graduation from high school, college, or university.[6]

In a discussion of who shall be educated, Warner, Havighurst, and Loeb sounded a note of caution contrary to unlimited education:

The fact that the educational system is a system of elections for positions of higher social and economic status makes it advisable to gear the selecting machinery to the demand and to the capacity of the social structure. If too few people are selected and promoted through the educational system, the upper levels will be filled through other agencies and perhaps not filled with people as well equipped by skill and training for the positions. If too many people are selected and pushed up through the educational system, competition will become fierce for the higher-level jobs, and some people will have to take positions below the level for which they have been trained. Doctors will have to take jobs as labora-

[6] James B. Connant, *Slums and Suburbs* (New York: McGraw-Hill Book Co., Inc., 1961), pp. 34–35 and 40.

tory technicians, engineers as factory workers, and teachers as clerks. This will cause feelings of dissatisfaction with the social order, and the social structure may be strained beyond its tolerance limit.[7]

It is apparent that education for what and for whom are not separate considerations. Under ideal conditions educational output and social need might match well enough, but conditions seldom are ideal and then not for long. What is ideal also constitutes an issue about which there is much argument.

## Education, the Individual, and Society

In speaking of the errors that help to account for the weakness of contemporary education, Highet said:

. . . Universal education is still a novel experiment in our culture; yet its gloomy obverse is already clear to see. All people do not want to be educated. Many resist education all their lives. When education is not a privilege, it easily becomes a burden. Teachers in the new state universities and the compulsory schools sometimes feel like doctors endeavoring to explain to an unwilling patient that pure food is better than tainted food, or to persuade mothers to put their children to sleep with milk rather than gin.

Now, in the Western world, there are three errors which help to account for the weaknesses of contemporary education.

The first is the mistaken idea that schools exist principally to train boys and girls to be sociable, "integrated with their group," "equipped with the skills of social living," "adjusted to family and community co-operation," and so forth. Obviously that is *one* of the aims of schooling, sometimes neglected in the past though usually emerging as a by-product. It was a necessary and valuable function of school and college at the most recent stage in American history to create a more or less uniform pattern of culture for the new middle class, and a stable social order in which the children of the unparalleled flood of immigrants who reached the country between 1880 and 1921 could find their place as Americans. But another aim of education, equally important or more important, is to train the individual mind as intensely and to encourage it as variously as possible—since much of our better and our more essential life is lived by us as individuals, and since (in the advancing age of mass-culture) it is vital for us to maintain personal independence.[8]

In the Eleventh Yearbook of the John Dewey Society, Counts suggested broad social reconstruction as a contribution of education:

The building of a world society will require a bold, resolute, and imaginative education. It will require an education that fosters a sustained sense

[7] Warner, Havighurst, and Loeb, *op. cit.*, p. 150.

[8] Gilbert Highet, *Man's Unconquerable Mind* (New York: Columbia University Press, 1954), pp. 75–76.

of necessity and concern, gives a clear view of the magnitude of the task, and prepares positively for participation in world citizenship. And for America it requires an education that will keep our country strong in every way during the period that must pass before a world order is established.[9]

Many persons take issue with the idea that the school should have an active role in shaping society at the local level, to say nothing of the international scene. Some imply that the school can only follow and never lead the society in which it exists. This argument sometimes waxes loud and long, particularly when controversial issues are proposed as desirable in the school curriculum.

## Technology and Talent

Admiral Rickover, an outspoken critic of American education, made many observations about strengthening our first line of defense. From these ideas the following were selected as provocative:

The consequence of technological progress is that man must use his mind more and his body less. We still think in terms of a more primitive era; we overvalue physical prowess and undervalue intellectual competence. This has a profound effect on our attitudes toward education. The kind of school which prepares young people adequately for life in a less complicated environment is of little use today. Nor do we need schools that concentrate primarily on adjusting the children of immigrants to this new country; on helping them become Americans quickly and painlessly. Today we must have schools which develop in all children—talented, average, and below average—the highest level of intellectual competence of which they are capable; schools that help young people to understand the complex world of today and how it came to be what it is. This means that our schools must return to the traditional task of formal education in Western civilization—transmission of the nation's cultural heritage, and preparation for life through rigorous training of young minds to think clearly, logically, and independently. . . .

American education in general emphasizes learning factual know-how at the cost of absorbing fundamental principles, just as it stresses conditioning of behavior at the cost of developing the ability to think independently. Most of our schools have lost sight of the fact that a well-trained mind can cope with many unforeseen problems. Instead, they try to foresee every possible future difficulty a young person may encounter and then give a special course in how to deal with it. This is hopeless endeavor, for in a rapidly changing world no one can foresee what future problems will have to be met. . . .

Apart from the life-adjustment fallacy so prevalent among American educationists, our schools seem unable to concentrate on training young minds because of partiality for so-called "useful" knowledge. This utilitarian concept of education is to be found among parents no less than

[9] Christian O. Arndt and Samuel Everett (eds.), *Education for a World Society* (New York: Harper & Row, 1951), pp. 4–5.

among educationists. It may be in the nature of a revolt against liberal-arts education which many consider suited only for gentlemen of leisure and hence out of place in a democracy. An extraordinary lot of nonsense is said and believed about European education which stresses the liberal arts. European education is dismissed as aristocratic and exclusive, perhaps in order to avoid having to stand the test of comparison which might necessitate eventual upgrading of American education. . . .[10]

Whether one accepts all that the Admiral said, and only a few statements are quoted herein, he is not alone in his views. As one reads the opinions of those who write, and thinks about them, both agreement and disagreement point up ideas that need additional study.

## The Intellect Is Not Enough

Few if any educators contend that the intellect is unimportant. But there are advocates whose words imply that education aimed at other than the intellect has little or no place in the schools. Two thoughts by a great philosopher merit attention.

In speaking of ideas and their preservation, Whitehead emphasized the importance of the discovery and glow experienced by the person involved.[11] The fervor for an idea and the adventure accompanying it lend a vitality that is essential. Extending the importance of what is done about the idea, Whitehead pointed out that 90 per cent of our lives are governed by emotion.

The association of adventure with ideas poses a challenge to every teacher. The relationship of emotion to the intellect creates no duality, nor does it suggest an either-or proposition.

## Looking Back and Thinking Ahead

Education is envisioned in many ways, as the few statements presented suggest. In reading and interpreting, the semantic problem is obvious, and the writers' words are not devoid of feeling that may speak more loudly than reason. The background of the reader and his personal beliefs also influence interpretation and reaction. The question of "Education for whom and for what" has not been answered, but its complexity has been amplified. Before our schools can serve effectively and economically, we must decide wisely on this question. The decision is a critical one. Its challenge must not go

[10] From the book *Education and Freedom* by H. G. Rickover, pp. 17–18, 23, 24–25. Copyright, ©, 1959, by H. G. Rickover. Reprinted by permission of E. P. Dutton & Co., Inc., New York.
[11] Lucien Price (recorder), *Dialogues of Alfred North Whitehead* (New York: Mentor Books, 1954), pp. 85–86.

unmet. Reappraisal of intent and effect is imperative in the present and most complicated of decades in which American schools have endeavored to serve the commonwealth.

## FUNDAMENTALS OR FRILLS

The educational program of the schools should be consonant with the purposes of education. Disagreement on the latter has already been noted. Agreement on content, method, and procedure is even less likely. Indeed, as one proceeds from the more general to the more specific, accordance is increasingly difficult to find. But, perhaps in a hopeful vein, it may be suggested that there is more than one road to the same goal. Or is there?

### The Larger Educational Environment

The importance of the larger educational environment and the many agencies working therein should not be neglected in thinking through the program of the schools. Something of the complication and contradiction that otherwise result was presented by Beals and Hoijer:

> In our own society, education is carried on by many agencies—the family, the age group, the school, and the mass media of communication—and these efforts are not infrequently unintegrated, confusing, and downright contradictory. The child is therefore often confronted with wide divergences between ideals and behavior, as when the ideals of cooperation and public service he is taught in school are found to conflict with competitive and individualistic ways of making a living. As Ruth Benedict has pointed out, we teach our children one set of values and then expect them to live by another. It is not surprising, therefore, that education in our society frequently fails to accomplish its ends, or that children emerge into adult life often unequipped either technically or emotionally to carry on successfully their adult roles.[12]

The coordination of the many educational influences in our modern society grows more complex decade by decade. At the same time, the value of such harmony of effort becomes more important than is often realized.

### Universals and Relatives

A search for fundamentals or universals motivates many who seek to establish the school program. Whether these values are subject

[12] Ralph L. Beals and Harry Hoijer, *An Introduction to Anthropology* (New York: The Macmillan Co., 1959), pp. 658–59.

to change is not always clear. One outspoken critic of the schools had this to say:

Certain intellectual disciplines are fundamental in the public-school curriculum because they are fundamental in modern life. Reading, writing, and arithmetic are indispensable studies in the elementary school because no intellectual life worthy of the name is possible or conceivable without these particular skills. Science, mathematics, history, English, and foreign languages are essentials of the secondary-school curriculum because contemporary intellectual life has been built upon a foundation of these particular disciplines. Some, but by no means all, of these studies can be described as "traditional." This fact, however, has next to nothing to do with the case. It is not tradition, but a realistic appraisal of the modern world, that points out these disciplines as fundamental.

In some far-distant future the list of fundamental disciplines may be somewhat different, just as it was somewhat different in the past. As the problems of a civilization alter—or, more accurately, as the methods available for solving them alter and advance and become more powerful—the course of study must inevitably change. Few thinking men would deny that this is true. From these simple and obvious facts, however, the most extravagant and unjustified conclusions about the school curriculum are often drawn. Change is exalted into a supreme virtue, on the tacit assumption that schools can keep abreast of the times only by engaging in a frenetic quest for novelty. No idea more disruptive of education can possibly be imagined. To recognize the fact of change is far from enough. Sound planning of education requires careful consideration of the direction and the rate of the changes that are occurring in intellectual endeavor.[13]

The change in the course of study suggested as inevitable by Mr. Bestor does not always take place, at least not in the views of many who work intimately with the school program. Perhaps the difference lies in what is considered to be change. In a delightful little book, Harold Benjamin captured the flavor of many a present-day argument about curricular change when he said:

As the knowledge of these new inventions spread, all the members of the tribe were engaged in familiarizing themselves with the new ways of living. Men worked hard at making fish nets, setting antelope snares, and digging bear pits. The tribe was busy and prosperous.

There were a few thoughtful men who asked questions as they worked. Some of them even criticized the schools.

"These new activities of net-making and operating, snare-setting, and pit-digging are indispensable to modern existence," they said. "Why can't they be taught in school?"

The safe and sober majority had a quick reply to this naive question. "School!" they snorted derisively. "You aren't in school now. You are out here in the dirt working to preserve the life and happiness of the tribe.

[13] Arthur Bestor, *The Restoration of Learning* (New York: Alfred A. Knopf, Inc., 1955), pp. 40–41.

What have these practical activities got to do with schools? You're not saying lessons now. You'd better forget your lessons and your academic ideals of fish-grabbing, horse-clubbing, and tiger-scaring if you want to eat, keep warm, and have some measure of security from sudden death."

The radicals persisted a little in their questioning. "Fishnet-making and using, antelope-snare construction and operation, and bear-catching and killing," they pointed out, "require intelligence and skills—things we claim to develop in schools. They are also activities we need to know. Why can't the schools teach them?"

But most of the tribe, and particularly the wise old men who controlled the school, smiled indulgently at this suggestion. "That wouldn't be education," they said gently.

"But why wouldn't it be?" asked the radicals.

"Because it would be mere training," explained the old men patiently. "With all the intricate details of fish-grabbing, horse-clubbing, and tiger-scaring—the standard cultural subjects—the school curriculum is too crowded now. We can't add these fads and frills of net-making, antelope-snaring, and—of all things—bear killing. Why, at the very thought, the body of the great New Fist, founder of our paleolithic educational system, would turn over in its burial cairn. What we need to do is to give our young people a more thorough grounding in the fundamentals. Even the graduates of the secondary schools don't know the art of fish-grabbing in any complete sense nowadays, they swing their horse clubs awkwardly too, and as for the old science of tiger-scaring—well, even the teachers seem to lack the real flair for the subject which we oldsters got in our teens and never forgot." [14]

## Minimums for All

In speaking of mass education and merit, Rickover proposed an educational program of given minimal requirements for all:

It is said that our public education must concern itself more with the average students who do not wish to become doctors, lawyers, or engineers. For these average students the situation is, if anything, worse. They must depend for competence in dealing with life's problems on what they have learned in the twelve years from age six to eighteen.

This is the time in a youngster's life when he can most easily absorb large numbers of facts and when his curiosity can be most readily stimulated to want to do so. This is the time when young minds should be filled to capacity with impressions; when they should be stretched to their maximum. Only the school can do this. It can do it for children of most varied natural endowments if it frankly recognizes these variations and devises curricula tailored to the capacities of the talented, the average, and the below-average child. Each group can then develop best at its own rate of speed. The same basic process of storing the mind with knowledge can be adapted for each group of students.

[14] Harold Benjamin, *The Saber-Tooth Curriculum* (New York: McGraw-Hill Book Co., Inc., 1939), pp. 40–42.

The above-average pupil who is from two to three years *ahead* of the average in mental age is able to move through the elementary and secondary schools in that much less time, given the chance to do so in a homogeneous group. The below-average child who may be an equal number of years *behind* the average in mental age will need longer. It may often be possible for him to absorb no more than is offered in the first eight grades and he may not be able to cover this before he is sixteen. But although he learns more slowly and cannot go so far as children with better minds, he, too, needs to be taught to think and to use the basic intellectual tools without which he would be helpless in today's world. With care and patience he can be taught at least the three R's, and he ought never to be rushed into vocational training at the cost of learning these three minimum requirements of civilized life. The educational process for all children must be one of absorbing knowledge to the limit of their capacity. Recreation, manual or clerical training, etiquette, and similar know-how subjects have little effect on the mind itself, and it is with the mind that the school must solely concern itself. The poorer a child's natural endowments the more he needs to have his mind trained.

Our elementary and secondary education should thus provide first, for the average and below-average student, a sufficiently broad terminal education to fit him into a modern technological society; and second, for the talented student, a solid base for subsequent professional education. Neither of these two objectives is achieved in the majority of American public schools.[15]

The reader is advised to review this quotation in the light of learning theory.

### The Liberal vs. the Practical

Reference was made earlier to Mr. Conant's support of vocational education. He did not propose such education as a substitute for essential general education, but saw it as complementary. Not all who have spoken in favor of the liberal education have been sympathetic toward vocational education. Witness the words of Keats, who wrote of "vocational training and other frills":

Conclusion: This need all youth share is not a need that can best be met *only* by the public school. Therefore, driver training must be put on the option list, and not on the necessary list. If there's money enough after the necessities have been cared for, then we might install a driver-training program in our school if we think it would be rather nice to have one.

If we go through the course offerings this way, we can eliminate countless programs offered in many schools that add greatly to the cost of public education, but which may have little to do with the role of the school in our community. Following this kind of thinking, we might want to

[15] From the book *Education and Freedom* by H. G. Rickover, pp. 132–34. Copyright, ©, 1959, by H. G. Rickover. Reprinted by permission of E. P. Dutton & Co., Inc., New York.

eliminate typing, bookkeeping, shorthand, shop, or any other form of vocational training. For instance, it is Mental Prep's notion that the school's first job is to ask each child to think as best he can, and that this is accomplished by exposing all children to work in what Mental Prep calls the "fundamental disciplines" of language, history, geography, mathematics, science, music and art. Mental Prep says these subjects demonstrate different orderly patterns of thinking of importance to everyone, and at the very least constitute the elements of a necessary general education. If we adopt Mental Prep's view of educational purpose, then it becomes increasingly difficult to justify any school program that does not serve it.

On the other hand, Pragmatic Tech says that minds cannot be trained by the so-called disciplines, and that whatever is taught should be immediately useful and up to date, taught wherever possible from the practical aspect of How To. Thus, the number of courses we might wish to install is limited only by the extent to which we wish to adopt Pragmatic Tech's view. In either event, we all know there is a limit to what is in the town till, and thus we might first want to restrict our school's offerings to what we all agree are universal necessities—subjects we think equally important to all children, regardless of differing "needs"—before considering any addition to the curriculum.[16]

After offering a few arguments in support of his point of view, Keats set forth what may be in the minds of many who view with concern any additions to the curriculum, although possibly for reasons different from those he gives:

In sum, we should regard vocational training coldly, remembering that the more difficult we make adoption of any addition to our school program, the better we preserve our sense of fundamental, universal values, and the greater the chance that whatever we add will be worth while.[17]

The element of educational costs is apparent in Mr. Keats's thinking. Probably this same concern is true of others who have spoken to the question, although perhaps they have not seen fit to discuss purpose and cost together. As one studies the question further, it is clear that the financial aspect of education often influences goals and program, frequently in an unfavorable direction.

### Subject Matter and Learning

More fundamental than content or subject matter per se is the concept held of these things in the teaching-learning situation. Some persons attribute almost magical powers to certain subjects. Others place less confidence in content and more in personnel. Still others

---

[16] Keats, *op. cit.*, pp. 113–14.
[17] *Ibid.*, p. 117.

believe that procedure and method are extremely important. Certain aspects of this relationship were summed up by Dewey:

From the standpoint of the educator, in other words, the various studies represent working resources, available capital. Their remoteness from the experience of the young is not, however, seeming; it is real. The subject matter of the learner is not, therefore, it cannot be, identical with the formulated, the crystallized, and systematized subject matter of the adult; the material as found in books and in works of art, etc. The latter represents the *possibilities* of the former; not its existing state. It enters directly into the activities of the expert and the educator, not into that of the beginner, the learner. Failure to bear in mind the difference in subject matter from the respective standpoints of teacher and student is responsible for most of the mistakes made in the use of texts and other expressions of preëxistent knowledge.

The need for a knowledge of the constitution and functions, in the concrete, of human nature is great just because the teacher's attitude to subject matter is so different from that of the pupil. The teacher presents in actuality what the pupil represents only in *posse*. That is, the teacher already knows the things which the student is only learning. Hence the problem of the two is radically unlike. When engaged in the direct act of teaching, the instructor needs to have subject matter at his fingers' ends; his attention should be upon the attitude and response of the pupil. To understand the latter in its interplay with subject matter is his task, while the pupil's mind, naturally, should be not on itself but on the topic in hand. Or to state the same point in a somewhat different manner: the teacher should be occupied not with subject matter in itself but in its interaction with the pupil's present needs and capacities. Hence simple scholarship is not enough. In fact, there are certain features of scholarship or mastered subject matter—taken by itself—which get in the way of effective teaching *unless* the instructor's habitual attitude is one of concern with its interplay in the pupil's own experience. In the first place, his knowledge extends indefinitely beyond the range of the pupil's acquaintance. It involves principles which are beyond the immature pupil's understanding and interest. In and of itself, it may no more represent the living world of the pupil's experience than the astronomer's knowledge of Mars represents a baby's acquaintance with the room in which he stays. In the second place, the method of organization of the material of achieved scholarship differs from that of the beginner. It is not true that the experience of the young is unorganized—that it consists of isolated scraps. But it is organized in connection with direct practical centers of interest. The child's home is, for example, the organizing center of his geographical knowledge. His own movements about the locality, his journeys abroad, the tales of his friends, give the ties which hold his items of information together. But the geography of the geographer, of the one who has already developed the implications of these smaller experiences, is organized on the basis of the relationship which the various facts bear to one another— not the relations which they bear to his house, bodily movements, and friends. To the one who is learned, subject matter is extensive, accurately defined, and logically interrelated. To the one who is learning, it is fluid, partial, and connected through his personal occupations. The problem of teaching is to keep the experience of the student moving in the direction of what the expert already knows. Hence the need that the teacher know both subject matter and the characteristic needs and capacities of the student.[18]

One of the critical challenges facing today's educator is that of defining for his own and the satisfaction of the general public the proper place of subject matter in the educative process. This must include, but also extend beyond, the identification of bodies of subject matter to be included in the curriculum. Until this clarification is accomplished, the question of fundamentals versus frills will remain unresolved.

### Learning by the Learner

In speaking of quantity and quality in higher education, Commager brought into focus another facet of educational challenge:

This means that we must free students for the enterprise of educating themselves and educating each other—in the library, in the clubs and societies that they maintain, even in the classrooms. It means that we should cease harassing them with endless requirements which tend to sap their intellectual independence and dampen their enthusiasm. We must cease seducing them with false standards of social and athletic success. We must cease to show our contempt for them by lecturing incessantly, as if the printing press had never been invented or libraries provided. We must cease trying to protect them from dangerous associations, activities, and ideas, and resolutely expose them to intellectual dangers as we expose them to physical dangers when we permit them to walk our streets or drive on our roads. We should take the position that the young are quite as capable of dealing with ideas as are their elders, and that it is not the children but their parents who are afraid of dangerous ideas: as you know all ideas are dangerous.[19]

Commager was speaking of students considerably more mature and older than those to whom Dewey was referring. Mindful of the differences, educators in all schools and colleges should heed Commager's counsel. The twin challenges of independent study and the freedom to learn have implications across all educational levels.

[18] Dewey, op. cit., pp. 214–16.
[19] Henry Steele Commager, "Quantity and Quality in Higher Education," Education in a Free Society, Pitcairn-Crabbe Foundation Lecture Series 2 (Pittsburgh: University of Pittsburgh Press, 1960), Vol. II.

## Commitment and a Crowded Curriculum

The need for a program planned in accordance with our basic educational commitments was recognized by Hullfish and Smith in a discussion of reflective thinking as aim and method in education:

These are not idle questions. A school program that left students with no guide lines to action would be a sorry one, indeed. But where are these guide lines to come from in a plural culture? Of the many which are available, is the school to make a selection and then arrange that students develop commitments to these? If so, will it wet a finger and hold it aloft, in the manner of a golfer, to see which way the wind of social emphasis is blowing at a given time? These are not idle questions, either. The fact is that an education appropriate for a democratic world is not easily fashioned. But one point seems clear. An experience in reflective valuing is at least as promising a base on which to erect the mansions of free men as is either an authoritarian control of the value experience or dependence at the point of decision upon a nonreflective, irrational quality of experience. The authors, of course, believe it to be more promising, holding the view that no culture has ever possessed too much intelligence.[20]

The importance of books and a liberal education for all is further stressed in several paragraphs from Hutchins:

What belongs in education is what helps the student to learn to think for himself, to form an independent judgment, and to take his part as a responsible citizen. Although I will admit that in the hands of Socrates any subject can be made important, even clowning, because any subject can lead to important questions, there was only one Socrates, and I know of none in any educational system today. We have to frame the course of study of American schools, colleges, and universities in the light of the capacity of ordinary teachers. If the object of the educational system is to help young people learn to think for themselves, it should help them to think about the most important subjects, and these are discussed in the greatest works of the greatest writers of the past and present. To destroy the Western tradition of independent thought it is not necessary to burn the books. All we have to do is to leave them unread for a couple of generations.

. . . If we can ever find out what the educational system should do, I am sure we shall discover that it will be so difficult as to demand all the time and attention we can give it. It follows that whatever can be learned outside the educational system should be learned outside it, because the educational system has enough to do teaching what can be learned only in the system. The words of Sir Richard Livingstone should be written in letters of fire on every schoolroom wall: "The good schoolmaster is

[20] Reprinted by permission of Dodd, Mead & Co., New York, from *Reflective Thinking: The Method of Education* by H. Gordon Hullfish and Philip G. Smith, pp. 261–62. Copyright © 1961 by Dodd, Mead & Co.

known by the number of valuable subjects he declines to teach." Even if
driving a car, understanding plumbing, and behaving like a mature woman
are valuable subjects, they can be, and therefore should be, learned outside the educational system.

   . . . When I urge liberal education for all, I am not suggesting that
all the people must become great philosophers, historians, scientists, or
artists. I am saying that they should know how to read, write, and figure
and that they should understand the great philosophers, historians, scientists, and artists. This does not seem to me an unattainable goal. If it
is, unless some better kind of liberal education can be invented than the
one that I have described, we shall be forced to abandon universal suffrage; for I do not believe that men can solve the problems raised by their
own aggregation unless they can learn to think for themselves about the
fundamental issues of human life and organized society. If anybody knows
a better way of helping them to learn to think for themselves about these
issues, I hope he will present it. It seems to me that we must agree at
least on this: the alternatives are democracy, with liberal education for all,
and aristocracy, with liberal education for the few.[21]

## Another Complicated Decision

   A second question has been raised and left unanswered. It relates
closely to the first question and is equally, if not more, difficult to
answer. Among those who have sought to give an answer, disagreement is apparent. It is obvious, however, that what is fundamental
and what is frill depends, at least in large measure, upon whom we
are educating and for what ends.

   Several ideas emerge from the various points of view as quite
relevant. These notions should be considered in the light of a vital
attribute of human experience that colors any decisions that we may
make—the rapid rate at which the funded capital of human experience
is accumulating. This characteristic complicates the problem of selecting educational subject matter and at the same time makes the choice
of experience increasingly essential. Curricular lag appears as a persistent problem confronting educators in every generation.

   The choices should be made in the light of the learner as well as
the society and the teacher. The manner of handling subject matter
influences outcomes. Learning can no longer reasonably be considered as limited to childhood and youth; it is a lifelong process to be
encouraged at all ages. Independent study and the freedom to learn
loom large as issues related to the selection of subject matter. These
factors also have a bearing on the organization and presentation of
materials, as well as on the involvement of the learner. Planning the

[21] Hutchins, *op. cit.*, pp. 13–14, 29, and 88.

curriculum in the light of all the forces and factors involved becomes a tremendous task.

## SENIORITY OR PERFORMANCE

It is generally conceded that the quality of education will never exceed the caliber of educators. How to recruit and prepare such persons is a great challenge, and the whole process is subject to much criticism. Also crucial is the performance of the educator on the job. The single salary schedule and teacher tenure have been fostered with the feeling that these measures would encourage capable and interested persons to enter and remain in education. But there are today many, both within and outside the profession, who believe that these conditions contribute to mediocrity in persons and in performance. Few issues in education today are more controversial; perhaps none is so far reaching in its possible impact on the profession and its future.

### Performance and Pay

Instead of basing teachers' salaries principally on seniority, various schemes have been devised to consider also the merit of the individual based upon performance criteria in terms of which he is rated. This idea is usually identified as merit rating. In noting the highly controversial nature of the topic, it may be appropriate to begin with statements in opposition, of which there are many. Citing the AFL-CIO position, Megel strongly contends that merit rating is unsound. A few excerpts from his presentation follow:

No other American institution is subject to so many nostrums and panaceas as the public school system. Large classes taught by television, the use of untrained teacher aides, and the revival of a previously discredited merit rating plan for determining teachers' salaries are among the most recent of these questionable remedies.

Basing teachers' salaries on a merit rating plan is educationally unsound. It was administratively impossible thirty years ago and school systems were unwise to try it; its use is even more unwise in our technological society today.

Basing teachers' salaries on a merit rating plan is educationally and professionally unsound for the following reasons:

1. Merit rating cannot fairly evaluate the true effectiveness of teaching.
2. Merit rating rewards conformity.
3. Merit rating similarly puts a premium on the absence of teacher problems.

4. Merit rating fosters a competitive rather than a cooperative spirit.

5. Merit rating strikes at the security of the teacher.

6. Rating systems disregard the type of environment in which a teacher teaches.

7. Merit rating cannot improve the quality of education.

8. Merit rating is a dangerous mirage and cannot and will not relieve the teacher shortage.

9. Merit rating plans do not reward good teachers for superior work.[22]

These are strong statements, and not everyone will accept them. But there is no question that many teachers not members of the AFL-CIO join with the membership in support of these allegations. Megel presented an alternative to merit rating as follows:

The American Federation of Teachers is advocating a realistic salary schedule which starts at $6,000 for all teachers and reaches a maximum of $14,000 in eight years with an additional spread up to $500 for training beyond the B. A. degree.[23]

Other suggestions were also made with the view of improving recruitment and the holding power of the schools in terms of qualified personnel.

### A Good Idea But a Bad Practice

Many teachers, probably an increasing proportion over past years, seem to favor the principle of recognizing and rewarding teacher performance. But the actual practice of merit rating is repugnant to some. Said one teacher about the idea:

Testimony that a merit pay plan is working successfully in this or that town leaves me unconvinced, no matter how eminent the witnesses. I prefer the evidence of my own knowledge of teachers and their superiors, and of my observation of how merit pay actually worked in one school system, my own. After functioning for about twenty years, it was scrapped about the year 1942, to the delight not only of the eighty per cent of the teachers who had been doomed to exclusion from the highest paid group but even of some of the other twenty per cent who had won their way into the favored circle. Indeed, principals and superintendents were reported glad to see the thing go.[24]

The fact that merit rating has been tried and abandoned is frequently cited as evidence of its fallibility.

These arguments in opposition to merit rating could easily be ampli-

[22] Carl J. Megel, "Merit Rating Is Unsound," *Phi Delta Kappan*, XLII (January, 1961), 154–56.

[23] *Ibid.*, p. 156.

[24] Irving Katz, "Why I Oppose Selective Merit Pay," *Phi Delta Kappan*, XLII (January, 1961), 161–63.

fied by others. There are also proponents of merit rating of equal fervor and sincerity who feel quite differently about merit rating and its future possibilities. One advocate, who was not always a proponent, spoke cautiously and encouragingly:

In the opinion of the writer, merit rating will continue to be studied and improved in the next five years and will be practiced in an increasing number of schools. Not all of these efforts will succeed. Although the programs may be similar, each district will develop its own. Both teachers and administrators will be rated on a merit basis. Caution, cooperation, evaluation, and periodic revision will characterize the development of programs that are successful. This kind of process aids in answering important questions, in allaying fears and suspicion, in eliminating inequalities and errors, and in encouraging essential mutual confidence among all those persons involved.

There is also a growing danger that merit rating may be imposed upon the schools. The motivation underlying this danger is varied; some of it is good, some is evil. It is to be hoped that administrators and teachers will be wise enough to avert this danger through constructive and positive action. To continue merely to decry merit rating is probably shortsighted and may seriously weaken the profession of teaching.

Merit rating is not a panacea for all the ills of education, but it will help to solve some of the fundamental problems. Among these are the recruitment and development of promising prospective teachers, increasingly effective utilization of teachers and administrators with rewards commensurate with performance, and the elimination of weak and ineffective administrators and teachers. Most important of all outcomes is the subsequent improvement of educational opportunity for our children and youth.[25]

## A State Supported Investigation

Also prudently optimistic are the general findings of the Utah School Merit Study:

*Merit Pay Is Feasible*

After studying and experimenting with teacher evaluation for six years, the Utah School Merit Committee again affirms the principle of compensating educators on the basis of the quality of their service as an additional factor in salary determination. On the basis of the Utah experience and from close examination of successful programs in other states, it appears that merit salary programs are feasible for school districts which establish the proper conditions for their success. Properly established programs should be beneficial to school children in terms of an improved educational program.

*Four Values Should Result*

It is the Committee's judgment that the recommendations which follow

[25] Stephen Romine, "Merit Rating in Colorado Schools," *Colorado School Journal,* LXX (May, 1961), pp. 319–20.

will meet the objectives of the original legislation which called for the study. Four major values should result. First, and most important, professional merit appraisal programs should improve the quality of teaching as a result of careful scrutiny of teaching functions. Second, information will be obtained that will improve the validity of administrative decisions regarding personnel employment, dismissal and retirement, inservice training, salaries and promotions. Third, a differential in salary would give deserved rewards to those who demonstrate superior quality service. Fourth, the teaching profession should achieve heightened status resulting from accepting quality of performance as an added factor in the determination of salary.

### Merit Programs Will Provide Additional Information

The Committee recognizes that complete answers are not available for all of the facets involved in merit appraisal programs for professional school personnel. However, enough is now known to warrant the establishment of merit programs in some school districts. It is the Committee's judgment that the application of merit appraisal programs should not wait until an ultimate program is developed through research. More practical information should be gained at this stage of development from experience with merit programs than can result from continued research alone.

### Recent Studies Further Substantiate Previous Reports

In the judgment of the Committee, the conclusions outlined in its previous Report and Recommendations, November, 1958, are still sound. These include: an enumeration of the potential values to be anticipated and hazards to be avoided in the operation of salary incentive systems; a list of nine basic conditions necessary for the successful implementation of merit appraisal programs; an outline of a professional salary plan to be considered in salary-incentive schedules.

The Committee believes that local school districts which adhere to these guide lines in the ·development of teacher appraisal and merit salary programs will meet with a success. Disregard of these principles will weaken the program and will likely lead to failure.[26]


## The Businessman's Viewpoint

In the discussion of merit rating, mention is often made of business and industry. Many persons apparently believe that such rating is more widespread than it actually is, according to a recent study.[27] And while the application to education of criteria designed for business and industry probably is indefensible, the point of view of a businessman deserves attention:

In this period of intense interest in education among many elements of

[26] Utah School Merit Committee, *Report and Recommendations,* Utah School Merit Study, November, 1960, pp. 2–3. (Mimeo.)

[27] "Merit Rating in Business and Industry," *NEA Research Bulletin,* XXXIX, No. 1 (February, 1961), 16–18.

the entire community, the point of view of at least some members of the business fraternity may be of interest to those whose careers lie totally within the field of education. With this thoroughly in mind, and writing from a background of personal and family association with school affairs, I should like to dedicate this article to a simple thesis: That the development of merit recognition (or, to use less controversial wording, performance recognition) is absolutely essential to the continued improvement of teachers' pay, performance, position in the social scale, and professional status.[28]

After mentioning one teacher who quit the profession because of a salary scheme that did not recognize performance, Hartsook said further:

Again, there is another side to this coin. I have talked with many teachers and administrators who are proud of their schools and of the product they turn out and yet are seriously concerned about the numerous teachers and administrators who are "just getting by." Unfortunately, it seems that many human beings will do no more in life than they have to—and this applies to teachers as well as businessmen, scientists, or common laborers. If you guarantee a job and fix the compensation exclusive of performance, there will be many who will simply drift along doing as little as possible. Admittedly, there are problems that go with competition, but unless there are some incentive drives it seems inevitable that performance will falter. So, without performance recognition, we continually risk the loss of highly competent, well-motivated people and a continual failure to meet the performance standards we desire to establish.[29]

The subjectivity of rating teacher performance is almost universally criticized, and reference is often made to business and industry as not having to face the difficulty of appraisal that is unavoidable if the measurement of teaching activity is to be accomplished. Said Hartsook about this:

It is also important to dispel one recurring but erroneous idea. There is a prevalent belief that industry merit evaluation is easier and fairer than evaluation would be in teaching because there are specific dollar-and-cents criteria to use in industry.

This is simply not true. Let us look at the points on which a typical industry evaluation is based. They include: knowledge of work, planning and organizing, analytical ability, judgment, alertness, initiative, dependability, volume of work, quality of work, safety, personality, leadership, development of men. To what extent are these criteria specific? To what degree do they avoid judgment and insure absolute fairness and lack of bias by evaluators? Or, in the case of a research scientist working in new conceptual areas, for example, how clear is the dollar-and-cents relationship to desired performance? Obviously, all of these factors are intangibles and

[28] E. A. Hartsook, "Merit Rating—Key to Better Pay and Better Teaching," Phi Delta Kappan, XLII (January, 1961), 157–60.
[29] Ibid.

subject to the same type of "can't do" arguments that are found in criticism of performance pay for teachers.[30]

## The Profession's Responsibility

One of the hallmarks of a profession is the effort made by the membership to upgrade the quality of personnel and performance. Teachers and other educational workers have not been unmindful of these matters. Thus far, however, major emphasis has been placed upon measures geared to security and similarity, to common denominators, so to speak. Attention has also focused on attributes assumed to be predictive of future performance. To a point this has been necessary and has been good. But the defining of excellence in teaching and the development of techniques appropriate to its appraisal have not received the consideration warranted.

As one approach to the related problems of pay and performance, merit rating is an educational "hot potato" that most school systems apparently prefer not to pick up. Approved in principle by some, it is condemned in practice by the same persons. Denounced officially by organizations, it is favored by individual members. Some advocates praise it uncritically, while opponents disclaim it bitterly. Still others grudgingly admit that the payment of equal remuneration for unequal performance is not right, but they prefer an evil with which they are acquainted in preference to one they suppose might be worse. Much emotion is generally associated with discussion of merit rating, and often more heat than light. Worse by far, however, is the apathy with which the issue is disregarded. Such conduct will not cause the ugly specter to go away.

## MIDDLE GROUND AND REASON IN EDUCATIONAL ISSUES

The issues presented above reveal the polarity of positions frequently taken by the critics, be they favorable or unfavorable in their appraisal of education. It has not been possible to consider all the critics or all the issues. Even had such consideration been possible, the same polarity would remain, with relatively few persons taking central positions.

In the great and continuing debate about education, it is easy to be misled on two points; namely, that all things are either black or white and that reason and a middle ground find no favor among those

[30] *Ibid.*

who debate. Actually there is much "grayness" about education, and there is sanity in a reasoned middle-ground position in many instances, perhaps in all. The schools have been accused of failing to do a high-quality job, of mediocrity in many things, and of neglect of the fundamentals. Guilty without a doubt, say some critics with thoughtless vigor. Completely innocent, scream defenders with equal volume and no more sense. All such claims should be weighed against the available facts. In the first place, the quantity and quality of education vary from system to system and from school to school. What is true in one instance will be only partially true in another and completely false in a third. Blanket approbation and damnation are equally absurd. Within the same school there are noticeable differences in strength and weakness, yes even in the same course and in the performance of an individual teacher or individual learner.

## Target for Extremists

Why, then, are the extremists so outspoken and those who advocate a middle position so quiet? Probably because of many reasons, only two of which are advanced at this time. First, one who takes a position midway in an issue is frequently a target for everyone and certainly for those at both extremes. The latter are more apt to respect one another across their great distance than to accord any friendship to the enemy nearer their positions. The man in the middle may also find it difficult to avoid being jockeyed this way and that, his very reasonableness often serving to erode away any solid singleness of position and denying him the security of being able to stand completely fast and unalterable. Many people tend to respect more highly the man who is not only forthright, but who is also very positive and unmoveable, than the one whose facts call for compromise and cautious conclusions that do not lend themselves to emotionally charged phraseology. Even facts sometimes fail those who marshal them.

Second, the "middle-of-the-road" is frequently occupied by persons who are going nowhere. Whatever their motivation, they simply do not wish to antagonize anyone, they really take no position, and they do not want to be identified as having a position, particularly not with either extreme. The presence of these neutrals, who are not where they are by virtue of reasoned acceptance of position, does not encourage the sturdy individual whose study of the issue seems to place him in the same camp. Often he will be unjustly criticized as a "Mugwump," and this accusation he rightfully resents.

### Educational Banners and Experts

It should also be pointed out that many of the banners run up the educational flagpole have had little or no influence on the troops. Many administrators and teachers who turn a deaf ear to the clamor about them are busily engaged in doing a fine job. They are committed to conducting a sound educational program *in toto,* and the battle of words seems unworthy of their time and energy. Education seems to suffer from a great many more or less isolated movements having virtue only if considered in perspective.

Increasing reliance on research should be of considerable help in resolving issues in the future. However, research will not yield a complete answer in every case. Some questions involve value judgments subject to little or no researching. The same variability in and among schools that complicates overall appraisal will not be eradicated by research. Parents whose experiences, real or imaginary, cause them to be critical of the schools are not likely to be persuaded by research done elsewhere; indeed, they may not even accept facts and figures presented in their own school. Educators, too, form and hold opinions that are contrary to demonstrable facts. There is no substitute for reasonableness in these matters; perhaps that is why reason is advocated by many as a primary educational outcome.

Another complication should not be forgotten. Nearly everyone thinks of himself as an expert on education. Persons who would never think of advising a mechanic how to repair their automobile, to say nothing of counseling their doctor or lawyer, have no hesitancy in telling educators what to do. This tendency, which undoubtedly relates to the manner of school organization and operation in our nation, is often annoying and discouraging. In some measure it has been accentuated by the occasional abdication of professionals in the educational decision-making process. On the whole, however, the values of lay participation probably outweigh the disadvantages, especially where wise school-community planning has been conducted.

## CHALLENGE AND CRITICISM REVIEWED

Only a limited number of issues have been presented briefly in this introductory chapter. This sample is sufficient to dispel any fears that education is a dull and vapid occupation devoid of adventure and suitable only for the meek and the mediocre. Quite the contrary, it is an endeavor demanding of those who really serve; and it yields satisfaction that gives one a sense of timelessness and achievement far beyond material gain. Its challenge can be met fully and its criticism faced adequately only by persons of ability, dedication, and persistence—persons who also have courage, faith, and vision.

The chapters that follow enlarge upon the nature of challenge and criticism. They seek to put the reader on the path to both questions and answers that are vital and sensible. The topics dealt with are of concern, or should be, to all citizens, as well as to those who are considering education as a field of study and work. If not surprising, the ignorance of the general public about education is discouraging and, at times, dangerous. Even within the ranks of educators, susceptibility to false doctrine or no doctrine at all and to the tendency of the extremes in theory and practice infer a lack of basic understanding.

More than this, the faith of the citizen in education is today denied in practice as regularly as it is affirmed in theory. We have inherited the idea of mass education, but it is clear that we do not always think of it with conviction and apply ourselves to its realization with enthusiasm. Our failure to support it adequately may well be our undoing.

In the initial section of this book attention has already been given to challenge and criticism. The second focal point is that of careers in education. A profession marked with conflict has need of the highest caliber people possible. The opportunities in education are many and varied.

The second section of the book deals with the foundations of education. Certain of these are alluded to in earlier discussion. Education is both social and biopsychological. The learner as an individual, and the mass of learners to be educated, cannot sensibly be disregarded in organizing and conducting the schools and related educational programs. Our schools of today and tomorrow emerge from schools of the past. It is wise, therefore, to consider the development of education in seeking to understand and improve what we have. Similarly, comparison and contrast with schools in other lands may help us to comprehend our own.

Following the survey of educational foundations, the third section of the book deals with instructional and related school services. These are presented in the light of the foundations upon which they rest. The task of seeking the knowledge of most worth is faced squarely. Purpose, program, issues, and trends are discussed in separate but closely related chapters dealing with learners of all ages from pre-elementary to adult learning. School services not strictly or even primarily educational are considered in their relationship to school goals and other forces and factors of educational and social origin.

The schools should be organized and operated in a manner facilitating the attainment of accepted goals through the pursuit of well-planned educational and related services. With this point in mind, the fourth section of the book describes the organization and operation of our schools, both public and non-public. Theory and practice are interwoven, and issues and trends are included. A look is also taken at the physical setting of school services, especially in relation to effective and efficient teaching and learning in an age of technology.

The importance of personnel to education is so obvious that it is not always accorded the attention deserved. In the fifth section of this book, the emerging educational profession is examined carefully. Recruitment, teacher preparation, advancement and rewards in the profession, and problems of the profession are included. Following, as it does, the earlier sections previously outlined, this section enables the thoughtful reader to reconsider his intentions regarding education and the schools, as well as study the nature of the profession and its problems in the light of challenge and criticism.

The final section is a single chapter focused on recapitulation and the future. Herein a look is had at vital and enduring challenges and problems against the background provided in earlier sections. This is done with the future in mind and with attention to the complex, expanding, and changing social setting in which opportunities must be seized and problems solved. It is also done hopefully in the firm belief that our nation has the resources and needs only greater will to help future generations realize through education the fullness of the American Dream.

# 1

# CAREER OPPORTUNITIES
# IN EDUCATION

These are exciting years in which to live. Unrest, individual and societal, is widespread. Knowledge is expanding as never before. Hopes are heightened, even in the face of adversity. The coloration of change, like the autumn hues, is everywhere apparent; and the rate of change is accelerating. To be challenged, confused, overwhelmed, and weary is easy. To be bored is difficult, unless one is immune to the surge of life around him.

In these days children and youth are responsive to a dynamic environment in which they live. Often they are thrust into a whirl that is largely not of their own doing. But their survival power is great and their enthusiasm, at least initially, is wonderful to behold. "Seldom a dull moment" is an apt phrase descriptive of life with younger children. Indeed, they may not be permitted enough free time in which to become a bit bored, and perhaps as a consequence, a bit more ingenious in entertaining themselves.

And what of the youth about whom so much that is not complimentary is heard today? For the most part, they are no more confused in their beliefs and behavior than the "mature" adults who set the common example and render judgment. Though perhaps hesitant to show it, they are concerned about their own and the future of the world in which they live. They have ideals. They are ambitious and can perform at high levels, often exceeding their own and the expectations of others. They need fine example and understanding more than exhortation.

These boys and girls and these young men and women, all too briefly and generally characterized here, are the greatest resource of our nation. This resource, like all others, can be wasted more easily than it can be developed, and it often is. At this point, the role of the teacher begins to take shape.

It is in this environment and with young people, whatever their age, that the teacher serves. Other educational workers also contribute to youth in various ways. This chapter was written primarily to help students view career opportunities in education, principally, but not exclusively, in elementary and secondary schools. It may assist them also in reviewing and perhaps revising conceptions that they hold. Self-appraisal and discussion with others are encouraged as valuable allied activities in reading and reflecting on what is written herein. Chapter 15 presents information on preparation for an educational career.

For both the prospective teacher and the reader who is making no vocational study or decision, this chapter presents current information on one of the most vital of all professions, that of education. No other enterprise touches so intimately and so persistently the lives and pocketbooks of so many.

## THE CHALLENGE OF AN EDUCATIONAL CAREER

Only the educated have a chance of enduring as free men in the world of today and tomorrow. Schooling and survival have become increasingly synonymous. In the never ceasing struggle of enlightenment versus ignorance and freedom versus slavery, the teacher is a cynosure. Our nation can and will prosper only as our teachers effectively instruct and our learners effectively learn. Herein lies the fundamental challenge of an educational career. For teachers are the foremost guardians of our cultural heritage and the principal progenitors of social evolution.

### Ideals and Hard Facts

Fortunately, youth tend toward idealism and optimism. Unless the power has been taken from them, most young men and women respond readily, if not always wisely, to the opportunity of making the world a better place in which to live. This contribution can be made in many ways. No single profession or vocation claims all of the interesting possibilities. None includes a majority of those persons whose primary motive is service. But few if any professions offer greater opportunity than education for response and service to the ideals underlying American democracy.

The significance and challenge of teaching lie in *service*. In this enterprise the teacher may wield tremendous power for good or for evil. In a complex world mankind is progressively dependent upon formal schooling as a means of social evolution and improvement. With the tools of annihilation in our hands, the power of intelligent control and decision making is a matter of life and death.

Schools and colleges are more than storehouses of knowledge. Teaching is more than the dissemination of information. Educational environment and influence encompass more than the academic and intellectual, as vital as these elements are. The role of the teacher has become increasingly complex and demanding in response to pressures outside our educational institutions. As life and learning have come into closer kinship, this development has taken place in schools everywhere. The cluster of complicated and changing conditions in which we live and learn calls for strong, stable, and intelligent teachers who will serve with courage, vision, and justifiable pride.

**Teachers Help To Preserve, Improve, and Extend the American Way of Life.** Education is the bulwark of American democracy. The primary basis of national well-being is a healthy and enlightened citizenry. Prosperity, world understanding, and peace are dependent upon this citizenry and the extension of individual and collective well-being around the globe. More than any other agency, our schools and colleges have been the melting pot from which the United States of America has emerged as a strong amalgam of many cultures. The preservation, transmission, and improvement of the human heritage has ever been and shall ever be an arduous and essential task to which teachers are dedicated. The extension of opportunities for a better life through education is the basic function of the teacher. Discussions of education and vocational opportunity in Chapter 2 and of education, earnings, and economy in Chapter 3 document the contention of this paragraph.

**Teachers Deal with Vital Problems of Living and Learning.** Teaching offers no escape from conflict or retreat from reality. It is not a refuge for the ailing or the weak. Those who really teach are in constant contact with the challenges, ideas, issues, and problems of this and other ages. Teaching and learning involve immersion in and reaction to these elements through which process are developed the attributes of an educated person. In the pursuit of truth with learners, the teacher cannot evade controversy, especially if the power of reasoning is to be fostered.

**Teachers Help To Expand Individual and Societal Horizons.** The concern and outlook of the child tend to be limited primarily to himself and his immediate environment. Such is true also of the uneducated youth or adult. Only through education is the individual led out of himself to envision the world and himself in proper perspective. The horizon of a society does not extend beyond the collective horizons of its members, but groups do display characteristics that are essentially collective rather than individual. For these groups, as well as for individuals, education opens doors to wide vistas and provides a means of social migration and improvement.

**Teachers Help To Raise Human Expectations.** Related to the expansion of outlook, education creates and sustains an expectation of a better life. Hopes as well as horizons are extended. Educational institutions generate within the individual the power that enables him to attain greater self-realization and to expect more of himself than would otherwise be possible. This influence is contagious. It spreads to others, gives rise to competition, and serves to elevate nations as literacy urges them on to higher levels of living. Teachers are architects of human destiny.

**Teachers Serve All the People and All Ages to Come.** Who can measure the extent and endurance of a teacher's influence? Great teachers of past ages are not forgotten. Though a teacher's name be lost, the learning he fostered lives on in others to give him a kind of unrecognized immortality. With their contact with practically all the children of all the people, teachers influence our total citizenry. Moreover, this influence is exerted during the formative years. Through the lives of learners, it extends to their children and their children's children. In times of illness, people call a physician. When they have legal difficulties, they employ a lawyer. For spiritual guidance, they consult the clergy. But compared with teaching, no one of these honored professions has the great and enduring opportunity for influential service that exists for those who make a career of education.

**Teachers Live Creative Lives.** Teachers are a creative force in the building of human lives. Their efforts serve to make of today's children and youth the adults of tomorrow. By means of the subjects they teach and in many different ways, teachers help to create attitudes, abilities, habits, ideals, understandings, and other attributes of behavior that characterize the well-educated person. In fostering individual creativity, the teacher also encourages a climate of creativity in the society wherein he works. This constructive activity also contributes to the development of the teacher, enriching his life as well as the lives of those he instructs. Creative living with ideas and people constitutes the adventure of teaching.

**Teachers Enjoy Teaching.** The feeling of satisfaction derived from one's job is important to his effectiveness on the job and to his well-being as a person. Many jobs today do not yield sufficient satisfaction. Some are fragmented. Others involve only casual relationships and endeavor remote from results. Most teachers, however, find their jobs challenging and satisfying. This statement does not mean that they are self-satisfied and not interested in improvement. Nor does it imply that all teachers are in love with their work. Many studies have indicated, however, that the great majority of teachers, especially those who make a career of education, derive much enjoyment from their work and feel that what they are doing is worthwhile. As the profession gains status, the satisfaction of those whose service contributes to such status will doubtless increase.

**Teachers Serve in Many Foreign Lands.** Prospective teachers usually think of teaching largely or only in the United States. Today, however, there are literally thousands of our teachers serving throughout the world. Many of these persons are employed in American Dependents' Schools where they teach the children and youth of American citizens serving abroad. Others teach in private schools or in the schools of the many foreign nations with which we have good working relations. Opportunity for travel and study often accompanies these teaching assignments. In recent years these doors to new adventure have attracted many youth into the profession.

## No Worthwhile Job Is All Roses

While teaching is a significant profession and yields many benefits and satisfactions, it is not without trials and tribulations. Teaching is often demanding and exhaustive. Success does not come easily nor without effort. Some of the difficulties and problems can be detected in earlier discussion herein; others will appear in subsequent chapters dealing with the educative process and the social setting in which schools and colleges are organized and operated. No person worthy of life and opportunity expects an easy carefree path to vocational success; indeed, he wants and chooses a way that tests his abilities and character as it makes of him an asset to himself and his country. Teaching is just such a profession.

The teacher is important in today's world. (Grosse Pointe, Michigan, Public Schools.)

## Only the Best Should Teach

Ideally, only the best should teach. So much that is important in learning is more a matter of example than exhortation. The manner in which subject matter is employed is very important to its educative value, and instructional procedures depend so much upon the teacher. The quality of an educational program will never exceed the caliber of those who conduct it. The high level of confidence and support basic to excellent schools will not be earned and maintained by mediocre teachers. Other reasons may be given in support of this point of view. To staff our schools and colleges with such persons will be costly. But it should be remembered that good education is expensive, and poor education is an extravagance that we in the United States of America cannot afford.

## Making That Important Decision

To teach or not to teach poses a serious question that should receive deep consideration by any who contemplate a career in education. One of the major purposes of this book is to help those who are interested in education to study the nature of teaching and what is involved in a professional commitment to it. No one should be talked into the decision to teach. That others wish one to teach is no reason at all. That some have entered teaching hastily or by accident should serve as a caution rather than an invitation. Anyone who wisely thinks about teaching, or any other vocation, will take his time in reaching a decision; and the latter will be based upon consideration extending beyond books and reading.

Introspection is useful to one who is considering teaching as a vocation. Reflection on past experiences as a pupil and about teachers one has had may be helpful. Interviews with teachers and administrators may give some insights. The counsel of those who have been quite successful in education is valuable. Visits to schools and classrooms offer opportunity to size up the job of teaching. Students in college who wish to know more about a career in higher education may talk with their professors. Participation in youth activities and in summer camp work provides another means of determining how well one likes to work with boys and girls or young people and a chance to see how the latter react to one's endeavor with them. Early in many teacher-education programs, opportunity is provided for observation in the classroom and other experience relating to teaching. Such experience is pertinent to decision making and adds meaning to subsequent professional study.

## Teaching as a Temporary Vocation

There are many persons who use teaching as a stepping-stone to other educational careers. Teachers often become counselors, supervisors, or administrators. They may also work in other professional capacities. High school teachers, following graduate study, move into college teaching. Some who are successful in counseling at the high school level find excellent opportunity in student personnel work at the college level. Other illustrations could be cited.

Some individuals who teach enter other vocations later. Many young women, for example, teach a few years before they marry and rear a family. Some re-enter teaching when their children are grown and gone from home. As long as high-level performance and personal satisfaction characterize the service given while a person is in the profession, his use of it as a stepping-stone is not objectionable.

Some who follow this path may later be of great value to the schools by virtue of their understanding of education. Working at any job gives one knowledge of it that is obtainable in no other way. But those who enter teaching reluctantly and suffer through it of necessity in reaching another goal, within or outside education, should not begin this route in the first place. Too much in the lives of others is at stake.

### The Career Person

Many who are teachers temporarily, or who serve for a time in other educational positions, contribute a great deal. *However, the strength and future of the profession rest with those who make a life career of education.* These are the men and women who, day by day, year in and year out, carry the brunt of meeting the grave challenges and the responsibility for improving the profession. Unheralded and unsung, they are heroes in the finest sense of the term. Only a school that has a preponderance of career personnel over the long run can cope with the needs that are to be met and garner the public support that is essential. There is also much waste of time, manpower, and money in preparing personnel professionally who subsequently teach not at all or only very little.

## TYPES OF EDUCATIONAL CAREERS

There are many different careers in education. Classroom teachers constitute the largest group of professional workers, but there are many other ways in which people serve in and through our educational institutions. Even among teachers there are variations involving grade level, subject taught, type of school organization, curricular pattern, composition of student body, nature of community, and other features that influence the position. Teaching and learning are the principal focus of those who occupy these instructional jobs, although they may have many other duties and obligations.

In addition to these professional personnel, great numbers of other persons contribute directly and indirectly to teaching and learning. More is said of such service later. In other professions too, for example, law, medicine, and nursing, many individuals are engaged in school or college related work.

## A Large and Growing Profession

There are probably close to two million persons employed in professional positions in our elementary and secondary schools today. In colleges and universities there are likely at least 175,000 full-time teachers and 70,000 part-time teachers. The profession is large and it is growing.

Accurate and up-to-date statistics are difficult to secure. However, for the school year 1959–1960 the number of persons employed in public elementary and secondary day schools was as follows: [1]

| | | | |
|---|---|---|---|
| Principals . . . . . . | 63,554 | Librarians . . . . . . | 15,816 |
| Consultants or supervisors | 13,775 | Guidance personnel . . | 13,119 |
| Classroom teachers . . . | 1,354,958 | Psychological personnel . | 2,054 |
| | | Other non-supervisory instructional personnel . | 755 |
| | | Grand total . . . . . | 1,464,031 |

In local school districts there were also 13,361 superintendents of schools plus more than 5,000 assistants to superintendents. There were also about 4,000 professional staff workers in state departments of education.

From the same source, a breakdown of teachers by sex indicates the following: [2]

| *Elementary Teachers* | | *Secondary Teachers* | |
|---|---|---|---|
| Men . . | 117,616 | Men . . | 275,054 |
| Women . | 716,156 | Women . | 246,132 |
| Total | 833,772 | Total | 521,186 |
| | Grand total . . | 1,354,958 | |

Estimates for 1963–1964 place the total instructional staff at 1,718,-832, an increase of 4.1 per cent over the figure for 1962–1963.[3] Distribution of personnel was as follows:

| | |
|---|---|
| Elementary school teachers . . . | 925,027 |
| Secondary school teachers . . . | 649,791 |
| Principals and supervisors . . . | 91,059 |
| Other instructional staff . . . . | 52,955 |
| Total staff . . . . . . | 1,718,832 |

[1] Carol J. Hobson and Samuel Schloss, *Statistics of State School Systems, 1959–60* (Washington, D.C.: U.S. Department of Health, Education and Welfare, Office of Education, 1963), OE-20020-60, Circular 691, p. 31.

[2] *Ibid.*, p. 35.

[3] "School Statistics, 1963–64," *NEA Research Bulletin,* XLII, No. 1 (February, 1964), 5.

Another interesting glimpse of the profession may be had in look-ing at the numbers of college graduates prepared to teach since 1950, for which data are presented in Table 1–1.

## Demand Exceeds Supply

The figures previously cited are impressive. When one considers mounting enrollments and the growing need for teachers and other professional workers in education, it is apparent that the demand is not being met. Automation and other technological advances; the growing interdependence and complexity of business, industry, and related enterprise; and the rapid pace at which our cultural heritage is accumulating all point to a need for more highly educated talent. Undoubtedly this means more schooling for more people than we have had in the past. It appears very probable that we will not be able to meet the demand for well-educated personnel for a long time to come.

As an example of the staffing problem that has been plaguing the schools, some figures by the National Education Association are perti-nent. The shortage estimated for September, 1963, was revealed as follows: [4]

Needs most likely to be met—
1. To replace those leaving ° . . . . . . . . . . . . . . . . 130,000
2. To serve increasing enrollment † . . . . . . . . . . . . . 35,000
Needs that have not been met, and are most likely to continue—
3. To relieve overcrowding and to eliminate part-time sessions ‡ . . 30,000
4. To give instruction and services not now provided § . . . . . 20,000
5. To replace the unprepared ‖ . . . . . . . . . . . . . . . 20,000

Total needed, September, 1963 . . . . . . . . . . . . . . . 235,000
Number of college graduates of 1962 likely to enter teaching (approxi-mately 74.5% of the new supply) # . . . . . . . . . . . 117,000

Net estimated shortage . . . . . . . . . . . . . . . . . . 118,000

° Larger than the estimate of 125,000 a year ago, owing to an increase of about 50,000 in total staff.

† Increased enrollment will occur chiefly in urban areas where overcrowding is now most prevalent, but some of the addition will be absorbed in classes not now overcrowded. If the expected increase were divided by the current pupil-teacher ratio, the indicated need would be 50% greater than this estimate.

‡ Based on the foregoing description (in the NEA Report) of class size in urban elementary schools, plus the findings of less comprehensive studies at both the elementary and high school levels.

§ This need is emphasized by the belated public recognition of need for trained counselors and adequately prepared teachers in some of the subject-matter fields.

‖ The current estimate of teachers holding only emergency certificates is nearly 92,000. More significant is the estimate of more than 100,000 persons now teach-ing who have completed less than four years of acceptable college preparation.

# Based on Part IV of the NEA Report.

[4] *Teacher Supply and Demand in Public Schools, 1963*, Research Report 1963–R4, Research Division, National Education Association, p. 20.

## TABLE 1–1

### College Graduates Prepared To Teach, 1950 to 1963 *

|  | 1950 | 1955 | 1960 | 1963 |
|---|---|---|---|---|
| Total receiving bachelor's de-degree † . . . . . . | 433,734 | 287,401 | 394,889 |  |
| Per cent change from 1950 prepared for high school teaching . . . . . . | – | –39.4% | –9.0% | – † |
| Grand total prepared to teach | 115,477 | 87,409 | 130,203 | 158,347 |
| Change from 1950 . . . . | – | –24.3% | +12.8% | +37.1% |
| Total prepared for elementary schools . . . . . . . | 28,587 | 37,712 | 52,630 | 61,979 |
| Change from 1950 . . . . | – | +31.9% | +84.1% | +116.8% |
| Total prepared for high schools | 86,890 | 49,697 | 77,573 | 96,378 |
| Change from 1950 . . . . | – | –42.8% | –10.7% | +10.9% |
| Agriculture . . . . . . | 3,294 | 1,430 | 1,379 | 1,084 |
| Change from 1950 . . . . | – | –56.6% | –58.1% | –67.1% |
| Art . . . . . . . . . | 2,225 | 1,930 | 2,719 | 3,575 |
| Change from 1950 . . . . | – | –13.3% | +22.2% | +60.7% |
| Commerce . . . . . . . | 7,235 | 4,434 | 7,106 | 7,205 |
| Change from 1950 . . . . | – | –43.7% | –1.8% | –0.4% |
| English . . . . . . . . | 10,709 | 5,507 | 9,295 | 14,209 |
| Change from 1950 . . . . | – | –48.6% | –13.2% | +32.7% |
| Foreign language . . . . . | 2,193 | 1,328 | 2,178 | 4,272 |
| Change from 1950 . . . . | – | –39.4% | –0.7% | +94.8% |
| Home economics . . . . . | 4,899 | 4,025 | 4,812 | 5,141 |
| Change from 1950 . . . . | – | –17.8% | –1.8% | +4.9% |
| Industrial arts . . . . . . | 4,890 | 2,177 | 3,785 | 3,518 |
| Change from 1950 . . . . | – | –55.5% | –22.6% | –28.1% |
| Mathematics . . . . . . | 4,618 | 2,155 | 5,652 | 8,123 |
| Change from 1950 . . . . | – | –53.3% | +22.4% | +75.9% |
| Music . . . . . . . . . | 5,296 | 4,499 | 5,200 | 5,778 |
| Change from 1950 . . . . | – | –15.0% | –1.8% | +9.1% |
| Men's physical education . . | 10,614 | 4,794 | 7,332 | 7,518 |
| Change from 1950 . . . . | – | –54.8% | –30.9% | –29.2% |
| Women's physical education . | 3,178 | 2,496 | 3,177 | 3,856 |
| Change from 1950 . . . . | – | –21.5% | – § | +21.3% |
| Social science . . . . . | 15,349 | 7,572 | 13,197 | 16,823 |
| Change from 1950 . . . . | – | –50.7% | –14.0% | +9.6% |
| Science . . . . . . . . | 9,096 | 3,754 | 7,119 | 9,344 |
| Change from 1950 . . . . | – | –58.7% | –21.7% | +2.7% |
| Other fields ‖ . . . . . . | 3,294 | 3,596 | 4,622 | 5,932 |
| Change from 1950 . . . . | – | +9.2% | +40.3% | +80.1% |

* Excludes students meeting certificate requirements at 90-, 60-, or 30-hour levels.

† From annual reports of the U.S. Office of Education.

‡ Data not available.

§ Minus less than 0.1%.

‖ Includes core teachers prepared in increasing numbers for junior high school service.

SOURCE: *Teacher Supply and Demand in Public Schools, 1963,* Research Report 1963–R4, Research Division, National Education Association, p. 12.

The Picture Is Complicated.  A few highlights from the NEA Report indicate the complex nature of the problem of supply and demand.[5] It appears that there will be an overall increase of 11.3 per cent in supply from 1962. For the elementary school this percentage is estimated as only 7.1 per cent, while for high school it is 14.1 per cent. This means about six new elementary teachers to each nine high school teachers, while the ratio of teaching positions is exactly the reverse or 9 to 6.

At the secondary school level, there is imbalance in need and supply. Foreign languages, a field of shortage, is estimated to be up 32.4 per cent over 1962. The fields of most acute shortage, sciences and mathematics, expect an increase of 19.7 and 18.8 per cent, respectively. English, which still is undersupplied, has a prospective increase of 19.5 per cent.

The fields of greatest shortage are women's physical and health education and home economics, with prospective increases in supply of 12.9 per cent and 7.4 per cent over 1962. Men's physical education continues to be the most obviously oversupplied field, with a likely increase of 7.4 per cent; the number of full-time positions in the field will probably not exceed one-third to one-fourth of the number of teachers prepared in 1963. Social studies is another field of prospective oversupply with an outlook of an increase of 14.3 per cent.

There is variation in demand and supply among communities in single states as well as among states. Rural areas remote from the "bright lights" often face a serious shortage of well-qualified personnel, while larger city schools may have more applicants than they can use. Prospective teachers should check their wishes against the supply-and-demand situation where they hope to teach.

Figures on supply and demand are also available at the college level, the following being taken from another NEA Research Report.[6] Figures from 1,565 collegiate institutions (out of a total of 1,946) revealed 158,884 full-time teachers and 64,700 part-time teachers in 1962–1963. For 1961–1962 or 1962–1963, 499 institutions reported having unfilled teaching positions in one or more teaching fields with a total of 1,306 unfilled positions. For the future, 782 higher institutions reported as probable a more acute shortage than now exists. Most fields seem to face shortages, some more serious than others, for example, the sciences and mathematics. The likelihood of not

[5] Ibid., p. 5.

[6] Teacher Supply and Demand in Universities, Colleges, and Junior Colleges, 1961–62 and 1962–63, Research Division, National Education Association, pp. 7, 23, and 27.

being able to secure persons with adequate preparation makes this whole picture less encouraging. Many administrative positions have also gone unfilled.

The seriousness of supply and demand in higher education is clearly presented in the following statements:

> How can a university or college obtain and hold competent teachers in the numbers needed to serve the steadily expanding enrollment? This is probably the most baffling of all the complex questions facing administrative officials today. Institutions of higher education of every type and in every part of the country now face sharp competition for the men they most want as members of their instructional staffs. And it appears almost certain that this competitive search for highly trained personnel will become more intense in the years ahead. . . .
>
> . . . Right now the total resources of the institutions of higher education are not equal to the total task which only they can perform. If they continue to be priced out of the market—as is now the case on many campuses—the tragic result is clear: the quality of their educational service will deteriorate at the very moment it should be further strengthened. In many instances the only course open to the employing officials will be to lower the standards, and thus concede the necessity for accepting a lower quality of teaching performance. In short, *this means second-rate education for a larger and larger number of our youth.*[7]

## Categories of Careers

For discussion purposes, career opportunities in education may be divided into six categories: (1) teaching, (2) administrative and supervisory, (3) counseling and student personnel work, (4) other educational specialists, (5) non-certificated educational workers, and (6) school-related work in other professions. Our principal concern here is for the first four groups.

**Careers in Teaching Normal Children.** Many choices are possible in teaching in terms of aptitude, interest, and preparation. The following list classifies teachers chiefly in terms of the grade level taught:

| | |
|---|---|
| Nursery and other preschool | Senior high school |
| Kindergarten | Junior or community college |
| Elementary school | College or university |
| Junior high school | Extension, correspondence, and adult education |

Although preparatory programs may focus on only one or two of these levels, it is often not necessary to pursue an entirely different curriculum in order to qualify for several grade levels or subjects. A

[7] *Ibid.*, p. 9.

common core of experience is typical of most programs at the under-graduate collegiate level. Minor variations in or additions to basically similar curricula enable one to meet requirements at several related levels or in several related subjects. Graduate work opens doors to opportunities in higher education, especially at the level of the doc-torate.

Nursery and other preschool opportunities are greater today than ever before and are likely to increase with growing urbanization. The same is true of kindergarten. Elementary school teachers are at a premium. It is not uncommon for teachers who prepared at the sec-ondary school level to be "retreaded" for the elementary school, espe-cially for the upper grades.

Preparatory programs for teachers of young children vary. Many colleges offer separate but not completely different programs that prepare teachers for nursery and kindergarten, for grades 1–3, and for grades 4–6. In some colleges the same general program prepares them for kindergarten through grade 6. Some elective courses may be available for certain options, such as teaching kindergarten.

Teachers in the kindergarten and elementary grades generally in-struct a group of children in all or most all of the subjects studied, whether these subjects are taught separately or in a more unified approach. Included are such things as language arts, reading, arith-metic, science, social studies, art, music, and physical education. The use of one teacher in one classroom in this manner is often referred to as the self-contained classroom. There may be some subject spe-cialization in the fifth and sixth grades of some schools.

Specialists in one or more subject areas are sometimes employed to assist the self-contained classroom teacher. For example, specialists in art, music, and physical education are fairly common. With the introduction of foreign language instruction, many elementary schools have found it necessary to employ specialists, as the supply of ele-mentary teachers with adequate training in a foreign language is quite limited.

In some elementary schools, particularly in grades 5 and 6, instruc-tion is handled by several teachers. A specialist in arithmetic and one in science, as an illustration, may do the teaching of these sub-jects in an approach to departmentalized instruction as found on the junior high school level. Much argument ensues in educational circles concerning departmentalization on the elementary school level, and the research seems to be inconclusive.

At the primary level (grades 1–3), there is emerging an ungraded plan in which pupils begin in grade 1 and remain together for three

These learners are the teacher's primary challenge. (Grosse Pointe, Michigan, Public Schools.)

years without the usual annual promotion. Generally, the same teacher remains with the class over the three-year period. Much attention is given to individualized instruction and to progression in accordance with individual rates of development and mastery. Such a plan is believed to foster improved articulation of the work covered during the three-year period and to challenge individuals more than in the traditionally organized school.

Many persons prefer to teach older children in one or perhaps two subject fields, such as art, English, history and social studies, mathematics, business, science, industrial arts, music, and other fields. The junior high school (typically grades 7–9) offers opportunities to teach young adolescents usually of ages twelve to fifteen. The high school (grades 9–12 or 10–12) caters to older adolescents normally in the age range of fourteen to eighteen. The aptitudes and interests of the prospective teacher help in determining a preferred subject and grade level for which to prepare.

Secondary school teachers (junior high and senior high school) generally receive preparation that is very similar, if not largely the same. There is disagreement regarding the nature of the preparation junior high school teachers should receive. Some preference has been expressed for persons having orientation and training similar to the elementary school teacher, usually with added subject specialization. Others prefer a program quite like that of the senior high school teacher with perhaps some special exposure to and study of the junior high age group.

Teachers in the junior high school work with an interesting and often restless age group. They have much challenge in helping pupils bridge the gap between the self-contained classroom in the elementary school and the highly departmentalized situation in the senior high school. Many junior high pupils have not mastered basic skills, such as reading and arithmetic; hence, familiarity with remedial and developmental procedures is important. In various ways the junior high school serves unique functions that make teaching at this level challenging and interesting.

There is also much opportunity for substitute teaching, especially in larger cities and in consolidated districts that employ many teachers. Rosters of qualified substitutes are often maintained; and frequently used substitutes sometimes receive a special designation, such as "supply teachers." These persons may teach for long periods of time while regular teachers are on leave or are assigned temporarily to other duties. Married women who are well prepared to teach frequently find employment of this type very rewarding, and they make a contribution that is important.

Careers for Teachers in Special Education.  At the elementary and secondary school levels, there are many opportunties for specialists to teach exceptional children. This latter category often includes the extremely able as well as the very dull, in addition to children and youth with a variety of disabilities and handicaps. Considered in the group are the blind, deaf, crippled, mentally retarded, home confined, cardiac, tubercular, and low-vitality cases. Increasing provision is being made for these persons needing special educational attention.  Some are handled in regular classrooms and schools; others are cared for in rooms or schools particularly adapted to their use. Working with these persons is often very challenging and equally satisfying.

Teaching at the College and University Level.  With the popularization of higher education, the need for teachers in colleges and universities is rising sharply. A high degree of subject specialization is commonly needed, even at the junior college level where a master's degree is normally required. A doctorate is usually expected of those who propose to teach in a four-year college or a university. Post-doctoral study is becoming common, especially in fields characterized by the rapid discovery of much new knowledge.

At the college and university levels, research, writing, and other creative endeavor are expected of the teacher, as well as instructional effectiveness. Promotion through the ranks of instructor, assistant professor, associate professor, and professor may depend as much, or even more, upon non-teaching contributions as upon classroom performance. Large multipurpose universities and graduate schools are particularly inclined to expect such productive scholarship. Unfortunately, too little attention is given to superior teaching in many collegiate institutions.

**Careers in Administration and Supervision.** Although fewer positions exist in administration and supervision than in teaching, there are many fine opportunities for able and well-trained personnel. These positions are generally more lucrative than classroom teaching in the schools; some pay excellent salaries extending above $15,000 to $20,000 a year. In addition, these positions involve much status and afford opportunities for highly rewarding professional service. The following list suggests the varieties of opportunities:

Department or division chairman
Vice-principal of elementary, junior high or senior high schools
Principal of such schools
Assistant and associate superintendent of schools
Superintendent of schools
Business managers of schools or school systems
Personnel director
Director of curriculum or instruction
Director of elementary or secondary education

Director of research
Coordinator or supervisor of instruction
County superintendent of schools
Executives in state departments of education
Executives in teachers' organizations, state and national
Executives in the U.S. Office of Education and other federal bureaus
Collegiate administration

The departmental or division chairmanship in secondary schools seems to be on the increase again after a period of decline. This position often includes part-time teaching. Chairmen give leadership in curriculum and instruction within their department (such as English) or division (such as humanities or sciences). As a group they may constitute a council on instruction for the school. If a coordinator of instruction is employed in the school, this person may serve to harmonize the various departmental programs and give leadership to the overall effort for the improvement of instruction. Varying operational patterns enable all these specialists to extend leadership and service beyond their own school.

The principalship in elementary, junior high, and senior high schools is becoming more professional each year. Increasing enrollments and school reorganization increase the number of schools in which part-time and full-time administrative positions are available. Vice-principalships, by several titles, are also more prevalent than in years past. Many states have certification requirements that tend to make these positions increasingly desirable. The opening each year of many new schools adds to the opportunities available to well-qualified individuals, especially men.

Larger school districts often have a central office staff of specialists in such areas as curriculum, instruction, personnel, business, and research. Included are such titles as Director of Curriculum and Instruction, Supervisor of Science Education, Director of Elementary Education, Assistant Superintendent in Charge of Personnel, and many others. The lines of responsibility and authority vary as do the total patterns of line and staff operation. Frequently, the occupants of these positions have had administrative or supervisory experience in one or more schools of the district. They may have been brought in from another school system where they held a comparable position. Graduate training is basic to advancement in positions of this type.

Traditionally, these specialists have been recruited from the ranks of teachers, although this situation is now changing somewhat. Directors of personnel and business managers, especially the latter, for example, may have had little or no instructional experience. Special preparatory programs involving interdisciplinary study are now available to prepare persons for these positions. It is common for school principals who are especially interested in business or personnel to complete such appropriate graduate study.

The school superintendency is evolving into a position of great magnitude in many communities. Persons in such positions often administer budgets running into millions of dollars and head up school systems employing hundreds of persons. Few jobs in our society involve greater responsibility or more far reaching and enduring influence. They require executive ability of highest order, as well as advanced graduate study. In very large systems, there may be a hierarchy of superintendents, each having a more specialized responsibility, under the direction of a general superintendent of schools.

Variation exists among states as to the status of the county superintendent. In many instances the position is elective, and political affluence is the primary requisite. Sometimes there is very little to the position, especially where reorganization eliminates many small rural school districts. The creation of county-wide reorganized districts results in a superintendency of the type previously discussed, a position different from the one described in this paragraph.

Another sort of county superintendency exists in California, which has a scheme of election for this position and for the county board of education. This organization has been known to afford excellent leadership and service, but does not represent a pattern likely to endure.

State departments of education offer a growing variety of positions; some are administrative and others are supervisory. Inspectorial, legal, leadership, and service responsibilities are vested in these state offices. Emphasis on leadership and service, plus growing professionalization of the positions, are resulting in contributions of a higher order than in years past.

The U.S. Office of Education in the Department of Health, Education and Welfare also employs specialists in education, both in Washington D.C. and in the several regional offices. As federal support of education increases, these opportunities are likely to grow. Cooperation with state departments of education probably will be expanded also in the years ahead, with a resultant increase of positions in both levels of operation.

Community or junior college administrators usually have been high school principals or superintendents of schools. This condition stems in part from earlier concepts of the junior college as an upward extension of secondary education. As these institutions are associated more and more with higher education, it is likely that junior or community college teachers will increasingly assume administrative posts.

With a few exceptions, four-year college and university administrators usually come from collegiate teaching ranks. In professional schools or colleges, such as business, education, law, medicine, and nursing, persons holding administrative or research positions outside these ranks not infrequently move directly into collegiate administration. College and university presidents may also come from outside the academic environment. Once considered as a scholarly seat, the college presidency is increasingly viewed as primarily an administrative job, particularly in large multipurpose institutions. Some such presidents are both administrators and scholars.

Academic deans, department chairmen, deans of students, admissions officers, and related administrative positions are also important at the collegiate level. Usually these positions are filled from collegiate ranks. Related also is the broad area of counseling and student personnel services at the college level.

**Careers in Counseling and Student Personnel Work.** Counselors and personnel workers are not new in education. However, the last two decades have seen a growing recognition of the need for more highly trained personnel in this area than ever before. Today, this field is one of the most rapidly developing of all areas of educational service. Increasing professionalization and healthy dissension characterize its development. Included among the many titles by which workers in this field are identified are the following:

| | |
|---|---|
| Counselor | School psychologist |
| Teacher-counselor | School social worker |
| Dean of boys or girls | Director of guidance |

Public school counselors are normally classroom teachers first. In many states teaching experience is prerequisite to certification as a counselor. Graduate study is generally required. Teacher-counselors frequently do more teaching than counseling. At the elementary school level, most of the counseling is done by teachers and the principal, none of whom may have had special training for this responsibility. Some school systems also use psychologists and social workers who have been trained especially to work with school-age children and their problems.

Persons in counseling and student personnel services may have associated administrative duties. For example, in small high schools the principal may also be the counselor. In larger schools, school systems, and collegiate institutions, many persons are employed to work with students in terms of testing, job placement, financial aid, extracurricular affairs, and related areas.

**Careers as Other Educational Specialists.** Persons with specialized training in various areas often find careers in education. Indeed, some of the positions mentioned earlier, particularly in student personnel services, might be placed in this category. More important than classification is the fact that satisfying careers and significant service are possible to appropriately prepared individuals.

The school librarian becomes increasingly important in the modern school setting with emphasis on independent learning and the wise usage of many learning resources. As the library becomes a laboratory for learning, materials other than books often are an added responsibility of the librarian. Generally found at the secondary level and beyond, school librarians are also on the increase at the elementary school level. Teacher-librarians are common in smaller secondary schools.

Specialized audio-visual and radio and television personnel are not uncommon in larger school systems and in collegiate institutions. Teachers with special interest in and preparation for such work frequently move gradually into positions of this type. Graduate study appropriate to leadership and service in these areas may be found in many colleges and universities.

Teachers' aids may become increasingly prevalent in a semiprofessional manner. If this development occurs, there may emerge a new field of endeavor related closely to the instructional process. Automation and the use of programmed learning, teaching machines, and computers will probably lead to the employment of persons in education who are skilled in these matters.

Careers in Non-Professional, Non-Certificated Educational Positions. Some of the positions already mentioned might properly be placed in this category, at least in some states. Many of them, however, involve a degree of professionalization not ordinarily found in the positions that follow. Any enterprise of the magnitude of education requires many workers whose contributions are essential, although they are neither professional nor certificated. The following are illustrative: clerks, secretaries, stenographers, bookkeepers, custodians, maids, firemen, electricians, carpenters, painters, plumbers, auto-mechanics, stockroom clerks, truck drivers, warehousemen, school bus drivers, cafeteria and lunchroom workers.

There may be others. The operation of our schools and colleges requires competent and efficient workers in these positions. It is quite important that they also be desirable persons in view of their close association with pupils in the educational environment. Their orientation to educational goals and problems is important, too, for these persons often wield more influence on the educative process than is recognized. Many times they are effective spokesmen for education in the community.

Careers in School-related Work in Other Professions. The broad scope of educational concerns and the magnitude of school and college operation in many communities call for highly proficient professionals outside the field of education, for example: physicians, dentists, dental hygienists, dieticians, nurses, school accountants, school architects, school engineers, and school attorneys. Sometimes these persons devote full time to the schools or colleges for which they work. In many instances they may also have other non-school related endeavor or private practice. The certification of school nurses is gradually creating a career in nursing associated solely with the schools. The utilization of these various personnel is most likely in larger schools and communities.

## CAREERS FOR MEN IN EDUCATION

Reference was made earlier to the need for excellence in teachers. It is also generally recognized that we need more men in education than we have, especially in the elementary and secondary schools. Such a statement does not depreciate women; and the caliber of women going into teaching has certainly been comparable to that of men, in fact exceeding it in many instances. In securing more men and better men for the profession, it is probable that schools will bring about conditions that are more attractive relatively than those made available to women. Higher salaries are one example.

### Leadership Opportunities for Men Are Excellent

Rightly or wrongly, the challenges and opportunities in education are probably greater for men than for women. With the exception of the very early years, men are increasingly welcomed in the elementary school. They are needed in an environment that tends to be more feminine than is desirable for pupils. Opportunities in elementary school administration were never better for men, especially as teaching experience on the elementary level increasingly is prerequisite. All conditions considered at present, able and ambitious young men probably can move ahead more rapidly in elementary education today than on any other level.

Secondary schools have long sought to staff heavily with men. Sometimes this effort has resulted in turning away better women teachers and hiring weaker men. With the exception of homemaking and girls' physical education, men have excellent opportunity in the

various teaching fields. In secondary school administration and supervision, they have a very definite advantage. Central office administrators and supervisors tend also to be men. Thus, a variety of fine non-teaching educational positions provide excellent opportunities to men. It has been suggested that women should have equal opportunities on the basis of competence, an idea that deserves study. But in fact, men seem to be preferred for various reasons.

At the college level men also have an edge on women. With mounting hordes on the higher rungs of the educational ladder, the opportunities on this level—for well-prepared men—in teaching, research, student personnel work, and administration will increase steadily.

### Financial Considerations Are Favorable to Men

Figures presented later provide an overall picture of salaries. The true situation is not revealed for men, however, since the great majority of teachers are women. If the data could be broken down by sex, the financial picture would be shown to be better for men than women. It is known, for example, that most administrative positions are held by men; and the higher paying extracurricular assignments usually go to them. There is also growing concern over the effect of the single salary schedule in holding salaries down, generally in terms of what it costs to employ women, many of whom do not become career teachers.

Thousands of administrative and supervisory jobs pay more than $10,000 per year, and many pay more than double this figure. Classroom teaching positions pay higher than ever, with an estimated average of about $6,200 for 1964–1965. At the junior college level and beyond, many thousands of positions pay more than $10,000 per year. While it is still true that teaching is not a profession for those who must have wealth to be happy, financial rewards are gratifying to those whose ability, preparation, and effort enable them to seize the many opportunities that exist. Ambitious men should not overlook teaching as a challenging and rewarding profession.

## THE ROLE OF THE CLASSROOM TEACHER

Later chapters in this book deal in detail with the educative process and the place of the teacher therein. The purpose of this section is to provide an overview of some of the major expectations of the teacher as a professional worker and as a person. The job and life

of the teacher have changed much in this century and are still under-going change.

## The Teacher in the School

The principal contribution of the teacher is made in the school through his activity in the educational program. This program often extends beyond the walls of the school; and outside resources, both material and personnel, are increasingly utilized in the classroom. Of all the many persons involved in some manner with the instructional job, teachers are in the most strategic position to foster effective learning. Indeed, the function of teaching is to stimulate learning and to carry it forward. This teaching-learning enterprise is central to many supporting endeavors carried on by teachers and by other professional and related personnel.

Said in another way, the promotion of learning is the teacher's principal objective. At times this objective may not be as obvious as it should, consequently educators are challenged now and again to

In a complex, changing world, there is much to teach and to learn.
(Chicago Public Schools.)

reiterate its primacy. As the schools and colleges become involved in activity ancillary to learning, or perhaps competitive to it, proper focus of attention and effort is often difficult.

Today, learning is conceived more broadly than in past years. Some critics say that this breadth has resulted in de-emphasizing intellectual outcomes. More correctly, the intent has been to modify the behavior of the learner, which activity resists dissection into discrete parts. Human behavior is a complex of physical, intellectual, and emotional factors that react constantly. The teacher who knows well his students and his subject, and who is talented in bringing the two together in pursuit of sound educational objectives, is a priceless person.

Teachers today work more often and more closely together than in the past. It is realized that significant long-range educational goals are attained only if the steps taken toward them year by year and subject by subject are characterized by continuity and progression. Thus, the planning of educational experiences involves cooperation horizontally across subject lines and vertically across many grade levels. In the actual teaching, there may also be much cooperation, for example, through team teaching, in which several teachers cooperate in offering a course. On both a small and large scale, this cooperative endeavor enables individuals to weave together their strengths into a fine instructional fabric. These efforts, if properly done, do not rob the individual teacher of opportunity for creative instruction on his own.

Teachers often engage in endeavor less central to instruction than teaching but not without educational value. Various extraclass activities, for example, serve to meet student needs and are sometimes related to curricular goals also. Occasionally, these "extras" are poorly handled and result in little or no benefit and are a waste of time and effort. A great deal depends upon the teacher and his ability and willingness in this endeavor.

Hall duty and the policing of the lunchroom represent another kind of teacher activity that is increasingly questionable. Further study and adjustment are likely to reduce the time teachers spend in these relatively unproductive and non-professional activities. At the same time schools today prize teachers who do these chores willingly and who extend themselves "to deliver" in every way on the job. One of the criticisms frequently voiced of new teachers is their lack of commitment in carrying through, without supervision and coaxing, on the multifold small obligations that schools and teachers are often expected to handle.

In the teaching-learning process, the teacher does many things. He studies his students so that he may motivate them and promote their proper growth and development. He informs them and assists them in informing themselves through various media. He encourages their active involvement in learning, knowing not only when to speak but also when to remain silent. He keeps up to date in his subject matter and in the more proficient ways of teaching and learning. Evaluation of pupil progress and of the instructional process marks his endeavor as he constantly seeks to challenge each learner to the level of his ability. In a sense the teacher is a dynamic conductor of a concert of teaching and learning. He is also a disciplinarian and a friend.

## The Teacher in His Profession

As a public servant the teacher is subject to many controls and forces that lie within and outside his job and profession. While his work is essential to individual and social well-being, the circumstances with which he contends are not always conducive to an effective and satisfying job. In order to improve their contribution and the conditions relative to their work and their profession, teachers associate together in many and varied professional organizations.

These organizations may consist of a broad cross-section of the profession, such as a state teachers' association or the National Education Association. They may be limited to those in a given field, such as teachers of English or elementary school principals. At the college level, there are also various groups and societies, for example, the American Association of University Professors. In many ways these groups, singly and in cooperation, seek to improve the service they render, increase the status and rewards of their membership, and influence public opinion and action. Often they seek objectives largely limited to themselves; on some occasions their goals are widely shared with other organizations.

Active participation is essential if professional membership is to mean very much to the individual and if his organization is to be influential. Too many teachers' groups focus effort largely on what they can secure for themselves, often fringe benefits, and give too little time, effort, and money to improving their service. Prospective teachers should study carefully the objectives and operation of groups they contemplate joining. Intelligent questions followed by active endeavor to improve professional groups are imperative if these organizations are really to be worthwhile. Prospective teachers should beware of all groups, professional and otherwise, that serve a divisive purpose within the ranks of the profession or seek to erode the ties of cooperation among professionals and between professional and lay interest in education.

## The Teacher as a Person in the Community

Schools tend to be more similar than the communities in which they exist, although there is variation in both. Urbanization and school district reorganization have resulted in the elimination of many small rural schools. Voluntary cooperation among schools in separate or overlapping districts has influenced many aspects of school operation. Yet differences are apparent, and teachers are subject to them. What is expected of the teacher, what he is permitted to do, and what his status is—these and other conditions vary from community to community.

The wise person inquires in advance of the community and school in which he is to live and teach. As a new teacher he is observant of reaction to his behavior and of the way in which other persons work and live. Teachers do not always reside in the school community wherein they teach, especially in cities and metropolitan areas. The teacher may find that he lives in but is not really part of the community to the degree that would be true in a smaller city or village.

Teachers who make the effort to live with others in a community are generally welcomed. Commonality of interest apart from the job; shared concerns; similar recreational, religious, and social participation—these and other factors are important. Over the years teachers have increasingly found ready acceptance as they have sought affiliation with others on the same general basis as do non-educational members of the community.

Because of their ability and background, teachers are sometimes asked to serve the community in ways traditionally expected of teachers. Smaller communities usually expect more such service of teachers than do larger ones and may be somewhat more restrictive in terms of social activity. In the main, however, teachers today are not expected to render non-school community service through churches and other agencies to the extent once common in the past.

Greater personal freedom is evident for teachers in most communities today than in the past. Such freedom is not an invitation to irresponsible behavior, however; and some citizens in every community look to teachers for an example they themselves cannot or will not set. The mores of a school, college, and community are not wisely dis-

regarded by those who would live happily and serve effectively therein. At the same time, teachers frequently attribute to others many
restrictions that are entirely or largely of their own imagination. The
teacher who is alert and friendly, who exercises common sense and
moves slowly, and who is receptive of others usually finds a warm
welcome in most communities.

## REWARDS AND STATUS IN THE PROFESSION

Matters of personnel administration, including salaries and other
benefits, are discussed in a later chapter. At this point it is appropriate to speak generally of reward and status for those in the teaching profession. Not the least of attractions is a growing opportunity
to earn a respectable income and build toward a decent retirement.

### Financial Rewards Are Increasing

The figures in Table 1–2 present a brief picture of estimated salaries for teachers and administrators. While the profession is not one
in which to amass wealth, it is clear that those who move ahead in an
educational career can do reasonably well. Gains in salaries have not
kept pace with those in some other professions, but the steady increase will likely continue longer and be more enduring in view of all
the forces at work in modern society.

Revised estimates for 1962–1963 and estimates for 1963–1964 reveal
the following figures: [8]

|  | 1962–1963 | 1963–1964 |
|---|---|---|
| All classroom teachers . . . . . . | $5,732 | $5,963 |
| Elementary school teachers . . . . | 5,560 | 5,797 |
| Secondary school teachers . . . . | 5,980 | 6,214 |

In terms of regions, classroom teachers' average salaries were estimated as follows for 1963–1964: [9]

|  | Elementary | Secondary |
|---|---|---|
| New England . . . . . . . . | $5,984 | $6,377 |
| Mideast . . . . . . . . . | 6,546 | 6,795 |
| Southeast . . . . . . . . . | 4,743 | 5,044 |
| Great Lakes . . . . . . . . | 6,113 | 6,561 |
| Plains . . . . . . . . . . | 5,111 | 5,836 |
| Southwest . . . . . . . . . | 5,440 | 5,631 |
| Rocky Mountain . . . . . . . | 5,418 | 5,713 |
| Far West . . . . . . . . . | 6,844 | 7,517 |

[8] "School Statistics, 1963–64," op. cit., p. 6.
[9] Ibid.

**TABLE 1–2**

### Salaries Paid to Classroom Teachers and Other Professional Education Personnel, 1962–1963

| | Estimated Total Number of Personnel, All Systems | Average Salaries Paid, by Enrollment Grouping of School Systems | | | Total for All Systems * |
|---|---|---|---|---|---|
| | | 25,000 or more | 3,000 to 24,999 | 300 to 2,999 | |
| Classroom teachers | 1,508,702 | $6,405 | $5,750 | $5,345 | $5,747 |
| Principals (supervising and teaching) | | | | | |
| Elementary school | 45,249 | $10,067 | $8,101 | $6,866 | $7,972 |
| Junior high | 6,494 | 10,981 | 9,311 | 7,708 | 9,176 |
| Senior high | 12,885 | 11,632 | 8,819 | 7,786 | 8,473 |
| Assistant principals | | | | | |
| Elementary school | 4,215 | $10,553 | $8,451 | $7,049 | $9,598 |
| Junior high | –† | 9,323 | 8,451 | 5,625 | –† |
| Senior high | 5,565 | 10,111 | 9,278 | 8,523 | 9,379 |
| Other instructional personnel ‡ | | | | | |
| School librarians | 17,760 | $6,456 | $6,252 | $5,755 | $6,145 |
| School nurses | 11,524 | 6,125 | 5,754 | 5,095 | 5,650 |
| School attendance officers | –† | 6,754 | 5,702 | 4,087 | –† |
| School psychologists | –† | 8,033 | 8,705 | 6,845 | –† |
| High school deans and supervisors of counselors | 1,731 | 8,125 | 8,990 | 8,455 | 8,677 |
| Junior high school deans and department heads | 1,399 | 7,955 | 8,269 | –† | 8,168 |
| High school department heads | 3,296 | 10,293 | 9,373 | 7,967 | 9,558 |
| Counselors | 18,894 | 7,704 | 7,578 | 6,825 | 7,390 |

* Weighted averages based on an estimated total of 28,738 operating systems in 1962–1963 of which 138 are in Group A, 2,402 are in Group B, 9,985 are in Group C, and 26,198 are in Group D. Average salaries in Group D school systems were computed only for classroom teachers, $4,604; elementary school principals, $6,056; and senior high school principals, $6,091. The average salary of both groups of principals was in the ratio of 1.32 to that of classroom teachers.

† Not computed.

‡ Limited to full-time personnel who do no teaching or who teach less than half-time.

SOURCE: "Salaries Paid Instructional Staff," *NEA Research Bulletin*, XLI, No. 3 (October, 1963), 67 (adapted).

Mounting enrollments and a continuing teacher shortage serve to bolster salaries. This influence is moving upward to the collegiate level and will continue to be felt at the elementary and secondary levels. We are not able now to meet the demand for first-rate teachers at any level, and this condition will not soon be remedied. As competition for qualified teachers involves business, industry, and government, an additional upward thrust will be felt.

While there are staffing and remuneration problems in higher education, financial rewards have been increasing in recent years. The data in Table 1–3 reveal the average salaries and fringe benefits by academic rank in 1961–1962.

## TABLE 1–3

### Number of Full-Time Faculty, Average Compensation, and Average Salary and Fringe Benefits by Ranks, 1961–1962

|  | Number Faculty | Average Compen- sation | Average Salary | Average Fringe Benefit |
|---|---|---|---|---|
| 545 institutions with professional rank | | | | |
| Professor . . . . . | 26,878 | $11,647 | $10,858 | $789 |
| Associate professor . | 24,484 | 8,875 | 8,309 | 567 |
| Assistant professor . . | 29,792 | 7,408 | 6,960 | 448 |
| Instructor . . . . | 17,889 | 5,976 | 5,647 | 328 |
| Lecturer . . . . . | 1,305 | 6,876 | 6,578 | 298 |
| All ranks . . | 100,348 | 8,639 | 8,094 | 545 |
| 43 institutions without professional rank: | | | | |
| one rank only . . | 3,568 | 7,701 | 7,544 | 157 |

Source: "The Economic Status of the Profession, 1961–62: Report of the Self-Grading Compensation Survey," *AAUP Bulletin,* Summer Issue, XLVIII (June, 1962), 120–54.

## Choice of Position and Location Is Improving

The conditions described above tend to assure able and well-prepared prospective teachers of a choice of position and location. Teachers are needed everywhere. States where salaries and working conditions are better usually have a larger reservoir from which to select. Persons prepared in one section of the nation increasingly find it easier to teach in another section. Opportunity for teaching in many foreign countries is good, and the chances for advanced study and travel there add to the attractiveness of such opportunity.

## Working Conditions Are Improving

Thousands of new school and college buildings dot the landscape from coast to coast. Thousands more are under construction, and the end is not in sight. Hence, while many old buildings are still in use, the chance of teaching in bright new surroundings increases each year. Improved facilities also characterize these new buildings, and some older schools have been renovated thoroughly. Large well-supplied libraries, well-equipped science laboratories, many instructional aids and services, teachers' lounges and offices, and other attractive and useful features are found in modern school buildings.

There is a new pleasantness to the surroundings in which teachers work. Color and lighting, plus arrangement, reduce the traditional rectangular drabness of earlier days. Even school furniture matches the new look, while serving better than ever before to seat pupils properly for learning. Many features of new buildings have come about because teachers wanted them and had a voice in school plant planning.

The job of the teacher is not easy. This statement has been made before, and it will be increasingly obvious in later pages. Teaching load continues to be a problem, especially in some schools, in some subject fields, and at some grade levels. The use of teacher aids and machines in instruction helps, but the need for a large number of qualified persons cannot be met by such approaches alone. Those who teach have much work to do outside of school hours, as is true of every other profession. But there is deep satisfaction in working with learners at all levels, and one's associates are usually intelligent and congenial.

Democracy in school administration and in education generally adds to the friendly atmosphere in which teachers work. Improvements in tenure, sick leave, retirement, insurance, professional advancement, and related conditions are also important. Vacations are more frequent and longer than in most professions, affording opportunity for recreation, study, travel, and other pursuits.

## Status Is Rising

Few jobs can compare with teaching in their impact on society. The consciousness of having done well something that is important to individuals and to the commonwealth is reward in itself. Gradually but perceptibly the significance of the teacher is growing. His social position is respectable, and he increasingly enjoys freedom to live his own life. Many teachers, professors, and administrators are prominent in community activities and social life. Progressively, they are members of service, social, and other groups. They serve on city councils and committees and in many ways give leadership and direction to civic affairs.

### Education as a Career Compared with Other Professions

One's ability and interest are of primary importance in choosing a career. Many of the qualities essential for success in one career are equally necessary in another. As one views the various possibilities, therefore, he considers himself and the conditions that characterize his opportunities. Much has already been said of conditions in teaching. A brief restatement and elaboration in comparative form may be useful as a summary.

1. In no profession is there greater need for first-rate personnel than in teaching, and in none is there greater opportunity for more significant service.
2. In no profession is there greater opportunity to work with ideas and people than in teaching, and in none is this relationship more congenial and conducive to creative living.
3. The profession of teaching affords as much or more variation in terms of specialty than is to be found in any other profession.
4. Few if any professions offer opportunities so easily grasped over the nation at large and on foreign shores as does teaching.
5. No profession affords a greater opportunity for continued study and growth than does teaching.
6. No profession today enjoys the rate of growth in prestige and status that is characteristic of teaching.

## QUESTIONS, PROBLEMS, AND PROJECTS FOR FURTHER STUDY

1. Draw up a statement of your expectations from the profession you eventually choose. Compare this statement with what a career in education seems to offer. Is a career in education a wise choice for you? Why?

2. Arrange opportunities, if you can, to observe some teaching at grade levels and in classes of interest to you. Discuss what you see and questions that arise in your own mind with persons in the profession. Are you encouraged at the prospect of entering teaching?

3. Interview several teachers or other career personnel that you know in the field of education. Ask them to size up the profession in terms of opportunities, challenges, problems, and rewards. Do their responses encourage you to enter the profession?

4. Suppose that you enter teaching and look ahead ten years at where and what you might be. From reading and discussion, what do you ob-

serve yourself as doing, and what satisfactions and rewards can you visualize as being reasonable expectations?

5. Discuss college teaching with several professors in fields that interest you. Check into opportunities, challenges, and problems in higher education. What advantages seem to be found in higher education in comparison with teaching on lower levels? Are there any disadvantages?

6. Look into opportunities for overseas teaching assignments, including requirements and rewards. Do such opportunities appeal to you? Why?

## SELECTED SUPPLEMENTARY READINGS AND FILM

BARZUN, JACQUES. *Teacher in America.* Boston: Little, Brown & Co., Inc., 1945. Discusses many problems of teachers and teaching, chiefly at the college level.

GROSS, CARL H., WRONSKI, STANLEY P., and HANSON, JOHN W. *School and Society.* Boston: D. C. Heath & Co., 1962. Chap. xii. Presents various views of teaching as a profession and a picture of the NEA and the AFT.

HIGHET, GILBERT. *The Art of Teaching.* New York: Alfred A. Knopf, Inc., 1951. Presents teaching as an art rather than as a science and provides examples of great teaching from the time of Socrates to the present.

HOLMAN, MARY V. *How It Feels To Be a Teacher.* New York: Bureau of Publications, Teachers College, Columbia University, 1950. Stresses the feelings of teachers in making adjustments that are essential to a happy and productive life in the profession.

LINDSEY, MARGARET (ed.). *New Horizons for the Teaching Profession.* Washington, D.C.: National Education Association, 1961. Chaps. ii and iii. These chapters present a picture of the profession in 1961 and point up the responsibilities of the profession in the sixties.

LIPSTREU, OTIS, and DOI, JAMES I. *Guidelines for the Aspiring Professor.* Monograph C–11. Chicago: Southwestern Publishing Co., 1963. Secs. I and II. These sections deal with the meaning of a university and the nature of the professor and his academic endeavor.

MERCER, BLAINE E., and CARR, EDWIN R. *Education and the Social Order.* New York: Holt, Rinehart & Winston, Inc., 1957. Chap. x. Deals with the teacher and his roles, prestige, and other facets of his career.

MOUSTAKAS, CLARK E. *The Alive and Growing Teacher.* New York: Philosophical Library, Inc., 1959. Discusses the growth of teachers in understanding themselves, others, and the nature and problems of education.

PETERSON, HOUSTON (ed.). *Great Teachers.* New Brunswick, N.J.: Rutgers University Press, 1946. Contains a series of short accounts about great teachers by their students.

### Film

*And Gladly Teach.* 27 minutes, color. Presents satisfactions of teaching and reviews the education of the typical teacher and behavior to be met in school. Washington, D.C.: National Education Association.

# II

# THE FOUNDATIONS
# OF EDUCATION

# 2

# THE BIOPSYCHOLOGICAL
# FOUNDATIONS OF EDUCATION
# AND THE SCHOOL POPULATION

The sociological foundations of education, which are discussed in Chapter 3, provide a perspective of education in terms of its interrelationship with the social order. Man is a social being. He is also a biological and psychological organism. Thus, while learning takes direction and substance from the culture, it is also governed in no small degree by the individual learner and by the total school population within which he lives and learns. Focus in this chapter is placed upon the biopsychological foundations as these are operative in individuals and in the masses who seek an education.

## ORGANIC AND SOCIAL EVOLUTION

Humanity abides and advances chiefly through two closely related major processes: organic evolution and social evolution. The first of these assures the biological or physical continuity of life. It provides the organisms in and through which the second process is carried on. By its very nature it affords advantages and imposes limitations. This organic process maintains the hereditary basis of human life.

The second process, social evolution, serves to maintain the humane and cultural continuity of life. It assures the transmission of man's social characteristics from one generation to another. It provides for the extension and improvement of these characteristics. While this process is social, it is also individual; and it relates closely to organic evolution. Indeed, neither process can continue alone. As the organic is fundamental to the physical spark of life, the social is basic in keeping this spark alive and in nourishing it into the warm flame of human personality.

## The Definition of Education

This process of social evolution is often called education. It is not entirely social, as has already been suggested, for the biological and psychological bases are fundamental. Broadly conceived, education permeates most of man's endeavors, which fact causes much controversy when attempts are made to determine what education should be and do.

For purposes of definition, *education is a biopsychological and social process involving many and varied experiences through which behavior is modified or strengthened.* The terms "learning" and "education" are frequently used synonymously in this book.

Education is the learning of correct and incorrect responses. It is memorization and more. Recitation is a part of it, but education extends far beyond the two covers of a book and the four walls of a classroom. The lives of every human being are touched by education of one sort or another. Neither the productive citizen nor the unproductive crook was born to his station in life; each became what he is through a process of education. The power of education is limited only by man's capacity and willingness to learn and to educate others.

## Education and Schooling

Education is more than schooling. It carries on wherever men congregate; indeed, it is not limited to man. Learning among animals is well known and has even been observed in one-celled organisms. Education is often incidental to other purposes and derives from experience as a by-product. It may be informal or formal. Countless agencies exert educational influence; for example, the home, school, church, business and industry, press, radio, television, fraternity or sorority, and many other groups. The teachings of these various agencies are apt to be inconsistent in part, sometimes creating conflict in the minds and souls of those affected.

Schooling refers to that part of education carried on by schools and colleges. It is usually formalized and structured to foster attainment of consciously sought goals. Schools and colleges exist to sort out and reorder experiences so as to make learning a primary concern and to give it prominence in the lives of those who are involved. These institutions foster economy and efficiency in teaching and learning. In this sense, as is implied elsewhere in this book, the school is a special, supplementary social agency whose primary function is schooling.

## Man's Genetic Advantages for Learning

Man's superiority as a learner derives from a unique pattern of genetic factors that provide an advantage not enjoyed by any other forms of life. This pattern not only makes high-level learning and culture possible, it renders them essential. This combination of factors is both a means and a motivational force. Included are:

1. A very highly developed nervous system, especially the brain
2. Complex and sensitive hands, including the opposed thumb
3. An upright position, which facilitates the use of the hands
4. Binocular vision
5. A flexible vocal mechanism
6. A state of plasticity throughout a prolonged period of infancy

Reflection on these conditions helps one to realize the tremendous potential for learning that man has. Perceiving, manipulating, discriminating, symbolizing, remembering, hoping, imagining, worrying, planning, communicating—all these and many other high-level activities are possible because of this unique combination. In the absence of these activities, human culture is impossible. Social man and his culture seem to have emerged together in the evolution of things; in a sense each is the creator of and the product of the other.

## Behavior and Decision

The high degree of decision making that man enjoys is potentially his most ennobling attribute. His pattern of genetic factors does not determine his specific behavior nor forever commit him to either good or evil. He enjoys great freedom in a wide latitude of behavior largely determined by himself. The importance of reason and responsibility thus appears in any consideration of education based on man's hereditary possibilities, as well as founded on his social opportunities and obligations. In every generation education is challenged to develop individuals appropriately so that their genetic possibilities become active realities supportive of a better life for themselves and others. The significance of teaching and learning that foster wise decision making is obvious, although not always properly handled in the schools. *Behavior* and *decision* are two key words for the teacher to recall frequently as he works with learners at every level.

### Education and Dependence

The prolonged period of human infancy and the dependency characteristic of this period necessitate education as well as care. The
family and the school owe their emergence largely to these conditions.
Immaturity is a primary condition of growth. It requires care or
guardianship of various types, the totality of these activities gradually
shifting responsibility from others to the individual. Education is
thus a means of accomplishing guardianship so as to foster increasing
self-direction and self-control.

Of course, infancy alone is not enough to make education possible;
and the genetic factors should not be forgotten. These conditions
and the nature of human growth and development are important in
organizing and conducting learning experiences. The teacher who is
unfamiliar with these matters is likely to find himself in difficulty,
and his learners are not apt to make the progress they can and should.

Informal education precedes formal education in the exercise of
guardianship. Informal education also preceded formal education in
the evolution of schools. Before there were schools among primitive
men, for example, children learned a great deal from play, work,
and other related activities in which they were associated with their
peers, parents, and other elders. Education was an integral part of
the ongoing activities of daily living, many of which involved teaching and learning, although they were conducted primarily for other
purposes. The disassociation of children and young people from
adults in modern society complicates certain learning and developmental activities. In a sense these learners are alienated from the
kind of environment in which they might easily and effectively be
taught. The transition from childhood to adolescence to adulthood
is often difficult as a result. A return to simpler days is unlikely in
today's complicated world, but increased attention to the induction
of youth into adult culture is needed.

As cultural evolution brought about specialization and related complexity, the school emerged and eventually became a highly structured
institution of levels and subjects. It served a special purpose in sup-
plementing the education provided by other living activities and other
social agencies. Over the years the range of educational endeavor in
schools and colleges has expanded greatly to meet emerging needs;
indeed, differing types of institutions have come into being for this
purpose.

From the beginning to the present day, one major purpose has been served by this whole social development. Education has sought and continues to seek to transmit the cultural heritage to each succeeding generation and to induct each individual into productive adult membership in the society involved. *Out of dependency, then, education seeks to foster self-dependency and interdependency.*

## VIEWPOINTS OF THE EDUCATIVE PROCESS

Conflict and contradiction have already been associated with education. Nowhere are these conditions more prevalent than in viewpoints of the educative process. As demands grow, expectations increase. As efforts are stepped up, dissatisfaction with imperfection is progressively apparent. Theory in education has not developed to the point of providing all the answers that are needed. Refusal to accept and act upon what has been learned, especially when it is contrary to popular belief (often dubbed common sense), has further handicapped the schools and confused teachers, learners, and laymen.

Disagreement over the biopsychological nature of education is apt to be especially disconcerting to prospective and new teachers. Parents, too, frequently have concerns, particularly at the time their first youngster goes to school or when a son or daughter is not doing as well as is expected. Both of these groups seek assurance or reassurance, one that it may teach well to produce sound learning and the other that it may understand what is being done, what is resulting, and why. Historically, a number of concepts of learning have developed as people have attempted either to understand or to give direction to schooling. These ideas are still evident today.

In considering the nature of learning, it is helpful to look at how people tend to view what is learned and how they value it. The expectations of persons served by the schools and colleges color what is taught and how it is taught. Attention to how learning takes place is also essential, for sound theory is basic to sound practice. These two categories of ideas are related; let us think of the first as concepts about learning and the second as theories explaining the learning process.

### Concepts About Learning

Time and circumstance influence very much the way in which people regard education or learning. What it does for them and what they believe it does may not be the same, but each condition bears on this concept of learning. As they find it necessary or desirable to make decisions, individuals frequently seek some criteria or bases that can be used. Logic is not always sought; indeed, satisfaction and support of preconceptions may be all that is wanted. Several concepts or sets of concepts about learning have been held for many years and figure in educational discussion today. These views offer little or nothing to explain how learning takes place, but some of them relate to such explanation as presented later.

**The Useful and the Preparatory.** Earlier peoples soon came to see the utilitarian in learning; it was essential to survival here and now. At the same time they recognized that they were preparing their youth for the future and adulthood. Much teaching was done by parental example, and much learning by emulation. Learning was by doing. The ideas of utility for the present and preparation for the future were not only consonant, they were sides of the same coin, which is what they should be.

This early education was comparatively simple. Rank and leadership were generally matters of inheritance and power. Gradually, however, learning and status became associated and the selective function of education came to be recognized. "Utility" was more and more connected with education for the essentials of life. "Preparation" was increasingly allied to learning that characterized the priesthood and other leadership somewhat removed from the rank and file and the purely utilitarian. The first of these types of learning culminated in practices of a vocational and physical survival nature. The second was more attuned to higher cultural activities, values, and religion. A dichotomy began to develop that was to sharpen and to appear and reappear, even unto this day. As conditions initially giving rise to educational experiences changed, the experiences that were no longer useful often held on through pressures from vested interests. The latter frequently justified these experiences as preparatory or, as we shall see later, as disciplinary.

Among our forefathers these viewpoints were prevalent, for example with the Puritans. Both ideas—utility and preparation—were known to them. They were practical people dependent upon themselves for so very much. They were also deeply religious and dependent upon the church. The present was viewed largely as preparation for the future, culminating in a heavenly hereafter or a horrendous hell. They prepared for a long, cold winter. They prepared their youth for adulthood. They prepared everyone to meet his Maker. They prepared the chosen few for leadership, civil and religious. They had a two-class educational plan. Their schools and colleges took on this coloration and separateness, which only several major educational battles were later to overcome. The idea of separateness is not dead even in this age of the comprehensive high school.

The conflict between the utilitarian and the preparatory continued throughout our history. The nature of pioneer life placed emphasis on the practical. The elementary school curriculum came to be the purveyor of practical education, which was preparation for an adulthood entered upon much earlier than now. This curriculum came later to consider the interests of children and economy and efficiency in learning. In the latter half of the nineteenth century, Pestalozzi, Herbart, and their disciples promoted this development. The movement of research in child study and development in the twentieth century also tended to foster the familiar, the meaningful and useful, and the present in education. Educational theory accepted and used in the elementary schools was not always accepted at the high school level. Nor is it necessarily used there today.

In the secondary schools, which initially developed only *to prepare* pupils for college, emphasis was placed upon studies believed to have value in subsequent collegiate endeavor. The *college preparatory concept* emerged as an expectation of people as well as a legitimate purpose. The college preparatory diploma became in some schools the desired graduation certificate with the greatest status. More is said on this point later as regards education and status symbols.

The college preparatory idea gave special significance apart from real value to certain subjects usually identified as being academic; for example, English, foreign language, mathematics, social studies, and science. College entrance examinations based on these subjects added to their luster. Early accreditation programs also favored the academic as opposed to the non-academic. No amount of research questioning the value of subjects per se and pointing to other predicative variables and important conditions has had the effect on thinking that is called for. The present trend toward greater use of entrance examinations leaves many of the earlier questions unanswered; but it satisfies many persons, nonetheless.

**Education as a Status Symbol.** As suggested earlier, certain kinds of learning became associated with the attainment of status. Education was recognized as a means of raising one's level of living, and it serves today in this manner. It became a badge of respectability to have an elementary school education, then a high school education, and now a college education. The popularization of education has extended upward to embrace the whole realm of learning, not merely to satisfy those who seek status, but also in response to a need for growing numbers of highly educated people. The *decorative concept* of learning came into being as a by-product of these developments.

According to this concept, which applied more to high school than elementary school, certain things were to be learned as evidence of cultural attainment. Those who learned them (or more accurately, were exposed to them) could feel the glow of superiority known only to persons whose learning was greater than the less schooled. Probably this feeling was at least as prevalent among parents as among sons and daughters. A high school diploma became a badge of distinction, a mark of merit, in short a decoration of attainment.

In attempting to meet the needs of mass education and high-quality education, the schools and colleges developed diverse programs. A high school diploma came to mean many things where it originally meant one. As increasing numbers graduated from high school, the decorative value of the diploma meant less in a "cultural" sense. Once desirable in a preparatory and decorative sense, the diploma has today become virtually essential in a utilitarian sense. Reconsideration is being given by some schools to the practice of granting several types of diplomas, which practice will result in renewed interest in the status value of the diploma.

Today, the decorative notion is increasingly attached to college attendance and a higher education. Not everyone should go to college. Some who go attend for the wrong reasons. Many drop out after being there only long enough to say honestly that they attended. The decorative concept is causing increasing harm and heartache today at higher levels. It has always operated there to some extent, but the condition is becoming worse. Even among some of the very able students and their parents, college going and/or graduation now means a great deal more if it involves one of the "status" institutions. Many persons refuse to believe that a good college education may be attained at any of several hundred higher institutions.

While the validity of this concept should be questioned, its power to affect people, schools, and colleges should not be underestimated. Some who read these pages will have been influenced by the seeking of status. Admittedly, education serves a useful end in elevating the individual and the masses. Most of these persons, it is hoped, will be seeking their education as a means to become productive citizens and workers in a chosen profession, not simply to gain whatever decorative status the degree may have in their own or the eyes of others.

**A Balanced Point of View.** Many people, perhaps the quiet majority, hold to no single well-articulated view about education or learning. They see the necessity for learning in helping their children or their pupils to live effectively, now as well as in the future. Both the useful and the preparatory are incorporated in their expectations, though probably in varying degrees. They see status as an outcome, not so much of merely earning a diploma or a degree, but as recognition for the life lived and the service rendered as a result of the education involved.

Educational improvement through a slow process of orderly and well-explained change is generally supported by persons who are balanced in their views and expectations of learning. But they are often silent in the councils where decisions are made. Consequently, teachers more commonly hear of and are influenced more actively by the vocal few who hold to some view suitable to their own ends. This latter condition makes it all the more essential that educators know how people are apt to feel and why.

## Theories Explaining Learning

Many theories have been advanced to explain how learning takes place and to offer guidelines for effective teaching and learning. Students of education usually study such theories in educational psychology, child growth and development, and in connection with practice teaching or the internship. A brief introduction to the topic is all that is consonant with the purposes of this book.

It will help the reader, both now and later, to remember that there are different types of learning and that a theory may be more applicable to one type than another. The teacher should understand the various major theories. More important, he should be able to translate these ideas into practices that facilitate the various types of learning that are included in schools and colleges. An eclectic approach that results in useful and effective practices is preferable to adherence to a single theory. Some of the theories presented herein are considerably more valid and useful than others, yet each has its adherents.

**Education as Mental Discipline.** Supportive of the decorative concept, the theory of mental discipline has been popular and continues to have many proponents. Those who supported this concept envisioned mental exercise as an intellectual counterpart of physical exercise. If muscular development is fostered by physical exercise, why mental development must, therefore, be facilitated by intellectual exercise. This view was based on faculty psychology, holding that there are a number of mental powers, such as remembering, reasoning, and judging. The mind, consequently, could conduct specific performances through these faculties that were sharpened or strengthened by exercise or discipline. Subject matter was believed to be important, not so much in itself, but in terms of its value in exercising or disciplining the intellectual powers.

Believers in mental discipline had faith in the general transfer of training. Reasoning, for example, was to be taught through the study of geometry and other mathematics. Once taught in this manner, a general reasoning power was thereby strengthened to operate in all manner of mathematical and non-mathematical thinking. Latin, as a tough and demanding subject, would foster intellectual toughness, persistence, and application—all of which would help in future difficult and uninteresting pursuits. If a subject was unpleasant, this very feature would add to its disciplinary value.

The relationship of the college preparatory, decorative, and mental discipline ideas should not go unnoticed. Separately and together, they have promoted important areas of learning but usually for false or wrong reasons. They have tended to support the status quo in school and college, without a recognition of changes that have been essential and have eventually come about in spite of opposition.

Many sincere persons testify as to the disciplinary value of certain subjects they studied in school. There is no question here that what they studied was valuable, but the *disciplinary* value theory bears careful scrutiny. In the first place, the passage of time lends enchantment and helps to create an aura of happy bygone days that is unrealistic but convincing. Few of these persons realize or are willing to admit that the values they recall, if they actually exist, came not from the discipline of the subject but from other factors in the teaching-learning situation that they have forgotten or of which they were never aware. Or having been told again and again, as many of them were, that certain subjects had much disciplinary value, they remember little else. It is comforting to remember kindly, particularly if memories suggest a certain Spartan quality in one's younger days!

The teacher's patience in explaining *why*, frequent and sound applications of theory, the requirement of *high-quality performance*, an *environment* at home and school *conducive to learning*—these and many other conditions not dependent upon certain subjects but present to influence whatever is being taught have a great effect on learning, retention, and subsequent use and value. All of this matrix often goes unrecognized by those who speak hopefully of mental discipline, and by those who nod affirmatively as they listen.

The concepts of preparation, decoration, and the theory of mental discipline helped to rescue the traditional classical education when its initial utility wore thin. Most roads lead into the school program; few lead out. Once a subject is included, for whatever reasons, it is seldom dropped. If the reasons no longer suffice, new reasons are thought of. Most of us are able to fool ourselves when we really want to do so. And often there is much more at stake.

### Education as Mind Storage.

One of the earliest and now generally discredited theories of learning was that of mind storage. It was thought that the mind was a kind of mental reservoir or storehouse ready and waiting to be filled. Those who learned most or best were those whose heads were crammed with valuable information that they could extract for use at a moment's notice. Those who were not so knowledgeable were referred to as "thick-headed" or "empty-headed," expressions that were descriptive, even though erroneous. The appeal of a simple sounding notion like "mind storage" is understandable.

This theory placed undue emphasis on memorization and rote learning, often destroying the virtue of meaningful memorization. The learner's role was relatively passive; he was the recipient of things to be learned and later recited. Meaning was secondary to "knowing," and the better pupils were those who could mentally ingest great quantities of material easily and reproduce the contents accurately and quickly.

In terms of this theory, the subject matter to be learned tended to become an end in itself, without sufficient regard to its value and to larger and more important educational goals. The compartmentalization of information was fostered by the theory and that of mental discipline, so that education came to be a series of capsules, doses, or exercises. By almost any means short of extreme violence, frequently through fear and force, knowledge was to be crammed, poured, pounded, drummed, or otherwise put into the learner's mind. Schemes for memorization were invented to produce a mental filing system from which needed bits of information could be drawn out at will. Outlining to save "mental space" was often utilized widely.

This theory placed emphasis on docility and receptivity of learners. They were to learn "what was good for them," an idea that carried over into mental discipline nicely. Quiet and orderly classrooms dominated by the teacher in an authoritarian role were consonant with this notion of how learning occurs. Such an idea promoted the conservative role in education but did little or nothing for the other roles.

**The Blank Tablet.** Also assigning a relatively passive role to the learner, the theory of the mind as a blank tablet (*tabula rasa*) is quite similar to that of mind storage. It was believed that the new born babe came into the world with a blank page upon which, through education, might be written those things believed to be important for him by his teachers and others.

**Education as Molding or Shaping.** Still another theory conceived of education as "doing something" to the learner. This was the idea of education as a molding or shaping process in which the individual, especially the young child, was thought of as a lump of clay, so to speak. Society and its various agencies, especially through the hands of the teacher, could shape the child gradually into the kind of adult desired. Similar to the other theories, this one also minimized the activity of the learner and gave emphasis to the activity of the teacher.

The reader should not conclude from this discussion that knowledge or information is not important, nor should he believe that memorization and the external influence of teachers and others are of no use in learning. But these theories tended to distort values and processes and failed to place the elements of teaching and learning in proper relationship. A few illustrations are pertinent. Meaning was often neglected in the memorization of information or process. The reaction of the learner, his curiosity and needs, and his readiness were inadequately considered. Relationships between elements common to several learning situations received little attention. Inference and insight generally were not thought of, nor was the creativity of the learner sufficiently considered. Adjusting the individual to external conditions and orthodoxy were encouraged by these theories. The influence of these views may be observed today in schools and colleges across the nation, indeed around the world.

**The Unfolding of Latent Powers.** Possibly a reaction to the inertness given to the learner by certain other theories, there developed a notion of education as a process promoting the unfolding or development of latent individual powers. That which was to be lay already within the learner, needing only to be drawn out rather than poured in or written on. Recognition was given to the individual as an active ingredient, indeed the primary one, in the learning process.

While the other theories credited the learner with too little, this one assumed too much of him. The idea of unfolding or developing did awaken attention to pupil freedom and responsibility. It assumed a sort of genesis of potential that was quiescent, awaiting only the proper time and conditions to spring forth in developed form. The importance of drive and need are recognized today in theories of learning, but not in quite the same simple fashion as was prevalent when this theory was popular.

In general, the pendulum of thinking swung from the one extreme of emphasis on the external in other theories to the extreme of focus on the internal in this theory. At the time the latter idea emerged, it was contrary to prevailing theories and to the generally accepted notion that children were born in and filled with sin that needed to be driven from them. As a result, its principal if not sole effect was to initiate some thought for the learner, which idea was later to bear real fruit.

## MORE RECENT PSYCHOLOGICAL EXPLANATIONS OF LEARNING

As the scientific movement began to influence education and outmoded theories of learning were discredited, newer and sounder psychological explanations were slowly forthcoming. Whereas earlier ideas had leaned toward the general if not the vague, the newer lines of inquiry were much more specific, perhaps too much so. But these newer ideas were to be more soundly based on research than older ones and were to give insight useful in improving the teaching-learning process.

### Learning as Conditioning

The conditioning theory of learning rests upon the idea that stimuli result in responses and that, therefore, we can control or elicit responses as we control the stimuli. Since each individual has some innate or acquired stimulus-response situations, we may develop others by learning as a process of conditioning. New stimuli may be substituted for those initially eliciting the response.

This theory, as did others that were psychologically and research based, recognized both the external or directive elements and the internal or responsive elements of learning. Learning was to be fostered largely by control of conditions outside the learners, and by persons other than the learners. This approach was not entirely contrary to earlier and less-scientific ideas, a fact that probably added to its general acceptability. The responsiveness of the learner and the attention given to his developmental behavior in the teaching-learning situation prompted by this theory represent a big step forward.

Timing and pacing in learning were also given attention in conditioning. Contiguity in teaching affords a means of building on the past and present to evoke future behavior changes, particularly as regards the overt actions of the learner. Retraining to obtain desirable responses or habits is often a matter of conditioning. Frequency and recency of experience are pertinent to learning and retention.

## Connectionism and Trial and Error in Learning

Some of the earlier psychologies dealt chiefly with establishing the existence of senses and discovering and verifying laws governing mental functions, such as perceiving and remembering. Thorndike was a major proponent of connectionism and trial and error in learning. This view involved a stimulus-response bond, as did conditioning, and focused on the reinforcement of desirable responses as a primary teaching-learning concern. Emphasis was to be placed upon stamping in and stamping out neural connections between stimuli and responses.

Trial and error is significant to such learning. Drill receives considerable attention as a means of establishing stimulus-response bonds and reinforcing them. Retention relates also to this practice and to the nature of rewards and punishment that may be used for motivation. The latter is a very complicated operation. Concentration on specific situations and skills is common, for example as regards arithmetic, handwriting, and spelling. Various rules appeared as guides to learning as a result of this theory, such as the laws of exercise and effect. More generalized and complicated forms of behavior and response subject to constellations of stimuli and other factors tend not to fit into this theory.

Later development and adaptation brought into the picture of learning such factors as drive, cue, response, and reward, relating these ideas to the elicitation and reinforcement of response. Inclusion of these conditions broadens the application of the learning theory, but does not explain adequately some of the higher forms of learning and some more generalized and variable behavior. Nonetheless, the theory of connectionism and the reinforcement of S-R bonds continues to have use and to exert influence in the classroom.

## Cognitive and Gestalt Psychology in Learning

From acceptance of specificity in human response and reliance on repetition of S-R situations, attention was shifted to the concept of more generalized response with the total organism as the reacting agent. The earlier theories failed to explain adequately the suddenness with which solutions to problems appeared and gave little or no attention to the symbolic perception or visualization a learner might go through between trials in learning. Ability to work mentally, anticipate, consider alternatives, speculate on probabilities, and make a judgment seemed to be left unexplained or unconsidered.

Cognition and insight are offered as another explanation of learning. These relate to structuring or conceptualizing as an intellectual or mental act, or series of acts, between stimulation and response. Having received a stimulus, the respondent, from past experience, visualizes and weighs mentally, perhaps drawing up some plan or scheme, before beginning to respond in a detectable manner. Understanding and insight sometimes are evident on the first attempt one makes to solve a problem. In other instances several attempts are necessary with such interspersed thinking as the learner wishes to involve and/or is capable of doing.

Gestalt psychology advocates that perception and learning are governed by the same general laws and that the total organization of experience is of fundamental importance. A learning experience is actually more than the sum of its separate parts. Meaning, organization, reorganization, and the relationship of old and new experience are stressed. Reinterpretation is important, as it is also according to the cognitive theory. The importance of trial and error is minimized, with greater attention being given to mental perceiving and patterning.

Drill as a process of repetitive establishment of connections is also devalued by Gestalt psychology. Proposed instead is the idea that there takes place in the learner a psychological process working toward a configuration, pattern, or organization (involving old and new learning) that is meaningful, understandable, simple, stable, and complete or whole.

## Human Growth and Development

If the teacher is to work effectively with people, especially children and young men and women, he needs to understand human growth and development. Whatever psychological theories impinge on the teaching-learning process at hand, the growth and development of those who are taught and learn is of much significance. Even among learners, there is need for self-knowledge and self-understanding, especially of certain changes in structure and function as these relate to one's perception of himself and his relationship to others.

As used here growth refers to an increase of the magnitude of some aspect of the individual. Size and weight and shape are good physical illustrations. One's vocabulary may also grow or his grasp of colors. Development, while it includes growth and often relates to it, is a larger concept and relates to organized sequential change, particularly as change of structure influences change of function.

Without a great deal of effort, the reader can, through introspection, list for himself numerous changes in growth and development that he has undergone. These changes affect learning in many ways. Perhaps the reader can also recall instances of this type of relationship. The needs and drives of children and youth vary, for example; and these also change in a developmental pattern. As this change occurs, readiness to learn is influenced. Maturation makes much difference in ability, interest, and effort. Means of motivation and effectiveness of such means depend in some degree upon these changes.

One who teaches should be familiar with the stages of growth and development common to the age-grade levels on which he works. He needs also to understand something of earlier and later stages, for variation is evident in most school groups. The objectives of teaching frequently focus some of the teaching-learning activity on the development of the individual and upon his perception of self in relation to others. Other objectives that are sought, and the effectiveness with which subject matter is taught, are dependent upon procedures consonant with the growth and developmental levels of the learners.

### The Individual and Learning

It should be clear by now that the individual is of paramount importance in learning. Yet many conditions and trends force attention away from him to groups and other masses of learners. The picture of educational challenge in the United States is tremendous; and its many facets, for example, numbers, need, and diversity, are all but overwhelming. So much pressure from "size" can blind us to the fact that no matter how many there are to educate, nor how far we must take them along diverse or similar routes, it is the individuals who count.

Only the individual can learn. While he can be taught in large groups, only he does the learning. His group has no learning apparatus as such, and an intelligent, well-educated society is one composed of intelligent, well-educated individuals. Most teachers take pride in doing a good job. They know their subjects and understand how to teach. Success of teaching, however, is properly gauged by success of learning; and only the individual pupil can accomplish the latter.

Other developments argue for teacher understanding of the individual. Articulation of educational experiences at given age or grade levels and over a period of years rests a great deal upon such knowledge. If progress is to be shown and understood, it can be accomplished only as teachers first know and understand individual learners. Rates of learning development, the fostering of independent learning, and the economy of teaching bear upon the grasp of the individual by those who teach him. No matter how many pupils a teacher may be assigned, he cannot escape the necessity of knowing each one well, although he may neglect to do so.

## THE PSYCHOLOGY OF EFFECTIVE TEACHING AND LEARNING

The teacher may derive much help from the biopsychological foundations of education. The nature of the educative process is significant. Study of the individual, including physical, mental, emotional, and social aspects, and of human variability is important. Consideration of the environment and its impact upon the learner and upon the educative process is also essential. From all of these matters and their dynamic interrelationship, there has emerged a view of education and some guidelines to teaching and learning that are very useful.

Education is increasingly viewed as a developmental process. The total development of the complete individual in his whole environment is the trinity of this view. Schools and colleges are charged with certain responsibilities that they are particularly fitted to meet. Wherever education is to be pursued, efficiency should be sought. As there are different types of learning, for example, motor skills, habits, ideals, and ideas, some principles of learning are more applicable in one situation than another. A skilled teacher knows how to use these principles, and he does so.

### Guidelines for Teaching and Learning

It has already been suggested that only the individual can learn. This point should never be neglected in applying guidelines for teach-

You may teach him, but only he can learn. (Albuquerque, New Mexico, Public Schools.)

ing and learning. What works with one pupil may not yield the same reaction or results with another. The teacher should also check the effectiveness of what he does as it influences learners or fails to do so. Constant evaluation of teaching effectiveness will do much in helping the teacher to become a professional of the highest order.

**Learning Is an Active Process.** As a first guideline it is appropriate to begin with the active involvement of the learner. Learning by doing is an old cliché, but it is true. A major criticism of earlier ideas of learning was their tendency to emphasize doing things *to* the learner and their failure to see the many ways in which he had to be an active ingredient of the process. Too much use of lecturing is an illustration of this type of teaching error.

Many ways of involvement are possible, such as reading, constructing, manipulating, imagining, reflecting, thinking, problem solving, and listening. *The keynote is thoughtful activity.* Merely doing something is not enough; doing and reflecting on the doing are essential. Vicarious and first-hand experience are useful and should supplement one another. Teachers should be careful that they do not do too much for pupils and thereby rob them of essential discovery, verification, application, and speculation as these and other activities enable the individual to learn on his own and to become effective at learning.

Readiness Is Basic to Effective Learning. There are times when the individual is better able to learn and times when he is less ready and able. Background, apperception, mind set, maturation, needs, drives, and many other interrelated factors influence the readiness of the learner for the activity proposed for him. Forcing pupils when they are not ready is often harmful; and the results are almost always discouraging to teachers, learners, and parents. Such pressure may retard the development of readiness and create feelings in the learner inimical to future study of the subject under consideration.

The teacher's initial work with pupils may well include checking on readiness and working to create it when it does not exist at an appropriate level. Developing reading readiness is an example. At the same time, one should not blame all failure to learn on lack of readiness nor use this condition to excuse learners from productive activity. Teachers should not use lack of readiness as a dodge, either. There are other types of roadblocks to learning, such as problems at home, non-school interests, or plain laziness, with which the teacher must learn to cope. Effectiveness of initial learning, retention, and application, and total economy of time and effort are affected greatly by the readiness of the learner and the ability of the teacher to create, maintain, and utilize it.

Background Is Fundamental to Meaningful Learning. Related to readiness, the background of the learner is important to new learning. In a sense it provides a foundation upon which to build, a base from which to range intellectually, and to which to fasten new ideas and practices. A frequent failure of new teachers is their assumption that learners have an adequate background because they studied the subject last year or last month.

Unless one has adequate background, he is not apt to see meaning in new educational experiences. It is helpful if the teacher will regard *meaning as a function of the learner* more than as a characteristic of that which is to be learned. Actually there is no meaning except as the individual comes to see it himself. Too much teaching today requires pupils to accept what is taught without meaning and understanding. This condition results in frustration and distaste, if not hatred, of learning. Teaching should take into account individual differences in background and build toward adequacy as a basis for effective and rewarding learning.

**Apperception and Mind Set Influence Learning.** One's attitude and mental and emotional outlook bear heavily on the learning process. Related sometimes to background, feelings of inadequacy may rest largely upon a recognition or belief of unpreparedness. The learner may also be intent upon some activity of his own that is not remotely connected with the proposed learning activity. In this case interruption will be unwelcome, especially if the individual's interests are high and his personal activity is satisfying. The young child engaged in play may not even hear the bell signaling the end of recess. The troubled adolescent worried by personal or home problems may resent having to put aside matters of vital concern to him for study of material in which he sees no possible value. Or he may want to put his troubles aside but somehow is unable to do so.

Individual and group expectancy also color the learner's reaction in a learning situation. The mood of the group may be contrary to settling down to work, especially if group leaders feel this way. An individual's feeling that he is likely to fail at what is proposed is apt to make itself felt in a negative attitude or possibly in evasive action, for example, misbehavior or truancy that removes him from the situation. Fear affects learners more than is often realized.

The learner's mind set influences the process of active involvement. If he is eager to get on with the job and has developed good attitudes toward himself and learning, the battle is more than half won. On the other hand, he may misread statements because of his frame of mind or react negatively to stimuli that usually elicit a favorable response. Seeking to succeed with confidence based on past success, his determination matches the challenge. Trying to succeed in the face of previous failure and/or present doubt, his spirits flag and his efficiency drops. Teachers face a regular and real challenge in properly committing pupils to the learning tasks at hand. To this end the apperception and mind set of the learner merit much attention.

**Interest and Effort Support Each Other and Foster Effective Learning.**[1] Effort is basic to effective activity in any endeavor. Without reason-

[1] For details, see: John Dewey, *Interest and Effort in Education* (Boston: Houghton Mifflin Co., 1913).

able effort there is likely to be no desirable development. Children and youth tend to shun tasks that are too easy. Prolonged exposure to such activity develops bad attitudes and lazy habits of acting and thinking. At the other extreme, learning that is too difficult and re- quires more effort than pupils can put forth (or more than is reasonable to expect of them) generally results in failure plus discouragement of all concerned. If quantity is mistaken for quality, as it often is, teachers may defeat the very ends they seek through senseless re- quirements that even able pupils will not meet.

Interest is vital and satisfying in its own right. It is also related closely to effort. The interested learner is better able to sustain effort than the disinterested one. Effort, especially if it is successful, gen- erates interest and the latter supports the former. One who watches learners at work in successful endeavor can see the levels of interest and effort fluctuate together.

Teacher concern for interest and effort is important. Determining individual interests, needs, and wants provides one base from which to move forward. The relationship of proposed learning goals to the learner's goals is helpful. Deferred goals may thus be brought into the picture more appropriately than otherwise, and horizons may be broadened. The development of each learner to his fullest requires constant use of interest and effort, even when discouragement and drudgery are encountered in learning. Teachers should set the tone and help with the pacing so as to assist learners in retaining faith in themselves and in what they are doing.

**Meaningful Drill and Spaced Repetition Are Helpful.** The newer psy- chologies do not eliminate the importance and usefulness of drill and repetition. It is essential, however, that these measures be handled appropriately. Drill that is not meaningful does little for the learner and may only aggravate him. Repetition that is not spaced with proper mental reinforcing in between may increase temporary learn- ing only to weaken retention.

Factors of recency and effect are involved in this situation. Recall of recent meaningful experiences is usually better than of those more distant in the past. The cumulative effect of spaced repetition is generally greater than that of one or two concentrated doses. The type of learning also influences the application of these factors. Re- learning is usually easier than initial learning, unless this first ex- posure was bad or the actual learning in error. If correction must be accomplished, a more complicated problem is involved. The importance of guidance to insure correct initial learning should not be overlooked.

The key words in this discussion are *meaning* and *spaced*, for these concepts give vitality and cumulative effect to drill and repetition. More is said later of cultivation and coverage as these ideas relate to learning and articulation.

**Association, Application, and Transfer Require Specific Attention.** Through proper association of old learning and new, the learner's concepts may be enlarged, modified, and strengthened. Varied application of what is learned serves to strengthen command of theory and may also help to develop the learner's ability to diagnose specific situations and employ proper principles and procedures. Within reason, the more one can associate and apply specifically what is learned, the better he learns it, and the more likely it is that transfer of training will come about. Teaching should aim to foster such transfer by attention to the specific situations in which it is expected.

Insight should be watched for and cultivated whenever possible. The structuring of learning situations so that the learner may look ahead, speculate on his own without too much or too little guidance, analyze and synthesize, and test out his own hypotheses is very important. Attitudes, skills, ideals, and other attributes of behavior should be sought when possible in situations similar to those in which it is expected they will subsequently be used.

**Purpose, Progress, and Motivation Are Interrelated.** Reference was made earlier to individual interests, needs, and purposes. These matters are important to the learner's activity and to the whole endeavor of teaching. The learner who believes that his own ends are being served by the learning activity is more apt to apply himself than is the learner who sees study as unrelated to himself. The former is intrinsically motivated, and this fact helps to sustain his effort. The latter will require motivation, probably of an external type at first, as the teacher seeks to initiate interest that will lead to intrinsic motivation.

Progress that the learner accepts and regards as desirable also helps a great deal in keeping him moving toward the purposes or objectives sought. Satisfaction and annoyance are involved, nothing probably being so ineffective in learning as an experience that neither satisfies nor annoys. *Knowledge of success and failure is important, together with reasons that are acceptable and meaningful.*

More success than failure is essential, otherwise discouragement develops and may lead to complete failure of the educative process. At the same time, some failure is probably good for all learners. They should be helped to learn from failure, which is a valuable lesson in itself. Able pupils who realize that they have done poorly should be helped to this realization by teachers. To credit them with a satisfactory performance in such circumstances is most unfair and unwise.

Grades, marks, warnings, threats, awards of various types, punishment, and other devices are often employed to motivate learners. Excessive and unwise usage is common, especially where pressures for scholarships are heavy. Threats are of dubious value at any time, and punishment for poor performance often serves to complicate its remedy. Care is essential in the use of all manner of external motivation, with the view of strengthening intrinsic motivation. This statement does not mean that external means should never be used, but rather that they be used when other appeals fail and in a manner leading toward eventual inner motivation of the learner by himself.

### The Roles of the Modern Teacher

The modern teacher plays many roles in facilitating learning. The guidelines offer much direction to his endeavor; indeed their effectiveness rests with his employment of them. Such application is more difficult than avowal in theory, and circumstances do not always help. The teacher must, therefore, have considerable courage and wise determination. Older and more experienced teachers sometimes try to "orientaint" new teachers in dissuading them from using what they have learned about teaching and learning. Initial attempts at using such knowledge are not always successful; but as he gains experience through sustained application, the new teacher will develop proficiency and reap the rewards that come with it.

Selection and Thoroughness in Learning. With each passing day, there is more to be learned. No one person can keep up with the rapidly accumulating human heritage. New knowledge changes old knowledge, often modifying the truth as it has been known. Old values no longer serve as well as they once did. Needs change, but the structures developed to meet them persist and often resist change. The importance of choice in learning and of thoroughness is highlighted against this background.

Teachers frequently feel pressured to complete a book from cover to cover or to run the full length of the course of study. Coverage is important to articulation and subsequent learning, but thoroughness should not be sacrificed. Superficial coverage is deceptive and results in so little retention as to be damaging in many cases. Substantial mastery of less and more important coverage is preferable. One cannot learn everything; but in learning significant things well, he becomes able to learn more on his own and develops the will to do so. To learn less and to understand more is a tricky thought worth pondering.

Gaps resulting from selectivity can be minimized if proper overall long range educational planning is accomplished. Broad superficial coverage does not eliminate gaps either; indeed it may loom a garment more noticeable for the holes than for the cloth. It is better that the gaps result from planning so that learners can be apprised as to what they have missed, rather than being misled to believe that they have encompassed a great deal more than they really have.

**Developing the Independent Learner.**   One of the chief hallmarks of a well-educated man is that he continues to study and learn regardless of the degrees he has earned. Whether he returns to school periodically or not, such a person seeks to learn on his own without having to be pushed and aided by others. His earlier schooling has laid a foundation and provided him with the will and the ways to learn lifelong. This objective should be a goal toward which every teacher moves his pupils while they are with him.

The effective independent learner has an educated curiosity and a high but reasonable expectation of himself as a scholar. The scholarship he practices is not necessarily remote from reality; quite the contrary, it is apt to be practical more than theoretical. He seeks excellence in his life—his home, his job, his recreation, his every endeavor. He learns about these things continually and uses what he learns in reaching decisions. Learning looms large in his life and gives him much satisfaction.

**Achieving the Highest Potential.**   Manpower needs and the quest for individual fulfillment call for education that helps each and every person attain his best. Attention to individual differences is imperative and should be followed up by teaching that is hopeful, encouraging, and insisting. Human resources are more valuable than any others. Probably developed and utilized, they yield a great dividend on the investment. Neglected, they become an expensive liability—

to self and others. We cannot afford the latter development, yet many conditions promote its existence. The challenge to able and dedicated teachers is tremendous.

**The Many Instructional Roles.** The teacher is first of all a *teaching scholar*. He continues to study, keeping up to date in his subject fields and in how best to handle them and his learners. He studies his pupils and the environment in which they live and learn, seeking to be of real professional service whenever he can. He cultivates other teachers and persons with whom he works, conscious of group impact and the need for articulation. His learning extends beyond his own field to the liberal areas close to men's living together, and he draws richness from all possible sources for wise use in his profession as a teacher.

The teacher is also a *planner, organizer, administrator,* and *disciplinarian.* To plan ahead—goals, appropriate content, useful materials for teaching and learning, schedule of activities, proper methodology, and so on—requires much time and effort. Some of this endeavor is done alone; much involves working with others. He arranges for others to help with teaching, for example, resource personnel from business and industry. He maintains order conducive to learning and uses discipline as a means of education rather than as a punishment. The records and reports for which he is responsible, and those which he uses, call for administrative as well as instructional ability. The managerial demands made on the teacher are many, both in curricular and extracurricular endeavor.

The teacher is also an *executor of plans,* an *instructor* who teaches in the finest sense of the term. He can lecture well when this activity is called for. He can work with small groups and with individuals. At times he is a *stimulator,* a *catalyst.* On other occasions he is a *troubleshooter,* or he may even be a devil's advocate or an obstructionist with a constructive purpose. He is a resource himself and a tireless worker in the instructional process.

The teacher is an *evaluator,* both of pupil development and the educative process, including his own roles and contributions. He utilizes pretesting as well as post-testing and knows what to do for relearning and for correcting errors in learning and in teaching. He is concerned with results and how to improve them, never denying his legitimate responsibility for lack of learning when it is revealed.

The teacher is a *friend* and a *counselor.* He likes people and seeks to help them, recognizing his own limitations and using other resources that are available. His interest is not limited to his subject

First-hand experiences add meaning to learning. (Alhambra, California, Public Schools.)

fields nor to what he can get learners to do for him. His relationships with pupils are proper; he does not impose upon them nor let them presume upon him.

The teacher is a *person and citizen* in his own right. He has a life of his own apart from the school or college and his job. He accepts his duties as a citizen and exercises his rights. He joins with others in endeavor vital to the commonwealth. He respects others who deserve it and conducts himself so as to be respected, and he lives fully within the law and social codes applicable to society. He does not put upon others nor let others mistreat him.

## THE SCHOOL POPULATION

No nation is as school conscious as is the United States of America. Nowhere has the popularization of education extended as far up the educational ladder as here. Our expectations of education are not exceeded anywhere. The need for highly educated talent is documented in this book. These interrelated conditions and the various manifestations of them combine to give us a higher percentage of population in school and college than can be found anywhere in the world.

With such a high percentage seeking an education, variation and diversity are inescapable. Healthy and unhealthy, bright and not so bright, eager and reluctant, with plans and without, able to afford schooling and not able, with home support and against home opposition—pupils with these and many other conflicting characteristics are crowding schools and colleges today. What they expect, what they are capable of, what the country needs of them, and what they are willing to make of themselves are all questions that complicate their own and the lives of those who seek to help them become educated.

## Population, Enrollment, Attendance, and Retention

Various sets of statistics are available on population, enrollment, attendance, and retention. These figures depend upon reports from various sources, and they are subject to error. Nonetheless, the available data today reveal a growing challenge of numbers in education at all levels.

Figures from Table 2–1 show that in 1960 the total population of the United States, excluding armed forces overseas, was 179,323,000. Of this total 24.5 per cent were school-age children (five to seventeen years inclusive) making a group of 43,881,000. For almost a century, the U.S. Office of Education has collected statistics, over which period there has been a tremendous increase in school-age population. In general, however, the relative increase in school-age population has not matched that of the total population, due to declining mortality at both extremes of the life span. Over this near-century the total population has multiplied by more than four, while the school-age population multiplied more than three times. The data in Table 2–1 reveal the growth of various features pertinent to population, enrollment, and attendance.

It is apparent that the percentage of the total population of school age declined steadily from 30.3 in 1869–1870 to 20.3 in 1949–1950. In the last two decades it has been increasing, the birth rate jumping upward immediately after World War II. The increase will likely continue through the present decade at a decreasing rate. An estimated enrollment in 1962–1963 of 39,700,000 pupils in public elementary and secondary schools presents the enormity of the educational task in terms of numbers.

## TABLE 2–1

Brief Historical Summary of Public Elementary and Secondary School Statistics, 1869–1870 to 1959–1960

| | 1869–1870 | 1889–1890 | 1909–1910 | 1929–1930 | 1949–1950 | 1959–1960 |
|---|---|---|---|---|---|---|
| Total population (thousands) | 39,818 | 62,948 | 90,492 | 121,770 | 148,665 | 179,323 |
| School-age population (5–17 inclusive, thousands) | 12,055 | 18,543 | 24,009 | 31,417 | 30,168 | 43,881 |
| Percentage of total population of school age | 30.3 | 29.5 | 26.5 | 25.8 | 20.3 | 24.5 |
| Total enrollment in elementary and secondary day schools (thousands) | 6,872 | 12,723 | 17,814 | 25,678 | 25,111 | 36,087 |
| Nursery, kindergarten, grades 1–8 (thousands) | 6,792 | 12,520 | 16,899 | 21,279 | 19,387 | 27,602 |
| Grades 9–12 and postgraduate (thousands) | 80 | 203 | 915 | 4,399 | 5,725 | 8,485 |
| Percentage of total population enrolled | 17.3 | 20.2 | 19.7 | 21.1 | 16.9 | 20.1 |
| Percentage of school-age population enrolled | 57.0 | 68.6 | 74.2 | 81.7 | 83.2 | 82.2 |
| Average length of school term (days) | 132.2 | 134.7 | 157.5 | 172.7 | 177.9 | 178.0 |
| Average number of days attended by each enrolled pupil | 78.4 | 86.3 | 113.0 | 143.0 | 157.9 | 160.2 |
| Percentage of enrolled pupils attending daily | 59.3 | 64.1 | 72.1 | 82.8 | 88.7 | 90.0 |
| Number of high school graduates (thousands) | – | 22 | 111 | 592 | 1,063 | 1,627 |

SOURCE: Carol J. Hobson and Samuel Schloss, *Statistics of State School Systems, 1959–60* (Washington, D.C.: U.S. Department of Health, Education and Welfare, Office of Education, 1963), Circular 691, p. 21 (adapted).

The percentage of school-age population enrolled in public schools reveals a steady increase from 57 per cent in 1869–1870 to 82.2 per cent in 1959–1960. If enrollment includes public and non-public schools, the figures are improved, reaching a total of 89 per cent in 1960. A breakdown of enrollment within the school-age population group is presented in Table 2–2.

### TABLE 2–2

Percentage of School-Age Population Enrolled in Public and Non-Public Schools, 1910 to 1960

| Age Group | 1910 | 1920 | 1930 | 1940 | 1950 | 1960 |
|---|---|---|---|---|---|---|
| Total: 5–17 years . . . . | 69.3 | 74.1 | 80.4 | 82.5 | 85.2 | 89.0 |
| Total: 5–13 years . . . . | 73.8 | 79.0 | 83.5 | 84.1 | 85.8 | 89.5 |
| 5 and 6 years . . . . . | 34.6 | 41.0 | 43.2 | 43.0 | 55.6 | 63.7 |
| 7 to 13 years . . . . . | 86.1 | 90.6 | 95.3 | 95.0 | 95.7 | 97.5 |
| Total: 14–17 years . . . . | 58.9 | 61.6 | 73.1 | 79.3 | 83.7 | 87.4 |
| 14 and 15 years . . . . | 75.0 | 79.9 | 88.8 | 90.0 | 92.9 | 94.1 |
| 16 and 17 years . . . . | 43.1 | 42.9 | 57.3 | 68.7 | 74.4 | 80.9 |

Source: Carol J. Hobson and Samuel Schloss, *Statistics of State School Systems, 1959–60* (Washington, D.C.: U.S. Department of Health, Education and Welfare, Office of Education, 1963), Circular 691, Table B, p. 6.

Statistics provided by the National Education Association reveal other interesting and noteworthy progress in education. For example, the number of high school graduates for each one hundred persons seventeen years of age has been increasing steadily since 1920,[2] as shown in Fig. 2–1.

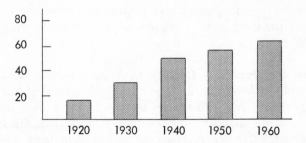

Fig. 2–1. High School Graduates Per One Hundred Persons Seventeen Years of Age

[2] "Interesting Facts and Figures on American Education," *NEA Research Bulletin*, XLI, No. 1 (February, 1963), 5.

As more youth complete high school, more are also going on to college. Of each 1,000 fifth-graders in 1951–1952, 604 completed high school and 319 went on to college in the autumn of 1960. Of the 417 (out of a thousand) graduating from high school in 1938, only 148 entered college the same fall.[3] The college-age population (ages eighteen to twenty-one inclusive) stood at 6 million in 1900. Reaching a peak of 9.7 million in 1940, it dropped to 8.6 million in 1955 and began a steady rise to 10.2 million in 1961. By 1970 it is expected to reach 14.4 million. Enrollment figures in higher education add to the magnitude of the total educational task: [4]

|                                        | 1900    | 1930      | 1961      |
|----------------------------------------|---------|-----------|-----------|
| Enrollment . . . . . . . . .           | 238,000 | 1,100,000 | 3,861,000 |
| Per cent of college-age population     | 4       | 12.4      | 37.7      |

It is anticipated that growth in terms of both numbers and percentage will continue to increase throughout the next several decades. High dropout rates in many colleges and universities are a cause for concern. This complicated problem should be studied nationally. Research of smaller scope is really inadequate to gaining a clear picture of what is happening and why.

### Factors Affecting the Attained Educational Level

Although high school graduation is now virtually a theoretical tradition in the United States, one in every three ninth-graders fails to graduate. Slightly more than half of our fifth-graders complete high school. These statistics are not encouraging in the light of the manpower needs of the country nor as regards the self-realization of individuals. Juvenile delinquency also causes great concern, and it is about 1,000 per cent more common among dropouts than among graduates.[5]

**Education and Vocational Opportunity.** The declining demand for unskilled labor and the growing need for highly educated talent exert much influence on youth to remain in school. More than this, these conditions call for diversity in education to meet diversity in needs and to encourage larger percentages to complete high school and college. Figures and trends make what should be a convincing case.

[3] *Ibid.*, p. 5.

[4] *Ibid.*, p. 7.

[5] "High-School Drop-outs," *NEA Research Bulletin*, XXXVIII, No. 1 (February, 1960), 11.

Trends in the occupational distribution of workers are shown in Fig. 2–2.[6]

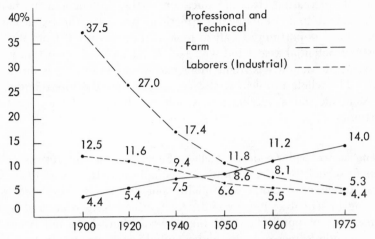

Fig. 2–2. The Vocational Distribution of Workers.

United States census reports for 1960 indicate that professional and technical personnel (the group requiring the most education) are increasing more rapidly than other categories: [7]

| 1950 | . . . . . . | 5.0 million |
| 1960 | . . . . . . | 7.5 million |
| 1970 | . . . . . . | 10.0 million (estimated) |

In 1950 these workers made up 8 per cent of the employed population, and it is estimated that by 1970 this figure will increase to over 12.5 per cent. Combined with the declining need for unskilled and uneducated workers, there is growing pressure for increasing education.

It is generally recognized also that individual income is related positively to educational level. A college graduate can normally expect to earn above $400,000 in a lifetime, while a person with less than an eighth-grade education is apt to earn less than $130,000. More details on income and education are given in Chapter 3.

[6] Data for 1900–1950 taken from David L. Kaplan and Claire M. Casey, *Occupational Trends in the United States, 1900 to 1950* (Washington, D.C.: U.S. Department of Commerce, Bureau of Census, 1958), Working Paper No. 5, Table 2, p. 7. Figures for 1960 and 1975 from U.S. Department of Labor, Bureau of Labor Statistics (actual 1960, estimated 1975).

[7] *Occupational Outlook Handbook* (Washington, D.C.: U.S. Department of Labor, Bureau of Labor Statistics, 1961), p. 24.

**Economic Status and Educational Progress.** The economic status of the pupil and his family has much bearing on his remaining in school, especially in the upper levels and in college. For this reason the currently increasing costs of education to the student and his family are a threat to a fundamental American principle—the extension of educational opportunity to all so long as they can profit from it. The waste of potential associated with lack of educational opportunity due to economic inability is tremendous and tragic; indeed, it is un-American. The whole problem is also complicated by the interrelationship of economic status, intelligence, scholastic ability, and vocational opportunity.

**Intelligence and Academic Ability.** Success in school fosters retention in school, but this condition is complicated by a variety of factors. Intelligence alone is probably not as closely correlated with staying in school as is supposed. As increases have occurrred in the percentage of pupils finishing high school, there have not been any corresponding increases in higher intelligence levels. It has been noted however that dropouts are, on the average, of somewhat less-measured intelligence and do less well in school. The average I.Q. also tends to be slightly higher from the seventh grade on through college.

Retardation, failure, discouragement, and other conditions that cause students discomfort and embarrassment also increase the likelihood of dropouts. Failure to challenge students, especially brighter ones, also encourages withdrawal. The importance of recognizing individual differences and of rich educational opportunity commensurate with ability is clear, but is not infrequently neglected in our schools and colleges.

**Health and Disability.** Also cogent to education is the health and vitality of the individual. While these conditions perhaps contribute alone to no significant percentage of dropouts, they do influence greatly the motivation of the learner and the satisfaction and success derived from school. And some who drop out do have health problems. Attention to mental health has become increasingly important as the tensions of living and learning have increased. A sane society cannot be made up of sick individuals. Provisions for the handicapped have served to help greatly in their education, but a much greater effort is called for today and in the years ahead.

**Home-School Conditions and Relationships.** Beyond the economic and occupational conditions that influence the home and its members, the climate regarding education is important. Family interests and expectations, the level of compatibility and affection, cultural interests, and related conditions serve to encourage or discourage school attendance and success. School conditions and programs are also very important. Attractive schools with adequate teaching-learning facilities and supplies, competent and interested teachers, challenging educational programs, and a total environment that is conducive to learning are quite significant. The relationship of home and school is also important. If both work cooperatively in demonstrating a personal interest in the learner and in his success, the likelihood of retention and progress is enhanced a great deal.

**Nationality and Race.** Both nationality and race relate to school attendance and vocational opportunity. Over the years, Negroes have not remained in school as long as whites, nor have foreign-born children remained as long in school as native white children. As both educational and vocational opportunity improve in relation to each other and are extended without discrimination, these children remain longer in school and tend to perform at higher levels. Social legislation that encourages school attendance has had definite influence also, but attending school and learning are not the same thing.

Pupils of different nationalities and races often have cultural differences that may cause some problem of assimilation, especially if these pupils are in great minority and are in school situations that do not provide for their needs. Differences in ability, interest, expectation, and so on, are the result, largely if not entirely, of environmental and cultural differences. The public schools serve as a great melting pot through the medium of which pupils from any and all backgrounds should have rich educational opportunity that provides for social migration and productive living.

**Other Influential Factors.** Where pupils live has some bearing on school attendance and the duration of their formal education. In the rural areas, there are still some pressures to free older children from school during planting, cultivating, and harvesting seasons. Legislation has helped some, but has not eliminated the basic problem. Migrant workers and others dependent upon seasonal labor often find school attendance and the need for children to work to be in sharp conflict.

In the upper years of high school, girls tend to persist somewhat better than boys. This situation does not obtain in higher education, although in some situations the number of young women exceeds that of young men. Compulsory school laws have great influence on attendance. When one views the educational developments of the past century, it is apparent that much progress in school attandance, length of school year, and related matters has been made. Higher-quality educational experience and more of it for greater numbers of people make up a requirement of modern living hard to refute, although it may not be met.

## Variation Among School-Age Personnel

Earlier sections of this chapter point to ways in which individuals differ. The social situations from which they come vary also and serve to enlarge upon the differences with which the schools and colleges must work. A few brief observations are pertinent on this point.

Differences in intelligence are usual and, within a single grade or class, may extend over a range of mental ages of five or six years, possibly higher in secondary schools and colleges. Homogeneous grouping and other measures to provide for differences of this and other types are employed in educational institutions at all levels.

Girls entering school are usually somewhat more mature than boys; and the early school environment, including teachers, seems often to be more attuned to them than boys. Differences in physical strength, interests, parental and pupil expectations, temperament, and related characteristics do exist between boys and girls, but also among the membership of each group. Cultural and other environmental and selective factors contribute to ethnic differences that are apparent in schools with a cosmopolitan student body. As an illustration, the great respect for education common to orientals, such as the Japanese, is observable in the behavior and accomplishment of their children in school.

While promotional policies have fostered homogeneity in chronological age among pupils at the same grade levels, there is often considerable difference in maturation and educational achievement. Girls usually mature earlier, possibly as much as one to two years. Brighter children mature somewhat earlier than dull ones. Negroes and children of Mediterranean nationalities also tend to mature somewhat earlier. Social maturity varies as well as physiological and emotional maturity. Various special aptitudes, for example, in art, music, reading, mathematics, or athletics, appear at different times, often as a result of opportunity or lack of opportunity. Home and school pressures influence these conditions and the attitudes of learners toward themselves and school.

Achievement in learning varies also, especially where mass education exists as it does in the United States. The operation of selectivity affects all kinds of variation. In European schools where selectivity is normally associated with elimination from school, the differences in scholastic ability and achievement in school would be reduced in comparison to ours.

The education of exceptional children extends the range of variation in terms of all manner of conditions, both positive and negative. Gifted children challenge the schools at one end of the spectrum. Some of these pupils are ambitious as well as able and need little motivation. Others are underachievers and may be retarded. Slow learners, handicapped children, and various combinations of abilities and disabilities make for a challenging situation as regards all learners.

The vitality of individuals varies a great deal. Nutritional and physiological conditions bear on the ability and interest of learners. Organic disorders and those related to emotional conditions influence the total behavior of children and youth, not just their learning.

In the detailed study of the learner and learning, the topic of variation should be stressed. Herein the significance of the topic lies in alerting the reader to the diversity that exists among those who attend school and college, and in pointing up the importance of dealing with individual differences wisely so that both individual fulfillment and the commonweal may be served.

## QUESTIONS, PROBLEMS, AND PROJECTS FOR FURTHER STUDY

1. Discuss the interdependency of organic evolution and social evolution, defending the thesis that each is essential to the other.

2. What are the major implications for education of the statement that man's hereditary background and makeup do not determine his specific behavior nor commit him to predetermined decisions?

3. It has been said that "universal values" relate closely to the biopsychological bases of life. Expand on this thesis and its implications for education.

4. Examine briefly the various concepts about learning and the outmoded theories of education in the light of more recent psychological explanations. How do you explain the persistence of the earlier ideas?

5. Look into human growth and development as it pertains specifically to an age-level group that you are interested in teaching. Characterize this group briefly as regards physical and mental maturation and suggest implications for teaching-learning.

6. Make a list of guidelines for teaching and learning in your own words. Develop each of these in terms of how you would apply it in teaching the age level and subjects that you propose to instruct.

7. Schools are frequently criticized for attending too much to non-intellectual matters and not enough to intellectual. Discuss such a criticism thoroughly in the light of teaching and learning.

8. It has been said by some sincere persons that knowing what to teach is important and that knowing how to teach accompanies the former. What is your reaction to such a statement?

9. What do you see as a sort of "triple threat" challenge to education as you study school population in the light of educational needs?

10. What specific suggestions can you offer to reduce dropouts and improve the holding power of secondary and higher schools?

11. What are some major implications of variation among learners for you as a teacher? Be specific in terms of your proposed grade level or subject.

## SELECTED SUPPLEMENTARY READINGS AND FILMS

BALLER, WARREN R., and CHARLES, DON C. *The Psychology of Human Growth and Development.* New York: Holt, Rinehart & Winston, Inc., 1961. Part I. Presents the teacher's need for psychology and discusses basic ideas in understanding learners; includes the nature of the scientific method in psychology.

BLAIR, GLENN M., JONES, R. STEWART, and SIMPSON, ROY H. *Educational Psychology.* New York: The Macmillan Co., 1962. Part I. Relates psychology and the work of the teacher and discusses biological and social bases of behavior.

COOPER, RUSSELL M. (ed.). *The Two Ends of the Log.* Minneapolis: University of Minnesota Press, 1958. Pp. 3–35. Discusses the student and how he learns at the collegiate level.

CRONBACH, LEE J. *Educational Psychology.* 2d ed. New York: Harcourt, Brace & World, Inc., 1963. Part I. Presents the contribution of psychology to education, sets forth the job of teachers, and provides an introduction to the learning process.

DEWEY, JOHN. *Democracy and Education.* New York: The Macmillan Co., 1916. Chaps. iv, v, and x. Deals with education as growth; presents fallacies of theories of education as preparation, unfolding, and formal discipline; and discusses interest and effort.

————. *Interest and Effort in Education.* Boston: Houghton Mifflin Co., 1913. This small book discusses interest and effort as interrelated aspects of the learning process.

FISKE, JOHN. *The Meaning of Infancy.* Boston: Houghton Mifflin Co., 1911. Presents the meaning of infancy in relation to the education and evolution of man.

FRANDSEN, ARDEN N. *Educational Psychology.* New York: McGraw-Hill Book Co., Inc., 1961. Part I. Deals with educational psychology in the learning process and offers an integration of theories of learning.

HIGHET, GILBERT. *Man's Unconquerable Mind*. New York: Columbia University Press, 1954. Deals with the powers and limits of the human mind and the importance of dedicated intellect to human progress.

*Learning and the Teacher*. 1959 Yearbook, Association for Supervision and Curriculum Development. Washington, D.C.: National Education Association. Part I. Discusses the facilitation of learning by the teacher and presents characteristics of the learner and his environment that influence learning.

McDONALD, FREDERICK J. *Educational Psychology*. Belmont, Calif.: Wadsworth Publishing Co., Inc., 1959. Part I. Deals with the nature of the educative process and the roles of the learner and the teacher.

WHITEHEAD, ALFRED N. *The Aims of Education*. New York: The New American Library of World Literature, Inc., 1929. Chap. ii. Discusses learning in terms of the rhythm of education from infancy to adulthood.

## Films

*Dynamic Learning*. 20 minutes. Professor Kilpatrick speaks on concepts of learning, authoritarian versus progressive, and their results. New York: Columbia University.

*Learning and Behavior*. 26 minutes. Reveals the measurement of learning and deals with learning as dependent upon reinforcement of a learned response; includes experiments. New York: Carousel Films.

# THE SOCIAL FOUNDATIONS
# OF EDUCATION

Intradependency and interdependency are conditions of life. It has been established that neither organic evolution nor social evolution can continue alone in the absence of the other. Numerous groups have been suggested as emerging in man's culture and serving the progress of civilization. The society of men and their educability thus triumph or fall together.

## SOCIAL ORGANIZATION AND EDUCATION

It is generally recognized that while man's biological basis is fundamental, his progress as a humane creature rests primarily in the social sphere wherein his native capabilities find expression and his needs are met. While some social contacts arise by accident, man consciously seeks to order his relationships with others. Elaborate schemes are built upon simpler ones, until today we hear and use such terms as "organization man" and "other directed." In various and effective ways, social organization and education are interrelated.

### Social Organization and Human Life

Group life is characteristic of most living things. Even among plants the solitary organism is less typical than those that grow in groups, however incidental or influential the organization may be among the individual members. Among animals the varying degrees of social organization are more obvious, for example, as regards colonies of insects, schools of fish, herds of deer or elk, flocks of ducks or geese, and families of apes. Groups tend to form in terms of common characteristics, tendencies, and needs, thus assuring the means of meeting the requirements of those included, such as food, reproduction, and protection. Both individual and social behavior are observable in the lives of those who live in such groups.

Of all living creatures man is the most social. Groups are not only possible because of man's dependency and pattern of genetic advantages, they are imperative to survival and development. In his being and responding, gregariousness is a universal characteristic common to all races, colors, and creeds. Simple or elaborate, the forms of social organization serve to develop man in accordance with the society in which he recognizes himself as living.

## Advantages or Benefits of Social Groups

Social organization exists to promote the well-being of the group and its individual members. Well-being is not defined the same in all societies, nor do these groups all aspire to the same goals. In complex societies membership may involve individuals in competing groups or in groups that operate differently. Exploitation of individuals by groups is not uncommon, and individuals frequently use groups for their personal advantage. The situation may be quite complex, and the advantages attributable to social groups depend upon the manner in which the membership is permitted to participate and does participate. Benefits are not usually automatic. Common to social groups, however, are certain related values and processes that provide a basis for accomplishments not otherwise attainable.

*Security* is a principal gain of social groups. This condition may be an inner personal satisfaction of the individual who, in allegiance with others, feels safer and more secure than when he is alone. It may extend beyond a few cronies to small group membership. In the process of social evolution, smaller groups have banded together to broaden the basis of security and to strengthen it. Such organization and reorganization has continued throughout history. Today, the United Nations is representative of an effort to unite in one group the family of man, as a means of extending security and providing a basis for other advantages of large social organization. But even this group limits membership in accordance with criteria and the disposition of the voting members.

Many kinds of security are involved in group membership; for example, physical, emotional, economic, and political. Individuals usually belong to more than one group. At times, internal conflict ensues as a result of the clashing of the differing objectives, views, or procedures of several groups to which one belongs. Conflict between groups also occurs as each is bent upon assuring the security and advancement of its membership.

*Cooperative endeavor* is also an advantage of social organization. Often, especially in our confused and rapidly changing world today, the welfare of one is dependent upon the well-being of all. This condition extends beyond security into many aspects of life. Within social groups differences must be minimized to the extent of promoting essential group solidarity. Beyond this cohesiveness, however, groups provide a means of broadening the basis of cooperation in working toward larger common goals. Monetary systems, schools, business, industry, government, trade, and many other ventures can exist only as there are groups through which cooperation is facilitated.

The complexity of cooperative activity increases with the number and size of groups and the consequent need for some central principles to which all groups subscribe. This endeavor relates to security and to other advantages that are possible of attainment through social groups. In a pluralistic society, such as that in the United States of America, cooperation that does not result in the extinction of all group differences has become a constant challenge. Conformity and orthodoxy result from extensive cooperation that permits no differences or deviations.

*Differentiation and specialization* are possible only in social groups. Creativity and invention are fostered in a society where a division of labor is possible. This differentiation focuses effort and releases energy to be concentrated in areas of special ability and interest. Balanced properly with other conditions possible through social organization, differentiation and specialization promote satisfying living and foster social evolution.

Together with cooperation, these activities permit the development of harmony among divergent groups or members of groups. The strengths of individuals are possible of greater realization, and even the collective strengths of groups may be utilized more fully in a society that properly utilizes differentiation and specialization. The exercise of these activities, in turn, promotes the development of types of social organization that facilitate or are believed to foster the development of differentiation and specialization. The danger of going to extremes faces any modern technological society.

*Competition and opposition,* possible among solitary organisms, take on new dimensions in the presence of and through social groups.

Both the nature and result of the process are altered as social organization is involved. Competition and other forms of opposition may be an advantage or a disadvantage, depending largely upon the purpose and manner of operation. As an illustration, competition may stimulate individual and group development. Carried to extremes, it can kill individual initiative and group interest.

Through social organizations man also exercises controls over competition and opposition, seeking to have each serve the members. Codes of ethics and values for living frequently reflect such self-imposed controls. Social groups are also used to provide desirable and constructive outlets for feelings of opposition and for the development of disciplines that enable individuals to harness the energy loosed by these feelings.

*Adjustment,* individual and group, is influenced by social organization. Whenever interaction is involved, the process of self-adjustment is both complicated and facilitated. Such adjustment is dynamic, not static. It does not imply, as many critics of adjustment infer, the willing acceptance of things just as they are and a leveling off of mental and physical activity on low planes of mediocre identity. Adjustment necessitates assessment of individual attributes in a social context and the use of these attributes in a constructive manner. It requires, also, that one be capable of remaining reasonably "adjusted" while being out of tune with some aspects of living. Both equilibrium and dis-equilibrium are involved.

Social organization broadens the framework in which adjustment is to be accomplished. Customs, mores, rules, values, and the like, call for individual and group adjustment. Indeed, a measure of conformity is essential to group solidarity as a basis from which differentiation may proceed. Other factors are closely allied.

*Culture* is also furthered by social organization. As used here, the term means the cumulative experience of man that adds to and enriches life. As man acquires social characteristics, he becomes cultured. Education is the principal force for culture, and through it the acquired characteristics of man as a social being are preserved and transmitted. Culture is, consequently, both the product of social man and the means by which man becomes social.

### The Family as a Biological and Social Unit

The child is born into social organization and begins life in one of the most significant social groups, the family. For years, if not for his entire life, this group influences his being, even after he grows up and leaves home. Teachers soon learn the importance of home-school cooperation in the education of children and youth.

The guardianship of the family emerged from the helplessness of the new-born child and the long period of infancy. The dependency that necessitates the family group early began to extend beyond matters of biological necessity. Social guardianship accompanied physical care; and much of the life of individual members, especially the younger ones, revolved about the family as a unit. Thus, the child and his parents constituted the basic group from which others evolved, these latter groups frequently changing the family relationship itself. The family of today in a complex total social setting, for example, is much different from the family of fifty or one hundred years ago. The family in fifty years will probably differ from that of today.

In the family the child first contacts the advantages, including restraints as well as freedoms, of social groups. Education, too, begins at an early age, the mother generally being the first teacher. The process of instruction is initially informal; but more formalized teaching and learning are common in many families, though less so today than in decades past. The beliefs of the older members of the family, their behavior and activity, the circle of immediate family friends, and many other conditions that constitute the larger family influence bear upon the child's learning.

Much basic education is still accomplished in the home today, although other agencies, to be discussed later, have come to accept a wider range of responsibility than in years past. Education in the home may facilitate or retard education in the schools. It may cause conflicts, for example, when what has been learned at home is not consonant with what is being taught at school. The schools are frequently expected, or think they are expected, to assume educational responsibilities that the home relinquishes.

As a biological and social unit, the family is still a significant educational group. The education of the child, including the attitudes toward and the foundations for subsequent learning beyond the home, is yet a paramount function of the family. Unfortunately, it is neglected in some instances. As the family has changed and as it continues to change, the effects will be felt by other agencies, especially by the schools, which are expected to provide the more formalized and higher forms of education. Knowledge of family life continues to be important to those who are to teach effectively outside the family.

## Other Forms of Social Organization

The rigors and uncertainties of life early brought into being social groups larger than the family. The clan and the tribe, for example, were prevalent in primitive societies and are still in existence today. These and the many additional groups and subgroups that have developed complicate social relationships as they extend the meaning of the benefits discussed earlier. The nature of education in the home has also been modified as more specialized people and agencies have assumed responsibility for teaching children and youth.

Within any larger social order many agencies or institutions are established. The complex of such social groups is, in a sense, descriptive of the social evolution that has taken place. The list of groups virtually defies identification. Some have been in existence for many years; others come into existence and die in a short period of time. Discussion here is limited to a few representative types that impinge directly on education.

The church is one of the well-established social groups that has long played a significant role in the education of its members. In some denominations, for example, the Catholic and the Lutheran, schools have been established to extend religious influence into the program of secular education. The recent problems and court cases bearing on religion in the public schools illustrate the conflict that sometimes arises between social groups. The line between moral and spiritual values, which are generally recognized as an important concern of the schools, and organized religious faith is often difficult to discern.

The impact of the mass media of communication on education is tremendous. The press rolls out daily, weekly, monthly, and less-regularly appearing publications of all types. Radio and television fill the air with voices and pictures. The competition for people's time and attention has never been keener. Children and youth do not escape the force of these media through which all manner of news, propaganda, and violence is placed before them. Thousands of groups utilize these media to tell their story and to enlist support of their views and their cause. Both positive and negative effects result.

Labor-management disputes are aired in the news. Legal cases are virtually tried by the press before they come to court. New cures for all manner of maladies are advertised. Countless contradictory versions of important events are given, each supposedly reasonably complete and honest. Theaters, in satisfying public taste, frequently subject youth to excesses of crime, horror, and sex. The values that apparently underlie much that is published, voiced over the air, or presented on the screen are frequently contrary to those taught in the schools.

Many groups, such as the American Legion, are actively concerned about the schools and influence both personnel and programs. Taxpayers' leagues frequently pressure for reduced school taxes and in so doing attempt to limit educational programs. More is said later of the numerous pressure groups that attempt to influence the schools. At this point it is important to realize that the many social groups in a modern society, and the manner in which they operate, greatly affect the educative process, both positively and negatively, in school and out. Teachers as well as learners are subject to the influence of and participate in many of these groups.

### The School as a Social Agency

Informal education preceded formal education in the evolutionary process and still plays an important role. In primitive societies, before there were schools, the child learned through play, work, other daily activities, and from his parents and other elders. As cultural evolution produced continuing complexity and specialization, the school gradually emerged as a special, supplementary agency with the primary purpose of education. More was said of this point in Chapter 2 dealing with dependency and guardianship.

The school thus issued from a supporting social order to which it was responsible. This basic relationship continues today. The nature and extent of school responsibilities vary from one society to another, but in each instance reflect the will of that society. At the same time, the school exerts an influence on society, especially through the children and youth who attend. This great interdependency has become a major social phenomenon; and education today is probably the largest single highly organized, complex human enterprise.

Reference was made earlier to security, cooperation, differentiation and specialization, competition and opposition, adjustment, and culture. Social organization makes possible these conditions, but does not automatically assure their proper balance and operation. One of the expectations of the school is the development of individuals who can and will, alone and in groups, promote the proper use of these factors. Social skills become increasingly complex and important as the world becomes a more complicated place in which to live.

## CULTURAL DEVELOPMENT AND THE SCHOOLS

Reference has been made to social organization and culture. Through involvement with these conditions, man has become a socialized being. Cultural attainment is recognized as a hallmark of civilization. It is known, too, that cultures once created do not necessarily endure. Cultural development and continuity are closely related to education.

### Man and Cultural Elements

Culture is cumulative. Every social order has a culture; some are dynamic and changing, others are relatively static. The culture is a complex collection composed of groups, beliefs, mores, values, habits, customs, language, tools, hopes, fears, machines, arts, crafts, music, literature, vocations, institutions, leisure activities, and many other attributes. These things characterize man as a social being. Indeed, only as man creates and continues a culture does he endure as a social being.

Among the important cultural elements, language is deserving of special mention. Its part in communication, thinking, planning, arbitrating, and related intellectual and social activity can hardly be overestimated. Not only does it permit precision of meaning, it affords a means of emotional influence that extends beyond its strict intellectual interpretation. The promotion of effective language usage is a major charge that society places upon its schools.

### Culture and Education

The cultural elements mentioned above are not part of man's innate equipment; he does not have them through his biological heredity. He comes to possess them only as they possess him. They exist only in and through him, and his humaneness lies in making them a part of his life. Education, therefore, is a major means of cultural evolution. It is the principal means by which a social order transmits its accumulated cultural heritage from one generation to another. Education serves also as a significant process through which the youth of a society are made fit for and inducted into adult membership. Not enough has been done with such induction in many years.

Culture is not only cumulative, it is also subject to change or modification. Confusion sometimes attends change. As old answers fail to satisfy continuing questioners, conflict and insecurity are likely to increase. Men in every society have known doubt as we are experiencing it now and have sought by various means to find better solutions to age-old problems. Perhaps major changes in values mark the beginning and ending of eras more than other more material evidences, for it is his sense of values that gives meaning to what man is and to what he possesses and does.

Clarity, understanding, order, reassurance, and a way out of dilemma are sought by individuals and groups. Some see in the return to the past a way toward salvation. Others seek new and better ways through exploration and experimentation. Many submit to the prevailing wind, or change the subject rather than face its realities. In any event, the dynamic character of culture is very significant to education and to the roles that are expected of the schools.

It was pointed up earlier that society originally created schools as a special supplementary educational agency. Changes in other agencies having an educational influence were also mentioned. The schools, consequently, face a complex task in dealing with an accumulative and changing culture in a social setting that is changing also its concepts of education, schooling, and the manner in which these processes are to be carried out.

### Education, Earnings, and Economics

A high educational level is fundamental to high individual earnings and a strong economy. Reference should be made to the discussion of education and vocational opportunity in Chapter 2 as bearing on additional statistics presented herein. It is obvious from the trend in the occupational distribution of workers that education is faced with a considerable challenge and opportunity.

The relationship of education to the type of work in which the individual engages is dramatically revealed in data from the U.S. Bureau of Labor Statistics, as portrayed in Fig. 3–1.

For many years it has been apparent that individual earnings are geared to educational level. Miller presented figures for 1958 that are revealing. In this year the earnings of males of age twenty-five and over were shown to be as follows in terms of schooling: [1]

| | |
|---|---|
| College of four years and more | $9,206 |
| College of one to three years | 6,966 |
| High school of four years | 5,567 |
| High school of one to three years | 4,618 |
| Eight years | 3,769 |
| Less than eight years | 2,551 |

[1] Herman P. Miller, "Annual and Lifetime Income in Relation to Education," *American Economic Review*, V (December, 1960), 966.

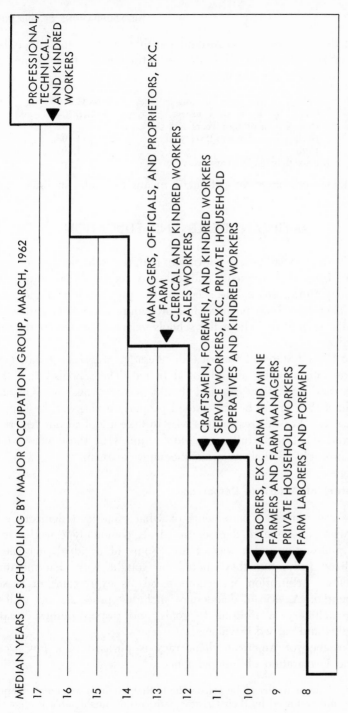

MEDIAN YEARS OF SCHOOLING BY MAJOR OCCUPATION GROUP, MARCH, 1962

PROFESSIONAL, TECHNICAL, AND KINDRED WORKERS

MANAGERS, OFFICIALS, AND PROPRIETORS, EXC. FARM
CLERICAL AND KINDRED WORKERS
SALES WORKERS

CRAFTSMEN, FOREMEN, AND KINDRED WORKERS
SERVICE WORKERS, EXC. PRIVATE HOUSEHOLD
OPERATIVES AND KINDRED WORKERS

LABORERS, EXC. FARM AND MINE
FARMERS AND FARM MANAGERS
PRIVATE HOUSEHOLD WORKERS
FARM LABORERS AND FOREMEN

17
16
15
14
13
12
11
10
9
8

Fig. 3–1. The Relationship of Educational Level and Vocation. Source: U.S. Bureau of Labor Statistics.

Using the same bases and recognizing that many factors other than education are involved, the following estimated earnings from age eighteen to death are also pertinent.[2]

| | |
|---|---:|
| College of four years or more . . . . . | $435,242 |
| College of one to three years . . . . . | 315,504 |
| High school of four years . . . . . . | 257,557 |
| High school of one to three years . . . . | 211,193 |
| Eight years . . . . . . . . . . | 181,695 |
| Less than eight years . . . . . . . | 129,764 |

These figures are based on arithmetic means for males in 1958.

## AMERICAN IDEALS AND EDUCATION

Within any social order, education and the schools derive much direction from the dominant political and social philosophies. One of the major purposes of the school is the preservation of the social order. Therefore, both purpose and procedure are influenced by the supportive society for whom the schools exist and to whom they are responsible.

In the United States of America, democracy—American democracy— is the keynote of political and social belief. The schools, what they are now, and what they can and should become, must be viewed in this light if they are to be understood properly and given the support they deserve. For this reason it is wise to take a look at our American ideals and what their full realization requires of those who would live accordingly, as well as voice allegiance to them.

### The Nature of American Democracy

There are numerous statements of what American democracy is. Those who subscribe to democratic ideals commonly consider it as both a philosophy and a way of life. Some of its ideals may never be realized fully; but they should be sought with determination, nonetheless. Arbitration and compromise, as expressions of reason, are essential. American democracy includes processes as well as ideals, machinery in addition to goals, and responsibilities equated with rights and earned privileges.

The essence of American democracy is phrased in a few words from the Declaration of Independence:

We hold these truths to be self-evident, that all men are created equal, that they are endowed by their Creator with certain unalienable Rights, that

[2] *Ibid.,* p. 981.

among these are Life, Liberty and the pursuit of Happiness. That to secure these rights, Governments are instituted among Men, deriving their
just powers from the consent of the governed.

Our way of life is an experiment in living based on a belief that
these statements are truths and upon the assumption that people can
be educated so that they will live by these precepts in governing
themselves.

Education is fundamental to the United States of America. (Yonkers, New
York, Public Schools.)

The vision and promise of American democracy merit continued
and wholehearted support. The venture in living upon which we are
embarked is really only in its infancy as man's social experiments
are dated and traced. What the future will bring with the greatest
of support can only be surmised. What it will bring without support
is catastrophe. Our failures and successes thus far do not reveal
clearly the probable outcome, but they do give reason for confidence
and hope, and they clearly reveal the importance of education.

### Fundamental Bases of American Democracy

Underlying the many pronouncements of democracy are two basic
ideas fundamental to all others:

1. American democracy is founded upon the worth and dignity

    of the individual and a firm belief in his improvability as a
means of attaining self-fulfillment, the general welfare, and
social progress.

   2. American democracy rests upon the exercise of intelligence and
reason as the best means of individual and collective decision
and action.

These statements embrace and support the many personal and civil
liberties that give our way of life a uniqueness among others. Included are the freedoms of assembly, speech, thought, religion, press,
person, property, fear, and want. No less important are the ideals
of justice, liberty, equality, and fraternity. For it is in the high regard for individuals that the hope and promise of American democracy lie. The people are the means of achieving what democracy
aspires to. The people are those for whom the benefits of democracy
are envisioned. American democracy is, as Abraham Lincoln so aptly
stated, of the people, by the people, for the people.

### Education for Democracy and the School Community

    American ideals are not sought in a vacuum, nor is the practice
of democracy isolated in the school environment from the realities
of life outside. For children and youth it is chiefly on the level of
the local school community that these matters operate. The relationship of the school to the local community is quite important, particularly in view of local school control.

    Community background influences education greatly. This control
is affected by the educational level of the community, the work in
which people engage, the abilities and aptitudes of pupils, the expectations of parents, the attitude of adults toward education, the
stability of the population, the religious beliefs of the people, the
home conditions, and many other factors. From a psychological as
well as a sociological point of view, it is essential to consider these
factors in establishing and operating the schools.

    In some communities much attention may be given to controversial
issues, and it will normally be expected that the school play a vital
role in dealing with community problems. In others, sentiment will
be against the inclusion of some or many issues in the educational
program; and the interest and participation of the school in political,
social, economic, or other problems will be considered as out of place
and will be opposed actively.

    An important concept of school-community relationship is captured in a statement by *The National Assembly on Teaching the Principles of the Bill of Rights:*

We say that schools are not doing what they should do in this field, but we do not suggest that this is solely, or even primarily, the fault of our school teachers and administrators. Schools are an organ of the community, and reflect the climate and disposition of the citizenry as a whole. In the long run, teachers cannot teach children what the parents do not wish to have them taught, nor can they withstand pressure to ignore or gloss over prickly and disagreeable questions unless they are given support by those who believe that education must stimulate the curiosity to wrestle with imponderables, and the boldness to grasp the nettles of controversy.[3]

It is not uncommon to find that social practice today violates democratic principles and that adult example is contrary to adult exhortation. Alertness to these conditions is wise, but discouragement should not be the result of awareness.

Schools that try to meet the obligations of education in a democracy may, therefore, find that this endeavor requires steadfast allegiance to basic principles in the face of local or larger opposition, and the exercise of much patience, wisdom, tact, and determination. To cut off one's nose to spite his face is not the answer, nor is abject acquiescence to demands that are contrary to American democracy. Only as the schools are aware of the ongoing turmoil of living on the community level and attentive to the responsibilities and requirements of an enlightened citizenry can they play a vital role in American life.

In later chapters attention is given to specific ways in which the schools attempt to assure the freedom of teaching and learning basic to the promotion of American ideals.

## Changing Currents in the American Scene

Scientific and technological advancement is on the cutting edge of change in our way of life. This type of change, often rapidly accomplished, sometimes results in dislocation because of our inability to accomplish social advances and needed adjustments at an equal pace. Currently, the nuclear threat cautions us to hurry with political, economic, and social advances so that we may avoid the holocaust that may come if we are long unable to keep pace with science and technology.

The direction of atomic power for purposes of peace and prosperity constitutes a challenge in a positive direction. Automation is moving rapidly into business, industry, and government in ways undreamed

[3] *The National Assembly on Teaching the Principles of the Bill of Rights* (Washington, D.C.: The Assembly, 1962), p. 10.

until recent years. Unemployment and related adjustmental problems are frequently involved in advances of the sort under discussion. In many less traumatic ways, science and technology influence our daily lives.

Urbanization is bringing many changes in living and working. Education, especially in the schools, is influenced greatly, as is housing, transportation, and other allied matters. The migration of people, including families with children, creates serious educational problems in many communities of many states. The education of migrant workers and their children is a special challenge. These conditions also add to the pressure for reasonable curricular uniformity. No longer can schooling be viewed sensibly as only a local or state problem. Men must set aside their differences across community and state lines and join ranks to meet needs that transcend artificial boundaries.

Federal projects of many types influence the concentration and movement of population. Large contracts granted to business or industry in a given area influence the economy in many ways. These operations also affect the educational situation. Loss of contracts once held create another and no less serious adjustmental problem. The movement of citizens abroad by the government, both civilian and military, has economic and educational implications that often go unrecognized. Even the voluntary increase in the travel of United States citizens abroad has a bearing on educational programs.

The birth rate and its impact on educational needs cannot be disregarded with impunity. The dropout rate, while improved in recent years, still poses a serious problem. Adult and juvenile delinquency constitute a threat of some magnitude. Often, the schools are criticized for this condition. Changes in the home, the church, and other agencies are cogent. In general, the social scene in which boys and girls are growing up today is one of turmoil and tension. Value systems are questioned; and individual and societal insecurity and fear are prevalent, especially among the less-fortunate members of society.

The cost of living and the cost of all manner of publicly supported ventures (such as schools, foreign aid, military establishments, fire and police protection, government agencies generally, hospitals, prisons, and so forth) create pressures that have an impact on education. Add to these costs those of social security, medicare for the aged, and other controversial projects that increases taxes, and the magnitude of concern mounts.

Living generally proceeds at an accelerating pace, rapidity of motion perhaps compensating for lack of purpose or direction in many cases. Sometimes the enduring and substantial satisfactions that people seek and need are not obtained. Frustration and a sense of hopelessness and helplessness are the lot of too many who strive in so many ways to attain happiness in living.

The maintenance of physical and mental health has become a critical national concern. Mental or emotional disorders and their influence on physical bodies fill the majority of hospital beds. Crime, divorce, and juvenile delinquency are linked to these conditions of disease. The effect on education and the challenge to education are tremendous. While much emphasis is being placed on the need for "rigorous" educational programs, the influence of such programs on physical and mental health must be considered. The schools face a difficult task in challenging all learners to high levels of performance commensurate with potential without adding to the disabling emotional and mental disorders already besetting society. Balance and reason, always hard to attain, were never more needed than now.

Unemployment.   One of the major adverse developments of recent years has been the growing problem of unemployment, especially among youth. Data presented elsewhere in this book reveal clearly the relationship of vocational opportunity and earnings to educational level and point up the manpower need for progressively higher education. As the need for educated talent grows, there is also a declining demand for the uneducated and unskilled.

This problem bears heavily upon individual and societal well-being, and it tends to be more serious in large cities than in smaller communities. Involved also are serious problems of discrimination and integration relating to both educational and vocational opportunity. The dropout situation is closely associated too, since unemployment among such persons is twice as high as among high school graduates. There is no doubt that an earned high standard of living for all peoples, regardless of race or color, would add greatly to our gross national product as well as reducing many serious social problems. The favorable impact upon individual living can hardly be overestimated.

The relatively uneducated and the unemployed youth are often alienated in other ways from society. They roam the streets, congregate in dives, and often cause trouble for themselves and others. They see no satisfying future ahead, and their understandable discontent provides fertile ground for ideas inimical to their own and the well-being of society. Schooling, as they have experienced it, has little or no appeal to them. Yet without it they are lost. Even with a high school diploma, not all would be assured of the vocational opportunity desired or deserved.

This complex family of conditions is probably the number one challenge to education today, and it will not soon be fully met. Schools and colleges, particularly high schools and junior colleges, are called on for imaginative leadership in fashioning and conducting programs fostering effective transition from school to work. Where education fails, delinquency and crime flourish.

**Integration in the Schools.**   Another of the developments calling for special attention is the move toward integration in the public schools. The 1954 decision of the United States Supreme Court has been far reaching and still constitutes a challenge to be more fully met than is currently true. Concluding that segregation on the basis of race deprives the children of minority groups of equal educational opportunities, this high-court action aroused a slumbering giant. The effects on education have been and will continue to be felt across the nation, particularly in the South where segregation is deeply entrenched as a social policy of a dominantly white society.

The readiness of both Negroes and whites for integration has bearing upon the rate at which this condition can be brought about successfully. White supremacists and others who oppose violently the admission of Negroes and whites in the same schools add to the dimensions of the difficult problem. So also do Negroes and whites who act as though this integration can and should be a successful *fait accompli* in a few months or years. The impact of the resultant conflict is not limited to education and the schools, although education is a principal force in resolving the conflict.

The problem of integration and the manner in which a solution is sought have international implications. In a world that is predominantly non-white, the surge of colored peoples for equality is not wisely neglected nor resisted. It does need direction and assistance. Educational and other resources should be brought to bear on the many facets of the problem such that a peaceful solution can be attained. Steady and visible progress is imperative in the years ahead until true equality and the conditions essential to sustain it are achieved.

**Religion and the Schools.**   A third major development is the renewed move to disassociate religion from the public schools. Numerous court decisions have given impetus to this action. Scripture reading, Christian holiday activities, and other events with a religious background or significance have been questioned in many communities beyond those in which legal action has occurred. Feeling has run high in many instances, and the effect of this conflict has split some communities.

The teaching of moral and spiritual values in the schools has always been a major problem. Early schools in the United States, in many cases if not most, were much concerned with this problem. The selection of teachers suggested the importance of character and morality, if not strict adherence to given religious doctrine. Even the doctrine of the separation of church and state failed to persuade the people that these values were not important in education. And today, many people expect the schools to do far more than is currently done with these values.

The line between religious doctrine and moral values is often very thin. In a nation whose tradition is basically Judeo-Christian, but which includes within this tradition many divergent beliefs, the possibilities for conflict are many. Add to this situation the numerous beliefs and values from other traditions and cultures and the whole decision-making process is complicated. Agreement on values and their sources is not always easily accomplished, especially in our pluralistic society.

Home and church have been argued to be the repositories for religious teaching and the values directly associated. Others criticize the schools as godless and point to the dissolution of the home and the ineffectiveness of the church. The influence of this struggle on school programs is one thing; the impact on young children and youth is quite another. And this impact reaches over into school finance and politics, often creating or adding to a problem of inadequate school support.

Citing the doctrine of the separation of school and state, as basically correct as it is, does not solve the problem of teaching values for living. The latter have never been more needed, nor have children and youth ever been more attracted to ideals in terms of which they can live. The fact that many such values and ideals have a religious background does not render them less important as part of our American heritage. This background should not be used to render these teachings improper.

At the same time the teaching of values must be accomplished in a manner that is not religious and does not offend the many religious and non-religious parents and children who are involved. Those of many faiths and those of none should attempt to agree on what they believe in as fundamental human values and how these things may be taught. Too much time and effort is probably concentrated on differences that tend to overshadow the common ground on which the nation rests.

**Education and the Doctrines of Hate.** The assassination of President John F. Kennedy brought into sharp focus a terrible and unfortunate development in our nation: the growing ascendancy of hate. There is no doubt that the condition relates to integration, religion, world relations, and other social problems. Individuals and groups, by action and apathy, have supported this development. We are now reaping the harvest of hatred from the seeds sown and cultivated in our midst.

Hate is a blinding passion that can only destroy. It resists reason and tends to consume all who are involved, especially its perpetrators. Extremists of the right and left find it useful in swaying opinion through highly emotionalized appeals. The fact that such activity of hatred is effective makes it no less despicable, but success encourages those who engage in and respond to it.

The schools face a grave challenge in resisting the forces of hatred, for these forces are not confined to the ignorant and the uninfluential. Countermovements of hatred are no answer; indeed these irresponsible reactions to deliberate and damnable provocation often lend credence to the initial deeds.

Resort to reason and continual belief in the worth and dignity of man stand in opposition to hate and offer the basic approach to the defeat of the latter. Schools and colleges are challenged to buttress the faith of individuals and groups against this destructive force of hate. In their educational programs and in their operation, attention to the significance of all men—regardless of race or color or creed or station—is imperative.

The confused, changing, and competing world of diverse ideologies in which we live provides a background that highlights this challenge. Our ability to destroy ourselves cannot remain controlled if the forces of hate are not defeated through education. It is to be hoped that the multifold agencies of society will join with education in this struggle for sanity and survival. Nothing less than a concerted social effort can succeed.

**Social Problems and Educational Endeavor.** The changing currents discussed in this section suggest the need for alertness to societal conditions in education. These conditions and currents are fit content for discussion in the school curriculum, and they also influence the operation of the schools. Social problems are a source of educational experiences that bridge the gap between the relative isolation of the school from life around it. Learning that stems from life problems and returns later to deal with such problems should be encouraged.

In addition to problems of larger social impact, there are many problems of a more individual and personal nature. The latter also have a place in the school curriculum. At times they are of much value in relating student concerns to school objectives and in motivating learners. If schools are to serve the social order, they can ill-afford to neglect the problems of any segment or any age group of the population.

## Tenets for Education in American Democracy

In the promotion of American democracy—its ideals and its practice—the schools and other agencies that have an educational influence should keep in mind certain basic tenets. Education should:

1. Strengthen our faith in man, in the integrity and moral worth of each individual as a person, and in the improvability of man.
2. Develop in our thinking and acting a recognition of and respect for the supremacy of human rights and freedoms and the placing of man above state, in the support and service of which ideal our codes, institutions, and processes are to be established and conducted.
3. Stress the necessity of the physical, mental, moral, and social well-being of all the people as fundamental to the well-being of any of the people.
4. Promote the active and enlightened participation of all the people in matters of common concern, recognizing the importance of the consent of the governed and the rights and responsibilities of majorities and minorities.
5. Develop human intelligence and promote its application in exploring and solving the many personal and societal problems confronting man in modern living.
6. Teach that every freedom has a responsibility and every liberty an obligation, that eternal vigilance is the price of maintaining our way of life against enemies from without and within, and that devotion freely given and duly reasoned is essential.
7. Provide not only for the preservation of our way of life, but for its peaceful and reasoned improvement, recognizing the ideals of democracy toward which we must ever strive.

8. Strengthen our belief in and dedication to these principles and others that underlie the American way of life.

9. Promote the development of behavior traits that make for active and effective citizenship on the part of all people.

### Devotion to American Ideals

The development of allegiance, devotion, and loyalty to American ideals is a grave and complicated challenge to be faced. Our nation deserves the loyalty of free men freely given. Such loyalty is reasoned and is reasonable; it emerges only as education enables it to do

Our flag has many meanings to be taught and learned. (Alhambra, California, Public Schools.)

so. Men believe and serve better when they understand and when they are equipped with the tools of learning such that they may intelligently face the future.

Safeguards must be maintained against those persons or groups, wherever they exist, that would abridge our freedoms or pervert our basic principles. Unfortunately, some among us are fearful of the truth and would deny others the right to seek truth wherever it may lead. Often these persons, however worthy or ignoble their motives, seek to place unreasonable restraints on the schools. The words of Thomas Jefferson, written of the University of Virginia, are appropriate to this issue:

This institution will be based upon the illimitable freedom of the human mind. For here we are not afraid to follow truth wherever it may lead, nor to tolerate error so long as reason is left free to combat it.

Sound and enthusiastic education, by word and vigorous social action, is basic to the devotion that our American ideals merit. Somehow we have gained much of the substance of these birthrights without catching the fervor essential to their effectiveness in living. The relation of knowledge and action as they pertain to the support of a nation is apparent in a statement prepared by *The National Assembly on Teaching the Principles of the Bill of Rights:*

We believe that the teaching of the Bill of Rights should constantly expose its dual nature, for while it declares individual rights, it also implies individual responsibilities. A free society cannot long endure unless enough of its members are able and willing to speak out in behalf of its principles when they are threatened. If the history of the Third Reich teaches us anything, it is that democracy in Germany fell victim to civic passivity, and the silence of those whose schooling and attainments ought to have made them leaders of an articulate and determined opposition to the encroachments of tyranny.[4]

## EDUCATIONAL CHALLENGE IN A CHANGING WORLD SCENE

The flames of the Cuban crisis still smolder today and have influenced brush fires in Latin America. India and Red China have fought bitter battles, and the unsettled conditions in Africa continue. Russia and Red China may or may not mend the rift that has been widening between them. In Panama people are still restive. France has recognized Red China. The wall in Berlin stands yet as an affront to humanity. In every quarter of the globe, there is human misery and an impatient longing and surging toward a better way of life, be it by accelerated evolution or revolution. Chester Bowles called this the Revolution of Rising Expectation.[5]

Education in these times is a most challenging and difficult en-

[4] *Ibid.,* p. 11.
[5] Chester Bowles, *Ideas, People and Peace* (New York: Harper & Row, 1958), p. 33.

deavor, full of excitement and adventure for those of ability and spirit. Reference has already been made to changing currents in the United States. Now a look at the changing world scene is called for. This scene is to be viewed in terms of the home front and the ideological struggle in which American democracy is involved around the globe.

## National Security and Education

As is true of foreign policy, education has a first loyalty to its supporting society. There is little doubt today that the schools are on the forefront of institutions fighting peacefully for the survival of our way of life. Insolation and isolation are no longer tenable, and in the educational process cognizance of world relations is important. Focus on local concerns to the neglect of larger national and international issues is blindness of the worst type.

American democracy cannot flourish in isolation from other ideologies and ways of life practiced by mankind. Indeed, it is increasingly questionable if any of these doctrines can long survive other than through intelligent cultural interaction. The concept of "one world" is gradually becoming a reality, particularly in a physical sense. A world society, however vague its direction, diverse its elements, and tenuous its ties, is in the making. Education, therefore, must attend to the preparation of people to participate in the building of this world society.

World conditions exert influence on all of us. No person escapes the destiny of his time, whether or not he is active in the direction of that destiny. Politically, economically, socially, psychologically, and in many other ways the world scene pressures the bodies, minds, and souls of men. Technological advances have given to the world terrible destructive power. It would appear, both at home and on the world fronts, that the disabilities and strains of modern living are accumulating more rapidly than social legislation, education, and all other agencies and processes for reform are managing to harness new knowledge and develop new attitudes and social skills for the reduction of such conditions.

## Individual Well-Being and the Commonweal

Well-educated, happy, and productive citizens are the heart of a secure nation and of a peaceful and prosperous world society of nations. Thus, in considering the commonweal the individual is a beginning point. He is the basic element of which all other social compounds are composed.

Security is a state of mind. It is bolstered by physical well-being and spiritual stamina. The bases of national security lie in the bodies, minds, and spirits of an enlightened and devoted citizenry. Each person contributes only as he possesses to the level of his ability the information, understandings, attitudes, skills, and other attributes essential to effective living. The promotion of such living for each individual is basic to national security, as well as to international peace and understanding.

Said in another way, neither a secure nation nor a peaceful world can be constituted of insecure individuals and groups. The integration of the individual personality is very fundamental, for one who is at war with himself can hardly be at peace with others. Education also helps to broaden the sphere of integration to include progressively larger and more diverse groups. Social psychology is pertinent to the wider concept of community that embraces all men as brothers though of different households.

## The Well-Being of All and the Well-Being of Any

Within a nation the well-being of any is dependent upon the well-being of all. The expansion of opportunity should embrace all, though many may not seize it. Discrimination and rejection lead to social as well as individual deterioration, and antisocial behavior is frequently the result., The freedoms and privileges of American democracy cannot reasonably be denied to any who are expected to uphold, with their lives if necessary, the security of our nation.

Human likeness knows no cultural nor physical boundary. Basically, human beings are a great deal alike. They share common needs and aspirations. Their problems are similar. The genetic advantages to learn and live are not a monopoly of a given race, color, or creed.

The manner in which needs are met and in which people live does vary. But this difference is a cultural product: it results from education and is not an organic or predestined necessity. Within our own nation, we have many cultures. A major challenge is the promotion of cultural pluralism. These cultures and their differences add spice and zest to living. The hope of American democracy, at home and abroad, lies in promoting unity among differing cultures within a large social framework. Only as progress toward this end is made within our own borders is it to be expected that nations can be brought together.

## Education for International Understanding and World Peace

World security is not incompatible with national security; it is only a logical extension of the concept of the well-being of one man to the well-being of all men. This has been in the thinking of great men of all ages and all cultures. Fundamental to American democracy is a belief that people can be educated to conduct and to govern themselves intelligently. Is it not reasonable to suggest that education can and should promote the peaceful interaction of the peoples of different nations?

War and strife begin first in the minds of men. Man is not committed biologically or genetically to a specific pattern of behavior. As we have been able to educate people to live together in smaller and then larger groups, we must also be concerned with the world group. Resort to war as a means of settling disputes has a long and bloody history that seems to have established a pattern that, at times, takes precedence over reason. This pattern is not inevitable, however; and the advances of science make modern warfare so devastating as to call for an urgent change. Not only with regard to international security, but for the very existence of individual nations as well, education faces a formidable task in promoting the peaceful settlement of world problems.

**More Social Tenets for American Education.** Suggestions were made earlier in furtherance of American ideals. These ideals may be reviewed as having a direct bearing on education for international understanding and world peace. In fostering both the former and the latter, education should also:

1. Promote individual and group security within our own nation and foster the extension of freedoms, privileges, and responsibilities to all groups of which it is composed.
2. Develop social skills and the art of living in groups, small and large, under varying conditions and in pursuit of a variety of shared objectives or goals.
3. Disclose the fallacy of the superiority of racial groups or nationalities and of other misconceptions regarding people and cultures.
4. Promote an understanding of the place of our nation among others in the world and of our responsibility in leadership and service.
5. Develop an understanding of other cultures and peoples and of our interdependence and interrelationship, including iden-

tification with institutions of a world society, such as the United Nations and UNESCO.

6. Support the ideal of a world community composed of many cultures, all of which cooperate as members of a world society.

# THE CONSEQUENT SOCIAL ROLES AND FUNCTIONS OF AMERICAN EDUCATION

In support of its sustaining society, education plays several roles and accomplishes several functions. Emphasis varies according to changing conditions and social trends, and depends also upon psychological factors that influence the teaching and learning process and those involved. The superior teacher is a sort of social engineer who creates conditions that facilitate learning appropriate to time and circumstance, always aware of the timeless and enduring challenge and responsibility of his job.

There are three major related roles of education: the conservative, the critical, and the creative. Each has a focus distinguishing it from the other, but none is independent. Their interplay is like that of an orchestra in which individual performance is significant but must be attuned to the concert effect.

## The Conservative Role of Education

The transmission, interpretation, and preservation of the social heritage is historically the predominant role in education. Schooling sustains society through this role, contributing to its unification in terms of distinguishing cultural characteristics. The conservative role provides the "social cement" that holds a society together and promotes social solidarity and continuity.

The conservative role tends to preserve the status quo. Emphasis is placed upon transmitting and interpreting in an orthodox manner those elements of the total culture already well accepted by the society. Effort is expended to instill ideas into youth and to induct them into the social order with a firm faith in the beliefs and practices of that social order.

This role generally looks more to the past than to the present for its substance. It deals with the accumulation of culture from which content is selected for educational purposes. This content is learned, that is, becomes a part of the young as they grow into membership in the society that gave them physical birth and now seeks to socialize them appropriately through education. Acceptance, belief, faith, and loyalty of an absolute and unquestioning nature are associated with this role, especially by those who affirm that the schools should preserve what society has and is, without thought to fostering social change.

The "universals" of learning, that is, those things that everyone should be expected to know or be capable of doing, are at the heart of this role. Emphasis is often placed upon memorization, although this can be carried to extremes detrimental to the conservative role. In fostering social solidarity, this role may overlook individual differences and injure cultural pluralism unless care is exercised. The tendency to propaganda is associated also with the conservative role, too, when it is improperly performed.

## The Critical Role of Education

Cultural accumulation increases the need for choices in education. No man can master the funded capital of human experience. Who is to decide what the so-called "universals" are to be? What content shall be utilized in performing the conservative role of education? For how long shall "acceptable" decisions stand? What conditions are sufficient to create a need for revision in education? These and other questions suggest the reason for another role—the critical or questioning role.

Cultural and social changes do occur; in fact, they are part and parcel of the same process. Principles already accepted and remedies practiced sometimes cease to serve as effectively as they once did. Circumstances change, different goals are sought, equilibrium is disturbed, and striving becomes prevalent in living. Social unification is weakened and continuity is threatened. The conservative role of education per se has not been enough alone to insure the social stability to which it is dedicated. The stability must be dynamic if it is to endure.

Acceptance, as a keynote of the conservative role, is not enough to assure social survival. Life and living, even in the most ordered households, are dynamic and changing. They are restrained only temporarily at best. The questing drive refuses forever to be restrained, but it may be given direction. Enter, then, the critical role of education.

With social change, especially progress, the gap between man's innate characteristics and his social possibilities and requirements is greatly extended. To bridge this gap, we have only education. The conservative role is helpful, but has not enough thrust alone to extend from yesterday through today and tomorrow. The critical or evaluative role is increasingly important under these circumstances. It places emphasis upon questioning, evaluating, and pondering. The "why" of things is sought. In short, critical thinking, which introduces reason as a basis for acceptance and rejection, is stressed.

This role is concerned with the status quo and with social change in at least two ways. First, it seeks to understand by searching for underlying reasons. Second, it supports those conditions that critical inquiry reveal as reasonable. The first of these endeavors is generally more acceptable than the second, for the latter often leads to a crusading spirit in youth that is threatening to the status quo and to those who support it. This threat is quite apparent when reason dictates the need to change long-established and comfortable social patterns.

Mere acceptance and adjustment are not tenable to the critical role. It teaches the learner to question, not in a cynical and dubiously distrustful tone, but with the view of buttressing acceptance of the old and choice of the new with reason. As older and socially acceptable values serve social advancement less well, they need to be modified in the light of such appraisal. Individual differences and cultural pluralism are likely to receive greater attention in the performance of this role. Social progress is recognized as a product of diversity as well as uniformity.

Those who object to the school having any role in the determination of social direction neglect a fundamental tenet of American democracy: the appeal to reason. The latter, as often as not, suggests the need for reaffirmation of old values that have been lost in the hustle of modern action independent of thinking. Utility and experimentation are important concerns of the critical or evaluative role of education. In a sense, this role is a balance to the conservative role.

## The Creative Role of Education

The creative role of education is the most dynamic of the three, although it often is performed in a slow subtle manner that escapes notice. Indeed, it may not be recognized as a role of education at all. This failure is most unfortunate for society, the learner, and the teacher.

The creative role is related to both the conservative and the critical, especially the latter. It seeks to develop fully in each individual those behaviors that his genetic advantages make possible. It is the nurture through which natural potential becomes living reality, particularly as relates to man's intellectual and volitional activities.

The conservative role may yield the solidarity and security of belief, both individual and group. The critical role may add reason to assent. But only the creative role enlivens the spirit and adds a cutting edge of productivity to reason. This latter role has its source in another basic tenet of American democracy: the worth, dignity, and improvability of the individual. Through creativity man has a means of solving his problems and satisfying his wants, and a mechanism to improve life for himself and others.

To illustrate, communicating and reasoning do not develop automatically because man is born with a genetic pattern providing a potential for them. In a real sense these activities of man result from *the creative force of education* working on and with these genetic advantages. Communicating and reasoning are a product of socialization, a humane and social attribute rather than an innate characteristic.

The creative role touches all learners and is especially attuned to individual differences. It recognizes that curiosity is the genesis of creativity and that human development is a long and continuous process. This role fosters the development anew in each generation of the skills of which man is capable. Without it the progress of man would cease.

Failure to recognize the creative role has serious consequences for the individual as well as society. Talents not developed and used are soon lost, often never to be regained. The creative urge that is unsatisfied or stifled frequently leads to frustration. The loss of individual self-realization contributes to social maladjustment. This role of education bears directly on the mental health of the individual and his relationships with others.

The teacher who is unaware of the creative role denies himself of deep satisfactions, as well as robbing those he instructs. The quenching of curiosity is a first step too frequently observed in the schools. Overemphasis on conformity often accompanies this stifling of individual initiative. The insecure teacher who is himself the epitome of conformity is one of the greatest offenders of this type, and his conviction and sincerity only makes correction increasingly difficult.

## The Functions of Education

In the performance of these roles of education, certain principal functions are accomplished. These are interdependent in the manner of the roles that they support. Some are more contributory to one role than another. Each and all relate to the dynamics of teaching and learning, as well as to the educational outcomes.

The *adjustive function* in education is overemphasized by some and misunderstood by a great many. It relates especially to the conservative role and the development of social likeness. The common core of an educational endeavor or the required studies, for example, tends to focus on content and experiences that provide a heritage to be shared and believed in by all. It is essential in assisting individuals to know and accept themselves in relation to others and the culture of which they are a part. The acceptance of values and other attributes of a society, including liberties and restraints, is part of the process.

*Diagnosis and direction* are part of this adjustive function. They are associated also with other functions mentioned subsequently. The adjustive function does not mean, as some critics contend, that the school "adjusts" individuals to a low common denominator of behavior and expectations. It does promote stability of a dynamic and societal variation. But it is not a harbinger of stagnation.

*Differentiation* is another important function of education. Sameness carried to extremes is monotonous and deadly. Through differentiation social evolution and progress may be brought about with both individual and societal satisfaction. If adjustment can be said to deal principally with the "universals" of education, differentiation attends to the "relatives." Individual fulfillment necessitates education that helps the learner to know his own strengths and weaknesses and to develop himself appropriately in the culture of which he is a member. The division of labor and specialization are based upon differentiation, as well as is cooperation. Both the critical and creative roles are served by this function.

Closely allied to adjustment and differentiation is the *integrative function*. It helps the individual, with his likenesses and differences, to achieve a sense of personal unity within himself. Further, it aids him in relating properly to others, thereby affording a kind of social unification, even though he may be a member of groups that are divergent in some ways. Much concerned with the psychological and the sociological factors influencing adjustment and differentiation and the resolution of individual and group conflicts, this function relates to guidance and counseling as well as to the more purely instructional aspects of education. What roles does such a function serve?

The *selective function* is more easily identified in certain foreign educational systems where early diagnosis and decision are prevalent.

But it operates in our schools also and is an important contribution. In some cultures selection is associated with elimination; that is, only those who are chosen are afforded extensive educational opportunity and the others are denied it. More is said later of this operation among foreign nations.

In the schools of the United States of America, there is some selection associated with elimination. For example, not everyone can profit sufficiently from a college education. Educational dropouts frequently disqualify themselves from further formal education. Among the critics of education are many who would support a more highly selective system, especially at secondary and postsecondary levels. But the concept of equality of educational opportunity is strong, and we are apt to operate the selective function in relation to the differentiative. In this way alternative educational opportunities are made available to those who do not qualify for, or perhaps do not want, a college education. Differences also exist among colleges such that a wide range of students can succeed in higher education if they choose wisely or are so chosen or guided. What role does this function seem to serve best?

The elective program in the schools relates to both the differentiative and selective functions, not only at elementary and secondary levels, but at the collegiate as well. The comprehensive high school recognizes selection and differentiation under one roof. Adult education also provides opportunities that serve these functions. The integrative function is related to these matters and is frequently served through the satisfactions attained in elective opportunities, either in required courses or in those courses that the learner chooses himself.

The *preparatory function* is another significant feature of education. It is possibly the most easily recognized function, although identification does not guarantee proper handling. Nonetheless, those who decry this challenge to education do us a disservice. The schools are rightly expected to prepare children, youth, and adults for living today and in the future. They should prepare us for lifelong learning, an essential in today's and tomorrow's world. Does this function relate to any one or to all of the roles?

### Needed: A Balance of Roles and Functions

The interplay of the roles of education and their supporting functions is observable in any good school or college. No one of these roles is self-sufficient. Nor is any one enough. No single function is sufficient alone, although each is significant. A balance and blend of roles and functions is imperative if education is to serve individual and society at home and abroad.

By itself the conservative role tends to foster social stagnation, possibly promoting the elimination of pluralism in favor of the majority. Alone the critical or evaluative role leads to social disintegration. Without a creative role education serves neither the conservative nor the critical, and all would be lost. Together in harmonious accord and intelligent dissent, these roles provide for a social framework within which individual and group differentiation are supportive of larger social unification.

In later chapters the purposes of education are related to roles and functions. As the teacher becomes skilled in the art and science of his profession, he is able to relate and use these guidelines effectively in promoting the education of learners at all ages and stages of development. Subsequent chapters should be read in the light of these roles and functions, for they are principal directional signals that chart the course of American education.

## The School as a Special Environment for Teaching and Learning

The school is a special, supplementary, social agency whose primary responsibility is the education of youth. It provides an environment in which learning can be accomplished more economically and efficiently than is otherwise possible. Detached somewhat from the activity of daily living outside its walls, the school must, nevertheless, retain connection with reality. Its effectiveness is evident in the behavior and performance of its charges out of school as well as in the classroom, and in their lives after they leave school.

In its detachment the school protects the learner while it nurtures him. But it must not shield him so unduly as to render him unaware, unwilling, or incapable of discharging his responsibilities in life beyond the school. Learners should also be weaned of this dependency upon the schools and teachers as a part of the educative process and made capable and willing of learning on their own. Each teacher should contribute in some measure to his own dispensability in the life of the learner.

Within the school and under its direction in the community, the educational program seeks to foster the American way of life. But the school cannot and should not attempt to do the complete job alone. Other social agencies have responsibilities, too. Far too often other agencies relinquish their obligations and the school too willingly assumes them. This leads to dispersion of efforts and reduces the school's effectiveness in many communities. School-community cooperation is essential.

### Faith in Education

This is the age of education. No other factor correlates more closely with the level of living than the level of learning. No other enterprise influences man and his future more significantly than that of education. It has become the principal hallmark of true cultural advancement, personal as well as societal.

Under these circumstances it might be supposed that education and the schools are held in the highest esteem by all. Unfortunately, this is not true. Many whose success rests upon the education provided in the schools consider themselves self-made men. The failures and those who seek a reason for their sad condition often find the schools a ready, if unwilling and innocent, scapegoat. And the danger of anti-intellectualism is growing, even as is also our need for intelligence.

It is imperative that education and the schools have the faith of the American people. This is an obligation of society and a challenge to educators. The schools cannot prove their worth without the sustaining faith of society basic to an educational investment in people. And this faith cannot be earned or kept alive unless the schools are productive.


## QUESTIONS, PROBLEMS, AND PROJECTS FOR FURTHER STUDY

1. In terms of the various social groups of which you are a member, draft a statement of the advantages or benefits that you enjoy, together with specific illustrations. What disadvantages and obligations does membership entail?

2. Relate physical and social dependency as they pertain to the family and the school. What aspects of dependency are primary to each agency? Should the school assume responsibilities relinquished by the home? What are the implications of your answer?

3. On what basis, if any, can you defend vocational education in the public schools? How does it relate to liberal education?

4. Draft a statement of American ideals in your own words. See if you can assign major responsibility for these to various grade levels or subjects. If subject matter is not enough, what else is necessary in fostering these ideals?

5. List some of the major social, political, or economic problems of a community with which you are familiar. Do you envision schools of that community as being able to utilize these problems for educational pur-

poses? If so, in what ways? Could the schools help with the resolution of any such problems? How?

6. Speculating on the major local, state, national, and international problems of today, characterize briefly the kind of education that seems essential to you in preparing citizens for effective living in our current world.

7. Review the proposed roles and functions of education and discuss briefly how your proposed teaching subject or grade level might contribute to these ideas.

8. What suggestions do you have for increasing the faith of citizens in public education and promoting greater willingness to support schools at higher financial levels?

## SELECTED SUPPLEMENTARY READINGS AND FILMS

BEALS, RALPH L., and HOIJER, HARRY. *An Introduction to Anthropology.* 2d ed. New York: The Macmillan Co., 1959. Chaps. viii and xx. Discusses the nature of culture and education in relation to the formation of personality.

CHANDLER, B. J., STILES, LINDLEY J., and KITSUSE, JOHN I. (eds.). *Education in Urban Society.* New York: Dodd, Mead & Co., Inc., 1962. Chap. i. Deals with the many forces influencing urban schools.

CONANT, JAMES B. *Slums and Suburbs.* New York: McGraw-Hill Book Co., Inc., 1961. Chaps. i and ii. Treats the problems of slums and Negro education and schools and jobs in large cities.

DOUGLAS, WILLIAM O. *America Challenged.* New York: Avon Book Division of the Hearst Corporation, 1960. This small book presents a challenge to education in terms of the individual, the crowd, the nation, and the world.

EDUCATIONAL POLICIES COMMISSION. *Social Responsibility in a Free Society.* Washington, D.C.: National Education Association, 1963. Discusses the nature of social responsibility, the role of the school, and implications for public policy.

FRANKEL, CHARLES (ed.). *Issues in University Education.* New York: Harper & Row, 1959. Chaps. i and iv. Deals with universities in the modern world and the democratization of educational opportunity.

GROSS, CARL H., WRONSKI, STANLEY P., and HANSON, JOHN W. *School and Society.* Boston: D. C. Heath & Co., 1962. Chap. v. Presents democracy as a way of life, including principles basic to education.

HAVIGHURST, ROBERT J., and NEUGARTEN, B. L. *Society and Education.* 2d ed. Rockleigh, N.J.: Allyn & Bacon, Inc., 1962. Interesting chapters on a variety of relationships between education and the society it serves, especially those on social mobility, social structure, and the social origins of teachers.

MERCER, BLAINE E., and CARR, EDWIN R. *Education and the Social Order.* New York: Holt, Rinehart & Winston, Inc., 1957. Chaps. vii and xii–xiii. Discusses the school as a social institution and its relationship to democracy, and to moral and spiritual values.

NATIONAL SOCIETY FOR THE STUDY OF EDUCATION. *Social Forces Influ-*

*encing American Education.* 60th Yearbook, Part II, 1961. Distributed by The University of Chicago Press. Chap. v. Presents social-class influences on education.

## Films

*Freedom To Learn.* 27 minutes. A high school teacher defends in open meeting the freedom to learn. Washington, D.C.: National Education Association.

*Freedom To Read.* 14 minutes. A librarian defends the freedom to read against community opposition. New York: Columbia University.

*Secure the Blessings.* 30 minutes. Dramatizes the role of public schools in a democracy through lives of people facing everyday problems; deals with learning to respect the rights and understand the problems of others. Washington, D.C.: National Education Association.

*The School and the Community.* 14 minutes. Deals with problems of school-community separation and shows benefits of school-community cooperation. New York: McGraw-Hill Book Co., Inc.

# 4

# BASIC THEORIES AND
# PHILOSOPHIES OF EDUCATION

## THE PROFESSIONAL TEACHER HAS A PHILOSOPHY
## OF EDUCATION

Back in the days when teachers were schoolmarms following established routines of textbook teaching, daily assignments, "discipline,"
and good relations with parents, with little understanding of what it
was all about, long-range goals were given little consideration, and
there was no need for having a carefully thought through philosophy
of education. Teaching was on the level of a skilled trade. The superintendent was the foreman; the state course of study and the textbooks were the content to be taught and manuals for procedure.
Little wonder that teaching as an occupation was not thought of as a
profession, and teachers had little more than average status in the
community. Teaching was not regarded as a profession.

Today, the *professional* teacher plans his teaching materials and
procedures, his counseling, and other work within the framework of
basic assumptions and professional knowledge of what he believes to
be sound. He is not working in the dark, going through a routine
with little promise of fulfilling potentialities.

### Levels of Objectives

There are several levels of objectives, and they constitute a hierarchy
of goals that must not be lost sight of if one is to do a high grade
of professional work in planning for the education of young people.
First, there are the ultimate objectives—envisaged in terms of the kind
of individuals we hope that our students will become, functioning in
life activities so as to give satisfaction and profit to themselves and
to society that finances their education.

In planning it is necessary to break these broad, general objectives down into more short-term objectives, something that we might wish to accomplish within a year, let us say, through the medium of the subject that is being taught; for example, arithmetic, chemistry, reading, or American history. Furthermore, the true educator then attempts to get in mind what specific growth; what information; what understandings; what intellectual, social, and physical skills; what social, physical, or intellectual habits; and what ideals, attitudes, and interests he will stress through well-chosen materials and teaching and learning activities.

## Working Without a Philosophy

To be sure, there are many teachers who merely assign lessons and attempt in some way to motivate the youngster through artificial incentives, proceeding with a naïve and partly correct assumption that if the youngster applies himself to learning, the study of the subject will be good for him and worthy of his time and efforts. Queried about the value of their subjects, particularly by one who seems to question their values, such teachers make rather unconvincing sales talk, such as "The study of algebra trains the mind," "The study of Latin enables one to speak and write better," "The study of modern foreign languages contributes to international understanding and peace and the understanding of peoples of other countries," or "By the study of science, children learn the scientific method of thinking."

If one visits the classroom of these teachers, the activities of the students and of the teacher would lead him to suspect that neither is conscious of the objectives the teacher claims for his subject. Definite, logical, practical work toward the attainment of well-conceived objectives is not a lick-and-a-promise, hit-or-miss type of working for goals.

Very few teachers leave college and begin teaching with a clear-cut and sound concept of either ultimate or mediate goals for children in general, or those of any particular subjects. The teachers who become most effective with years of experience are those who continually improve their concepts of goals and their efforts to keep both types of goals in mind. They are alert to exploit, utilize, and capitalize upon whatever opportunities present themselves so that the learners will have had experiences that will result in growth toward the goals and objectives. This growth separates the educators from the schoolmarms, male and female.

Many teachers, on the other hand, discover that they can get by without a professional approach by following a sort of catch-as-catch-can philosophy of what they are attempting to accomplish. They labor along, avoiding controversial situations, buttering up the parents and their superior officers, and doing a mediocre job. They get on the permanent salary schedule and move toward the maximum salary along with the teachers whose work is of a professional character. They are, however, rarely promoted to positions as supervisors or administrators or have their applications accepted for more desirable positions in larger and better-paying school systems. It is tragic that so many of them are confused and leave the profession for other work or marriage with the rationalization that administrators do not appreciate them, that children are spoiled by their parents, and that parents in general are not grateful for what is done for their children.

### A Confusing Myriad of Philosophies

Through the ages there have developed scores of philosophies and "isms" that are overlapping, inconsistent, and incomplete. They are almost invariably couched in rather unusual words of many syllables, studded with words used in an unusual sense. Long involved sentences do much to raise the question as to whether the author was scholarly or whether he sought refuge in vagueness, unusual vocabulary, and complicated expressions. Nevertheless, at least a considerable number of these philosophies of life and of education need to be examined and evaluated for whatever they may be worth in this day and age as guides to planning education of young people for life in the United States as they will find it. In the next few pages the reader will find a very concise description of the essence of a few of the most commonly accepted philosophies that have definite implications for education. For simplicity they are grouped into major categories.

## ESSENTIALIST POSITIONS

There have always been educated leaders who believed that there is considerable subject matter that is essential to a good education. The philosophy of the *essentialists* exists in a number of forms and has a number of names, e.g., the storage concept, the formal discipline concept, the classicalist concept, the "passing on the heritage" concept, and humanistic realism. Perhaps the clearest concept exponent of this type of philosophy as applied to American education was William Chandler Bagley who unlike many philosophers had the desire and ability to express himself specifically in generally understandable language. In essence, it is the philosophy that education is primarily for the purpose of passing on to young people the knowledge that was accumulated over the centuries, with some attention given to the selection of knowledge that might be of most value to the student but, in general, attaching importance to its age.

Among those who have been vigorous in pressing the essentialist assumption has been Dr. Robert M. Hutchins, who for several years was Chancellor of the University of Chicago. He took the position that the school should be chiefly concerned with the great writings of the past—especially the "Great Books." While many lay people and some educators were impressed, most of them after careful thinking became conscious of important limitations of such material for the education of the great majority of young people. No matter how scholarly and able the authors of past centuries may have been, their ideas were formed and written in the days of authoritarian governments and authoritarian church, in times when the practice of democracy and of a Christian attitude toward one's fellow man had not gotten beyond a very primitive stage. Consequently, they have serious limitations as materials for the education of young people for life in a highly automated and industrialized economy and highly organized democratic society. The problems with which we contend today were not even dreamed of by the learned and able writers of the "Great Books." While it is true that practically every individual should have some knowledge of the classics, regardless of their practicability for life today, certainly it should not constitute more than one aspect of a truly effective, modern education either for practical life or for intellectual development.

All essentialists either state or imply that there is educational subject matter that ought to be taught, since it has been taught for generations and "has stood the test of time." The very endurance of these bodies of knowledge is attributed largely by essentialists to their intrinsic merits. Some of the clearer thinkers of the essentialists agree at least in part with William Chandler Bagley, who took the position that it is really necessary for us to examine carefully the possible essentials and to determine what is truly "essential."

Some forty years ago, an outstanding English scientist and philosopher, H. G. Wells, wrote a series of articles in the *Saturday Evening Post* that later became published as a book, *Salvaging Civilization*. He suggested that surely there must be a "best" curriculum, an essential and enduring curriculum; and it should be determined once and for all. Surely, he wrote, there are "best" methods of teaching, which should be identified; and the school should be put on the basis of the *best* curriculum and the *best* methods throughout the English-speaking countries. He suggested that departures from them should be challenged and compelled to prove their worthiness. This type of approach created quite a stir among thinkers about education, and a considerable amount of amusement as well as rather general and devastating opposition. His naïve oversimplified concept of learning is shared by a great many Americans, who in their ignorance greatly oversimplify the problem.

## Subject-Matter-centered Schools

Since the time of the Renaissance and the Reformation and the rediscovery of and increased attention to Greek and Roman classics, there has persisted the practice in secondary schools, though waning in recent decades, of having young people study and master the content of books of the great writers of previous generations. For example, when Johann Sturm was brought to Strasbourg in 1576 from his professorship of classics at the University of Paris to reorganize and to administer the Gymnasium, he developed the curriculum around Latin, Greek, and Hebrew authors, since most of what he had learned had been written in those languages. The Strasbourg school influenced the secondary schools in Europe of the seventeenth, eighteenth, and nineteenth centuries.

When our first schools were established in the United States, this type of curriculum was transplanted initially in our Latin grammar schools; and the general content and idea persisted and influenced the curricula of the later academies and the early high schools. People of this generation were not the first to be thoughtful about status symbols in connection with education. For generations, those who had given much time to the study of Latin, French, physics, or literature were likely to bring into their conversation evidence of their acquisitions, however superficial, of this sort.

Out of this idea there naturally developed a philosophy of education that has been given various names, among them being "mind storage" or filling the mind with essential things. This point of view naturally favored a curriculum made up of what its proponents of essentialism thought was essential, usually largely "traditional," or "decorative" contributing to status among one's friends and acquaintances. Fathers and mothers, as well as students and former students, began to raise embarrassing questions as to the limitations of a program built on this philosophy of subject matter for the preparation for a rich and useful life. But for generations the majority of secondary school teachers felt much safer in teaching the traditional subjects and supported their position by statements of a greatly exaggerated doctrine of formal discipline or transfer of training as it had been expounded by John Locke and others.

As early as 1761 in his *Emile,* Jacques Rousseau, a great French philosopher and author, said: "Children reason about matters related to their immediate experience and interests, and hence the reasoned solution of small scientific problems should be part of their education. The premature memorizing of words spoils the child's judgment." [1]

The very large majority of outstanding leaders in educational theory in the past century have expressed similar views.

Nevertheless, on the part of most people including educators, there was an awful respect for the printed word until well into the twentieth century. Doting parents felt that their children were being educated as they learned to repeat words from books, even if they knew not their meanings.

It is true, too, that in this country to a far greater extent than many people have ever realized, the teacher at all levels has until recently relied heavily upon the textbook. His goals and aims tend to consist largely of the "covering" of materials in the textbooks, even though it may result in little understanding or intellectual interest or permanence. Someone has characterized the philosophy behind this textbook covering practice by relating the story about a moron who was accosted at a crossroads by an automobile driver, who asked the way to a village somewhere in that part of the county. It became apparent that the retarded boy could not read well, if at all. The driver asked him if he could read the highway signs, to which he replied, "Yep, I can read some of it. I can read how fur but I can't read where to."

Unfortunately, there are still many teachers who have an eager eye for a simple, easy way to make a living and do not want to be compelled to rely upon creative imagination in planning learning materials. They are very quick to accuse the teacher with modern concepts and theories of education of being anti-intellectual or relatively uncultured. This type of attack has frightened and made cautious a great many teachers, who by reason of low salaries and low economic and social status have assumed an inferior role reminiscent of Uriah Heep, the servile character in Dickens' *David Copperfield.*

[1] As quoted in Samuel Chester Parker, *A Textbook in the History of Modern Elementary Education* (Boston: Ginn & Co., 1912), p. 181.

# PROGRESSIVIST POSITIONS

## The Child-centered Position

In the first few decades of this century, there could be observed a rather strong trend to think about education in terms of child growth and development, and in terms of growth of the individual child. More educators began to adopt or lean toward the pragmatic and experimental philosophies, as well as toward the acceptance of the Gestalt concept of the human being. They began to support more widely the activity or "learn by doing" movement, reinforced by the development of individual psychology. Many leading educators were primarily concerned with providing an educational situation that would enable each child to develop all his potentialities for growth. Among those who were outstanding in this field was Colonel Francis Parker of the University of Chicago, a Rousseauvian disciple, who greatly influenced the outstanding educational philosopher of the present century, John Dewey. The proponents of the extreme child-centered point of view were little concerned with setting up goals for growth in terms of life needs and life activities. Instead, they were believers in the importance of assisting learners to unfold like a plant in the way made possible by nature, and to grow as much as they might in attaining self-realization.

Today, the planning of course of study materials and of teaching procedures attaches great importance to assisting the child, especially those with creative talents and propensities, to grow and develop without excessive frustration. Much importance is given to identifying, encouraging, and guiding the development of creative abilities; special attention is paid to youngsters of unusual abilities, and those of lower abilities, the handicapped, and those with few social and economic advantages. Pretty much discarded and forced largely out of modern practice are the discredited concepts of formal discipline, lock-step methods, the common fare for all, and impractical disregard for the interests and propensities of growing young people. In this group, there have been many extremists who were responsible for misleading many parents and teachers into overindulgence and a lack of leadership with young people as they grow up.

## The Society-centered Position

Always in the background of thinking of the American people was the belief that the schools existed to produce young people who would make good citizens and provide us with good leaders, and in other ways contribute to the health and the advancement of our society. The schools were generally thought of as being the place for passing on the social heritage, although many intellectuals conceived the social heritage to consist chiefly of the facts in books, particularly in those written by intellectuals. Nevertheless, an increasing proportion of people became much interested in the passing on of our heritage of ideals, of interests, of attitudes, and ways of behavior as they have developed in our society and proved to be worthy and necessary.

It is hardly fair to accuse the great John Dewey, who believed in this position, as being a straddler in American education; it is much better to say that he was an open-minded individual seeking the truth and that he could see no wrong in the necessity for having the educational program of the school both child-centered and society-centered. This idea of a society-centered school he added to Colonel Parker's idea of child-centered education in the nationally famous laboratory elementary school of the University of Chicago in the 1890's.

As the result of World War I, the depression, the New Deal, the development of foreign trade, the development of gigantic firms such as General Motors and General Electric, World War II, and the extension of welfare plans, along with the great expansion of taxes, people throughout the country, including not only educational leaders but leaders in all walks of life, began to think of the need for and the possibilities of education of citizens who would be much better able to understand and to cope with the economic, political, and international problems that had come to confront us. Increased prosperity of and the greatly increased enrollments in schools and colleges also contributed to the spread of the society-centered idea of the purpose and nature of education.

A number of books appeared stressing the part that education would play in enabling us to solve our national, state, and local problems and to continue our economic and political progress. Professor George S. Counts, then of Columbia University, in his *Dare the Schools Build a New Social Order?* [2] pointed out the possibilities of educating young people so that they might understand and contribute to our social and economic progress, and play a more active part in it.

Counts and his book were vigorously attacked, as were Professor Harold Rugg of Teachers College of Columbia University and his social studies textbooks, which went much further into the immediate

[2] Essentially the "Great Society" concept of today.

and practical problems of American government and American economic and political life than textbooks had done previously. There were many influential people with vested interests of one kind or another who wished to turn the clock back to the days of William McKinley and Grover Cleveland and who wanted no questions asked by young people coming through the schools. While Counts and Rugg suffered rather severe verbal castigation by the McCarthyites of their time and their dupes, the general idea they expressed continued to find acceptance.

There has developed a fairly general feeling that schools should prepare for citizenship, not merely by emotional patriotism but also by knowledge, by interest, and by appropriate attitudes and behavior. The schools must develop people who are willing to conform to the laws of society and the rule of the majority. The school must help develop individuals who have new ideas and originality to bring about reform in those aspects of our life that prevent further progress and that are liabilities rather than assets to democratic American ideas of freedom, free enterprise, and our republican form of government. Various philosophers in education have developed this idea, notably Theodore Brameld, first at the University of Minnesota and later at New York University.

In *The Education of Henry Adams,* Mr. Adams complained that he had been educated to live in the time of Julius Caesar. He insisted that the schools should not educate for the past but for the present. It has become evident to the majority of leading thinkers in American education that we must educate not entirely for the present but we must definitely make adequate and effective provision of education *for the future.* In other words, young people must be educated to understand and to adjust to change and occasionally to oppose it and to lead or assist in bringing about change and determining the nature of change.

The great English philosopher Herbert Spencer (1820–1903), in his discussion of what knowledge is of most worth, urged the consideration of the importance of society-centered schools and education for participation in the activities of the times. He identified the principal areas of life activities, and upon this background was issued the statement of the National Commission on Reorganization of Secondary Education under the title "The Cardinal Principles of Secondary Education" in 1917, which took the position that education should prepare young people to engage effectively in activities as citizens, as home-members, in leisure life, in maintaining health, and as workers. The basic ideas and concepts of this statement and the "education of all American Youth" were at the heart of the "education for life adjustment" movements that sprang up in the 1940's. The misunderstandings of this philosophy of education and misapplications by superficialists and extremists were seized upon and built into a ludicrous helpless straw man by critics of the American schools, but the central ideas survived.

As a part of this general idea of the society-centered school, there were people like Franklin Bobbitt of the University of Chicago and W. W. Charters of Ohio State University in the 1930's and 1940's who attempted to determine what should be taught in the schools by an analysis of the activities of people in various walks of life, as citizens, as readers, as homemakers, as users of leisure time, as workers in each of a number of different vocations, by means of observation and questionnaires. This approach has been called the *activity analysis* approach to curriculum building. It is of course a society-centered type of approach.

## SOME FORMAL PHILOSOPHIES OF EDUCATION

### Idealism in Education

It would be only natural that as man became more intelligent and learned more, he would seek to answer the question of what really is *best*, and which are the highest values, as determined by religious, intellectual, or social considerations. As a result, one finds as far back as Plato the development of idealism as a philosophy of life; this philosophy was carried forward with some variations by Immanuel Kant and George Wilhelm Friedrich Hegel in the latter part of the eighteenth century, and in the nineteenth and early twentieth centuries by William Torrey Harris, Ralph Waldo Emerson, Josiah Royce, and others. According to this philosophy, the aim of education is the realization of an ideal.

This school of thought is in definite opposition to the development and spread of materialism and extreme ivory tower intellectualism that Arnold Toynbee, the great English historian, believes so definitely characterizes Western civilization. Toynbee suggests that Western civilization is in a period of decay and on its way out following twenty-three other civilizations that have each in turn displayed these characteristics and subsequent decline. Oswald Spengler set forth much the same idea in 1918 in his book *Decline of the West*.

## Nationalist "Idealism"

Followed by practically all rulers, but emphasized on a large scale in the latter half of the nineteenth century in Germany under Bismarck and William I and in Italy under Victor Emmanuel II, Garibaldi, and Cavour, there has existed a belief that citizens should be trained to be unquestioningly loyal to their rulers and their way of life. This has included among other things acceptance of belief in the *divine right* of kings to rule, and the divine destiny of a particular nation.

In the present century excellent examples of this policy and belief are the indoctrination of the people of Germany by Hitler and his lieutenants into naziism, the delusion of belonging to a superior race, the devotion of Italians to fascism inculcated by Mussolini and Giovanni Gentile, and the belief in the divinity of the Divine Emperor of Japan. More recently, excellent examples are the programs of indoctrination in communism by the ruling dictators of Russia and her satellite nations; and even more recently in China and Cuba, and the strong-man dictatorships in Latin America, Africa, and Asia.

In an address to school administrators gathered at Harvard University in 1960, Neil McElroy, Secretary of Defense in the Eisenhower administration, declared:

We are in a great, long-range struggle to determine whether our free society shall survive. In this struggle, the basic source of our strength lies in the education of our people.

We must provide not only more education for more children; we must be sure to identify early and guide the special talents of *each* child, so that each may make the most of his or her abilities, whatever these may be, both for individual achievement and for the progress of our society.

Without question it is desirable to have as a principal aim of education the development of patriotism and bias in favor of one's own government, rulers, and way of life; and this is done to various degrees in practically all modern nations, including the United States.

Max Lerner had this to say about the goals and values of American civilization:

I think we ought to be very clear about just what the nature of this educational crisis is in which we are caught, because there have been several distortions of its nature that have been used by well-meaning but perhaps hysterical people for dubious educational ends.

Let me first say that what we are engaged in now educationally is not a weapons race with Russia, nor a technological race to turn out scientists as if from an assembly line.

If it were either of these, I suppose that the most efficient thing to do would be to turn over the educational system of America to the Pentagon to be administered by one of those assistant secretaries of defense, with periodic interservice quarrels as to whether students would be educated to be air-minded, land-minded, or water-minded.

Our problem is to think in terms of what we want our society to be and to shape our young people with that in mind. That means shaping them primarily as valued creators in a democracy, as young people who can develop their own kind of personality, their own kind of thinking in a society where our principal weapon is freedom.

They have to do with something that has emerged very recently in our civilization: an understanding on our part of the needs of the child's personality, not just his mind, not just his literacy, not just learning crafts, but his mental health, the health of the personality itself.[3]

## Naturalistic-Sensationist Theories

Going back more than two centuries, there has been a group of people who believed very much in what might be called *giving nature its course*—or the *self-realization* theory of education: the realization of man's potentials through natural methods of development. These philosophers wielded much influence upon elementary education in the past century: Jean-Jacques Rousseau (1712–1778), Johann H. Pestalozzi (1746–1827), and Friedrich W. Froebel (1782–1852). With the exception of Rousseau, who was essentially a non-conformist and an individualist, they were Christian-idealists with respect to objectives and developed and spread to their students what has often been called the child-centered theory of teaching methods.

Rousseau argued that the child came naturally into this world with all the possibilities for perfection if given the opportunity to develop without being spoiled by his unfavorable environment. Froebel said that the child instinctively seeks "union with God." They were all very much opposed to highly organized, formalized, intellectual education; and they might well be said to have been in a way the prophets of progressive education in the United States.

Later, around the turn of the century and early in the twentieth century, important aspects of their views were put into effect and spread by Colonel Francis W. Parker of the University of Chicago (experimental elementary school) and popularized by G. Stanley Hall of Clark University, who was the first outstanding student and authority on the nature and the education of adolescents, and by

[3] Max Lerner, "American Civilization: Goals and Values," *NEA Journal*, XLVII (October, 1958), 18–19.

John Dewey, who had a very comprehensive and cosmopolitan view of education.

Dewey and Hall were much influenced by Darwin's theory of evolution and the idea of individual growth. Along with others, they preached the culture-epoch theory, which in substance held that in the growth of the child, there was recapitulated the history of the race, and different stages in his development corresponded to different stages in the evolution of man. They tended to believe in what was called a *cathartic* idea—that since the children were passing through these stages, their behavior would frequently be of a type not socially acceptable or desirable as a permanent characteristic. They urged that it should not be taken too seriously, but that it be permitted to run its course, and that under favorable circumstances, it would decline and disappear. The idea of the operation of the principle of catharsis in behavior is as old as Aristotle and has never had wide acceptance except in a very modified form.

Overlapping these beliefs were those of *scientific realism* with respect to education—the belief in the scientific approach to the real nature of human growth—later followed by long-term child-growth studies of Anderson, Baldwin, Dearborn, Terman, Gesell, and others in the second quarter of this century.

## Sense Realism and Social Realism

In western Europe, there developed a definite feeling that education had given far too much attention to form and words, and too little to content and meaning—too much stress on verbalism, not enough on social relationships. Several types of philosophies of realism developed, including the *sense-realism* of Comenius and others. An interesting but somewhat ephemeral offshoot of it is still influential in certain types of schools in the United States as well as throughout the world, such as various forms of child-activity education, field trips, and learning-by-doing.

The idea of *social-realism* was expressed well by John Locke in England in the latter part of the seventeenth century who advocated that young people be given a type of schooling that would enable them to participate effectively in the activities of upper-class society.

Michel de Montaigne of France in the latter part of the sixteenth century was also a social-realist. Montaigne, a member of the social upper crust of France, studied much and hard and became a person of superior intellectual tastes. He went even further than that in recommending that the young people of "class" be sufficiently well educated that they could move with ease, and some of them with a considerable degree of superiority, in the social and intellectual circles in the capitals of the civilized world.

## Pragmatism, Instrumentalism, Experimentalism

With the development of scientific approaches to the acquisition and extension of knowledge in many fields, including psychology and education, there began to be leaders who insisted that "The proof of the pudding is in the eating." In other words, all things should be put to test through trial and experimentation—controlled as far as possible, but at any rate to an experimental test. Many leading thinkers became somewhat bored with efforts to discover by mental manipulation alone *general absolutes,* which had intrigued the ancients. They began to analyze and evaluate critically various hypotheses and theories on the basis of how well they seemed to work, pragmatic leading in practice—the *pragmatic* approach. Among the experimentalists of one type or another were William James, John Dewey, Boyd Bode, J. L. Childs, and William Heard Kilpatrick. Characteristic of the thinking of these thinkers about the nature and goals of education is Dewey's classic definition of education as "the continuous purposive reconstruction and reconstitution of experience" to solve problems and to meet felt needs.

In recent years, there has been a vigorous assault upon these philosophers and upon this point of view, especially by some emotional business and religious leaders and their followers. Its logic and its appeal to practical minds attracted a majority of the leaders engaged in planning curricula and instructional methods, despite vigorous and vicious attacks. John Dewey particularly was attacked because of his views about the progressive nature of our social institutions and the social responsibility of all of us for each other. He was accused somewhat unfairly as advocating a "welfare state." His position and his ideas on equality and the worth and importance of every individual were attacked viciously by influential conservative business groups and "patriotic" organizations, and by individuals who were their agents.

In addition to these critics, there were many people of sincere, deeply religious thought and emotions, who believed that the pragmatic and progressive approach with goals of improvement through change would probably lead young people away from the fundamental doctrines of the church.

## PHILOSOPHICAL CONSIDERATIONS IN
## EDUCATIONAL PSYCHOLOGY

### The Human Wants or Good Life Theory

This theory has not often been referred to as a separate and distinct philosophy of education, but as a phase or version of an idealistic or perfectionist philosophy. It has had much influence on thinking about the purposes as well as on the materials of education in the United States. Furthermore, it grew up rather definitely out of the thinking of the specialists in philosophy through the centuries who were attempting to arrive at general principles that they called *universals*, which would give us a vision of the type of life that we should try to develop through thinking, education, and religion.

It is interesting to note that outstanding educational psychologists of the period 1920–1940, Edward Thorndike of Columbia University and Charles Hubbard Judd of the University of Chicago, the great scientist Albert Einstein, and many, many other scientists, turned in their later years toward a social-philosophical type of thinking. In his advanced years, Professor Thorndike set forth the following as examples of the things that make up a good life:

1. Maintenance of the inner causes of the joy of living at or above one's present average.
2. Food when hungry, and drink when thirsty.
3. A diet that is physiologically adequate.
4. Protection against pain-causing animals.
5. Protection against disease-causing organisms, poisons, and other causes of disease.
6. Protection or insurance against accidents and disasters, such as floods, earthquakes, wars, for which the person in question is not responsible.
7. Protection against extreme shocks, fear, and strains.
8. Some room or place for undisturbed rest, protected from the elements and from bad or uncongenial men.
9. Enjoyable bodily activity, especially when one is young.
10. Enjoyable mental activity, including esthetic pleasures.
11. Opportunity for human society.
12. Opportunity for courtship, love, and life with one's mate.
13. Opportunity to care for children and to be kind to human beings and animals.
14. The approval of one's community, or at least the absence of scorn or remorse.
15. The approval of one's self, self-respect, the absence of shame and remorse.
16. Opportunity to have friends and affection, if deserving of them.

17. Opportunity to be a friend and give affection.
18. Opportunity to exercise power over some persons, animals, things, or ideas, making them do one's will.
19. Opportunity to serve a worthy master.
20. Opportunity to participate effectively as members of organized groups.
21. Opportunity to compete successfully with one's peers.
22. Opportunity to compete with one's own past record, and, if deserving, to have the pleasures of achievement and success.
23. Occasional opportunities for adventure, risk, and danger.
24. Something to be angry at and attack.
25. Protection by society (via customs, laws, and government) in what is regarded by the existing moral code as a good life.
26. Freedom to discover and publish verifiable truth.
27. Enjoyment of the happiness of others.[4]

The "good life" philosophers usually stress general and cultural education that would enable one to enjoy enriched experiences and were in general opposed to the harsh ascetic education and to strictly materialistic vocational education. They stressed the importance of developing in each human being a set of values, i.e., a desire and appreciation of higher and nobler things. In some ways, these people approach in their thinking the idealistic moral thinking of G. W. F. Hegel (1770–1831) and W. T. Harris (1835–1909), although the latter in his later years divorced his ideals from religious coloring.

### Behaviorism and Atomism

With the development of scientific methods and scientific knowledge, it was natural that some thinkers would take the position that beliefs about human nature should be based not upon basic philosophies or biases, but upon observation of human behavior. Professor Edward R. Thorndike, eminent educational psychologist at Teachers College, Columbia University, circa 1910–1940, especially in his earlier years espoused this philosophy and moved ahead on what has been referred to as the "stimulus-response theory of learning." Following the lead of the physical chemists who were intent upon breaking things down into smaller units, into molecules, into atoms, and then splitting the atom, Thorndike and his followers moved in the direction of splitting human behavior similarly into smaller and smaller units. It was only when there seemed to be a preponderance of knowledge and related theory demonstrating the unity of and the interrelationships between various aspects and facets of the human

[4] E. L. Thorndike, *Human Nature and the Social Order* (New York: The Macmillan Co., 1940), pp. 405–16.

being that this approach came to be more or less abandoned as a general approach.

The "atomistic" theory grew naturally out of the ideas of the English associationists of the eighteenth and nineteenth centuries who developed the ideas that whatever were associated together in the experiences of an individual, particularly if they were associated in the same place or at the same time, tended to be related to each other in the learning apparatus of the individual so that when one was recalled the other was likely to be recalled too—whether it happened to be ideas or physical behavior. In spite of the excesses to which this theory was carried by behaviorists, including Thorndike, John B. Watson, and others, especially between 1910 and 1930, and the degree to which it has since been discredited or limited, it very definitely has influenced our thinking and fundamental theory about learning.

### The Learner-Activity Principle

Inspired by Froebel and Pestalozzi, and in the early part of this century by Junius L. Meriam, of the University of Missouri, and William Heard Kilpatrick of Teachers College of Columbia University, this principle is what may be called "the learning by doing" principle or the activity type of education. An application of it may be seen in the project method popularized by Kilpatrick but which had been used previously in agriculture and home economics education, and in shop classes.

It was essentially a type of sense-realism. The general principle is still rather widely accepted and is a part of the repertoire of practically all of the most effective teachers at the elementary and secondary school levels.

### Gestalt-Wholeness Psychophysical Philosophy

Coming to a head in the early 1920's, there developed what was most frequently called the *Gestalt* or "field" concept of learning. As set forth in the early part of this century by Wolfgang Koehler and Kurt Koffka of Germany, it set up a major premise that the human being behaved as an interrelated, unified organism; and that as a whole, it possessed characteristics not to be found in any of its constituent parts. This theory has stood up rather well, not only in the field of learning, but also in the field of medicine—psychosomatic medicine. It has become increasingly evident that any experience that affected one part of an individual was very likely to have some if not very important effects upon many of the other parts of the individual.

This idea later on was developed in a practical way by William Heard Kilpatrick of Columbia University who formulated the phrase "concomitant" or "incidental" outcomes of learning situations. They may be good, bad, or indifferent, but frequently are bad with the types of motivation commonly employed by poor teachers. This idea was very much opposed to the atomistic, stimulus-response theory advanced by the behaviorists; and it has rather generally replaced that fragmentized concept.

### The Principle of Apperception

While perhaps not deserving at all the name of a distinct philosophy of education, an idea advanced by Johann Friedrich Herbart (1776–1841) has influenced educational thinking very greatly. This was the principle of *apperception*, namely that what one understood and how one behaved depended greatly upon what one knew and understood, and how one had previously felt, thought, and behaved. This concept of course made a good foundation stone for the development of the concept of individual differences among learners, and the belief that every individual responds somewhat differently to learning materials. It was not, however, until the development of tests for the measurement of intelligence and other human traits that the possibilities of Herbart's idea of apperception began to be influential in adapting instructional and learning materials and methods to the individual learner, including the concept and importance of "readiness."

He believed, as did John Dewey, strongly in the doctrine of interest—that *interest* previously acquired is the power behind *effort*. Inconsistently, however, he advocated a formal teaching procedure, the "Five Formal Steps," adapted to high school teaching procedure by Henry C. Morrison of the University of Chicago in the 1920's. The Morrison procedure, too, was very definitely structural and left little to the originality of the teacher to survive in a period of better educated teachers and a growing belief in the concept of teacher-planning and the teacher as an artist.

## A MODERN, ECLECTIC, BASIC, AND FUNCTIONAL PHILOSOPHY

As it became evident to John Dewey and many other leading thinkers about the problems of American education, neither the child-centered school nor the society-centered school is an adequate vehicle for preparing young people for a rich and satisfying and useful life.

1. It has become increasingly evident that to be effective in preparing young people for life today, the school must develop its program in light of the conditions and the needs and the current changes and changes likely to take place in society in various aspects of its life.

2. Furthermore, it is evident that these goals may be achieved only if the program of preparation for life is worked out in terms of just and soundest knowledge of the nature of child growth and development. It is clear that one's growth and development is conditioned very greatly by experiences that can be organized as a basis for his behavior.

3. It is also clear that a quality education can be achieved only if the learner is brought into contact with subject matter appropriate for the learner's age and stage of development as well as for the social objectives of education.

It also became evident that no one philosophy is a complete foundation on which to build a sound program for the young people of today for the world of tomorrow. The modern, comprehensive, eclectic philosophy of education so widely accepted as a basis for modern education promises a freedom from the provincialism of those individuals who like the blind men and the elephant see education from only one point of view and have a narrow philosophy of education as expressed in a great many statements of the objectives of education. Rather commonly held today in education is a comprehensive philosophy by leaders that envisages the child as he now is with his potentialities for growth and looks ahead to the type of individual that the school should attempt to bring about for effective and satisfying life in modern and future American society. This philosophy contemplates that the teacher will attempt to provide and arrange learning materials and activities for experiences by the learner that will result in growth toward the broad long-range objective.

The modern eclectic philosophy of education encompasses most of the sound principles of progressive education and the John Dewey philosophy, though quite dissimilar to some of its weaknesses, misapplications, and excesses of its superficial practitioners. It is also quite dissimilar to the image of progressive education that has been presented to the public by many of the most voluble, biased, and relatively uninformed critics of modern education, such as Adler, Smith, Woodring, Bestor, Lind, Rickover, and minor agitators, who generalized from examples of misapplication of sound ideals of progressive education by superficialists, faddists, and band-wagon hoppers. It is a successor to, and outgrowth of, many of the philosophies of education mentioned earlier, including sense-realism, the good life, self-activity, and pragmatism. As Mehdi Nakosteen, outstanding scholar in the field of the philosophy of education, explains:

> The eclectic view does not necessarily imply accepting all opposing philosophic and psychological positions, for this may lead to accepting diametrically opposed views that cancel each other and leave the would-be eclectic with nothing to hold onto save conflicting and confusing ideas. A distinction should be made here between the eclecticism based on the formulation of a point of view by addition of a number of conflicting views, and that based on making one's outlook large enough to incorporate the good elements of other philosophic and psychological positions without damaging one's own central position. Just as in political parties we have narrowly defined positions or liberal positions regardless of the label we may attach to the party, so also in philosophic positions we may have provincialism or universalism of outlook. One may be a narrow realist, rationalist, or idealist to the complete exclusion of whatever may be worthwhile in other positions, or one may be liberal enough to hold to the core of a given position but widen the circle of belief to allow for inclusion of ideas from other camps without damaging one's identification with that central position.[5]

> He drew a circle that shut me out—
> Heretic, rebel, a thing to flout.
> But love and I had the wit to win:
> We drew a circle that took him in.
>
> EDWIN MARKHAM

In conclusion it should be borne in mind that the superior educator and the most effective teacher today is not essentially a scientist or a philosopher, but is more of an artist working with human materials. He has in his mind, though maybe a bit vague at times, long-term social and child-growth objectives as well as immediate subject-matter objectives. He is constantly thinking in terms of promoting the potential growth of the young people in his classes—their present educational status, bearing in mind their hopes, their interests, the ways in which they learn. He keeps in mind the great variation that exists among the youngsters and their great desire for individual recognition. He does not blindly or slavishly follow any textbook or course of study; he examines his repertoire and background of subject matter (the greater it is in supply, the better) and exercises his judgment, discretion, and creativeness in selecting and organizing learning materials and activities. He functions as an artist in planning learning situations.

An excellent statement growing out of the eclectic philosophy of

[5] Mehdi Nakosteen, *The History and Philosophy of Education* (New York: The Ronald Press Co., 1965), p. 566.

education was recently issued by the American Association of School Administrators as follows:

We Believe This Philosophy About Our Schools

We believe our schools are our one best hope for individual attainment and for national strength and welfare. Without appropriate education of children, youth, and adults, our values will be lost, our economy and productivity famished, our vision blurred, and the individual obscured.

Without education of an ever-growing scope and quality, our nation will become feeble, and the individual will fail of his destiny. Either we disavow faith in free men, free enterprise, and a government of free men, or we retain and strengthen our faith in education as the means by which we conceive, attain, and protect them.

Schools now affect the welfare of the United States more than ever before in history, and this new importance of education has been dangerously underestimated for a long time. . . . The schools have become the chief instrument for keeping this nation the fabled land of opportunity it started out to be. . . . As long as good schools are available, a man is not frozen at any level of our economy, nor is his son.[6]

## QUESTIONS, PROBLEMS, AND PROJECTS FOR FURTHER STUDY

1. Many teachers instruct their classes daily without too much thought of the ultimate philosophy or intermediate objectives of secondary education. How has it been possible that so much has been accomplished and graduates of our secondary schools are so well educated?

2. To what extent do you agree with this statement that one outstanding educator made? "Since teachers are so poorly prepared and have such a dim view of the ultimate objectives of education, they should stick to the 'essentials' as outlined for them by leaders in education."

3. Be able to state in class the principal arguments in favor of using the Great Books as a major part of the high school curriculum, and the limitations of such a policy.

4. Be able to state in class what is the (a) child-centered position, (b) society-centered position.

5. Do you think that schools should be child-centered or society-centered? Do you believe that schools exist primarily for the children or for the benefit of the society that established the schools and supports them?

6. Be able in class to speak from notes, giving a five-minute talk on what teachers in the schools can contribute to the moral and spiritual education of young people as a means of combating materialism, juvenile delinquency, and crime.

7. Do you think that idealism and intellectualism are opposed? Be able to support your position.

8. To what extent do you think it is necessary for every country to operate

[6] *This We Believe* (Washington, D.C.: American Association of School Administrators, 1963), pp. 3–4.

its schools in a way that will indoctrinate the young people in the form of government, the prevailing economic system, and its way of life in general?

9. Sum up in a few words what Max Lerner said in the October, 1958, issue of the *NEA Journal*.

10. Do you see any signs of application of the naturalistic-sensationalist theory in educational practices today?

11. Sum up what you think were the major beliefs of John Dewey with respect to the purposes and nature of education.

12. Someone has said that Professor Thorndike's statement of the good life smacks of education for life adjustment. What do you think of that?

13. Be prepared to give in class your evaluation of an "eclectic," basal, and functional philosophy of aims and nature of education; and state what you think are its good points and its weak points.

## SELECTED SUPPLEMENTARY READINGS AND FILMS

BRAMELD, THEODORE. "World Civilization: The Galvanizing Purpose of Public Education," *The Phi Delta Kappan* (November, 1962), 58–65. A very modern, international point of view.

COMENIUS, JOHN AMOS. "Instruction for the Present and the Future Life." In *Prologue to Teaching* by SMILEY and KIEKHOFF (eds.). Fairlawn, N.J.: Oxford University Press, 1959, pp. 269–73. A concise statement of the principal educational theory of Comenius.

CUBBERLEY, ELLWOOD P. "New Ideas from Herbartian Sources," *The History of Education*. Boston: Houghton Mifflin Co., 1948. Pp. 759–64. The influence of Herbart upon American educational thinking.

DEWEY, JOHN. *Democracy and Education*. New York: The Macmillan Co., 1916. Chaps. iv and xiv.

GORDON, JULIA W. "Values in the Classroom," *The National Elementary School Principal*. LIII (November, 1962), 30–34.

GWYNN, J. MINOR. *Curriculum Principles and Social Trends*. New York: The Macmillan Co., 1960. Chap. ii.

HILGARD, ERNEST R. "The Place of Gestalt Psychology and Field Theories in Contemporary Learning Theory," *Theories of Learning and Instruction*. Chicago: The University of Chicago Press, 1964. Pp. 54–77. By an outstanding authority of the theories about learning.

LEE, GORDON C. *An Introduction to Education in Modern America*. New York: Holt, Rinehart & Winston, Inc., 1953. Pp. 61–81, 82–95, and 96–115.

MACLEAN, MALCOLM S., and LEE, EDWIN A. *Change and Process in Education*. New York: The Dryden Press, 1956. Chap. xi. Many types of emotional development are described and their relation to democratic classroom procedure are discussed.

MCDONALD, FREDERICK J. "The Influence of Learning Theories on Education (1900–1950)," *Theories of Learning and Instruction*. Chicago: The University of Chicago Press, 1964. Pp. 1–26.

MOULY, GEORGE J. *Psychology for Effective Teaching*. New York: Holt, Rinehart & Winston, Inc., 1960. Chap. xiii.

PARKER, J. CECIL, EDWARDS, T. BENTLEY, and STEGMAN, WILLIAM H. *Curriculum in America.* New York: Thomas Y. Crowell Co., 1962. Chaps. ii, iii, and iv.

RICHEY, R. W. *Planning for Teaching.* New York: McGraw-Hill Book Co., Inc., 1959. Chaps. v and xvii.

RISK, THOMAS M. *Principles and Practices of Teaching in Secondary Schools.* Cincinnati: American Book Co., 1958. Chap. v.

RIVLIN, HARRY N. *Teaching Adolescents in Secondary Schools.* New York: Appleton-Century-Crofts, Inc., 1961. Chap. ix.

THOMAS, R. MURRAY. *Ways of Teaching.* New York: David McKay Co., Inc., 1955. Chap. iv. An excellent brief review.

THUT, I. N. *The Story of Education: Philosophical and Historical Foundations.* New York: McGraw-Hill Book Co., Inc., 1957. Chaps. vi and xxi. Excellent discussion of these topics.

WATKINS, RALPH K. *Techniques of Secondary School Teaching.* New York: The Ronald Press Co., 1958. Chaps. vi, vii, and ix.

## Films

*American Teacher.* 15 minutes, "March of Time" film. Describes modern theories of education and the work of today's teacher. New York: McGraw-Hill Book Co., Inc.

*Your Educational Philosophy: Does it Matter?* 40 frames, filmstrip. Presents a number of views of the classrooms of two teachers. Compares similar situations in these two classrooms to indicate how the teachers' educational philosophy affects the types of classroom activities planned for pupils. Detroit: Wayne State University.

# 5

# THE GROWTH AND
# DEVELOPMENT OF
# AMERICAN EDUCATION

The epic story of American education cannot be encompassed by a single chapter. However, a rapid survey of the main threads of that development will help one understand better than he would otherwise the origins of our educational beliefs and practices. Even a modest acquaintance with changes that have been wrought in three and a half centuries by the currents and cross-currents of innumerable ideas and forces affords some perspective and balance with which to contemplate the contemporary scene, and the future. As Walter Lippmann has said, "We shall never imagine the present nor make any sense of it until we have explained our past well enough to imagine our future."

For the sake of convenience and an easier grasp of the material, this historical summary is divided into three parts. The first deals with the Colonial and early national period, from the Puritan settlement of Massachusetts to about 1800, dominated largely by European thought and practice. The second period embraces the nineteenth century, during which most of the features of our present educational system were shaped, many of them along distinctively American lines. Finally, a look is taken at the modifications and innovations that have occurred during the two generations since 1900, a period of unprecedented expansion and change, and, hopefully, progress. This last is dealt with only very briefly, as much of the development since 1900 merges into the contemporary and is treated better in other chapters than it could be here.

History is not made, of course, in neatly bounded intervals such as these three periods. Granted that there is some carryover from one period to another and even further (which is true of history

1790-1830

generally), sudden changes in the character of events and ideas did not occur between 1800 and 1801, or between 1900 and 1901. Nevertheless, it is helpful to break the study of history into "manageable wholes." And it is also perfectly possible, without doing violence to the truth, to discern certain characteristics that distinguish an era from other eras.

## THE COLONIAL AND EARLY NATIONAL PERIOD: LAYING FIRM FOUNDATIONS (1620–1800)

The period extending from the coming of the Pilgrims in 1620 to 1800 is just about equal to the time that has elapsed since Washington took office as president in 1789—the beginning of our national existence under the Constitution. As one reviews the educational developments of the early days, he is impressed with their very small scale, and the slow headway made against many serious obstacles. In comparing this period with later periods, one may readily see that a greatly accelerated pace characterizes the latter. It would be easy to write off as having slight significance the sometimes reluctant and fumbling efforts of the Colonial and early national era, and enthusiastically acclaim the progress achieved in later times, particularly the decades of the twentieth century.

However, some of the most important principles underlying our vast and complex educational enterprise were enunciated during those early times, as will be shown. Undoubtedly, our forebears had no conception of the influence that their beliefs and laws would have on succeeding generations. But it is fair to say that both the philosophy and practice that we believe distinguish U.S. education and schooling largely stem from decisions taken and certain convictions and attitudes held by those influential in the settling and creation of the new nation.

### Diverse Backgrounds of Early Education

The most favorable seedbed for popular education was the New England colonies, because they happened to be settled by people with strong convictions on the importance of at least a little education for all. These convictions were partly religious in origin, and partly economic and political. Massachusetts, by action of some of the early settlements and by acts of its legislative body, was the leader in this early movement for education and the establishment of schools; and for more than two hundred years exercised great influence on the pattern and character of American education. Other New England colonies more or less followed her example.

The very first school—the Boston Latin Grammar School, still a flourishing "academic" secondary school—was founded as early as 1635 by a vote of the town. The town also donated some land, the income to supplement private pledges by which the school was mainly supported.

Only a few years later, in 1642 and 1647, the General Court (legislature) of Massachusetts Bay colony enacted the first two school laws in America. It is in these two acts that the important principles referred to a moment ago have their inception; and they also reflect the combination of motives—religious, economic, and political—behind the impulse for education. James Russell Lowell alluded to these two early laws in his essay *New England Two Centuries Ago* when he wrote: "It was in making education not only common to all, but in some sense compulsory on all, that the destiny of the free republics of America was practically settled." The first law held parents and masters of apprentices accountable to the civil authorities "concerning the calling and implyment of their children [teaching a suitable trade]," and especially "their ability to read & understand the principles of religion & the capitall lawes of this country. . . ."

The second law required townships of fifty householders to appoint teachers of young children to read and write, and townships of one hundred families to set up grammar schools to prepare youth "so farr as they shall be fited for ye university." The teachers were to be supported by the "parents or masters of such children, or by the inhabitants in general." This famous law of 1647 exemplified again strong religious inspiration. The preamble held that it was "one cheife project of ye ould deluder, Satan, to keepe men from the knowledge of ye Scriptures"; hence, all children must learn to read so that Satan could be foiled.

The heavy weight given to reading originated in the Protestant Reformation, whose leaders argued that every person should be able to read God's word for himself. By an accident of fate, people of this persuasion settled New England and governed the various colonies. Thus, this important conviction was incorporated into the political structure. Later, when civil and religious authority was divided, the control of education that early legislative bodies had assumed remained with the civil government.

This became the rule throughout our country, and even today the fifty states control education. Church-related and other non-public schools have never been prohibited, however, and today they comprise a significant and vital element in the scheme of American education. But even they are subject to the authority of the several states, so long as the Constitution is not contravened.

One other important event of those very early times in New England must be mentioned. The founding of Harvard College in 1636 showed that colonial Massachusetts was interested in higher as well as in elementary and secondary education. Originally, its main purpose was to prepare ministers, the founders "dreading to leave an illiterate Ministery to the Churches, when our present Ministers shall lie in the Dust." They also wished "to advance learning, and perpetuate it to Posterity." In the Royal Charter granted in 1650, Harvard's purposes were stated as "the advancement of all good literature, artes and sciences," and making "all other necessary provisions that may conduce to the education of the English and Indian Youth of this Country in knowledge [and] godlines."

This was the first of nine colonial colleges. All were set up under private auspices, and all but one of them (Pennsylvania) were church-related. It is clear, though, that their founders considered colleges an essential element of a civilized society and were interested in promoting the advancement of knowledge, albeit their ideas about the scope of higher education were rather narrow and dominated, as the grammar schools were, by the classics. Higher education was limited to a minute proportion of the population. It remained for much later generations to liberalize college and university studies and to make them available to more than half the graduates of secondary schools.

Popularly referred to as the "Ivy League," these colonial institutions are all flourishing today as never before; and two of them have been designated in recent years as state institutions. In addition to Harvard they are: William and Mary, Virginia, 1693; Yale, Connecticut, 1701; Princeton, New Jersey, 1746 (originally the College of New Jersey); Columbia, New York, 1754 (chartered as King's College); Pennsylvania, 1755; Brown, Rhode Island, 1764; Rutgers, New Jersey, 1766; and Dartmouth, New Hampshire, 1769.

The two other major areas of colonial America had quite different educational beginnings. To the middle colonies—New York, New Jersey, Maryland, Pennsylvania, and Delaware—came settlers from several different countries of northern Europe, in contrast to the British origin of most New Englanders. They also possessed several different faiths, including mainly Lutheran, Mennonite, Presbyterian, Anglican, Quaker, and Roman Catholic.

Church-related parochial schools operated by the various congregations were one type of educational effort. Private schooling for their own children was financed by wealthy families; and charity schools for the poor were supported by such organizations as the Society for the Propagation of the Gospel in Foreign Parts, an Anglican missionary enterprise based in England. In some places, public provision for children of the poor was also made in pauper schools. This philosophy prevailed for a long time. Pennsylvania, for example, did not create a state public school system until 1834, and New Jersey about 1840.

The southern colonies in general possessed a third outlook on education. Typically, schooling was provided for privately by the families who could afford it; those who could not afford it might send their children to pauper schools, or to church-sponsored schools as in the middle colonies. Education was not provided for Negroes; for the station in life to which they were assigned, education was not deemed necessary or desirable.

## Elementary Schooling: Religion and the Three R's

While today the term "The Three R's" is still used to some extent, it seldom carries the literal meaning it had in the early days. Now we usually mean "the fundamentals," which may include several elementary school subjects not covered by the Three R's, e.g., social studies, science, health and safety, music, and art. But originally the term meant just what it stood for and no more: reading, 'riting and 'rithmetic.

In the seventeenth century, writing and arithmetic were, more often than not, taught apart from reading, in separate schools; and a little music was taught in singing schools. During the eighteenth century, however, children were increasingly brought together for all studies in one school. About 90 per cent of school time was devoted to the Three R's, in contrast to about 50 per cent in our day. This reduction was a natural result of the need to accommodate new subjects added from time to time in the elementary school curriculum.

Reading served as the primary vehicle for the teaching of religion. This was regarded as extremely important in New England. The heavy weight given to religion in children's schooling lasted a long time, but began to be tempered by secular itnerests about the middle 1700's. Yet it was a good hundred years more until the public schools became generally free of religious control or domination and took on more or less their secular characteristics, leaving the field to parochial and other non-public schools.

At first, schoolbooks were not available; but for beginners, a device called a hornbook was widely used. It consisted of a sheet of parchment (later paper) fastened to a thin wood paddle and protected by a thin sheet of transparent horn like plastic. On the parchment were hand lettered the alphabet and the Lord's Prayer. Toward the end of the seventeenth century, however, textbooks began to arrive from Europe, and American authors also commenced to write for the domestic market.

One of the best examples showing how religion and reading were tied together is the first American schoolbook, *The New England Primer*. This little book, about the size of a 3 × 5 card, less than a hundred pages, was published in Boston in 1691; and it came out in successive revised editions for more than a century and a half. Most of its contents during the colonial period consisted of religious selections such as the Lord's Prayer, the Apostles' Creed, the Ten Commandments, an alphabet in doggerel (A: In Adam's fall / We sinnèd all), and the like. Some editions included a woodcut of John Rogers, a London minister, burning at the stake, with a long rhymed sermon, "Advice to Children," which the martyr left to his wife and large family. The "Shorter Westminster Catechism" (which one of the authors of this textbook studied as a boy) was a major feature of the Primer, along with another treatise with the unusual title "Spiritual Milk for American Babes, Drawn out of the Breasts of both Testaments, for their Souls Nourishment." The Primer was said to have taught "millions to read, and not one to sin." It probably did but in a dreary and melancholy fashion, for there was really little or nothing in it of juvenile interest. It was adult religious matter watered down to make it appear superficially interesting to youngsters.

After the Revolutionary War, reading books included more patriotic selections and less religious emphasis. In 1785, Noah Webster, of dictionary fame, published *An American Selection*, the first reader completely an American product, and also the first of a long series mostly or entirely secular that had wide use. This book was commonly called the Third Part Reader, as it was the third volume in a set of three. The first volume was Webster's *American Spelling Book*, the famous "blue-backed speller," issued in 1783. It went through hundreds of editions, selling a million copies a year in the 1840's; and by 1880 estimated to have exceeded eighty million. The second volume in the series, not so well known, was a grammar. Other authors also contributed textbooks in these and other subjects.

Writing was second in importance to reading until about 1750. One of the first penmanship books was published in 1730 at Boston with the title *The Young Secretary's Guide.* The handwriting manuals of those days emphasized "artistic" writing with elaborate flourishes as much as legibility, and this emphasis continued right down to the late nineteenth century with its "Spencerian hand" that our great-grandparents probably were taught.

Arithmetic was not taught much in the early Colonial period; but it was more common in the southern and middle colonies than in New England, to prepare boys for commercial occupations, especially trade with Britain and Holland and their possessions. Its popularity as a school subject grew rapidly during the eighteenth century. In 1745, Yale College began to require it for college entrance. In 1789, it was made a legally required school subject in Massachusetts and New Hampshire, and in 1797 in Vermont.

The first arithmetic books were brought over from England or reprinted from English works. As early as 1729, however, a Harvard professor, Isaac Greenwood, published the first American arithmetic, whose practical outlook is reflected in its title, *Arithmetic Vulgar and Decimal, with the Application thereof to a Variety of Cases in Trade and Commerce.* One of the most popular arithmetic textbooks remained, nevertheless, one first published in London in 1743, *The Schoolmaster's Assistant,* by Thomas Dilworth, a famed schoolmaster. For fifty years this was a leader in the field, until challenged in 1788 by the appearance of another American arithmetic written by Nicholas Pike. (Dilworth's book was called *The Schoolmaster's Assistant* because it had the answers as well as the problems.)

There are many interesting and amusing social and economic sidelights in these old books. In Dilworth's book, for example, this problem is given:

A gentleman's servant went to the market with an order to buy 20 fowls for 20d. [pence]; he did so; and brought home pigeons at 4s. a-piece, larks at a half-penny a-piece, and sparrows at a farthing a-piece;—I demand how many there were of each sort?

Pike's book had twenty-one pages of rules for reducing different kinds of money to American dollars and cents, an important subject in a new nation whose citizens transacted business with many foreign countries. Continuing well into the nineteenth century, many problems involved dealings in brandy, wine, beer, lotteries, and even piracy, which would be shocking if they were found in today's arithmetics—can you imagine the furore that would be aroused! For example:

A vintner hath 4 sorts of wine, *viz.* Canary at 10s. [shillings] *per* gallon, Malaga at 8s. Rhenish at 6s. and Oporto at 4s. and he is minded to make a composition of 60 gallons, worth 9s. *per* gallon.—I demand how much of each sort must he have.

Ans. 45 gallons of Canary, and 5 gal. of each other sort.

For "mental discipline" hundreds of problems of a puzzle type were set for the pupils. These problems sound practical; have a kind of everyday, even casual tone; but they did not have any application to actual needs. Problems like these, set in 6-point type, probably stump a good many students using this book:

Two men talking of their ages, one said he was $37 \dfrac{3847}{14783}$ years old, and the other said he was $64 \dfrac{213}{250}$ years old. What was the difference of their ages?

Seven gentlemen, who were travelling, met together by chance, at a certain inn upon the road, where they were so well pleased with their host, and each other's company, that in a frolic, they offered him 30 £. [30 pounds] to stay at that place so long as they, together with him, could sit every day at dinner in a different order: The host thinking that they could not sit in many different positions because they were but a few of them, and that himself would make no considerable alteration, he being but one, imagined that he should make a good bargain; and readily (for the sake of a good dinner and better company) entered into an agreement with them, and so made himself the eighth person;—I demand how long they staid at the said inn, and how many different positions they sat in?

Ans. The number of positions were 40320; and the time that they staid was 110 years, 142 days; allowing the year to consist of 365 days, 6 hours.

Other subjects were added to the elementary school curriculum from time to time. The first geography textbook was published in America in 1783, written by the Reverend Jedediah Morse, father of Samuel F. B. Morse, artist and inventor. Here and there schoolmasters taught a little history, science, and drawing. Generally during the Colonial and early national period, these subjects were not taught; the elementary school curriculum as we know it did not begin to take shape until after the Civil War.

It will be recalled that the law of 1642 charged parents and masters to teach children a suitable trade, as well as the Three R's. Apprenticeship was an important element in the training of children of the poor and orphans and abandoned children. Although it fell far short of being universal and desirable, apprenticeship was a kind of compulsory schooling for the groups mentioned. Laws governing apprenticeship were enacted by most of the colonies and later the new states well into the nineteenth century.[1]

Another kind of effort, chiefly in New England, to bring children into some contact with the rudiments of learning was the so-called dame school. This was not really a school, but only a group of youngsters taught informally by a housewife while she went about her household tasks. A small fee, perhaps a penny a day, was paid for each child. Elementary schooling was also afforded by private tutors, parish priests and ministers, and missionaries employed by such organizations as the Society for the Propagation of the Gospel in Foreign Parts.

Schooling was, however, far from universal; although the early enactment of school laws and the variety of educational effort might give a different impression. It is known that all through the early period many children did not attend school, and that most girls received little schooling. The typical length of the "school year" in 1800 has been estimated as only four months.

In general, boys and girls must not have had a very happy time in school. Discipline was harsh, sometimes cruel, for teachers were expected to be masters in the literal sense, and one who lost the upper hand was a failure. The school day was often seven or eight hours, compared with five to six now. Schoolrooms were crudely furnished with benches, a high teacher's desk and stool. Such conveniences as cupboards, blackboards, good lighting, heating, toilets, drinking fountains, and so on were, of course, unknown. Playgrounds, especially in town schools, were extremely small or non-existent.

### Secondary Education: Classical and Selective

In the Colonial and early national period, there was a widespread conviction that the main if not the sole purpose of secondary education was preparation for admission to college. Indeed, this attitude persisted throughout the nineteenth century, with some notable exceptions that will be mentioned.

During this early era, three main types of secondary school can be identified. The Latin grammar school was a direct importation from England, spreading from New England through all the colonies except Georgia. While the law of 1647 gave an impetus to grammar schools, some towns took the easy way out and simply paid a fine of £5 to a

[1] An interesting document is the apprenticeship agreement entered into for twelve-year-old Benjamin Franklin by his parents and elder brother James, a printer, in James Parton's *Life and Times of Benjamin Franklin* (Boston: Houghton Mifflin Co., 1882), Vol. I, p. 53.

neighboring town rather than set up a grammar school of their own.

But the grammar school never became a popular institution. Its curriculum consisted almost entirely of Latin and Greek and some-times Hebrew—subjects deemed of most importance in the training of clergymen and lawyers. Girls were not admitted. By the end of the eighteenth century, the grammar schools had almost all folded. They failed to meet the needs of the people; they were too far re-moved from the pressing concerns of life as it was lived, and catered to too small and select a segment of the population.

In the first half of the eighteenth century, this out-of-touch char-acter of the grammar schools had already given rise to two other kinds of secondary schools: the private "English" school and the academy. Both offered a much more liberal program of studies than did the grammar school, emphasizing also the use of English, although most academies retained the classics as part of their pro-gram. They added other practical and up-to-date subjects, such as mathematics, science, modern languages (especially French, some-times Spanish and German), navigation, commerce, history, agricul-ture, and surveying. Girls were usually admitted along with boys, making these schools far more democratic than the grammar schools. In many private schools, girls could study dancing, needlework, music, and drawing.

Private schools were, as their name indicates, supported by fees paid to the master or owner. Most academies also required fees, but during the eighteenth century some began to receive aid from local public funds. They were boarding schools, as a rule, and were re-garded as a good thing for a community to have. The academies displaced the private schools pretty largely by 1800, partly because they did not depart so radically from traditional subject matter or from the college preparatory goal. They served a broader range of interests, were better managed, and in many cases were backed by churches.

One of the most notable academies was founded with Benjamin Franklin's help at Philadelphia in 1751. During the preceding ten years, he had worked on proposals for a new type of school with a modern curriculum alongside the classical. His aim was that students would be taught "everything that is useful and everything that is ornamental. But," he added, "art is long, and their time is short. It is therefore proposed that they learn those things that are likely to be most useful and most ornamental, regard being had to the several professions for which they are intended." Of the three divi-sions set up, the Latin, Mathematical, and English schools, the first was soon converted into the University of Pennsylvania (1775), and the other two were subordinated to carry on as prep schools for half a century. This and other academies assisted in liberalizing secondary education as it developed in the nineteenth century.

In those days, the idea of secondary education for all was not even a dream. One must not be misled by the variety of secondary schools mentioned, and by the limited extension of opportunity to more boys and girls. Not for another hundred and fifty years after the opening of Franklin's academy would secondary education enter a period of rapidly increasing availability. The American people were not ready for popular secondary education—socially, politically, or economically. But new forces were beginning to operate toward this end.

### A Caste System for Teachers

Quite a contrast prevailed between secondary teachers and those of young children in this early period. While almost all teachers were men (except in the dame schools), those in the common schools—the primary or elementary level—were far inferior to those in secondary schools—in training, status, personal character, and pay. Or so it seems from reading the sources.

One writer states that the elementary school teachers were as good as the times demanded, but this seems like a rather shallow judgment. No recognized preparation for teaching was available (and would not be until well into the nineteenth century) either in subject matter or methodology. There was no certification or licensing procedure; although in some places, especially in New England, ministers had to give their approval before teachers were hired. Anyone who wanted to teach could do so if he could just find someone to sign him on, and teaching was often the last resort of ne'er-do-wells and sickly men. Some teachers were even indentured servants who paid for their passage to the New World by contracting to teach for a given number of years.

Socially and economically, the elementary school teacher's status was very low, as a rule. His pay was often "in kind," that is, in the form of firewood, potatoes, apples, wheat, etc.; often, his meager salary was supplemented by "boarding 'round" with different families—a custom not beyond the memory of persons living now. To eke out their livelihood, and frequently as part of their duties, teachers did many odd jobs for church and community: grave digging, bell ringing, janitor work, choir singing or directing, serving as town crier, and letter writer. Such responsibilities were sometimes attached to secondary school teaching too.

On a much higher plane were the early day secondary school masters, particularly those in Latin grammar schools. Many were graduates or former students of Oxford and Cambridge. They were better paid than teachers in the lower schools, even though their salaries came in whole or in part from the precarious source of tuition fees. Their social status was, on the whole, high; and they were recognized as "career educators," which was seldom true of the lowly schoolmaster who taught the Three R's.

A few influenced their schools by such outstanding work over so many years that their schools became, as Emerson said, "the lengthened shadow of one man." Notable both for the quality of their teaching and for their longevity, for example, are Ezekiel Cheever (1614–1708), who taught seventy-one years in New England, thirty-eight of them as head of the Boston Latin School, and Elijah Corlett (1611–1687), who was headmaster of Cambridge Latin School for forty-three years.

### State and Local Control Originated

In the early period, schooling was of necessity largely a local matter, with only general oversight being exercised by first the colonial and then the state governments. The pattern of control that was later to become dominant had its beginnings in New England. We have seen that an attempt to establish central authority was made in those two laws of 1642 and 1647. However, the isolation of settlements, the poor roads, and the lack of rapid communication forced local communities to take charge.

In 1766, Connecticut legalized the creation of local school districts and empowered the voters to elect their own school trustees, appoint teachers, and levy taxes. Massachusetts followed suit in a series of laws between 1789 and 1827. In the South, where settlements were more widely separated and large plantations were developed, counties became the basic unit of local control. However, the typically small district of New England, as small as 3 or 4 square miles, was the model carried west as the country expanded.

During Colonial times, the governing board of a school was ordinarily a committee of the town council, until as noted above separate boards were elected just for schools. In some eastern states, the board is still called the school committee.

The small districts and local boards noted here not only evolved into a unique feature in the structure of American government, but also gave rise to many serious problems in the nineteenth and twentieth centuries, as we shall see later in this chapter and in Chapters 12 and 13.

## New Vistas at the Close of the Eighteenth Century

Toward the end of the early period, changes of great magnitude were foreshadowed. Events occurred, proposals were made, and pronouncements issued that during the next century and down into our own time proved to be of immense influence in shaping American education in both philosophy and practice. At the time, these far-reaching effects could perhaps not even have been imagined. Today, it would be impossible to exaggerate their wisdom and applicability for a nation destined for world leadership. The first U.S. census in 1700 reported only 3.9 million inhabitants, and the census of 1800 about 5.3 million. For such a small population, the infant nation was richly blessed with men of unusual ability, vision, and idealism, the like of which has never been seen.

The crucial importance that the new nation's leading statesmen attached to education is vividly reflected in a few short quotations.

WASHINGTON: "In proportion as the structure of a government gives force to public opinion, it is essential that public opinion should be enlightened."

JEFFERSON: "If a nation expects to be ignorant and free, in a state of civilization, it expects what never was and never will be."

MADISON: "A popular Government, without popular information, or the means of acquiring it, is but a Prologue to a Farce or a Tragedy: or perhaps both. Knowledge will forever govern ignorance; and a people who mean to be their own Governors must arm themselves with the power which knowledge gives."

JOHN ADAMS: "The whole people must take upon themselves the education of the whole people, and must be willing to bear the expense of it."

Such pronouncements have been echoed and reinforced down through our history by our presidents and other statesmen as well as by a long succession of men and women of letters and leaders in business, industry, labor, and other fields. There can be no doubt that American educational thought was initially so well shaped and given so strong an impetus in the eighteenth century that the ideas and ideals then expressed still control.

Even before the ratification of the Constitution, there were signs and portents of the great importance that was to be attached to education. In 1779, Jefferson introduced in the Virginia legislature a bill proposing a complete state system of education from primary school through the university. The only part that he lived to see was the creation of the university; but the idea of universal, secular, and free elementary education that was part of his proposal did persist and was largely achieved in the nineteenth century.[2]

Two statements of national policy reflecting concern for popular education were enacted by the government while it was still operating under the Articles of Confederation. The Ordinance of 1785 provided for the surveying of public lands, established the 6-mile-square township as the unit of territorial measurement, and reserved in each township 1 square mile the sale of which should be used for support of common schools.

Only two years later, the government passed the famous Ordinance of 1787 setting forth the plan for organizing and creating states from the Northwest Territory (Ohio, Indiana, Michigan, Illinois, Wisconsin, and part of Minnesota). This act confirmed the land-grant policy of 1785 and proclaimed that "Religion, morality, and knowledge being necessary to good government and the happiness of mankind, schools and the means of education shall forever be encouraged." This land-grant policy has continued throughout our history to suit changing conditions as new states in the West were admitted to the Union. It culminated in the most vast endowment ever given anywhere for any purpose.

In secondary education, as we have seen, there were changes already being wrought before the end of the early national period. The academy embodied in greatest measure the most widely approved practices in secondary education; but early in the nineteenth century, it was to be challenged and soon supplanted by the high school.

Reforms in elementary schooling were slower in appearing. Incipient dissatisfaction on several counts was apparent, however. Too many children were not attending schools, and universal schooling seemed beyond reach. There were more religious influence and control than many thought was proper for a public school system. Teaching methods, relying largely on rote memorization and strict discipline, were sterile and incapable of meeting the needs of pupils ranging from five to twenty-one years of age, gathered higgledy-

[2] For the main provisions of Jefferson's plan, see E. E. Brown, *The Making of Our Middle Schools* (New York: Longmans, Green & Co., 1914), pp. 206–8. Jefferson Seminary (and University of Louisville) was founded in 1798 on principles advocated by him.

piggledy in one schoolroom. Immediately with the dawn of the nineteenth century, new ways of conducting elementary schooling were tried, eventually leading to pretty much the pattern with which we are familiar.

## THE NINETEENTH CENTURY: OPENING THE DOORS OF EDUCATIONAL OPPORTUNITY

Vast changes that took place in U.S. education during the nineteenth century were just one phase of the growth from a small agrarian nation to a lusty industrial society. As the West was settled, new currents of thought and action flowed through American life. Many new social, political, and economic problems arose, among which were problems of education. It was truly a period of extraordinary ferment—the adolescence of a mighty nation.

Mechanization of agriculture and manufacturing led to stepped-up production, giving Americans an ever higher material standard of living. It also made possible the withdrawal of children from the labor market, although the fruits of this movement were and still are being realized more in our time than in the preceding century. Labor leaders had an ardent belief that "knowledge is power." The early associations of workingmen, antecedents of modern labor unions, during the middle of the century regarded equal, universal educational opportunity as a chief plank in their platform of social goals.

Another important influence operating to make more schooling more accessible to more children and youth was the breaking down of old class distinctions. The people who settled the West, in particular, would not tolerate the class system of education found in some of the older states, which provided free schooling only for paupers. Nor did they favor giving as much weight to the classics as did the Latin schools and many academies. More attention was demanded for practical arts and sciences, the knowledge and skill needed for mastering the vast empire reaching to the Pacific.

Accelerated urban growth brought a mixture of advantages and serious problems to public education. During the century, the population not only grew from about five million to seventy-six million, but also its urban ratio changed from about 5 per cent to 40. This increasing concentration in cities—reaching unprecedented levels today —made possible longer school terms and greater flexibility in grouping and scheduling pupils. On the other hand, problems of keeping schoolhouse construction in pace with growing enrollments became acute, and problems of delinquency and the use of leisure time were multiplied.

Two other changes during the century had high social and educational significance. In 1800, there were few educational opportunities for girls and women and practically no vocational outlets except as domestics, seamstresses, teachers, and of course housewives. But by 1900, most barriers to educational opportunity and taboos against admission to most types of vocational and professional work had been broken or at least battered. The status of girls and women underwent a radical change during the period.

The other change referred to was the titanic flow of immigrants from Europe to the United States, which went on during most of the nineteenth century, bringing some twenty million foreign-born to our shores. At the end of the century, about 14 per cent of the population was foreign-born. In cities of more than 25,000, the ratio was 26 per cent; in cities of more than 100,000, 35 per cent, with a few of the largest cities having in excess of 50 per cent.

Assimilating such large numbers of immigrants, who came from many different countries, was urged by proponents of universal education as an important task of the schools. Free schools were needed, it was argued, to help the children of immigrants become good American citizens; and in the cities adults were also offered many opportunities by the schools to become "Americanized."

The "forward surge of democracy," it is clear from just these few examples, was greatly furthered by the evolving educational system. Of many changes experienced in the American educational system during this exciting, restless, tragic, and booming period, those that seem to have contributed most to our thought and practice are noted in the next few pages.

## European Models Discarded in Elementary Schooling

During the first half of the nineteenth century, attempts were made to improve and extend common schooling by importing four schemes from Britain. The Sunday School was the first of these, a secular school conducted on Sunday for children who worked the other six days. By 1824, it was largely taken over by churches for religious instruction. Schools supported by private subscription were a second type of effort, conducted by "school societies" similar to those in England. They catered to children whose parents were not declared paupers, or who were not entitled to send them to parochial schools, or who were not wealthy enough to have their offspring privately educated. In the cities they were fairly successful; in New York these schools enrolled more than half a million pupils between 1805 and 1853 when they were turned over to the city school system. DeWitt Clinton was president of the New York Free School Society for many years.

The plan known as monitorial schools was brought over by one of its originators, Joseph Lancaster. Its central idea was the use of teen-age pupils to teach younger children. Thus, one paid schoolmaster could take charge of several hundred children, seated in groups of ten on benches ranged in a large hall. Each day's lessons were taught by the master to the "monitors," who in turn were supposed to impart the same information to their charges. In the cities, these schools achieved meteoric popularity; but by 1830, they had mostly died out.

Finally, the Infant School was given a whirl. Robert Owen, its originator, was a wealthy Scottish cotton mill owner of philanthropic and humanitarian bent, who believed that education was one of the main avenues for improving the lot of working people. He conceived the idea of giving little children three to six years old some rudiments of schooling before they had to go to work in mills and mines and on the farms. (Owen is best known in this country for his ill-fated attempt to found a utopian colony at New Harmony, Indiana.) By 1840, the societies that supported the infant schools folded; the older pupils were absorbed by the expanding public school system.

It would be easy to dismiss lightly these four kinds of educational effort. They were all short-lived, their aims were low and missed by a wide margin meeting children's needs, and there was too much emphasis on mechanics of operation and low cost. Yet they were symptomatic of a growing interest in making more education available to more children. Since they were believed for a while to yield good results for little expense, they helped mightily in spreading the idea of universal education. People began to believe that it might be within the realm of possibility to get and keep more children in school and for more years.

## Emergence of American Concepts of Education

Through about the middle fifty years of the nineteenth century, a transformation in education was effected that brought American schools to essentially the form we have now. Many refinements and changes were to occur after 1875, to be sure; but by that time the graded, free, universal, and secular character of public elementary (and within a few years secondary) education had been firmly grounded in theory and in law if not equally in practice. The completion of the "ladder system," a sequence of educational opportunity in public schools from kindergarten through high school, was attained by 1875, and through college by the dawn of the twentieth century. Perhaps it is in order to sound here a note of caution that none of these gains and improvements has been literally and fully put into practice even today (and they may never be) except the organization of schools by grades—and on this there is currently some movement back toward "ungraded" schools! However, the principles involved are widely accepted, and ever more generally actualized, even though they continue to be debated with varying degrees of intensity as new problems arise and as waves of public opinion rise and fall.

The "common school" of the colonial and early national period was an ungraded school, it will be recalled. As pupils enrolled in greater numbers, some convenient way of grouping them seemed necessary. The eight years of the elementary level, as it was then defined, were first divided into "primary" and "grammar" groups of four years each; but soon an "intermediate" stage was created, the three groups embracing respectively what we would call grades 1–3, 4–6, and 7–8. These designations are still used more or less informally today, although the junior high school has nearly obviated the term "grammar grades."

In the 1830's, the Prussian Volksschule ("people's school" or "common school") was the subject of enthusiastic and widely circulated reports by such eminent American educational leaders as Horace Mann and Calvin E. Stowe, and by an outstanding French educator, Victor Cousin. These reports hastened the adoption of the eight-grade elementary school, the pupils normally advancing one grade a year, in the United States as well as throughout Europe.

The abolition of tuition fees was a major victory for the advocates of universal education. Through the first half of the nineteenth century, it was common practice for public school authorities to charge parents of pupils a fee geared to the number of their children enrolled and the number of weeks they attended. Other sources such as lotteries, philanthropic grants, and state aid supplemented the fees. These "rate bills," as the fees were called, were the subject of a struggle whose bitterness is hard for us to understand. Free schools were regarded as subversive of American principles and ideals by many wealthy, or childless, or foreign-born, by farmers, southern whites, social and political conservatives, and by the unschooled, of whom there were many. In fact, it seems that those who would have benefited most from tax-supported schools were most numerous and vociferous in opposing them. General taxation for school support was an unpalatable idea, and free schools had for a long time been thought of as pauper schools. But the battle for tax-supported elementary schools was won by the middle of the century.

Another controversy, and one not concluded even today, raged around attempts by some to make public schools secular, that is, free from church control or sectarian influence, and attempts by others to perpetuate the strong religious influence of colonial times. The general principle that tax-supported public schools in the United States must be free of sectarian control or influence finally won out. From 1850 on, the states provided in their constitutions or statutes that public (tax) funds could not be used for sectarian purposes. The Constitutional guarantee of religious freedom made such an outcome inevitable. However, the definition of what is religious or sectarian influence or control is still not completely forged—it is the subject of a whole series of Supreme Court decisions in our own day. It is also safe to say that few, if any, schools are completely secular in the literal sense, for observance, for example, of Christmas and Thanksgiving is commonplace. The part that religion should play in education and the relations of public and parochial education are still the subject of much study and discussion.

The latter half of the nineteenth century brought major advances in compulsory school attendance. Along with all the other changes going on, the conviction grew that every child was entitled to an elementary education. Commencing with Massachusetts in 1852, all the states except those in the South by 1900 enacted laws requiring parents to send their children to school, usually to age fourteen or sixteen, or through the eighth grade. (All the southen states enacted attendance laws by 1918; but Mississippi, South Carolina, and Virginia repealed theirs as part of their resistance to racial desegregation, following the Supreme Court decision of 1954.) While we tend to take compulsory attendance for granted, it is almost impossible to ascribe too much importance to this single feature of our educational system. A large majority of the world's nations still either lack such laws or fail to enforce them.

Some changes in secondary education were also in the making. From its heyday in the 1850's, the academy gradually gave ground to the public high school. This new institution, born in Boston in 1821, experienced slow growth for some forty years due in part to the same kind of opposition as was directed at the elementary school.

The American people were not quite prepared for secondary education on a big scale—they had yet to popularize elementary schooling—although Massachusetts did enact a law as early as 1827 requiring every town of five hundred families or more to provide a high school. But the wave of popular demand for extension of free elementary education widened during the latter half of the century to engulf secondary education.

In 1874, the principle of tax support was applied to high schools in the famous Kalamazoo case. Justice Cooley cited in the decision such weighty precedents as the Massachusetts laws of 1642 and 1647 and the Ordinance of 1787. Public high schools were soon established in all states to satisfy growing demands for more education for both girls and boys, more comprehensive programs of study, and less emphasis on preparation for college entrance. From approximately 400 high schools in 1860, their number grew to 6,005 in 1900. In the latter year, about three-fourths of the enrollment in all types of secondary schools were in public high schools, with about 520,000 pupils. However, only 15 per cent of the children fourteen to seventeen years old were enrolled, a fact indicative that the high school still fell far short of being a truly democratic or popular institution.

## A New Outlook on Philosophy, Curriculum, and Methods

For almost everyone who lived during the last century, schooling ended somewhere in the course or at the completion of their elementary education. Little more than literacy was the objective; secondary education was the privilege of a very small proportion of the population. Toward the end of the century, however, demands for free schools open to all became more and more insistent, first at the elementary level, and then in the nineties at the secondary level.

Accompanying the popularization of education, there were the beginnings of a marked shift from personal to social values. Pestalozzi, Spencer, and Herbart, for example, emphasized the improvement of society along with personal growth. During the last decade of the century, John Dewey, one of the greatest American philosophers and teachers, began to develop this social philosophy and continued to refine it for half a century. Now it is agreed by educational leaders and statesmen that a publicly supported, free system of schools and compulsory attendance at either public or private school are justifiable mainly because of their contribution to our society. Within this framework, there is still much stress on and opportunity for individual improvement. This change in the philosophical underpinnings of American education accounts in large part for the fantastic progress that has been made since the turn of the century.

School curricula underwent considerable shaking up, too, partly by revision of content and partly by addition of much new content. In the lower schools, for example, about 1800, more than 90 per cent of a child's school time was devoted to the Three R's. Little by little, through the efforts of such enlightened men as Horace Mann, James G. Carter, and Henry Barnard, new subjects were added—history, geography, sewing, and nature study. By 1850, the time spent on the Three R's declined to 70 per cent; and with the further addition of new content—science, drawing, physical training, music, cooking, manual training—by 1900, it was down to 60 per cent. The increasing availability of textbooks by American authors helped this new movement. Very important also in creating a favorable milieu for educational change and progress was the gradual but continuing freeing of the United States from political, economic, and cultural dependence on Europe. All through the nineteenth century, our people increasingly turned their attention to the problems of a new and growing nation and, hampered relatively much less by tradition than were the peoples of Europe, more readily accepted new ideas and content. A fair conclusion would be that there were more changes in and more ventilation of elementary and secondary school curricula in the United States during this century than there had been anywhere in the previous thousand years.

New ideas and practices related to philosophy and curriculum naturally were reflected in methods of teaching and discipline. Beginnings were made that, while modest, were to evolve in our century into a veritable revolution in education.

To teaching methods three solid contributions were made. One, originating in the work and thought of Pestalozzi, influenced by Rousseau, was insistence on supplanting rote learning with firsthand experience, so far as possible. Pestalozzi believed that children should have contact with nature and things, not just read about them in books. This line of thought was followed by Edward Sheldon and others in training teachers at the state normal schools at Oswego, New York, from 1860 on. In the 1890's, the German philosopher-educator Herbart further refined Pestalozzi's conclusions and formulated an instructional method that was known as "the five formal steps." The present-day National Society for the Study of Education was originated by his American disciples as the National Herbart Society in 1892. The method's emphasis on literature and history, the social conception

## OF EUROPE

Q. What are the minerals?

A. Silver, quicksilver, copper, lead and iron; coal, freestone, gypsum and alum.

Q. What is the religion of France?

A. The Roman Catholic. By the new constitution all religions are tolerated.

Q. What is the government?

A. A limited hereditary monarchy. The legislative power is vested in the king, a house of peers, and a house of delegates chosen by the people.

Q. What is the population?

A. In 1812, the population of the present limits of France was 23,397,-215; making 175 to a square mile.

Q. What is the military strength?

A. A standing army is now maintained of about 200,000 men. At the present time France has but a very small number of veteran troops. Her old army was wholly destroyed in Russia, in Germany and at Waterloo.

Q. What is the naval strength of France?

A. In 1809, it amounted to 40 sail of the line and 30 frigates. A considerable part of it has since been captured.

Q. What is the revenue?

A. It amounts to about 600 million francs or nearly $120 millions. The national debt in 1807, was about 2000 millions of francs. The arrears since that period are stated at 1305 millions; making a total of more than 3,300 millions.

Q. What is the national character?

A. The French are remarkable for quickness of apprehension, vivacity and gaiety; and for taste in dress and in equipage. They are at the same time generally immoral and unprincipled; and, within the last 25 years, have discovered a ferocity, cruelty, and thirst of blood, unrivalled in the annals of human crimes.

Q. What is the language?

A. The French is a corruption of the Latin, intermixed with the Gothic. On the coast, between the Seine and the Loire, remains of the Celtic are obvious in the vernacular tongue.

Q. What is the state of literature?

A. Since the revolution the French have been distinguished for their progress in mathematics and physical science. Learning, properly so called, can hardly be said to exist in France at the present time.

Q. What is the capital?

A. Paris, on both sides of the Seine, 150 miles from its mouth, in 48° 52' north latitude. . . .

Fig. 5–1. Reproduction of Page 55 from A System of Universal Geography for Common Schools in Which Europe Is Divided According to the Late Act of the Congress at Vienna, by Rev. Nathaniel Dwight (Northampton: Simeon Butler, 1817). (This is one of three pages on France.)

of education, and the scientific approach to the solution of educational problems are still of much significance today.

With the adoption of graded classes, pupils were taught in groups somewhat more homogeneous than formerly. Textbooks began to appear for specific grade levels, like the famous McGuffey series of readers. Efforts were made to include material in the books that was more appealing and appropriate to the children for whom they were intended. The old catechetical style of question and answer (illustrated in Fig. 5–1) was suited to the rote method but not to newer methods whose goal was learning with comprehension. In the illustration, one can note also the sweeping characterization of a whole people in most unfavorable terms, something that would never be tolerated in the latter part of that century or in ours.

The scientific movement, which is one of the major attributes of twentieth century education, had its inception in the closing years of the nineteenth century. It stems from the work of both European scholars like Wundt and Herbart and Americans like G. Stanley Hall, who led the way in child study, and J. M. Rice, who pioneered standardized testing.

Changing concepts of discipline made obsolete the stereotype of the teacher as a master who was expected to maintain physical as well as moral ascendancy over his pupils. Although great teachers of all ages, clear back to ancient times, have counseled mild discipline, this was certainly not the rule a hundred years or so ago (Fig. 5–2). A long list of offenses and penalties quoted below from 1848 rules of an academy in North Carolina is vivid testimony of what was regarded as bad conduct and how it was dealt with. The lashes prescribed were strokes with a switch or a cane.

### Rules of School

Boys and Girls Playing Together, 4; Quareling, 4; Fighting, 5; Fighting at School, 5; Quareling at School, 3; Gambleing or Beting, 4; Playing at Cards at School, 10; Climbing for Every foot Over three feet up a tree, 1; Telling Lyes, 7; Telling Tales Out of School, 8; Nick-naming Each other, 4; Giving Each Other Ill Names, 3; Fighting Each Other in time of Books, 2; Swaring at School, 8; Blackgarding Each Other, 6; for Misbehaving to Girls, 10; For Leaving School Without Leave of the Teacher, 4; Going Home with each other without Leave of the Teacher, 4; for Drinking Spirituous Liquors at School, 8; Making Swings & Swinging on Them, 7; For Misbehaving when a Stranger is in the House, 6; For waring Long Finger Nails, 2; For Not Making a bow when a Stranger Comes in or goes out, 3; Misbehaving to Persons on the Road, 4; For Not Making a bow when you Meet a Person, 4; For Going to Girl's Play Places, 3; Girles Going to Boys Play Places, 2; Coming to School with Dirty face and Hands, 2; For Caling Each Other Liars, 4; For Playing Bandy, 10; For Bloting Your Copy Book,

Fig. 5–2. A Schoolmaster of a Hundred Years Ago (an old print of unknown origin)

2; For not making a bow when you go home or when you come away, 4; For Wrestling at School, 4; Scuffling at School, 4; For not Making a bow when going out to go home, 2; For Weting Each Other Washing at Play time, 2; For Hollowing & Hooping Going Home, 3; For Delaying Time Going home or Coming to School, 4; For Not Making a bow when you Come in or go Out, 2; For Throwing Any Thing Harder than your trab ball, 4; For Every Word you mis In your Hart Leson without Good Excuse, 1; For Not Saying yes Sir & no Sir or yes marm or no marm, 2; For Troubleing Each others Writing affares, 2; For Not washing at playtime when going to Books, 4; For Going & Playing about the Mill or Creek, 6; For Going about the Barn or doing any Mischief about the Place, 7.

November 10, 1848.                         Wm. A. Chaffin, Master.[3]

[3] C. L. Coon (ed.), *North Carolina Schools and Academies, 1790–1840—a documentary history* (Raleigh, N.C.: North Carolina Historical Commission, 1915), pp. 763–64. Reprinted by permission.

In Edward Eggleston's folk masterpiece, *The Hoosier Scholmaster*, published in 1871 but with its setting a score of years earlier, one can discern the beginnings of a change from the use of force and brutality toward what might be called the modern mental hygiene approach to discipline problems. While teachers and psychologists have not always agreed on definitions of "good" and "bad" conduct, since Eggleston's time less effort has been expended on enforcing rigid conformity to teachers' conceptions of "good" behavior, and more on getting at the roots of unsatisfactory performance and behavior of children in school. With this change of attitude, the child was not always looked upon as invariably in the wrong; it might be any one or a combination of causes related not only to the child himself, but also to the parents, the home situation, the teacher, the school, other children, and other factors of society.

The growth of kindergartens helped bring a more humane spirit into the educational system by its emphasis on wholesome environment and gentle treatment of little children. The first U.S. kindergarten was set up in 1855 by Mrs. Carl Schurz in Watertown, Wisconsin, who brought from Germany the pattern of Froebel's "garden of children," in which play and instruction were intertwined. This was a private, German-language kindergarten; but the idea caught on fairly quickly. The first public school kindergarten was opened by the St. Louis school system in 1873; and its teacher, Susan Blow, spoke and wrote prolifically on the subject. By 1900, most large cities included it as a regular part of the elementary school level.

### Beginnings of Teacher Education

For two centuries after the first colonists came to the New World, there was no formal provision made for the preparation of teachers. Finally in 1823, the twenty-eight-year-old Reverend Samuel R. Hall, who headed a small private academy at Concord, Vermont, had the happy inspiration to offer "Lectures on Schoolkeeping" in the third and final year of his three-year course for those of his students who planned to teach. He also had them observe at nearby rural schools, the forerunner of student teaching. James G. Carter began as a young man of thirty-two similar work at his academy in Lancaster, Massachusetts, in 1827.

Teacher education remained very small potatoes until Massachusetts established several state institutions for the purpose, beginning in 1839. Carter and Mann, who helped pioneer so much that was good in American education, were instrumental in this work too. By

1860, there were a dozen teachers' colleges in various states; and in another twenty years, the recognition of teacher education as part of college and university programs was rather widespread. The licensing or certification of teachers remained on an informal and local footing until the end of the century. A sample document of the mid-century, issued by the "Instr. of the Nash. Lit. Institution," is shown in Fig. 5–3.

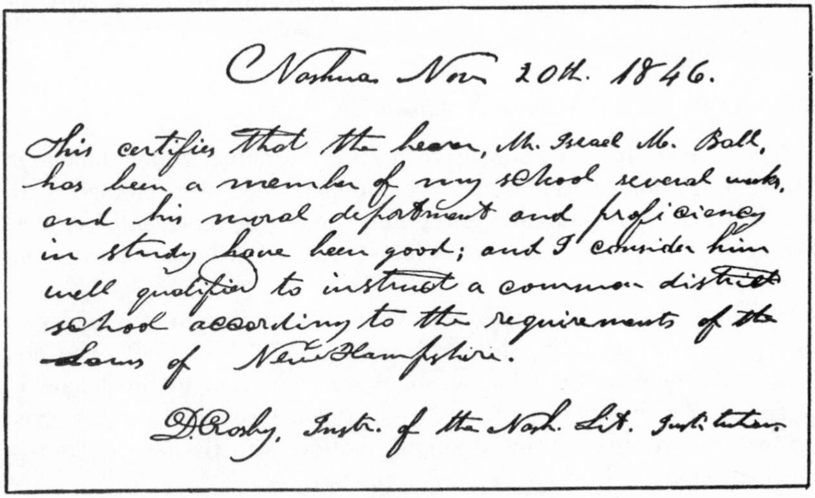

Nashua Nov 20th. 1846.

This certifies that the bearer, Mr. Israel M. Ball, has been a member of my school several weeks, and his moral department and proficiency in study have been good; and I consider him well qualified to instruct a common district school according to the requirements of the Laws of New Hampshire.

D. Crosby, Instr. of the Nash. Lit. Institution

Fig. 5–3. Facsimile of a Note Issued as a Teacher's Certificate in 1848

Important in helping to make teaching more nearly professional, in enhancing the status of educators, were the many teachers' associations. The vast majority of them were short-lived; but they were the antecedents of more permanent organizations at local, state, and national levels. Many published journals and sponsored "institutes," what we would call workshops or conferences. Only one national teachers' organization, the National Teachers Association (now the National Education Association) survived to emerge in the twentieth century as notably influential. Its long, feeble infancy may be inferred from the fact that after forty-three years, its membership in 1900 was only 2,300. In 1867, school superintendents formed an organization to promote the professionalization of school administration, support measures for improvement of public education, and oppose harmful legislation. The first city school administrators were appointed in 1837, and it took about fifty years for this position to be generally recognized in the city school systems throughout the nation.

The small association of those days grew into the present American Association of School Administrators.

Improvement not only of preparation and certification for teaching but also of working conditions have continued to be major concerns of teachers' organizations. They helped start retirement systems, promote tenure legislation, support research on curriculum and instruction, work for higher salaries, and so on. But it must be conceded that most of these efforts did not bear much fruit until well into our century.

### Broadened Federal Interest in Education

The interest in education professed by the national government in the period immediately following independence was clothed with reality by many federal laws and grants during the nineteenth century. Three of the most important are cited here as evidence of this continuing concern.

In the first decade, land grants were inaugurated to give effect to the policy announced in the Ordinances of 1785 and 1787. The first state so benefited was Ohio, when it was admitted to the Union in 1803. This policy was continued right down through the years, even to our own times, with more liberal allotments in the less-productive western states.

Another manifestation of national concern was the passage of the first Morrill Act in 1862, granting to each state 30,000 acres for each senator and representative in Congress for the support of one or more colleges to teach agriculture and mechanic arts, as well as liberal arts. In some states, this endowment or the proceeds from its sale was used to create new institutions; in others, it was given to an existing university that added an A. and M. division. The institutions were required also to teach military science, the origin of the R.O.T.C. programs. In 1890, the second Morrill Act was passed, providing for small annual money grants. Other acts and amendments have been enacted from time to time to strengthen or broaden land-grant college programs, especially research and extension services. The first Morrill Act was perhaps the greatest boost to higher education ever made by any government, inspired, as has been said of the founding of Massachusetts Institute of Technology in 1861, "by a revolt against the concept that literature, the arts, and Greek and Latin were the [sole] mark of an educated man."

Finally, Congress created in 1867 a Department of Education, without Cabinet rank, to carry out a limited assignment. Since education was then and still is regarded as a function properly administered by the states, the Department was charged with three duties that would not encroach on state authority: (1) to collect educational statistics and facts, (2) to publish information on organization and administration of schools and on teaching methods, and (3) to promote the cause of education. The last clause could, of course, by liberal interpretation, allow the agency great leeway in its operation, subject to congressional appropriations. Until the end of the century, the work of the Bureau of Education (as it was termed from 1870 to 1929) was generally along the lines indicated; but thereafter an increasing amount of administrative responsibility was assigned in connection with a wide variety of federally supported educational programs.

## Notable Advances in Higher Education

Finally, among the many extensions of educational opportunity that marked the nineteenth century, one that must be mentioned was the swelling tide of higher education that during the mid-twentieth century was to reach the proportions of a tidal wave. For a country of small population, there seemed to be an inordinate zeal for the founding of colleges and universities, although their enrollments remained very small until well into our century.

By 1860, the number of institutions had grown to about two hundred and fifty, including twenty state universities and a dozen teachers' colleges. Religious denominations were extremely active in this movement, impelled by the urgency of propagating their faiths as well as by the conviction that the youth of the land should have more opportunity for higher education. During the latter part of the century, several hundred colleges were founded; but very few institutions had enrollments exceeding four to five hundred. The total college and university enrollment in 1900 was less than 250,000, about 4 per cent of the college-age population.

Besides the impetus given to higher education in general and particularly to the liberalization of curricula by the Morrill Act and other legislation, several other crucial developments occurred. One was the revolution in opportunities for young women. At the beginning of the century, no girl could go to college. At the end, women constituted 24 per cent of college and university enrollment. This tremendous gain was won only over bitter opposition, especially sharp in the first half of the century. Opponents (mostly men, of course) contended that the intellectual demands of higher education would undermine women's health, reveal "their innate mental inferiority," "rob them of all feminine charm," and "lead them to neglect home and children in feverish pursuit of Greek roots or the intricacies of quadratic equations."

While many academies for girls were established in the half-century after the Revolutionary War, the beginnings of higher education for women took place in a handful of "seminaries," some of which became top-rank institutions. Outstanding were the Troy (N.Y.) Seminary founded in 1821 by Emma Willard after fourteen years of similar work in Vermont; Mount Holyoke (Mass.) Seminary, founded by Mary Lyon in 1837; Hartford (Conn.) Female Seminary, 1825, and Western Female Institute (Cincinnati), 1832, both founded by Catherine Beecher.

Oberlin College in Ohio is given credit for being the first coeducational institution, admitting women on the same basis as men when it opened in 1833. Only seventy-nine women had earned bachelor's degrees there by 1865, about two a year; but the ice had been broken. Gradually, professional study was opened to women. Elizabeth Blackwell was the first woman to earn a degree in medicine (1849), Antoinette Blackwell (no relation) in theology (1851), and Ada Kepler in law (1870). By 1900, women were studying in every professional field except veterinary medicine.

Several universities pioneered in affording opportunities for graduate study in America. The Johns Hopkins University in Baltimore was opened in 1876 with the specific aim of providing staff and facilities for graduate study and research. Clark University in Massachusetts was founded in 1887 and the University of Chicago in 1891, both with strong emphasis on research and graduate work. Existing institutions rapidly added professional and research divisions, which in only a few decades became very important aspects of higher learning; and some notable institutions enrolled more students than the undergraduate and preprofessional divisions.

## THE DRIVE FOR EXCELLENCE IN THE TWENTIETH CENTURY

As the nineteenth century was characterized by an unparalleled movement to lower barriers to educational opportunity, so the twentieth century, particularly in its middle decades, has seen a great surge toward the achievement of excellence.

Many of the strenuous efforts made prior to 1900 to open schoolhouse doors to all children and youth, to reconstruct curricula and improve instruction, to place on more secure footing the financial support of education—all these continued to bear fruit after the turn of the century. In turn, gains along this broad front have called for innovations to meet phenomenally increased demands on the American educational system.

New emphases have been generated by two major contemporary developments: the emergence of the United States as an undisputed world power, and its acknowledged leadership of the free world. These have brought home to Americans as never before the crucial importance of high quality in education, the urgent need to challenge our most able and ambitious children and youth, to demand and reward excellence in those who are capable of high performance. At the same time, it has been seen that those of average and lower ability must continue to have appropriate opportunities to make the most of themselves, and to grow up to be decent men and women, participating in the various roles and relationships belonging to citizens of a great free nation.

Because the movements for change and improvement in the twentieth century are still in process, they must be treated as contemporary rather than as past. Hence, in many other chapters of this book, they are discussed in more detail and with more documentation than can be done in this chapter's panoramic view of our educational history. From the data summarized in Table 5–1, one can gather a pretty good idea of the ferment that characterized American education in the period from 1900 to the sixties, and of the tremendous advances that were made in this short period. These facts seem to report very largely, at first glance, gains that are only quantitative in nature, not qualitative. Yet it must be recognized that many of the items indubitably have an important bearing on the quality of education, for example, the lengthening of the school year and the higher levels of teacher preparation. This table is worth considerable study. As new data are published, the student will be able to extend the period covered and see if changes occur in the trends indicated by the figures. While many of the items listed in Table 5–1 are discussed in later chapters, it is appropriate to submit here a few generalizations on the changes that have taken place since the beginning of the century.

1. There has been a substantial rise in the American expectation of what constitutes a child's "educational birthright." In 1900, the completion of eighth grade was about as high as most children aspired, and their parents for them. Some years later, in the twenties, this rose a year to completion of ninth grade, as the spread of the junior high

**TABLE 5–1**

## Significant Statistics of Educational Change in the United States, 1900–1965

| | 1900 | 1930 | 1960 | 1965 (est.) |
|---|---|---|---|---|
| 1. Enrollment in elementary and secondary schools (public and private) | 16,961,000 | 28,552,000 | 42,012,000 | 47,000,000 |
| 2. Per cent of population five to thirteen years enrolled | 73.7 (1910) | 83.5 | 95.1 | 96.0 |
| 3. Per cent of population fourteen to seventeen years enrolled | 11.4 | 51.4 | 86.1 | 88.0 |
| 4. Number of high school graduates | 94,883 | 666,904 | 1,769,000 | 2,000,000 |
| 5. Enrollment in colleges and universities | 238,000 | 1,100,000 | 3,861,000 | 4,500,000 |
| 6. Per cent of population eighteen to twenty-one years enrolled | 4.0 | 12.4 | 37.7 | 40.0 |
| 7. Median years of school completed by adults twenty-five and over | no data | no data | 10.6 | 11.1 |
| 8. Per cent of illiteracy * | 11.3 | 4.8 | 2.4 | 2.0 |
| 9. Length of school term (number of days) | 144 | 172 | 178 | 180 |
| 10. Number of school districts (basic units) | 185,000 (est.) | 127,531 (1932) | 40,520 | 28,000 |
| 11. Total tax receipts for public elementary and secondary schools from federal, state, intermediate, and local sources | $220,000,000 | $2,088,557,000 | $14,756,618,000 | $22,000,000,000 |
| 12. Expenditures per pupil in average daily attendance, public elementary and secondary schools † | $20 | $109 | $487 | $600 |
| 13. Income of higher education institutions | $41,000,000 | $494,910,000 | $7,334,000,000 | $9,000,000,000 |
| 14. Average salary of teachers (public elementary and secondary schools) | $325 | $1,420 | $5,174 | $6,200 |
| 15. Per cent of teachers with four years of college preparation or more: | | | | |
| Elementary | —‡ | 12 | 76 | 85 |
| Secondary | —‡ | 87 | 98 | 99 |

* For 1900 and 1930 for population fifteen years and older; for 1960 and 1965, fourteen years and older.

† In addition to current expenditures, these figures also include capital outlay, debt retirement, and interest (chiefly for new buildings and equipment). Capital outlay, debt retirement, and interest are usually about 20 per cent of total expenditures.

‡ For the years around the turn of the century, the typical elementary school teacher received preparation distinctly below the equivalent of high school graduation, according to the National Survey of the Education of Teachers (1935). High school teachers received more preparation, but probably not more than half had completed college. Exact figures are not available.

SOURCES: For 1900, 1930, and 1960, chiefly *Digest of Educational Statistics* (1963 ed.; Washington, D.C.: U.S. Government Printing Office, Office of Education, 1963), Bulletin 1963, No. 43, supplemented by various other reports. Estimates for 1965 by the authors, based on preliminary statistical data published by Office of Education, National Education Association, and other sources.

194

school tended to keep pupils a year longer (Chapter 9). Still later, in the 1950's, the completion of high school became the normal expectation. As the table shows, a great increase has been experienced in the number and per cent of children who go on to high school and who graduate from the twelfth grade.

We are now at a point in this upward movement where completion of junior college is coming to be recognized as a reasonable minimum for a majority of young people. Enrollment in institutions of post–high school level has already seen unprecedented expansion, and the end is by no means in sight. In the age group eighteen to twenty-one, more young men and women and a larger per cent are entering institutions of education beyond the high school, and more are completing two and four years of study than ever before. More than half the population over twenty-five has completed twelve years of school, the first time any nation has achieved this mark. In just one generation, according to Census Bureau reports, the percentage of high school graduates in the population twenty-five to thirty-four years of age exactly doubled: from 32 per cent in 1932 to 64 per cent in 1962, and it is still going up.

Such impressive gains and others noted in the table are a reflection of deep-running social, political, and economic trends. They are a reflection of our society's need for better educated people to produce more and better goods and services on the one hand, and to consume them on the other hand. Not so many illiterates buy and use high-fidelity stereo equipment, records and tapes, for example, as do high school and college graduates. In two other ways, these data reflect a high standard of living: (a) the ability of our society to get along without depending on the labor of children and youth, and (b) the ability to allocate a hefty percentage of the labor force (for education about 4 per cent) to teaching and administration in schools and other educational institutions, and to allied services of many kinds (book publishing, schoolhouse construction, manufacturing and selling an endless list of supplies and equipment, and so on). A society has to attain a fairly advanced form of economy, especially industrialization, before it can do these two things.

An increasing interest in improving the quality of formal education has been manifested in a variety of ways, a few of which are cited here to illustrate the point.

2. Shortly before and after the turn of the century, regional accrediting associations were formed, such as the North Central Association of Colleges and Secondary Schools and the Southern Association of Colleges and Secondary Schools. Originally, these or-

ganizations, six in number, of which the N.C.A. blanketing nineteen
states is the largest and most influential, worked chiefly to rate high
schools on their fitness to send well-prepared graduates on to college
without entrance examinations. They also rated colleges and universities for the transfer of credits. In recent years, however, accreditation (getting on the approved list) has dealt more with improvement of faculties, curricula, administration, libraries, financial
support, etc. The accrediting associations are really self-help, voluntary improvement societies. In some states, the state departments
of education follow similar procedures; and in a few states, elementary schools are included in the accreditation program.

3. Requirements for certification to teach have been stepped up.
"Normal training" in high school has all but vanished, as has the two-
year college course that used to be thought sufficient for elementary
school teachers. Now most states require at least a bachelor's degree
for initial certification for either elementary or secondary school teaching, and a few require a fifth year of college or a master's degree.
There are more teachers with master's degrees now than there were
with bachelor's degrees in the 1920's. A great impetus was given to
the improvement of teacher education by the widespread adoption
of the single-salary schedule. This provided for paying teachers in
accordance with the number of years of college completed or degrees
earned, and with credit for teaching experience. Since grade and subject taught and the sex of the teacher are not given any weight in a
single-salary schedule, teachers in elementary and secondary schools
were paid alike if they had equivalent education and experience.
This had the effect of materially raising the status of elementary school
teachers.

4. From extensive curricular expansion and revision during the
twentieth century, there emerged the "comprehensive high school,"
with all pupils, regardless of their future goals, in one school. At the
beginning of the period, high schools were definitely conceived of as
"college prep" schools. Most boys and girls who were not destined
to go to college went to work after eighth grade; a few attended vocational or trade schools, most of them of a caliber definitely inferior
to the regular academic high schools. The Smith-Hughes Act of 1917
made vocational education respectable by providing for federal grants
for it, to be matched by state funds.

Along with this development, subjects were added so that pupils
could include some electives in their programs of study. Typically,
ninth-graders used to take English, algebra, Latin I, and ancient history; Sophomores took English, plane geometry, Latin II, and world

history or European history. About forty years ago, this strait jacket of four required subjects gave way to allow for some freedom of choice along with certain required subjects; in the eleventh and twelfth grades, some electives had customarily been allowed, but the choice was broadened. In brief, high school came to be regarded not exclusively as preparation for college; but, while for many this function still remained, the school became more widely and properly conceived of as preparation for the various roles young men and women occupy in adult life at home, at work, and in their civic responsibilities.

5. While we are on the subject of high schools, mention should be made of the Advanced Placement Program. Since 1950, several hundred high schools have developed or adopted college-level courses for their more able and ambitious students. Upon completion of these courses with a satisfactory mark, the students earn not only high school credit, but also in many cases college credit, or are excused from the beginning college courses entering students ordinarily take. Advanced Placement courses are available in schools that have joined the program in all the traditional academic fields: English, foreign languages, science, mathematics, and social sciences. Although this interesting feature of high school life was initiated before the U.S.S.R. orbited Sputnik I in October, 1957, this spectacular event certainly accelerated the adoption of advanced placement courses in many schools, along with other measures for the better identification and schooling of bright and diligent youngsters.

6. While vast increases in the dollar amount of financial support are apparent in Table 5–1, changes in methods of raising and distributing the school money are not apparent. Early in our century, the concepts of state support and "equalization" were promulgated and rapidly gained acceptance. State governments increased their share of support for public education from less than 10 per cent to about 40 per cent.

They also began, about 1920, to take cognizance of variations in the ability of communities to raise taxes for the support of education. Eventually, all the states adopted the principle of equalization referred to above, whereby districts of low financial resources are given more state aid than are more favored communities. No similarly significant change was wrought in the participation of the federal government, although considerable funds exceeding in some years $3 billion are now expended by the government for a wide variety of educational enterprises and aid for specified services.

7. Changes of greater or lesser degree in the administration of education have been made at state and local levels. State depart-

ments of education have been strengthened and somewhat more professionalized. Emphasis has been shifted from regulation, direction, and statistical reporting to leadership and counseling. Not much gain has been reported in state-level research, but it is recognized as an important function with great potentiality for improvement of state school systems.

One notable departure from the pattern of 1900 and 1930 is the reduction in the number of school districts. During these thirty years, the number climbed to approximately 130,000, each unit independent of others, operating under a board of education. By 1965, the total had declined to about 30,000. In most states very small districts have been combined to make larger administrative units capable of offering a complete elementary and secondary school program.

8. Finally among these few generalizations should be mentioned our contemporary preoccupation with self-appraisal and self-criticism of the schools. Perhaps this should be taken for granted, since schools, as we have seen in Chapter 3, are one of our most important social institutions, and the systematic study of society (the social sciences) has flowered only in the last half-century or so. However that may be, it is doubtless true that during no like period anywhere has there been such a searching evaluation of education, by those who work in the field as well as by parents and citizens in general. Despite the vitriolic character of some of the criticism, the net effect has probably been a strengthening and upgrading of every aspect of educational service. It is a curious thing, however, that European schools, held up as a model by some critics, tend little by little to adopt American practice and philosophy.

From the foregoing paragraphs, the student should not gain the impression that all our educational problems have been solved, that all is well in American education. Undeniably, great progress has been made in both the extent and quality of schooling at all levels, contrary to what some critics would have us believe. Yet grave problems on a broad front remain, which are in part the subject matter of the final chapter of this book.


## QUESTIONS, PROBLEMS, AND PROJECTS FOR FURTHER STUDY

1. In addition to the generalizations given near the end of this chapter on the period from 1900 to 1965, formulate three others and present facts to support them.

2. Compare a school textbook of a hundred years ago or earlier with a

contemporary book in the same subject and for the same age level. Note the contents, organization, vocabulary, use of pictures, and format.

3. What were the advantages claimed for organizing elementary schools by grades about the mid-nineteenth century? Now about a hundred years late, why do some educators advocate ungraded schools? What is your own conclusion?

4. Write a research paper on the influence of labor organizations on the democratization of educational opportunity during the latter half of the nineteenth century.

5. Prepare a chart, with appropriate explanatory legends and text, to show the expansion of higher education between 1900 and now. Consider whether or not to classify institutions as public and private, junior colleges, liberal arts colleges, and universities; also whether or not you want to report enrollments by sex and percentage of relevant age groups. Consider also whether or not financial data should be included, and if so, which kinds?

6. Arrange for a debate between two teams composed of members of the class on this proposition: Resolved, That the typical curriculum of the academy at the height of its popularity in the 1850's was suited to the needs of the times better than the typical senior high school curriculum of the 1960's is suited to the needs of our times.

7. Collect statements on education made by great American statesmen, beginning with Franklin, Jefferson, Madison, and continuing to the present. What are the reasons they give for attaching much importance to education? (This might well be done as a group project, starting with the listing of statesmen to be included.)

8. Trace the development of higher education for women from the early nineteenth century to our own generation. This subject might well be treated by certain periods, e.g., 1820–1860, 1860–1900, and 1900 to the present.

9. Compile a well-organized statement of the special contributions to education and the values stressed by parochial schools that distinguish them from public schools. Or, if you prefer, do this for independent (private) schools.

10. Select an educational leader in American history and write a biographical sketch of some 2,500 words, including particularly an appreciation of his or her contributions to educational thought and practice.

## SELECTED SUPPLEMENTARY READINGS AND FILMS

ALLEN, HERMAN R. *Open Door to Learning.* Urbana, Ill.: University of Illinois Press, 1963. Based on twelve reports celebrating the centennial of the Morrill Land-Grant College Act of 1862. Part I relates the expansion from an original rural U.S. constituency to an all-inclusive and worldwide scope. Part II tells of the new emphasis on liberal arts, graduate study, and research.

BUTTS, R. FREEMAN, and CREMIN, LAWRENCE A. *A History of Education in American Culture.* New York: Holt, Rinehart & Winston, Inc., 1953. A well-written work that interprets the story of American education as a persistent "search for freedom." Fundamental questions related to the development and maintenance of a free society and the ways they were faced at different periods in our history are well documented.

CUBBERLEY, ELLWOOD P. *Readings in Public Education in the United States.* Boston: Houghton Mifflin Co., 1934. A collection of laws, documents, speeches, and other source materials arranged about a series of major themes in chronological order. Supplements CUBBERLEY's *Public Education in the United States* (1934).

COMMAGER, HENRY STEELE. "Our Schools Have Kept Us Free," *Life,* XXIX (October 16, 1950), 46–47. A classic statement by an eminent historian of four major contributions of the American school system to the progress and well-being of our country and the people who have come to it from many lands.

EDWARDS, NEWTON, and RICHEY, HERMAN C. *The School in the American Social Order.* 2d ed. Boston: Houghton Mifflin Co., 1963. Especially good for its scholarly treatment of trends in U.S. culture since the Civil War and their impact on educational thought and practice.

ELSBREE, WILLARD S. *The American Teacher.* New York: American Book Co., 1939. Recounts the social, economic, and professional status of teachers from Colonial to modern times.

HOFSTADTER, RICHARD. *Anti-Intellectualism in America.* New York: Alfred A. Knopf, Inc., 1963. Part V is of particular interest here, for the author's views of the problem of maintaining respectable standards in an educational system that attempts to educate the whole population.

GOOD, HARRY G. *History of American Education.* 2d ed. New York: The Macmillan Co., 1962. A comprehensive survey. With emphasis on the twentieth century, it examines factors in the social, political, and economic institutions of our society that have affected the development of the U.S. educational system.

MONROE, PAUL. *The Founding of the American Public School System.* New York: The Macmillan Co., 1940. A history of the schools from the beginning to the Civil War. Many interesting examples and some pictures of practices not included in other books.

NEWCOMER, MABEL. *A Century of Higher Education for American Women.* New York: Harper & Row, 1959. Traces the gradual breaking down of barriers from the time of the "female seminaries" to our own day with its more nearly open-door access for women to higher education.

ROSSITER, CLINTON. *The First American Revolution.* New York: Harcourt, Brace & World, Inc., 1963. The author's thesis is that the American Revolution took place in men's minds long before Lexington and Concord. The facts he cites on university development and the ideas that have heavily influenced our particular needs and methods are clearly presented.

## Films

*Education in America: The 17th and 18th Centuries.* 15 minutes. From the early New England school laws to the educational provisions of the Northwest Ordinance, the beginnings of American education are re-enacted in actual locations of dame schools, Latin grammar schools, church schools, and pauper schools. Along with colonial colleges, these were the foundations of education in the United States. Chicago: Coronet Productions.

*Education in America: The 19th Century.* 15 minutes. The development of free public school systems, including the westward movement, the change to secular education, rise and decline of the district schools, the struggle for tax support and state control, effect of the Civil War, compulsory attendance laws, and the rise of teachers' colleges. Contributions of Webster, McGuffey, Hawley, and Mann are touched on. Chicago: Coronet Productions.

*Education in America: 20th Century Developments.* 15 minutes. Presents the effects of the Industrial Revolution on education in America and the influences of Herbart, Binet, Dewey, Thorndike, and others. The appearance of the junior high school, expansion of graduate study, school consolidation, federal aid, the G.I. Bill, and recent Supreme Court decisions are included. Chicago: Coronet Productions.

*Horace Mann.* 19 minutes. Portrays important episodes in the life of "the father of the common school." Reviews his work as teacher, lawyer, state senator, secretary of the Massachusetts state board of education, and college president. Emphasizes Mann's great work in making known the need for well-built schools, good textbooks, democratic methods of teaching, special preparation for teachers, and universal education. Wilmette, Ill.: Encyclopaedia Britannica Films, Inc.

*Our Schools Have Kept Us Free.* 30 minutes, color. Starts with Massachusetts Bay Colony, proceeds through the Revolution and Civil War, and the movements of population west and south. It sweeps from Ellis Island to the Americanization of immigrants, and explores the unity produced in people widely differing in national origin, customs, religion. Based on the reading of same title listed above. Produced in 1964 by the National Education Association, and is available through state education associations.

# 6

# EDUCATION IN OTHER COUNTRIES

Americans who travel abroad almost always say that what they see in other countries and what they learn about other peoples' way of life help them better understand their own country. They see things "with new eyes," returning home with a keener perception of life in the United States and its institutions. A small percentage return with an outlook highly critical of America; most can hardly wait to set foot again on their own shores, fed up with other countries. The great majority return with a heightened appreciation for living in America, at the same time acknowledging that no one country or people has a monopoly of all that is good.

In this chapter an attempt is made to give a general picture of how education is carried on in some other countries. It is the writers' aim to enable students to grasp the outlines of a few national education systems, and how they seem to resemble or differ significantly from our system. Books and statistical reports are available on education in almost every country; and students may find it interesting to make a comparative study of one major topic for the United States and some other country, e.g., the structure of the system, how it is financed, intergovernmental relations, higher education, teacher education, the school year, home and school relations, educational opportunity.

## HOW SHOULD ONE LOOK AT EDUCATION ABROAD?

We are sometimes admonished not to judge educational systems in other lands except in the light of their own philosophy. A nation's provisions for and management of education can be evaluated fairly, it is said, only in terms of that nation's goals, of what it expects its schools and higher education institutions to accomplish or contribute.

According to this view, education in China for forty centuries before the establishment of the Republic in 1912 was eminently successful, for it achieved the aim of perpetuating the status quo in general. Traditional Chinese aims were to cultivate the familistic conception of society, both economically and socially; to harmonize individual thought with established mores; to perpetuate and honor the wisdom and way of life handed down from the past. The schools lent their help by not interfering with this process; less than 5 per cent of the population was literate, and formal education was conducted privately and for boys only, who advanced through a severe examination system. The goal of a young scholar was a government position. The "system" accomplished what the rulers intended it to do, and might thus be thought of as highly effective. It produced a race of people the great masses of whom were stable, peaceful, and content.

### No One "Best" or "Only" Way

However, this way of looking at things, while it may be theoretically appealing, is of little practical use, for a person can scarcely disassociate himself from the matrix of the culture he has grown up in. Hence, one inevitably does make judgments or assessments of other countries, their institutions, and way of life in part, at least, in the light of his own background and knowledge. Furthermore, the educational systems of nations are not geared nicely but only in a most general sense to the dictates of a national philosophy or outlook. Procedures and beliefs emerge gradually, as a rule, and arise from a variety of causes: as response to changing conditions, as the result of one or more influential leaders or groups (usually groups in our time), in response to pressures of many different sorts. It is not simply a matter of a national philosophy (if there can be said to be one), governing organization, curriculum, and teaching in the national educational system. Few if any countries have any clear-cut base of philosophy on which to erect an educational system. Even the U.S.S.R., monolithic as it appears to be and probably largely is, is subject to some local and regional variations; major changes seem to sweep through the whole system from time to time as the ruling party makes adjustments in the vast interlocking machinery of the state. Referring again to Chinese education, most of us would condemn it as atrocious, because our thinking is influenced by values that we have been reared to cherish. But our aim is not to sit in judgment. It is to understand how other countries meet problems as they see them, and to learn from them something of value for us in meeting our problems.

The longer one studies education in the world scene, the more strongly he becomes convinced that no one country has discovered the "best," the "only" way. Each system has some characteristics or qualities that appear to us admirable, and each has some that seem backward or negative. Some U.S. critics of American schools discern more favorable points abroad than at home. Admiral Rickover, for example, seems to find general superiority to American schools in each of the three other national systems he has thus far claimed to examine: Russian, Swiss, and British. It is strange that three such different educational systems should all be so superior to U.S. schools as the author reports; although each may, of course, possess certain attributes that we could adopt with profit. It is worth noting in this connection, however, that most of the reforms either agitated or undertaken in various countries from time to time tend to bring them closer to American practice, not farther removed from it. (Europeans are quite critical of the very characteristics of their schools that Rickover praises.) There will always be many different approaches to the solution of educational problems, for each country has its preferred way of doing things. This makes life much more interesting than if all nations were pretty much alike.

## WORLDWIDE INTEREST IN CHANGE AND REFORM

For us who have grown up in a land with less than two hundred years of history as a nation and little more than three hundred since the arrival of the earliest colonists, it may be difficult to appreciate the vast weight of history and tradition that older countries carry. This has made it difficult to effect change until pent-up forces were released in a violent upheaval or even revolution. In the United States, the federal government is more able than some of our states, especially the older ones, to get some things done because it does not have to cut through a heavy growth of legislation, tradition, and historical precedents. Perhaps for this reason and because of a long-time emphasis on constitutional government and orderly processes of change, our history has been generally evolutionary rather than revolutionary, and particularly so in education.

### Emphasis on Education in New Countries

During the twentieth century and especially in the middle years of the century following World War II, many new nations have been created and many former colonies have won independence. As these new entities have assumed the responsibilities of freedom and self-government, their statesmen immediately grasped the importance of education for national development. Every new country has taken steps to extend and improve its system of education at all levels. While to Americans some of these efforts seem pitifully inadequate, one must remember that in a relative sense this is not so. Per capita income, for example, is less than $100 a year in many underdeveloped areas; and the level of illiteracy is as high as 80 or 90 per cent. They must cope not only with these staggering difficulties, but also with the problem of making fundamental changes in the entire fabric of their society to move it into the twentieth century. The work of the Peace Corps is primarily directed toward the solution of such problems, in those countries that request assistance, half of the members of the Corps serving as teachers.

## Catching Up with the Atomic Age

In addition to the numerous bootstrap operations of new countries in several continents, manifold problems also beset well-established societies everywhere. For during this century the production and application of knowledge have increased at a pace and in volume far exceeding anything the world has seen; and this has given rise to all kinds of new problems, or has led to new awareness of old problems, in every sphere of thought and action.

It is not to be wondered at, then, that all round the world an unprecedented interest in educational reform, or agitation for reform, is one of the distinctive characteristics of the mid-twentieth century. The extent of interest and improvement is uneven; but the value of education for advancement on all fronts—economic, political, social, moral or ethical, and so on—is no longer doubted. Forces opposing reform must be contended with in most countries, and in some they do slow it down to what we think is a snail's pace. But such reactionary influences are fighting a losing battle. Worldwide interdependence and communication are growing so close-knit that even comparatively laggard areas are being swept into the movement of educational upgrading.

# EDUCATION AND THE ECONOMY OF NATIONS

Economists have only recently fully awakened to the importance of economic aspects of education. Many studies have been made in the last two or three decades and important ones are in progress, analyzing the effects of expenditures for education on productivity, consumption, standards of living, and related subjects. The general conclusion is that educational expenditures are a form of investment that yields a high rate of return. While the measurement of the rate of return still lacks precision and is the object of extensive research, there is enough evidence to warrant this conclusion.

## Educational Opportunity Essential for Economic Progress

It is clear that if a nation increases its outlays for education, at the same time making educational opportunities available to a greater proportion of the population, and for more years of schooling, great benefits result. Production of goods and services is increased, standards of consumption are elevated both in quality and quantity, and the general standard of living rises. The people learn, as their educational attainment rises, how to capitalize on human and material resources and how to conserve them.

The contrasts between underdeveloped countries and advanced ones are apparent when one considers such different living standards as, say, those of the Scandinavian countries and of India. Or one may look at two countries not far apart, both poor in natural resources, but with widely differing living standards: Switzerland, which supports education well and where the people have excellent educational opportunities, and Spain, where education is neglected and the doors of opportunity are closed to most. A new investigation of education and economic growth reports a high correlation (a coefficient of 0.89) between educational level of the population and gross national product. Many other factors enter into a nation's economic progress, including its natural resources, foreign markets, and outside assistance. However, the researchers who made this study of seventy-five countries conclude that the best single indicator of a nation's wealth in human resources (the key element) is the proportion of its young people in secondary schools.[1] They cite the example of Israel as an outstanding example of how "a well-educated and motivated people will do extraordinarily well" with very limited natural resources. As history has shown repeatedly, education sows seeds that "can inspire and energize" whole peoples.

## Educational Opportunity Overcomes Disadvantages of Poor Natural Resources

Economists are joining educators in conducting research and publishing convincing data that show that the extent and quality of

[1] Frederick Harbison and Charles A. Myers, *Education, Manpower, and Economic Growth* (New York: McGraw-Hill Book Co., Inc., 1964).

educational opportunity are closely correlated with standards of living. Table 6–1, based on recent statistics, shows that even with poor natural resources a nation of advanced educational development can attain high levels of income that make high living standards possible.[2]

## TABLE 6–1

| Nation | Endowment in Natural Resources | Educational Development | Ratio of Income per Capita (using base of 1.0 for Nigeria) |
|---|---|---|---|
| Nigeria | High | Low | 1.0 |
| Mexico | High | Low | 4.4 |
| Brazil | High | Low | 4.6 |
| Colombia | High | Low | 5.0 |
| Denmark | Low | High | 15.0 |
| Switzerland | Low | High | 20.2 |
| United States | High | High | 37.4 |

SOURCE: Adapted in part from data by John K. Norton, "Education Pays Compound Interest," *NEA Journal*, XLVII (November, 1958), 47.

Similar comparisons can be made among states of the United States. States whose provision for education is evaluated as poor have a failure rate on selective service mental tests eight to ten times as high as states whose education systems rank high. The same relative positions are found when other items are considered, such as per capita income, amount of life insurance owned, and quality of housing. This whole subject has a sort of chicken-and-egg character: which comes first, good education or the wherewithal to provide it? Probably there is no need to try to find a cause-and-effect relation, but at least the two seem to be closely associated and to operate in a reciprocal fashion on each other. It is vitally important that a lagging nation or state make considerably more than ordinary effort to prime the pump. And some of the underdeveloped new nations are doing that, allocating huge proportions of their national budgets to education in an effort to make a beginning of catching up on accumulated deficiencies of generations.

## AIMS OF EDUCATION: LIKENESSES AND DIFFERENCES

It is not simple or easy, and in fact it may be impossible, to summarize in capsule form such a complicated subject as the purposes

[2] See Harold M. Groves, *Education and Economic Growth* (Washington, D.C.: National Education Association, 1961) for a concise treatment of this and related items.

of education of any one country, much less of several. Much caution must be exercised to avoid oversimplification, for educational aims are the product of both history and contemporary forces, of governmental and private interests, of the play of internal and external conditions to which peoples must react. With these warnings in mind, the writers submit in the next few pages some examples of the forces and spirit that seem to underlie or motivate selected national systems of education. Students will find further study of education in one or more other countries, or certain facets of those systems, an interesting project, especially if they have traveled or studied abroad, or plan to do so.

## Promotion of Nationalism or National Identity

All countries seek through education to foster love of country, the maintenance of national identity, the retention of and loyalty to their forms of government. In this sense, education may be thought of as an expression of national policy, or as an instrument of national philosophy. But national policy or philosophy in turn usually means the policy of the ruling group or political party, or in a few instances perhaps of a ruler, at a given time. It is not always clear whether what looks like national policy is a true reflection of the whole people's thought.

In any event, all countries that may be said to have a system of education do utilize it to promote certain national objectives, the United States along with others. And no government tolerates the operation of schools designed to undermine or weaken it. Children and youth are taught to love and defend their country, and in some places to believe in the superiority of its way of life and to undergo privation and sacrifice, if necessary, against real or imagined threats from beyond its borders. To what degree a nationalistic spirit is fostered appears to be related to the degree of insecurity felt by the governing powers and ambitions for continental or even world domination. Whipping up strong nationalistic feelings and preparing for defense against aggression from abroad is a favorite device of dictatorships, the ultimate exemplars of nationalism. After taking over the armed forces, dictators always take over the schools next. The entire educational system of Germany under Hitler, from the nursery school through the university, was prostituted to the building up of a strong nationalistic state, and is the best example of this in history, rivaled only by the Communist party's monopoly of education in the U.S.S.R. In Red China likewise education is exploited to further the ruling party's control. Only the most "politically reliable" students win advancement to desirable posts. The country is so badly in need of workers that since 1961 enrollment in secondary and higher education has actually been cut as much as 20 per cent a year. The "Great Leap Forward" launched in 1958 collapsed, partly because of successive crop failures and a breakdown of farm collectivization, and partly because of a critical shortage of technological workers in all fields. Education is the chief means of expanding a trained labor force, so present policies curtailing education seem peculiarly inappropriate and are probably only temporary. For in the decade of the 1950's, China expanded elementary school enrollment threefold, secondary ninefold, and higher education sixfold. According to Harbison, writing in 1963, total enrollment at all levels is more than a hundred million, about the same as in the United States and U.S.S.R. combined.[3] More than 55 per cent of the students in higher education are studying science and technology, compared with 25 per cent in most other countries. Ninety per cent of China's engineers and scientists have been trained since 1950.

## Preservation of the Status Quo

Closely related to the promotion of nationalism is the interest, found to greater or lesser degree among all peoples, in preserving things as they are. The reader will recall the example of China a few pages back. Except in the most stable and tolerant or long-suffering and downtrodden societies, conflicts frequently arise between those who welcome change and those who oppose it. Very often these conflicts occur about political affairs and class structure; but many others originate in problems of language, race relations, labor-management relations, and so on. Conflicts may persist for many years, as solutions are gradually worked out, which might be called an evolutionary method such as we favor in the United States. Or the resolution of major conflicts may be suppressed; and then there is oppression, as in the U.S.S.R. where a party in power consisting of 2 or 3 per cent of the adult population rules the entire country. Having won its position by violent revolution, the party cannot tolerate any widespread or serious expression of opposition to its despotism. The Russian educational system is exploited as an engine to further the party's grip on the country.

In India conflicts rage around class structure, although the na-

[3] Frederick Harbison, "Education for Development," *Scientific American*, CCIX, No. 1 (September, 1963), pp. 140–47.

tional constitution does not recognize the caste system. Italy, in the view of some observers, is also beset by problems of class structure, the elite trying to hold on to their privileged position against the rising tide of demands for greater opportunity for the whole people. An astute American professor observed in 1963 during a professional tour of Italy, "Education really is for the elite in Italy. It is almost impossible for a young person to move up the social ladder even though he may be brilliant. This situation is worse in Italy than in any other country in Europe, with the possible exception of Spain."

We generally think of Great Britain as being a leader among the democracies; and it is in many ways, despite its clinging to a form of government—its constitutional monarchy and Parliament—which we Americans do not quite understand. Yet even that enlightened people has a predilection for preserving the status quo. There is a good deal of educational reform going on in Britain, but the following interesting quotation shows how very difficult it is to effect change in an old society with long-established patterns of relationships.

As I look back on the period from 1945 to 1951 I consider that the outstanding failure of the Attlee government was its inability to realize that the wartime Education Act [1944] would give Britain neither a democratic nor even an adequate education system. Almost twenty years after the war, close to four-fifths of British children are excluded from the approaches to higher education by the age of eleven, and segregated in dead-end inferior schools. Even the privileged remnant are further sorted, and forced into increasing competition for the scarce places in higher education itself. Britain has had relatively fewer such places than any other advanced country.

In October last year [1963], the committee of inquiry headed by Lord Robbins reported that what is needed is a dramatic expansion of the college population, an increase in the proportion of science and technical students, and at least a doubling of university facilities. But even this reform would not really meet the problem. The crying need is for a thoroughgoing overhaul of the school system, both to meet Britain's demand for skilled people and to insure social justice. Today, Britain has effectively three school systems. The "modern" school for the majority; the "grammar" school for most middle-class and a small proportion of working-class children; and the elite "public" (independent and private) schools which, at a given moment, educate the 12,000 boys who will later claim a disproportionately high percentage of the places in professional education and in politics, business, and the public service.[4]

In France, endless educational reforms have been proposed and agitated for many years, particularly since World War II. One of the chief obstacles seems to be the insistence of successive Ministries

[4] Norman MacKenzie, "Harold Wilson's Britain," *Harper's Magazine*, CCXXVIII, No. 1365 (February, 1964), pp. 76, 78. Quoted with permission.

of Education on preserving a highly academic education for the few, selected by a rigid examination system, with very strong emphasis on preservation of the purity of the French language. For the great majority of the people, elementary education to the age of fourteen or fifteen is deemed sufficient. Innumerable articles may be found in French educational and other journals, in newspapers, and in magazines of more popular appeal on the glories of the French language and the dire necessity of guarding against its corruption, especially against the popular adoption of English and American terms resulting in what to an academically respectable Frenchman is a revolting patois called "franglais."

## Education for Social and Individual Progress

In contradistinction to the two general aims discussed above—promoting nationalism and guarding against change—a third important aim of education is the improvement of personal and social life. The weight given to this aim varies tremendously among the nations of the world, inversely in relation to their emphasis on the other two aims. Countries are not motivated by a single aim, of course, but by a combination of aims varying in importance and in the extent of their implementation.

The United States is probably second to none in devotion to education for social and individual improvement. At the same time, Americans believe strongly that their schools are one of the chief agencies, second only to the home, for the preservation and transmission of long-cherished values and mores. Another outstanding illustration of reliance on education for social and personal uplift is furnished by Mexico. Its foremost objective since 1933, according to official documents, is to improve standards of health, home life, work, and recreation through education. In the rural schools, teachers spend half or more of their time helping adults learn better farming, homemaking, and craftsmanship.

Britain and the U.S.S.R. afford two more examples of education's importance as an engine of improvement, although we in America think that both countries are handicapped by certain political, social, and economic conditions that seem inconsistent with and retard the progress they seek. The Soviet Union's leaders have announced in unmistakable terms that the aim of education is "to master the knowledge of all races," and to catch up with and surpass "in the shortest possible period the most advanced capitalistic countries." The Soviet Union goes further than any country in providing the full cost of tuition, board and room, supplies, health, and travel expenses for students who are selected by a system of examinations to attend a variety of postsecondary institutions and universities. Students are not free to study what they choose, however, since the objective is to supply the state with the professional and technological personnel the Communist party calls for. In the process, however, many individuals do gain academic advantages that they would not have access to without financial aid.

Great Britain during the 1960's has felt a new wave of concern for the creation of better educational opportunities for more people. The government has financed several major studies, including a monumental inquiry into higher education,[5] published in 1963–1964 in a series of seven volumes, calling for a very large expansion of higher education, from places for 216,000 students in 1962 to 344,000 by 1970 and 560,000 by 1980. These figures include places for admission of students from overseas equal to 10 per cent of the total enrollment. This proposed expansion stems from a conviction that Britain keeps too many of its able young people from developing their talents, to the serious detriment of the nation domestically and in the world community. It is also illustrative of a rising crest of demand by young people all over the world for a chance to sample higher education, for the abolition of social, political, and economic barriers to access to opportunities for advanced study. By way of comparison, if the number of places in U.S. higher education were estimated in the same proportion, we would have in 1970 about three and a half million students instead of the estimated six million.

There is ferment in Britain in secondary education, too. Many people believe that there is "an urgent need" to raise the school-leaving age from fifteen to sixteen, as provided in the famous Education Act of 1944 but never implemented, and that better provision should be made for pupils in the lower half of the ability range.[6] There is a ground swell of opinion that "comprehensive" secondary schools should largely replace the three types now in vogue: grammar (highly academic), secondary modern (general secondary), and technical (vocational) schools, not, however, without encountering some pretty solid resistance. The comprehensive secondary school and the

[5] Committee on Higher Education, *Higher Education* (London: Her Majesty's Stationery Office, 1963). (Commonly referred to as the Robbins Report for Lord Robbins, chairman of the Committee.) A series of five appendices on different aspects of the inquiry was published in six other volumes.

[6] Central Advisory Council for Education (England), *Half Our Future* (London: Her Majesty's Stationery Office, 1963). (Commonly referred to as the Newsom Report, for the Council chairman, John Newsom.)

"eleven-plus" examinations have even got into politics, Labor advocating the former and decrying the latter. In several populous counties, the eleven-plus examinations, customarily given to all children at about the age of eleven as an aid in deciding to which type of secondary school they should be sent, have been abolished. Parents and teachers make the decision that seems best for each pupil.

## EXAMPLES OF ORGANIZATION AND ADMINISTRATION

From such a grand arena as education in other countries, only a few examples of how national school systems are organized can be selected for inclusion here (Figs. 6–1 to 6–5). The authors' aim was not to identify the unusual or rare, but to illustrate various patterns characteristic of a few major countries. Every country has many special provisions within the framework of the main structure of its system of education that cannot be shown in such figures. Accompanying the charts are observations on a few of the important aspects of education that cannot be seen in the charts: administrative control, teacher education and status, progress of children and youth through the school system, and the curriculum. Students are urged to look up more details in the many excellent books and reports published nowadays on education in other countries. The cultural affairs officers of most embassies in Washington will, on request, send information on education in their respective homelands.

### Administrative Control: Centralization vs. Decentralization

Of all national systems of education, that of the United States is probably the most decentralized in administrative control, with its fifty state systems and 28,000-odd local school systems, while that of the U.S.S.R. is probably the most centralized. In between there is every conceivable pattern of local, provincial (state or regional), and national relationships. Whether or not a national government exercises strong central control is not always readily apparent. In the U.S.S.R., for example, there is no national ministry of education, contrary to popular belief, but central control is very strong. In Britain, on the other hand, there is a national Ministry of Education endowed with great authority; and the government bears about 60 per cent of the cost of education; but in practice the Ministry delegates much of its power to the L.E.A.'s and is noted for its self-restraint in educational control. The United States has a Cabinet education officer, too, in the Secretary of Health, Education, and Welfare; but he has

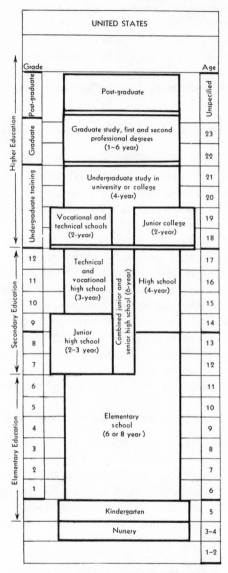

Fig. 6–1. Organization of Education in the United States. Source: Nicholas Dewitt, *Education and Professional Employment in the U.S.S.R.* (Washington, D.C.: U.S. Government Printing Office, 1960).

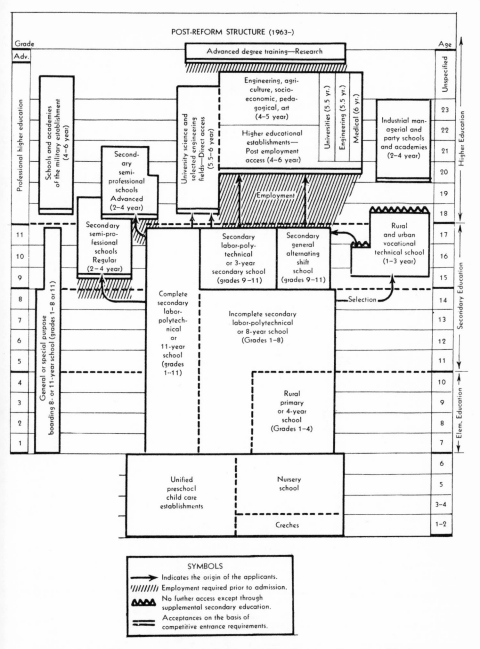

POST-REFORM STRUCTURE (1963–)

Grade
Adv.

Advanced degree training—Research

Professional higher education

Schools and academies of the military establishment (4–6 year)

Secondary semi-professional schools Advanced (2–4 year)

University science and selected engineering fields—Direct access (5.5–6 year)

Engineering, agriculture, socio-economic, pedagogical, art (4–5 year)

Higher educational establishments— Post employment access (4–6 year)

Universities (5.5 yr.)

Engineering (5.5 yr.)

Medical (6 yr.)

Industrial managerial and party schools and academies (2–4 year)

Employment

Higher Education

Unspecified
23
22
21
20
19
18

11
10
9
8
7
6
5
4
3
2
1

General or special purpose boarding 8- or 11-year school (grades 1–8 or 11)

Secondary semi-professional schools Regular (2–4 year)

Complete secondary labor-polytechnical or 11-year school (grades 1–11)

Secondary labor-poly-technical or 3-year secondary school (grades 9–11)

Secondary general alternating shift school (grades 9–11)

Rural and urban vocational technical school (1–3 year)

Selection

Incomplete secondary labor-polytechnical or 8-year school (Grades 1–8)

Rural primary or 4-year school (Grades 1–4)

Secondary Education

17
16
15
14
13
12
11
10
9
8
7

Elem. Education

Unified preschool child care establishments

Nursery school

Creches

6
5
3–4
1–2

Age

SYMBOLS
→ Indicates the origin of the applicants.
/////// Employment required prior to admission.
AAAA No further access except through supplemental secondary education.
=== Acceptances on the basis of competitive entrance requirements.

Fig. 6–2. Education in the U.S.S.R., 1963. Source: Seymour M. Rosen, *Higher Education in the U.S.S.R.* (Washington, D.C.: U.S. Government Printing Office, 1963). (From Nicholas DeWitt, *Education and Professional Employment in the U.S.S.R.*, 1960.)

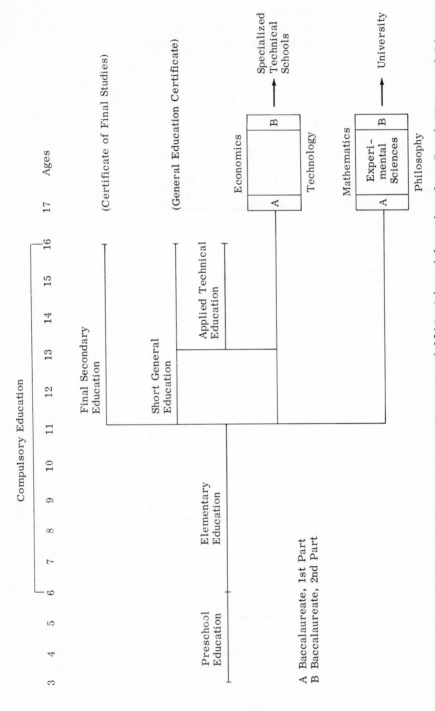

Fig. 6–3. General Educational Organization in France As of 1964. Adapted from data from French Ministry of Education and the Centre International d'Etudes Pedagogiques de Sevres.

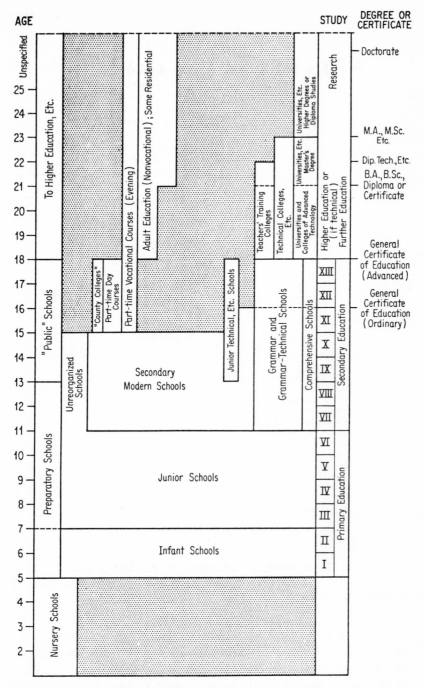

Fig. 6–4. Educational System of England and Wales. Reproduced with permission from Edmund J. King, *Other Schools and Ours* (New York: Holt, Rinehart & Winston, Inc., 1963).

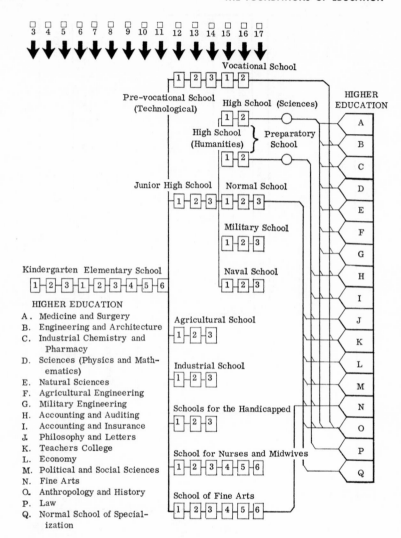

Fig. 6–5. Organization of Education in the United Mexican States.
Source: *The Educational Situation in Latin America* (published by UNESCO
in 1960). Reprinted by permission.

no administrative authority at all over the general system of elementary and secondary education or over higher education; only over
specific, grant-aided programs that schools and institutions may choose
to join or not does federal authority exist (school lunch, N.D.E.A.,
vocational education, and the like). Germany has no national edu-

cation ministry, but the ministers of education of the states comprising the Federal Republic work closely together through their Permanent Conference of Ministers of Education. France has a Minister of National Education and Mexico a Secretary of Public Education. All these and probably every other country have commissions, boards, and various directorates for designated services. Examples are Indian Affairs (United States), School Building Program (Mexico), Libraries (France), Culture (U.S.S.R.), University Grants (Britain), Scientific Research (Germany). The structure of education in no country is completely monolithic, even though it may be a government monopoly. That this is so might properly be interpreted as an indication that the education of nations is too complex to be harnessed under the control of one neatly streamlined, straight-line organization.

Two of the most highly centralized national school systems are those of Soviet Russia and France, but they work in different ways. Central control in France seems to be about as tight as in Russia, except that criticism seems more free in France and opponents of national educational policy and practice are not liquidated or sent to labor camps in Siberia. In the U.S.S.R., each of the component Republics has its own Ministry of Education, a system that allows for some adaptation to regional conditions and needs. For example, where Russian is not the native language, school is taught in the local tongue, but Russian is required as a subject of study as a second language. Financial and other requirements are compiled from documents prepared by the various Republic ministries, and on major items the central government sees that provisions are made for meeting needs. The republics finance and maintain their own teacher-education institutions for elementary and some secondary school teachers, but academic standards are watched over by the U.S.S.R. Ministry of Higher Education.

The real locus of control is the Communist party, although it is not always out in the open. Directives of national significance promulgated by the Supreme Soviet and the U.S.S.R. Council of Ministers (e.g., changes in school organization, curriculum, compulsory attendance) always represent the party's will. The party controls the entire governmental and bureaucratic structure, and no directive would or could be issued unless the party approved it. Thus, a high degree of uniformity in outlook and practice is achieved.

In France the Ministry of National Education issues directives also, working through the heads (recteurs) of nineteen large administrative districts called académies. Since the government puts up about 85 per cent of the money for education, pays the teachers (in public schools), and employs six or seven hundred inspectors to see that the Ministry's directives and suggestions are carried out, there is a high degree of control. Private schools (enrolling about 18 per cent as compared with 15 per cent in the United States) are subject to inspection the same as public schools and must receive permission to operate; in return for submitting to government supervision, they receive partial support. Control is also exercised by the examination administered at the end of the compulsory eight years of elementary schooling, covering the syllabuses issued by the Paris office. One interesting little example of the Ministry's control is the schedule of school vacations for 1963–1964 for the entire country:

Toussaint (All-Saints Day): beginning Wednesday evening, October 30, and ending Tuesday morning, Nov. 5, 1963.

Christmas: begins Friday evening, Dec. 20, and ends Monday morning, Jan. 6, 1964.

Mid-year vacation: begins Saturday evening, Feb. 8, and ends Monday morning, Feb. 17, 1964.

Easter vacation: begins Wednesday evening, March 25, and ends Monday morning, April 13.

Summer vacation: in the pre-elementary schools (kindergartens) and the final grades of the primary schools, classes will end the evening of Wednesday, July 1, and resume the morning of Sept. 21. For all others, classes will end the evening of Saturday, June 27, and will resume the morning of Sept. 21, 1964.

The Ministry specifies that examination schedules will not necessarily coincide with the beginning of the vacation periods.[7]

Agitation for educational reform is a perennial feature of French society. It is hard to achieve changes because of a prevailing belief that there must be a uniform and centralized school system in order to build and preserve cultural solidarity.

### Teacher Education and Status

For many years there has been a sharp distinction between elementary and secondary school teachers, in training programs, salaries, and status. In progress toward placing all teachers on the same footing in these matters, the United States definitely is the leader.

The general rule, even in the advanced countries of Europe, is to prepare teachers for elementary (primary) schools in separate teacher training colleges offering a two- or three-year program of studies beyond secondary school. In some countries prospective elementary school teachers are admitted to the universities for a special program

[7] *Education in France* (New York: Cultural Services of the French Embassy, December, 1963), No. 23, p. 11.

of academic and professional studies, but it is always shorter than the requirements for secondary school teaching by at least a year. Salaries are also lower; and this fact combined with the less-academic requirements results in the lower esteem in which elementary school teachers are almost everywhere held, compared with high school teachers.

An announcement by Germany at the XIVth International Conference on Public Education held at Geneva in 1951 by UNESCO was regarded as conferring a notable rise in status for elementary teachers because they were to be admitted to the universities as well as to teacher training colleges and institutes. This was acclaimed as "bridging the social gap" between elementary and secondary school teachers even though the training course was still to be only two or three years, and not culminate in a university degree.

In England the required period of training for elementary school teachers was two years until 1960, when it was raised to three years. The approximately 170 training colleges (for elementary, housecraft, physical education, vocational education, and art) average less than 400 enrollment. For secondary school teachers, the almost invariable requirement is a university degree (B.A. after three years' study), plus one year of professional study. Similar provisions obtain in most other countries of the Western world.

In the United States, the rapid spread of the single-salary schedule (discussed in Chapter 16) probably did more to help toward equalizing the status of elementary and secondary school teachers than any other single factor. Because the amount of college study is one of the two main bases of a single-salary schedule (the other one being years of teaching experience), elementary school teachers were encouraged to complete B.A. and M.A. programs. More high school teachers actually have M.A. degrees and hence receive higher salaries, but elementary school teachers may also qualify by completing master's degree studies, and both categories may proceed beyond that.

### Limitations on Secondary and Higher Education

We in the United States have become so accustomed to the "educational ladder," by which any child may normally progress from kindergarten through the university, if he can "make the grade," that we forget the severe limitations in other countries. No other nation yet regards secondary education as universal education to the degree we do, although Soviet Russia is in process of extending its compulsory seven-year school to eleven years. Enrollment in practically every country is limited if not by social or financial conditions then by a series of examinations designed to keep the number of entrants to a desired level.

It is also true that few countries have arrived at a stage in economic, social, and political development where they feel they can begin to adopt measures that look toward universal secondary education. Most of the world's nations have not yet achieved universal five- or six-year primary education. These statements are not made in any spirit of criticism. Societies must reach a certain stage of development in order to release children and youth from the labor force to go to school, and adults to teach them.

In our own history, the work contribution of children and adolescents was so valuable that not until about 1920 did all forty-eight states require compulsory school attendance to at least age fourteen. (Massachusetts was the first state in 1852.) Rapid industrialization made it possible within a few decades to keep adolescents in high school. But as is shown in Chapter 9, it was not really until after 1920 that U.S. high schools began to broaden their outlook from that of being merely college prep schools, and to welcome boys and girls from the entire spectrum of society. More than two million people in the United States are full-time teachers, professors, and school administrators; and perhaps an equal number earn all or a major part of their living in school-related employment. Few nations have arrived at the point where they can dedicate 5 per cent or more of their working population to the function of education. These and similar considerations have to be kept in mind when one looks at the extent of educational opportunity afforded in different countries. The research reported by Myers and Harbison, cited earlier in this chapter, and several of the supplementary readings listed at the end of this book should be consulted on these points.

### Progress of Children Through the Schools

Comparative educational statistics are not completely reliable, and countries define certain terms in different ways (e.g., what comprises elementary or secondary education). However, the general conformation of education can be seen in the proportions of appropriate age groups in the three main segments: elementary (primary), secondary, and higher education. The latest data available at the time of writing are reported by Harbison and Myers for seventy-five countries. They grouped the countries into four levels according to criteria established for their study: I, underdeveloped; II, partially developed; III, semiadvanced; and IV, advanced. The following estimated percentages (rounded) of relevant age groups enrolled in countries at each level of development are reported: [8]

|  | Level I | Level II | Level III | Level IV |
|---|---|---|---|---|
| Primary schools . . . . . . . | 22 | 42 | 62 | 73 |
| Secondary schools . . . '. . . . | 3 | 12 | 27 | 59 |
| Higher education . . . . . . . | 0.2 | 2 | 5 | 11 |

Most impressive in the foregoing figures is the large decline that occurs between elementary and secondary school enrollment. This is a cause of deep concern in many countries, and it will take time to achieve marked improvement because of a shortage of teachers and facilities. But the notable gains in education in China during the 1950's, cited by Harbison (*supra*) should encourage others to recognize that much can be done even when the obstacles seem to be insuperable. They do not have to imitate China's totalitarian approach and methods, but they do have to be strongly motivated.

As a sort of base point from which some meaningful comparison may be drawn, recent data for the United States on percentage of various age groups enrolled are: elementary grades (ages five to thirteen), 95+ per cent; secondary (ages fourteen to seventeen), 87+ per cent; higher education (ages eighteen to twenty-one), 38 per cent.[9] United States experience over the last forty years is shown in another way in Fig. 6–6, where fifth-grade enrollment (practically 100 per cent of the appropriate age group) is used as the base.

A movement to extend the free, public, and universal school system in the United States for two more years, through grade 14 or junior college, has taken hold since 1963. Late that year the Educational Policies Commission (an agency of the National Education Association and the American Association of School Administrators) issued an influential statement advocating such an extension. Since more than a million students are already enrolled in two-year postsecondary institutions, it is likely that this proposal will be rapidly adopted in the next few years.

### The School Curriculum

Differences in school studies are not as marked as people in many countries have been led to believe. In all countries with fairly well-developed school systems, elementary or primary school curricula are

---

[8] Harbison and Myers, *op. cit.*, p. 38. For detailed explanation see their Chapter 3, "Quantitative Indicators of Human Resource Development," pp. 23–48.

[9] *NEA Research Bulletin*, XLI, No. 1, February, 1963.

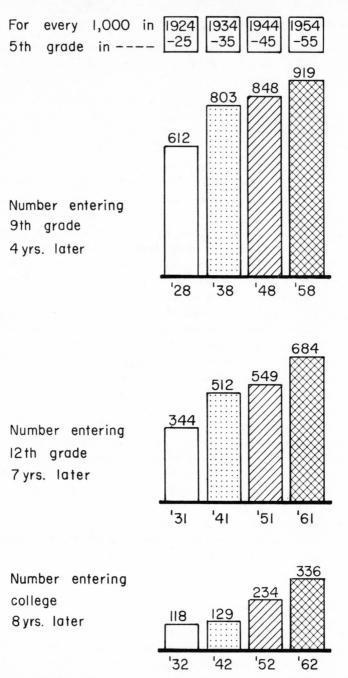

For every 1,000 in 5th grade in ---- | 1924-25 | 1934-35 | 1944-45 | 1954-55 |

Number entering
9th grade
4 yrs. later

612  803  848  919
'28  '38  '48  '58

Number entering
12th grade
7 yrs. later

344  512  549  684
'31  '41  '51  '61

Number entering
college
8 yrs. later

118  129  234  336
'32  '42  '52  '62

Fig. 6–6. Holding Power of U.S. Schools, 1924–1962. Source: *School Life* (official journal of Office of Education), XLV, No. 2 (November–December, 1962), 35.

remarkably similar, including approximately the same kinds of subjects as we have in the United States. The mother tongue and related
skills, some social studies (usually history of the homeland), elementary science, music, art, physical education, and crafts—these are
almost universally taught. There are differences in methods, amount,
and quality of facilities, and so on; but basically elementary education
is elementary education wherever you find it. The number of hours
per week in school does not vary much, either, centering closely
around twenty-five hours. Even the number of school days per year
is much the same. One reads reports of school years of 205, 215, or
even 230 days per year; but when all the holidays and holy days are
deducted, practically all are reduced to between 180 and 190 classroom days. In the United States, the average is about 180. Universities abroad typically have a considerably shorter academic year
than those in the United States, opening later in the fall and closing
earlier in the spring.

At the secondary level, more significant differences exist than at
the primary. Pupils study more subjects in any given year; classes
do not all meet every day, which is the general rule in the United
States; and there is almost invariably more homework. The actual
number of hours in school per week is about the same everywhere here
and abroad.

Earlier specialization is the rule in other countries, beginning at
about age thirteen or fourteen for most pupils who are destined to
go on for secondary education. In the United States, we emphasize
that so far as possible every boy and girl should become acquainted
with the major fields of human knowledge, which we call "general
education." This is continued right up through the first two years
of college, after which students concentrate most of their work in a
"major" field and one or two "minors." This would be unthinkable
and does not make sense to most educators in any other country;
but there are signs of incipient interest in some, for example the
United Kingdom and France. In those countries, doubts are beginning to be expressed over too-early specialization. Relative merits
of "depth" vs. "breadth" will probably never be agreed on, nor is
there any reason why they should be.[10]

Another difference, one that can be seen in the charts of national
school systems in Figs. 6-1 to 6-5, is the larger number of types of
secondary and higher institutions. In the Mexican plan, for instance,

[10] An interesting article on this point: Geoffrey Crowther, "English and American Education: Depth vs. Breadth," *Atlantic Monthly*, CCV, No. 4 (April, 1960),
pp. 37–42.

every major professional specialty has its own institutions; and this is true of other Latin American countries. Numerous ages and stages of progress for entering and leaving a variety of secondary and post-secondary institutions seems to be the rule in most countries. The relatively simple plan of the "educational ladder" prevailing in the United States is made more clear by examining the structure of other systems.

One controversial subject is argued all over the world, or so it seems: How much and what kind of vocational education should be offered, when should pupils begin it, and how should it be conducted? The U.S.S.R. has answered this in the most sweeping fashion. Since 1962, all pupils, boys and girls alike, at all levels of education, must learn some trade or profession; and much of the trade training is carried on in cooperation with industry and business. Everyone must also learn to work with his hands, even though he may not be intended for manual labor; and he must also do some regular physical labor.

Finally, among these few observations, it should be noted that for able and ambitious university students, other advanced countries do far more than is done in the wealthy United States. Not nearly so many young people go on to university, it must be conceded; but many of those who do receive not only full tuition, but also room and board, books and supplies, and even travel expenses if they need them. While a great deal of scholarship money is available in the United States, it does not provide aid anything like this for the most promising students.

## THE AMERICAN PREDILECTION FOR SELF-CRITICISM

It seems fitting to conclude this chapter with a few paragraphs on the American people's dedication to "progress," and the tendency to underrate what in our hearts and minds we know is one of the great achievements of our society: the educational system from kinder-garten through university oriented to an "open society." No other people is so strongly gripped by the belief that practically everything, including the conduct of education, can be done better, more efficiently, cheaper, or all three together. This idea of progress, as J. B. Bury called it in his book of the same name, is a fairly recent concept, emerging almost entirely within the last two hundred years.

When our citizens criticize their schools and universities, they exemplify this deep-rooted attachment to progress, along with exposing what they believe are weaknesses that should be remedied. Sometimes criticism points toward an experimental or "try-out" approach to improvement; sometimes it demands the adoption of the philosophy and practices of education in other countries.

## Criticism Construed by Visitors from Abroad as Insecurity

Educators from abroad who observe American schools, as exchange teachers and professors, researchers, and plain citizens, and thousands of students, seldom understand our predilection for self-criticism and improvement. They tend to interpret it as a sign of insecurity, a lack of confidence in our great institution of education. They exploit our self-depreciation as an invitation to inform us what our weaknesses are and how to cope with them. As they warm to the task, in all courtesy some of our guests really let us have it between the eyes.

Eventually, it dawns on us that they by no means have the background for understanding America that we assumed. They have some of the words but not the music. And how could they? One has to live with and experience American education for more than a few weeks or months, if not indeed be brought up in it as a child and youth to know it. We who study education professionally are so close to it that we see more of its qualities, good and bad, than any visitor possibly can. But furthermore, we forget that he looks at us and our institutions from a quite different background. What he sees may be the same as what we see, but it is filtered to his mind through a lifetime of different experience.

## Objectivity Hard To Maintain

Naturally it is difficult for persons on either side to be objective. While we may like to point out our good features and even some not so good, we get defensive when visitors identify what they regard as soft spots. Could this originate from a sneaking suspicion that there is a grain or two of truth in the newcomers' impressions?

Seasoned travelers in both directions have given sound advice: When one is in a foreign land, he should listen and look more, speak less. Honest questions to elicit information are rarely resented; but freely offered opinions, comparisons, and suggestions for improvement are just as rarely welcomed. It is axiomatic that no educational system can successfully be borrowed by one country from another, although some aspects of it may be adapted with profit. Probably every country can learn something of value from every other country.

However, the American people should not be blind to the virtues of their educational system. They can with propriety be proud that more than 70,000 students per year come to the United States to study in institutions of higher education, the capstone of the whole system. If our schools are weak, how could our institutions of higher education be so strong? America still affords asylum for hundreds of thousands of refugees from oppression; it is still the land of freedom and opportunity for people from many lands. These things could not have occurred in the absence of a vital, progressive, comprehensive system of education.

## QUESTIONS, PROBLEMS, AND PROJECTS FOR FURTHER STUDY

1. Do you see any inconsistency on the part of some U.S. critics of education in advocating the adoption of certain educational standards and practices of the U.S.S.R., a nation whose political and economic systems are repugnant to us?

2. How are the relations of religion and education managed in the English, French, Mexican, and Russian educational systems?

3. Explain the U.S. educational system in the form of an article for publication (perhaps in translation) in some other country. You decide for which country your paper is intended, and include reference to similarities and differences as an aid to your intended readers' understanding of our system.

4. In the early history of our country, as shown in Chapter 5, European thought and practice were understandably very influential in education. Can you discern any influence from abroad now? If so, describe it.

5. Try to find data on the economic status of teachers in three or four other countries and compare it with the status of U.S. public school teachers. Can you arrive at any general conclusions?

6. Interview two or three teachers who have served as exchange teachers and summarize their views on (a) the educational systems of their host countries, and (b) American education as it looked to them from abroad. Prepare a good outline for the interview, with the assistance of two or three classmates.

7. Arrange for a visit to the class by two or three students from abroad, who are attending your institution, to hear their impressions of American higher education (and schools, too, if they feel qualified). Brief them in advance, perhaps at a small coffee party, and go over points that you would like to have included, but avoid highly structuring their observations.

8. Examine several issues of the weekly Education Supplement of *The Times* of London. Compare the subjects that appear to be of most interest to the British with those currently discussed in the United States.

9. What are some important differences between universities in other countries and those in the United States? You may want to investigate this in two parts: (a) control, administration, and finance; (b) academic program, student-faculty relations, and student activities.

## SELECTED SUPPLEMENTARY READINGS AND FILMS

BEREDAY, GEORGE Z. F. *Comparative Method in Education.* New York: Holt, Rinehart & Winston, Inc., 1964. By selecting specific educational problems that cut across national boundaries and cultures, the author illustrates how comparative study of education may best be done, and how lessons can be deduced from variations in different societies.

BRADBURY, MALCOLM. "The Rise of the Redbrick," *Holiday,* XXXIV (November, 1963), 84–87 ff. An article on the expansion of higher education taking place in Britain through the "provincial universities" (a term that covers all those except the ancient universities of Oxford and Cambridge and London University), their character, and some of their problems.

CHETWYND, H. R. *The Comprehensive School: The Story of Woodberry Down.* London: Routledge & Kegan Paul, Ltd., 1960. This little book, by a headmistress, reports the founding and first four years' life of the first coeducational comprehensive secondary school in London.

CROWTHER, SIR GEOFFREY. "English and American Education: Depth versus Breadth," *Atlantic Monthly,* CCV, No. 4 (April, 1960), 37–42. A pithy explanation of a major difference in English and American education: earlier and more narrow specialization there, in contrast to emphasis on general education and deferment of specialization here.

DENT, H. C. *The Educational System of England and Wales.* 2d ed. London: University of London Press, Ltd., 1963. A brief yet comprehensive description, prefaced by a short historical survey.

DIVISION OF INTERNATIONAL EDUCATION. *Education in the USSR.* U.S. Office of Education, Bulletin 1957, No. 14. Washington, D.C.: Government Printing Office, 1957, 1960. An excellent, detailed study of Soviet education. Since its publication, some changes have occurred in the structure of Soviet education and in statistical data, but the major conclusions appear to be still valid.

ELAM, STANLEY E. (ed.). "Problems and Promises of Education in Latin America," *Phi Delta Kappan,* XLV, No. 4 (January, 1964), 161–229. Fifteen articles, book reviews, and an annotated bibliography of twenty-seven doctoral dissertations on all phases of education in Latin America.

FRASER, W. R. *Education and Society in Modern France.* London: Routledge & Kegan Paul, Ltd., 1963. Treats chiefly of the many efforts over a long period to reform the French educational system. Administrative, professional, cultural, religious, political, and financial obstacles to reform are discussed against a background of historical and contemporary events.

HARBISON, FREDERICK, and MYERS, CHARLES A. *Education, Manpower, and Economic Growth.* New York: McGraw-Hill Book Co., Inc., 1964. A "global analysis," both quantitative and qualitative, of the significance of educational opportunity for human resource development and economic growth in seventy-five countries. Expansion and improvement of education are pre-eminent among the "appropriate strategies" suggested for countries at various stages of development.

HEATH, KATHRYN G. *Ministries of Education: Their Functions and Organization.* U.S. Office of Education Bulletin 1961, No. 21. Washington, D.C.: Government Printing Office, 1962. This report was compiled thirty years after the first similar study, and, as one might expect, it records many changes. The first five chapters constitute a "multinational comparative analysis," followed by short sections on sixty-two countries.

JOHNSTON, MARJORIE C. *Education in Mexico.* U.S. Office of Education Bulletin 1956, No. 1. Washington, D.C.: Government Printing Office, 1956, 1962. The complex educational system of Mexico is well explained. A sympathetic view is gained of the formidable problems of providing education for a people ethnically and culturally exceedingly disparate.

KING, EDMUND J. *Other Schools and Ours.* Rev. ed. New York: Holt, Rinehart & Winston, Inc., 1963. This book by a professor at London University deals with six countries (Denmark, France, Great Britain, United States, the U.S.S.R., and India), each selected for "the distinctiveness of its educational system." The organization charts are rather useful except that they are somewhat oversimplified and (for France and the U.S.S.R.) a bit out of date. The chapters on the United States and U.S.S.R. leave little doubt as to the author's bias.

LINDEGREN, ALINA M. *Germany Revisited: Education in the Federal Republic.* U.S. Office of Education Bulletin 1957, No. 12. Washington, D.C.: Government Printing Office, 1957, 1960. Includes interesting background material on education under the Empire, the Weimar Republic, and National Socialism, and extensive data for the Federal Republic. Progress toward equal educational opportunity is shown to be the general goal of the present system.

MALE, GEORGE A. *Education in France.* U.S. Office of Education Bulletin 1963, No. 33. Washington, D.C.: Government Printing Office, 1963. Includes a good, brief, historical survey of French education. Administration, structure, curricula, and recent developments from nursery school to higher education are covered. (See also *Education in France,* a quarterly available on request from French Cultural Services, New York.)

RELLER, THEODORE L., and MORPHET, EDGAR L. (ed.). *Comparative Educational Administration.* Englewood Cliffs, N.J.: Prentice-Hall, Inc., 1962. The administration of education in sixteen countries, representing all continents, is explained. Trends, problems, national purposes, and control are discussed in a series of chapters at the end. Included are Australia, Brazil, Canada, China (People's Republic), Germany (Federal Republic), Great Britain, India, Japan, Mexico, Netherlands, Philippines, South Africa, Spain, United Arab Republic, U.S.S.R., and the United States.

"The Times Educational Supplement" of *The Times,* London. Published weekly since 1910, the Supplement presents a highly diversified, worldwide and unusually interesting coverage of educational problems, practices, and trends. While nations of the British Commonwealth receive the greater attention, others are given a reasonable share.

ULICH, ROBERT. *The Education of Nations: A Comparison in Historical*

*Perspective.* Cambridge, Mass.: Harvard University Press, 1961. After four chapters on cultural and historical foundations, there is a series of penetrating chapters on England, France, Germany, United States, and the U.S.S.R. The "persistent problems of education" are identified in a concluding chapter as (1) nationalism vs. humanity, (2) state vs. individual, (3) the role of religion, and (4) tradition vs. reform.

UNESCO. *World Survey of Education.* Vol. III. *Secondary Education.* Paris: United Nations Education, Scientific and Cultural Organization, 1961. Includes charts and text on most of the world's national educational systems, with emphasis on but not limited to secondary education. A companion volume is Vol. II: *Primary Education,* 1958. Books may be ordered and a list of publications obtained from Columbia University Press, New York.

WEBER, DEL. "Education as a Tool of Power," *Phi Delta Kappan,* XLI (June, 1960), 388–93. Based on original sources, this report clearly shows how the educational system of a country is seized and exploited by a dictatorship to strengthen its control. The author states that the government now finds "centralized leadership with decentralized management" of education preferable to highly centralized control, but that the Communist party completely dominates the entire system.

## Films

*Cambridge and Oxford.* 10 minutes, color. A study of the architecture and life of the two universities. Evanston, Ill.: Contemporary Films.

*How Do American Schools Compare with Yours?* 29 minutes. A forum discussion by representatives of Australia, Guatemala, Norway, and Turkey, comparing their schools with those of the U.S. National Educational Television.

*It's a Small World.* 45 minutes. Impressions of the daily life and routine in a London nursery school, from morning until the children's departure in afternoon. Children's reactions to the surroundings and the school program are depicted without the use of the spoken word by hidden cameras. New York: Columbia University.

*Le Lycée sur la Colline.* 20 minutes. In French. Description of a French secondary school. New York: Society for French American Cultural Services and Educational Aid.

*Learning To Live.* 28 minutes. The pattern of school life in Britain from primary to high school, designed to give Americans an idea of Britain's educational structure and a glimpse of British youth at work and at play. Includes interviews with children. Evanston, Ill.: Contemporary Films, Inc.

*Russian School Days.* 70 minutes. Soviet film with English subtitles, prepared for showing in U.S.S.R. Ann Arbor: University of Michigan.

*The Schoolmaster.* 20 minutes. Portrait of a young teacher in a small country town in the Scottish hills. An insight is given into the workings and atmosphere of a typical British country school, and a good idea of the respect and affection with which the teacher is regarded. Evanston, Ill.: Contemporary Films, Inc.

*Schools of Mexico.* 10 minutes. A view of educational institutions from the ultramodern Ministry of Education in Mexico City to remote, one-room, adobe schools far removed. Includes normal schools, vocational and agricultural institutions, and kindergartens. Chicago: Coronet Productions.

*Schools to the South.* 12 minutes. An accurate picture of the educational systems in operation in Latin American countries. Washington, D.C.: U.S. Office of Inter-American Affairs.

# III

# INSTRUCTIONAL
# AND RELATED
# SCHOOL SERVICES

# EDUCATIONAL SERVICES
# AND THEIR ORGANIZATION

Earlier chapters have exposed the reader to the foundations of education and something of the challenge and conflict characteristic of educational theory and practice. This chapter introduces a section of the book dealing with the educational and related services provided by schools and colleges. While it seems logical to expect that primary emphasis be placed upon educational activity, one cannot always be sure. Custodial and housekeeping duties sometimes interfere. The entertainment of the student body and of the public, for example through interscholastic athletics, may assume undue proportions. Public service enterprise often requires time and effort. Both teachers and learners are occupied in many ways, some central to their major purposes, others only ancillary, and a few perhaps inimical to these purposes.

## A FUNDAMENTAL EDUCATIONAL QUESTION

What knowledge is of most worth? This age-old question is asked repeatedly by educators seeking to provide experiences consonant with the roles and functions of educational institutions. They turn to many sources for satisfying answers, and the latter are increasingly difficult to obtain and progressively in need of periodic re-examination. The wise teacher is both conservative and progressive in seeking solutions to educational problems. He tests all proposals, holding to those that prove to be good; and he attempts to find better answers whenever needed and possible.

### Human Experience and the Necessity of Choice

Man's knowledge is accumulating at an unprecedented and accelerating rate. The knowledge that exists today is tremendous in breadth and depth. Libraries of a million or more volumes exist, and no one of these is said to encompass all knowledge. New books are turned out by the thousands each year, not all of them adding to enlightenment, of course. They do complicate the problem of choice, however. The world into which each succeeding generation is born offers a greater accumulation from which to choose the knowledge that is of greatest worth.

The problem is complicated in another sense, namely, that what was true yesterday is not necessarily true today; and the latter truth may be false tomorrow. New discoveries are ever being made, especially in the biological and physical sciences and in mathematics. What was only a vague hypothesis a year ago may be accepted as a proven theory today, and on rechecking again and again is discarded next year as better theories emerge. Truth is often elusive, and the pursuit of it a hectic as well as an exhilarating experience.

Furthermore, the learner needs to experience for himself the thrill of discovery. Too many choices made for him tend to weaken his power of decision. Merely to be fed partially or wholly digested bits of information, however true and significant they are, is not to experience a very nutritious and healthful educational diet. Consequently, the appropriateness of knowledge in terms of its meaningful handling with and by learners enlarges the problem of selection.

The migration of families today adds still another element to the complex situation. Pupils frequently attend many schools before graduating from high school and college. If articulation is to be fostered under such conditions, the need for reasonable agreement across school, community, and state lines has to be faced. The tendency for some pupils to drop out of school adds to the complexity of the grade placement of experience. In other ways the reader may think of, the need for choice is evident, and the difficulty of making one is obvious.

One of the major problems of the schools and colleges is thus the selection and ordering of knowledge most suitable for education. Within the individual classroom, the teacher faces this problem, and so also do his pupils. The choices made are governed to some extent by decisions made elsewhere. Members of a single department, for example social studies at the senior high school level, usually have ideas as to what should be taught and when. What has been taught, or is supposed to have been covered in the elementary and junior high schools, is pertinent to their decisions. Community conditions may impose limitations or favor certain views while opposing others. Much time and effort is currently given to the selection and ordering of curricular experiences in an attempt to answer the age-old question that has been posed. Today's answers will not likely suffice for to-morrow.

## Bases of Educational Choice

In establishing criteria for the selection of educational content and experience, reference should be made to the foundations of education and to the roles, functions, and purposes to be served by schools and colleges. The application of criteria necessitates the use of subjec-tive judgment. Not all content chosen for use will meet every cri-terion, and each of the various criteria may be met in varying degrees.

Often the principal, if not the sole, basis for choice lies in the text-book or textbooks adopted for use with a class. That is, what the book includes is taught; what it does not include is apt to be neg-lected. This reliance on textbooks relates also to another determining factor—the courses or subjects that are included in the educational program. Courses of study and the opinions of teachers are also in-fluential, the latter often being based largely on past experience. Tradition is a factor, too; and state or city courses of study and text-book adoptions affect content a great deal.

The following criteria provide some specific considerations that are useful in the selection process. These questions suggest also that the manner of handling the content has a bearing on the decisions to be made.

1. Is the proposed content significant, valid, and useful in inter-preting, understanding, and appreciating contemporary life?
2. Does the proposed content relate definitely to one or more of the pertinent areas of life problems with which the curriculum should deal?
3. Will the proper use of the proposed content promote the well-balanced growth and development of boys and girls in terms of stated educational objectives (abilities, attitudes, habits, sensitivities, etc.)?
4. Is the proposed content important in terms of its contribution to the overall roles of the curriculum—conservative, critical or evaluative, and creative; has it real significance in human ex-perience?
5. Does the proposed content have use in satisfying the immediate challenges, interests, needs, and problems of boys and girls?
6. Is the proposed content consonant with the maturity level and the experiential background of the learner?

7. Is the proposed content readily capable of adaptation to meet individual differences?
8. Does the proposed content contribute to a continuous and inter-active learning situation that promotes the progressive growth and development of the learner?
9. Does the proposed content permit effective associations and has it useful application in present-day situations pertinent to the learner?
10. Does the proposed content have sufficient intrinsic motivational power to encourage satisfying learning activity?
11. Will the inclusion of the proposed content promote a well-balanced curriculum free of unnecessary repetition, and does it take into consideration other educative agencies and forces?

The importance to the teacher of a broad liberal education, knowledge of subject matter, and professional competencies (including knowledge of children and youth) is apparent as one views the job of selecting appropriate educational content. Within the framework of the educational program, teachers and pupils often plan and choose together. Factors promoting successful teaching and learning, as discussed in Chapter 2, are cogent to this process.

## The Process of Selecting Educational Experiences

In making choices it is not feasible for teachers or learners to approach the total culture as an entity and attempt to appraise it all in terms of criteria. Some of the influences likely to reduce the breadth of the search have already been suggested, such as subjects to be taught, adopted textbooks, courses of study, and tradition. Usually, therefore, the selection is confined to some less-inclusive area with which the teacher is familiar, if not the learners. While human experience has thus been classified for convenience, there is need to be careful lest such departmentalization does not destroy the unity of knowledge or render it inert.

**Means of Selecting Content.** In actually making choices, by use of criteria suggested earlier or by other standards, several means are employed. Teachers, individually or collectively, often turn to that knowledge that is familiar from past experience; or they may choose from among many unfamiliar possibilities. They may, for example, select a *textbook* that seems, among those examined, to be the one best suited to their purposes. Perhaps several books have been recommended to them. Sometimes various units, topics, or texts are submitted to a group, and choice is made through a *survey of opinions*.

*Curricula* or *courses of study* from other schools are frequently examined, and ideas are picked from them by teachers for use in their own program. The *errors* that students make or that are common in adult endeavor may be analyzed to discover content and activity needed for remedial or developmental purposes. Spelling words may be chosen partially on such a basis and on an analysis of usage. An *analysis of activity* (adult or youth) provides another way of determining educational experiences. Study or analysis of broad social activity or of youth interests and needs gives other clues. Reference to the criteria offered earlier will reveal that some precedures are more useful with certain bases of selection than with others.

The use of many resources enables teachers to enrich educational experience and to broaden the exposure provided for students. Supplementary reading; outside speakers; visits to business, industry, and museums; audio-visual materials; laboratory experiences; and other possibilities are appropriate, depending on the purposes sought and the nature of the group taught. The skill of the teacher in making choices, alone and with others, is quite important in determining what is learned and how well it is learned. Attention is given to the organization of teaching-learning content and experiences in a later section of this chapter.

## EDUCATIONAL ROLES, FUNCTIONS, OBJECTIVES, AND OUTCOMES

This chapter might properly have opened with a discussion of educational purpose. When a question of worth is raised, the answer invariably depends upon purpose; indeed interdependency of value and purpose is apparent. Roles, functions, objectives, and outcomes are of primary significance in education. One of the major weaknesses of teaching, at all levels, is the failure to relate these things properly and regularly in the total educational process.

In Chapter 3, roles and functions are discussed. Brief reiteration is provided here as an approach to dealing with directional signals more closely associated to daily teaching and learning.

| *Roles of Education* | *Functions of Education* | |
|---|---|---|
| Conservative | Adjustive | Integrative |
| Critical | Diagnostic | Selective |
| Creative | Differentiative | Preparatory |

Educational objectives range from those of immediate concern associated with a single teaching-learning experience to those of ultimate concern relating to a comprehensive series of experiences. As one illustration, in an arithmetic lesson the teacher may be seeking to have pupils develop the ability to read points on a line graph. This immediate objective, with others to follow, contributes to the larger ability of interpreting graphic data (an intermediate objective); and the latter purpose relates to the ultimate objective of thinking. This ultimate objective of thinking serves several of the functions and contributes significantly to at least one major role of the school. What functions and role(s) do you believe are involved?

Concomitant objectives or outcomes may derive from a teaching-learning situation in which completely different objectives are being sought. Such concomitant outcomes may be desirable or undesirable. For example, in seeking to teach pupils how to understand and appreciate literature, the procedures employed may result in active dislike of literature. Repeated overemphasis on literary dissection may drive pupils away from reading. On the other hand, the study of trees as a biological plant may yield an appreciation of beauty and utility. The wise teacher anticipates and is alert to signs of all manner of outcomes as he teaches.

Objectives are sometimes classified as teacher or pupil objectives in terms of their origin or source. Teachers have objectives they wish pupils to attain. Pupils often have their own objectives, not always in agreement with those of teachers. Their purposes may be contrary to the education proposed for them. It is important that objectives relate in terms of ultimate to immediate and that teacher and student objectives be brought into agreement. Otherwise, effective teaching and learning are not apt to be accomplished.

## The Use and Value of Educational Goals

Educational objectives are useful and valuable as they provide:

1. Direction to teaching and learning
2. Continuity of effort
3. Bases for evaluation
4. Motivation of endeavor

Education is a value process. There are always some goals sought, although these goals may be inconsequential and understood neither by teachers nor learners.

Carefully related immediate, intermediate, and ultimate objectives help to keep teaching and learning moving forward with continuity. They guard against irrelevancy and sidetracks. Serving as directional mileposts, they make it possible to evaluate progress and to appraise the teaching-learning methods that are used. If well accepted, educational objectives draw the learner on, stage by stage, just as a distant peak, bold and sharp against the sky, pulls the mountain climber toward its summit. The actual magnetism, of course, lies in the learner and the climber as much or more than in the goal or the peak. To create or sustain motivation in a learner is a significant accomplishment.

## The Formulation of Educational Objectives

Educational objectives should be stated in terms of the behavioral outcomes that pupils are expected to attain. The following are illustrative components of behavior that such outcomes may voice:

Abilities, such as the ability to study, read, or think
Attitudes, such as the attitude of optimism or sincerity
Habits, such as the habit of dependability or punctuality
Appreciations, such as appreciation of beauty in nature
Understandings, such as understanding of a scientific theory or
a historical event
Ideals, such as the ideal of extending equal opportunity to all
Sensitivities, such as sensitivity to injustice and a desire to remedy
it

Other phraseology may be used, but the essence lies in stating objectives such that they relate to what is expected of the learner rather than to what the teacher is to do. Occasionally, one sees statements of teacher objectives and student objectives in parallel; but the real outcomes sought lie in the attainment of the latter.

Teachers should not assume that valid objectives are inherent in the courses they teach or in the materials they use. There is nothing automatic about this relationship. Much depends upon the manner in which the courses are developed and in which the materials are prepared and are subsequently used. The new teacher usually goes into a school or college situation having some overall philosophy and goals. Courses in educational theory and the student teaching experience help in this regard. The persons with whom he teaches may aid him in seeing his courses in the larger perspective, or he may be left on his own to develop specific course objectives appropriate to the larger situation. Having studied the subjects earlier himself, he likely relies on this experience unless he has been taught other ways of doing things.

The cooperative development of objectives is recommended. On the level of a school or college, the broad ultimate goals should reflect the sweep of experience that only a concerted, cooperative effort can yield. Agreement is usually difficult to obtain on other than general statements. On a given grade level, or within a given department, somewhat more specific objectives should be stated, hopefully in relation to the ultimate goals. Smaller groups of teachers having similar assignments may give greater specificity to objectives, and the individual teacher with his learners sharpens these statements to give vitality to the specific teaching-learning situation. Various combinations of approaches are used with attention being directed to the roles, functions, and areas of life problems appropriate to the subject and grade level, and the resources available. Just as objectives suggest the nature of content, the latter also indicates objectives appropriate to its usage.

## THE EDUCATIONAL PROGRAM OF THE SCHOOLS

The multifold activities by means of which the primary job of teaching and learning is fostered constitute the educational program. Two or three related divisions comprise this program: the curriculum, extraclass or student activities (sometimes called extracurricular), and counseling and student personnel services. Some concepts of curricular include the extracurricular, as will be noted later. Of these divisions, the curriculum is most central to formal teaching and learning; and it is with this phase of the educational program that this chapter is principally concerned. Student activities and counseling and personnel services are valuable and serve also in other than instructional ways. More is said of these programs later.

### The Nature of the Curriculum

Both narrow and broad concepts of the curriculum exist. It is viewed by some persons as being as broad as life itself and as including *all* educative experience, formal or informal, within or beyond the school or college and their control. Others conceive the curriculum as composed only of the formally organized subjects taught in the classroom, such as reading, spelling, arithmetic, U.S. history, English, biology, history of Western civilization, anthropology, and physics.

Definition of Curriculum. A workable definition that avoids the enormity of the first view and the undue restrictiveness of the second identifies the *curriculum as those educative experiences that learners have under the direction of the school or college.* Included in this concept are the subjects studied, the books read, the games engaged in, and other educative activity carried on under the direction of the educational institution. Extraclass or student activities under school sponsorship are curricular according to this view. Some counseling and personnel services are included also. However, because these latter activities and services range from rather definite bearing on formal teaching and learning to almost no relationship at all, the discussion to follow immediately excludes them and focuses on subjects and courses comprising the central core of the curriculum.

**Curricular Bases and Goals.** The curriculum should be thought of as a means and not an end. Its development and use should be consistent with the social and biopsychological bases of education already discussed. Including goals, content, methodology, and materials, the curriculum provides a framework that fosters economy and efficiency in teaching and learning. From one point of view, it consists of what and how the pupils *are to study and pursue truth,* and what the teachers *are to do* with them. There are those also who say that the curriculum is what learners and teachers *actually do,* rather than what is written down for them to do. The degree to which advance structuring of teaching-learning is and should be accomplished and followed remains a controversial matter among educators. In general, advance structuring should be sufficiently flexible to make needed adjustments as teaching and learning proceed.

As suggested earlier, educational objectives are vital. The form taken by the various aspects of the curriculum, the content to be used, the methodology to be employed, and the materials to be drawn upon are determined in no small degree by the purposes sought. Review should be made of the earlier section in this chapter dealing with philosophy and objectives.

**Types of Curriculum and Courses.** Most elementary schools operate on a self-contained classroom basis in which one teacher handles all or most all of the subjects taught, such as reading, writing, spelling, arithmetic, social studies, science, art, music, and health and physical education. Each of these studies is frequently allotted a given period of time in the daily or weekly schedule. Sometimes these subjects are combined or unified into units that deal with some aspect of life or an era. For example, in a unit dealing with "Community Helpers," many of the separate subjects would be brought in and taught as needed.

Some departmentalization exists in many elementary schools, at least in grades 5 and 6. At the junior high level, usually grades 7 through 9, and in the senior high school, course structure by departments or divisions and with different teachers is basic to the typical curriculum. The term "curriculum" is also used in a less-inclusive sense than defined herein. One hears reference to a *college preparatory curriculum,* for example, or to a *general curriculum,* or a *vocational curriculum.* In each instance the curriculum identified consists of those courses (such as English 9, Algebra I, Physics, American Literature, Speech II, College Grammar, Typing and Shorthand III, or Advanced Machine Shop) of which it is comprised.

Some schools, usually smaller ones, offer only a single curriculum with enough courses to afford students only limited choice beyond the courses required of all. Usually this curriculum is the college preparatory or the general. Larger schools offer multiple curricula. In all high schools, there is usually some overlapping of courses across curricular lines and of students in courses and curricula. The same course may enroll pupils in several curricula. More is said in a later chapter of grouping, tracks, and other arrangements used within these basic curricular plans.

**Curricular or Course Types.**    The courses that comprise the one curriculum or several curricula are of various types according to organization. *Subject-centered* courses focus on selected content in a single subject field, such as Latin I, Chemistry I, Plane Geometry, or U.S. History. *Fused courses* represent a move toward combining elements in a single field, once offered in separate subject-centered courses, into a broader course. For example, biology as taught today usually includes elements from botany, zoology, and physiology, once commonly taught as separate courses. Newer fused courses in biology include some chemistry and/or physics. The idea of *fusion* is also carried further to result in *broad-fields* courses that sample from many separate courses in a large field, such as general mathematics, general business, and intrdouction to the social studies.

*Correlation* is an idea similar to fusion except that it pertains to relating common elements usually taught in subject-centered courses in different fields rather than in the same field. *Correlated courses* are separate courses, but in them this relationship is sought. As an illustration, American history and American literature have much in common. Courses in each subject could well be correlated so as to reinforce and give larger meaning to both. They might take their chronology from the history and bring in literature appropriately, in terms of events, themes, or periods. One or more teachers could be involved in handling the two separate courses.

This idea of correlation is sometimes carried to the point of actually combining two correlated courses into a single *core course*. Referring to the earlier example of history and literature, a two-period block of time might be set aside in which one teacher would handle both subjects in a completely correlated fashion, essentially teaching them as one subject. There are various kinds of core courses, among which the type illustrated is most common and is identified as a *unified studies core*.

At the college level, the *subject-centered* courses are by far the most common. Increasing specialization in higher education fosters extreme compartmentalization. It has been said that this development is a principal source of inadequacy, especially as regards the general or liberal education of college students.

Certain of the other types of courses are found in collegiate institutions seeking to provide a broader approach to general education than through an elective sampling of introductory courses basic to each of many subjects. A biological science course or a physical science course, for example, may represent *fusion*. A course in the humanities may combine elements from art, literature, and music in a *correlated* offering. Not so much is done with broad-fields courses, although a few examples exist. In colleges and universities, one also finds an extension of the use of curriculum as identifying a program of courses leading to some special outcome, such as a liberal arts curriculum, a teacher education curriculum, a basic science curriculum, and a premedic curriculum.

**The Elective System and Course Identity.** Another means of identifying courses is employed in terms of their importance in one or in several curricula. In high schools and colleges of the United States, the elective system through which pupils are given considerable choice has led to a classification scheme that is fundamental. Both secondary school and college courses fall into the following groups:

1. Constants, prescribed, or required courses that are essential to graduation in the given institution or curriculum
2. Limited, qualified, or restrictive electives, that is, courses from among which some choice must be made, for example, in satisfying the requirement of one year or eight semester hours in social studies

3. Free electives consisting of those courses that students may choose as they please so long as they meet the prerequisites, if any exist

The term "curricular prescription" is also used to identify courses variously required for given curricula. Courses that are required of some pupils may be among the limited and free electives for others.

**Curricular Evolution and Revision.** The curriculum has grown ever since the establishment of schools and colleges. The evolutionary process has been characterized by three related tendencies:

1. An increase in the number of courses with marked compartmentalization of knowledge
2. An increase in the content of each course, often resulting in unnecessary duplication among courses
3. A pushing down of courses or elements therefrom to lower grade levels

Harvard once taught the arithmetic subsequently offered in the academies and later in the high schools. By 1910, arithmetic was strictly an elementary school subject, grades 1 to 8. Countertrends developed also, as was the case in mathematics with the movement to postpone the more formal number of concepts and processes. Now the "modern mathematics" is slowly revising many aspects of mathematics instruction in elementary, secondary, and collegiate schools. Advanced placement programs operate to move Algebra I to the eighth grade and biology to the ninth grade, each typically offered a grade higher. Other illustrations may be provided by the reader. The pendulum and the cycle are characteristic of curricular movements. In some respects schools and colleges that have resisted change and continued the status quo have been in fashion periodically over a number of years. This fashionability does not mean that they have been excellent schools, however.

Curricular revision has been accomplished largely through a process of addition. As new needs have arisen or old ones not well met, the easiest change has been to expand existing courses and add new ones. It has been the authors' experience that, with a few exceptions, the curriculum is like the fox's den in one of Aesop's fables, of which the rabbit said in declining to enter, "All tracks lead in, none lead out." Much of the curricular content remains today as it is because, once included, no one could or would remove it. An analysis of the courses offered in secondary schools and colleges, particularly the latter, will reveal the extravagance with which curricular empire building has been accomplished in many places.

Other characteristics of evolution and revision also merit attention. Initially, college preparatory, the secondary school, curriculum slowly added other courses as it came to serve pupils not going on to college. Supplanting followed supplementation in a few instances, for example, as modern foreign languages displaced Latin and especially Greek. Parallel curricula developed with a variety of names, although careful analysis reveals that there was often only a basic curriculum plus a number of additional courses. The elective system ran its course, turned the corner, and gave way partially to renewed prescription. Balance is always difficult to maintain, especially in periods of accelerated evolution or change.

In the elementary school content, studies in social sciences, literature, and science were added to the basic drill subjects of earlier days. The arts and crafts and some physical education also expanded the total offerings. The "practical" came to be considered as well as the "disciplinary"; and with the popularization of education, verbalization was often accepted as a substitute for reasonable mastery. Attempting too much and not doing it well has been a long-standing criticism of the curriculum, not without cause in many instances.

Change in theory has been much greater than modification in practice. Renewed attention has been given periodically to various groups of learners; for example, the able and ambitious, the large average group, and the slow learners. With the popularization of education moving upward from the elementary years to the college years, diversity and flexibility in offerings and performance have become increasingly evident.

Curricular decisions were initially made and modifications brought about largely by individual teachers and single schools. Small-scale revision was the usual type. In time, however, more people became involved as school systems undertook broad-front revision projects, such as the development of curricular guides in subjects from the kindergarten through the twelfth grade. Statewide programs have focused on given subject areas or grade levels and sometimes on special projects such as driver education in the high school or conservation in the elementary school. National professional groups, such as the National Council of Teachers of English, have also made pronouncements and offered specific ideas for curricular revision.

Currently, national groups working with foundation or federal support strive to bring about modifications in such subjects as English, biology, chemistry, foreign languages, physics, and mathematics.

Such endeavor exerts influence from the elementary through the college levels. Money seems to make a great difference in overcoming apathy and inertia, even among educators!

## Curricular Determiners

The preceding discussion opens the door to a look at some of the principal determiners of the curriculum. At the college level, much is left to the discretion of departments, schools, and colleges within the framework of administrative and board of trustees control. The latter boards have the legal authority, sometimes subject to statewide or "super" boards. The legislature frequently has more control than it exercises due to its role in the funding of higher education. Unfortunately, the exercise of legislative control is growing in some states.

Education is normally viewed as a function of the state. State legislatures typically delegate much authority to such agencies as state departments of education and local boards of education, although state laws may require certain courses. While these agencies support curricular change or resist it, the actual work is usually done by professionals: supervisors, teachers, administrators, and other specialists working with them. At the level of teaching and learning, the teachers have principal responsibility for curricular determination. At the college level, professors may resist any outside control of what they teach as an abridgement of academic freedom.

Colleges and universities exercise much influence through entrance requirements, the preparation of teachers and other educational workers, and their position at the apex of the educational pyramid. The lay public has been increasingly articulate in recent years and is often involved actively in educational decision making. Other groups referred to in the previous discussion serve also as determiners of curriculum as well as agencies of evolution and revision.

The idea of a community-centered curriculum has given rise to controversy in many quarters. In general the elementary and secondary school programs have in recent years become increasingly responsive to parents and others, particularly to vocal minorities. Two major sorts of such influence are felt on the curriculum. First, there are those who wish something added to the curriculum, such as health and physical education, art and music, more math, foreign language, science, or guidance services. Or they wish some aspect improved, such as reading instruction or the program for superior or for retarded children.

The second group consists of people who would restrict what the schools do. They often wish to limit academic freedom, deny the right to discuss controversial issues, remove certain courses and books from the school, and in other ways limit or reduce the schools' sphere of influence. Sometimes people in these groups act as individuals; often they exert pressure as a group. The reduction of educational costs sometimes motivates their restrictive endeavor. The activities of such groups were mentioned in an earlier chapter and more is said in a later one.

The study of community, state, and national problems in the curriculum provides meaningful ways of relating schooling to life here and now. Surveys focused on some segment of life or of a community or state may serve to determine in part what is subsequently studied, as well as identifying areas in which service to the community may be rendered. For example, the following problems are illustrative of conditions that may be disclosed and subsequently studied:

1. Inefficient use of and failure to develop and conserve material resources—land, water power, timber, and minerals, for example
2. Undemocratic perversion and exploitation of democratic processes and control of the community by a few for the interests of a minority
3. Absence, incompleteness, or mismanagement of social institutions and equipment such as those for public health, education, leisure, and recreation
4. Problems relating to wasteful and undemocratic division of the community into religious, economic, occupational, or social factions, and the treatment of minority ethnic groups
5. Problems relating to unemployment and adequate income
6. Problems related to consumer exploitation, monopolistic prevention of free competitive enterprise, misleading or untruthful advertising
7. Problems related to community care for the ill, the aged, the orphans, the crippled, the feebleminded and insane, the blind, and the hard of hearing
8. Problems related to community beauty—community housekeeping with respect to streets, lawns, parks, playgrounds, and so forth
9. Community leisure and recreation—parks, playgrounds, art museums, musical programs, sports programs, libraries
10. Problems relating to adequate housing, health inspections and control of food, waste disposal, water supply, and communicable diseases
11. Juvenile delinquency

These conditions are not necessarily limited to local communities. National and international concerns may exert influence on the curriculum, causing attention in specific courses to be focused on such matters as loyalty, the space age and race, unemployment, integration, and growing nationalism. Assent and dissent at home and abroad impinge on the curriculum in a world and era in which isolation and insulation are no longer possible or desirable.

## Trends in Curricular Development

The curriculum today is under constant scrutiny, out of which some revision slowly comes about. Generally, we have lagged behind at least a generation in accomplishing changes to meet needs. Teacher turnover, undue conservatism, sporadic and poorly planned revisions, and uncertainty have plagued the schools and the colleges. In the latter institutions, curricular revision has seldom received the attention it deserves. Overall, however, there are discernible trends in curricular development that warrant discussion.

The nature of trends is important to those who seek to trace and evaluate them. Certain conditions seem generally to characterize trends, often making it difficult to determine either the validity or vigor of what is proposed and what actually is happening. Theory leads action, often by a generation. What is advocated as a trend, therefore, may be chiefly a recognition by most people of what should be done, and may be practiced as a course of action by very few. Studies of proposed trends frequently reveal that while some schools are moving with the trend, others are moving against it, and the majority moving not at all. Consequently, a small minority may be all that determines the trend. The pendulum or cyclical effect mentioned earlier is important to remember also. Sometimes countertrends develop rapidly if a strong trend becomes threatening to many people or to a few who are in a position to react vigorously. Advocates of trends and countertrends are sometimes guilty of overemphasis or undue optimism.

With these statements in mind, the following major general trends merit careful consideration, for they reflect response to developments in and beyond the schools:

1. The curriculum is viewed more broadly than ever before as the growing need for all manner of education becomes apparent, especially at and beyond the secondary school years.
2. Both high quality and diversity are increasingly recognized as

essential in a curriculum for mass education faced with many and varied challenges.

3. The importance of individual differences is highlighted in a curriculum that is giving renewed attention to a general or liberal education for all pupils to the level they can profit from.

4. Participation in curricular building is broader than in the past, but there is also growing recognition of the leadership and decision-making roles that professionals must play.

5. The range of resources used in developing and teaching the curriculum is increasing as science and technology have growing impact on the educational process.

6. The fundamentals are being reconsidered, often in a different light than in the past, as growing emphasis is given to discovery, meaning, and useful application in the curriculum.

Specific curricular innovations also reflect the characteristics of trends previously indicated. The following items suggest something of the current ferment in specific aspect in the curriculum:

1. Growing emphasis is apparent in the communication arts, including oral as well as written language, and foreign languages as well as our own.

2. Geography is receiving greater attention as a separate subject and in connection with other physical and social sciences at elementary and secondary levels.

3. Many new ideas are being incorporated into certain subjects as national movements and money are brought to bear; for example, in biology, mathematics, foreign language, chemistry, physics, earth science, counseling, and audio-visual education.

4. Attention to social problems and international relations is growing as these matters are increasingly brought to public attention daily and because they affect our national budget so greatly.

5. Education to ease the transition from school to work is receiving renewed attention, especially in larger cities where unemployment, large groups of underprivileged peoples, dropouts, and delinquents are prevalent.

6. The fine arts and the humanities are enjoying a somewhat less-active resurgence than the sciences, but more schools are making better provisions for them than in the past.

7. Outdoor education is spreading, together with camping, as an activity allied to the schools, particularly at the elementary level.

8. There is growing admission of the importance of moral and spiritual values, but this area is involved also in the religious

controversy. The need for education for citizenship and American ideals is also receiving growing recognition, although it remains subject to much criticism from the right and left.

### Extraclass, Extracurricular, or Student Activities

Additional attention is given to this topic in Chapter 11, but some aspects are properly discussed in relation to the educational program of the schools. The extensive provisions for these activities, especially at the secondary school level, is peculiar to the United States of America. In some foreign countries, one also sees this idea slowly taking root, as pupils are given more choices and a freer role in the schools. The exchange of students has done much to sow some of the seeds that are beginning to grow in lands from which we have had pupils and to which our own students and educational consultants have gone.

**Curricular or Extracurricular?** The distinction between extracurricular and curricular is not always clear. In a sense the latter encompasses the former, at least as defined herein. At the same time, some extraclass or extracurricular activities are more "extra" than others. They differ in a number of ways from the formalized courses that constitute the core of curricular offerings. It may be useful to explore the relationship further since each has contributed to the other and both foster the same and similar educational objectives.

The academic curriculum of earlier high schools has grown by a process of addition in which extracurricular activities have often represented the first stage. By way of illustration, arts and crafts, music, dramatics, speech, and physical education were first offered in many schools as a kind of student activity held before or after school hours, for which no credit was earned, and in which little attention was given to the specific qualifications of the sponsor. These were "extra" activities in a very real sense. Gradually, however, and not on a uniform front, a movement developed that slowly brought them into the curriculum with regularly scheduled periods, credit, fully qualified teachers, and special facilities and materials for instruction. In periods of depression, these subjects are among the first to be dropped or put back on an "extraclass" basis.

Another related development has taken place. In the so-called extraclass activities where credit was not given and only interested students were involved, teachers felt freer to do such things as the following:

1. Utilize pupil interests and needs, attend to individual differences, and give pupils a more active and responsible teaching-learning role
2. Draw upon experiences outside their subject fields, correlate learning across departmental lines, and make use of a wider range of resources—material and personnel
3. Establish less formal and more functional learning situations involving the immediate present and giving much attention to pupil self-direction and self-appraisal

As teachers became secure in these matters in extracurricular situations, they began to use the same ideas in curricular courses. Thus, while there was a trend to curricularize the activities, there was also a trend to use what had been successful in these activities within formal courses where they had not been so widely used previously.

### The Nature and Value of Extraclass Activities

For purposes of convenience, these activities may be classified as follows: athletics, assemblies, clubs, dramatics and speech, honorary groups, music organizations, pupil government, school publications, and social events. Sometimes there is overlapping. Practically all secondary schools have some of these activities, and in large senior high schools extensive programs are found with numerous groups in each of the various categories. Colleges, too, offer much of the same opportunity.

These student activities serve in many ways the same objectives as do the formal courses that are offered. A few illustrations clarify this point. Social science courses aim at developing, among other things, understanding of the democratic process and skill in making it work. Student councils, homeroom organizations, and other associated student groups (even on the collegiate level) provide actual experience contributing to the same outcomes. The wise use of leisure time is served by both literature classes and various clubs, such as the English Club, the Drama Group, and the Science Club. Health and physical fitness are fostered in various formal courses and also in various athletic activities. In other ways a fine student activity program adds to pupil morale and serves interests and needs not so easily dealt with in "curricular courses." At the collegiate level, the support and interest of alumni often depends more upon these activities than on the curriculum proper.

The experiences that teachers and pupils share in these student activities also provide opportunities for each to know the other better, completely apart from the formal learning situation. A common activity may serve to motivate a pupil or interest a teacher in a pupil. Clues as to social maturation and rapport with peers may be observed more readily in the less-structured student activities than in formal courses. Properly handled, extraclass activities add to the impact of the school or college. They may also be a source of difficulty, for which the solution is usually improvement rather than elimination.

## Counseling and Student Personnel Services

This topic is also treated in its broader sense in Chapter 11, reference here relating chiefly to counseling and the curriculum. With the popularization of education, the student body of all schools, especially at the secondary and higher levels, has become increasingly variable. Educational offerings beyond the elementary school have also increased greatly. Shifts in the job market have complicated school-to-work transition. Increasing emphasis on health and well-being and an expanding concept of what education entails have broadened the concerns of educational institutions. Pressures in life have added to the personal-social responsibilities of the schools and colleges. All of these developments, and others too, have increased the need for counseling and related student personnel services, especially beyond the elementary school level.

Counseling and the Curriculum. The elective system, with opportunity to choose among a growing variety of courses, soon demonstrated that pupils needed help. College entrance requirements written in terms of specific subjects sharpened this need. Counseling activity, often identified as educational guidance, grew and is today recognized as a very important area of work in which highly trained counselors serve at both secondary and higher educational levels.

Vocational guidance also emerged as high schools began to serve growing numbers who were not going on to college. Job analyses provided patterns of qualifications. The testing movement developed examinations that made increasingly useful personal inventories possible. Counseling, both educational and vocational, came to be a process of helping individuals make choices consonant with their own attributes, the requirements of education and vocation, and existing opportunities available to them.

In this endeavor classroom teachers were among the first to aid pupils. From the beginning, teachers have counseled pupils on many

matters. The counseling movement gave impetus to the development
of theory and practice appropriate to a higher degree of specialization
and a more adequate counseling job. In time the personal-social needs
of pupils were recognized, as well as the educational and vocational.
Attention to individual differences in the classroom also helped to
bring about counseling and personnel services. As teachers learned
more about pupils, they recognized symptoms and conditions beyond
their knowledge, skill, and the time at their disposal. Expert help was
needed, and not even the high school principal could care for all
the demands. Teacher-counselors, with definite amounts of time for
counseling, were employed and were followed by full-time counselors.
Specialists were trained to meet the growing need in larger schools
and colleges. The movement is still underway, and there is considerable controversy today as to many aspects of counseling and how
appropriate guidance service should be provided in the schools.

Counseling and instruction touch and overlap in the educative
process. Consequently, changes in and additions to the curriculum
were brought about in the counseling movement. Units with titles
such as the following were developed and taught as part of the coun-
seling-instructional effort:

Orientation to Educational Opportunities
The World of Work
Understanding Human Behavior
Making a Personal Inventory
Dating and Marriage
Managing Personal Finances

Some persons would contend that little counseling and much unimportant instruction were involved in this endeavor. By whatever
title, these units focused attention on pupil concerns and brought resources to their aid. Group guidance and individual counseling were
often related to this instructional approach.

Individual counseling is the heart of the program. Classroom
teachers do much of this activity in proportion to their ability, interest, and rapport with pupils. Perhaps beginning with academic or
other study interests and problems, the scene often shifts to more
personal concerns. It is not difficult to understand how the need
for more highly trained personnel arose, and one of the most vital
areas of opportunity in education today lies in counseling and personnel services.

**Counseling and Personnel Services Beyond the Curriculum.** The evolutionary development of specially trained counselors has been touched

(Albuquerque, New Mexico, Public Schools.)

(Albuquerque, New Mexico, Public Schools.)

Modern schools provide a variety

(Detroit Public Schools.)

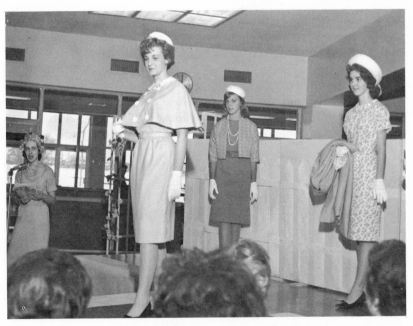

(Maine West, Des Plaines, Illinois.)

of rich educational experiences.

upon very briefly.  Personnel services associated with counseling have come to include testing, informational services, records and reporting of various types, referral services, placement, and follow-up.  Sometimes related research is included.  These services, like others, are intended to help each student make the best of himself within the limits of his ability.  In this sense they are often considered as part of the educational program.

## THE AMERICAN EDUCATIONAL LADDER

It is often said that the educational system in the United States of America is a single educational ladder.  Just what does this statement mean and what is its significance?  Chapter 5 provides some of the historical background.  In Chapter 6 a look at education in a few other countries reveals differences in the alignment of educational opportunities.  It was not easy to develop what we have today, and its maintenance and improvement constitute a task of great magnitude.

### Structure To Serve Need, Clientele, and Program

The founders of this nation imported with themselves all manner of hopes, fears, dreams, institutions, and ways of doing things.  Early elementary and secondary schools were not part of a single educational ladder.  A two-class idea was prevalent.  Opportunities offered to some children and youth were not available to all who might have profited and served society better.  Much struggle ensued and many years were to pass before the single ladder concept became a reality, even in theory.

Only slowly and against much resistance and indifference did it become generally apparent that the young struggling nation of states needed a different system of education than was found in Europe.  Leaders were essential in greater abundance than in less democratically operated nations.  Decisions made by the few who controlled the many in Europe were every man's right here.  Freedom and opportunity in many areas called for greater educational opportunity.  Battle by battle, free state supported schools came into being, particularly in the north.  Even so, it was 1860 by the time that the idea of a single educational ladder including elementary, secondary, and higher education was established in principle.

This structure, since embellished in various ways, developed to serve people who increasingly believed that everyone should have a chance to work himself up by dint of ability and effort. The educational ladder is not and was not meant to be an escalator. This structure made sense also in that the several levels of educational programs (elementary, secondary, and higher) were gradually aligned to represent progression from bottom to top. No two-class or multiclass educational system was acceptable to the great bulk of the people who aspired to a scheme that was meant to be truly democratic, a system that would foster unity among peoples from many and diverse backgrounds and serve the new and emerging nation. That the idea did not become wholly acceptable is apparent, especially in the south, even today. And there are persons across the nation who feel that the function of social unification has been served and is no longer a legitimate primary concern of the schools.

## Popularization, Diversification, and Other Developments

There is no doubt that the single educational ladder contributed to the growing popularization of education in the United States of America. This movement continues today with growing hordes of young men and women mounting the higher rungs of the educational ladder. New needs, personal and societal; greater expectations, individual and collective; and a growing recognition of education as a means to emancipation brought more and more children to school as the nation grew and as the schools served individual, state, and national ends.

Diversification was unavoidable as mass education moved ahead. But it was accomplished largely if not entirely within the single educational ladder. At the elementary school level, the range of mastery increased as the numbers grew. Such a development moved up with the pupils promoted to higher levels. The maintenance of quality became a great problem, indeed remains a problem to this very day. The elective system, still within the single ladder concept, afforded broader opportunities. Performance equated with potential came to be sought across the wide range of pupil ability, background, interest, and need. The comprehensive high school, with general education and a host of elective possibilities involving both breadth and depth, came to be the most generally accepted secondary institution.

Today higher education is undergoing much that has already happened in the secondary schools. Quantity, quality, and diversity pose problems. Postsecondary education of a non-collegiate degree type is needed and is only slowly being provided in most places. In a sense the ladder is being spread outward at its upper reaches. Graduate study, postdoctoral work, and lifelong learning at advanced levels also extend the ladder upward. The opportunity to climb and to attain the heights is a great contribution of American education.

## NEEDED IMPROVEMENT IN EDUCATIONAL SERVICES

The doctrine of mass education was not easily developed in the United States of America, although it now flourishes here as in no other nation. Many years were required to establish this idea as a tradition to be supported by public taxation. Even today the faith of the American people in mass education is not uniformly great, nor should this faith be thought of as unshakeable. There are some forces that favor restriction of educational opportunity.

Over a period of many years during which the popularization of elementary and secondary education was increasing, the focus of educational achievement tended to be on minimal levels attainable without undue effort by the "average" pupil. Keeping pupils in schools and providing what they could handle without too much objection were important considerations in selling the nation on mass education. Quality was not willingly sacrificed, nor were educators unmindful of high standards. Often they were overwhelmed, however, by the magnitude of the task they faced. Able students, it was expected, could learn on their own more than was required. Many of them did. But it is true also that despite the generally acceptable job being done and the gradual improvement of standards of performance over a long period, many pupils were not sufficiently challenged and did not develop as they should have.

Attention was also needed in large measure for weaker pupils who required much individual help. Fear of being undemocratic in expecting, urging, and requiring too much often resulted in equally undemocratic practices of expecting, urging, and requiring too little. These were years in which much trial and error was evident, mistakes were made, and yet the schools were laying a foundation upon which to erect an improved program for all in the future. Higher education today faces some similar problems. It is hoped that important lessons may be learned from the experience of secondary education, an expectation that will probably not be realized completely.

## Programs and Services To Challenge and Develop All

The major overall improvement needed today is perhaps properly stated in saying that our greatest need is for programs and services that will enable each and every pupil to realize fully his complete potentiality. There is no choice between quantity and quality. We cannot educate only the best and eliminate or neglect the rest. Nor dare we fail to challenge the best. Every child born is potentially good or evil. Properly educated he becomes as self-dependent and productive as his strengths and limitations permit. Ignored or uneducated he becomes a social liability. To provide education is costly, but not nearly so much as is the consequent cost of neglect.

The need to educate more people to higher levels has been documented earlier. A resultant major challenge is that of enriching and accelerating educational programs for those who can accomplish high-quality learning rapidly. Where this action has been taken, the overall effect has been to raise the general level of scholarship and satisfaction derived therefrom. The Advanced Placement Program of the College Entrance Examination Board is an illustration of what can be done.[1] Many other provisions adding depth and breadth to learning are needed and have often been provided.

The early identification of able and ambitious pupils and programs appropriate to encouraging their development are basic. Found in some places, these programs are needed everywhere. The same conclusions are true of less-able, handicapped, and retarded learners; indeed no segment of the school population can wisely be neglected. We must begin early and continue throughout their schooling to do our utmost that all learners achieve their maximum. This effort calls for balance and reason, as well as total development—physical, mental, emotional, and social.

## Articulation Is Essential

High levels of expectancy and of challenge are not likely to yield results unless the educational programs and services are properly articulated. Progression from one level to another is best accomplished when these levels are carefully related and properly bridged. There has often been too little attention to such articulation, espe-

[1] See the following: A Guide to the Advanced Placement Program (New York: College Entrance Examination Board) (published annually); Advanced Placement Program: Course Descriptions (New York: College Entrance Examination Board) (published regularly).

cially in matters of curriculum and instruction. The junior high school developed, in part, to help bridge the chasm between self-contained classroom instruction in the elementary school and highly departmentalized instruction in the senior high school. One unfortunate result in some communities is the creation of two chasms where only one previously existed. This condition is not an argument against the junior high school, but it does suggest the importance of care in making modifications and the ever present need for attention to articulation.

Horizontal articulation that relates and unifies learning across subjects and other divisions at the same grade level is also quite important. Fragmentation may foster depth in selected topics, but relationship is also an essential feature of sound education. Growing attention is needed if articulation of this type is to be preserved at a time of increasing compartmentalization of teaching and learning.

Administrators and counselors often get together across departmental and school or college lines. More such cooperative endeavor should involve classroom teachers. There is no good reason why these teachers should not do much planning and appraisal together. They share common goals and work with the same pupils. The success of those who work with pupils later in their educational career depends in no small measure upon the earlier teachers. And the direction and stages of attainment early in the program relate intimately to these matters in later phases.

### Flexibility Is a Necessity

In dealing with mass education and the large numbers involved, there has been an understandable tendency to categorize, quantify, and otherwise organize and order learning experience. Time of exposure, for example, has become a measure of learning, as expressed in the Carnegie Unit, semester hours, or quarter-hours. Subjects offered in the elementary and secondary schools are taught in periods of given length and for a given number of periods each day or week. Colleges and universities utilize a similar approach. In general a rather rigid framework has resulted; indeed the lock-step structure often hinders rather than fosters effective teaching and learning.

Increasing flexibility with less attention to exposure and related endeavor and with greater concern with outcomes is needed. Some pupils come to school and college better prepared initially than others. Some pupils learn more rapidly, and others learn more slowly. Not all subjects are necessarily best taught in periods of the same length nor with the same interval of time between class meetings. Different starting points are needed with freedom to move more rapidly or to take longer as required. Flexible scheduling is basic to such endeavor, and greater use of pretesting and posttesting is essential. Credit for demonstrated performance is more important than credit for being in a class or with a group. Opportunity to "test-out" of requirements makes good sense, but is too seldom practiced.

## Newer Approaches to Teaching and Learning

The increased and accelerated learning possible through flexibility is fostered also by newer instructional approaches properly utilized. Large-group and small-group instruction are appropriate in serving different goals. Class size standardized at some given ratio is often difficult to justify in specific situations. Team teaching provides a means of utilizing strengths of teachers and combining talents.

Teacher aides reduce routine and other semiprofessional chores, thus saving time and energy of the teacher for high-level individual and group activity. For example, a reader to assist an English teacher likely means that pupils will write more papers and have the benefit of more correction and instruction on writing improvement than would otherwise be possible without the reader. Smaller classes also enlarge certain types of individual instructional activity.

Language and other laboratories encourage a type of learning that enables pupils to gauge their own progress, detect individual errors, make and check appropriate corrections, and in general assume much responsibility for their own learning. This outcome is to be desired. Increasing emphasis upon independent learning and its promotion is called for as the pupil progresses through school and college. High-quality performance, for which the individual learner feels a personal responsibility, requires constant attention.

## Programed Instruction and Teaching Machines

Programed instruction and the use of teaching machines offer still another approach to the improvement of curriculum and instruction. These things are not intended to replace teachers, but are instead useful to them and to learners who are capable of doing much learning on their own. Two basic steps forward are taken in the programing of instruction.

First, educational objectives are defined very carefully at the operational level and are related specifically to content and activity that will further their attainment, afford evidence of accomplishment, and suggest needed remedial activity to correct errors. This relationship of purpose, content and procedure, and evaluated result is often not well done in typical instruction. In programed instruction it is a must. Second, this latter type of instruction is highly individualized, places responsibility directly on the learner, involves him actively, and provides him with clues as to his progress and need for improvement. It can be seen, therefore, that the programing has focused attention on sound theory long recognized but often neglected.

This type of instruction is carried on through textbooks or workbooks that are programed and through the use of teaching machines. These machines may be relatively simple and inexpensive or quite complex and costly. The more complex ones provide for a wider range of resources, higher levels of learner motivation, and richer teacher-learner involvement in classroom situations. Much experimentation remains to be done, and costs will likely need to be reduced, before machine teaching will be widely utilized.

There is need now, however, for more schools to become involved in programed instruction. The invigorated activity of the learner, pacing himself, responding to his successes and failures, and generally assuming the initiative in the learning process, is wholesome. The use of such programed instruction may also foster useful attention to other instruction in which many of the same principles and problems are involved. There is need also to relate programed instruction to ultimate educational goals and to determine more widely than is now apparent what its possibilities are with differing types of learners, with different subjects and teaching-learning situations, and with other independent study activity. These things, and the promise shown thus far, suggest that further use and experimentation should be tried.

## A National Curriculum: Pro and Con

Proposals to develop a national curriculum or to establish national standards of scholastic performance are met with mixed reception. Population mobility; the difficulty of interpreting diplomas, degrees, and transcripts; the varying and often discouraging performance of graduates; the great amounts of time, effort, and money put into curricular revision (often with little tangible improvement in learning); the movement of teachers across state lines; the great variation in curricular offerings and educational opportunity; mounting enrollments and educational costs; the teacher shortage; and other conditions have been considered as arguing for such a proposition. Individual and community differences, cultural plurality, local and states' rights, fear of undue outside control, the danger of narrow and restrictive programs, the imposition of undesirable external examinations, dislike of wide scale textbook adoption, fear of the routinization of teaching-learning, the abridgment of academic freedom, and other arguments are advanced to thwart any move toward centralization, even within a single state.

Neither extreme is wise—that of complete localism nor that of complete centralism. There are strengths to be realized and dangers and weaknesses to be avoided in compromise. Voluntary cooperation is much preferred to legal or other coercive action. The broad framework of the curriculum should provide sufficient uniformity to insure proper attention to basic educational needs broadly defined. Local authority should not be exercised in ways that cheat children or rob them of needed educational opportunity. Nor should centralized prescription place local schools in an educational strait jacket.

As national groups of educators work together with laymen in curricular research and development, the results should be utilized in schools across the nation. To do otherwise is to further the existing lag of practice behind theory. One major challenge today is that of expediting sound change nationwide, knowing that if only a few schools move ahead, the full benefits possible will not be realized, and the whole movement may be so out of step as to fail. Factors of articulation are involved in the assurance of success.

## Vision and Daring: Experimentation and Exploration

Balance and sanity are terms often associated with enduring programs that serve well their constituency. In addition to these characteristics, however, there is need for vision and daring in facing the future. A nation or an enterprise that loses its sense of adventure and its vital forward thrust is on the road to defeat and extinction. Old curricular patterns are not good simply because of age, nor are new ones inevitably better. Evaluation is important, and efforts are needed in exploring new ways that have possibilities for improvement. Only persons of vision and daring are likely to be willing to undertake experimental and exploratory programs. And it is exactly such programs that pave the way to progress for the great bulk of our educational institutions.

The need for experimentation, exploration, and improvement is great at all levels, including the collegiate. Individual teachers should face their endeavor with a searching attitude. Colleagues need to look together at what they are doing, department by department and division by division. Interdisciplinary enterprise is also important as ways and means of improvement are actively sought.

## QUESTIONS, PROBLEMS, AND PROJECTS FOR FURTHER STUDY

1. As you reflect upon man's life in a rapidly changing and confused world, what knowledge seems to you to be of most worth? Justify your answer.

2. Look over several textbooks published for use in the subject and grade level in which you are interested. Apply the criteria listed under bases of educational choice and evaluate the books accordingly.

3. How might you and your colleagues in a subject department or on a grade level utilize the various means of selecting educational content?

4. Working with some classmates, attempt to formulate some ultimate educational objectives. Relate these to more intermediate and immediate objectives appropriate to given subjects and grade levels.

5. Discuss the interrelationship of curriculum, extracurriculum, and counseling and personnel services.

6. There are various types of curricula and courses. Define and illustrate these types, noting relationships. Develop the ideas of fusion and correlation.

7. Write a brief essay (four hundred words) on curricular revision.

8. Check into your own proposed field and list six or more of the major trends that are apparent.

9. Discuss the classroom teacher as a counselor, noting strengths and limitations of this position in the counseling service.

10. Write a brief essay (four hundred words) on the development of the single educational ladder and its implications today.

11. What do you see as major challenges to the educational program of our schools in the decade immediately ahead?

## SELECTED SUPPLEMENTARY READINGS AND FILM

BENJAMIN, HAROLD. *The Saber-Tooth Curriculum.* New York: McGraw-Hill Book Co., Inc., 1939. Presents a series of brief, satirical, and witty lectures on curriculum change from the beginning of time.

BENNETT, MARGARET E. *Guidance and Counseling in Groups.* 2d ed. New York: McGraw-Hill Book Co., Inc., 1963. Chap. i. Discusses group procedures in the guidance activity.

COUNTS, GEORGE S. *The Challenge of Soviet Education.* New York: McGraw-Hill Book Co., Inc., 1957. Chap. iii. Presents a challenge to American school services in a discussion of Soviet educational objectives.

DOUGLASS, HARL R. (ed.). *The High School Curriculum.* 3d ed. New York: The Ronald Press Co., 1964. Chap. xxvi. Discusses the extrasubject curriculum in terms of values, characteristics, and types and makes reference also to guidance.

FREDERICK, ROBERT W. *The Third Curriculum.* New York: Appleton-Century-Crofts, Inc., 1959. Chaps. i–iii. Provides definitions and classification of student activities and discusses the historical development of these activities.

*Guidance in the Curriculum.* 1955 Yearbook, Association for Supervision and Curriculum Development. Washington, D.C.: National Education Association. Chaps. i–iii. Relates guidance and instruction, characterizes teachers who integrate the two, and offers suggestions on educational objectives.

MATHEWSON, ROBERT H. *Guidance Policy and Practice.* 3d ed. New York: Harper & Row, 1962. Chaps. i–ii. Provides perspectives on guidance, deals with needs of individuals, and gives focus to counseling services.

MILLER, FRANKLIN A., MOYER, JAMES H., and PATRICK, ROBERT B. *Planning Student Activities.* Englewood Cliffs, N.J.: Prentice-Hall, Inc., 1956. Chaps. i and vi. Suggests a point of view of the cocurriculum, including functions and guiding principles; deals with guidance through the cocurriculum.

RAGAN, WILLIAM B. *Modern Elementary Curriculum.* Rev. ed. New York: Holt, Rinehart & Winston, Inc., 1960. Chap. i. Discusses the need for curriculum improvement and presents a historical chart of curriculum development.

*The Bulletin of the National Association of Secondary-School Principals,* XLVII, No. 284 (September, 1963). This issue deals with aspects of guidance and counseling in secondary schools and provides an approved list of national contests and activities for 1963–1964.

WHITEHEAD, ALFRED N. *The Aims of Education.* New York: New American Library of World Literature, Inc., 1929. Chap. i. Suggests challenging educational objectives and the proper handling of appropriate subject matter.

WOODRING, PAUL, and SCANLON, JOHN. *American Education Toady.* New York: McGraw-Hill Book Co., Inc., 1963. Part V. Presents a series of articles on innovations as edited from *The Saturday Review*'s education supplement.

## Film

*Teaching Machines and Programmed Learning.* 28 minutes. Deals' with the theory of programed learning, a variety of machines and materials, and the implications for education. New York: Norwood Films.

# 8

# CHILDHOOD EDUCATION: PRE-ELEMENTARY AND ELEMENTARY SCHOOLS

The development of our superb system of public elementary education is a blessing, unique to the United States, that the very large majority of Americans take for granted. As described in Chapter 5, we had in our Colonial period (1620–1780) very weak, short-term schools taught by poorly prepared teachers with methods that would not be tolerated in any school today—the very cheapest of buildings, no free transportation, what public schools there were being in most states charity schools for paupers or the very poor.

Since then, elementary education in the United States has steadily developed and improved until practically every child has an opportunity not only to attend throughout the elementary school years, but for a term of not less than nine months and in many districts more, usually with transportation where transportation is really needed, with a modern and comprehensive curriculum, taught by teachers who are college graduates and in most instances have a year of study after that and who, for the most part, employ modern methods with a modern philosophy of what education ought to be and with at least a fairly good knowledge of the nature of child growth and development.

## EDUCATION OF YOUNGER CHILDREN

### The Boundaries of Elementary Education

The boundaries of elementary education are not clearly defined. The beginnings are made in the nursery school and the kindergarten, and the secondary and high schools continue the functions and the objectives of elementary education. There has been in recent decades much debate on the question whether the seventh and eighth grades are elementary education or secondary education. It is not essential that this question be answered unequivocally. Perhaps the best practical answer is that grades 1 through 6 are predominantly elementary education, that grades 7, 8, and 9 are both elementary and secondary education, and that grades 10, 11, and 12 are predominantly secondary education.

It is interesting to note that in school systems of other countries, what is called secondary education usually begins in separate schools, ordinarily at the age of eleven or twelve, and even earlier in some. As a matter of fact, while some subjects usually thought of as secondary education, such as foreign languages, are begun earlier than is typical in the United States, much of the curriculum of the first few years of foreign secondary schools includes a considerable amount of what is ordinarily considered elementary education. The early beginning of secondary education is in reality a provision for segregation of the children of the upper classes, and the providing of special training for the brighter elementary school children who would, unlike the majority, go beyond elementary education. Those who do not go on to secondary schools attend elementary schools in leading European countries until the age of fourteen.

## Important Variations in Elementary School Children

To an extent with respect to interest, there are no really important differences between present day boys and girls in early childhood. Children of each sex have potentialities for learning in every subject that are approximately the same as those of the other sex. To be sure, interests of boys and interests of girls are somewhat different in some respects; and the most alert teacher gratifies and exploits most of them in getting learning activities performed in a way that will make major contributions to growth and learning.

At no age is there greater desire on the part of most youngsters for expressions of their ideas, especially with their hands and body. It is indeed unfortunate that the classes are so large to restrict possibilities in these directions. The superior teacher, however, plans carefully to provide considerable opportunities for expression and for distribution of opportunities among the various youngsters and avoiding monopoly of opportunities for aggressive boys and girls.

In many districts the children come to school from homes that are greatly different from each other with respect to the following:

1. Opportunities for growth and learning that have been had in the home and through the education of their parents and the books and other materials available for learning
2. The type of training with respect to social behavior and responsibility for property that has existed in the home
3. The attitude of parents toward the school and teachers and the confidence that they have developed in the child, in the school, and in his ability to do well in school
4. The language and skills developed in the home, particularly in those homes in which a language other than English is spoken at least part of the time
5. The degree to which the parents cooperate with the teachers, supporting them in the home with the children and exchanging information about the children so that the parents and the teacher may work together as a team

## Important Formative Years

It should be remembered that experiences in these early years are tremendously effective in the formation by the child of his ideals, attitudes, and character. This fact constitutes a very definite challenge to the teacher, both on the positive and on the negative side. It is also a critical period for the development of social skills and social adjustment, and the superior elementary school teacher takes this responsibility and this opportunity quite seriously.

As indicated by thousands of schoolchild "howlers" or "boners," this is a very important period for the development of precision of vocabulary, meaning of words, and fundamental concepts that are tremendously important to their further education and in conversation with people outside of school and in their reading. The superior teacher makes it a point to see that important meanings are cleared up and makes much use of concrete materials in teaching and learning activities. In fact, teaching for meaning has in recent years become very much more prominent in the practice of the superior elementary school teachers.

While the little boy and the little girl upon first coming to school are somewhat proud of any recognition of their growth and maturation, and are pleased by the opportunity to have new experiences along with their age peers, many of them come with fears, uneasiness, and shyness, and most of them have a strong desire and need for affection. It is the first responsibility of the nursery school, kindergarten, and first-grade teacher to give the child confidence and assurance and indeed clearly observable affection. There must be developed a feeling of security and belonging and definitely one of acceptance, particularly by the teacher.

## KINDERGARTEN AND NURSERY SCHOOL EDUCATION

Until the present century, there were very few nursery schools and few kindergartens in the public schools in the United States. Prior to that time, even going back to the seventeenth century, however, there were in many communities women who gathered about them in the living room or kitchen a few young children and gave them some fundamental training in the ideas of Christianity, in social adjustment, preparation for learning, and the simplest beginnings of reading, and some of what we might call nature study.

In later years, particularly in the well-to-do families of the South, governesses, tutors, or adult "baby sitters" were employed for many youngsters of this age, while the early schooling of others was what they received in the home from their parents or from relatives. It was not until the last quarter of the nineteenth century that kindergartens began to be established in the United States.

### Beginnings Abroad

Ideas and practices of the early education of children were influenced very much by a German, Friedrich Froebel, who established a little private school at Blankenberg, Germany, in which children from three to seven years of age, were taught to play and to sing simple songs and to make simple things with their hands including drawings. He had had a very unhappy childhood and after studying under Pestalozzi, he conceived a plan for a more pleasant and effective type of educational experience. This he called a "kindergarten," which in German means a "child garden." His ideas did not spread widely at first; they were definitely contrary to the old ideas of strict discipline and authority that existed in the homes everywhere among more civilized people and especially in Germany. However, just before his death, Baroness Bertha von Marenholdt Bulow-Wendhausen studied with him and became very much impressed with the values of his approach to education of childhood and spent the rest of her life, some thirty years, in drawing the attention of the world to the kindergarten ideas that were a composite of Froebel's, Pestalozzi's, and her own, but mostly Froebel's.

Kindergarteners have wonderful imagination to build upon. (Yonkers, New York, Public Schools.)

Although vigorously opposed and forbidden for a while in Germany, indeed prohibited by law for a while in Prussia, the kindergarten idea spread to several countries in Europe, particularly France, Italy, Switzerland, Belgium, and Holland, and later upon being translated into English spread to the United States.

### The Beginning in the United States

In Boston in 1860, Miss Elizabeth Peabody established a private kindergarten and some ten years later established a training school for kindergarten teachers. In 1873, Superintendent William Torrey Harris of the St. Louis, Missouri, public schools engaged Miss Susan Blair, a graduate of the school for training kindergarten teachers in New York City, to come to St. Louis and open what came to be the first public school kindergarten in the United States. The kindergarten idea spread slowly at first and then more rapidly.

The fundamental idea of the kindergarten is founded upon emphasis on the principle of much student self-activity as opposed to the "learn-off" and "say-back" practice that had been prevalent for so long, and on assisting and directing a child in exploring in play activities and awakening the ideal side of his nature. Learning activities consist largely of directed play, singing, the use of color, storytelling and listening, and small-group social activities as well as motor activity.

Much attention is given to the diet and physical care of children with the cooperation of parents. More emphasis is placed upon social education, particularly in group play and work. Emphasis also is placed upon developing a love for nature—flowers, plants, insects, and animals—and for beauty, particularly in school surroundings. Only in kindergartens operated by inferior teachers is there failure to attempt to develop pupil initiative and to provide for much free activity, particularly physical activity. Considerable time is given to storytelling and the simpler creative arts. In an increasing number of kindergartens, some attention is given to beginning reading, handwriting, numbers, and viewing television; and in an increasing number, specially adapted workbooks are being used.

The number of school systems providing kindergartens has steadily increased until today it is the exceptional community in which kindergarten facilities are not available. In 1962–1963 more than two and a quarter million (nearly 60 per cent) of five-year-old children were in attendance in kindergartens, 82.5 per cent of them in public kindergartens. The percentage of five-year-olds attending kindergarten has more than doubled since 1947.

A century ago in Italy under the leadership of Dr. Maria Montessori, a somewhat different type of kindergarten idea began to spread all over the world and had much influence in the United States. After having lost ground in recent decades, the idea has again begun to be employed by more and more kindergarten teachers, especially in private schools in the United States. This idea laid great stress on the freedom of the child and individual attention, but it also made a very special contribution in the field of the development of the so-called subnormal child. It placed much emphasis upon moral education and upon the idea of education through use of the senses, as compared to the older emphasis upon verbal training. All of these early schools emphasized hand training of one type or several, including basket weaving, woodcarving, some metal work, and drawing.

In recent decades there have been established in many schools and colleges of education a special curriculum for the training of teachers for teaching in kindergartens, and many young women find it a most pleasurable type of activity and enjoy it greatly.

### Early Nursery Schools

The kindergartens of Froebel and Montessori enrolled children younger than the conventional five and six years. So did many in the Dame schools in our Colonial period. "Baby-sitting" with small groups of children came into the picture later. In England and in the United States, "nurseries" for young children of working mothers were operated by employers and others for decades before such facilities came to be thought of seriously as educational agencies.

Kindergartens operated by public schools in the United States usually refuse to enroll children under five years of age, and private nursery schools for the younger children became more popular. During World War II, public nursery schools for the children of female workers in industry related to the war effort were established in a great many places; and the idea stayed on after the war though the number did not materially increase until the 1960's when it became evident that nurseries were very valuable social institutions in school districts in which there was a fairly large number of families of very low economic and cultural status, especially in cities where there were large numbers of recent immigrants.

The typical nursery school ordinarily takes children of the ages of three and four and handling them in groups contributes to their social and play development ideas very similar to those of the kindergarten except that in few is there any attempt made for formal instruction in reading, numbers, or any other subject except oral language and simple art and construction. In recent years there have also been thousands of so-called nursery schools established privately by women who feel that they would enjoy the work and wish to supplement their income. These vary in character and quality from merely places where small groups of children are supervised in play activities to schools that are in the charge of trained educators who provide a wide and rich program of activities.

### The Future of Nursery Schools

It seems only logical to expect that publicly supported nursery schools will be established increasingly each year, until they will be found in practically all but rural schools, and in areas in the South and sections of the prairie states where income is markedly below national levels.

The increased employment of mothers; the greater importance attached to proper emotional, social, and health training in the early years; and the increased recognition of the educational significance of an unfortunate environment in crowded homes with relatively ignorant parents of low economic and cultural levels combine to make compelling in the social interest the case for establishing public nursery schools.

## Objectives of Nursery School and Kindergarten Education

The educational objectives of the nursery school and kindergarten may be set forth as follows:

1. To train children in proper attitudes. and habits of emotional response to their environment, particularly the human environment
2. To train in good health habits and tastes
3. To develop muscular coordination and basic big-muscle skills
4. To provide good social training in play and work
5. To provide appropriate food, rest, and premedical attention and examination
6. To assist in the formation of correct pronunciation and language skills and habits
7. To provide, by example, conferences and supervised assistance for training mothers in child care and upbringing
8. To provide opportunities for young children to learn to express themselves orally and by simple arts and crafts
9. To provide experiences that strengthen readiness of the child for learning to read and for thinking about numbers and number relationships

Beginning in the late 1950's, experiments have been conducted in a number of cities that provide especially adapted preschool facilities for children three and four years old who live in homes of very low economic and cultural level, especially those in which parents are (1) recent immigrants, (2) functionally illiterate, (3) on relief, and (4) who have bitter resentment of the middle class. These experiments have been conspicuously successful, particularly in Detroit, where especially trained teachers are employed.

# ELEMENTARY EDUCATION

## Expanded Programs Today

In the elementary school today, there are taught more subjects than previously, including in many schools the following: speech training; a modern language other than English; and very great additional amounts of material in the fields of elementary science, in arts and crafts, and in physical and health education.

In the past few years, there has been a tendency to push subject material down earlier in the grades, a procedure that has been overdone in some schools with very poor results for a large portion of the students. The policy has been abandoned, and in its place there has been substituted a plan of providing special instruction for the very bright children who move on more rapidly to subject matter of higher levels. Nevertheless, with the length of the school year and the increased length of the school day and the great desire parents have for their youngsters to learn as much as possible, the content of various subjects in the elementary school has been definitely expanded. This has brought about special provision for the youngsters of definitely less than average learning ability who would otherwise be swamped by the tidal wave of additional material.

### The Non-graded Primary Unit

In recent years, there has been an idea that has been rapidly spreading and indeed a related practice that has been spreading widely toward the abolition of grouping of youngsters into the old idea of graded levels such as the second grade, the sixth grade, or the ninth grade. At the elementary school level, this is taking place more commonly and with much more success in the lower grades. In many schools, it is called the primary non-graded unit. The non-graded primary plan places children in flexible groups and allows each child to progress at his own optimum rate. It avoids gaps in learning and unnecessary repetition.

There are two general types of ungraded primary plans, one in which all the youngsters follow the lock-step pattern of a grade a year and are deceived into thinking that they made a grade a year. These students, with very few exceptions, are dumped into the fourth grade at the end of three years regardless of their reading ability or knowledge of basic number facts. Unless this ungraded plan is carried on through the intermediate grades—where it can be done with great difficulty—the idea breaks down and has not worked out well.

Where the plan has been much more successful, in spite of opposition by some parents, some teachers and by a few leading educators and writers who have not yet adapted their thinking to changed conditions of American life, the youngster enters the fourth grade not before he is ready for it. This means that some youngsters spend four years and an occasional youngster five years in school before

A library is more than books. (Newark, New Jersey, Public Schools.)

he enters the fourth grade. On the other hand, some youngsters will be ready for the third grade at the end of the second year. Ordinarily, no provision is made for going on to the fourth grade in the middle of the year.

This plan of acceleration does not preclude enrichment. Indeed, where it is done most effectively, it will involve changes in the curriculum. It may be adapted to those who progress very slowly and also to those who progress very rapidly.

### Education in Culturally and Economically Deprived Neighborhoods

There has in recent years been a great increase of population in metropolitan centers. As the better educated whites have moved to the suburbs, families from Puerto Rico and other countries, without having first mastered the English language, have come to the city, as well as more than two million poorly educated Negroes from southern states. Some four to five million employable people are unemployed at any given time, and another two or three million are employed only part of the year, with still another several million employed at what is barely subsistence wages. Because of these developments, there has developed all over the United States, but particularly in the East and South, neighborhood pockets in or near our larger cities consisting of a considerable number of families with children of school age who are not able to provide their children with the various types of backgrounds that contribute to their success in school. Children coming from these homes are likely to be ashamed of their parents and their surroundings; they are embittered by the discouragement and bitterness of their parents; they are required to work whenever they can and attendance in school is low; for linguistic and other reasons, their ability to learn verbal material is in a large majority of cases much below the average of youngsters in their classes; their clothes are not as attractive as those of many other children; they are discouraged by their parents to participate in any of the clubs or extracurricular activities; in some instances their food, nutrition, health, and sleeping conditions are not conducive to good feeling tone or learning effectiveness.

This condition is being rapidly recognized by business, educational, and social leaders; and in many places, particularly in Detroit, Kansas City, New York, Chicago, as well as many smaller places, developments have gone on that offer at least a partial solution to the problem. Common among these are the following:

1. A closer relationship between representatives of the schools and parents involving home visitation and the offering at school of various types of recreational entertainment and educational projects for the parents of the lower cultural and economic levels.
2. A much better and comprehensive guidance program involving special counselors for these groups.
3. The formation of special classes for those badly in need of it, certainly in the fundamentals.
4. The retraining of many of the adults so that employment and more lucrative employment may be obtained.
5. The relocating of many of these families and destroying the slum buildings and areas.
6. The establishment outside the school but with the cooperation of school authorities, school counselors, and teachers of various types of centers for recreational and social activities by the youngsters. These have been promoted by municipal, civic, religious, and educational leaders.
7. The use of textbooks with materials and vocabulary especially adapted to previous and present out of school experiences of the children.

## Rural Elementary Schools

Except in very sparsely settled communities and areas where year-round transportation is impossible, the small rural school—"the little red school house"—with only one or two teachers has all but disappeared.

The following features are characteristic of the rural elementary school.

1. Not all of the subjects are offered that are in the larger city schools because of lack of time and lack of training of the teacher.
2. A great many subjects may be offered, but classes do not meet every day.
3. The amount of time available for students in class for each subject is definitely too limited.
4. The lack of appropriate housing and equipment make it impossible to teach some of the things that are taught in schools in larger places where there is a teacher to a grade, such as laboratory work, library work, and audio-visual aid.

There has been a very pronounced trend toward consolidation of smaller school districts into larger ones that can provide adequate equipment, housing, and supervision where teachers may be assigned to not more than one grade and transportation is furnished students who have to come from some distance. Teaching in a consolidated school is much more pleasant for many reasons, particularly with the better equipment and housing, not only because of the opportunity to do better teaching, but also by reason of the association with larger numbers of teachers and the stimulation for professional growth. Furthermore, there is much more opportunity for satisfaction as regards social life in such centers, and this will continue particularly as the population of the nation increases.

Also it should not be overlooked that with consolidation, teachers have been relieved from the irritating and disappointing experiences with members of boards of education in small districts who in large numbers have been individuals lacking in vision and possessed of greater propensity for interfering in the work of the teacher and in her private life.

## The Church Affiliated Elementary School

By far the greatest number of children attending church affiliated elementary schools attend Catholic schools in which the teachers are largely from Sisters' organizations such as the Sisters of Charity, the Sisters of the Sacred Heart, and Sisters of St. Dominic, and from the Christian Brothers organization in the Order of the Jesuits. The Catholic population has increased so rapidly, however, and enrollments of the schools are so great, approaching five million in elementary and high schools in 1964, that Catholics have had to rethink their program in the direction of something like the shared-time program in which the students are in public schools on half-time and the parochial schools on half-time.

The Catholic leaders are very desirous that their children attend a school in which they will recieve education along Catholic lines, as indicated by the following quotation by Rev. Paul C. Reinert, an outstanding educator and President of St. Louis University.

Historically we have had and, please God, probably always will have a diversified system of education in this country. As American citizens, therefore, and especially as American educators, we must be interested in the improvement not only of our own unique kind of education, but of all kinds of education—public, private, denominational—whatever it may be. . . . The public schools, as a complementary system to private education, are absolutely necessary for the thousands of Americans who are content with the purely secular educational pattern. Such schools deserve the interest and support of our Catholic population.[1]

The Protestant schools are of a wide variety, none of them enrolling a very great many students. In the more than three thousand Protestant Day Schools, there are now only slightly more than 200,000 pupils. These are chiefly in schools of the Christian Reformed Church, Missouri Synod Lutherans, the Seventh Day Adventists, the Mennonites, the Episcopalians, the Latter Day Saints, and Seventh Day Baptists. In general, the Hebrew population has preferred to send its children to public schools and avoid any tendency toward segregation by race or religion for reasons that are not difficult to call to mind. There are only about two hundred elementary and secondary Hebrew Day Schools in the United States, about half of them being in the New York metropolitan area. Less than 50,000 people attend all of these, and it is probable that they are on their way out and those who wish their children to get instruction and indoctrination in the Jewish faith will provide out-of-school religious education of one type or another.

Taken as a whole, the non-public schools serve very valuable purposes; the principal ones may be summarized as follows:

[1] The Very Reverend Paul C. Reinert, S.J., "American Catholic Educators Face New Responsibilities," *Proceedings and Addresses*, 49th Annual Meeting of the National Catholic Association, 1952, p. 59.

1. The further preservation and strengthening of the cherished American ideals of freedom of choice and of the pluralistic philosophy that nourishes that ideal.
2. The support of non-public schools has definitely decreased the burden of support of public schools.
3. Some of the non-public schools have made distinctive contributions to improved educational practices. More radical experimental work can be and has been carried on in non-public schools than can be done in the public schools. Many of the best ideas of the public schools have been borrowed from the more progressive and experimental non-public schools, particularly at the elementary school level.

## THE MODERN CONCEPT GOALS OF ELEMENTARY EDUCATION

### Ultimate and Immediate Goals

There have been scores of statements of the goals of elementary education. These tend to fall into three groups as follows:

1. Goals that emphasize the growth of the child, e.g., the development of his potential powers, character, habits, skills, ideals, interests, attitudes, and fund of information and understanding
2. Goals that emphasize the ultimate aims, i.e., good citizenship, ability to earn a living, good character, good health, and preparation for establishing effective and happy homes; and preparation for advanced learning
3. Goals in terms of the mastery or accomplishment of achievement in various subjects or at least passing through the subjects with study of them, such as, for example, learning the words most commonly employed in writing in the United States and the ability to perform accurately and reasonably quickly fundamental operations with whole numbers, common fractions, decimal fractions, and percentages

Many of the statements seem to be a somewhat confusing combination of the objectives of both systems or categories: (1) the immediate aims in terms of growth, and (2) the ultimate goals in terms of responsibilities and activities in life that must be performed.

It should be seen that *immediate* goals must be selected so as to make important contributions to *ultimate* goals that must be definitely and constantly envisaged and used as criteria for selecting subject matter and learning activities. There must also be a breaking up of immediate goals into subdivisions of immediate goals. For example, to be a good citizen, which must be thought of as a citizen in the home, in the coummunity, in the state, in the nation, and in the world, there is the necessity for the development of appropriate forms of information; understanding; intellectual, social, and physical skills; intellectual, social, and physical habits; interests; ideals; and attitudes.

## Social vs. Personal Goals

Many point out that the goals of education should be thought through in terms of interests of the nation and of the taxpayers who support the public schools as well as the goals that benefit the individual learner directly. In any system in which the schools are supported by taxes of those who have no children as well as those who have, of those who send their children to non-public schools as well as those who send them to public schools, and of those who pay taxes in very great amounts although having no more than the typical number of children, it is evident that the schools exist for the benefit of the society that establishes and supports them as well as the individuals to be educated. To be sure, the benefits of the individual in many cases in many areas contribute to the social benefit.

## Objectives and Functions of Elementary Education

The objectives and the functions of elementary education are much the same as those for the entire school system. Nevertheless, the relative emphasis upon the different objectives and functions, as well as the means of achieving them, is somewhat different at the various levels. In the elementary school, of necessity much greater emphasis must be placed upon the Three R's. Below are listed some of the distinctive characteristics of the elementary school with regard to its peculiar emphasis upon the objectives and functions of education.

1. To develop fundamental intellectual skills:
   a) By learning to get adequate meaning with reasonable speed from printed material
   b) By learning to spell correctly the commonly used words
   c) By learning to express facts in reasonably correct and clear language, orally and in writing
   d) By developing habits and skills in clear thinking
   e) By acquiring reasonable speed and accuracy in fundamental arithmetical processes and in the ability to solve quantitative problems

2. To lay the basis for intelligent citizenship:
   a) By developing ideals and attitudes favorable to political, economic, and social democracy
   b) By developing appreciative cooperative attitudes toward others of different national and racial origins and to other countries
   c) By gaining an understanding of the simpler facts and an appreciation of community, city, state, and national governments
   d) By acquiring familiarity with and appreciation of the more important facts and lines of development in the history of our nation
3. To assist in the development of a high degree of social character and responsibility, including moral and ethical concepts, attitudes, and habits:
   a) By developing ideals, habits, and attitudes of fair dealing, cooperation, responsibility, respect for the rights of others, and self-reliance
   b) By developing prejudices against such attitudes and habits as lack of cooperativeness, excessive selfishness, dishonesty, and unwillingness to assume responsibility
4. To contribute to the development of the tastes and practices that are conducive to use of leisure time in such ways as to bring satisfaction and that are harmonious with the welfare of society:
   a) By developing interests and appreciation of a wide variety of games, sports, reading materials, hobbies and work experience, social activities, music, and arts and crafts
   b) By developing appropriate interests and attitudes toward physical well-being of one's self, community, and society at large
   c) By encouraging the development of habits of living known to have high health values and by avoiding those likely to be inimical to health
   d) By providing physical and health examinations and by encouraging corrective measures
   e) By providing (1) efficient supplementary services, such as school lunch and medical and dental service, to children unable to pay for them; and (2) special attention for those suffering from remediable health and physical defects

## Recent Thinking About Objectives

In recent years there has been much thinking about reassessment of the objectives as well as the program of elementary education.

The basic skills are vital. (Detroit Public Schools.)

Many parents are pushing for a more rapid and earlier mastery of the fundamentals. The use of teaching machines has invaded the elementary school. Resulting from pressures from without, there are dangers of shifts in objectives, materials, and procedures that may produce unfortunate by-product growth on the part of many children.

A sound statement relative to important aspects of this problem was made by Dean Harold Shane of the College of Education of Indiana University, as follows:

If it is true—as certainly seems to be the case—that the aims of elementary education have become more forthrightly academic, does this increased intellectual emphasis threaten sound practice? Several points seem relevant.

*First*, and obviously, there is nothing inherently wrong with a judicious increase in the tempo of attempts, through education, to improve the intellectual powers and extend the information of children. Any argument to the contrary is fatuous.

*Second*, there is a real and present danger that elementary teachers may become so mesmerized by the magic of technology, the appeal of novel grouping plans, and the respectability of more challenging content that they overlook the fact that these elements are means rather than ends in education.

The use of technology, for instance, is not a goal. It is a procedure in attaining a goal. Even mastery of content per se is relevant to aims only as it motivates the child to continue his education and to use his knowledge. In Alfred North Whitehead's well-known phrases:

Culture is activity of thought, and receptiveness to beauty and humane feeling. Scraps of information have nothing to do with it. A merely well-informed man is the most useless bore on God's earth. What we should aim at producing is men who possess both culture and expert knowledge in some special direction.

*Third,* increased interest in the goal of enhanced academic achievement should be characterized by teaching that is stimulating and challenging rather than merely harsh and onerous. Standards are not improved by requiring that pupils engage in increased busywork. There is little or no point in their doing busywork in the first place.

*Fourth,* it is incongruous for elementary education to seek to improve itself by an all-out effort to ape the programs and practices of the junior or senior high schools. Such mimicry is not only foolish but ironic as well during a time when secondary school teaching is being influenced by instructional policies and by research in learning which were initiated in the elementary school.

Certain established objectives of elementary education should be preserved. Changes in the educational climate of the United States, as already noted, have generally reaffirmed devotion to intellectual growth and indicated the vitality of the school's concern for basic skills, problem-solving ability, and rational thinking. These are goals of long standing that merely have been restated with vigor. Plainly they are worth preserving.

Other outcomes that merit our best efforts include the following durable goals: improved physical health, mental and emotional well-being, the cultivation of individual talents and ability through equal opportunity, the development of social and economic literacy and of moral values, improvement of skills in the realm of human relations, the achievement of an understanding of the workings of practical democracy, and an awareness of and loyalty to the ideals of democracy at the child's level of ability to understand them.[2]

## THE ELEMENTARY SCHOOL TEACHER

### Sex

Up until recent years, teachers in grades 1 through 6 were largely women, at one time 95 per cent of them being women. In recent years, however, there have been many more men going into the elementary school classrooms. This has been partly because of the fact that elementary school teachers in more and more districts, in fact the great majority, are now being paid the same schedule of

[2] "Objectives of Elementary Education," *Journal of the National Association,* II, No. 6 (September, 1962), p. 42.

salaries as secondary school teachers—in other words, the same salary for the same number of years of experience and the same amount of collegiate training. It is also true that since the salaries of the teachers themselves have gone up so greatly in recent years, men have found that they can support a family from an elementary school teacher's salary at the level of the average family and a little better if they work in the summertime or have some other way of earning a little more during the regular year. Furthermore, the fact that many men have been given preference for promotions to principalships over women of equal or better ability and training and success has attracted many young men to come into elementary school teaching with a view of becoming a principal and later a superintendent.

## Education

A half-century ago the typical elementary school teacher was no more than a high school graduate with two years or less of normal school training. Today, the typical elementary school teacher has a bachelor's degree, and a large and increasing number have a master's degree. There are more elementary school teachers today who have training beyond a bachelor's degree than there are who have training of less than a bachelor's degree. Teachers in elementary schools who do not possess four years of college training are either in the upper age brackets or in the very poorest schools where salaries are exceedingly low.

There has been some talk and a slight trend in the direction of having elementary school teachers have an academic subject major in their preparation. It is not likely that this trend will become a general practice. Instead, there has been another trend that seems much more sound—the insistence upon subject-matter training to the level of about that of a minor in several fields including history and the social studies, English, science, physical health education, art, or music. In spite of the severe criticism—often unfounded and inaccurate—over the amount of time given to the study of methods in the training of elementary school teachers, it seems rather clear that not only is there a definite necessity for some training in the teaching of each of a number of fields, particularly arithmetic, reading, art, music, physical education, and so on, but institutions preparing teachers will continue to see that they get some background in the fundamental principles and procedures of teaching the subjects that they will be called upon to teach.

## Departmentalization vs. the Self-contained Classroom

The great majority of the teachers are assigned by grade on what has come to be called the self-contained classroom basis. Departmentalization is found only in a minority of schools. There was developed in the first decades of this country and practiced in many cities what was called a platoon system under which a teacher of a given grade, let us say the fourth grade, taught two groups of youngsters, one in the morning and one in the afternoon. She gave them their instruction in their fundamental general subjects; but in the afternoon they were taught other subjects by specialists, including music, art, and physical education. The platoon system seemed to break down, but just why it has almost disappeared is not clear to close students of elementary school organization.

There has developed in recent years a movement toward departmentalization in the elementary schools. Indeed in a very small percentage of elementary schools, there is a considerable amount of departmentalization down as far as the fourth grade with a home-room teacher in charge of the class for two or three subjects. The great majority of educators, however, do not favor extensive departmentalization in the elementary school. What is taking place in a much larger number of schools with the blessing of educational leaders is lightening of the self-contained classroom teacher's load by at least one period in the day, and in many schools one period in the morning and one period in the afternoon, during which her class is taught by a specialist in some field in which the teacher is not strong: e.g., music, physical education, art, modern foreign language, arithmetic, or reading.

There is much to be said for a limited degree of departmentalization in the form of informal exchange of classes between teachers—a type of team-teaching—and the relief of each elementary school teacher of instruction in one or two fields in which the teacher is least well prepared. It is the general opinion of principals, supervisors, and superintendents that elementary school teachers who have their load thus lightened do better work and make more careful preparation, have more time for conferences with parents, etc., while instruction in the specialized courses is better given than was possible before the introduction of this limited degree of departmentalization. It is likely that differing patterns of departmentalization and self-contained classroom instruction will continue.

### Increased Number of Positions in Elementary Education

The number of elementary school positions for teachers, administrators, and supervisors has increased tremendously since the middle 1950's by reason of the very greatly increased birthrate starting back in the middle 1940's. This increased demand will continue by reason of the fact that a large number of youngsters who were born in the 1940's are now or soon will be married and producing children who will begin entering the schools in large numbers by 1970 and swelling the enrollment in elementary schools beyond that of any previous time by the latter 1970's.

There is also a definite increase in employment of specialized elementary school teachers in the fields of physical education, modern languages, teaching of the dull and the handicapped, teaching of the bright, teaching remedial reading, and other specialized divisions.

With the increase of national prosperity and the increase in national income, parents are beginning to demand, or are at least willing to support rather generously, various types of specialized and improved services for their children in school. Indeed, there never has been a time in which the parents were more keenly interested in seeing that their children are well educated than the present.

### New Teaching Materials, Technique, and Equipment

A teacher who goes into elementary education today should be well equipped with the knowledge and, in many fields, the skills for using newer materials and methods of teaching. Like many other things, developments in these areas have shot upward in recent years, including dozens of important innovations such as team teaching, teaching by machines, the use of tapes and recorders, the use of television and other audio-visual approaches, newer procedures in evaluation and reporting techniques of counselling, working along the lines of improving mental hygiene of their children, and closer ties with parents and the community.

## QUESTIONS, PROBLEMS, AND PROJECTS FOR FURTHER STUDY

1. In what rather important ways do children in the elementary school differ from one another? How may the teacher quite early in the school year get information about each child with respect to the important characteristics in which they differ significantly?

2. Do you believe in the nursery school that little boys and girls should be taught to read and be taught the beginning of arithmetic?

3. Assuming that the children learn very little about school subjects in the nursery school, do you believe that the nursery school should be a part of the school system? If so, what type of education should little ones receive in a nursery school?

4. How far down in the elementary school should teachers be assigned on a departmentalization basis? Do you believe that they should be relieved of some classes in which they are not well specialized?

5. Do you believe that elementary school teachers should have a major in some such subject as English, physics, or music, or that they should be broadly educated instead?

6. Be prepared to give in class the story of some of your reactions of surprise or amazement with respect to the character of the early elementary schools in this country.

7. Write a list of twenty of what you think to be the more important goals of elementary education.

8. There are people who believe that one- and two-room rural schools should not be abolished and that schools should remain close to the homes and parents of the children. What do you think are the relative advantages and disadvantages of small, rural schools?

9. Do you think that the trend of more men going into elementary education is good? Be able to defend your position effectively.

10. Draw up a list of what you think to be the five most important ways in which elementary education should be improved in the next few years.


## SELECTED SUPPLEMENTARY READINGS AND FILMS

Frasier, George Willard. "The Nursery School and Kindergarten," *An Introduction to the Study of Education*. New York: Harper & Row, 1956. Pp. 335–54.

Shane, Harold G. "Elementary Schools Changed Only a Little During the Fabulous Fifties," *The Nation's Schools*, LXV, No. 4 (April, 1960), 71–73.

—————. "Objectives of Elementary Education," *The Education Digest*, XXVIII, No. 3 (November, 1962), 29–31.

Thomas, Lawrence G., Kinney, Lucien B., Coladarci, Arthur P., and Fielstra, Helen A. "What Are the Elementary Schools Trying to Accomplish?" in *Perspective on Teaching*. Englewood Cliffs, N.J.: Prentice-Hall, Inc., 1961. Pp. 5–31.

Van Dalen, D. B., and Brittell, R. W. *Looking Ahead to Teaching*. Rockleigh, N.J.: Allyn & Bacon, Inc., 1959. Ch. ix.

Warner, Ruby H. *Elementary School Teaching Practices*. Washington, D.C.: Center for Applied Research in Education, 1963. Pp. 90.

## Films

*Effective Learning in the Elementary School.* 20 minutes. Shows a fifth-grade teacher and her class as they plan their daily work for the study of a unit on pioneer life. New York: McGraw-Hill Book Co., Inc.

*From Ten to Twelve.* 26 minutes, black and white, and color. Ten- to twelve-year-olds are no longer boys and girls, but instead, young individuals who are independent, sometimes responsible, often discerning, always testing, striving, living to the hilt, with deep currents of feeling often hidden from view. In the Jones family, we observe the problems of discipline, guidance, and understanding that confront most parents and see how much of the conflicting behavior of preteens is actually a normal part of their growth and development. National Film Board of Canada. New York: McGraw-Hill Book Co., Inc.

*Frustrating Fours and Fascinating Fives.* 22 minutes, black and white, and color. This film, by following a small boy's cheerful, zigzag course through stages four and five, shows us a modern nursery school in operation; takes up problems of discipline, and shows what may be expected of and explained to a child at four and five. National Film Board of Canada. New York: McGraw-Hill Book Co., Inc.

*Guiding the Growth of Children.* 18 minutes. Shows how a teacher may work to understand each child and to guide him in his growth and development. New York: McGraw-Hill Book Co., Inc.

# 9

# EDUCATION OF ADOLESCENTS

## EARLY ADOLESCENCE AND THE JUNIOR HIGH SCHOOL

### The Movement Toward Reorganization of Secondary Schools

With the accomplishment of the graded, elementary school of eight grades and articulation with the four-year high school, it would seem that by the beginning of the present century that the 8-4 plan of organization would be a permanent plan. However, even before 1900 there were rumblings of discontent with the 8-4 plan, particularly on the part of college and university presidents who felt that secondary education should not be deferred until the ninth grade and that secondary school subjects should be begun earlier.

There was also dissatisfaction with the teaching staff, most of whom were not college graduates but teachers with little more than a high school education plus sixty or more hours of normal school professional training. It was also the belief on the part of many that teachers in grades 7 and 8 should be assigned at least somewhat on the basis of departmentalization according to their special fields.

Still another reason for demanding reorganization was the fact that with greatly increased knowledge about the psychology of adolescents and young people in their teen and preteen years, it was felt that they should be sent to a school separate from the younger students where there could be somewhat more social life, much better organization, and a wider variety of clubs and student activities, and a better program of counseling and guidance. It was further advocated that ninth-grade students were somewhat too immature to attend school with the much more greatly sophisticated boys and girls in grades 11 and 12. It was also realized that a rich curriculum including household arts for girls and shopwork for boys and other electives could be offered in typical elementary schools only at greatly increased cost.

So it was that in about 1910, there began to be established first on the West Coast and then later in the North Central states what was called in some instances intermediate schools, although later generally given the title of junior high schools. At first there were more of the intermediate schools consisting of grades 7 and 8 only, largely by reason of the local building situation. With the great increase in the number of students persisting in schools through grades 7, 8, and 9, there had developed a housing shortage. Superintendents and boards of education were importuned to establish new elementary schools and new high schools, and the question often arose as to which should come first. A Solomon-like decision was made in many districts to build a new junior high school, relieving the pressure at the elementary school level and at the high school level.

While in 1920 there were less than two hundred of these intermediate or junior high schools, by 1930 there were nearly two thousand, by 1940 approximately three thousand, and in 1960 more than four thousand. In the fall of 1963, approximately 60 per cent of boys and girls attending grades 7, 8, and 9 in public schools were in junior high schools, and another 20 per cent in six-year high schools, including grades 7 through 12, leaving only 20 per cent to be attending grades 7 and 8 in districts maintaining the 8-4 plan. The 8-4 plan has almost disappeared in most states, persisting chiefly in California and Illinois where there are township high school districts and union high school districts that are separate from elementary school districts with separate boards of education.

In most of the districts with schools of grades through 8 only, grades 7 and 8 are organized somewhat on the junior high school plan; and much of the junior high school curriculum and methods of teaching, counseling, and other services are provided for them in an attempt to offer instruction in harmony with the modern philosophy of the junior high school.

### The Phenomenon of Pubescence

Boys and girls do not enter the period of pubescence (the early stage of adolescence) at the same age, even within the same sex. Girls start to mature about a year and a half earlier than boys, usually at the ages of eleven, twelve, or thirteen. The large majority of boys, on the other hand, remain immature until they are thirteen, many of them until they are fourteen, and some fifteen and sixteen. The junior high school age then is primarily an age of early adolescence and an age in which there are great differences in the maturity of different individuals. A glance at the student body of any junior high school will reveal these facts. There will be included sometimes within the same class some boys of 6 feet and many boys and some girls of more than 5 feet 8 inches while alongside them in the halls or in the classroom may be observed both boys and girls barely 5 feet, and some even shorter. It is in this period that very pronounced changes take place that are quite important for teachers, parents, and counselors.

Socializing with his own age-mates has been a part of the child's experiences from his earliest years. All through his early and later childhood, the child has been part of a neighborhood group or gang. Until adolescence, group activities were accepted as natural or routine with little consciousness of the relation of himself to the group. But with the coming of puberty, belonging to a social group acquires real significance. Social consciousness is developed. This is due in part to an awakening of the expectations of society that he will put aside childish play and interests and will develop social skills more allied to the adult pattern of behavior, and in part to his own intensified need to "belong" and to be an integral part of a group of his peers. New patterns of behavior must be learned and adjustments must be made. These new and radically different adjustments in activities and interests and habits increase emotional tension and may result in feelings of which in turn cause overt expressions of jealousy and anger.[1]

Young people of both sexes tend to have an increased interest in the other sex and a greatly increased interest in mixed social life. At this age, too, vocations and vocational choice beckon more vigorously and clearly for boys, and the idea of marriage will enter more definitely into the consciousness of girls.

Constituting a great challenge and difficulty is the greatly accelerated desire of young people for independence from adults—their parents, their teachers, or any other adults. This has become more pronounced in recent years than formerly. Young people at this age, partly because of the lack of attention and comradeship of their parents, begin to live more completely in the world of their age peers and to listen to the values of their age peers rather than to take on those of adults of the previous generation.

As they go from immature to mature individuals, they begin to

[1] David Segel, *Frustration in Adolescent Youth* (Washington, D.C.: Government Printing Office, U.S. Office of Education, 1951), Bulletin No. 1, pp. 35–36, reprinted 1954.

give much more attention to physical appearance and to dress. It is also a period in which the rapidly growing boy is confronted with a responsibility of developing better control and coordination of his body, particularly his legs, feet, arms, and hands. It is a clearly recognized fact, although not adequately taken into consideration in planning the educational program in many schools and in many classrooms, that many individual differences among the youngsters are not confined to their height and weight, but that they develop greater individual differences in their interests, in their capacity for intellectual growth, in plans for future education and for vocations, and in out-of-school experiences that influence not only their interests but their background for the assimilation of new ideas and new information.

### The Objectives and Functions of the Junior High School

While the general objectives for the junior high school are the same as for those of the elementary school and the senior high school, some of them need greater and special emphasis. The junior high school should function in certain ways that are characteristic of its program and challenge the boys and girls of that age to be educated.

Dr. William T. Gruhn of the University of Connecticut, with the cooperation of several hundred junior high school principals and thirty-two recognized authorities in secondary education, developed a statement of the special functions of the junior high school—a statement that has become a classic. It is as follows:

#### FUNCTION I: INTEGRATION

To provide learning experiences in which pupils may use the skills, attitudes, interests, ideals, and understandings previously acquired in such a way that they will become coordinated and integrated into effective and wholesome pupil behavior.

To provide for all pupils a broad, general, and common education in the basic knowledges and skills which will lead to wholesome, well-integrated behavior, attitudes, interests, ideals, and understandings.

#### FUNCTION II: EXPLORATION

To lead pupils to discover and explore their specialized interests, aptitudes, and abilities as a basis for decisions regarding educational opportunities.

To lead pupils to discover and explore their specialized interests, aptitudes, and abilities as a basis for present and future vocational decisions.

To stimulate pupils and provide opportunities for them to develop a continually widening range of cultural, social, civic, avocational, and recreational interests.

## Function III: Guidance

To assist pupils to make intelligent decisions regarding present educational activities and opportunities and to prepare them to make future educational decisions.

To assist pupils to make intelligent decisions regarding present vocational opportunities and to prepare them to make future vocational decisions.

To assist pupils to make satisfactory mental, emotional, and social adjustments in their growth toward wholesome, well-adjusted personalities.

To stimulate and prepare pupils to participate as effectively as possible in learning activities, so that they may reach the maximum development of their personal powers and qualities.

## Function IV: Differentiation

To provide differentiated educational facilities and opportunities suited to the varying backgrounds, interests, aptitudes, abilities, personalities, and needs of pupils, in order that each pupil may realize most economically and completely the ultimate aims of education.

## Function V: Socialization

To provide increasingly for learning experiences designed to prepare pupils for effective and satisfying participation in the present complex social order.

To provide increasingly for learning experiences designed to prepare pupils to adjust themselves and contribute to future developments and changes in that social order.

## Function VI: Articulation

To provide a gradual transition from preadolescent education to an educational program suited to the needs and interests of adolescent boys and girls.[2]

In addition to these six special functions, the junior high school of today must make unusual and somewhat unique contributions to preparation for senior high school and preparation for college. It is becoming increasingly recognized that success in later years of education depends tremendously upon the development of the skills and habits in learning, including particulary reading skills, computational skills, skills in reasoning and problem solving, skills in making accurate generalizations, skills and habits in deriving the principal ideas from printed materials, skills in the location and use of books and other materials in the library, skills in oral and in written expression, habits and disciplines in the matter of effective study, and the development of interests.

[2] William T. Gruhn and Harl R. Douglass, *The Modern Junior High School* (2d ed.; New York: The Ronald Press Co., 1956), pp. 31–32.

## Advantages and Disadvantages of Junior High School Organization

While there has been a very pronounced trend toward the organization of schools on the 6-3-3 plan in all but the smaller communities, and of the 6-6 plan in those, there has always been opposition to these plans of organization and a demand for a retention of or a return to the 8-4 plan. These objections to the junior high school have not been too articulate but center their opposition around the idea that ninth-grade youngsters can be held to higher standards in the four-year high school and that better preparation for college can be made under the 8-4 plan. Some, too, have objected to the increased socialization of young people in grades 7 and 8.

Below will be found a statement of the conclusions that careful students of various plans of organization including the 6-3-3, 6-6 and the 8-4 plan have made. It should be noted that the advantages of the 6-3-3 plan are, as far as the junior high school is concerned, not related to improved achievement in the academic school subjects as judged by whatever is measured by standard tests, but by enrichment of curriculum and through other services such as socialization, counseling, and guidance.

I. *Conclusions relative to instruction*

1. The curriculum of the junior high school is broader and provides for more enriched learning experiences than does the 8-4 system, especially for pupils in grades seven and eight.
2. It is easier to introduce changes in the curriculum, especially when the junior high school is first introduced.
3. A broader program of extraclass activities can be provided. This is possible for ninth-grade pupils as well as those in grades seven and eight.
4. Teachers with better preparation, particularly in the special subject fields, can be attracted.
5. It is easier to attract men teachers than in grades seven and eight of the elementary school.
6. The supply of well-qualified administrators, supervisors, and teachers for the junior high school has been increasing in recent years.

II. *Conclusions relative to pupil achievement*

7. Pupils in junior high schools do as well in the fundamentals as pupils in schools under the 8-4 plan, even though they spend less time on these subjects because they take a number of new subjects and participate in extraclass activities.
8. Pupils from junior high schools do as well as those from other schools when they enter the senior high school.

III. *Conclusions relative to guidance, meeting pupil needs, and retention of pupils*

9. Better guidance personnel, facilities, and activities are provided.
10. It is easier to make provision for individual differences in the junior high school because the number of pupils in grades seven and eight is larger than in an elementary school.
11. There are usually more opportunities in both the curricular and the extraclass programs for pupils to explore their interests, abilities, and talents.
12. Pupils tend to remain in school longer, usually through the ninth grade.
13. There are fewer failures and less retardation in the junior high school, especially in the ninth grade.
14. Articulation between the elementary and the secondary school has improved in most communities where the junior high school has been introduced. However, much still needs to be done to achieve satisfactory articulation.
15. Although evidence is lacking on this point, many educators believe that the disciplinary situation, both in the elementary school and in grades seven and eight of the junior high school, is better when the older pupils are separated from the younger ones.
16. Ninth-grade pupils are less likely to develop early sophistication because they do not have contact with older high school pupils. Furthermore, they can usually participate more fully in pupil activities in the junior high school than in the four-year high school.

IV. *Conclusions relative to housing and costs*

17. Better building facilities, equipment, and athletic fields can be provided, especially for seventh- and eighth-grade pupils.
18. The cost of providing an adequate educational program for young adolescents is less in the junior high school. If comparable facilities were provided for grades seven and eight in the elementary school they would need to be duplicated in every school.[3]

# LATER ADOLESCENCE

## The Characteristics of Later Adolescence

Most boys and girls entering the tenth grade have definitely entered upon the adolescent period and many of them are well along, and some of them indeed are well advanced in it. Some of the characteristics started in the early years now become stronger. There is very definite increased interest in intersex social life and companionship. There is also much keener interest in the selection and preparation for a vocation; and on the part of most of them, there is a preoccupation with the decision of whether to go to college and if

[3] *Ibid.*, pp. 57–58.

so how to get admitted into the college of their choice, how to select a college, and what type of work to take while there.

The desire for independence from adult domination becomes quite intense with most youngsters at this period, particularly as they become more and more enmeshed in the peer-age association, activities, and cultures. This finds expression in many ways, including rebellion against authority, destruction of property as an exhibition of their contempt for adult standards as well as an expression of their own individual hostility, and a determination to play a larger part in the management of their own affairs. They wish to manage their student clubs and activities and plan their own learning activities, along with a propensity for doing no more than is absolutely necessary in the way of doing activities and studying materials assigned by teachers. It is a period in which there is also much more thinking about marriage, including early marriage and indeed about sex and sexual intercourse.

As may readily be seen, this period—and it is probably much more so today than in previous decades—is one that constitutes very definite challenges to teachers as well as to parents.

Mathematics is the language of science. (Springfield, Massachusetts, Public Schools.)

## Developmental Tasks of Adolescence

Professor Robert Havighurst of the University of Chicago formulated a widely accepted statement of what he referred to as "the developmental tasks of adolescence" as follows:

1. Achieving new and more mature relations with agemates of both sexes
2. Achieving a masculine or feminine social role
3. Accepting one's physique and using the body effectively
4. Achieving emotional independence of parents and other adults
5. Achieving assurance of economic independence
6. Selecting and preparing for an occupation
7. Preparing for marriage and family life
8. Developing intellectual skills and concepts necessary for civic competence
9. Desiring and achieving socially responsible behavior
10. Acquiring a set of values and an ethical system as a guide to be-behavior [4]

## A Rapidly Growing Serious Problem

In recent years on the part of a considerable minority of adolescents, especially those who come from underprivileged homes such as the slum or low-economic areas in cities but also generally throughout the country, there has developed a feeling of aloofness and nonbelonging. They feel that life in this country, if not in the world in general, has moved into a period in which there is little place or little chance for satisfactory life for young people of their economic status and little opportunity for employment except in the armed forces.

These young people, particularly boys, are resentful and are not easily interested in schoolwork, although they have begun to realize rather generally that it is difficult to get any kind of desirable position without having graduated from high school. They resent the adult world in general and have become, as Professor Havighurst and others have put it, "alienated youths." Their inability to earn money and participate in other luxuries of life in which they see adults participating rather generally—the use of cars, extensive entertainment, alcoholic drinks, etc.—has embittered several million young people to a degree characteristic of only several hundred thousand in previous decades. The tendency for adults to strongly encourage remaining in school until graduation from high school and the recog-

[4] Robert J. Havighurst, *Developmental Tasks and Education* (New York: Longmans, Green & Co., Inc., 1952), pp. 31–71. Courtesy of David McKay Co., Inc., New York.

nition of young people that only poorly paid blind-alley jobs can be counted on by dropouts have caused a much larger percentage of this type of youngsters to remain in senior high schools and constitute a very great challenge to teachers, counselors, and administrators.

# PREDECESSORS OF THE HIGH SCHOOL

## The Latin Grammar School

As pointed out in Chapter 5, the primary purpose of our first type of secondary school, the Latin grammar school, was to prepare youngsters to enter college, particularly Harvard College, but also to bring them in contact with the learning of the time, which was very largely written and printed in Latin. In the middle state colonies where there were many more Catholics, they wished their schools to be Latin grammar schools, too, because a very great part of the religious ceremonies of the Catholic church was carried on in Latin.

It was found necessary for young people attending Latin grammar schools, at first almost exclusively boys, to have some knowledge of English, so many of the abler boys were sent to a Latin grammar school where they were also provided basic elementary education as preparation for the study of Latin and Greek.

The following is a description of the content of a curriculum in a typical Latin grammar school of the seventeenth century and the early part of the eighteenth century.

> 1st Class—Cheever's Accidence. Corderiou's Colloquies—Latin and English. Nomenclator, Æsop's Fables—Latin and English. Ward's Latin Grammar, or Eutropius.
> 2nd Class—Clarke's Introduction—Latin and English. Ward's Latin Grammar. Eutropius, continued. Selectæ Veteri Testamento Historiæ or, Castilio's Dialogues. The making of Latin, from Garretson's Exercises.
> 3rd Class—Cæsar's Commentaries. Tully's Epistles, or Offices. Ovid's Metamorphoses. Virgil. Greek Grammar. The Making of Latin from King's History of the Heathen Gods.
> 4th Class—Virgil, continued—Tully's Orations. Greek Testament.—Horace. Homer.—Gradus and Parnassum. The Making of Latin continued.[5]

[5] Alexander Inglis, *Principles of Secondary Education* (Boston: Houghton Mifflin Co., 1918), pp. 164–65.

## The English Grammar School

The Latin grammar school was not popular with the boys. They could not see that it would enable them to protect themselves against the Indians or to work out a living in the rocky soil or in limited trade opportunities in New England; and then, too, there were those particularly among the women who thought some provision for secondary education should be made for girls. In New York City in 1732, there was established an English grammar school offering, in addition to Latin, instruction in writing, arithmetic, geometry, algebra, geography, navigation, and bookkeeping. Not only were there other English grammar schools established in New England and the middle colonies, but the Latin grammar schools began to reshape their curriculum toward the "modern" side, although it was definitely over the opposition of the conservatives (then as now), and most of the Latin grammar schools disappeared.

There were not too many competent teachers available so that the staffs of the Latin grammar schools in most instances left much to be desired. Not enough teachers were available to teach in the Latin grammar schools who had an adequate or nearly adequate command of the subject. There was very little in the matter of requirement for prospective teachers other than that they be firm in the faith. The methods employed were ineffective, cruel, and inhuman; and the Latin grammar school was destined fortunately not to be the type of secondary education in the United States, although it has influenced our secondary schools even down to the present time.

### Typical Curriculum of the English Grammar School.

1st Class—Composition; reading from the most approved authors; exercises in criticism, comprising critical analyses of the language, grammar, and style of the best English authors, their errors and beauties; Declamation; Geography; Arithmetic, continued.

2nd Class—Composition, Reading, Exercises in Criticism, Declamation; Algebra; Ancient and Modern History and Chronology; Logic; Geometry; Plane Trigonometry, and its applications to mensuration of heights and distances; Navigation; Surveying; Mensuration of Surfaces and Solids; Forensic Discussions.

3rd Class—Composition; Exercises in Criticism; Declamation; Mathematics; Logic; History, particularly that of the United States; Natural Philosophy, including Astronomy; Moral and Political Philosophy.[6]

[6] Report of the Sub-Committee quoted in *Catalogue of the English High School* (Boston, 1890).

## The Academy

The grammar school was never popular in the southern half of the country, and it eventually lost its popularity in the northern half. While some grammar schools broadened their curriculum, there was a demand for a new type of school. Academies sprang up in many sections of the states. At first the academy put much less stress on Latin and Greek and taught more of the modern subjects, such as science, history, and English, and was in general supported at least in part by taxes.

In the nineteenth century, the establishment of academies spread like wild fire until at one time there were about six thousand academies in a nation of less than twenty million people. Many of these academies were not public academies but were established by religious organizations, which wanted to make sure that their children would be brought up well doctrinated in their particular sectarian creed and beliefs. Chambers of Commerce (or what functioned as such in those days) generally wanted to have academies in their towns, so there were many schools that enrolled only a few students and had a faculty of two or three teachers. Academies remained for the most part non-public or independent schools, although many received some form of public support from the local community.

SUBJECTS OFFERED IN NEW YORK ACADEMIES IN 1853 [7]

| | |
|---|---|
| Arithmetic; geography | Natural theology |
| Spelling | Evidences of Christianity |
| Reading; pronunciation | Moral philosophy |
| Grammar | Intellectual philosophy |
| Writing | Political economy |
| Declamation | Bookkeeping |
| Composition | French |
| Rhetoric; elements of criticism | Spanish; Italian |
| General history | Greek |
| Mythology | Latin |
| Astronomy | U. S. History |
| Analytic geometry | Drawing |
| Mensuration | Algebra; logarithms |
| Descriptive geometry | Plane geometry |
| Conic sections | Trigonometry |
| Natural philosophy | Surveying; leveling |
| Logic | Navigation |
| Electricity | Optics |
| Magnetism | Mechanics |

[7] Francis Spaulding, *Historical Development of the New York State High School System* (Albany, N.Y.: Williams Press, Inc., 1922), p. 81.

| | |
|---|---|
| Chemistry | Law and government |
| Anatomy; hygiene | German |
| Botany; natural history | Principles of teaching |
| Greek antiquities; Roman antiquities | Geology; meteorology |

A typical offering of a large eastern academy is shown below:

First Year    Mental Arithmetic, Elocution; Rhetoric; Geometry; Geography of the Heavens; Bookkeeping; Botany; Political Economy; Astronomy; Governmental Instructor [probably a civics manual].

Second Year   English Composition; Analysis of Words; Ancient Geography; Universal History; Geometry, completed; Trigonometry; Mental Philosophy; Elements of Criticism; Evidences of Christianity; Natural Theology.

Third Year    Modern Geography; History of the United States; Surveying and Navigation; Mental Philosophy; Logic; Agricultural Chemistry; Animal Chemistry; Analogy and Religion; Geology; Mineralogy.

Fourth Year   English Grammar; Analysis of Language; Written Arithmetic; High-Arithmetic; Elementary Algebra; Higher Algebra; Anatomy and Physiology; Natural Philosophy; Chemistry; Drawing; Painting; Music; Greek; Latin; French; and German.[8]

Throughout the nineteenth century the academies found it difficult to find teachers and funds for offering a wide range of subjects, particularly since the number of students was usually small—most of them enrolling between fifty and one hundred and fifty students. There was, therefore, a tendency for the academy to teach only subjects that were most cheaply taught and by means of textbooks. That meant, of course, English, history, mathematics, and Latin, and in many schools what was purported to be science.

There were academies for boys, academies for girls, and academies for both boys and girls. The age range of students varied greatly from academy to academy. Some academies received students as early as eight or nine years of age as did the early Latin grammar schools, particularly in places where parents were not satisfied with the local schools. They kept them on, if they would stay, until somewhere between sixteen to eighteen years of age; although many students were nineteen or twenty before their teachers thought they were adequately prepared for college or university. Later on in the

[8] S. L. Kandel, *History of Secondary Education* (Boston: Houghton Mifflin Co., 1930), p. 415.

nineteenth century, the academies became schools of three, four, or five years in length and had some type of articulation with the public elementary schools that were then seven, eight, or nine years in length; although the articulation was quite incidental and informal.

According to W. J. Gifford, in 1853 the 167 academies in New York State offered a bewildering array of subjects. The tendency to make secondary education more practical is evidenced by the addition of so many new applied subjects. Offered in at least 30 per cent of these academies in New York State in 1853 were the following list in the order of the per cent of schools offering: English 100 per cent, arithmetic 97 per cent, geography 97 per cent, natural philosophy (science) 90 per cent, Latin 97 per cent, astronomy 90 per cent, French 90 per cent, Greek 80 per cent, general history 70 per cent, rhetoric 63 per cent, intellectual philosophy (psychology) 58 per cent, moral philosophy (ethics) 50 per cent, mensuration 32 per cent, electricity 31 per cent. No other subject was offered in more than 80 per cent of the academies. Later many academies offered some types of manual training for the boys and home economics for the girls.[9]

Some of the academies established for girls were of a distinctly inferior character to those for boys and emphasized particularly the "polite accomplishments" of the period. Foreshadowing these schools was a school such as that whose announcement is quoted by Monroe for the Armston School (1772), in which such subjects as the following were offered:

Petit Point in Flowers, Fruit, Landscapes and Sculpture, Nun's Work, Embroidery in Silk, Gold, Silver, Pearls, or embosed, Shading of all kinds, in the Various Works in Vogue, Dresden Point Work, Lace Ditto, Catgut in different Modes, flourishing Muslin, after the newest Taste, and most elegant Pattern Waxwork in Figure, Fruit, or Flowers, Shell Ditto, or grotesque, Painting in Water Colours and Mexxotinto; also the Art of taking off Foliage, with several other Embellishments necessary for the Amusement of persons of Fortune who have Taste.[10]

Such a school was the prototype of the later "finishing school."

Many of the academies were boarding schools, and young people learned some things that were not in books that contributed to their maturation and socialization. There was definitely a tendency to emphasize the traditional subjects as instructors were able to per-

[9] E. P. Graves, *A History of Education in the United States* (New York: The Macmillan Co., 1904), p. 173.
[10] Paul Monroe, *Cyclopedia of Education* (New York: The Macmillan Co., 1924), Vol. II, p. 120.

suade the leaders in their community that the traditional subjects that had been transplanted from the older secondary schools in Europe were much more respectable, had much greater values for training the mind, and made much better preparation for college than the newer subjects, which were usually more expensive to teach anyway.

## Sabotage by the Conservatives

Illustrative of this regressive influence is the subject of a story told of Benjamin Franklin—a self-educated man—who persuaded the academy in Philadelphia to put in a modern curriculum that was subsidized by funds from some of the VIP's in that region. This modern curriculum went the way of many others; and when Benjamin Franklin came back from an extended stay in Europe and visited the academy, he was horrified, disappointed, and angry. How indignant he was is indicated by the following quotation from a review of a book written by Thomas Woody, *The Educational Views of Benjamin Franklin.*

Versatile and lovable old Ben, so Dr. Woody reminds us, held a life-long contempt for the system of higher education which wastes upon Latin and unapplied mathematics the time that could have been devoted to preparing youth to serve the public. Among the Franklin experiences, assembled in this volume of the McGraw-Hill education classics, the academy adventure reads like educational fiascoes of here and now. Franklin was the father of the project. He drew the prospectus and gathered the money. Here was to be an institution released from tradition and conditioned by public need. Life was too short and obligations too pressing to permit youth to devote precious time to dead languages and unapplied science. However, trustees of wealth and position must be got on the board. They are for the good old curriculum suitable for a gentleman and a scholar. Franklin, according to his life-long principle, takes half a loaf as better than no bread. He compromises on a school with two courses—a classical, and English. Then follows the oftplayed educational game of putting the prospectus in the cupboard and throwing away the key. Like Ezra Cornell's or Jacob Tome's educational purpose, Franklin's, in the hands of educators, gets more and more moulded into the traditional pattern until it is hardly recognizable.

Absent in Europe and busied with the affairs of the Revolution, Poor Richard scarcely knows what the old-timers are doing to this project. But old, sick and within a year of his death, the philosopher wrote one of the most scathing reports ever submitted to a school board. It consists of a series of minutes from the board records, exposing a startling contrast of resolutions with performances. "From the beginning, the contempt of your employees for the new, the English, course has been allowed to damage it. They get you to give the Latin master a title. You gave none to the English principal. To the Latin head you gave 200 pounds: to the English, one half as much money and twice as many boys. You voted 100 pounds to buy

Greek and Latin books, nothing for English. I flatter myself, gentlemen, that from the board minutes it appears that the original plan has been departed from; that the subscribers have been deceived." [11]

With few exceptions teachers in the academies had no training in psychology or in education. Many of them were excellent teachers; most of them were mediocre; and a considerable number of them were very inferior, resorting to excessive appeals to fear of failure and physical punishment.

## THE HIGH SCHOOL

### Two New Democratic Ideals

In the nineteenth century, it became more and more evident that the academy was not the solution to the problem of providing appropriate secondary education for young people in this very greatly developing nation. There was a desire for education to be available to more people than would be possible through the academies, which

Young adolescents love activity. (Atlanta Public Schools.)

[11] William McAndrew, *School and Society*, XXVIII (September, 1932), 18–19.

in practically all instances charged tuition. It was also believed that secondary education should be provided for girls as well as boys. Furthermore, it was very definitely felt that more modern curricula should be developed. In 1821, there was established in Boston a public high school, the first in the world of this type of secondary school—an institution toward which secondary education is trending in most countries today. There were not many others developed prior to or during the War Between the States, as shown in Fig. 9–2. Beginning in the 1870's, high schools began to be established throughout the country and enrollments began to increase so greatly that the number of students enrolled in grades 9 through 12 in the United States doubled every ten years from 1870 to 1930 and since 1940 has increased from approximately seven million to approximately nine and a half and will exceed eleven million in 1970—the probable peak for some years.

## The Slowly Developing Curriculum

Primarily because of the expense involved, the curriculum of the high schools was not much more appropriate for secondary education in this country in our times than was that of the academy. But gradually, particularly between 1870 and 1900, new subjects began to be introduced, such as courses in physics, chemistry, physical geography, civics, home economics, shopwork, and agriculture. For the first twenty-five or thirty years of the present century, these subjects were expanded and improved and additional subjects were included, such as typewriting, shorthand, various types of shopwork, and auto mechanics.

In 1925, it was quite clear that we were headed in the direction of secondary education for all boys and girls who could profit from it and for various types of curricula that were suitable for those not going to college as well as those going and that provision for secondary education must be made everywhere even for the youngsters who lived in rural areas.

It was not the wealthy or cultured class of New England that pushed the public high school forward. The well-to-do parents could send their boys and girls to non-public schools, and in general they opposed the public high school because it would result in greater tax burdens. To insure nationwide establishment of high schools, the efforts of the masses were needed—the farmers, the laborers in the factories, and the struggling middle class from many occupational fields.

In 1830 in Philadelphia, a workingmen's meeting resolved that "there can be no real liberty without a wide diffusion of real intelligence—that until means of equal instruction shall be equally secured to all, liberty is but an unmeaning word, and equality an empty shadow." For the poor, middle class, and the laborers, the only school that was self-respecting for their children was one supported by the state and open and free to everybody alike. There must be no class distinction, sectarianism, or charity. The first public high school law was passed in Massachusetts in 1827, but it was in the frontier states that the high school made its greatest strides, and it was certainly in these states that the curriculum was liberalized. Its purposes were not realized satisfactorily, however, until 1850, when the modern public high school evolved.

## GOALS AND FUNCTIONS OF SECONDARY EDUCATION

Prevailing concepts of what are the aims and functions of secondary education in the United States have always been and still are in the process of change and modification. There has always been disagreement as to what are the purposes and the objectives of the American secondary schools, and disagreement has never been more prominent than in recent years.

### An Important Transition

After the abandonment of the Latin grammar school and the academy, the high school more and more broadened its purposes and its offering. Nevertheless, in its early history as nowadays, educational conservatives and those with vested interests both among educators and lay people opposed the broadening of the curriculum and were able to persuade many of the people that only the older, more academic subjects were respectable, would convey status upon their sons and daughters, and would prepare them for college, and furthermore that these subjects possessed mystical potentialities for training the powers of the mind.

Gradually, but slowly, the high schools added new subjects, including new courses in science, the social studies, and history, and in some vocational fields as well as in music and in art. Later in the nineteenth century and the early part of the twentieth century, additional vocational subjects were added, particularly in the field of business and shopwork, and courses in home economics, physical and health education, and the social studies were included. But the conservative forces among teachers and parents fought all these additions, and the adaptation of the curriculum to modern needs and modern constituency was very slow until well into the twentieth century. In other words, while the expansion of the concepts of purposes and objectives of secondary school to preparation for life grew and spread, they were not greatly realized.

As more and more young people—both boys and girls—went on to colleges of one type or another, the college preparatory objective remained paramount until the 1920's and 1930's when education for responsibilities and activities of life, broadly conceived, began to be the focus of thinking about the purposes of American secondary schools.

## Modern Concept of Goals for Secondary Education

In 1912, there was appointed a committee that was to exert great influence on thinking about the goals and other aspects of secondary education; this committee was called The Commission on the Reorganization of Secondary Schools. While the report of this committee, *Cardinal Principles of Secondary Education,* was in some way a compromise between tradition and forward-looking, this group of educators, for the first time in the history of American education, started as a base with an analysis of activities of life somewhat after Herbert Spencer's approach. The seven areas of life designated were as follows: (1) health, (2) command of the fundamental processes, (3) worthy home membership, (4) vocation, (5) civic education, (6) worthy use of leisure, and (7) ethical character.

This milestone in the development of practical thinking about education for the modern times has gradually and slowly but definitely spread until it is today, by far the most commonly accepted type of statement of goals. The following is a rather faithful summary of the thinking of leaders in secondary education with reference to the areas of life for which adolescents should be prepared.

1. *Citizenship:* involving one's participation in all social groups outside the home, including the neighborhood, work groups, leisure groups, city, county, state, region, nation, and world
2. *Earning a living:* including selection of a vocation, economic understanding, and acquiring vocational job skills, information, and attitudes
3. *Enjoyable use of leisure:* rich enjoyment of all non-vocational life experiences in ways conducive to the common welfare
4. *Home living:* including relationships of married people, rearing of children, leisure life in the home, and consumer activities of various sorts

5. *Mental and physical health:* including activities related to diet, exercise, dress, first aid, self-care, care of others, mental hygiene, and personal development

6. *Skills in fundamentals and preparation for further learning:* including skills in reading, spelling, oral speech, written composition, numerical computations applied to whole numbers, fractions, decimal fractions, percentage, and formulas; propaganda analysis and critical thinking, problem solving and decision making, and study habits and skills

This broadened concept of the objectives of secondary education and the consequent broadened curriculum contribute heavily to the increase in the number and per cent of boys and girls remaining in high school until graduation. In 1964, approximately two million boys and girls graduated from public and non-public secondary schools—nearly two-thirds of all eighteen-year-olds.

With the increasing difficulty of finding steady employment, a very large number of boys and girls of types who once quit school at sixteen years of age now remain on for study in the senior high school. To accommodate them, and other less-able students, special sections of subjects, sometimes called "basics," have been provided in the great majority of schools in the fields of English, social studies, history, biology, physics, chemistry, and mathematics.

Likewise, special sections often carrying college credit have been formed in a great many schools for students of definitely superior ability in academic learning.

## "THE IMPERATIVE NEEDS OF YOUTH"

A very concrete and influential statement of the most important needs of adolescents that should guide the thinking of those teaching them and those planning education and guidance for them was "The Imperative Needs of Youth" as set forth by the National Association of Secondary School Principals and the Educational Policies Commission of the National Education Association (Fig. 9–1).

## GROWTH OBJECTIVES OF HIGH SCHOOLS

In order to achieve ultimate life objectives—good citizenship or vocational competence, for example—a student must grow in a variety

All youth need to develop saleable skills and those under-standings and attitudes that make the worker an intelligent and productive participant in economic life. To this end, most youth need supervised work experience as well as education in the skills and knowledge of their occupations.

All youth need to understand the methods of science, the influence of science on human life, and the main scientific facts concerning the nature of the world and of man.

All youth need to develop and maintain good health and physical fitness.

All youth need opportunities to develop their capacities to appreciate beauty in literature, art, music, and nature.

All youth need to understand the rights and duties of the citizen of a democratic society, and to be diligent and competent in the performance of their obligations as mem-bers of the community and citizens of the state and nation.

All youth need to be able to use their leisure time well and to budget it wisely, balancing activities that yield satisfac-tions to the individual with those that are socially useful.

All youth need to understand the significance of the family for the individual and society and the conditions conducive to successful family life.

All youth need to develop respect for other persons, to grow in their insight into ethical values and principles, and to be able to live and work co-operatively with others.

All youth need to know how to purchase and use goods and services intelligently, understanding both the values re-ceived by the consumer and the economic consequences of their acts.

All youth need to grow in their ability to think rationally, to express their thoughts clearly, and to read and listen with understanding.

Fig. 9–1. The Imperative Needs of Youth—The Common and Essential Needs That All Youth Have in a Democratic Society

of ways, involving principally the following types of growth acquisitions as a result of his experiences in contact with his environment.

1. Factual information, understandings, meanings, vocabulary, principles, and laws
2. Intellectual, physical, and social habits of behavior as associated with types of situations that he is likely to find himself facing many times
3. Intellectual, physical, and social skills that may be employed, for example, in home living, in maintaining mental and physical health, in vocational life, in citizenship, and in leisure activities
4. Interests in appropriate activities and important areas of life, of knowledge, and of leisure
5. Attitudes that make for character, worthy home living, vocational success, mental and physical health, and effective good citizenship
6. Ideals that provide inspiration for an individual to think and act in ways that will contribute to good citizenship, good health, vocational success, effective home living, and socially accepted leisure pursuits

Many of these types of psychological outcomes, for example, skills, habits, and ideals, are not developed in one subject field alone, but are outcomes from learning activities and materials in a number of subject fields, for example, the ideal of service, the attitude of open-mindedness, skill in problem solving, and the habit of courteous and thoughtful social behavior.

Because these things are so, the curricular materials and learning activities must be selected and planned with a view to *providing experiences that will result in students' acquisition, as far as possible, of psychological growth outcomes of the types mentioned above, which are necessary or at least desirable for effective participation in various areas of life activities.*

## Functions of Secondary Education

Various authorities in the field of secondary education have made statements of what they think to be the more important functions of secondary education. While these statements are not identical by any means, there is some common agreement among them and a consensus may be formulated as follows:

1. *Integrative function.* It is exceedingly important that secondary education include subject matter, methods of instruction, learning, guiding, counseling, and extrasubject student activity that will tend to bind people together with basic general funda-

mental ideals, appropriate in a democracy such as ours and with a common language and a common culture and background in literature or music, and other common interests such as those in the field of recreation.

2. *Differentiative function.* It is very desirable that the program for secondary education identify the interests and special abilities of students and provide preparation for the development of specialized abilities as a means of providing leaders and workers in all of the various important aspects of American industry, culture, and work.

3. *Propaedeutic or preparation function.* While every secondary school should provide a program that is prepared primarily for the students who will not continue in formal schooling after graduation, the secondary school should very definitely and effectively prepare students to continue their education in universities and in junior and senior colleges. It should also prepare them for continuing to learn through informal means such as reading, listening to radio and television, in civic, industrial, and social activities.

4. *Socializing function.* Both by means of instruction and by means of guided group activities of students, definite provision should be made for growth on the part of the students, which will enable them to participate more effectively in all types of group activities—both as leaders and as followers. This program should include in addition to the group activities related to the subjects taught other group activities in connection with clubs, homeroom, and teams.

5. *Exploratory function.* The school should enable its students to explore and to discover higher activities of an increasingly differentiated type in the major fields of the racial heritage of experience and culture, their significant values for social living, the problems in them of contemporary life, the privileges and duties of each person as an individual and as a member of social groups. It should also explore and reveal to the students their potential interests, aptitudes, and capacities, looking toward the direction of them into avenues of study and of work for which they have manifested peculiar fitness.

6. *Guidance and counseling function.* The superior modern secondary school should provide the personnel and the facilities for the guidance and the counseling of young people—both individual guidance and group guidance—in connection with the increasing problems that they face, such as:

*a*) Selecting and planning to prepare for suitable vocations.

*b*) Planning an appropriate program of education.

*c*) Developing a wholesome and satisfying philosophy of life as a basis for thinking about participation in various kinds of life activity.

 d) Wise thinking about relationships with other individuals, including, in the home, social relationships with peers of each and both sexes and with adults in general.

 e) The problem of planning for military service in connection with plans for education, vocation, and married life.

 f) Problems related to mental health and the development of a healthy and satisfying personality.

## The Development and Spread of High Schools

As indicated in Fig. 9–2, high schools spread somewhat slowly before the War Between the States and very rapidly after. While in

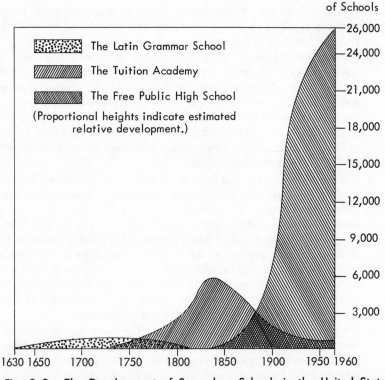

Fig. 9–2. The Development of Secondary Schools in the United States. (Extrapolated from a similar diagram prepared by Ellwood P. Cubberley for 1630 to 1930, *Public Education in the United States* [Boston: Houghton Mifflin Co., 1934], p. 173.)

1900 there were less than two thousand secondary schools in the United States, by 1965 this had grown to more than twenty-six thousand.

The increase in the number of students was even greater. Doubling approximately every ten years from 1880 to 1930, enrollments grew as shown in Fig. 9–3 from approximately 250,000 in 1880 to more than 2,000,000 in 1920, after which enrollments increased very rapidly

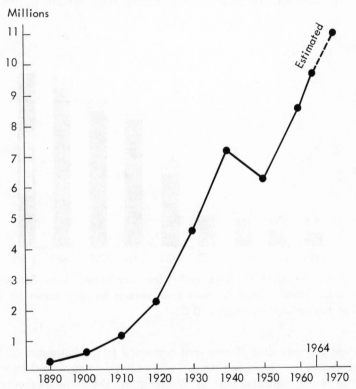

Fig. 9–3. Number of Students Enrolled in Grades 9–12, 1890–1970. (Based on data from several bulletins issued by U.S. Office of Education, Washington, D.C.)

reaching more than 7,000,000 in grades 9 through 12 in 1940. Because of the war there was a slight decrease in enrollment between 1940 and 1950, and then it shot up again reaching approximately 9,000,000 in 1960, and it is estimated that it will reach at least 11,000,000 by 1970.

Of the boys and girls in the fifth grade in 1944–1945, 85 per cent reached the ninth grade, 75 per cent the tenth grade, and a little more than 50 per cent graduated. Of those in the fifth grade in 1954–1955, more than 90 per cent remained to enter the ninth grade, 86 per cent the tenth grade, and 64 per cent graduated (see Fig. 9–4). It should be kept in mind that these figures are averages; in some states, in some cities, and with some races, percentages remaining beyond the ninth grade were much less, and in others substantially more. In Evanston and New Trier Township High Schools in Illinois,

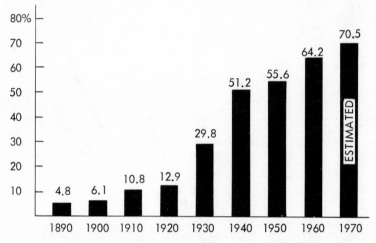

Fig. 9–4. Per Cent of Boys and Girls Graduating from Secondary School Since 1890. (Based on data from several bulletins issued by U.S. Office of Education, Washington, D.C.)

for example, more than 80 per cent remained to graduate and 85 per cent of those (nearly 70 per cent of all) entered some sort of college; while in South Chicago and in Washington, D.C., the percentages were less than half; and in many districts in Mississippi, Georgia, South Carolina, Arkansas and Alabama, even less.

It is estimated that throughout the remaining 1960's, these percentages will increase slightly as follows: by 1980 they will reach a more or less permanent maximum of 95 per cent remaining through the ninth grade, 90 per cent through the tenth grade, and 75 per cent remaining to graduate. While great efforts are being expended to reduce the number and percentage of students who do not remain to graduate from high school, it seems quite unlikely that more than

75, or at the very greatest 80, per cent will remain to graduate from high school.

The better educated the father, the more likely it is that the son is better educated. Census Bureau's figures show that 55 per cent of men who were between the ages of twenty and sixty-four in 1962 were high school graduates. Only 24 per cent of their fathers had high school diplomas. Among men whose fathers had completed high school, but no more, nearly half of the sons of white collar workers had gone to college. The percentage fell to 32 per cent in the case of fathers engaged in manual and service jobs, and 28 per cent in the case of farm families.[12]

The library is useful for independent study. (Houston Public Schools.)

### The Six-Year Secondary School

The large majority of the school districts in the United States do not enroll more than three or four hundred students in grades 7 through 12; and in these village and smaller consolidated districts, there has been a very strong trend in the direction of substituting a

[12] *Education U.S.A.*, October 8, 1964, p. 22.

6-6 plan instead of the 6-3-3 plan for the 8-4 plan.[13] It is uneconomical to attempt to operate both the junior high school and a senior high school in the smaller districts. By 1960, this type of organization had become definitely the most common, there being approximately 12,000 schools of the six-year secondary schools, some of which are operated somewhat as separate units or schools within a school and others especially in the smaller districts are operated as a single unit—practically all the teachers teaching classes in both divisions. Because of the smallness of most of these schools, they enroll only about 20 per cent of the students going beyond grade 6.

There are definite disadvantages and limitations of six-year schools, being principally those that pertain to all small secondary schools. The economic resources of these communities are in terms of assessed valuation; and income per student is definitely smaller than in larger districts, which are usually organized on the 6-3-3 plan. As a consequence, the curriculum is somewhat limited, the teaching staff is somewhat inferior in the amount of training and years of experience and in other respects, the housing and equipment is inferior, as are such services as guidance and counseling, and health service. In addition, grades 7, 8, and 9 tend to be neglected as compared to grades 10, 11, and 12 with respect to extrasubject activities, equipment, and "guidance."

### The Small High School

As indicated, the small high school is not as effective as the large one. Beyond this it has been increasingly recognized not only by educators but by the students and their parents and other lay people that consolidation has gone on in many areas of the country for several decades. District consolidation and the greatly improved and expanded highways as well as the greater population and the disappearance of the sparsely settled areas have led to free transportation, and to the establishment of larger schools including secondary schools. In the Conant report, *The American High School Today*, it was advocated that great effort should be expended to build up high schools to a size that would include one hundred students in the twelfth grade. Schools of this size may provide a much more varied curriculum, more and better guidance service, and for the formation of sections for students of definitely limited learning ability and also sections for the abler and creative students who are outstandingly superior.

[13] It was originally proposed in the 1890's that we move to a 6-6 plan of organization—the 6-3-3 idea coming later.

# THE UNIQUE CHARACTER OF SECONDARY EDUCATION IN AMERICAN SOCIETY

Far more than most Americans and even many teachers realize, secondary schools in the United States are quite different in many important respects from those in any other country; although, since the close of World War II, the secondary schools of most countries have become somewhat more like those in the United States. In the majority of those countries, however, the gap has been lessened only a bit; and the differences are still very great and important. In large part, our schools reflect the nature and fundamental philosophy of American society.

## Fundamental Differences

The principal differences are the following:

1. Secondary schools in the United States are planned for all the boys and girls who complete elementary school, while in other countries pupils are admitted usually only after written examinations.

2. The program of the American secondary school is very comprehensive, including in the same school vocational and academic subjects as well as new subjects not offered in foreign schools at all.

3. A great many parents do not believe as strongly in hard study for a long school week and a long school year as do parents in European countries.

4. The American secondary school is controlled almost entirely by elected officials in the local community.

5. The American secondary school is a democratic social institution; and employed in connection with it are various types of democratic rather than authoritarian procedures affecting lay people, students, teachers, and administrators.

6. The objectives of the American secondary schools are much broader, including preparation for various areas of life, and are less concentrated upon preparation for college. Also, they are concerned with developing all aspects of human growth and not merely the intellectual asset.

7. The teaching and administrative staffs in American secondary schools are quite differently prepared, have less university preparation, and are composed about equally of men and women, as contrasted with the great majority of men in secondary schools in other countries.

8. School housing and equipment for secondary education in the United States are much more modern and much more expensive than in Europe.

## QUESTIONS, PROBLEMS, AND PROJECTS FOR FURTHER STUDY

1. Which do you think would be better for the typical ninth-grader: the 6-3-3 plan of organization, the 8-4 plan, the 6-6 plan, the 6-2-4 plan, the 6-2-2-2 plan, or the 5-3-4 plan?

2. Quite recently there has been a small trend toward the 6-2-2-2 plan, which provides something like the junior high school for grades 7 and 8 but splits up grades 9 through 12 into two separate schools with different buildings and different staff. What advantages do you see, and what disadvantages?

3. What differences do you see in the nature of the boys and girls who are in the pubescent stage, e.g., through ages thirteen and fourteen, as compared to the adolescent stage, ages fifteen, sixteen, and seventeen?

4. After comparing Professor Havighurst's statement of the developmental tests of adolescents with the statement of ten imperative needs as set up by the Educational Policies Commission, what common characteristics do you find? What may be found in one statement and not in the other? What inconsistencies can you find?

5. For what students going to high school today would you find the curriculum as offered in the typical Latin grammar school of the seventeenth century good? The English grammar school?

6. How do you account for the fact that so many different subjects were offered in a few academies?

7. How do you account for the fact that so few of these subjects were offered in high schools in the nineteenth century?

8. How do you account for the fact that the number of high schools increased so rapidly between 1900 and 1960, but tend not to increase so rapidly since 1960?

9. How do you account for the fact that enrollments in secondary schools have increased so rapidly in the twentieth century?

10. Which of the goals and functions of secondary education do you think have been neglected or given less emphasis than others?

11. Do you believe that secondary schools exist primarily for seeing that young people learn a set body of subject matter, or do you believe that subject matter is a means to an end? How can you justify your position?

12. Do you believe that there are areas of life other than those mentioned in this chapter for which young people should be prepared? Do you believe the areas listed in this chapter tend to overlap each other? Which ones?

13. Do you believe that some high schools should be set up to prepare students for college and others set up to prepare them for jobs? Do you

believe that practically all high schools should make provisions so that students may prepare for jobs and prepare for college at the same time?

14. Why are there so many six-year secondary schools? Why are not all schools of that type? What are the advantages and limitations of the six-year secondary school?

15. How are the secondary schools in the United States different from those in England, France, Germany, or Russia?

16. There are people who have insisted that we should pattern our secondary schools more like those in the countries of Europe, and there are those that say that the schools in Europe are becoming more and more like those in the United States. What do you think of this matter?

## SELECTED SUPPLEMENTARY READINGS AND FILMS

ALBERTY, HAROLD B., and ALBERTY, ELSIE J. *Reorganizing the High School Curriculum.* 3d ed. New York: The Macmillan Co., 1962. Chap. ii.

ALEXANDER, WILLIAM M. "The Junior High School: A Changing View," *The Bulletin of the National Association of Secondary-School Principals,* No. 290 (March, 1964), 15–24. Detailed practical suggestions for "middle schools."

ANDERSON, VERNON E., and GRUHN, WILLIAM T. *Principles and Practices of Secondary Education.* 2d ed. New York: The Ronald Press Co., 1962. Chaps. ii, xviii, and xx.

BENJAMIN, HAROLD. *The Saber-Tooth Curriculum.* New York: McGraw-Hill Book Co., Inc., 1939. A satirical myth illustrating resistance to curriculum improvement.

BENT, RUDYARD K., and KRONENBERG, HENRY H. *Principles of Secondary Education.* 4th ed. New York: McGraw-Hill Book Co., Inc., 1961. Chap. ii.

BOHRSON, RALPH G. "The Small High-School—Its Strengths and Limitations," *The Bulletin of the National Association of Secondary-School Principals,* No. 282 (April, 1963), 106–18.

CONANT, JAMES B. *The American High School Today.* New York: McGraw-Hill Book Co., Inc., 1960. Pp. 96. Recommendations resulting from a nationwide study. "A must."

————. *The Child, the Parent, and the State.* Cambridge: Harvard University Press, 1959. Chap. iv.

————. "The Public High School and the National Interest," *The Bulletin of the National Association of Secondary-School Principals,* No. 237 (April, 1958), 343–56.

DOUGLASS, HARL R. *Modern Administration of Secondary Schools.* Boston: Ginn & Co., 1963. Pp. 588–608.

————. *Modern Secondary Education.* New York: The Ronald Press Co., 1964. Chap. iv.

DUBRIDGE, LEE A. "The Best Freshmen Are Getting Better." In *American High School Graduate.* Washington, D.C.: National Education Association, 1962.

GWYNN, J. MINOR. *Curriculum Principles and Social Trends.* New York: The Macmillan Co., 1960. Chap. xii.

HEELY, ALLAN V. "The Private School in American Education." In *Public Education in America,* George Z. F. Bereday and Luigi Volpicelli (eds.). New York: Harper & Row, 1958. Pp. 50–61.

HUGHES, JAMES MONROE. "The Non-Public Schools." In *Education in America.* Evanston, Ill.: Row, Peterson & Co., 1960. Pp. 324–44.

KAMINETSKY, JOSEPH. "The Jewish Day Schools," *Phi Delta Kappan,* XLV, No. 3 (December, 1963), 141–44. A short objective statement relative to their place in American education.

KVARACEUS, WILLIAM C. "Social Stresses and Strains on Children and Youth: Some Implications for Schools," *The High School Journal,* XLVII, No. 4 (January, 1964), 140–45. A reliable, modern, important statement.

LATHROP, IRVIN T., and KIEFFER, THOMAS J. "College Achievement of Public vs. Private High School Graduates," *The Clearing House,* XXXIII, No. 5 (January, 1959), 299–302. A surprising discovery.

ZAKIS, OTT, and COLLINS, CHARLES C. "The German School System: A Capsule Description," *The Bulletin of the National Association of Secondary-School Principals,* No. 273 (April, 1962), 162–86. A complete modern description of a compromise of the old caste system type and the struggle to modernize it.

## Films

*Broader Concepts of Curriculum.* 21 minutes. Points out the changes in the high school curriculum necessitated by the great increase that is taking place in enrollments in secondary schools and some of the causes for this growth. New York: McGraw-Hill Book Co., Inc.

*James B. Conant.* 30 minutes. Reviews important educational problems and presents some of the conclusions of Dr. Conant's book, *The American High School Today.* Chicago: Encyclopaedia Britannica Films.

*Counselor's Day.* 29 frames, filmstrip. Shows the work of a school counselor. McGraw-Hill Book Co., Inc.

*Meaning of Adolescence.* 16 minutes. Describes the problems in gaining physical, social, sexual, religious, and moral adjustment, and explains how adolescents attempt to meet their needs. McGraw-Hill Book Co., Inc.

# 10

# HIGHER AND
# ADULT EDUCATION

## THE COMMITMENT OF OUR AMERICAN DEMOCRACY

The President's Commission on Higher Education included in their report in 1947 the following epoch marking statement that seems to express the beliefs of most leading educators today.

It is a commonplace of the democratic faith that education is indispensable to the maintenance and growth of freedom of thought, faith, enterprise, and association. Thus the social role of education in a democratic society is at once to insure equal liberty and equal opportunity to differing individuals and groups, and to enable the citizens to understand, appraise, and redirect forces, men, and events as these tend to strengthen or to weaken their liberties. . . .

It is essential today that education come decisively to grips with the world-wide crisis of mankind. . . . But the scientific knowledge and technical skills that have made atomic and bacteriological warfare possible are the products of education and research, and higher education must share proportionately in the task of forging social and political defenses against obliteration. . . .

In the light of this situation, the President's Commission on Higher Education has attempted to select, from among the principal goals for higher education, those which should come first in our time. They are to bring to all the people of the nation:

> Education for a fuller realization of democracy in every phase of living.
> Education directly and explicitly for international understanding and cooperation.
> Education for the application of creative imagination and trained intelligence to the solution of social problems and to the administration of public affairs.[1]

[1] President's Commission on Higher Education, *Higher Education for American Democracy* (Washington, D.C.: U.S. Government Printing Office, 1947).

This commitment and these goals have their seeds in the thinking of leaders in the United States more than a century ago. To some extent they go back to the voice of Thomas Jefferson in the first decade of the nineteenth century.

### Growth of Higher Education in the United States

In 1910, there were only about 240,000 students in colleges and universities of all types. By 1930, this had increased to 1,100,000; in 1940, 1,500,000; in 1950, 2,300,000; and to approximately 4,000,000 in 1960. In the fall of 1964, approximately 5,000,000 students enrolled in some kind of college or university; and by 1970, it is estimated that this figure will approach 6,500,000. Also, in the fall of 1964, it is estimated that 40 per cent of young people of the ages eighteen, nineteen, twenty, and twenty-one were enrolled in postsecondary schools of some sort; and by 1975, that proportion will exceed 50 per cent and include approximately 8,000,000 students, more than 2,000,000 of which will be in junior colleges.

In no other country does the number of students in institutions of higher education approach those in the United States. The percentage of young people going on to college in the United States is from two to five times the percentage of that in western European nations, Russia, and Japan, and from five to twelve times the percentage of those going on in eastern European nations and in China. It is from ten to twenty times the percentage in Latin American nations, and from fifty to a thousand times that in nations of Asia and Africa, other than Japan and China.

### Reasons for This Tremendous Growth

It is not difficult to discover why the provision for institutions of higher education and enrollment in them has gone on so rapidly in the United States and so much more rapidly than in any other country. The more important reasons are as follows:

1. In the first place, no country has become sufficiently prosperous economically so that it is able to support higher education and provide institutions of higher education as has the United States.

2. In no other country can the people afford to spare from production their young people and to send them to institutions of higher education in nearly as great numbers as in the United States.

3. The expansion of business, technology, education, and agriculture in the United States as well as the amount of legal, medical,

nursing, and other personal services bought by this people and the demand for scientists, technologists, physicians, and teachers have increased very greatly in the last few decades and consequently the number of opportunities for college graduates has increased far more rapidly than in other countries.

4. There has been going on in the United States (and in the world) not only a population explosion but a very great and significant *knowledge* explosion. Not only has the amount of knowledge increased at an accelerating rate in the past half-century, particularly in the last few decades, but much of what was thought of as accurate knowledge in previous times is no longer accurate, being either false or only partly true and needing modification.

Buildings cannot be authorized and constructed fast enough to accommodate the avalanche of students. Many colleges and universities have put into effect practices to help meet the situation by (1) keeping the institution operating the year around with three semesters or four quarters a year and reducing the time necessary in college to earn a degree, and (2) reducing the amount of time necessary to obtain higher-level degrees, e.g., Doctor of Philosophy, Bachelor of Laws, Doctor of Medicine, and Doctor of Education. It seems obvious that these trends will spread.

## TYPES OF INSTITUTIONS OF HIGHER EDUCATION

In recent decades, it has become quite difficult to classify the different types of institutions of higher education. No longer can a college be definitely catalogued as a liberal arts college or a teachers' college or an agricultural and mechanical college, or a university. Many of the teachers' colleges have become state colleges; and in many of them, there are five-year programs leading to a master's degree; and many colleges have become "universities."

Colleges other than junior colleges, which are not universities, may be classified with respect to the agency providing control and support: (1) state colleges; (2) municipal colleges; (3) independent colleges operating largely through endowments and tuition, such as Oberlin College in Ohio; and (4) denominational colleges, principally Catholic, Presbyterian, Lutheran, Baptist, and Methodist, which are supported in part by funds from affiliated churches.

These colleges emphasize general education or liberal arts programs, though in many of them there are specialized curricula such as professional courses for teachers and for secretaries.

## The Junior College

The most rapidly growing type of institution for higher education is the junior college of which there were in 1964–1965 nearly eight hundred, enrolling nearly one million students. Approximately three-fourths of them are public junior colleges operated by local districts with state assistance. About one-fourth of them are independent or non-public institutions primarily operated by religious organizations. Between 85 and 90 per cent of the junior college students are enrolled in public institutions.

Early in this century with high school enrollments doubling and high school graduates tripling every decade, there began to develop a demand for some sort of post-high school education close to the homes of the students. A number of high schools offered what was called "post-high school" or "graduate" courses for high school graduates, but this did not satisfy the public demand. A number of weaker four-year non-public colleges had already pruned their offerings back to two years when at Joliet, Illinois, there was established in 1902 the first *public* junior college. While the movement was slow getting under way, by 1925 junior colleges, both public and private, were being established in large numbers in every section of the country, particularly in California and Texas.

With the great increase in the number of students graduating from high school with meager opportunity for employment, and the great stress and strain put upon colleges to take care of those who want to attend and with increased entrance requirements and tuition, the present trend toward a large number of junior colleges and a much larger number of students attending them is going to continue for many years.

The Educational Policies Commission, an important body set up by the National Education Association and the American Association of Administrators, issued a report late in 1963 in which they took a definite stand for two more years of free public education for all American youth after high school graduation. They were not thinking entirely of vocational education but emphasized general education aimed at intellectual growth and a greater understanding of self and the world.

As more and more boys and girls went through high school who were not what was thought to be the "college going" type, there developed a greater demand for terminal courses. In the 1940's, there was a big movement toward what was called the "community institute" type of junior college. The junior college teachers and administrators, however, did not want to be referred to as an "institute"; the chief administrative officer wanted to be called a "president," or at least a "dean," and the instructors preferred to be called "professors," so that the "community institute" idea was adopted in not more than a small fraction of the institutions, and in most of those the term "institute" has been dropped. Indeed, in many of the institutions many of the junior colleges do not use either the word "institute" or "junior" but merely the word "college," such as Mesa College in Colorado.

## The Technical Institute

There are in the United States approximately one hundred technical institutes or colleges that enroll students who have completed high school. About sixty of these might be thought of as technological colleges. They enrolled somewhere in the neighborhood of one hundred fifty thousand students in 1963–1964.

The curricula are largely in the fields of industrial education, including, of course, various aspects of electronics; and they do not attempt to offer the curriculum found in the engineering schools and colleges of the universities. They are for young people with somewhat less than the average ability to master mathematics and science who do not wish to attend a four-year engineering school or college. It is obvious now that there is need for many more technical institutes.

## Colleges

Four- or five-year colleges constitute a variety in themselves. Their status, purposes, and programs have been for a considerable time, and still are, in a rather fluid state. Some of them are teachers' colleges, most of them operated by the states; many of them are four-year liberal arts colleges some of which offer a master's degree, established and supported by the state or established and supported by some religious organization. A small percentage of them are technical colleges, usually giving courses in one or more forms of engineering.

## The College of Arts and Sciences

As the college grows larger and the number of departments and the number of courses increase, and the opportunities for specialization become greater, there is more or less a departure from the fundamental concept of a well-rounded liberal general education. The idea of a liberal education (the word "liberal" derived from Latin meant "free") is to prepare the mind, through facts, ideals, attitudes, and intellectual skills, to evaluate facts and ideas in an unbiased and objective manner. A liberal education should develop appropriate appreciations of the free mind, open-mindedness, and the revolutionary nature of human knowledge and social progress.

Since the courses in liberal arts are with few exceptions taught by individuals who have specialized in one branch (sometimes quite narrowly) of academic learning, there is a tendency for the instructor in liberal arts colleges to think of the aims of the college very largely in terms of the mastery of the facts, ideals, attitudes, appreciations, and intellectual skills, especially facts and skills in his particular field of specialization.

In the larger colleges, the courses offered for freshmen and sopho-mores in various departments are for the very large part such as will provide adequate foundation and preparation for those who wish, in the third and fourth year and in graduate work, to specialize in major and minor fields. There has been in the past quarter of a cen-tury a countertrend in the direction of attempting to rescue liberal education from this digression and to restore it to its early intention with respect to the liberal education of the student. This may be seen in the form of various general courses, interdepartmental courses and curricula, and the reorientation of the faculties of many of these colleges through such studies and publications as *A Liberal Educa-tion in a Free Democracy*, the Harvard College faculty report on that subject.

### The University

There is not complete agreement on what constitutes a university. Originally, a university was a "community of scholars," e.g., at Oxford, Paris, Bologna, and other cities. In the Western Hemisphere, there were the University of St. Marcos at Lima and the National University of Mexico, both of which opened their doors in 1553, eighty-three years before Harvard College was established. These were not uni-versities in the sense that we think of universities today, but they were certainly much more advanced than would be indicated by the use of the word "college" to designate them.

The true university exists to improve and expand knowledge by research and to give instruction to those wishing to become specialists in various fields. In the beginning, they had very meager buildings and were poorly supported, the support being largely from tuition and from the communities in which they were located, although in some instances the university had a church affiliation that supplied funds and in some instances instructors.

It is difficult to say just when some of the early colleges of the United States arrived at their true university status, but it is certain that those that were called universities before 1875 were not universities in the sense that we know them today.

There has recently come to be a rather great diversity of types of universities. The highest type includes strong professional schools, e.g., law, medicine, dentistry, and education, which require at least two years of college work for entrance and which support strong graduate programs in many departments, offering the doctor of philosophy degree and at least one other type of doctoral program. There are now many colleges that are midway between a college and a university and have been given or have assumed the title of "university." Approximately 40 per cent of the institutions with the title of university are supported by the state; and about 25 per cent by non-public sources, principally endowments and tuition, although to some extent by funds from religious denominations. This is particularly true of Catholic universities. Enrollments today are divided approximately equally between the public and the non-public institutions of this category.

## Professional Schools

Professional schools of the collegiate or university level are parts of colleges and universities. For a long time, particularly in the latter part of the nineteenth century and the first part of the twentieth, there were law, medical, and engineering schools operated independently of any state control and of any institution of higher education. They were conducted primarily for profit. Practically all these dental and medical schools have disappeared, as their graduates were discovered to be greatly inferior to those coming from the schools of dentistry and the schools of medicine of the university.

Engineering education of a university grade really started in a modest way at the Rensselaer Polytechnic Institute at Troy, New York, in 1825, supported by state funds. Later, throughout the latter half of the nineteenth century, engineering schools and colleges were established in a large majority of the universities.

Professional education in agriculture at the university level began in the late 1850's in Michigan, Maryland, and Pennsylvania. Soon after the passage of the Morrill Act providing large areas of public land as an endowment, in 1862, separate colleges of agriculture were established in twenty-eight states and as parts of state universities in fifteen states.

## Teacher Education

In recent years, the discussion of teacher education has been characterized by poorly supported sensational attacks by sensationalists, and by some teachers and educational politicians, along with very reliable presentations by fully informed people whose bias and vested interest consisted largely in improving the quality of education.

This unfortunate condition has grown largely out of four elements in the situation:

1. The more or less futile attempt to prepare a teacher for superior service in the junior and senior high schools in four years of work beyond the high school and the consequent struggle between the subject matter departments and the departments of schools and colleges of education
2. The great variety of practices and standards among teacher training institutions, including institutions of very low standards, for admission and graduation of students with respect to the amount of time, effort, and ability required for better than average grades in the courses in education
3. The depressing spectacle of men outstanding in their own fields of specialization, such as science, in the armed forces, or in American history, writing like charlatans in the field of education—misstating facts and using epithets and wisecracks along with fragmentary quotations out of context in their efforts to discredit professional education of teachers
4. The lack of coordination and articulation among courses in education

The situation has been greatly improved in recent years as a result of the following developments:

1. Moving to five-year programs for the education of teachers, which will enable the subject matter departments to enroll more students in the more advanced courses, and will permit prospective teachers to prepare better for teaching by reason of additional available time
2. A general awakening of the public to the degree to which they had been misled by sensationalists, publicists, and authors motivated primarily if not entirely by political and commercial interests

3. The improvement of the content and the coordination of courses of education—to provide better articulation and to prevent duplication
4. The pressures brought to bear upon the weakest institutions through accreditation standards and procedures, though much progress is yet to be made in this field

With the increased amount of knowledge available to be learned by students in both junior and senior high schools and by teachers, and with the great responsibility of teachers and the greatly increased amount of professional knowledge available, it is quite clear that five years for the preparation of teachers is not too much. And it should be supplemented by additional course work to fill in the gaps and to keep up with the development of subject matter in the fields they teach and in the new sound practices in the schools.

It has also become quite clear that professors and instructors in subject-matter courses must address themselves more vigorously to the task of participating effectively in the education of teachers. Most of them need to know more about the types of services rendered by teachers and their problems as they exist today rather than to rely so heavily upon the tirades of former teachers who were not successful and found it desirable to attribute their mediocre performance to some things or persons other than themselves.

These institutions have an important part to play in the preparation not only of engineers and agriculturalists, but in teachers of agriculture, home economics, science, and industrial arts.

## Municipal Colleges and Universities

Particularly in the latter part of the nineteenth century and the first few decades of this century, there were established in many cities municipal colleges and universities. Prominent among them are the University of Pittsburgh and the five City Universities of New York, enrolling more than 100,000 students. In recent years, there has been a trend for these institutions to become a part of the state university system.

## Graduate Schools

Until about a century ago, there was no thought of graduate work in the universities of the United States. Those who wanted to do graduate work usually went to some European university. However, in 1876 at Johns Hopkins University in Baltimore, Maryland, there was established a graduate school offering work in several departments toward master's and doctor's degrees. Soon thereafter, other universities, including particularly Harvard, Princeton, Yale, and Michigan, established graduate departments or graduate schools, and later created the position of dean of the graduate school with more or less authority over all the various departments of the university offering graduate degrees. Particularly in the present century, graduate courses, graduate schools, graduate students, and graduate degrees have multiplied and mushroomed until there are more students registered in graduate schools in the United States today than were registered in all the colleges and universities in the United States in 1900.

A very illuminating statement about graduate education was made in 1964 by an eminent authority on the subject, as follows:

The graduate schools are grappling with a triple-headed monster—the research needs of the country: for teachers, for pure scientists, and for an almost limitless number of applied scientists in business, industry, and government.

For many years the doctor of philosophy degree has been considered the normal qualification for a teacher in colleges and universities. Yet the present annual output of the American universities supplies only about 20 per cent of the number needed to fill vacancies in the faculties of higher education.

This much is certain: the Ph.D. degree is no guarantee that its holder is qualified to give instruction in the liberal arts college. The nature of researches performed even in the basic subjects is often unrelated to liberal education and, as such, is not satisfactory preparation for college teaching.

A criticism of the modern university education is that it no longer asks the important questions or deals with fundamental issues.

The graduate faculty is usually the ablest of the university staff, the cost of graduate education is greater than any other except medical education, and the need for its products—Ph.D. graduates—is unparalleled. Yet graduate schools are more confused, ineffective, and inconsistent in their practices than any other school or college in the university.

The emphasis on current humanistic research appears to be on analysis, just as it is in the natural sciences; but humanistic-social studies should involve synthesis as well. One result of attempting to apply scientific methods rigidly to humanistic-social science research is that it turns out to be research *about* the humanities or social sciences rather than research *in* these fields.[2]

Several of the conclusions of Berelson pointed up a need for renewed attention to ways of helping new college instructors assume the varied responsibilities of their positions. His specific recommendations with regard to achieving this goal included the following:

[2] Oliver C. Carmichael, *Saturday Review*, 1964.

1. Give all doctoral candidates who intend to teach in college some actual teaching experience (as teaching assistants) while doing graduate work —at least half-time for a year, supervised by an interested senior staff member.

2. Systematically vary this teaching experience so that it involves contact with more than one area of the curriculum.

3. Set up in the graduate school a course or seminar which deals with the character, problems, and goals of the liberal arts college for those who intend to enter the field of college teaching.

4. Encourage the first employing institution to take increased responsibility for educating the new faculty member with respect to effective methods of teaching—as part of an in-service program guided by staff members who know and care about good instructional practice.[3]

## HIGHER EDUCATION FOR ALL?

### The Incredible Increase in College Enrollments

For at least three centuries in the United States, from the beginning of higher education in European and other countries, higher education has been thought of as something for the select few, presumably those of superior capacities for the type of learning that takes place in colleges but also for the children of the upper economic and ruling classes and for the priesthood.

It was very natural that in the United States with its advanced ideas about democracy and equal opportunity for all that gradually there would develop a feeling that opportunities for higher education should be open for all. This idea has flourished recently because of increased prosperity of the country and of the majority of its families, the greater desire for higher learning, the decreased opportunities for employment for young people, and the decreased necessity for utilizing young people in work incident to production of foods and other necessities of life. It was stimulated also by the very greatly increased demand for teachers, physicians, attorneys, pharmacists, nurses, engineers, scientists, business employees, executives, and investment specialists.

There has been an increased realization that the present criteria and practices employed in choosing prospective students admit a large number of students who cannot or will not do well in their courses, and also operate to exclude many who would be superior students and many whose work makes outstanding contributions to so-

[3] Bernard Berelson, *Graduate Education in the United States* (New York: McGraw Hill Book Co., Inc., 1960), pp. 248–50.

ciety, more than 25 per cent being dropped in the first two years for poor scholarship. Consequently, there has been considerable experimentation in connection with admissions to college. Some colleges admit students of special types who give evidence of unusual promise, even though they have not scored well on paper-and-pencil tests or have not made outstanding grades in high school. This type of procedure apparently is spreading.

### Protests Against Mediocrity and Anti-Intellectualism

With the greatly increased enrollments in colleges, there has been opposition on the part of the intellectuals, particularly the intellectual aristocrats, real and pretended, who felt that admission of average and mediocre students would tend to impair the quality of higher education. These individuals have failed to realize the fact that not only can the large majority of young people profit from education beyond the high school, but that there exists a great difference among colleges with respect to the amount and the pattern of learning abilities that are necessary for successful completion of courses and curricula required for a degree.

As a matter of fact, with respect to academic learning ability, the upper quartile of some colleges in the United States is at about the same point as the lower quartile of a number of other colleges. Likewise, differences in the pattern and amount of the capacity for learning differs among the various schools and colleges comprising a university and the different departments within schools and colleges of the university and with departments in colleges. In determining whether a given high school student is "college bound," one should first decide what type and level of college he is bound for.

Among those apparently most concerned is Robert Hutchins, former Chancellor of the University of Chicago, who maintains that the problem of higher education in America is not a problem of quantity. Whatever our shortcomings in this regard, we have a higher proportion of our young people in higher education than does any other country. He points out that we have more teachers and more square feet per student in bigger, newer buildings than any other nation in the world.

This statement, though seeming very plausible at first, seems to smack of days gone by. It is focused upon the welfare of a given institution and overlooks the fact that there is a great need for continued education of the great mass of young people in this complicated and rapidly changing world, as well as the fact that there are greatly decreased opportunities for employment of people with no more than a high school education.

Others have made similarly authoritarian and undemocratic statements, which definitely imply that our national culture is not something for the great mass of people, but a privilege for those who happen to be born with high I.Q.'s. It is encouraging that within recent years, a number of important national educational organizations have made statements, which have been supported by people in education and in business, to the effect that we have now reached a period in which we should expect all but a small percentage of young people to complete high school. There should be available for all of them at least two years of post-high school general education, vocational education, or both.

While there was for a period in the late 1950's and early 1960's an orgy of giving and taking paper-and-pencil examinations with the will-of-the-wisp hope of being able to select students who could profit from a college education, investigations of the validity of such claims and wishes have shown that it is now a relatively futile and impractical approach to the problem. Success in college courses cannot be estimated with considerable degree of accuracy.

The National Merit Scholarship Committee a few years ago concluded rather that it was not practical from the point of view of their objectives to select students for scholarships on the basis of their showing on paper-and-pencil examinations. Important consideration should also be given to evidences of drive, ambition, special qualities of leadership, and other matters. After thirty years of ignoring research studies relative to the matter, it is becoming more and more obvious that success and happiness in life and the value of contributions to society are not in proportion to the ability to pass examinations and to receive grades assigned by a classroom teacher.

Investigations reveal that as compared to individuals who possess only qualities and abilities that are thought of as related to scholarship, those of approximately equal academic ability who participated widely in social and extrasubject activities not only succeeded as well or better in receiving good grades in college, but the proportions of those graduating from college were larger. Furthermore, the proportions of those going on for graduate school were definitely larger, especially for master's degrees; and the proportions of those receiving some sort of distinction in a creative way in literature, music, or science, etc., were definitely much larger. Naturally, it goes without saying that those possessed of these other interests, capacities, and identities received much greater annual incomes.

It is clear that, regardless of the protests of individuals who like to be thought of as intellectuals, the institutions of higher education in the United States are going to enroll increasingly larger and larger numbers of students until at least three-fourths of those graduating from high school go on to some sort of college.

## Higher Education for Women

Following slowly but surely on the heels of pioneer work at Mt. Holyoke, the admission of women to Oberlin College in 1833,[4] Antioch in 1853, several universities including Iowa, Wisconsin, Michigan, Maine, and Cornell in the 1860's and 1870's, higher education for women has been freely provided; and women have been enrolling in larger and larger numbers, particularly in the twentieth century. One by one, various professional schools have opened their doors to women until at present there are few if any professional curricula not available to qualified women students.

The resistance to this movement was not based upon any feeling that women students might not do as well in college as their male counterparts. The general feeling was that coeducation provides the distraction of one sex by the other, that the college courses were designed for men in the professions, and that to some extent the professions for which training was given were not sufficiently open to women to justify their preparing for them.

By 1900, about 20 per cent of the students in institutions of higher education were women; and by 1964, this had increased to about 45 per cent. Originally established for men, great universities such as Columbia and Harvard set up coordinate divisions for women. Very recently, dividing lines have been broken and these institutions are well on their way to becoming coeducational institutions.

In some areas it may be said that we have almost reached the status where coeducational institutions are the rule except for a small number of Catholic colleges. Furthermore, they are moving in the direction of obtaining a situation in which higher education for women is almost as well suited for their needs as is higher education for the needs of men:

1. The needs of women and men are becoming more and more alike.
2. More emphasis is being placed upon courses and curriculum for women in coeducational institutions to prepare them for

[4] Oberlin was also the first college to remove all social bars to admission.

useful activities broadly conceived of adult women in American life.

While there is narrowing difference between the interests and activities of adult men and women, there is nevertheless a definite problem of providing a type of education in our colleges and universities that will prepare women for participation in various activities in American life, in the home, in the community and nation, as a large and increasing number will be involved.

Extension of the suffrage to women in 1919 and breaking down the barriers to various types of occupations for women have resulted in a a tremendously increased necessity for citizenship and vocational education at all levels for women. Automation and the relief of women from household duties by the development of various types of household appliances and the increased extent to which food and clothing are produced cheaply and sold in the stores have increased the amount of leisure for women, thus proportionally increasing the necessity for education of women for leisure and civic activities.

## Higher Education for Negroes

In the Colonial period of our life and for the first century at least of our National period, Negroes did not attend college. In fact, less than one hundred Negroes graduated from college before the end of the War Between the States in 1865. In the North, there were few Negroes; and most of them did not aspire to higher education. In the South, Negroes did not enter college primarily for two reasons: (1) they were not permitted to enroll, and (2) they were not given any type of secondary education as preparation for college.

Before the War Between the States, a few beginnings were made, such as the establishment of Avery College in Pennsylvania in 1849, and in 1851 the Miner Academy for Negro Girls in Washington, D.C., the founding of the Ashmand Institute in Pennsylvania by a Presbyterian group in 1814, and Wilberforce University in Ohio by the Methodists in 1855. After the war, more beginnings were made, particularly in the reconstruction period. The Freedmen's Bureau and numerous church organizations attempted to establish colleges in the South; but then as now this sort of progress was opposed by certain types of southern white people by law and by violence, which included the killing of the president of one of the Negro colleges.

There did develop out of this turmoil a few important colleges for Negroes, such as Atlanta University in Georgia, Hampton Institute in

Virginia, Fisk University in Tennessee, Howard University in Washington, D.C., and Tuskegee Institute in Alabama.

While Negroes were not especially encouraged to attend the colleges and universities of the northeastern states, they have for some time been admitted to most of them; and in the higher educational institutions of the Rocky Mountains and far West after about 1860, they were admitted freely; although there were some problems of obtaining meals, rooms, and personal services. The increase in the number of Negroes attending colleges and universities and the improvement of the attitudes of white people toward their admission and attendance were handicapped by the fact that Negroes both from the North and from the South were very poorly prepared in their inferior elementary and secondary schools, and on the average they did inferior work in college or university.

Since the United States Supreme Court Decision in 1954, which held that racial segregation in the schools violates the Constitution of the United States, token admission of Negroes to southern colleges and universities has gone on. Many colleges previously open only to Negroes accept white people as well. The better educated and the more social minded leaders in the South have moved more and more in the direction toward gradual desegregation, and it is only a matter of a few decades until the colleges and universities of the South will be enrolling rather large numbers of Negroes. Large funds have been provided in the past few years for scholarships for Negroes.

## SOME IMPORTANT SERVICES AND OPPORTUNITIES OF HIGHER EDUCATION

### Counseling and Guidance

Practically all colleges and universities today at least attempt a program of guidance, although the quantity and quality of the service vary greatly from institution to institution. In the institutions with presidents and deans who have a modern philosophy of education and up-to-date knowledge about modern problems of young people and the world that they face and where ample funds are available, a considerable number of counselors adequately trained are placed in various types of positions in the college or university—in the office of the various deans, in the president's office, in the office of student affairs, in the office of the appointment agency, to say nothing about those who are part of the staff and of course university counselors.

Much useful counseling still is done by those without special training in departments of education and in subject-matter departments, but a great deal of advice and counseling that is needed by students as such lies beyond the experience and knowledge of these individuals.

## Research Service

In all of the universities, and indeed in many of the larger colleges, members of the faculty are expected to carry on investigations that are supposed to expand the amount of knowledge in their field. In many institutions one may not obtain the rank of a full professor without having produced and published some meritorious research. This is not true in colleges where the greater emphasis is upon teaching; indeed, there has been in recent years a movement to increase the relative emphasis upon teaching so that the quality of teaching might be improved rather than neglected as is done by many college teachers who prefer to spend the greater share of their time on research or who are compelled to do so in order to obtain promotion to full professorship.

A very great amount of the knowledge available today in all fields has come about through research by members of college and university faculties, although in recent years the amount of money expended by industry and government in research has mushroomed greatly until now in some fields more research comes from those sources rather than from the efforts of college faculties.

## Field Service

Another area in which faculty members increasingly have worked in recent years has been what may be termed as field service. This takes on many forms, including extension courses; giving lectures at various places in the state or region; serving on the state or national committees; and acting as consultants to industrial, business, agricultural, educational, and political groups and agencies.

## Educational Experimentation

In recent years there has been carried on a great amount of experimentation with new and different ideas with respect to curriculum and with respect to teaching. It has taken a great variety of forms, including building courses around great national and world issues, the "Great Books" idea, work-study plans, special provision for the abler independent student, and the giving of courses by television.

## MAJOR PROBLEMS, ISSUES, AND TRENDS

For the last quarter-century, higher education in the United States and in many other countries has been in a state of excitement and ferment as the result of recognition for the need for improvement in the adjustment to the greatly increased and new types of student clientele, the great changes in life all about us in all fields, and in the great increase in the amount of knowledge as well as the discovery of the inaccuracy of much thought to be accurate knowledge in previous times.

In the following paragraphs, an attempt will be made to present a brief description of the major, more important problems, issues, and trends.

### Liberal vs. Specialized Education

As indicated previously in this chapter, there has been a trend for a great many years, as the colleges have increased and the universities have become larger, away from the broad, general, liberal education with much of it required for all students and with a minimum of electives for specialization.

This is a result of several developments such as:

1. The increase in emphasis being placed on college and university education as preparation for a profession or other vocation
2. The increased amount of knowledge available in each of a considerable number of fields and the consequent tendency of teachers in those fields to wish to make room for it by condensing or displacing class work in other fields.
3. The exaggerated importance that has been attached to "specialization" in American life

Naturally, the scientists have even greater difficulty in discussing their new knowledge and fields even with those in the humanities and with others. It was once said that Einstein said, perhaps facetiously, about a matter, "This scientific development is of such a complex nature that only God and I can understand it, and sometimes I am not too sure about Him."

C. P. Snow, the great English writer who is well trained both in the humanities and in the sciences, discussed that situation in a small book, *The Two Cultures and the Scientific Revolution*, in which he said, "Constantly I felt I was moving among two groups [scientists and writers] comparable in intelligence, identical in race, not grossly different in social origin, earning about the same income *who had almost ceased to communicate at all."*

## The Oversized University

Universities have become so large as to alarm many of the students of higher education, including presidents and deans as well as the faculty of these large universities. The belief is held by many that when a university gets to more than eight or ten thousand students, certain very definite values begin to be lost, for example, teaching suffers, individual personal relationships between student and teacher are lost, greater emphasis is placed upon research, and many problems of discipline and morality become greater. The outstanding university presidents of the early part of this century, for example, President Jordan of Stanford, President Harper of Chicago, President Angell of Michigan, and President Folwell of Minnesota, anticipated and advocated that as the university became larger, presumably more than eight or ten thousand students, it would drop the lower two years and permit junior colleges to take over in that area. Under pressure of alumni and ambitious faculty members and deans, presidents and boards of regents have permitted the universities to become unfortunately large.

President Clark Kerr of the University of California, which is one of the two largest universities in the United States, is very much interested in the problems of the "multiversity," and in an article in *Harper's Magazine* in November, 1963, suggests the strong possibility that the university be split up into units or colleges something like the schools-within-a-school plan of large senior high schools. Indeed, in California there is under way an experiment to set up a campus of some twenty different colleges somewhat like Oxford and Cambridge Universities in England.

## The Stake of American Society and That of the Individual Student

The individual attending a college or university has the greatest stake in his own education. Most people rate the monetary vocational objective at the top of the list of the reasons why they are in college. Nevertheless, the state and society also have very important stakes, particularly in state and municipal institutions. It follows naturally that these institutions have as one of their most important and fundamental obligations to give those people going through the institutions, paying only a fraction of the cost, training and education that will enable them to understand the problems of community, state, and nation, and to participate in a solution of them in an intelligent and effective way.

Furthermore, the institution has an obligation to the individual, which he or she may not fully recognize at the time, of preparing that individual for a much richer type of life; richer types of experiences; and richer enjoyment of leisure in at least several fields, including music, fine arts, literature, science, and others.

The following quotation supports the foregoing ideas:

> Human personality cannot, however, be broken up into distinct parts or traits. Education must look to the whole man. It has been wisely said that education aims at the good man, the good citizen, and the useful man. By a good man is meant one who possesses an inner integration, poise, and firmness, which in the long run come from an adequate philosophy of life. Personal integration is not a fifth characteristic in addition to the other four and coordinate wtih them; it is their proper fruition. The aim of liberal education is the development of the whole man; and human nature involves instincts and sentiments as well as the intellect.
>
> Two dangers must be mentioned. First there is the danger of identifying intelligence with the qualities of the so-called intellectual type—with bookishness and skill in the manipulation of concepts. We have tried to guard against this mistake by stressing the traits of relevant judgment and discrimination of values in effective thinking. Second, we must remember that intelligence, even when taken in its widest sense, does not exhaust the total potentialities of human nature.[5]

## Independent Study

In recent years, much more emphasis is being placed upon independent study on the part of the more capable, the more industrious, and the more interested and creative student. In the upper division of a large and increasing number of colleges and departments and schools in universities, special plans are being developed for honors courses and other types of study that put more responsibility upon the students, and give the students much more opportunity and responsibility for direction of their own learning activities.

## Special Programs

In very greatly increased numbers in recent years, the colleges have been developing and putting into operation special programs. One of the first of these was Antioch College at Yellow Springs, Ohio, which developed what is called the "work-study" and "the community program." Students' time is divided between study of subjects, work experience along some vocational lines, and experience in service to

[5] Harvard Committee, *General Education in a Free Society* (Cambridge, Mass.: Harvard University, 1945).

communities. That plan has been spreading somewhat in recent years and no doubt is followed in some form by some one hundred colleges.

Bennington College at Bennington, Vermont, has been successful in adapting entrance requirements so that they are not based entirely upon the grades made in high school or scores on college aptitude tests, but also include drive, sustaining power, independence and creativity, attitudes toward self and other people, genuineness of interest in college, and the validity of their interest in a school such as Bennington. They are interested particularly in getting women students who have or wish to develop particular talents or skills. The college year consists of three terms, two of which are spent in residence and one in non-resident work. While there are general broad requirements for graduation, there is great flexibility; and each student with the advice of a counselor draws up a program for herself. Many of the students work at least nine weeks in factories, stores, government and social agencies, research laboratories, hospitals, museums, and schools and offices.

Blackburn College at Carlinville, Illinois, also has a work-study program and devotes itself especially to the training of Presbyterian ministers.

Monteith College at Detroit, Michigan, is an autonomous unit of Wayne State University. This new college already has twelve hundred students who take basic courses in a four-semester sequence in natural science, a three-semester sequence in the sciences of society, a three-semester sequence in humanistic studies, and a two-semester integrated course for seniors. These courses are somewhat organized especially for this college, although much of the contents taught in similar courses in other colleges and universities is included. Logic and mathematics are included in the first semester course in natural science. The faculty advisor is called a *don*. While the student has considerable freedom, the *don* must approve variations that seem to be in the interest of the student, or disapprove those he thinks to be unsuitable. This plan also features individual conferences with the student at least once every two weeks. The college specializes in painting, sculpture, design, theater, dance, music, writing, and similar creative fields.

Stephens College at Columbia, Missouri, is an outstanding junior college for women. It has developed its program on the basis of a very careful analysis of the needs of the adult woman, and it attempts to prepare students for the three periods of later life—the period of working life, following graduation from college; the years of wifehood and motherhood; and the period that begins when the children are educated and gone from the home and she has time to pursue her own interests and make new contributions to society.

At Stephens courses are given in the field of consumer problems, child study, personal appearance, fashion design, marriage and the family, basic beliefs in human experience, communication, general biology, general humanity, and contemporary social issues. The school is not intended for preparation for the upper division, although students do transfer without loss of much credit.

### Year-Round Plans

In a small but increasing number, colleges and universities, in order to accommodate and graduate more students, have adopted four-quarter or trimester plans, enabling students to complete requirements for bachelor's degrees in three years.

With the gradual extension of the years of study required for degrees in medicine and law and for the Ph.D. degree in most fields, it is very desirable that young people with definite evidence of superior abilities should be graduated from high school not later than their seventeenth birthday, and that they should be able to enter a professional school or graduate school at the age of twenty. Otherwise, valuable years of their productive life are lost.

### Cooperative Plans

Cooperative programs have developed in some colleges in recent years. In general, it means the cooperation of a number of colleges that are located close to each other in the development of programs to be offered partly by one college and partly by another. A degree may be offered by one or both of the institutions, as at Vanderbilt University and the Peabody College of Teachers at Nashville, Tennessee. This plan enables the colleges to specialize somewhat and avoid distributing funds and faculty over too wide an area to be effective.

### Faculty and Student Exchanges

Stimulated especially by the passage of the United States Congress of legislation called the "Fulbright Act" which gave subsidies to carefully selected people who wished to teach and study abroad, students and faculty members from the United States have been going in increasingly larger numbers to other institutions of higher education in other countries. Likewise, a very great number of students and faculty members from other countries have come to us.

# PROFESSIONAL OPPORTUNITIES FOR TEACHERS IN HIGHER EDUCATION

## The Need for More Teachers

It is quite clear that there will be far more positions available for college teachers in the next few decades than there are competent teachers to fill them. Already there is a great shortage of college teachers, particularly in the fields of science, engineering, education, mathematics, and foreign languages, somewhat in that order. In 1964, there were approximately five million students enrolled in various types of institutions of higher education; it is estimated that by 1970 there will be six and a half million, by 1975 more than eight and a half million.

These additional three and a half million students together with the replacement of professors who retire because of ill health or age, or resign to accept other kinds of positions, and those who die will indicate a need for two hundred thousand additional college teachers. Approximately seventy-five thousand will be needed in junior colleges, twenty thousand in various types of professional schools and graduate departments, and the other one hundred thousand as teachers in undergraduate schools and colleges.

In 1963–1964, salaries for teachers in the four- and five-year colleges for the most part were between $6,000 and $10,000, with an average of about $7,800—in junior colleges about a thousand dollars less. These salaries are ·certain to go up for at least another quarter of a century, and it is very likely that by 1980 teachers in four- or five-year colleges will be employed at salaries for the most part between $7,500 to $12,000, with the average between $9,000 and $10,000 a year.

In universities, salaries vary greatly from institution to institution and with academic ranks. The great majority receive between $8,000 and $12,000, with many as high as $15,000. Salaries vary a great deal among colleges and universities; some small non-public colleges being at the bottom and some larger non-public universities like Harvard, Yale, and Chicago being at the top. Some state institutions, for example, New York, Illinois, and California, pay more than those located in the South and in North Dakota and South Dakota. To obtain a position in the stronger and better-paying colleges or to get beyond an instructorship in a university, a minimum of six years of college education is almost always required; and preference, of course, is made to people with a Ph.D. or Ed.D. degree. Most college and university presidents receive between $15,000 and $25,000, though a few receive as much as $40,000 or more.

## Other Rewards of College Teaching

College teaching is a vocational field much to be desired. The rewards are varied and many, including the following types:

1. *Professional advancement.* Promotion in rank; increase in salary; appointments to higher positions such as head of departments, deanship, presidency, etc., are possible.

2. *Security in the position and academic freedom.* In a large majority of colleges as well as universities, the college teacher may be quite confident with respect to his being continued in that position unless he becomes guilty of some flagrant violation of moral and professional code.

3. *Retirement and other fringe benefits.* The great majority of colleges now have funds for annual payments until death for former members of the faculty who have retired. These vary a great deal with respect to the number of years of status in the institution and with the financial resources of the institution. Funds for retirement have been materially increasing year by year in the United States until the typical college or university today is able to pay upon retirement an annual pension of between 40 and 50 per cent of the average salary received in the last few years of teaching.

4. *Leaves of absence.* The majority and an increasing number of colleges and universities now provide a sabbatical leave with at least half pay. The individual teacher after having taught six years in most colleges may be relieved of his duties for a year, or at least a semester, without loss of pay for purposes of travel, research, study, but ordinarily not for accepting another type of position. In many institutions, temporary leaves are usually available to individuals who wish to engage in some form of study, research, or employment related to his profession. Individuals not eligible for sabbatical leave or who do not want to utilize their privilege in that respect may obtain a leave on little or no pay. There are, of course, generous sick leaves available in most colleges.

5. *The joy of teaching and the association with young people.* While rewards of this sort vary a great deal from individual to individual, a great majority of college teachers enjoy very much their positions of importance and leadership in guiding young people through the upper levels of learning and their association with their students.

6. *Teaching load.* In many colleges and universities, the teaching load is light enough so that the individual teacher will have time to do an excellent job of preparation for his classes, for conferences with students, and other aspects of his work; and consequently there is indeed keen satisfaction and good morale resulting from the possibilities of doing high-quality work. In many institutions, the teaching load and other responsibilities are in need of reduction.

7. *Other benefits.* Among the other benefits might be mentioned the following, which are variable in a great many colleges and universities: reduced rate for medical expenses, accident insurance, hospitalization, life insurance, discounts on purchasing costs, loan funds, and recreational facilities. A definitely important advantage is the opportunity to live in a community with unusual cultural opportunities and one that is especially favorable for rearing children.

## Faculty Personnel Problems and Procedures

While there is considerable variation with respect to practice in the employment of members of the faculty of institutions of higher education, there is also considerable uniformity. The usual procedure is as follows: The department head very frequently with the cooperation of a committee of members of his staff submits to the dean of the college in which the department is located the name of the individual they wish to recommend (sometimes the procedure is to recommend two or three names). Unless the dean has good reason to do otherwise, he then passes on to the president the recommendation with his approval who unless he has good reason to withhold his approval submits it to the governing board.

In better colleges and universities, the possession of a doctor's degree, if not actually required for appointment, is necessary to obtain promotions or substantial increases in salary. The large majority of teachers in colleges and universities begin with the rank of instructor or assistant professor. Promotions depend upon teaching performance, research, and publication, in addition to possession of a doctorate.

The requirement of a doctor's degree is not necessary in schools of law, schools of medicine, and other professional schools with the exception of the school of business and the school of journalism. In these schools, the individual may have the appropriate professional degrees and outstanding experience accepted for qualifications rather than the doctor of philosophy degree. For example, in the school of medicine, the M.D. degree is always a requirement as usually is the completion of several years of successful practice. In schools of law, the best positions are frequently reserved for those having the doctor of jurisprudence degree.

In most colleges and universities, the faculty member has a permanent position; although in many institutions, the appointee must serve a period of years on probation before being given this status, which is spoken of as "permanent tenure." Tenure is to protect the individual not only in his academic freedom but from administrative caprice by his head of department or dean. Nevertheless, although many relatively incompetent college teachers are protected in their positions by tenure, it is generally regarded as a desirable protection from interference from off the campus. An individual who is outstandingly insubordinate, immoral, or of course incompetent may be dismissed upon action of the governing board, although this is usually avoided by pressuring the teacher to resign.

## ADULT AND CONTINUATION EDUCATION

### Need for Continuing Education

There are many types of students who need to take up education again after having not been in a formal institution for many years and some who need to continue their education beginning immediately after their dropping out of school.

Included in the first group are the following types of people:

1. Women who have brought up their children and now have more time on their hands and desire to know more, to live more richly, and to participate more intelligently in the citizenship and other social activities, and women who for one reason or another—divorced, death of the husband, or because of family expense—must prepare to become a breadwinner
2. Individuals who have become unemployed by reason of automation or other cause and need retraining for the particular industry in which they work or for another type of job entirely
3. Students who dropped out of school before preparing well for any vocation and after a few years of discouraging attempts to find satisfying employment have come to see the need for additional training
4. Individuals who realize that they do not understand or know much about the world or what is going on in it outside of their homes and who wish to carry on studies that will enable them to become more knowledgeable

5. Individuals who find either that they were inadequately prepared for leisure pursuits or that they were prepared for pursuits in which they are no longer able to participate

There are many young people who drop out of school before completing high school, or who after having completed high school become married or go to work or both rather than go to college, who should continue their education both along vocational and general education lines. But more and more of them have been staying in school in recent years as the futility of attempting to make a good living without continued education has become clear to everyone.

Adult education is not restricted to academic studies. (Yonkers, New York, Public Schools.)

## Beginnings of Adult Education

Adult and continuation education is not at all new, although it has grown and has changed greatly from the type of adult education that existed in the eighteenth and nineteenth centuries. In the eighteenth century, adults met in the churches and other places for discussion, particularly in town hall meetings in New England.

In the nineteenth century, lyceums and chautauquas were organized and conducted particularly in the New England and Middle State areas but later on in the Middle West and to a lesser extent in the South. Toward the end of the nineteenth century, various colleges and universities began to offer instruction to people who did not reside on the campus. For example, in the 1880's and the 1890's, many colleges and universities began to offer courses in cities other than the one in which the institution was located in which credit might be earned to count toward graduation as well as courses in which no credit was offered. About 1890, there was established a correspondence school at Ithaca, New York, later taken over by Cornell University. Soon thereafter a number of correspondence schools were established, including one that was very famous for several decades at Scranton, Pennsylvania—The International Correspondence School. This stimulated the colleges and universities to put in correspondence courses so that in the first few decades of the present century, correspondence divisions were developed in practically all the state institutions and in the majority of state colleges and independent universities.

## New Attitudes

Two sound statements relative to the need for adult education today were made by two very eminent university presidents as follows:

> Education should be a life-long process, not education in vocations and professions alone, but education for citizenship. Effective citizenship tomorrow will demand broader knowledge and deeper understanding than ever before.
>
> Education can at best only help a student lay the foundation on which he can afterwards build a life that is effective, rewarding, satisfying, and useful, whether judged from the personal point of view or that of the society of which he is a part.
>
> More than a hundred million dollars a year has been spent in the last few years on correspondence courses sold by proprietary schools. There is no reason why individuals wishing to have the equivalent of a secondary, or a vocational, or a college education should be put to such an expense in a nation which assumes a great responsibility for education of its future citizens.
>
> Several of these correspondence school concerns emphasize in their advertising that students may get their high school diploma and that their high school diploma is worth tens of thousands of dollars to them. Employment and personnel officers in business and industry as well as admission officers at colleges and universities attach little importance to the possession of correspondence high school diplomas and the student not only has

been deceived with respect to money spent on it but also with respect to time.[6]

When president of the University of California, Robert Gordon Sproul declared:

> Nothing has handicapped the American educational plan more than the tendency of American citizens to think of schooling as a kind of vaccination against ignorance, and to consider that a concentrated dose of it in youth makes one immune for a lifetime. Actually immunity lasts only a few years, and unless it is renewed by periodic inoculations in study and thinking, one falls victim to a chronic type of ignorance which is often more dangerous than the acute form, because the patient, incompetent to recognize the symptoms, doesn't know he has the disease. We meet such chronic sufferers from ignorance everywhere. They look all right on the outside . . . But inside, their minds are suffering from atrophy. Instead of thinking through problems in the light of all available facts, they merely supply a pattern of opinions based on facts that went out of date along with their yellowing diplomas, and liberally garnished with prejudices that have accumulated in their minds like broken furniture in an attic.[7]

### Types of Organization for Adult Education

As indicated previously, most of adult education is carried on through extension instruction and correspondence courses by institutions of higher education. Another very important type of provision for adult education is through schools in local communities and in schools where there are junior colleges; programs of adult education are taught largely by members of the faculty of the junior college. Where there is no junior college, courses are offered by high school teachers and others in the community. At first this was organized by the individual local high school. More recently where there is more than one senior high school, there has been set up a division of adult education in the city school system that has the responsibility of organization and management of courses for adults.

The old idea that adults of middle age and beyond cannot learn well has been pretty generally discredited. Whether or not it was ever true, certainly with increased opportunities and with increased health, the percentage of adults who cannot learn well has been found to be very small; and in the main those who do not do well are individuals who have gotten out of the habit of self-discipline necessary for study. With the increased adaptation of materials and methods of instruction for adult education courses, even many of these individuals have been able to get back into the groove and to profit from

[6] President John A. Hannah, Michigan State University, "Education for the Jet Age," *The Education Digest*, XXIX, No. 5 (January, 1964), 3.

[7] Robert Gordon Sproul, *Lifelong Learning*, XXI, No. 5 (May, 1940), p. 7.

courses. It is amazing that studies by psychologists have indicated that the power to learn declines very little with age until after sixty or seventy, and even then there is great variation among individuals.

Research proves that some individuals in their sixties and seventies not only can continue to learn, but they do learn in the formal college and university courses and receive degrees, some of them with high honors.

Art is fun for all ages. (Fresno, California, Public Schools.)

### Types of Adult Education Programs

A considerable variety of adult education programs has been developed for special purposes by various agencies. In addition to courses in literacy education for the purpose of developing sufficient literacy so that a person may qualify as a citizen of the United States and for voting, among these programs enrolling most students are the following:

The Army Literacy Program. The army has developed very successful programs of literacy training both for the purpose of developing literacy of inducted men and improving literacy among those who are barely able to pass the literacy test.

**Americanization Program.**  This has been extended beyond the bare literacy and involves knowledge of the elements of the United States Constitution as evidence of qualification for naturalization and receiving citizenship.

**Vestibule Education.**  Many industries and businesses have set up plans and programs for giving to their workers training in knowledge and skills and attitudes that are needed in the duties that they will perform in the industry or business and relative to which the new employee is not sufficiently well trained.  This type of education has been extended much in recent years as the nature of the activities in a great many jobs has changed with the passage of time and the incorporation of automation.

**Adult Clubs.**  Spreading widely has been the phenomenon of voluntary organization of clubs for discussion and learning among adults in communities in the United States.  With the increased amount of leisure time, the number of people participating in these clubs has increased rapidly and very greatly.  There are probably hundreds of these types of clubs.  Among the more important are The League of Women Voters, Business and Professional Women's Club, the Junior League, and the American Association of University Women.

**Alumni Education.**  As the result of the rapidly increasing amount of new knowledge, and techniques in medicine, law, dentistry, engineering, and business, there has developed what is frequently called a provision for alumni education in which graduates of various professional schools in the university are brought back for bringing their training up to date.  In recent years, however, this type of training is being given in metropolitan centers for doctors, lawyers, businessmen, dentists, and so on, who feel the need for catching up and keeping up with new knowledge and practices.

## QUESTIONS, PROBLEMS, AND PROJECTS FOR
## FOR FURTHER STUDY

1. How do you account for the great increase in college enrollments since 1945? Is this likely to continue? Do you believe that all or practically all boys and girls should have some education beyond the twelfth grade?

2. Do you think the junior college or community college as it is called in many places should be primarily for preparing students to go on with

their college work, to prepare them for jobs, or to give them general education even though they may not go on for further education?

3. What do you think the technical institute is, and do you believe that there should be many more technical institutes, or should they be replaced by junior colleges?

4. How do you account for the fact that so many college professors seem determined to have young people specialize in their work for the bachelor's degree rather than to see that they get a good general comprehensive liberal education?

5. Do you believe that professional schools such as law, medicine, engineering, pharmacy, and education should all have as an entrance requirement at least two, preferably three, years of general liberal education? Do you believe that the years spent in a liberal arts college should be spent in pursuing courses that are not so much for liberal education as for preparation for the professional school in which the student will go?

6. What is your opinion of the degree of liberal education that is possessed by the typical engineer? Typical doctor? Typical teacher? Typical lawyer?

7. In the five-year program for the preparation of secondary school teachers, what proportion of the five years of study should be given to a subject field? A general education? Professional education?

8. What courses in professional education do you think should be required of secondary school teachers?

9. What courses in professional education do you think should be required of elementary school teachers?

10. Dr. J. B. Conant, in his treatise on the education of teachers, advocated the practice of letting each institution certificate its graduates, and he was opposed to having any national accrediting association set standards for institutions educating teachers. What in your mind are the strong points and the weak points in this position?

11. Bitter complaints have been made that the graduate schools tend to prepare people for research, but that they do not make any definite preparation for the education of college teachers. What is your opinion?

12. Do you believe that college enrollments can continue to increase without lowering of the standards of quality in the schools? How if at all could this be done?

13. Do you believe that liberal arts colleges should have the same curriculum and requirements for graduation for men and for women?

14. There are great differences among colleges and universities with respect to the academic ability of the student body and their entrance requirements. Do you think it is bad or good?

15. There have been those who have insisted that colleges and universities should not spend money on separate counseling and guidance services, but that the counselors in a subject-matter department, the dean of men or the dean of women, and the health service can do all the counseling that is necessary. What is your opinion?

16. Billions of dollars have been given in recent years to both private and public universities to finance research carried on by members of the faculty. What are the good features and the bad features of this?

17. What do you think should be done about a trend toward very large universities?

18. Tuition for students has gone up tremendously, being five to ten times as much in some institutions as it was a half-century ago. What is one of the unfortunate effects of this great increase in cost to the students, and what do you think ought to be done about it?

19. Does the prospect of teaching in college appeal to you? If not, why not?

20. Quite often recently, people have made statements that education in the United States is moving toward a situation where it will begin at the cradle and stop only at the grave. Does this seem to be true? What advantages or disadvantages would accrue from such a trend?

21. Do you believe that adult education should be at public expense, or that those who receive adult education should pay for it? Maybe you will have a different answer for different types of adult education.

## SELECTED SUPPLEMENTARY READINGS AND FILM

BROWN, JAMES W., and THORNTON, JAMES W., JR. "Preparing To Teach." In *College Teaching: Perspectives and Guidelines.* New York: McGraw-Hill Book Co., Inc., 1963. Pp. 105–32.

EDUCATIONAL POLICIES COMMISSION, *Universal Opportunities for Education Beyond the High School.* Washington, D.C.: National Education Association. A report pointing out the need for and the probability of providing close-to-home two years of education beyond high school graduation.

————. "Higher Education," *Education in American Society.* Boston: Houghton Mifflin Co., 1961. Pp. 241–80.

HILLWAY, TYRUS. "Cooperative and Adult Education," *The American Two-Year College.* New York: Harper & Row, 1958. Pp. 117–41.

LITCHFIELD, EDWARD H. "Colleges *Can* Operate All Year," *Saturday Review,* XLV, No. 50 (December 15, 1962), 50–55. Plans for year-round operation.

MEDSKER, LELAND L. *The Junior College: Progress and Prospect.* New York: McGraw-Hill Book Co., Inc., 1960. Chaps. ii–iv and viii. A comprehensive discussion of the purposes of the public junior college, its curriculum, and growth in the United States.

RADCLIFFE, SHIRLEY A., and HATCH, WINSLOW R. "Advanced Standing," *New Dimensions in Higher Education,* U.S. Office of Education. Bulletin No. 8. Washington, D.C.: Government Printing Office, 1961. Pp. 24.

ROGERS, FRANCIS M. *Higher Education in the United States: A Summary View.* 3d ed. Cambridge: Harvard University Press, 1960.

Rosecrance, Francis C. *The American College and Its Teachers.* New York: The Macmillan Co., 1962. Pp. 27–56, 87–104, and 105–37. Purposes, types, and new plans.

Taylor, Harold. "On the Education of Women." In *On Education and Freedom.* New York: Abelard-Schuman, 1954, pp. 165–203.

## Film

*Adult Education.* 19 minutes. Depicts night classes and activities attended by adults at Bryant School, Woodside, Long Island. Arts and crafts, mathematics classes, shop courses, and other activities are pictured. Students in a public-speaking course describe the benefits of adult education. New York: United World Films, Inc.

# 11

# THE SCOPE AND TYPES
# OF SCHOOL SERVICES

## GREAT DEVELOPMENTS IN RECENT DECADES

There are many important services rendered by schools today that were unthought of or at least not in existence at the beginning of the century, even some time later in many schools. For example, at that time in a four-year high school in a county seat town in Missouri, population 4,000, there was no library and only a very primitive laboratory that served all the science courses. There was no auditorium; and when a meeting of all the students was called, it was held in a large study hall. Classes were held in the front of this same study hall most of the day, while students studied in the back section.

There was no cafeteria or food service, and most of the students walked back and forth for lunch the year around; some brought their lunch with them, especially when the weather was bad, and it was eaten at school; a few walked downtown a half-mile away to a restaurant usually to get soup, a sandwich, and a piece of pie. There was no transportation; most of the students walked to school and back home, covering a distance of up to 3 miles. A few rode horseback, and a few others came by horse and buggy.

There were no clubs or student activities except two literary societies, to one of which each student was compelled to belong and to perform once a year at a program during the last hour of school on Friday afternoon. Eventually, a football team and a baseball team were organized, but there was no coach except an encouraging mathematics teacher who had never played football and very little baseball. The student manager of the team scheduled all the games and took care of all business matters with some help from members of the team.

Guidance and counseling as a technical service were as yet unheard of; although almost every teacher attempted to render counseling service, some of which was quite valuable. There were no physical or health checkups or records, nor was there any immunization of children against contagious diseases—only the barring of children from the school who came from homes where a serious contagious disease was known to exist. If several cases of smallpox developed in the community, all students were required to give evidence of having been vaccinated against it.

The public schools of the United States have in a half-century come a long way in extending the scope and improving the quality of services to their students and to the community.

### Equipment and Supplies

In practically all junior and senior high schools and in the majority of elementary schools, there are provided laboratory facilities of some sort. These in the senior high school include benches, tables, and equipment and materials for individual laboratory training; and in the junior high school and elementary schools, materials that permit demonstration by teachers and students and possibly some individual small group experimentation.

Also, in practically all senior and junior high schools, there are provided shops for various kinds of arts and crafts and vocational education and materials that are sold at cost and often at much less than cost to students who are unable to pay for them. In these schools, there has come to be a great deal of expensive equipment that students use at no expense to themselves.

Similarly, in home economics there will be found in junior and senior high schools and to a limited extent in elementary schools a great variety of equipment particularly related to preparation of foods and clothing construction and repair. In most schools, too, there is provided, and usually below cost, materials for use in these home economics laboratories.

In business education, services usually include typewriters for which little or no rental is charged and in many schools a variety of business machines.

## COUNSELING AND PLACEMENT SERVICES

From the very beginning, teachers have given young people advice and attempted to inspire them and to assist them in solving their problems. Particularly in recent decades, this has become recognized as a very important guidance and counseling service that the school can render its students. This is done by teachers, sponsors of activity groups, and administrators; and in recent decades, there has been added to the staffs of schools, including elementary schools in recent years, individuals who are trained especially in guidance and counseling and who spend full time or a majority of their time in individual and group guidance, including conferences with students and conferences with parents.

In many homes today, both mother and father are working, and children have developed a social life that requires a considerable amount of time, to say nothing of a large amount of time spent viewing television. Along with the disappearance of the necessity of young people working in the home alongside mother and father, this development has increased the desirability of providing guidance services by someone outside the home. Since the lines of communication between parents and young people are not as great and not as naturally available as in former generations, the opportunities and responsibilities of the schools have increased greatly.

## Types of Guidance Services

The principal areas of guidance and counseling service have expanded, including today a variety of types of counseling and guidance, as indicated in the following list of types served.

1. Vocational guidance
   a. Furnishing the pupil with knowledge of occupation, particularly relating to rewards, conditions of employment; opportunities for advancement, and requirements for entrance to, and success in, occupations.
   b. Furnishing the pupil with opportunities to discover and reveal to himself his general and special capacities and aptitudes, his interests, and his traits of personality and character as related to vocational life.
   c. Furnishing the pupil with a point of view and a method of study of occupations which will assist him in making his vocational decisions.

2. Educational guidance
   a. Furnishing the pupil counsel and the opportunity to discover his interests, abilities, and capacities in various studies.
   b. Furnishing counsel as to what studies will contribute best to the realization of his probable vocational and educational plans and where such studies may be best pursued.
   c. Providing courses of study adapted to the abilities of atypical children, as well as guidance in electing such courses.
   d. Furnishing pertinent information concerning the possibility and de-

sirability of further schooling and stimulating the pupil to consider these carefully.

e. Acquainting the pupil with the curricular and extracurricular opportunities of the school and with conventions relative to the life and management of the school.

f. Acquainting the pupil with the opportunities and methods of using the school library most effectively.

3. Leisure or avocational guidance

a. Providing opportunities, curricular and extracurricular, for the pupil to discover or develop tastes and interests which will provide avenues or fields of reflection, enjoyment, and recreation and thus make life more worth while to the individual and the individual more worth while to society.

4. Moral and social guidance

a. Furnishing counsel, example, and learning situations in private conference, in the classroom, or by means of extracurricular activity which will contribute to the development of right ideals and habits of conduct and living.

b. Furnishing opportunities for training in extracurricular group situations, which will result in information, attitudes, habits, and abilities which will contribute to the tendency and ability to work and play effectively with other people with satisfaction—as leader, follower, or colleague—in the home, in school, at work, or at play.

c. Furnishing training in correct social conventions.

d. Developing adjustments to other people, particularly young people of both sexes of the pupil's own age.

5. Health guidance

a. Providing situations which will call attention to any infirmities, defects, or tendencies that should be corrected or removed.

b. Developing an interest in health and in a strong, healthy body.

c. Developing interest, habits, and skills in games and other activities which will operate to promote health.

d. Assisting the pupil to develop sound mental and emotional health and hygiene, partly through expert counseling in this field.

6. Miscellaneous personal guidance services

a. Providing, under favorable conditions, hints or suggestions that are likely to make for improvement of personal appearance and traits of personality.

b. Providing advice and counsel on personal problems of all sorts which the boy or girl may desire to receive: sex problems, problems of family relationships, etc.

c. Providing the inspiration and encouragement which come from personal interest of an older individual who "understands" and is "interested."

7. Military-service guidance

a. Assisting the boy in senior high school to become informed about his responsibility for military service.

    b. Assisting the boy in senior high school to understand the nature of and the opportunities in the various armed forces.

    c. Assisting the boy to approach the problem of deciding what time in his life to give the required military service.[1]

Because of the small amount of time available for the professional education of prospective teachers, most of them go out into the schools poorly prepared to do some of the duties assigned them, especially counseling. Teachers need to know what are the types of problems with which they are prepared to cope, and they need to refrain from attempting to give counseling service in areas and on problems in which they are not competent to advise. They need to be trained to make use of referrals.

Since the beginning teacher usually assumes his first year of teaching without any adequate preparation for counseling, he should obtain immediately a book on guidance and counseling at the level at which

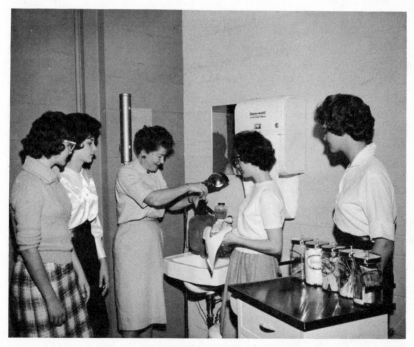

School services often supplement learning. (Dwight D. Eisenhower High School, Blue Island, Illinois.)

[1] Harl R. Douglass, *Modern Administration of Secondary Schools*, 1963, pp. 262–63. Reprinted through the courtesy of Blaisdell Publishing Co., a Division of Ginn & Co., New York.

he is to teach; i.e., the elementary school, the junior high school, or the senior high school. There are excellent books available at each of these levels. Quite early in his teaching career, a young teacher should take at least one course in counseling and guidance in summer school. In addition to counseling individuals in most secondary junior and senior high schools today, the teacher has responsibilities and opportunities for service in connection with group guidance if he is given responsibility for homeroom, core programs, large block teaching, or sponsorship of extrasubject student activities.

### Placement and College Admission Services

Most four-year high schools and senior high schools now operate a placement service that assists students, graduates, and dropouts, to obtain positions. Usually counseling goes along with the conferences in connection with placement. Many junior and senior high schools render service in assisting young people to get jobs while in school and summer jobs, operating a placement bureau for that purpose. In most schools today, there is at least one counselor who uses the opportunities he has in assisting students to get employment and to give counseling and advice, particularly in connection with planning for future education and selection of a vocation.

High school principals furnish to colleges and universities complete records of their seniors who apply for admission. In recent years, the school also sends along to college admission officers and counselors useful information about their schools as indicated in the following statement from a large Midwest school.

NEW TRIER TOWNSHIP HIGH SCHOOL

WINNETKA, ILLINOIS

William H. Cornog, *Superintendent*

*INFORMATION FOR COLLEGE ADMISSIONS COUNSELORS*

*School*

New Trier is a comprehensive Chicago suburban high school of 4687 students—grades 9 to 12. It is governed by its own Board of Education and serves six underlying elementary public school districts which also have their own Boards. Parents of the community are in large proportion college graduates with a high percentage of business executives and professional people. There is a strong public school tradition and support.

*Faculty*

318 certificated members—the great majority with master's degrees and beyond. Average teaching experience about 12 years—one-third over 20

years. One certificated faculty member to each 15 students. Typical teacher load 4 classes of 26 each and one adviser room.

### Student Leadership and Responsibility

Student organizations operate over 90% of study halls, administer honor system on examinations, provide traffic controls, ushers, lunch hall supervision, and many other services.

After-school activities are largely student operated and include athletics, publications, drama, music, student council, boys' and girls' clubs, student opera, talent show, service groups, and special interest clubs—all of which develop student responsibility and leadership through direction and participation.

Effective parental cooperation is notable in all student and faculty affairs.

### Subject Level Grouping

We have practiced ability grouping for 40 years. Basically there are four groups in academic subjects: superior, 15-20%; above average, 50-55%; normal, 25-30%; limited, 2-3%. Advanced placement classes are regarded as fifth group. Student may work at different levels in different subjects. Grades in each level are based on the work required in that level.

### Class Rank—Weighted Average

In computing senior class rank $A = 4$, $B = 3$, $C = 2$, $D = 1$, on the normal level. On other ability levels values weighted by following multipliers: Advanced placement (for courses in the senior year only)—1.8; superior—1.5; above average—1.2; limited—.8.

### Guidance

Comprehensive guidance—157 advisers on a one-fifth time basis; eight adviser chairmen (class deans) and a dean of students; three full time college counselors; eight school social workers; a psychologist; a test director; a vocational counselor; two reading consultants.

## OTHER TYPES OF SERVICES

### Extrasubject Activities

In no other country are equal provisions made for assisting students to develop valuable qualities such as leadership and fellowship, developing and extending interests, habits, and skills in group effort, and other attributes for which study of the subjects taken leaves much desirable educational growth to be stimulated and guided.

Schools in the United States provide housing space and qualified sponsors and guides for from eight or ten to upwards of forty different extrasubject organizations and activities. The role of the teacher in this area of service was discussed in Chapter 1.

### Transportation

With the increased size of school districts as the result of the consolidation of small districts into larger ones and as the size of population has increased the size of cities, there has developed in every section of the country planned systems and services for transportation of students who live beyond easy walking distance, usually about three-fourths mile for elementary school pupils and two miles for senior high school pupils. Except on a very small scale in a few countries, public transportation in school buses is available only in the United States.

### Health, Safety, and Food Services

Even in the small, rural school and even in impoverished areas, schools are rendering valuable service in connection with matters of health, involving in the great majority of them periodic if not annual routine health and physical examinations and every few years a somewhat more thorough examination by a physician. From the results of these examinations, reports are sent home to parents, particularly in cases where the physical condition of the child should be remedied and where there is reason to believe that the parents are not aware of the situation or of the significance of it. In many school systems, there is opportunity for immunization at nominal cost against influenza, polio, smallpox, and several other contagious diseases.

The school has also assumed in recent decades much more responsibility for the health of the students involving prevention of accidents in the school, on the playground, on the schoolbuses, and in the neighborhood of the school. School authorities are very active in getting traffic regulations in the neighborhood of the school that tend to be of a protective nature. School sites are selected today very definitely with a view to safety.

At the beginning of the century, there were very few schools providing food service for students. It has within the last few decades become to be the regular thing that the secondary schools and a great many of the elementary schools provide warm food for sale at cost or even less than cost. Even in many elementary schools, cafeterias are being provided and in the smaller ones some sort of lunchroom. The federal government is of much assistance in this connection by supplying at very low cost to the schools for lunches materials and foods from the surplus that the government has accumulated in food products in an effort to prevent undue lowering of prices for foods generally.

The National School Lunch Program made approximately 2.7 billion

Today's schools sustain the body as well as the mind and the spirit. (Atlanta Public Schools.)

lunches available in 1963. The lunches were eaten by 16 million children in 68,000 schools throughout the nation. Approximately 10 per cent were served to needy children at free or reduced rates.

By having lunch at school, not only is the school able to operate with more of the day given to educational activities, but many parents are relieved of their responsibility for the preparation of food, and the children are not subjected to the hazards of the journey home and back at lunchtime. Furthermore, through the food service, there is some control of diet, which in the case of many youngsters is a distinct improvement in the possibility for good health. Another side effect of the school lunch program is the development of ideals and habits of good table and dining-room manners.

## Provision of Housing for Community Meetings

In most communities today, school buildings are available to the community for various kinds of civic and other community meetings for which there are not appropriate buildings. In many communities this is a great saving in the matter of costs of building construction and maintenance.

It is true that the school authorities have a problem in connection with decisions relative to permission to use school buildings for various purposes. In the first place, they must decline permission to some individuals or organizations who wish to use the school for purposes for which the community would not approve. Profit-making organizations should be charged a fee, and this requires some clear thinking, and in many instances courage. In most districts the board of education has adopted a sliding scale of fees, ranging all the way from a very nominal fee confined to costs of lighting and janitorial service on up to a fee that would be of a magnitude charged by a non-public organization for renting a building. The size of the fee is set in view of the purpose and nature of the organization or individual requesting permission.

In many ways the school exerts a cultural influence on the community, not only on the children who bring into the homes cultural interests and attainments, but through the types of cultural programs that the school is able to sponsor and to admit the public, including of course plays and musical entertainments put on by the students and members of the faculty but also in connection with television programs and with speakers, musicians, and artists whom they bring in from outside.

### Home-School Contacts

In the majority of schools today, there is provided at least some type of home visitation. Often, this has to do with guidance and counseling and with conferences about problem children; but it also has to do with reporting to parents about the progress of their children in school. In some instances, it has to do with the problem of the health of the child. In many schools today, teachers are required to hold an office hour at least once or twice a month, if not once a week, and to inform the parents about the hours so that conferences may be held at school on such subjects.

In recent years, an increasing number of elementary school teachers, early in the fall, have made it a point to visit the homes of each of their pupils; or parents have accepted an invitation sent to the home to call on the teacher at a designated office hour. While appointments are not generally considered necessary, they may save time in the case of working mothers. Some teachers prefer to call by appointment in the evening when both parents are at home.

Reported in the March, 1964, issue of *It Starts in the Classroom*,[2] a teacher at Stevens Elementary School in Aberdeen, Washington, visited the home of each of her thirty-nine students. Her decision to go unannounced proved successful. She found that making appointments meant delays and allowed the mother to worry.

Schools today also provide people in the community with a variety of types of public information about the schools—its programs, its problems, its opportunities, and changes in its plans. In many schools there is sent home to parents periodically some sort of bulletin, either printed or mimeographed information of one or more of these types. In practically all communities, the local school system operates some sort of publicity release source giving information about the school, its problems, its programs, its achievements, and the achievements of the students through local newspapers.

## Additional Community Services

Schools render many other services to the community, including preparation of skilled workers in business, in shops, and salespeople; in spreading information concerning activities of the government in connection with business, the draft, and armed services; and in publicizing scientific knowledge that may be applied to problems of production and distribution of consumer goods.

It has also been brought out several times by the U.S. Chamber of Commerce and many educational agencies that education increases the productive and consumer capacities of the people. The U.S. Chamber of Commerce has pointed out that:

1. Education is an essential instrument through which commerce, industry, and agriculture can be expanded. A rather close relationship was found between the amount of educational attainments and retail sales, income, magazine circulation, and salaries paid various workers.

2. Regardless of the abundance of natural resources, there is evidence both in the United States and abroad that economic well-being reflects a high level of education.

3. Since education has been and should continue to be a local function —at least on the state level—every community exerts itself to utilize education as a lever for its own advancement and should join in a state program for similar advancement.

4. The cost of adequate education is an investment that local citizens and business can well afford in increased measure, when related step by step to the improvement of local economic conditions.

2 Published by the National School Public Relations Association, a department of the National Education Association, Washington, D.C.

5. The quality of education is not the same in all areas. Educational programs must be made to apply more directly to the needs of the people.

6. Mere technical education is not enough. Cultural education must accompany technical training to develop the appetite of the people for better living.

## SERVICES TO THE NATION AND ITS PEOPLE

In many ways schools serve the people of the nation, including the following:

1. The preparation of men and women physically fit for national defense
2. Improving knowledge of the fundamentals of reading, writing, and arithmetic so that they may discharge their responsibilities in the armed forces
3. Providing understanding of various scientific things related to national defense
4. In developing patriotism and a spirit of cooperation

In every community schoolteachers and school administrators are always among those most active in various types of civic enterprises and community improvement projects. It should be recognized, too,

Hobbies and individual interests are important to the teacher. (Mount Vernon School Library, Newark, New Jersey.)

that perhaps among the best informed, the most and least biased citizens and leaders of the community are those employed in its public schools.

The nature and importance of the service of schools to the nation was set forth in the following excerpts from an unpublished address given at Harvard University, July 14, 1960, by a former Secretary of Defense and very successful businessman, Neil McElroy, whose theme was "Education Is the Key Weapon."

In our relatively short history, we have made remarkable progress— progress to which many factors have contributed. We think of our natural resources, the characteristics we have developed as a people, the system that encourages initiative, and the incentive inherent in our kind of society. These are essential elements in the story of our growth.

But there is another of pervasive importance. It supports all of these. It gives vitality and purpose to each of them. It is at the heart of all we have done—all we hope to do.

It is our American system of education.

If our educational system functions at or near its optimum, our nation will thrive and grow. If we allow this system to fail to achieve its potential, we must expect to decline as a free society.

Our people have not only willed the growth of education but have taxed themselves to finance it. They have done this by free determination. In education, as in all else of importance, we have forged our decisions in the fire of public opinion.

By contrast, public debate is unknown in the authoritarian system. The state sets the norms and directs every resource—including the lives of its people—toward their accomplishment. As skills are needed by the state, education serves as the tool to produce them. The only choice for the individual is a dictated choice.

The ruthless efficiency of the pragmatic approach of the U.S.S.R. destroys any grounds for complacency on our part. However, although we may despise this system, we must recognize the intensity of its competition with our own. And as you know, you do not beat a competitor simply by deploring him, but by outdoing him.

Education is the source of our economic strength. If we are to succeed, we must continue to apply technological advances widely, and bring these to bear in the form of efficient production and broad distribution of goods and services. We must constantly sharpen our management techniques. Greater employee skills at all levels of industry will be essential.

The urgency of our needs for economic and military defense, however, should never lead us to compromise our concept of education. Solutions based purely on expediency could never have brought us to our present position.

Our purpose goes far beyond the sufficient supply of technically capable people. The opportunities of a free society are many and complex. We shall take advantage of them only as our education develops broadly, in all fields of human knowledge.

This is education that can equip future generations for greater participation in both the responsibilities and rewards of our society. Moreover, it will bring the greatest satisfaction to the largest number of people.

We must develop talented leaders in every field of activity. We shall need many people prepared to guide the evolution of an expanding economy: able, thoughtful, dedicated educators, writers, politicians and diplomats, clergymen, businessmen, labor leaders and legislators. All will be essential, and all will be capable to the extent of the quality of the educational system which produces them.

We must have a citizenry able to cope with increasingly complex issues. Our people must be familiar with the development of our free society, so that they may apply the critical lessons of the past to problems of the present.

We must have an electorate which recognizes the need to participate in political activities—an electorate that, by virtue of its intelligence and courage, can make the wisest and soundest decisions.

When national leaders talk, our people must be able to grasp the matters presented and relate them to an effective course of action.

Obviously, the further development of our educational system, to gear it for such demanding needs, is a responsibility of our entire society.

Parents, clergymen and national leaders all have a part. But it is in the school—in an atmosphere that encourages learning and stimulates young minds to inquire—that constant, day-by-day progress can best be made and where the early groundwork can best be prepared.

The nature of the educational process inevitably means that the already heavy burden of responsibility borne by our educators will be increased. It will involve not only rising enrollments, but the utter necessity of giving each young man and young woman his best opportunity to realize on his own capacity. It will concern the importance in both the private and the national interest that every individual participate in our society to the fullest extent of his ability and effort.

These goals, of course, are well known to you, but you will agree that still today we are seeing an appalling waste of youthful talent. We are familiar with the fact that too many young people who do not go to college are entirely qualified to do so. It is impossible to assess the loss to the nation through our failure to cultivate their intelligence and abilities. Certain it is that a measure of our future progress will be our success in devising means to encourage and to enable them to seek higher levels of attainment.

Most importantly, the educational system faces the responsibility of providing highly capable *leaders* for the most efficient functioning of our nation in every branch of its activity, in every walk of life.

The guidance at an early age of gifted young people into channels of their special aptitudes will increase their capacity to give true leadership—intellectual and cultural, as well as economic and military. This will be invaluable to the free world over the years ahead. We cannot afford to waste or to use ineffectually a single mind of leadership quality.

We are in a great, long-range struggle to determine whether our free society shall survive.

In this struggle, the basic source of our strength lies in the education of our people.

## QUESTIONS, PROBLEMS, AND PROJECTS FOR
## FURTHER STUDY

1. There are those who insist that the school has gone much too far in rendering certain types of services for students and the community and that it should have stuck to its original purpose of classroom instruction. What is your position in this matter? If you believe that some of the services should be very greatly diminished or omitted, which ones do you suggest?

2. After a careful review of the types and areas of guidance service, which ones listed under the seven different heads do you think are most important for senior high school, and which most important for junior high school?

3. Which guidance services are least important for senior high school, and which for junior high school?

4. What are the additional guidance services that are not mentioned in this chapter that you think are important?

5. How do you account for the fact that most colleges set up their entrance requirements in terms of the accumulation of credit in certain preferred fields such as mathematics, science, and foreign languages when it has been shown over and over by careful reliable research that grades made in college are correlated only to a very small degree with the subjects taken in high school?

6. Do you believe that each high school should furnish every college to which a student goes with a statement such as that furnished by the New Trier Township High School of Winnetka, Illinois, or do you believe that is carrying it too far?

7. What use would college admission authorities make of such information that is contained in the New Trier Township High School statement?

8. Do you believe that transportation of students to public schools is a service that ought to be extended also to students attending non-public schools? If you believe that it should, on what basis should it be organized?

9. How do you think a health program at public schools, including physical examinations, reports to parents, etc., at taxpayers expense can be justified? Do you believe that school children should be immunized against contagious diseases without cost to the student or parents?

10. What is your reaction to the requirement of many schools that all students eat their lunch at school? Do you believe they should be required to patronize the school cafeteria or that they should be permitted to bring their own lunch with them?

11. What is wrong with the practice followed by some schools of letting such students who want to go home for lunch to do so?

12. In some communities that are of very low cultural and economic status, particularly those in large cities, there has been provided through public funds special services that involve having youngsters in the schools with special help and after school hours and on Saturdays and having the parents come to the school and participate in and enjoy some of the ad-

vantages of the school. While this seems to go a long ways in solving the problems of juvenile delinquency, dropouts, etc., there are conservative taxpayers who insist that schools are going into areas for which they were not established and that this is a type of socialism. What is your reaction?

13. To what extent do you think that the schools should plan their program so as to make various types of valuable contributions to national security and national welfare rather than pattern them entirely upon improving the student for his own benefit?

14. Evaluate the statement made in 1960 by the then Secretary of Defense Neil McElroy.

## SELECTED SUPPLEMENTARY READINGS AND FILMS

BUNDESEN, HERMAN N., and BERGMANN, JOHN C. "A Dental Health Program in a Large Mid-West School System," *American Journal of Public Health* (March, 1955), 67–71.

COX, PHILIP W. L., and MERCER, BLAINE E. *Education in Democracy: The Social Foundations.* New York: McGraw-Hill Book Co., Inc., 1961. Part VI, chap. xviii.

KLAUSMEIER, HERBERT J. *Teaching in the Secondary School.* New York: Harper & Row, 1958. Chap. xv.

MILLS, HUBERT H., and DOUGLASS, HARL R. *Teaching in High School.* 2d ed. New York: The Ronald Press Co., 1957. Chap. xxvi.

THOMAS, LAWRENCE G., KINNEY, LUCIEN B., COLADARCI, ARTHUR P., and FIELSTRA, HELEN A. "What Is the Role of Guidance in Education?" In *Perspective on Teaching.* Englewood Cliffs, N.J.: Prentice-Hall, Inc., 1961. Pp. 89–111. A scholarly analysis.

YEAGER, WILLIAM. *Administration of the Non-instructional Personnel and Services.* New York: Harper & Row, 1959. Chaps. xiv, xv, and xvii.

### Films

*Crises in Education.* 34 frames, filmstrip. Reviews the significant causes of the critical problems facing educators in the public schools in the United States. Detroit: Wayne State University.

*Schools.* 33 frames, filmstrip, color. Points out that instead of lunchrooms, libraries and gymnasiums, the early settlers' children had to sit on benches and write on birchbark with goose-feather pens and homemade ink. Today's schoolchildren learn about the world, they learn to think, and they have teachers who help them to work alone and with others. Detroit: International Visual Education Services, Inc.

# IV

# ORGANIZATION AND MANAGEMENT OF THE AMERICAN EDUCATIONAL SYSTEM

# 12

# EDUCATION AND GOVERNMENT:
# THE LOCAL SCENE

There is literally no such thing as an American educational system
in the sense of a unified, coordinated scheme with a minister in the
national government at its head.  One of the truly distinguishing characteristics of education in the United States is its high degree of decen-
tralization.  Some writers use the term "dispersal of powers" to indicate
the extensive participation of the states and of local school districts in
every aspect of educational service.  In addition to public education,
there are many schools and institutions of higher education that are
under religious and other non-public auspices.

All these efforts collectively are called the American educational
system.  It is the purpose of this chapter and the next to explain how
the whole thing is organized and administered, how it hangs together.
The third chapter in this series of three deals with the physical setting
of educational programs—the buildings, equipment, and grounds as
they are, and the directions in which they seem to be evolving.

## THE SCHOOL AS A COMMUNITY INSTITUTION

The concept of the school as a distinctively local enterprise has been
held tenaciously by Americans since the early Colonial period.  Colonial (and later, state) legislatures enacted the laws by which towns
were required to provide schools, as noted in Chapter 5, thereby exercising authority over the local units in the field of education.  However, long before the end of the Colonial period and continuing at a
faster pace through half of the nineteenth century, the legislative bodies
delegated more and more duties and powers to local school officials.
Thus, the real relationship to state government of school districts at
the local level tended to be blurred or lost sight of.  Towns and cities
and even one-room school districts came to be thought of as pretty

much in control, under only general regulation and supervision, of state government.

## Proliferation of Districts

During his distinguished service as secretary of the Massachusetts state board of education, 1837–1849, Horace Mann came to the conclusion that the proliferation of districts had gotten so bad that it was the worst condition in the country's whole educational structure. Ironically, this had occurred in an effort to bring schooling within reach of families living in scattered small villages or sparsely settled farm lands, in a period when roads and the means of transportation were very poor or lacking. But by 1850, the process had gone so far in all the northern states that it had become a real detriment to progress. In the South, counties were the main political subdivision of the states; the plantation system was not conducive to the creation of many small units. Down through the years, nearly all the southern and "border" states have continued this practice, the county in this case being the local or basic school district.

Mann's condemnation of the "small-district system" did not suffice to curb it. The westward movement of population and the admission of many new states west of the Mississippi naturally led to the creation of thousands of new local school districts. So it was a good eighty years later before the upward climb finally took a downward turn. This is reserved for some further discussion near the end of the chapter.

Henry Barnard, one of Mann's contemporaries and the first U.S. commissioner of education (1867), once said, "The schools are the people's own work." By this he meant to emphasize the closeness of their schools to citizens' interests, and the fact that citizens could fashion the schools in any way they wished by their financial and moral support. While Barnard referred to the public schools, his pronouncement was equally applicable to non-public schools; and it is just as valid today as it was a hundred years ago.

## The "Community School" Concept

In our time the word "community" has taken on hitherto unheard of meanings. When we speak of a "community school" or the school as a "community institution," we usually mean a neighborhood school, or a school or school system serving one town or city. Yet we often hear such phrases as "Atlantic Community," "European Economic Community," even "world community." These extensions of the original meaning are used to focus attention on common interests, but they do not fit the concept under discussion in this chapter. However, it must be admitted that communities served by individual schools or school systems are becoming larger and ever more complex, as the population grows and becomes more urban and more mobile. The former relatively simple and stable idea of "community" is fading, and concurrently it is becoming more difficult for schools and school systems to keep in close touch with their constituents.

## DANGER OF OVEREMPHASIZING COMMUNITY ADAPTATION

This is one reason why it is futile to try to preserve an extremely local quality in our educational institutions. The population served is not as homogeneous as it used to be; it is larger, and there is more turnover of pupils as families move about. In many city neighborhoods, it is not unusual for 25 to 50 per cent of the pupils to move away and be replaced by newcomers. In some the rate is between 50 and 100 per cent, the school ending the year with less than half or none of the pupils who began in September. In conditions of such transiency, one can readily see how adapting the curriculum and activities to a particular neighborhood would not only be difficult but also foolish, because the girls and boys are likely to be in new surroundings very soon. Only so far as general community characteristics are roughly similar does the idea of community adaptation make sense.

### Basic Needs of Children Are Universal

Related but perhaps more fundamental is the fact that the needs of children and youth are everywhere more similar than dissimilar. Because a school is in a farming community, should the staff attempt to prepare the pupils for life as farmers? Or in a coal mining area, for life in the mines? Or in a factory district, for a future in the factories? This is patently absurd, besides its being an indefensible limitation of opportunity. Few of any given group of children remain in their hometown or area to work and raise a family. The "basic needs" of children and adolescents throughout the world are much alike.

On the other hand, the community school idea need not be completely tossed out. In two particular respects, it can and should be observed. Teachers ought to tie in local history, conditions, and problems with instruction so far as this is possible. This is mostly a matter of curricular content and is applicable to varying degrees in different subjects of study, but more applicable than many teachers think. It takes a little imagination and effort. Methods are also concerned, for example, in the scheduling of field trips, overnight or one-day camping, and use of persons in the community who can add something of interest and benefit to the regular teaching out of their experience or specialized knowledge.

Second, schools everywhere should make an effort to serve their communities—their neighborhoods and towns and cities—insofar as it is compatible with the primary job of teaching. Adult education is a good example of such a service (Chapter 10), and another example is a school board policy making facilities generously available for a variety of local, non-profit activities.

## THE SCHOOL BOARD: CONTROL AT THE LOCAL LEVEL

The instrument that the American people devised for the local management of public education is the board of education. In some states it is called a board of trustees or school directors, or a school committee; but whatever the name, the functions in all states are much the same. (In Hawaii the entire state is organized as one school system, and so there is a single board that serves in the dual capacity of state board and district board.) Through school districts created as units of government for educational purposes alone, governed by a board of citizens elected or appointed from among the residents, the American people have endeavored to keep their schools close to the people, to provide for an interplay of varied interests, and to preserve initiative and responsibility.

### Characteristics of School Board Members

Membership on boards of education is made up almost entirely of men and women elected by a vote of their fellow citizens of the school districts; only about 10 per cent are chosen by some other method, for example, appointment by the mayor of a city. By tradition, or in some states by law, very few are professional educators, which preserves the lay character of community educational control. It is generally held that persons who are not on the school payroll can deliberate and arrive at decisions more objectively than those who work for the district. Also, it seems illogical for district employees to serve on a board under whose policies they work. Only twenty-five years ago it was estimated that there were 400,000 school board members in the United States, about four board members for every ten teachers. With the rapid decrease in the number of school districts since then, the number of board members has fallen to a bit under 200,000, for a ratio of a little more than one for every ten teachers; the number of board members has been cut in half while the number of teachers has almost doubled in that period.

In non-public schools, boards are usually self-perpetuating, new members being appointed by carryover members whose terms have not expired. In the case of schools with a religious affiliation, members are appointed by a church board or other ecclesiastical authority; and they serve more in an advisory capacity than in one of responsible authority.

A very large majority (85 per cent) of school boards have five to seven members; in rural school districts, the number is often three; in some cities, it may be a dozen or more. Ninety-six per cent have terms ranging from three to six years, the most common being three or four. The average length of service on a board is about seven years, which would lead one to think that there is pretty good continuity or stability of board membership, along with a fair degree of opportunity for induction of new members.

Recent studies of school board membership show that the median age is about fifty, half are college graduates, and about two-fifths are high school but not college graduates. As a group, school board members are drawn mostly from among owners or executives in business and industry, and professional people such as doctors, dentists, lawyers, scientists, and engineers.

## Extensive Local Control Through School Boards

Some writers in the last few years have tried to make a great point of the "myth of local control," the "folklore of school board responsibility," and the like. In part this attitude has been engendered by examples of incompetence, cynicism, and partisanship that can be found among the many thousands of school board members. However, such writers reveal a large gap in their knowledge of the achievements of the "school board system," and how it stacks up in comparison with the conduct of education in other countries. As one might gather from Chapter 6, there is nothing just like the American school board in any other country, although there are some near approaches. What is it that makes this humble body so remarkable? What does it do, and how does it do it?

Originally, it may be recalled, school boards were subcommittees of town or city councils. As both municipal government and educational responsibilities became more complex, during the nineteenth century state laws were changed to provide for election of boards just for education. These boards served in an administrative as well as a policy-making capacity, because there were no superintendents of schools. The boards worked directly with principals and head teachers. In turn, when the management of educational affairs came to demand more time and specialized knowledge, school boards began to appoint superintendents of schools as their professional executives; the first ones were so designated in 1837 in Louisville and Buffalo. This arrangement became the standard in most cities by 1890, and within two more decades practically universal except in one-room and very small village districts.

### Mandatory and Discretionary Areas of Board Work

While this familiar pattern has entirely or nearly freed the school boards from direct administration, each state does still hold school boards responsible for carrying out the state's mandates as expressed in constitution, statutes, and regulations. Thus, a heavy charge is laid on local boards as agents and officers of the states. To help them the states offer varying degrees of financial and professional assistance (as noted in the next chapter). This legal responsibility is not the whole picture, however; there are two other elements that by their nature are perhaps more difficult to perform, and that are discretionary with the boards—that is, they may do as much or as little as they see fit, so far as the law is concerned. (California is the only state in which discretionary action by a local board is extremely limited.)

One of these two elements is ascertaining and being responsive to community desires and interests so far as they relate to education and do not contravene state requirements. Since many conflicting and differing interests and preferences abound in every community, some vehemently championed and others scarcely formulated, it is extremely difficult for a school board to decide what to do. Some aid is given them by the administrative and teaching staff and by citizens' advisory committees that thousands of boards enlist, but in the end the school board usually finds itself castigated by some and lauded by others no matter what it does.

The remaining demand on school board ability, interest, and time is that of keeping reasonably well abreast of current educational thought and practice. When one bears in mind that board members as a rule serve without pay, have full-time occupations of their own, and are not presumed to be specialists in education, he must concede that the ideal of keeping informed and up to date can at best be only to a rather moderate degree achieved. Assistance from the superintendent and other professional employees of the schools is essential. To provide an avenue of communication, a great many boards now devote one of their regular meetings each month to hearing reports from committees of teachers and principals on curriculum, methods, pupil progress, national and state trends of various kinds, and the like. Increasingly, boards hold regular meetings twice a month or once a week; and scheduling such discussions for one meeting a month is becoming popular as a means of focusing attention on the work actually going on in the schools, and problems related to it. Otherwise, there is a tendency for boards of education to be preoccupied with the more concrete aspects of a school system such as finances, buildings, and equipment.

## HOW SCHOOL SYSTEMS AND SCHOOLS ARE ADMINISTERED

While legal responsibility for the operation of schools and school systems is delegated by the states to boards of education, these boards do not themselves administer or manage either individual schools or groups of schools to which the term school system is applied. (The only exceptions to this are the one-room and other small rural or village schools.) Principals and superintendents who as a rule have had some years of teaching experience and professional preparation for administration are employed for this work. Only a few states provide for such positions in the law; but necessity, long-standing practice, and the influence of accrediting associations have caused them to be universally adopted. Every city and practically every town has a chief administrator as superintendent of schools, and nearly every school with eight or more teachers has a principal as its full or part-time head. In very small elementary schools, frequently one of the teachers is designated as head teacher and carries only limited administrative responsibility, since his regular (and usually full-time) job is teaching.

### Origin and Development of the Principalship

The principalship has much the longer history, extending back to early Colonial times. The heads of the Latin schools, our first secondary schools, were scholarly men of considerable stature and influence, as shown in Chapter 5. The elementary school principalship evolved during the second half of the nineteenth century, when the organization of schools by grades was widely adopted, and in the cities school enrollment became so large that head teachers could not handle all the work of management.

Principals and head teachers were responsible directly to boards of education before the position of superintendent was created and widely recognized, as noted above. The appointment of superintendents relieved school boards, first, of the supervision of instruction and, later, of other administrative responsibilities such as finance, business management, personnel administration, and schoolhouse planning. Boards were at first reluctant to permit educators to serve as their executive officers for non-instructional services and activities. Until well into the twentieth century, it was common practice for the superintendent to have charge of all instructional matters (curriculum, methods of teaching, selection and appointment of teachers, classification, promotion and failure of pupils, and so on), and for the secretary of the board or a business manager appointed by and working directly under the board to have charge of all other matters. This is still the rule in a small minority of city school systems, and it is known as "dual control." In a few places, three or more such coordinate chief executives are appointed; this is called "multiple control."

### The Superintendent as Executive Officer

Gradually, it became clear to most boards of education that a school system with two or more chief officers could not be as efficient as one with unified control. It did not seem logical to hold the superintendent responsible for good educational results and improvement when, for example, the business manager made decisions on the amount and quality of instructional supplies to be ordered, the upkeep and operation of schoolhouses, and in fact the entire budget. Even though his decisions or recommendations were subject to final action by the board, they could and did give rise to much friction. Within the last thirty or forty years, the office of superintendent of schools has become very widely recognized as the single top executive position, under the immediate control of the board of education, and responsible for putting into effect policies and regulations enacted by the board.

How elaborate the administrative organization of a school system is depends on its size. In small school systems, the superintendents head up all the services of instruction and the business office. For the former he works largely through the principals; for the latter through persons appointed as directors or supervisors of business affairs, buildings and grounds, food service, and so on. When a school system exceeds about one hundred employees (teachers, custodians, nurses, and others), it is very common practice for the board to appoint an assistant superintendent as business manager to manage all non-instructional services. He works under the general supervision of the superintendent, with whom remains the chief responsibility for instruction and allied services. When still further division of labor is necessary, an assistant superintendent in charge of instruction is usually the next major appointment.

A plan of administrative organization recommended for a school system of ten to fifteen thousand pupils is illustrated in Figure 12–1, but there is no fixed pattern followed throughout the country. Under each assistant superintendent, there would be appropriate bureaus headed by directors to carry on the work of the division. For example, under the assistant superintendent for instruction, there might be a director of elementary education and a director of secondary education. The number and kind of bureaus would depend on the work load and the division of labor decided upon, the standards of performance required or expected, and the qualifications of the personnel.

### Main Duties of the Principal

The role of school principals probably should be given more weight than the public or even the principals themselves ordinarily ascribe to it. For the principals are right on the firing line, so to speak, and are, or should be, collaborating closely with the teaching staff in the classrooms. Principals are almost without exception regarded by experts in school administration as the chief supervisory officers for the carrying on and improvement of instruction. They do not all measure up to this expectation, of course, for various reasons, including lack of adequate preparation for the work, failure to keep abreast of educational research, lack of interest and enthusiasm, and unsuitable personal qualifications.

In large secondary schools, there seems to be a revival of departmental organization, such as English, mathematics, and science, with an especially capable teacher as chairman. A reduction in teaching load or a modest addition to salary or both are often attached to such appointments. This practice is beginning to be followed also in large elementary schools, but for the most part city school systems appoint supervisors working out of the central office to assist principals with instruction.

One recent development in large junior and senior high schools (and in some cities in large elementary schools) is the employment of "coordinators" as instructional heads of the schools, under the general supervision of the principal. The principal and his assistants, however, have as their chief concern all other school services and activities be-

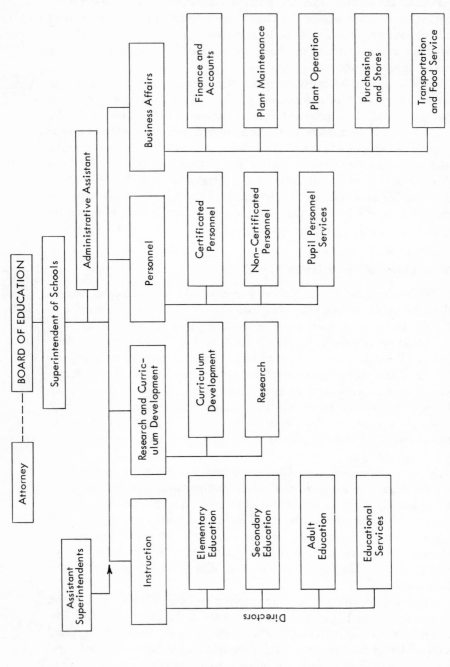

Fig. 12–1. Suggested Central Administrative Organization for a School System of Approximately 15,000 Enrollment

sides instruction. This is not a good arrangement in the opinion of some experts and many critics of public education, who believe that the head of a school ought to retain instructional leadership himself and be the kind of person by temperament, experience, and professional training who is fit for it.

## Complexity of a Modern School System

The foregoing description of school system administration is of course much simplified. It is really a skeletonized version of what is one of the most complex enterprises in our society. A moment's reflection may make one wonder how a school system achieves as much as it does. Ideas, laws, state regulations, research, curriculums, courses of study, pupils of different age levels, abilities, and interests, teachers and administrators, secretaries and other classes of personnel, books and supplies, money, buildings, grounds, parental support—all these elements and many others must be brought to bear on the instruction of pupils, at appropriate times and in harmonious relationships.

The participation of citizens as school board members, and of educators, specially prepared as administrators, in the direction and management of U.S. schools is a unique combination of lay and professional interests and abilities. In some other countries, there is also shared responsibility involving laymen and professionals, as may be recalled from Chapter 6. However, in no other is there so much authority delegated to community school boards, or so much latitude allowed by central agencies for the exercise of local discretion. Both strengths and weaknesses no doubt inhere in this way of running schools, but most of those who study it thoroughly and compare it with the philosophy and practice in other lands believe that the strengths outweigh the weaknesses. Among the fifty states, there are many differences in the statutory allocation of powers and duties to boards and administrators; but one may think of these as minor variations of a main theme rather than as entirely different patterns.

The next chapter shows how the roles of state and federal governments in providing for education are conceived and their relation to each other and to school districts.

# THE COMMUNITY SUPPORT OF EDUCATION

Because of the premium placed on local participation in making available educational opportunities, financial and moral support by the community are of essential importance to the health of the schools.

### Great Dependence on Local Financial Support

Historically, the financing of public schools has been largely delegated by states to their school districts. More than half the funds have and still do come from local taxation, for the nation as a whole. Highest reliance on the local property tax for school support is found in Nebraska, with a figure of approximately 95 per cent; lowest in Delaware with about 10 per cent. The southern states rely less than other regions on local resources, state appropriations in most of them running over 50 per cent. For the whole country, however, local funds (including county school taxes where they are levied) constitute about 55 per cent of the total, state support 40 per cent, and federal aid 5 per cent. These ratios fluctuate a little from year to year. For 1929–1930, they were 82.7, 16.9, and 0.4, respectively; and in 1945–1946, 63.8, 34.8, and 1.4. A general trend in the direction of less local support and more state and federal support has been experienced during the last half-century. Now the ratios seem to be changing more slowly, but still in the same direction. Local funds consisting almost entirely (98 per cent) of taxes imposed on property are still the mainstay of school support in most areas, and are likely to remain so for many years.

The determination of how much money should be raised for schools each year and how it should be spent rests with the school board of each district. Boards do not have complete freedom, as a rule, because, at least in most cases, they must observe certain state laws and regulations such as those on minimum salaries and number of days to be taught, and there are some other limitations noted below that apply in many places. Nevertheless, there is still much leeway for decision making on these matters.

### The Budget as a Financial and Educational Plan

Usually, school boards receive recommendations from their superintendent on financial planning, in the form of a school district budget. This document is a sort of blueprint for an entire twelve-month fiscal year, translating into dollars the services, materials, and activities to be provided, and submitting careful estimates of how the needed funds are to be raised. The board reviews the proposed budget several weeks or months in advance of the new fiscal year. After such hearings and other public discussions as may be required by law or by board policy, the budget is adopted as finally approved by the board. Changes may be and often are made by the school board in adopting the final budget, as the board attempts to make the educational pro-

gram fulfill community needs and interests and bring the whole program within financial reach of the district, as they see it.  One can see
here that what a board of education chooses to support, and the level
of that support, is some indication of the relative weight it gives to
the many items that appear in a budget.  Some boards may think it is
important to support a kindergarten program, even though the state
may not require it and may give no state aid for it; others will not make
such provision, preferring rather to put that money into some other
service.  Teachers' salaries may take 75 per cent of the budget in one
district, 65 per cent in another, partly because of different priorities
assigned this particular budget item, and partly also because of other
conditions, such as long or short average tenure, or less comprehensive
or more comprehensive programs of services and activities.  Schoolbus
transportation may be very extensive in one district, but not needed in
another; and these conditions would, of course, be reflected in the
budgets.

No one criterion can be set forth on just what percentages of a
budget should be allocated to the various categories of expenditures.
It is easy for boards and superintendents to obtain state and national norms for educational expenditures, and make comparisons
with local fund distribution. If a marked departure from average
practice is apparent, this does not necessarily mean that it is better or
worse; but it may properly lead to a review of local practice to see if
the difference is justified.

## Limitations on Local Financial Planning

After the budget is approved, a school board certifies to the proper
authority (usually a county officer or board responsible for the actual
levying of taxes) the amount needed.  In most states, this authority
is then obligated by law to impose the tax, provided that no state controls are violated.  These limitations on a board of education's freedom
take many forms, and some kind of budget review or approval is applicable in about 40 per cent of the nation's school districts.  Actually,
such review is performed in most cases in a perfunctory manner.  Two
kinds of restraint are most common and make educational planning
more onerous than it would otherwise be.  One restraint is found in
some large cities, mostly in the East, where the board of education
must submit its budget to the city council for approval.  This type of
fiscal dependence, as it is called, is gradually passing out of the picture, and a good thing too, for such a requirement denies the historic
position of school districts as agents or arms of state government, mak-

ing them subordinate to municipal government. Furthermore, it is illogical to require a budget, adopted after careful preparation by professionals and board members, to be submitted to a city council not responsible for or even well informed about the schools; not involved in all the preliminary study, consultation, and figuring that go into making a budget; and thus ill-qualified to evaluate it in whole or in part.

The other kind of limitation found in some states is the imposition of a ceiling on the amount or per cent that a budget may exceed the preceding year's figures. In one state, for example, only a 5 per cent increase in the amount is permitted from one year to the next, except by special approval of the state tax commission; and the commission may approve only up to a certain fixed limit, no matter how serious the need. Rapidly growing school systems such as are found in many cities and suburbs these days cannot operate on a 5 per cent annual increase without serious deterioration. Generally speaking, only a school system with a declining school population can operate within such a limit. Several other kinds of control are utilized, such as absolute ceilings in tax levies, a referendum election to give citizens an opportunity to approve or turn down a proposed tax increase, and submission of proposed budgets to the state education department for approval.

These last two paragraphs put the district board of education in a distinctly circumscribed position. It appears to be hemmed in by so many restrictions that possibly an impression quite contradictory to the emphasis on local responsibility has been gained by the reader. Notwithstanding the existence of these controls, the fact yet remains that a very large area of discretionary action is open to local districts. The enforcement of such restrictions as do exist is, moreover, rarely carried out in an arbitrary or authoritarian way. It may be appropriately mentioned, by way of reminder, that states do legitimately exercise such control over their school districts as they see fit, so long as the Constitution is not violated; but they usually do it in a reasonable way, and largely through the advice and leadership of state education departments.

### Moral Support Essential to Success of Schools

Important as financial support is, a school system would have rough going without winning also what one might call the moral support of the community. And whether such support is given depends on a number of factors, among which probably ranking first is community confidence in the schools. This one element has several components:

confidence in the board of education and in the administrative staff employed to carry out the board's policies and decisions; confidence in the teaching staff, and in the non-teaching employees whose work facilitates instruction; and the conviction that the schools do afford good opportunities for all children to make the most of themselves and to grow up to be decent young men and women. Other items will readily come to mind. The point is that if a community's schools are really going to have an impact on the lives of pupils, and also in different ways on the lives of adults and out-of-school young folk, people have got to "believe in them," believe that they make an important contribution to standards of personal and social life. Mere apathetic toleration or passive acceptance is hardly the climate in which a school or school system can thrive.

To foster confidence and enlist active support, most public school systems engage in three specific major activities, all calculated to bring the citizenry into close relations with the schools, and to inform them on what the schools are attempting to do, what they are achieving, and problems and needs that still require attention. These three activities, briefly commented on below, are: (1) the Parent-Teacher Association, (2) citizens' advisory committees, and (3) reporting to the public.

## The Parent-Teacher Association

The PTA was established in 1897, and now enrolls about 12.5 million members in forty-seven thousand local units (in individual schools). The National Congress of Parents and Teachers, whose headquarters are in Chicago, has state branches in all states and in more than a dozen far-flung areas outside the United States, including Mexico, Singapore, Japan, the Philippines, Labrador, and Marshall Islands. There are even local units for junior colleges, colleges, and universities, although they make up a very small part of the total. The Congress publishes the *PTA Magazine,* a first-rate journal from the standpoint of both content and editing. Each local unit has its own characteristics, of course; and they change from time to time, depending on the school principal's attitude, the ability and interest of the officers, and the spirit of the school parents who make up the membership.

The "Objects of the National Congress of Parents and Teachers," a sort of platform for the organization, supplemented in the official Manual by eleven "principles," are as follows:

To promote the welfare of children and youth in home, school, church, and community.

To raise the standards of home life.

To secure adequate laws for the care and protection of children and youth.

To bring into closer relation the home and the school, that parents and teachers may cooperate intelligently in the training of the child.

To develop between educators and the general public such united efforts as will secure for every child the highest advantages in physical, mental, social, and spiritual education.

**PTA Strengths and Weaknesses.** No one can quarrel with these laudable aims, although critics have pointed out that they are very general, even vague. But the PTA is probably the butt of more "school jokes" than any other facet of education, some probably deserved and some not. In the authors' opinion, the potentialities of the PTA for fostering good home and school relations are immeasurable, but they are rarely realized fully. Critics emphasize the preponderance of female membership and management as a source of weakness, the dullness of the monthly meetings, the middle-class orientation, the tendency to encroach on territory properly regarded as that of the administrative and professional staff. Teachers and parents alike often feel compelled, say the critics with some truth, to make a show of interest for fear of being criticized for not being sufficiently dedicated to their respective roles.

Non-public schools may organize local units of the PTA, but often they have their own "Home and School" organization or "Parents' Association," or in parochial schools, they affiliate with their own church-related parent-teacher organization. There is no significant difference in their aims and practices.

The weaknesses that may be discerned in all these organizations are not irremediable. It must be recognized that parental interest seems to be highest at the elementary school level, and these units are the most active and the most generally successful. Interest progressively decreases at the junior high and senior high school levels, as the pupils begin to be less dependent on their parents and teachers, and as the "neighborhood" served becomes larger—so large, in fact, that it is no longer a neighborhood. As an organization for the study of child growth and development and for parent education, which it mainly centers on today, the PTA stands pre-eminent, and it would be hard to find an adequate substitute for it. On countless occasions, it has come to the aid of boards of education at local and state levels, when grave decisions were hanging in the balance. The one qualification the authors would make is that the PTA is the best available organ for maintaining wholesome and fruitful relations between schools and their communities—if it is "run right," i.e., in accordance with the recommendations of the National Congress of Parents and Teachers.

## Citizens' Advisory Committees

There have been advisory committees of one sort or another to assist school boards for more than fifty years, chiefly in the field of vocational education. It was not until after World War II, however, when educational finance lagged seriously behind rising costs, that a small number of leading business and professional men and women saw in citizens' committees a hope of generating more interest in and better support of public education. In 1949, at the time they founded the National Citizens' Commission for the Public Schools, it was estimated that there were 150 local advisory committees. Under Commission stimulus, boards of education created about 1,500 advisory committees within three years; and by 1960, there were some 18,000, two or more in many school districts. There has been a slight decline in the total number since then, but thousands of school systems solicit help from citizens' committees as a normal part of the problem-solving activity.

Today, most of these committees, appointed from among citizens whom the school boards and administrative staffs deem to be well qualified, normally tackle local problems of finance, curriculum, physical facilities, and personnel. They are utilized because some problems require more time than the board itself can devote to them, and because the board wants a somewhat broader sample of community opinion than the board and administration themselves represent.

In general, the outcome of such committee work has been very good, so good, in fact, that county, state, and even national advisory committees have become almost commonplace. The White House Conference on Education in 1955 and the White House Conference on Children and Youth in 1960 are examples; both these conferences were preceded and followed by hundreds of study and discussion sessions at state, county, and local levels.

Criteria for Citizens' Committees. Several well-recognized criteria have been developed out of experience (given in most textbooks on school administration and school public relations) to help committees succeed. Of most importance are these:

1. A committee should be carefully instructed by the board on the work it has been asked to do; it should report only to the board;

and its report, consisting of findings and recommendations, should be regarded as advisory only and not binding on the board.

2. A committee should be small enough to work effectively, yet large enough to be fairly representative of the community, so far as possible, and to allow for some subcommittees to be appointed for specially assigned inquiries. Usually a minimum of twenty-five and a maximum of fifty are suggested.

3. A citizens' advisory committee is preferably created to study certain definite problems confronting the school system, and for a definite term such as three or six months. After reporting, the committee should be discharged with thanks.

4. In order to facilitate committee work, factual data, previous studies, and a clear statement of problems should be furnished by the school administrative offices. Suitable meeting places and secretarial assistance should also be provided by the school district. Regular meetings should be scheduled, about twice a month, and for about two hours, such a routine allowing for subcommittee work between sessions.

### Numerous Channels for Reporting to the Public

Throughout the school year and increasingly during summer months, there are school-related events that are widely observed by public and non-public schools. They are all intended to cultivate friendly, understanding, and mutually supportive relations between school and community. Such major occasions as high school commencement, "Back-to-School Night," and American Education Week are probably well known to most if not all users of this book. The last named has been sponsored since 1921 by four national organizations: The American Legion, the National Congress of Parents and Teachers, the National Education Association, and the United States Office of Education. A general theme is adopted for the second week of November, with specific topics suggested for each of the seven days. Many ministers plan sermons around the Sunday topic, business and professional clubs hear speakers on various other subjects through the week, and special assemblies in elementary and secondary schools are held. Through the N.E.A. office in Washington, free and inexpensive materials are available. This autumn event is supplemented in some cities by a similar "Public Schools Week" in April.

Exhibits of schoolwork in the spring, science fairs and more recently social science fairs, concerts and recitals, plays, debates and other speech events, athletic contests, publications, and other school activities, if well planned and carried out—not as professional performances or accomplishments, but as reflections of schools in action—are all valuable aids to building cordial community relations. If mismanaged or shoddy, they can backfire, of course. Budget hearings or neighborhood meetings for explanation of a proposed budget are helpful in cultivating popular understanding of a rather complex subject. Printed reports to the public, annually and at appropriate times in between, radio and television programs and instruction, interesting news stories and pictures all are much used. One measure that is widely used and appreciated by the public is the free use of school facilities for adult education and free or low-cost use for non-profit community recreation, entertainment, and public information. Bringing qualified residents into the schools as visiting lecturers and to assist with vocational guidance is another good way of relating school and community, not for pay but merely as a contribution on their part; they get as much good out of it as the pupils. The employment of well-qualified residents as teacher aides, cafeteria and noon hour supervisors, school crossing guards, and as readers for English classes is recommended. It not only helps get the various kinds of work done—its primary purpose—but it also brings quite a few people into direct contact with the schools. This practice has not been widely adopted but is growing. Excursions, field trips, and camping, planned well in advance and conducted in strictest accordance with school district regulations on safety and care of the pupils, are acknowledged almost everywhere as highly valuable for their instructional effects as well as for cementing school-community ties. Unfortunately, these last three activities are not utilized nearly so extensively as would be desirable, and far less than in several European countries, notably Britain, Germany, Switzerland, and the Scandinavian countries.

## IMPROVEMENT OF LOCAL UNITS

For an institution to maintain its vitality and its ability to contribute to the well-being of the society of which it is a part, it must be subjected to constructive criticism and be capable of change. Otherwise, it will be unable to fulfill new demands made upon it and weather new conditions. The school district, as an instrument evolved by our society for carrying on education, has been the focus of three kinds of efforts not only to help it survive, but also to make it function better.

### Reorganization of School Districts

Although the weaknesses of small independent local units have been pointed out for more than a hundred years, the number of districts continued to increase until 1932. During the preceding two decades, well-organized plans to consolidate small districts and schools had made some slight headway; but in spite of it, the total number continued to increase. The aims of consolidation were to bring together in one school building the pupils of small rural elementary and high schools. The lack of good roads and dependable, economical transportation equipment, along with a prevailing intensely local viewpoint, stymied any large-scale improvement. By 1940, however, roads and vehicles had been vastly bettered; and a new plan of reorganizing schools had emerged. This plan called for the combining of *districts* rather than *schools,* thus enlarging the basic administrative units but preserving such attendance centers (schools) as were desirable. The state of Washington in 1941 enacted the first such plan into law, and its example was followed in the next few years by about twenty states where the small-district problem was serious. Eight states, all in the Midwest, have about half of the total number of districts in the United States and still are in need of an aggressive program of reorganization.

The advocates of reorganization claim that if it is done wisely, both educational and financial advantages ensue. On the educational side, it is likely that extremely small schools, except in isolated areas, will be brought together to form larger schools, although this does not necessarily occur. Where larger schools can be set up, they can offer better study programs (especially in junior and senior high school grades), more incentive to pupils, better library, laboratory, shop, and other facilities. Instruction can be improved because teachers can be assigned to classes in their major fields of study. In small schools, teachers often are required to work in fields where they have had insufficient preparation. In general, the opportunities for pupils to mingle with more schoolmates; to have contact with a larger and more specialized staff; and to have available a number of special services such as guidance, health services, psychological testing and evaluation, and schoolbus transportation have also been shown by research to yield better educational outcomes.

### Why Reorganized Districts Increase School Expenditures

From the financial point of view, seldom if ever is less money spent by a reorganized district than has previously been spent by the original units. More productive use of funds is, however, definitely achieved. For example, one district can provide transportation more economically than seven or ten or fifteen small ones serving the same area and population. Instead of average classes of ten to twenty in secondary schools, classes of fifteen to twenty-five or thirty make for better use of staff. Fewer facilities like gymnasiums, heating plants, toilets, laboratories, home economics suites, athletic and other play fields are needed for one school of eight hundred or a thousand than for four or five separate small schools. Of great importance also is the creation of a single large school taxing area, where the people pay for schools at the same tax rate, in place of a patchwork of small districts with different tax levies. The reduction of bookkeeping and paper work at local, county, and state levels must be impressive, for example, in Illinois where the number of districts was reduced from more than 12,000 to about 1,500 between 1930 and 1960, or in Colorado, from about 2,000 in 1940 to fewer than 200 in 1965.

One great benefit that neither advocates nor opponents of reorganization have ever seemed to foresee but which clearly flows from it almost without exception is the general raising of educational sights and standards. Of the former separate districts, the one with the reputation for best schools becomes the pacemaker; all the other areas want for their schools the same quality in teaching staff, textbooks and libraries, curriculum, physical plant, and so on. This costs more, naturally, and is the main reason why reorganization usually results in larger budgets. But few people want to see the educational standards of the best schools lowered. Most residents prefer to bring the lagging schools up to the best, even if it increases taxes.

### Efforts Made To Improve Small Schools

Since 1955, several "small school projects" have been carried on, e.g., the Catskill Area Small Schools Project in New York State, and the Western Small-Schools Project in five Rocky Mountain states. Their object is to improve small rural schools through the development of specially adapted methods and materials of instruction, and the preparation of teachers for small schools, with the emphasis on high schools. In part, these attempts are viewed as alternatives to reorganization; but even in reorganized areas, some small schools will always have to be retained. So it is well to see what can be done to raise their standards. During this same period, the so-called "intermediate district" has received considerable but largely misguided support. Such a unit is created when several basic local districts pool their resources for certain purposes, such as audio-visual instruction, psychological and counseling services, pupil transportation, and purchasing school supplies and equipment. In the authors' view, this superimposed entity is actually an avoidance of reorganization. The time, money, and effort devoted to the formation of intermediate districts would be better spent on getting along with the reorganization of small districts into larger, viable, functional districts.

How far the process of making big districts out of little ones should go, no one can say with certainty. Those who specialize in such matters suggest that the entire country could manage very well with 5,000 to 8,000 districts. In thirty-five states, there is no crucial problem; although some improvements could be made. In the other fifteen states, there are far more districts than are required; in fact, the large proportion of small units is a detriment to public education in those states. Each state must, however, forge its own standards, taking into account the size and distribution of the population, the roads, existing school buildings, and finances. Experts say that a good minimum enrollment for a district is approximately 10,000, but in many states this would have to be lowered in view of the geography and population of various areas. On the other hand, in some populous states the base might be increased, although the danger of districts getting so large as to be unwieldy (like New York, Los Angeles, Chicago) should be guarded against.

### Upgrading School Board Competence

The attitude of some persons toward the competence of school board members and what they do ranges from amused indifference to utter contempt. It is probably safe to say that most citizens give little or no thought to their school board or its activities and decisions except when taxes are increased. When they do think on these things, they vastly underrate their importance. This is nothing new; it is almost proverbial for Americans to treat cavalierly their public servants, and school boards are no exception. Some contemporary writers like Lieberman and Rickover seem to be quite impatient with them, and argue that the best thing to do is abolish them. This is a remedy generally known as throwing the baby out with the bath.

Boards of education actually do carry much responsibility for the education of children and youth, much more than is delegated to education committees and governing boards in other lands. It is no exaggeration to say that the quality of community educational services and activities depends greatly on the fitness of board members for their office—their level of interest in education; their ability and willingness to devote much time to meetings and the study of conditions and problems on which policies and decisions have to be made; their sensitivity to community needs and interests and the larger needs and interests of the state, the nation, and the world. They must be able to work as members of a board and to support fully decisions made by this group, even though personally they may disagree with them. They must be willing to learn what being school board members means, how to behave as members of a policy-making body exercising general oversight of a school system, but not itself administering the system. And above all, their integrity must be without blemish.

It has been recognized for a long time that some persons will not fit these specifications, but that it is possible to help school board members improve, barring defects of character. It is fortunate that the very nature of school board work, however, commands the interest of a generally public-spirited and unselfish type of person who "believes in" education. With such good prospects to work with, those concerned about school board improvement need not be discouraged.

## State and National Associations of School Boards

State school board associations (now found in all the states except Hawaii, which has only one board) are one of the most useful sources of help. Through state conventions and workshops, publications, advisory service, legal assistance, legislative activity, and other means, they inform their members, stimulate interest, and in general exercise considerable influence for educational improvement. Tax-supported and independent universities and some colleges have faculty members who lend assistance in research, by speeches, articles, and even as officers or committee members of school board associations. State education departments conduct conferences, issue helpful suggestions and handbooks, and provide many kinds of services to aid school boards in discharging their duties. One of the most important responsibilities of a superintendent of schools is assisting the board to work intelligently and productively, by transmitting information; making recommendations for action; and participating with the board in discussions of educational objectives, achievements, problems, and needs.

The National School Boards Association, a federation of state associations, is of doubtful value in upgrading school board competence and sponsoring national legislation on education. Since education is so universally regarded as a responsibility of the states, it is uphill going for an "action group," as the NSBA likes to think of itself, to be effective as the voice of American school boards. However, its annual conventions draw five to seven thousand participants, who hear and discuss speeches by educators; leading state and district board members; and leaders of government, business, and labor. Undoubtedly, the national association has contributed to improving public opinion about the importance of school board work, and given much-needed recognition and status to board members themselves.

Two factors are of more than ordinary significance in the upgrading of school board service. One is the retention (or recapture where they have been lost) of separate elections for school boards, apart from city, state, and national elections. There is a running fire of attack on separate school board elections, carried on chiefly by teachers' unions who see in a change to combine school board with municipal or general elections a better chance of electing representatives of organized labor. It is true that separate elections do not draw as big a voter turnout, but the interested voters will turn out, and school board candidates are not relegated to some obscure place on the ballot.

The other key factor is the nominating procedure, on which little progress has been made. About two out of every three school districts rely on either a petition signed by a would-be candidate's supporters or announcement of their candidacy by individuals. In these methods there is no preliminary screening of possible candidates by a community school board election convention or caucus. It is of the utmost importance that none but excellent candidates be nominated, for only by this means can there be assurance of excellent board members.

### Professionalization of School Administration

Higher standards of professional preparation and performance have, in the last forty years, gone hand in hand with increased responsibilities. Among principals and superintendents, it is commonly held that the professionalization of educational administration has not yet matured; but they and the universities and colleges that offer such preparation are convinced that the profession is approaching maturity. Since 1950, many millions of dollars probably in excess of $25 million, have been channeled by foundations, institutions of higher education, state and city school systems, and professional associations into research, experimentation, and a variety of field services to improve school administration. The W. K. Kellogg Foundation alone has contributed more than $10 million.

Most states require at least one year of graduate study for a superintendent or principal; and a few require superintendents to have two years or a doctor's degree, the latter ordinarily necessitating three or more years of graduate work beyond a bachelor's degree. The North Central Association of Colleges and Secondary Schools and other accrediting associations and agencies uphold similar requirements for their member schools or school systems. One of the most influential agencies in the improvement of the teaching and study of educational administration during the sixties is the University Council for Educational Administration, a voluntary association of some sixty major universities. Its purposes are to help professors improve their own competence (through seminars, conferences, and "task forces"); to sponsor and conduct research on content and experiences of student programs; and to prepare for classroom use films, tapes, case studies, and carefully designed simulations of actual administrative situations.

## Professional Standards in Advance of Legal Minimums

It is interesting that most of the impetus for improvement issues from professional organizations. The law, of course, represents a crystallization of public opinion that is not usually very advanced. Professional organizations should by their very nature operate at the "growing edge" of their field.

Led by the American Association of School Administrators (superintendents), other national professional organizations for secondary and elementary school principals, supervisors, and counselors have taken steps to raise qualifications for membership, generally in terms of more and better graduate study in universities. The A.A.S.A. made effective in 1964 a requirement for new members of two years of graduate study in programs designed to prepare school administrators. Other organizations are tending in the same direction for their respective spheres of service.

Not only has the period of professional preparation been lengthened, but the quality has also been and is being improved. Heavy emphasis is placed on the importance of a good solid liberal education at the undergraduate level, and the continuation of academic interests into the graduate level. The professional program itself is less weighted than formerly with techniques, more with the study of theory and principles. Practical experience in the field by means of surveys and internship is required or recommended in all graduate administration programs.

Higher ideals of service are gradually being attained, and this results in attracting more able persons to the profession of educational administration.

## QUESTIONS, PROBLEMS, AND PROJECTS FOR FURTHER STUDY

1. Write an explanation in about two thousand words of the "school district system," as it operates in the United States, in the form of a letter to a teacher in some other country (you select the country) who is going to come to your hometown next year as an exchange teacher.

2. Interview a school principal (elementary, junior high, or senior high school) to get figures on and discuss reasons for pupil turnover for the last five years. Arrange with your instructor to report the findings in class.

3. What are the advantages and disadvantages, as you have been able to gather from your reading and observation, of keeping school board elections separate from other elections, or holding them at the same time?

4. Write to your hometown superintendent of schools for a copy of a current school budget. What per cent of the school money comes from (a) school district and county taxes, (b) state appropriations, and (c) the federal government? How is the local and county money raised? Is the presentation of facts on these items clear; or if not, which points are not clear; and how could you as a citizen find out what you want to know?

5. Find out exactly how the members of the board of education in your hometown (or the community where you are now living) are designated: by election or appointment, their terms of office, and whether they are paid or not. If possible, interview two or three members about their views of the school board's main duties and powers. Compare these responses with what the local superintendent of schools thinks the board should do.

6. Arrange to attend a regular meeting of a school board, remaining for the entire meeting. Summarize your observations and conclusions in a short report to the class, or in a paper to be handed in, as your instructor and you decide.

7. What qualifications should citizens have, in your opinion, to serve well as school board members? Should there be established by law any educational requirements or other standards to be met by candidates for election? Should a plan be followed for having representatives of various community groups or interests on the board of education?

8. Should there be a concerted effort to get more women on school boards? Is there any evidence that women are better board members? Or any that men are?

9. Write to the National School Boards Association, Evanston, Ill., for information about the main purposes of state school board associations, and

the activities and services they undertake to achieve their goals. At the same time, inquire about what the N.S.B.A. stands for, and how it operates.

10. Attend one or more PTA meetings, preferably at different levels (elementary, junior high, or senior high school), and report your observations and conclusions, relating them to the treatment in this chapter.

11. Why do some rural school board members strongly oppose district reorganization? If the circumstances permit, arrange with one or two class members to interview six to ten rural board members on this subject; and report your experience to the class or to your instructor. Take care to formulate the questions carefully.

## SELECTED SUPPLEMENTARY READINGS AND FILMS

ALFORD, ALBERT L. *Nonproperty Taxation for Schools.* U.S. Office of Education Bulletin 1964, No. 4. Washington, D.C.: Government Printing Office, 1963. An investigation of possibilities for local district use of various non-property taxes to relieve the typical heavy reliance on property taxes for school support.

CHAUNCEY, HENRY (ed.). *Talks on American Education.* New York: Bureau of Publications, Teachers College, Columbia University, 1962. James B. Conant, Lawrence Cremin, Robert J. Havighurst, Francis Keppel, and other notables discuss American education in a series of broadcasts for foreign audiences.

*Education U.S.A.* A sprightly four-page weekly report of news and views, issued September through May by National School Public Relations Association, Washington, D.C.

FOSHAY, ARTHUR W. (ed.). *The Rand McNally Handbook of Education.* Chicago: Rand. McNally & Co., 1963. A "fact book" or almanac of education in three parts: organization and administration of education in the United States, the curriculum, and education in England, France, and the U.S.S.R.

GRIEDER, CALVIN, PIERCE, TRUMAN M. and ROSENSTENGEL, WILLIAM EVERETT. *Public School Administration.* 2d ed. New York: The Ronald Press Co., 1961. See chap. i on the local school district. Other chapters deal with such topics as finance, community relations, the school board, and other major aspects of American education from the viewpoint of administration.

MACHLUP, FRITZ. *The Production and Distribution of Knowledge in the United States.* Princeton, N.J.: Princeton University Press, 1962. This is a scholarly report showing that the rate of knowledge production exceeds that of anything else included in the Gross National Product, and how occupational distribution changes with the creation and distribution of new knowledge. It suggests far-reaching reforms in elementary, secondary, and higher education, compressing elementary and secondary education into ten years, with high school completion at age fourteen.

NATIONAL CONGRESS OF PARENTS AND TEACHERS. *PTA Manual, 1964–65.* Chicago: The Congress. Published annually. A complete guide to the purposes, structure, procedures, and activities of the Congress, its state branches, and local units. Many helpful suggestions for planning interesting programs for local PTA units, and for conducting meetings. See also *The PTA Magazine;* ten issues a year.

RAYWID, MARY A. *The Ax-Grinders.* New York: The Macmillan Co., 1962. A pungent exposé of critics of public education and their purposes.

*Saturday Review.* The third week's issue each month includes a review of current events in U.S. education, articles of timely interest, and reviews of books related to education.

WHITE, ALPHEUS L. *Local School Boards: Organization and Practices.* U.S. Office of Education Bulletin, No. 8. Washington, D.C.: Government Printing Office, 1962. The report of a nationwide survey of 4,000 school districts enrolling nearly 75 per cent of all public school pupils. Facts are tabulated for boards classified according to enrollment and four major regions, on methods of selection and characteristics of board members, organization and meetings, policies, and problems.

WOODRING, PAUL, and SCANLON, JOHN (eds.). *American Education Today.* New York: McGraw-Hill Book Co., Inc., 1963. An interesting collection from the Education Supplement of the *Saturday Review.* It includes facts, articles, and observations on the many kinds of schools and institutions, public and private, that comprise the U.S. educational establishment. Critical issues are also discussed.

## Films

*A Desk for Billie.* 59 minutes. The true story of a migrant girl (Billie Davis), who found opportunity in the public schools across America. It pays a real tribute to those teachers who gave her consideration and encouragement under very adverse conditions of the Great Depression. This film is a classic of its kind. Washington, D.C.: National Education Association.

*How Good Are Our Schools?* 28 minutes. A documentary produced by Columbia Broadcasting System and narrated by Ralph Bellamy. Based on report by James B. Conant, *The American High School Today.* Washington, D.C.: National Education Association.

*School and the Community.* 25 minutes. Compares a school more or less isolated from the community it serves and a school closely integrated with its community. Examples of school-community cooperation are given. New York: McGraw-Hill Book Co., Inc.

*Schoolhouse in the Red.* 42 minutes. Describes a typical rural community debating whether to change from a system of small rural schools to a larger district system. Discusses the sociological and psychological factors, and pictures actions and opinions of local citizens. Battle Creek, Mich.: Kellogg Foundation.

# 13

# EDUCATION AND GOVERNMENT:
# STATE AND FEDERAL RELATIONS

Much that has been said in Chapter 12 may lead one to think that communities have almost complete independence so far as education is concerned. It is true that school boards, most of whom are elected by fellow citizens in their own school districts, do have much responsibility for the conduct of public education. However, one should not overlook the fact that the powers and duties they have are delegated to them by the state governments. The states are responsible for education in the United States; and each state runs its schools as it sees fit without accounting to any other authority, so long as it does not contravene the Constitution.

Not all the educational activity, however, is under the auspices or control of the states. About 15 per cent of elementary and secondary pupils are enrolled in parochial and other non-public schools, and about one-third of the students in higher education attend privately controlled institutions. There are school systems under federal government control in the District of Columbia and in our territories and possessions such as Puerto Rico, American Samoa, Guam, Virgin Islands, and Canal Zone. The federal government also conducts or assists in the operation of nearly three hundred other educational programs and activities. So it can be seen that when one speaks of "the American educational system," he refers to a very large and complex enterprise to which all levels of government—local, state, and federal—are a party, but of which a significant part is under nongovernmental auspices.

## THE BASES OF STATE CONTROL

In our day and age, it is practically axiomatic that education is a responsibility of the fifty states, and is subject (non-public as well as public) to state control. The degree to which responsibility and control are practiced varies greatly among the states, but the principle is well established. This principle was evolved over a long period reaching clear back to early colonial times. The four bases on which it now rests are described briefly in the following paragraphs.

### Reservation Implied in the Tenth Amendment

There is no reference to education in the Constitution. Several explanations have been offered by historians for the omission of such an important subject. One of the most credible reasons is that the education of children was regarded by those who drafted our basic law as a responsibility of the home and the church. Furthermore, several of the new states had already made provision for education in their constitutions, and the leaders from those states were opposed to the federal government's interference. There was also a disposition not to grant the national government any more power than necessary, as the United States had only recently freed themselves from a central government that they viewed as tyrannical. In any event, education is not consigned to the care of any specified level of government. The belief that it lies within the province of the state governments stems from the reservation stated in the Tenth Amendment: "The powers not delegated to the United States by the Constitution, nor prohibited by it to the States, are reserved to the States respectively, or to the people." Recent decades have seen a liberal interpretation of the Constitution, and a departure from the conception of the federal government as a government whose powers are delegated by the states. Yet the Tenth Amendment, despite the ambiguity of the last phrase, "or to the people," is relied on by those who subscribe to state and local responsibility as a safeguard against federal control of public education. There is no national code for, and no national administrative control of, education, except for specific services such as Smith-Hughes vocational education, the school lunch program, and financial aid for certain districts enrolling a substantial proportion of children of resident federal employees.

### State Constitutions and Laws

In Chapter 5 it was seen that the antecedents of state law on education were the famous laws of 1642 and 1647, enacted by colonial Massachusetts. When the colonies became independent, some states incorporated provisions on education in their constitutions; although by 1820, when there were twenty-three states, the constitutions of ten made no mention of education. As new states were admitted after the middle of the nineteenth century and into the twentieth, Congress required them to make constitutional provisions for education. The modern trend is to include a mandate to the legislature to establish and maintain a system of free, public, non-sectarian education, and to provide also for institutions of higher education. Details are properly reserved to statutory law, so that changes may be more readily made to fit changing times.

State school laws, often referred to as education codes, vary a great deal in degree of specificity. In all the states but one, however (the exception being California), the statutes leave considerable latitude to local school boards in how they conduct public education. School legislation covers a wide range of subjects, as one would expect for a service as complex as education. Important among them are the state education department, district organization, elections, finance and taxation, teacher preparation and certification, school construction, pupil census and attendance, bus transportation, curriculum, and state colleges and universities.

Since about 1910, appropriations for education have vastly increased. This expansion of state support has been accompanied by an increasing number of requirements that local districts must fulfill as a prerequisite to receiving funds, an effective method of exercising state control. Non-public schools are, of course, not subject to such action, in accordance with the general rule that public funds cannot be granted to non-public undertakings. (This is being tested now in several states, notably in Maryland, where a law was passed granting financial aid to non-public institutions of higher education for buildings.)

### Court Decisions Consistent on State Authority

For three-quarters of a century, the highest state courts have uniformly upheld state control of education. One of the earliest and likewise one of the most frequently cited decisions was given in Indiana in 1890, holding that "the schools . . . are matters of state and not of local jurisdiction. In such matters the State is a unit and the Legislature the source of power." (*State ex rel. Clark v. Haworth*, 1890.) The Colorado Supreme Court in 1937 ruled that "the establishment and financial maintenance of the public schools is the carrying out of a state and not a local or municipal purpose." (*Wilmore v. Annear.*) And the same strong support of state control is echoed in a famous opinion of the state supreme court of Washington: "Local subdivisions of the state can be created by the sovereign power of the state without solicitation, consent, or concurrent action by the people who inhabit them. This being so, it follows that legislative authority over school districts is unlimited except as that limitation is found in the state constitution." (*Wheeler School District v. Hawley*, 1943.) Many other decisions could be cited, but these suffice to illustrate the point under discussion. One must also remember that the federal Constitution, as well as a state constitution, limits both state and local freedom of action in certain respects that are touched on later in this chapter.

### Long-standing Exercise of State Authority

In more than three hundred years of legislative history, the American colonies first and then the states have always held education as an important function of government. For the first two hundred years, until the time of Horace Mann, local school districts were assigned the main responsibility for setting up and operating schools. Mann's brilliant work as secretary of the Massachusetts state board of education, 1837–1849, led to a reawakening of the states to their responsibilities and greatly strengthened state educational administration. Since then the states have exercised gradually more and more control over education, and new laws have endowed their state boards and departments of education with more powers as well as more duties.

Although we read fairly often of the "threat" or the "need" of federal control of education, for more than a century and a half the federal government has, with few exceptions, helped firm up state control. The first instance, in 1803, was assigning to the states the title to "school sections" granted by the Ordinance of 1785 to townships for the benefit of local schools. With the admission of Michigan in 1837, the school lands were given to the states for the benefit of all schools, not limited to schools in the township where the school sections were situated. In Supreme Court decisions, also, state authority has been upheld except where it has been used to deprive citizens of Constitutional rights. And in most major federal programs, most recently the National Defense Education Act, the government has worked through regularly constituted state educational agencies.

# THE PARTNERSHIP CONCEPT OF STATE
# AND LOCAL RELATIONS

Postponing for the moment the educational relations of the federal government to state and local agencies, let us consider the role of the latter two. While their spheres of responsibility and action are not the same in all states, there has evolved a widely accepted idea that the states and their school districts are or should be partners in the conduct of education. Granting that state authority is pre-eminent, and that some areas must be reserved to the states, there are yet some operations that can be better managed by local units, or that it is wiser to share with them.

Attesting to this is the fact that no state, except Hawaii, administers public education directly without the help of school districts. Any state has the power to abolish all its districts, raise all necessary school funds by state taxes, construct the required buildings, employ, assign, and pay all personnel, and prescribe *in toto* the curriculum and extracurriculum; but no state operates this way, with the exception noted. (In Hawaii the present system was inherited from territorial times, when the Islands were admitted to the Union in 1959 as the fiftieth state.) Many states have made significant moves to enlarge their share of cooperative responsibility. As examples, the number of school districts has been much reduced in about three-quarters of the states since 1920; the percentage of school money raised and distributed by state governments has more than doubled in the same period; and steps have been taken to strengthen state school administration by removing it in part from party politics and providing professional leadership, better qualified staff, and better financial support.

## States Set the Basic Standards

What has emerged is a workable arrangement whereby the states, as a general rule, prescribe minimum or basic standards that all districts must meet or exceed. This leaves to the districts a large area of discretionary power in all states except California and Hawaii, as noted previously.

States establish standards through constitutional provisions and by statutory enactments of their legislatures. These are referred to collectively as the mandatory area of public education; local school boards have no choice but to obey, and are subject to penalties for not doing so. Among the most common items so mandated are compulsory attendance and ages it covers, minimum number of school days per year, minimum salaries that teachers may be paid, standards of safety and sanitation for schoolhouses, the conduct of school board elections and the terms and duties of board members, and taxation and budgets. In many states, certain subjects are required to be taught in all public schools, although educators are doubtful of the qualifications of legislators as curricular planners.

Along with such legal mandates and having the same force are directives, rules, and regulations promulgated by state boards and departments of education. It often happens that the law is silent on a given problem of educational administration or service; often, too, problems can be handled better by an administrative directive or regulation. A good example is the forms to be used for the school budget, financial, attendance, and other reports from which state and eventually national statistics on education are compiled.

In summary it may be said that states establish standards, or a "floor," of educational service below which no district is authorized to operate. The term "foundation program" is often used to convey this idea.

### Discretionary Powers of Districts for Local Adaptations

The foregoing discussion may leave the impression that local school districts are only mere lifeless instruments of state government. Indeed they have been described by various courts as "arms," "creatures," and "mere instrumentalities of the state." However, the districts nevertheless do possess quite a range of latitude or discretion in how they carry out state requirements. The requirements must be fulfilled, but in many cases there are different ways by which the letter and spirit of the law can be observed. Of more importance in this connection is the fact that minimum standards may be exceeded, that local educational efforts may and do generally go far beyond statutory or mandatory prescription. In practically all the states this is true. (In California, the state has followed a quite different path, permitting local boards to do only what the Education Code says they may do, thus severely limiting or attempting to eliminate the area of discretionary power. This is a major problem in California, and is the focus of strenuous efforts to liberalize the school laws.)

Numerous illustrations of the exercise of local discretion are to be found in nearly every community. It is almost impossible to find teachers' salaries at the minimum level prescribed by law; they have generally risen far above it. Curriculums embrace far more than the subjects prescribed by various states. Buildings and other physical facilities are better, in general, by a wide margin than building code requirements. It should be noted, nonetheless, that the unique freedom that American communities possess for educational experimentation, innovation, and adaptation to local conditions is not capitalized upon to a sufficient degree. During the decade of the 1960's, a more venturesome spirit has appeared; but there is a long way still to go in freeing our schools of inertia, apathy, and fear of breaking new ground.

## Conflict of "Centralist" and "Localist" Philosophies

How to strike the proper balance between centralized state control on the one hand and community control on the other hand is a perplexing problem. Each position has its strong advocates. Some contend that state governments should "put flesh on the bones of state responsibility," put the theory that education is a state function into practice. Others emphasize that "the schools belong to the people"; control must be vested largely in the community so that schools can be responsive to the needs and desires of the people.

The centralist is on.the firmer ground historically and legally, and the localist perhaps has tradition and sentiment on his side. The crux of the matter is how the enterprise of education can be carried on most effectively. If strong central administration tends to kill off community interest, support, and initiative, then it is too strong. Conversely, if a high degree of control is delegated to local school systems, absolutely unacceptable inequalities of educational opportunity for children and tax burdens for adults are almost sure to become widespread. For these reasons the partnership of state and local units, a sort of functional middle of the road, has evolved, as explained at the beginning of this section. Thus far it has served well, and further clarification of the respective spheres of state administration and school district operation will unquestionably strengthen it. This relationship, as also that between the states and the federal government, will always be in process of evolving, and never arrive at a fixed, immutable, final state.

# HOW STATES ORGANIZE TO CARRY OUT
# THEIR RESPONSIBILITY

Machinery has been created to enable each state to discharge its educational responsibility, as it is conceived by the people. About 350 state boards oversee a variety of educational enterprises. All but three states (Illinois, North Dakota, and Wisconsin) have a board for the general supervision of public elementary and secondary education; half of them are provided for in state constitutions and the rest by statute. Other services and activities are overseen by other boards, which in most cases are appointed for some specific program, such as education of the handicapped, library service, higher education, teacher education, certification of school personnel, textbook selection, and school building finance. To carry out or execute laws of the state and policies of state boards, a department of education has been set up in every state, headed by a chief state school officer, with the title of superintendent of public instruction or commissioner of education. Our concern in this section is with the general type of board referred to above, the chief school officer, and the department of education.

### State Board Membership

The first state board of education dates from 1784, when the Board of Regents of the University of the State of New York was set up. (The term "university" in this name is roughly equivalent to "state school system"; but in the beginning the Regents dealt only with King's College, now Columbia University, and academies chartered by English kings during the colonial period.) Other states that at an early date incorporated education in the structure of state government are North Carolina, Vermont, Michigan, Kentucky, Massachusetts, Connecticut, Missouri, and Tennessee.

Of the approximately four hundred members of state boards of education, 60 per cent are appointed (by governors usually); 35 per cent are elected by popular vote; and the rest hold office *ex officio*, by virtue of occupying some other office. The term of office ranges from three to nine years in all states except New York where it is thirteen. As a general rule, the members serve without pay; all are reimbursed for expenses incurred in attending meetings of the board.

While no one argues for ex officio membership, a good case can be made for either of the other two methods of selection. The current trend of thought favors appointment by the governor, preferably from a panel of nominees submitted by a special commission. Terms of seven to nine years are advocated, one expiring each year. It is believed that by appointment, rather than by popular election, better qualified persons can be selected for this important work.

In most states the qualifications for office are not elaborate. They may specify that one member must be chosen from each Congressional district; that one or more members, or on the other hand that no members, be engaged professionally in education; that not more than a given number may be members of the same political party; and so on. No educational attainment is prescribed in any state, but recent surveys show that about 85 per cent have attended or graduated from college.

### Duties and Powers of State Boards

A fairly close analogy can be seen between a state board and a city school board. At both levels the boards are concerned primarily, or should be, with policy making and general oversight of their respective educational enterprises. Administrative responsibilities are in both cases assigned to professionally qualified executives, the state superintendent or commissioner and the city school superintendent. There is a difference, of course, in that a state board typically is not immediately or directly responsible for the operation of any local units or institutions, while a local board is.

Experts in educational administration define state board responsibilities as in part directive or regulatory and in part advisory. The board is charged with seeing that the school laws embodied in the constitution and enacted by the legislature are complied with. It must approve rules and regulations whereby the state's will can be implemented. These matters are in the directive and regulatory sphere. Of an advisory nature are the exercise of leadership, encouragement, and cooperation in connection with local school systems. Most of this is done through the chief state school officer and the department of education, but the posture of the state board is of great importance in the improvement of educational service. The board should stand for and represent the aspirations of the people so far as educational matters are concerned. This is a high calling, and challenges the best abilities that can be marshaled for service on the board. It should take an active part, too, in interpreting the aims, achievements, and needs of education in the state. This is largely neglected now.

There are undoubtedly more state boards of various kinds, in addition to the type discussed here, than are needed. For greater effectiveness, all services at the elementary and secondary levels of education should be under one board. Probably, higher education can be better managed under a different board or separate institutional boards.

### The Chief State School Officer

This position has a surprisingly long history, for the first state superintendent was provided for by law in New York State in 1812. After nine years, the office lapsed and was not again established until 1854. Michigan claims the honor of having longest continuous history, dating from 1829. Since 1900 all states have had such an office under one or another title, about two thirds using "state superintendent of public instruction," or a very similar term, and one third "commissioner of education." At latest count (1964), twenty are elected by popular vote at general elections and thirty appointed—in all but five states— by the state board of education. The trend toward appointment and longer terms (or indefinite tenure) is quite pronounced. In 1940 only eight chief state school officers were appointed. Persons of better professional qualifications can probably be procured by appointment, and it is very likely that by 1980 few states will cling to the elective plan. For this is essentially a professional position, not merely a political post that the most successful vote-getter wins. Strong support was given to this view by the White House Conference on Education held in 1955, in referring to the chief school officer:

> His true functions are to provide leadership to the state's educational program and to serve as the chief executive officer of the state's school policies. Unfortunately, the circumstances under which this position exists in some states has made it difficult and sometimes impossible to realize the high potentialities. It is an important and encouraging fact that the trend is distinctly toward selection of the chief state school officer by a state board of education. This is preferable to popular election and other methods of selection.

### Duties and Powers of the Chief School Officer

At the state level, the superintendent or commissioner's work corresponds rather closely to that of a city school superintendent. He is the state board's executive, responsible for carrying out the duties given him by the board, or by the law, including putting into effect policies adopted by the board. With few exceptions, he must delegate the actual work to appropriate divisions of the state department of education, of which he is the head. But he cannot delegate responsibility for seeing that things are done.

One big difference between a state commissioner and a city superintendent is that the latter actually has schools operating under his immediate charge and for which he is accountable, while the state officer does not. The state man works through the education department with school districts, school systems, and higher education institutions, but is not their head.

## State Department of Education: The Operating Unit

Two main functions are carried on by state education departments, although there is quite a bit of variety in the way they are organized and staffed. These two dominant areas are usually referred to as regulation and leadership. The relative emphasis given to each depends somewhat on the philosophy or tradition of administration. In some states of strong, centralized administration, more emphasis is likely to be given regulation; in states with decentralized authority, more emphasis on counsel and assistance, although there is no clear-cut grouping possible. There is, however, a definite movement toward rendering more service to school systems and playing down control and direction.

The regulatory function serves at least five purposes: (1) protection of children's lives and health, (2) assurance of safety and prudence in use of school funds, (3) promotion of efficiency in educational management, as for example the reorganization of school districts, (4) maintenance and improvement of at least a reasonably satisfactory basic program of instruction throughout the state, and (5) development of an educated citizenry through enforcement of compulsory attendance laws and like matters. The leadership function includes (1) planning, (2) research, (3) advice and consultation, (4) coordination, and (5) fostering constructive relations between the state school system and the people of the state, especially their elected representatives in the legislature.

The area most in need of expansion in state education departments is research. Not only is there a generally naïve conception of what educational research consists, but there is also a shamefully inadequate commitment of funds and staff to research. Less than 5 per cent of state department activity is devoted to research, if one omits routine statistical studies. One way in which states could unquestionably make worthwhile contributions to educational thought and practice is financing and cooperating with "pilot programs" in school systems ready and willing to be designated as research centers. Little is being done now along this line, but there is more promise for the future.

Staffing state education departments has been a serious problem for many years, partly because of low salaries and partly because of their ineffectiveness in making any real impact on schools and school systems. While these frustrations have not been completely overcome, improvement in the last decade has been noteworthy. Better qualified personnel than formerly is now generally employed, and more of it. The staff is still too much tied down to the desk. A state education department probably should be administered much as a university is, with a high degree of freedom within a framework of institutional coordination.

## HOW THE STATES FINANCE EDUCATION

In Chapter 12 it has been shown how large a part local school districts play in financing public schools. The share that the states furnish is somewhat small, for the nation as a whole, but important for its effect on equalizing educational opportunities and reducing inequalities in taxation. Before an explanation is given of how the states raise and distribute school funds, however, a resumé of educational expenditures and reasons for their continued rise is submitted. Reference to Table 13–1 (p. 419) as the next few paragraphs are studied will help the reader get a clear understanding of the changes and trends mentioned.

Education constitutes a substantial financial enterprise. In the last few years, total annual expenditures for education—elementary, secondary, and higher, public and private—have been approaching $30 billion and now exceed that figure. For public elementary and secondary education, which takes about 65 per cent, the latest estimate, for 1964–65, is $22 billion. For non-public elementary and secondary education, $3.5 billion is spent. Higher education requires $9 billion, in the ratio of about 60:40 for public and private institutions. These amounts include expenditures for capital outlay such as land, buildings, and equipment, which in public schools is about one-fifth of total outlay. Of the gross national product, education now requires about 7 per cent; public elementary and secondary education, approximately 5.5 per cent. These ratios are the highest for many years.

## Reasons for Continued Rise of Expenditures for Education

Five factors are responsible for most if not all of the increases that are characteristic of educational expenditures decade after decade. This has been going on since financial statistics were first collected, in the 1870's; and the end is not in sight.

1. Increased school attendance at all levels. More children are in school and college, more days per year, and staying more years than formerly. With the exception of a ten-year period in the latter 1930's and early 1940's, when depression and war caused a decline in school enrollment, there has been for many decades an upward trend. About one in every four persons in the total U.S. population is enrolled in school or college. The next few years will probably give an indication of whether this ratio will change, for the children born at the beginning of our record high birthrate period since 1945 will begin having their families.

The median level of educational attainment of persons twenty-five years old and over continues to rise, and is now a little beyond eleventh grade. In 1950 it was only 9.3 years of schooling; in 1940, 8.4 years. Since about two-thirds of all pupils now finish high school, the typical level of education completed by the adult population twenty-five and over will very soon exceed twelve years. Substantially more than half of high school graduates go on to higher education, double the ratio of only a quarter-century ago. In the states with highest expenditures per pupil in elementary and secondary schools, more children enter college and more stay on to receive degrees than is true in states of low expenditures.

2. Improvement in the status of teachers. As teachers have become better prepared, their salaries have risen, although an undetermined fraction of such gains must be ascribed to the nationwide trend toward higher pay levels generally. In 1930 the average teacher's salary was only $1,420; in 1950, $3,010; and in 1963, $5,735—all a little below the average of all employed persons. However, teachers' pay is now about at the average of all employed workers, and will probably exceed it soon.

Levels of education have improved notably. In 1930, 88 per cent of elementary school teachers did not have college degrees, and 13 per cent of high school teachers lacked degrees. Today, less than 1 per cent of the total teaching force have no degree, while about 30 per cent have master's degrees or higher. With society's demands for better and better educational service (of which teaching is the very heart), inevitably higher levels of teacher education will be needed.

Higher pay will surely accompany this movement. More is said about these matters in Chapter 16.

3. Another major cause of increased expenditures is the addition, extension, and improvement of various school services. Nobody except a rare type of reactionary today advocates a literal return to the Three R's—reading, 'riting, and 'rithmetic. Most people, on the other hand, call on the schools to do more and more. Both elementary and secondary school curricula have been expanded every decade as the schools try to meet new demands. New services are added from time to time: health services, school lunches, guidance and counseling, pupil transportation, etc. Just the one item of transportation alone is almost unbelievable, for about thirteen million children are transported to and from school every day in tens of thousands of school buses. Class size has been declining slowly for many years, although research on it is inconclusive. Teachers prefer classes of twenty-five to thirty; and except in some very large city school systems, this is the rule in most school systems. Team teaching and other modifications permit large classes up to two or three hundred for some purposes, but it also calls for very small groups of five to fifteen, so usually there is one teacher for about every thirty pupils on a school staff regardless of the type of instructional program.

4. Making tax-supported schools really free for pupils is another significant item. At the moment, we seem to have reached a plateau, for not much progress is being made to free the schools of quite a wide assortment of fees, admissions, club dues, activity costs, and the like. The problem exists mainly at the high school level, where various kinds of costs borne by the pupil (or by his parents in addition to their taxes) total as much as $200 a year. Textbooks are rented or a fee paid for them and other instructional materials; even in elementary schools about one-third of the states do not require textbooks to be furnished free of charge. Users of this book may cast their minds back over their own experience and then ask if their schools were really free. How literally this should be interpreted has often given rise to hot debate. Historically, however, the scope of free schooling has grown mightily and contributed to the need for increased financial support.

5. Finally, the effect of inflation has been a quite serious reason for increased school expenditures since 1940. For the same goods and services, it would take about three times as much money now as it did then. The pace of inflation varies from year to year; but stabilized prices, wages, and salaries seem definitely to be features of the past, not the present or the future. People forget how large an element in-

flation, or the decline in purchasing power of the dollar, is in their education bill, as in every other field.

## "Holding the Line" an Unrealistic Cliché

Some critics, like one of the state governors who called education a "sacred cow" in 1963, are alarmed by the continuing rise of educational expenditures. But when one considers the combination of reasons back of it, he would, in all likelihood, be unable to suggest a remedy that would be generally acceptable to the American people. The critics also forget, or perhaps disagree, that schools and higher institutions are established to spend money, not save it, and that the level of expenditure is correlated closely with the quality of services rendered. No one has yet defined the point of diminishing returns. Most school systems are so far below the level of good support that reducing or stabilizing expenditures is simply not realistic. Even if the amount spent per child per year were held constant, increasing enrollments by themselves would, of course, require proportionately greater funds. The effects of inflation, higher standards of service demanded by our culture, and other items mentioned above would be impossible for any one state or school system to escape. Actually, when the purchasing power of the dollar is kept constant, there has been a few cents decline in the expenditure per pupil per day since 1900.

One must also ask if we as a people want education to take a smaller part of our financial resources, in a nation that boasts of being the richest and most advanced in the world, where the average citizen lives on a standard that is described as luxurious by other peoples. "Holding the line" either on dollar amounts spent per pupil or on per cent of tax funds used for education would hurt education in comparison with other public services unless *all* held the line. And that does not seem to be in the cards.

## The Extent of State Support and Method of Distribution

On the average the fifty state governments contribute about 40 per cent of the current cost of operating public elementary and secondary schools, and thirty make loans or grants to assist local districts in providing buildings and grounds. However, in several states the extent of state support for current expenditures is less than 20 per cent, and it is more than 70 per cent in several others, so that considerable differences exist. Most school finance experts believe that a state should participate at somewhere near the 50 per cent level, which sixteen states already exceed. There is also a consensus that buildings and equipment, along with needed sites, should be included in the budget supported by the state.

Equally important as the proportion of state support are the methods by which it is distributed. All the states impose some qualifications that local school systems must meet in order to receive state funds. Such requirements are intended not to penalize communities, but to assist in preserving local initiative, and to encourage communities to strive for higher standards. Most of the requirements relate to the number of days that school must be in session, paying at least specified minimum salaries to teachers, employing only properly certified personnel, and the like. In some states, the local districts must show that they have levied the tax required by the state as a condition of receiving state money, as a sort of proof that reasonable local effort is made to meet the cost of a basic program of education. This last point is especially important in fund distribution and explains why so much weight is placed on state support.

In a district or county with many pupils but low property valuation, the required local tax levy will not raise much money toward the cost of the basic program. In a community or county with relatively few pupils and a high property valuation, the tax will raise nearly or more than enough for the basic "foundation program." Therefore, by a formula that takes account of the number of pupils (or in some states the number of teachers required), and the taxpaying ability of the district, the state gives more help to the needy areas and less to the more favored. This method of fund distribution is called "equalization," because it helps communities of below-average levels of taxpaying ability and above-average levels of pupil population offer reasonably adequate educational service, with a reasonable taxpaying effort.

Suppose a state legislated that for every twenty-five pupils (defined as a classroom unity), each school district would be guaranteed $7,500 for its current expenditures. In this state, let us say that each district was required to levy 20 mills in order to qualify for state aid. A mill is one-thousandth part of a dollar and is often used to indicate the *rate* of taxation. A tax of 1 mill is a tax of $1.00 on every thousand dollars worth of property subject to taxation. Thus a tax of 1 mill on a house and lot assessed at $5,000 would equal $5. A tax of 20 mills would be $20 on every thousand or, in this case, a total of $100 on the house. (In some states, the term "mill" is not used, but rates are calculated in terms of dollars and cents per $100 valuation. A rate of $1 means $1 tax on every $100 property value, or $10 per $1,000 value. This is the same as a 10-mill tax. A rate of $2 is the same as 20 mills, etc.

It's merely a matter of different terminology.) In Table 13–1, an example is given to show how districts of above-average, average, and below-average taxpaying ability would receive different amounts of state support. This is a highly simplified, fictitious example; but it does show how the principle of equalization might operate.

**TABLE 13–1**

|  | District A | District B | District C |
|---|---|---|---|
| 1. Cost of basic or "foundation" program that is guaranteed by state for each classroom unit of twenty-five pupils . . . . . . | $7,500 | $7,500 | $7,500 |
| 2. Number of classroom units | 400 | 400 | 400 |
| 3. Total guarantee . . . . | $3,000,000 | $3,000,000 | $3,000,000 |
| 4. Assessed valuation of property to be taxed . . . . | $150,000,000 | $100,000,000 | $50,000,000 |
| 5. Yield of uniform tax of 20 mills ($20 per $1,000 property) . . . . . . . . | $3,000,000 | $2,000,000 | $1,000,000 |
| 6. Balance the state is required to pay to fulfill guarantee . . . . . . | None | $1,000,000 | $2,000,000 |

Since it is a relatively wealthy community, District A would receive no state support; it could raise the guaranteed amount by the required levy of 20 mills. Without state support, District B would have to levy 30 mills; and District C, 60 mills. In actual practice, states usually see that every district, no matter how well off it is, receives some state money. Usually, too, counties raise some school money, which is distributed to their districts and counted as part of the local effort. In a few states, a state grant is made at a given amount per pupil, for instance, $200 per pupil, which is then supplemented by funds raised by local and county taxation.

The basic or foundation amounts used in state support formulas fall considerably short of what schools actually spend. The U.S. average annual expenditure per pupil (excluding the cost of buildings and interest on bond issues for buildings) is about $500. Thus a "classroom unit" of twenty-five pupils would cost $12,500, not $7,500 as shown in Table 13–1. In some states, about 40 per cent more than the national average is spent; in others, little more than half the average.

### Support of Higher Education

There are about 2,100 institutions of higher education in the United States, including some six hundred junior colleges. Of this large total, one-third, including 60 per cent of the junior colleges, are under control of state governments, cities or counties, or school or college districts. All the rest, except twelve operated by the federal government, are under church or other non-public auspices. More than $6 billion a year is expended from public and private sources for higher education. The figure is rapidly mounting as college and university enrollments each year set new records.

The non-public institutions receive no tax support; but depend on tuition and fees paid by students, earnings of endowment funds, gifts, foundation grants, and earnings of auxiliary enterprises. Publicly controlled institutions rely on some tax support from the governmental unit they are responsible to. The per cent of funds derived from public funds ranges from 30 to more than 90 per cent, but tends to center around 60 to 65 per cent. Student fees and tuition, gifts and grants, earnings from invested funds, and income from auxiliary enterprises (bookstores, food services, and the like) make up the balance. For all institutions, public and private, student fees and tuition supply about 25 per cent of the operating funds (not including funds for construction); state funds about 30 per cent; federal sources (of which research grants constitute 90 per cent), 25 per cent; with the remaining 20 per cent coming from endowment earnings, gifts and grants, auxiliary enterprises, and miscellaneous sources.

An interesting segment of American higher education is the sixty-eight land-grant colleges, provided for by the first Morrill Act in 1862 and subsequent laws. Each of the fifty states has at least one of these institutions, seventeen states have two, and Puerto Rico has one. One-fifth of all higher education students attend these institutions, many of which are state universities of the first rank. The main difference in their financing, compared with higher education as a whole, is much less reliance on student fees and tuition, which constitute only about 10 per cent of their income. Earnings from "related activities" and "auxiliary enterprises" are higher than average, but federal and state funds are close to average.

## TWO CENTURIES OF NATIONAL GOVERNMENT INTEREST IN EDUCATION

Federal control of education would be totally unacceptable to a vast majority of American citizens, including the authors of this book. However, as leading political scientists for many years have well said, education must be the first concern of a modern nation. Our national government's concern for and interest in education are the burden of this last portion of the chapter, concluding with a brief discussion of major issues related to the role of the federal government in education. It is news to many people that encouragement of education by the federal government has an unbroken history of nearly two hundred years. Some demagogs would have us believe that the manifestation of our national government's interest in education is a monstrous thing that only recently appeared on the horizon as a deadly threat to our way of life.

## Land Grants and Other Forms of General Aid

During the Colonial period, several colonies, including Massachusetts, Connecticut, and New York, developed a policy of making grants of land for the benefit of local schools and churches. Taking a cue from this practice, with respect to schools, the Congress under the Articles of Confederation adopted the great Ordinance of 1785 (referred to in Chapter 5), which laid the foundation of what was probably the greatest endowment for any purpose anywhere. Thirty-one states have received grants of land ranging from 1 to 4 square miles in each township for the benefit of public education. All these grants reached a total of about 150,000 square miles, three-quarters the size of France, or equal to the combined areas of Indiana, Illinois, and Wisconsin. The states that did not receive school lands were the original thirteen in which there was no federal land; states carved from them (Vermont, Maine, and West Virginia); states admitted before Congress actually enacted laws making the policy effective (Kentucky and Tennessee); and Texas, which was an independent republic when it was annexed in 1845. Much of this splendid endowment was dissipated through the years by selling off the land at prices that now seem ridiculous, e.g., $1.25 an acre in Illinois (what would a square mile in Cook County be worth now?), and by mismanagement and graft. The value of the lands, if all had been retained by the states for the benefit of their schools, would today probably be several billions. Other smaller land grants were made until 1866, mainly saline and swamp lands, sometimes as payment to the states for funds spend in reclamation work. Small amounts of money have been granted from time to time, in some cases a percentage of the price received from sale of government land, or of forest and grazing income, or leases and royalties from mineral lands.

Additional land grants were made to the states (or "land scrip" to states with no federal land) under the famous Morrill Act of 1862 for colleges of agriculture and mechanic arts, the land-grant colleges mentioned above. More than 11 million acres were distributed this way; and various other grants for normal schools, universities, schools of mines, and so on, bring the total to about 15 million. The grand total of all land grants for education is approximately 175 million acres, or 273,000 square miles, a little more than the area of Texas.

### Financial Grants for Specific Programs

Many billions of dollars have been appropriated by Congress for education, in addition to the land grants. Small amounts were paid under various acts, beginning in 1836 with the Act to Regulate the Deposit of Public Money down through the rest of the nineteenth century. Aid for land-grant colleges in the form of small money grants was provided by the second Morrill Act in 1890. This has grown from such nominal sums as $15,000, then $25,000 per institution, to much larger amounts through legislation, now exceeding half a billion dollars annually, or an average of more than $8 million per institution.

Since 1917, when the Smith-Hughes Act for vocational education below college level was passed, the government has been engaged in quite a wide variety of aid programs, some of them of large proportions. Since the amounts vary from time to time, generally increasing, the major programs are named here to illustrate the range of national interest. The federal government actually engaged in about three hundred educational programs, many administered by cabinet departments and independent agencies, others in cooperation with state and local units.

The depression of the 1930's gave rise to four large programs that continued until 1942–1943, after the United States had entered World War II. These were the Work Projects Administration (WPA), the Public Works Administration (PWA), the National Youth Administration (NYA), and the Civilian Conservation Corps (CCC). These were designed to relieve unemployment and stimulate the economy in many ways, and were not primarily intended as aid to education. But there were also numerous benefits to state and local school systems and to institutions, a few of which are indicated.

Tens of thousands of high school and college age youth were assisted in continuing their education by providing part-time employment. To show how desperate were the times, the million and a half high school students who were aided received $6 and the 620,000 college students $25 a month; these wages made the difference between being able to stay in school or not. Through the WPA, 6,000 schools were built and 33,000 enlarged or remodeled. Millions of adults were enrolled in many kinds of classes, and many types of employment were partly financed. At one time in 1937, approximately two million adults were enrolled in adult education classes. School lunches, book repair, nursery schools, and numerous other educational activities were important facets of this largest of all the depression relief programs. The PWA concentrated mostly on educational and other public buildings to bolster the far-flung construction industries. The CCC was administered mainly by the War Department, with certain aspects under the Departments of Agriculture, Interior, and Labor. Its efforts were focused on getting unemployed youth below age twenty-five off the streets. They were put at useful work in national parks, on soil and water conservation projects, and the like, and offered a chance to take vocational courses in order to learn some employable skills. In its nine years of operation, the CCC enrolled about 3.2 million young people.

Near the end of the war, in 1944, the Servicemen's Readjustment Act (GI Bill) provided for educational benefits for war veterans. Amended several times, the act was kept in force until the sixties, and extended to include veterans of the Korean War. This is one of the largest educational programs ever approved by Congress, running to some $15 billion and assisting hundreds of thousands of veterans to attend colleges and other institutions.

The federal school lunch program, operating under a 1946 act subsequently amended, assists school districts to provide wholesome, inexpensive lunches for millions of elementary and secondary school children in public and non-public schools. Surplus commodities and small cash grants are made available. Aid for communities overburdened by an influx of population associated with federal installations began as an emergency program during the war (Lanham Act). It has been continued and expanded ever since under two labels: Public Law 815 to finance construction of schoolhouses, and Public Law 874 for current operating expenses. Communities near large military centers, federal construction projects, and various other kinds of large government operations have been enabled to cope better with enrollment increases by these acts. The government does not furnish enough aid but it helps.

In just the last few years, some new federal ventures into education are especially noteworthy. The National Defense Education Act (NDEA) was approved in 1958, and about one billion dollars authorized for the first four years. It has since been extended with increased funds provided, embracing a number of different purposes. Matching funds from the states are required for some phases, continuing a principle embodied in the Smith-Hughes Act of 1917. The NDEA helps finance loans and fellowships for college and university students; instruction and equipment in mathematics, science, and certain foreign languages; improvement of guidance, testing, and counseling services; and some aspects of vocational education. The idea behind the original NDEA, passed shortly after the U.S.S.R. launched its first Sputnik into orbit, is that in a free society well-educated individuals are the first line of defense.

In 1964 a $2 billion plan for grants and loans for college and university construction was approved to help institutions accommodate the unprecedented rise in enrollments that by 1970 will reach an estimated seven million. Vocational education funds for secondary schools were approximately doubled to more than $100 million annually. Other acts provided for aiding medical education, and combating the dropout problem. But Congress has never in this long history, or in the most recent flurry of new and expanded aids for education, ever made appropriations for the *general* support of public elementary and secondary education. Every dollar is appropriated for a designated *specific* purpose, such as school lunches, science education, or school construction in "federally-impacted" localities. This point is brought into the discussion again in the last section of the chapter.

### The U.S. Office of Education

Perhaps the reluctance of the federal government to become active in the field of education explains the fact that not until three-quarters of a century after the election of Washington was a national agency for education set up. No nationwide statistics were collected; no data were available in any one place on the status or progress of education in the several states. The National Teachers Association and the National Association of State and City School Superintendents (now respectively the National Education Association and the American Association of School Administrators) played a leading part in working for a national agency. James A. Garfield, then a member of the House of Representatives, introduced the bill and President Andrew Johnson signed it, creating a Department of Education in 1867. It was changed to a Bureau of Education in 1870 and placed in the Department of the Interior, where it stayed until 1939. Then it was transferred to the Federal Security Agency, which in 1953 became the Department of Health, Education, and Welfare. Since 1929 this agency has been known as the U.S. Office of Education.

Originally, the Office was charged with three duties: (1) to collect facts on the condition and progress of education, (2) to disseminate such facts, and (3) to "promote the cause of education throughout the country." This charge is broad enough to allow for considerable latitude for the Office to engage in a wide variety of activities. The scope of its work has been greatly expanded by assignments from Congress, such as supervision of the allocation of funds to land-grant colleges, administration of vocational education and vocational rehabilitation, the NDEA, a huge "Cooperative Research Program," and numerous other activities. Hundreds of publications issue from the Office over a broad spectrum of educational interests. Some of the most useful are the *Biennial Survey of Education*, reports on educational systems in other countries, the monthly journal *School Life*, and an annual *Digest of Educational Statistics*.

The U.S. Office of Education is headed by a Commissioner of Education appointed by the President. About 1,500 persons are employed, and annual appropriations for salaries and expenses are in the neighborhood of $15 million. While the internal organization of the Office undergoes changes with each new commissioner, in general the work is carried on through major divisions, such as Elementary and Secondary Education, Vocational and Technical Education, Educational Statistics, Educational Research, International (or Comparative) Education, and College and University Assistance. The latest plan of organization had eleven divisions.

## The Supreme Court's Far-reaching Decisions on Education

A few examples of the influence of U.S. Supreme Court decisions should be mentioned as an avenue for the expression of national interest. The Court is one of the chief bulwarks of our Constitutional system; it has consistently upheld state control of education within a framework of individual and group rights guaranteed by the Constitution. While it speaks with authority, even to the extent of redefining the functions and limits of public education from time to time, the Court's decisions always reflect Constitutional authority, and no grant of power has ever been made to Congress for the general control or administration of the public schools.

The famous Dartmouth College case of 1819 was the first education case to reach the Court. The New Hampshire legislature had tried to take over the College for a state university, but the Court upheld as inviolable the royal charter issued to the College. This outcome encouraged donors to support private institutions more liberally than they might otherwise have done. Most of the cases reaching the

Court have originated since 1930. Many of them relate to racial segregation of schools and to matters of religious import, but there are other extremely significant decisions also. A few interesting examples are given.

On segregation the Court in 1896 (*Plessy v. Ferguson*) held that "separate but equal facilities" were not in violation of the Constitution. On May 17, 1954, however, this position was reversed in a historic decision (*Brown v. Board of Education*) and a series of later cases. Segregation on racial grounds was struck down, the Court branding it as inevitably resulting in unequal facilities and opportunities and inherently wrong on social and psychological grounds. In 1925 the Court ruled that the state of Oregon could not require all children to attend only public schools, overruling a barefaced attempt by the legislature to liquidate non-public (mainly Catholic) schools. (*Pierce v. Society of the Sisters of the Holy Names of Jesus and Mary,* and *Pierce v. Hill Military Academy.*) This decision did not question a state's authority to require parents to send their children to school, but it held that a state cannot decide for the parents which school.

In 1943 the Court ruled that pupils cannot be required to salute the American flag or recite the pledge of allegiance as conditions of attending public school. This reversed a 1940 decision. (*West Virginia State Board of Education v. Barnette,* 1943, and *Minersville School District v. Gobitis,* 1940.) A great stir was created in 1963 by a decision declaring unconstitutional a prayer composed by the Board of Regents of the state of New York for use in opening exercises in public schools. Such an action conflicts with the Constitutional prohibition on establishment of religion. The Court said, in effect, that no official body has the right to compose a prayer for school use even though pupils are permitted to be excused at their parents' request from reciting it. A great many people set themselves up as better judges of the Constitutional question involved than the Supreme Court, which seems to be a favorite pastime when a decision goes against people's special interests.

The Court has been diligent in these and about a hundred other "school cases" in preserving Constitutional rights and liberties, and in interpreting the complex relationships of local, state, and federal governments. It is interesting to read decisions on the extremely important cases heard by the Court and to follow the reasoning by which the justices reach a conclusion. Split decisions are not infrequent in cases relating to education, which illustrates a characteristic of the social sciences in general: that questions can rarely be settled in a categorical or absolutist fashion.

## Questions Frequently Raised About Federal Relations

Most of the questions on federal relations to education revolve around two points: (1) federal aid and (2) federal control. In the following discussion, a few of the topics most frequently encountered are briefly covered.

**Is Education a Proper Concern of the Federal Government?**  Those who ask this question seldom answer it in the affirmative, arguing on the contrary that education is solely a matter of state and community interest. Some go so far as to hold that it is a matter of purely local interest. Perhaps the most compelling evidence that the federal government properly may be, indeed must be, concerned about education is the record of its interest extending for nearly two centuries, antedating the Constitution itself, as noted a few pages back. If the mature judgment of leading statesmen and scholars is added to this, then assuredly a very strong case for the federal government's participation in education is obvious.

**Should the Government Appropriate Funds?**  One of the best ways, in the authors' opinion, for the government to demonstrate that its concern for education is not merely lip service is to appropriate money to help finance it. Here again there is a long history of financial aid, which has certainly helped states and communities to some extent, and served a wide variety of needs. One might ask why education is singled out by critics as not needing federal aid when dozens of other state and local services are aided, some on a very big scale. Two questions dealt with next are closely associated with this one.

**Should the Government, in Making Funds Available, Include Non-Public Schools in the Distribution?**  This is a widely debated question, and intense interest has been generated on both the negative and affirmative sides. While many states prohibit in their constitutions the use of tax money for non-public schools of any kinds, the question of direct or indirect federal aid has not been settled. Pupils in non-public schools do benefit from such tax-supported services as school lunches in all states, free provisions of textbooks and school bus transportation in some states. These are deemed to be benefits to the children, not to the institutions, and hence have been held to be not in violation of the U.S. Constitution. A state may, however, prohibit free books and transportation for pupils in non-public schools. The U.S. Constitution does not require them to be provided.

**Can the States Receive Federal Aid Without Giving Up Control of Education?** In all federal aid acts that provide for grants of funds to states and school districts, some degree of control is present. What one considers as control depends on the rigor of his definitions, and there are some conditions attached to grants that may be more tolerable than others. Experts on school finance and taxation agree, however, that the method Congress uses to distribute aid, for the support of specific services or activities, encourages and opens the door to federal control. The Smith-Hughes Act is sometimes cited as a prime example; and if one reads the text of that 1917 act, he will find at least a dozen conditions or restrictions with which a state or school district must comply if it wants federal funds. The NDEA is another more recent example of restrictions on the way grants may be spent.

While Congress has never approved a bill for lump-sum grants to the states, requiring only an audit to show that the funds are spent for public education and not some other purpose, this is the way recommended by those who study the problem, if federal control is to be avoided or reduced to the very minimum. Grants should be made to the states, based on their relative taxpaying ability (as measured by the income tax), and the percentage of population of school age; and the states should be free to distribute such funds as they distribute other school funds. A few who call themselves realists do not believe Congress will ever make such lump-sum grants because representatives and senators feel that they must be able to show their constituents something more tangible than just "aid for education." The next best thing would be grants earmarked for teachers' salaries and schoolhouse construction, which together take 75 per cent or more of the typical school budget. This would come close to "general aid."

Of course, a few people agree that a nationalized or "federalized" school system would be better than the decentralized state-and-local system we now have. When one looks at the experience of other countries with a highly centralized national system, however, he cannot be very sanguine about its fitness for the United States. It is quite doubtful if we would want to adopt the monolithic pattern of the U.S.S.R., the highly centralized system of France, or the monopoly of education exercised under such dictatorships as those of prewar Japan, Italy under Mussolini, or Germany under Hitler. The authors are convinced, and they believe most Americans take the same position, that our society benefits from the diversity inherent in our decentralized system, and that it is a good thing to have many citizens participating in decision making at local and state levels. Federal control could not enforce uniformity in such a vast and vital country, but it could and probably would reduce citizen initiative and participation.

## Four Chief Reasons for Advocating Federal Aid

It seems well to conclude this discussion with a brief note on four reasons in support of federal aid, which seem to the authors quite persuasive.

1. Among the states there is a wide spread in the number of school-age children per thousand adults. In some states there are more than six hundred children per thousand adults, while in others there are only three to four hundred. Thus the former have nearly double the load to provide for.

2. Per capita income likewise extends to a large range. In some states per capita income is about twice as much as in other states; in recent years the highest being approximately $3,500, and the lowest in the vicinity of $1,500 to $1,800. Now, most of the states with the relatively greater load in terms of school-age children are at the low end of the income distribution, which compounds their difficulty in financing education. These first two reasons are often cited as showing a need for federal funds to help equalize the taxpaying effort among the states, to give more aid to the needier states, and less to those more able to finance schools.

3. The population of the United States is very mobile. Each year about 20 per cent of the population moves, and about one-fourth of these move across state lines. So the quality of schooling in any state is of concern to other states; in other words, it is a national concern.

4. The federal government's tax-collecting machinery has become so efficient that it now takes in about 75 per cent of all taxes collected, while the states and all their subdivisions combined take in only 25 per cent. This is just the reverse of thirty years ago. Therefore, finance experts argue, if the federal government does not materially reduce its tax take to allow the state more leeway in taxation, then it should return some of its funds to the states for education, as it does for many other purposes.

## QUESTIONS, PROBLEMS, AND PROJECTS FOR FURTHER STUDY

1. Should non-public schools be required by state law to meet the same standards as public schools, e.g., on number of days per year, educational qualifications of teachers and principals, and adequacy and safety of buildings and equipment?

2. Compare the national concern for education in the United States with that in one other country (selected by you), showing how this concern is manifested in each nation.

3. Should the members of state boards of education be required to have high school or college diplomas? What reasons can you give either in favor of or against such a requirement? Should other qualifications be prescribed?

4. In connection with the continuing rise of school expenditures as discussed in this chapter, some critics hold that school boards can keep expenditures from rising if they really want to. To what extent do you agree or disagree, and for what reasons?

5. Are school fees for textbooks, activity tickets, student activities, etc., incompatible with the American ideal of free public education? Should all fees and costs assessed to pupils be abolished? Or, if not, which ones should be kept and why?

6. In the latest edition of the government's biennial report, *Federal Funds for Education*, look up expenditures for five or six major federally aided programs and the total for all federal aid for all purposes. Compare this last figure with total educational expenditures for the whole country, available in various U.S. Office of Education reports. In the report, *Federal Funds for Education*, note the many different kinds of educational endeavors in which the government is involved and the numerous departments and agencies concerned.

7. Arrange for a debate by members of the class on the proposition: Resolved: That one state board for the entire public educational system (including elementary, secondary, and higher education) would serve the interests of the state better than the present arrangement.

8. Why does it make any difference if state support of education is at the 20 per cent level or the 50 per cent level, since all public funds come out of "the taxpayers' pockets" in either case?

9. For which side do arguments on federal aid seem the more persuasive to you, for or against? Give reasons why, and conditions that might make you change your position.

## SELECTED SUPPLEMENTARY READINGS AND FILMS

ALLEN, HOLLIS P. *The Federal Government and Education*. New York: McGraw-Hill Book Co., Inc., 1950. A standard work on the subject. Although many of the data are out of date, the problems and issues identified have remained much the same.

BEACH, FRED F., and WILL, ROBERT. *The State and Education.* U.S. Office of Education, Misc. No. 33. Washington, D.C.: Government Printing Office, 1955. Focused on the structure and control of public education at the state level, this report also identifies changes that should be made to cope with expanding responsibilities and rapidly increasing enrollments. It does not, however, deal with all agencies involved in education, e.g., retirement boards, library commissions, and apprenticeship councils. There are individual sections on the several states.

*Biennial Survey of Education.* Washington, D.C.: Government Printing Office. Issued every two years by the U.S. Office of Education, this publication includes a wealth of statistical data on public and nonpublic education. An especially useful part, "Statistics of State School Systems," may be procured separately. See also the excellent annual *Digest of Educational Statistics,* issued by the U.S. Office of Education and published by the Government Printing Office.

*Federal Funds for Education.* Washington, D.C.: Government Printing Office. For more than thirty years this report has been issued by the U.S. Office of Education every two years. It gives detailed, reliable statistical data on federal participation in financing a vast array of educational activities.

GRIEDER, CALVIN, PIERCE, TRUMAN M., and ROSENSTENGEL, WILLIAM EVERETT. *Public School Administration.* 2d ed. New York: The Ronald Press Co., 1961. Chaps. ii and iii deal with state and federal relations to education.

NATIONAL EDUCATION ASSOCIATION. *Financing the Public Schools, 1960–1970.* Washington, D.C.: The Association, 1962. Report of a committee on rapidly expanding U.S. school and college enrollment, and amount and methods of financial support needed to provide for it. Designed as a source book for the public as well as for teachers' associations, it includes a wealth of facts and projections on many phases of educational finance.

NORTON, JOHN K. *Changing Demands on Education and Their Fiscal Implications.* Washington, D.C.: National Committee for Support of the Public Schools, 1963. Concerned primarily with "the interrelations of education and economics," as they affect the well-being of individuals and the nation. In twelve short chapters this booklet presents essential data and interprets them in plain language.

RESEARCH DIVISION OF THE NEA. *Rankings of the States.* Washington, D.C.: National Education Association. Published annually. In this interesting and useful compilation of latest available facts, the states are ranked in about one hundred tables on population, school enrollment, teachers, educational attainment, finances, and other subjects.

SCHULZ, THEODORE W. "Education and Economic Growth." Chap. iii in *Social Forces Influencing American Education,* Sixtieth Yearbook of the National Society for the Study of Education, Nelson B. Henry (ed.). Chicago: University of Chicago Press, 1961, pp. 46–88. An exploratory study of the economic returns to U.S. society from its investment in education. By means of a lucid text and twenty-four tables, it leads the student to an appreciation and introductory grasp of the "exceedingly complex connections" between education and economic growth.

See also by the same author, *The Economic Value of Education*. New York: Columbia University Press, 1963.

SPURLOCK, CLARK. *Education and the Supreme Court*. Urbana, Ill.: University of Illinois Press, 1955. Discusses decisions rendered by the Court in cases relating to education.

THURSTON, LEE M., and ROE, WILLIAM H., *State School Administration*. New York: Harper & Row, 1957. A comprehensive treatment of the history, growth, and current status of state administration of education.

## Films

*Design of American Public Education*. 16 minutes. An animated film showing the structure of American public education, first as it might be if it were an "assembly line" process centrally controlled, then as it actually is in a democratic society. New York: McGraw-Hill Book Co., Inc.

*Do You Approve of Federal Aid to Education?* 26 minutes. Relevant facts pro and con concerning national issues are submitted to audience for evaluation. Facts Forum (film available from Brigham Young University, Provo, Utah).

# 14

# THE PHYSICAL SETTING
# OF SCHOOL SERVICES

Schools and school systems are made up of many components, of which physical facilities are one rather large and inclusive type. Covered by this term is a bewildering variety of school grounds, buildings, fixed equipment, and movable equipment and furniture, which take on the average 15 to 20 per cent of school funds each year. Not a great deal of exact knowledge is available on the effects of sites, buildings, and equipment on the learning process. But it is firmly believed by nearly all educators that the physical environment and the many kinds of equipment used in modern instruction can either facilitate or hinder pupil achievement, depending on their suitability and on teacher ability to make intelligent use of them. Such research as has been done—and its volume is growing—supports this conviction.

Teachers are at the very heart of the instructional effort. Highly intelligent, imaginative, and ingenious teachers can no doubt teach well even in discouraging circumstances. They do even better with superior facilities, although ordinary teachers are probably benefited more. In any event, modern science and technology have produced so many advances in all the accoutrement of education—in materials, design, beauty, and usefulness—that it would be a shame not to capitalize on them. The purpose of this chapter is to summarize contemporary thought on the school plant, illustrate trends, and give some concrete examples of new developments. Naturally, many readers using this book will recognize some of the items mentioned as having been a part of their own experience, but others will perhaps be new to them. Visits to newly constructed schools are a good way to see firsthand the application of contemporary ideas and findings to the improvement of the teaching and learning environment.

## SYMBOL OF COMMUNITY ASPIRATIONS

In some communities, the vaunted "American faith in education" is not readily apparent. However, if one travels about the country and takes the trouble to get off the bypasses of the superhighways, he cannot fail to see the prominent place accorded to elementary and secondary schools. While older schools, especially in large cities, are not so favorably situated, schoolhouses erected in the last thirty or forty years (and particularly within the last ten or fifteen years) are typically placed on generous sites that allow for landscaping and playgrounds. Architects cooperate with school boards and teaching staffs, frequently assisted by citizens' committees, to design schools that exemplify community ideals and aspirations. School buildings and grounds are conceived of as far more than custodial institutions or as mere containers for the meeting of highly regimented classes. Planners hold that the school should enhance the quality of living, should be a place of beauty outside and inside, a source of community pride, and a mark of their high regard for education.

### Schools Not Hidden Away in the United States

As the importance of education has become better recognized in our society, interesting changes in attitudes toward physical facilities have occurred. One change has resulted in allocating for school use not vacant lots that nobody wants, badly located, cramped in size, and expensive to improve, but carefully selected sites of generous proportions. (In metropolitan school systems, large sites are inordinately expensive, and schoolhouses may have to be several stories high. Yet even here strenuous efforts are made in most cases to provide enough ground for suitable landscaping and some play area. In the most congested areas, play spaces are provided indoors and on roofs.) In short, the controlling idea is to display schools prominently and advantageously, and not segregate them from the mainstream of community life.

Anybody who has traveled abroad, especially in Europe and Latin America, and has tried to visit schools, will recall how hard it was to find them. Often schools are secluded behind high walls, with locked gates attended by a porter. In the cities, it is difficult to distinguish schools from neighboring structures. The universities are like this too, except those few that have been recently rebuilt at new sites or those newly established, as in Britain (Chapter 6). The term "campus" is not generally used in connection with European universities or those modeled after them; in the United States, it is very nearly universally used when speaking of colleges and universities. In recent years, even secondary and elementary schools have been designed on the "campus plan," with several structures connected by walkways. More compact buildings, however, are again coming back into favor, partly because it is simpler and a little less expensive to install mechanical services such as heating and ventilating, air conditioning, and lighting.

### Old and New Schoolhouses a Study in Contrast

No aspect of the American scene has changed more, perhaps, than its school buildings. If one can find late nineteenth or early twentieth century schoolhouses for a tour of inspection, and then follow up with a tour of schools designed to current standards and concepts, he will see almost incredible contrasts. To begin with, school grounds have become much larger than the acre or two regarded as sufficient in the old days (sometimes less than an acre). For elementary schools 5 acres plus an acre for every one hundred pupils of building capacity is now the minimum acceptable size. Recommended for junior and senior high schools, respectively, are 20 and 30 acres plus 1 acre for each one hundred students. Many secondary schools now have 40 to 60 acres or more.

Inside the schools similar startling differences are observable. Typical of our grandparents' schools were 15- or 20-foot ceilings, long flights of stairs, dark halls with few exits, ill-lighted classrooms with tall, narrow windows and a single gas or electric light, unventilated basement toilets, classroom seating firmly fixed in rows, and an overall color scheme of "schoolroom brown." Wood floors darkened by years of improper care added to the generally depressing atmosphere. The classrooms of elementary schools were large, even by the modern standard of at least 900 square feet; but sixty or more children were assigned to each room, so quarters were not so commodious as one might think.

Today's schools differ in almost every respect. Fire-resistant materials make them safer and also easier to keep clean and in good repair. Much attention is given to pleasing architectural design, to proportion and line, and use of a variety of building materials. The rooms and equipment are planned, so far as possible, to fit the type of instruction to be accommodated. Lighting, heating and ventilation (or year-round air conditioning in many new schools), acoustical treatment, sanitation, color schemes—all are continually subjected to extensive research; and the latest findings are incorporated by architects who specialize in school building planning. Often they point out that an expertly planned, beautiful, functional schoolhouse costs no more, and usually less in the long run, than an unimaginative, ordinary one; and this has been repeatedly demonstrated in practice. The key concept today is functionalism, discussed in the next section, but not a cold, forbidding sort of functionalism. Schools of today are colorful, light, airy, and generally delightful places in which to live.

## EDUCATIONAL SERVICES THE CONTROLLING FACTOR

Extraordinary care is given today to planning schools that will afford the best accommodation, so far as possible, of the activities and services that are to be carried on. This concept of functionalism —"the program determines the plant"—is the chief consideration; but it does not, of course, preclude the incorporation of beauty, harmony, and taste in schoolhouse design. It does mean, though, that ornamentation merely for its own sake is played down; and if it does not contribute to functional use of the building, it will be omitted. That is why we do not see, for example, new schools whose entrances are approached by imposing flights of broad stairs and flanked by stately columns.

### Regimentation Yields to Flexibility

Evidence of better planning at both the elementary and secondary levels can be seen in the way floor space is allocated and in the relationships of various instructional areas. Seldom seen in recent years are orderly banks of more or less uniform classrooms with a corridor down the middle—the "egg-crate plan," as some architects have derided it. In many elementary schools, the customary rectangular shape of classrooms has given place to trapezoidal, pentagonal, and (best liked of all) hexagonal rooms. In high schools adapted to team teaching, as well as in many others, spaces ranging from study cubicles or carrels for individual students to lecture rooms seating 150, 200, or more are provided. Other rooms of appropriate sizes are included for small discussion groups of ten to fifteen, and for classes of twenty-five to thirty.

The development of effective materials and machinery for soundproof, movable partitions now makes it quite feasible to divide large rooms and even auditoriums into smaller units. Such flexibility is

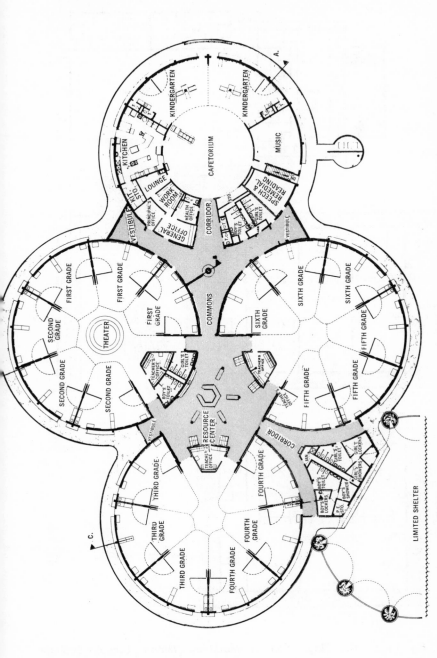

Fig. 14–1. General Floor Plan of Sherwood Elementary School Built at Greeley, Colorado, 1963–1964. Note the grouping of grades in different units, the unusual shape of the rooms, the movable partitions by which several rooms may be converted into one, and other provisions for functionalism. Reproduced by permission of Shaver & Co., Architects, Salina, Kansas.

437

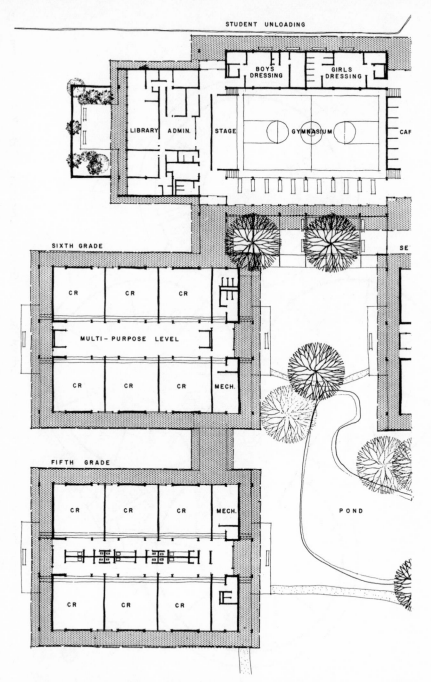

Fig. 14–2. The Floor Plan of Mackinaw Middle School, Saginaw, Michigan, Built in 1961 To House Grades 5–8. This plan, selected by famed architect W. W. Caudill as one of his favorite projects, is a "de-

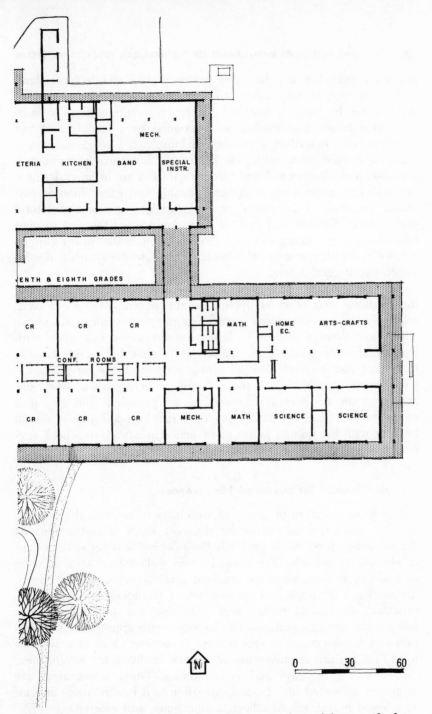

MECH.

ETERIA    KITCHEN    BAND    SPECIAL
INSTR.

ENTH & EIGHTH GRADES

CR    CR    CR    MATH    HOME    ARTS-CRAFTS
EC.

CONF. ROOMS

CR    CR    CR    MECH.    MATH    SCIENCE    SCIENCE

N

0    30    60

centralized school," with connected units that are planned for specific functions. Reproduced by permission of Caudill, Rowlett, and Scott, Architects,
Houston.

best managed when it is included in the original architectural plans, so that lighting, heating and ventilation, seating, television, and other systems will be properly installed. So much weight is given to flexibility that in one mammoth school designed by a leading architect that has been described as history making, not a single cabinet is fixed to a floor or a wall. All laboratory furniture is completely movable, and all electrical and mechanical lines are in an under-floor arrangement to make room changes possible and easy. Interior partitions are easily disassembled and relocated by use of a structural grid system. Figures 14–1 to 14–4 give some idea of the way modern schoolhouses are being planned, but a much better grasp can be gained by visiting some new schools. The state department of education can suggest a few.

Mention should be made of another kind of flexibility: adapting the furniture and other equipment to the pupils. In the old days, relatively little attention was given to proper seating for pupils above and below average size, or to fitting out lavatories and toilets with fixtures of appropriate sizes. Today, it is regarded as inexcusable to neglect such matters. Special provisions were made for physically handicapped pupils only in the big cities, where schools were built just for them, or specially furnished rooms provided. But now it is recommended that, so far as possible, handicapped pupils should be kept with the normal groups; and hence in any given school, special equipment may be required in any or all classrooms.

### Schools "Zoned" for Increased Effectiveness

The gross structure or group of structures of individual schools is usually subdivided into areas for different kinds of instruction. At the secondary level this is generally the rule, but it is not so important in elementary schools. For example, one well-defined area or wing or building is designated for practical arts: home economics, crafts, various kinds of shops, and the like, where considerable noise can be expected, or special wiring and plumbing are required. Science laboratories are grouped in a similar way, with appropriate preparation and storage rooms in connection. Sometimes classrooms for subjects that require extensive use of library facilities are located near that unit, e.g., English and social studies. Other major areas are ordinarily allocated for physical education and health, vocal and instrumental music, school offices, auditoriums, and cafeterias.

In very large high schools, the student body may be organized into "houses," or "schools within the school," and partial or complete

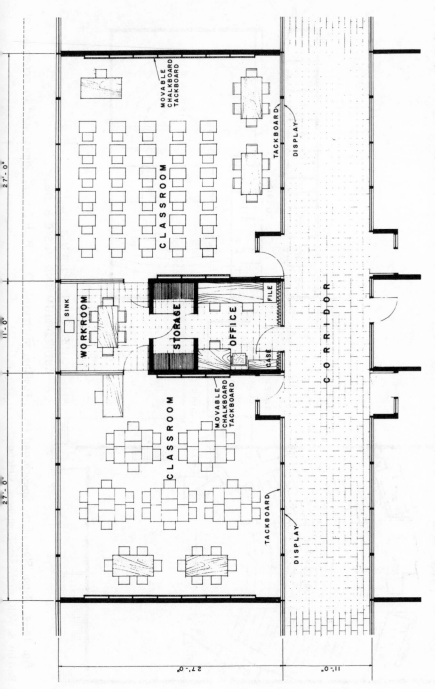

Fig. 14–3. A Typical Classroom Unit Plan of Newark, Ohio, High School. Reproduced by permission of Perkins & Will, Architects-Engineers, Chicago.

441

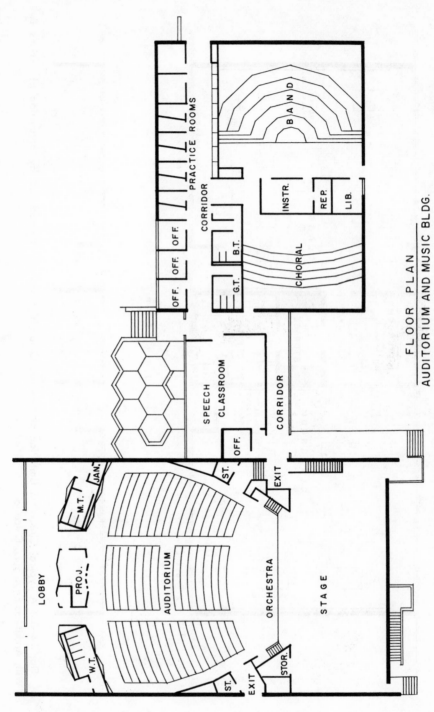

FLOOR PLAN
AUDITORIUM AND MUSIC BLDG.

Fig. 14–4. Floor Plan of the Speech and Music Facilities of Newark, Ohio, High School. Reproduced by permission of Perkins & Will, Architects-Engineers, Chicago.

442

quarters allocated to each unit just for its use. Each "house" or "little school" is limited to several hundred pupils, in an effort to mitigate the impersonal effect of bigness. A school to be operated along these lines is best provided for when its organization is incorporated into the original architectural plans, but sound original planning will make many different adaptations possible.

School boards, administrators, and architects responsible for the wise and economical expenditure of building funds, which total from $3 billion to $4 billion a year, have been unexpectedly successful in keeping construction costs within reasonable limits and at the same time providing excellent schools. School costs have risen less than any other major type of building costs since 1940. For this immense and varied undertaking, the governing principle is to take into account everything that is to be carried on in a given building, and then figure out how it can be best provided for within financial and other limitations that may be present. No one can predict the changes that the future will bring during the normal life expectancy of a schoolhouse (fifty to sixty years); hence, great importance is attached to generous space allotments and flexibility.

## A FEW OTHER PROMISING INNOVATIONS

Outside and inside, other changes are being wrought in school plants to make schooling more effective, and also in response to new conditions in our society and new demands from it. The unceasing flow of newly developed building materials and techniques and new inventions for school use, and the venturesome spirit of schoolhouse planners and teachers willing to utilize them, also represent no mean contribution to the notable advances in American school and college buildings. A number of the more interesting and significant innovations, in addition to those already touched on, are mentioned in the next few paragraphs.

### Schools Without Windows

At first blush, most people react to the thought of a windowless school with consternation. Who ever heard of such a thing! Yet as a matter of fact several schools without windows have been built and are so well liked that opinion polls of parents, pupils, and teachers have been unanimously favorable. One of the first such schools was constructed in 1961 at Artesia, New Mexico, as an experimental combination of elementary school and fallout shelter. (A Strategic Air

Command base at Roswell is about 30 miles away. The federal government contributed about one-third of the cost of this building.) Not only is this school completely without windows, but it is also completely underground, roofed over by a two-layer concrete slab 21 inches thick for protection from radiation.[1]

Several other schools without windows but above ground have been built; still others have windowless classrooms but some glass in corridors, entrance ways, and toilets. When the advantages and disadvantages of windowless schools or classrooms are weighed, the former seem, at least to the authors, to outweigh the latter. The chief objection to absence of windows is esthetic (occupants cannot see the sky, clouds, trees, grass, birds) and psychological (pupils and teachers may get a feeling of being closed in, akin to claustrophobia). On the other hand, the most vexatious design and engineering problems of sun, light, heat control, and acoustics are easily solved by having no windows; and, in addition, all classroom walls are usable for instructional purposes. Instant darkening is possible at the flip of a switch for films and slides without the bother or expense of window shades or shutters.

Most people would probably feel oppressed by a feeling of being too confined if care were not taken to safeguard against it by pictures, variations of wall patterns and surfaces, a floor plan that affords certain vistas, and of course by scientific lighting, heating, and ventilation. We forget that millions of people work every day in windowless offices, stores, research centers, and factories without suffering any known ill effects. If such a school is within convenient travel distance, students should make a special effort to visit it before coming to conclusions.

### The High School Enters the Motor Age

When the location of new secondary schools a generation ago was plotted by school authorities, the general rule called for junior high schools to be situated approximately 3 miles apart and senior high schools 4 or 5 miles apart. By being so placed, the schools were believed to be within reasonable walking or cycling distances from students' homes, not more than 1¾ and 2 or 2½ miles respectively for junior and senior high. Somehow the idea of walking has mostly faded away, and at the senior high level bicycles have largely given way to cars. Even the recent emphasis on physical fitness has not restored walking and cycling to popularity.

[1] See "Underground Abo School Is the Most—in Air Conditioning and Light Control," *Nation's Schools*, LXXI (January, 1963), 80–86.

Parking lots for student cars at high schools have become a pretty well-accepted fact of life, partly to get the cars off the streets and partly to bring them under closer school supervision. At colleges and universities, it may be remarked, the problem of parking is even more acute, for faculty, staff, students, and public. To the authors, high school parking lots for students (except in case of hardship or handicaps) still seem like a misuse of money and space. However, large schools need parking lots for the convenience and safety of the public who attend meetings and a variety of school events; thus student parking is really provided for incidentally or as a by-product. (In heavily populated urban areas, where space limitations make parking lots unfeasible, public transit services are relied on by those who do not walk.)

## A New Look in Classrooms and Laboratories

It seemed almost too revolutionary when in the early sixties a few schools carpeted their classrooms. Prior to this, carpeting had been used on a small scale mainly in kindergartens; and it still looks luxurious for use in classrooms, offices, and corridors. However, principals and teachers report that carpeted buildings are much quieter and pupil behavior seems to be markedly improved. Custodians relate that the new kinds of carpet material and methods of cleaning make carpeted floors easier to keep clean than other types. Financially, carpet costs about the same as other kinds of floor treatment over the long run. When one recalls the extensive use of carpet in hotels, restaurants, department stores, and other areas that have heavy traffic, the use of carpets in schools does not seem so unusual. New things like this often arrive at the schools near the end of the line: theatres, stores, offices, homes, dog kennels, churches, and schools were air conditioned in about that order. Now carpeting has finally been accepted, at least on a small scale.

New layouts for science laboratories make such rooms more convenient and more economical of space. One good plan has the lab tables around the perimeter of the room instead of in the center. Another provides for sort of Lazy Susan units, with work space for five or six individual students arranged around a revolving core fitted with shelves and small cupboards for supplies and equipment. The laboratory concept is being extended to other fields besides science, with emphasis on individual and small group learning activities. Probably the most notable is the rapid growth of language labs, financed in part by the federal government under the provisions of the National Defense Education Act.

## Programmed Instruction via New Media

As indicated in Chapter 7, individual progress is the chief objective of programmed instruction, as a variety of self-teaching methods are usually termed. Programmed materials of instruction are arranged by small parts in a sequential order, so that a pupil progresses from each part mastered to the next. One important element of programmed instruction is teaching machines. These range from very simple, hand-operated devices, which can be purchased for two or three dollars or made in a school shop, to complex electronic units costing $2,000 or more. The main advantages of teaching machines are the flexibility they give teachers in the use of their instructional time and effort, and the freedom they give pupils to progress at various rates. Research has not so far conclusively demonstrated that teaching machines improve pupil achievement, or that they reduce the need for teachers. However, it is highly likely that they will be found increasingly valuable as supplements to regular instruction, particularly for pupils at the upper and lower ends of the ability range.[2]

Programmed instruction, while still in its infancy, utilizes also such other new media as "scrambled textbooks" and televised units of subject matter. The latter are ordinarily used with learning groups, as are films and slides. Some of the more sophisticated self-teaching units actually do make it possible for individual pupils to tune in on televised lessons, see films, and listen to tapes and recordings.

## New Functions Assumed by School Libraries

For many years libraries have been given lip service as the central facility for instruction. In practice they have not been financed or staffed well enough, and their chief use has been as a repository for books and as study halls. Now at long last it seems that the school library is being accorded its proper role in the instructional program. Besides books, files of magazines, and other printed materials, recordings, photographs, drawings and paintings, and tapes and films are all considered parts of a first-rate library collection. Even where an audio-visual department is set up to facilitate the distribution, use,

[2] For a different view, see Sidney L. Pressey, "A Puncture of the Huge 'Programing' Boom?" *Teachers College Record*, LXV, No. 5 (February, 1964), 413–22. The "dean" of American educational psychologists, who is credited with inventing the teaching machine, takes a jaundiced look at both programmed learning and its underlying theories.

and maintenance of films, slides, and other A-V instructional tools, it must work closely with the library.

Book stacks and reading rooms retain, of course, their important place in new school libraries; but they constitute a much smaller part of the total resources than was true formerly. Auxiliary spaces of several kinds are incorporated, such as rooms large enough for classes of twenty-five to thirty students, small conference or committee rooms for group library projects, small rooms for listening to tapes and discs, and, above all, individual carrels for independent study. Of the almost infinite variety that characterizes carrels, two styles are shown in Fig. 14–5. The work cited as the source of this figure is a veritable mine of good ideas for the secondary school and college library, illustrated with dozens of sketches and photographs. Adequate work space for the librarian and library assistants is essential for the efficient operation of a library, but it tends to be quite inadequately provided.

For elementary schools of more than about three hundred enrollment, central libraries (supplemented by classroom collections) are recommended, less elaborate and with less emphasis on individual pupil work than in secondary schools. For smaller elementary schools, a central library is not usually advocated, but larger classroom collections are generally recommended. In the latter case, centralized services are rendered by the school system to change the collections of books and other materials as required; it would be inordinately costly to provide for permanent allocation of large collections to individual small schools.

### Teachers' Offices and Workrooms

Two features of contemporary schools best-liked by teachers are faculty offices and workrooms. A real need for these facilities exists in both elementary and secondary schools, to give teachers some degree of privacy and for the planning of their work, reading and marking papers, and counseling and conferring with students. They need a place to keep their books and other paraphernalia brought to school for use in their work.

In elementary schools the self-contained classroom plan, where teachers ordinarily teach in the same room all day and keep the same room year to year, is still the most common. The most appealing arrangement for office space here is to provide a small room for each pair of classrooms. Most teachers prefer to have a private office even if it must be small, rather than share an office, so the space be-

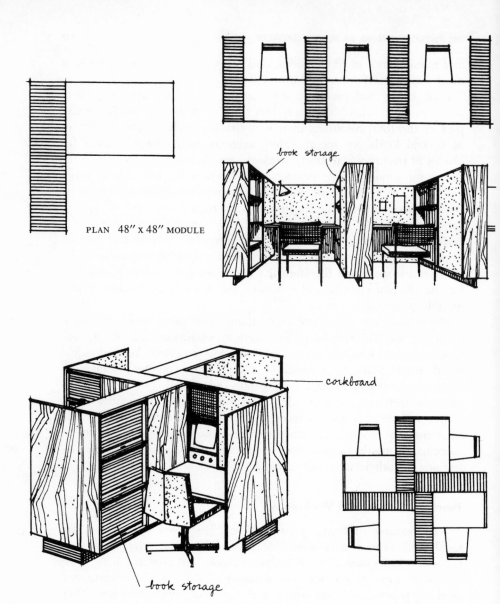

PLAN 48" x 48" MODULE

book storage

corkboard

book storage

Fig. 14–5. Two Plans for the Arrangement of Carrels for Individual Students by Using Tables, Bookcases, Storage Cabinets, and Side or Back Panels. These units can be made simply, from the standard tables and bookcases that may already be available in a school, or from manufactured modular units intended for easy assembly in numerous arrangements. From *The School Library* by Ralph E. Ellsworth and Hobart D. Wagener (New York: Educational Facilities Laboratories, 1963), p. 64. Reproduced by permission.

tween each of the two classrooms can be divided to form two offices. At the high school level, it is more common for teachers to use different classrooms. In schools or departments organized for team teaching, individual room assignments do not fit at all. Hence in secondary schools, teachers' offices are really necessary to provide them with a home base. Such units in large schools are probably best arranged in suites or clusters by departments, not attached to individual classrooms. Teaching teams absolutely require this kind of space for effective performance.

Workrooms for such typing as teachers want and need to do, and for preparing materials for classroom use, are highly favored by teachers. (Laboratories require their own connected preparation and storage rooms, as noted earlier in this chapter.) Both elementary and secondary school teachers need and should have some kind of workroom equipped to meet the demands of their work, kept in good order, conveniently located. Sometimes workrooms in older schools are so poorly lighted, heated, and ventilated, and so ill-arranged and equipped that they are of little value and reflect badly on the school.

The fact that well-equipped work space is provided does not obviate the need for competent clerical and secretarial help. It is a waste of money and professional skills to require teachers to do all their own office-type work. School clerical and stenographic work should be performed to the greatest possible extent by well-trained staff, affording attractive career opportunities as pointed out in Chapter 1. However, in practically every teacher's work week, a lot of things come up for which some suitable work place is needed. As the incipient movement for an eight to five school day gains ground, and it appears to be doing so, such facilities as offices and workrooms will be not only a convenience, but also a genuine necessity.

## GENERAL SERVICE UNITS FOR SCHOOL AND COMMUNITY USE

An intimate and constructive relationship between schools and the communities they serve is assiduously cultivated in the United States; and in the view of most Americans, its advantages are clear. For in spite of a number of problems that it creates, the public's conviction that the schools are theirs, to serve and not to dictate to them, does foster community initiative and a feeling of responsibility, and redounds to the benefit of the schools. This does not mean that the public should dictate to the schools, either, which European critics think is a rather typical weakness of American education. There need not be dictation from either of the two parties of the educational enterprise—the professional or expert side (staff, administrators, state and federal agencies, university and college educators) and the public.

## The Main Question and How It Is Answered

One chief problem connected with school buildings does arise frequently, and that is to what extent facilities should be planned and constructed both to house educational programs and to accommodate community activities. A whole chain of subsidiary questions is exposed when concrete decisions must be made:

Should the school system alone be responsible for raising the necessary funds, or should part of the cost of facilities for shared school and community use be chargeable to the city? Does it make any difference?

What does the term "educational program" cover? Is adult education, for example, included?

How is the term "community activities" to be interpreted? Should all community activities be eligible to use school facilities, regardless of whether they are school-related, non-school but of public interest, non-school and private, or commercial in nature? Should political, religious, or promotional meetings and enterprises of various kinds be entitled to such use? Should fees be imposed by the school district for some uses and not for others?

Liberal policies prevail, in general, on such matters; but there is a great variety of arrangements on specific items. On the main problem first raised, the common practice is for school districts to build auditoriums, gymnasiums, cafeterias, playing fields and stadiums, and in rare instances libraries, pre-eminently for school and school-related uses, but also with an eye to the convenient accommodation of the public. Most towns never have enough gyms, auditoriums, and playing fields. Infrequently, municipal bodies put up part of the money; but this may lead to legal and management complications, so it is simpler just to forget about it. The best example of municipal and school district cooperation is the development of adjoining park and school sites. This is done widely throughout the country.

Most boards of education adopt policies allowing school-related activities and youth-serving organizations (PTA, Boy Scouts, and the like) free use of school facilities. For private undertakings of public interest, such as meetings on political affairs and discussion groups, only nominal fees are assessed. And for money-raising events or commercial enterprises (e.g., a cooking school sponsored by the local electric or gas company, or a play produced by a local club), a schedule of fees is used so that the cost of heat, light, custodians' wages, and other expenses are taken care of. The trend is toward ever more liberal policies, especially for events of public interest and for non-profit undertakings. State education laws typically allow wide discretion to local school boards on decisions relating to building use, so long as such decisions are not discriminatory, arbitrary, or contrary to sound public policy.

### Are School Activities Too Commercialized?

Unresolved still are questions of whether students are being exploited for purposes of public entertainment and, if they are, how serious the problem is. In the author's judgment, there is considerable overemphasis on public entertainment and on gate receipts. It is hard to justify huge bleachers for spectator seating in gymnasiums and stadiums on the grounds of educational values. School boards, superintendents, principals, and teachers have let themselves be pushed by the public into condoning and even encouraging practices that are not defensible on educational bases. Students who read these lines should think over their own secondary school experience; and from the vantage point of greater maturity, consider whether or not their schools ran an entertainment business under the guise of education.

## CAMPS AND OTHER EXTENSIONS OF THE SCHOOL

A small number, estimated at about a hundred, of alert school systems own and operate one of the most interesting and highly valued types of facilities as part of their educational plant: school camps. Only twenty years ago the opinion prevailed that school districts were too hard-pressed financially to embark on such ventures as school camps. It was left to other child- and youth-serving organizations to provide camping experiences: 4-H Clubs, Scout Councils, churches, and others; and camps were operated almost solely as summer projects. The pioneer school camps were launched largely through gifts of funds or land or both, among the leaders being Battle Creek, Michigan, Tyler, Texas, and San Diego, California.

At first they, too, were limited to mainly summer programs, with perhaps some week-end or Christmas holiday excursions. A few camps were carried on in connection with school farms operated for vocational agriculture classes. We in the United States have been tardy in recognizing the values of camping as part of children's educational experience, in comparison with European peoples. As for the expense, we are seldom concerned about that if we really want something badly; and reports of school camps leave no room for doubt as to their important contribution in the educative process.

Typically, the school systems that operate camps endeavor to give all pupils (except those excused at parents' request or for health reasons), usually in the fifth and sixth grades, a week at camp during the school year. Summer camp provides additional opportunity, and with more emphasis on recreational aspects of camping. Facilities include bunkhouses, a lodge for cooking and serving meals that doubles as a meeting room, toilets and showers, provisions for picnicking, and if the situation allows, for boating, swimming, ice skating and other activities. The grounds may run to several hundred acres, or with luck adjoin state or national park or forest land.

### The Community as an Educational Facility

Several years ago a midwestern city school system published a report under the title, "School Is Everywhere." It spotlighted the many public and private enterprises in the city that welcomed school field trips as supplements to schoolroom studies. In a real sense they may be thought of as educational facilities, and add immeasurably to the learning experiences of children and youth. No school system could even approximate remotely the richness of their collective resources: museums, art galleries, libraries, stores, factories, mills, banks, theatres, and so on.

## A SUMMARY OF CURRENT THOUGHT ON THE SCHOOL PLANT

To recapitulate this discussion of the physical setting of educational services, it may be said that eight concepts guide the planning and construction of school facilities in our time. They have evolved gradually through more than a century, increasingly reflecting higher standards of educational effort, expanded knowledge of the nature of teaching and of learning, and discovery and refinement of architectural and engineering advances. The importance attached to most of these concepts varies somewhat in different communities, so that it is impossible to list them in a firm order of priority. It is likely that fairly high agreement would be expressed by professional educators, school architects, school boards, and citizens' committees that none of these eight items can be ignored in providing the best possible school buildings, grounds, and equipment.

1. *Safe and hygienic.* The school plant should be so designed, built, and operated that it is a safe and wholesome place for children and staff. Since parents are required to send their children to school, it is of utmost importance that this injunction be observed to the fullest. The occurrence of two to three thousand school fires a year is just one kind of evidence that there is some improvement needed.

2. *Functional.* The school plant should be suitable for the educational program to be carried on. It should be functional, facilitating the instructional program, not hampering it.

3. *Flexible.* Flexibility should should be built into school facilities so that the arrangement of instructional spaces and equipment can be modified quickly, easily, and inexpensively.

4. *Adaptable.* Since a school building is expected to give good service for at least fifty years, it should be so planned originally that additions and changes may be easily made to fit major changes of program and increases in enrollment. A site should be large enough to accommodate such additions in case enrollment increases require them, without impairing the adequacy of playground and other outdoor areas.

5. *Beautiful.* An educational center should be beautiful and reflect good taste. Its proportions and lines should be pleasing, and it should exemplify high ideals and standards of our culture.

6. *Homelike.* Rather than standing as an imposing, forbidding edifice of monumental character, a school should be inviting; and especially at the elementary level, it should have the atmosphere of a good home.

7. *Useful to the Community.* If it is to be of maximum benefit, a school should be so located and designed that appropriate services to the adult population can be conveniently housed and carried on.

8. *Economical.* And finally, wise economy should be practiced in the use of building funds. The objective should be to provide what is needed without cutting corners on space allotment or in the quality of materials and construction. An eye should be had for economy in heating and ventilating, housekeeping, and so on, and for economy of maintenance (keeping the building in first-class condition). Cheap materials and construction, and skimping on space are universally condemned as false economy.

## RECEPTIVITY TO INNOVATION

In this atomic age, when new discoveries and inventions are reported in incredible volume, it would seem almost gratuitous to admonish students on being open-minded to innovation. Yet in the field of educational facilities, it has been slow going to win acceptance or even a fair trial of promising new ideas, inventions, and improvements. Sometimes the public is too complacent or the school board "too conservative" to subscribe to any schoolhouse or schoolroom plan that deviates from the ordinary, "the tried and true." Teachers and administrators, too, may lose the student attitude, the zest to try the untried, to know the unknown.

As a rule, the innovations in school plant planning and construction of the last couple of decades have produced very good results. They have given more facilities for the money spent, and have tended to improve both teaching and learning. Certainly, no one can point to any harm done. In view of these conditions, teachers are fully justified in lending their full support to the adoption of new developments in buildings and equipment. The pace of change in education is characteristically so deliberate that educators are justified in assuming a rather radical position to help speed things up a bit.

## QUESTIONS, PROBLEMS, AND PROJECTS FOR FURTHER STUDY

1. Read up on the meaning and practice of "shared time" in connection with the use of school facilities by public and parochial schools. Summarize the case for and against it.

2. With one or two classmates, make a fairly detailed inspection of an elementary school built about forty years ago and one constructed within the last five years. (Get permission from the principal to do this. A letter of introduction from your instructor would be helpful.) Present a well-organized report of your impressions to the class.

3. Visit a windowless school, if you can find one in your area. Prepare a written report on it, including your opinion on the advantages and disadvantages of this type of school as discussed in education journals. (An inquiry addressed to your state education department may help locate schools of this type. In some areas there may be none close enough to visit.)

4. If you have had any personal experience in your career as a student with TV instruction, language laboratories, tape recordings, films, teaching machines, programmed instruction, etc., write a paper of about 2,500 words

on the value of such facilities. In addition to drawing on your own personal knowledge, read up on the subject, and be careful not to draw sweeping conclusions from just your own experience.

5. Prepare a sketchbook of changes in schoolhouse and schoolroom design that have occurred in about the last hundred years. Show a few features typical of certain periods, such as size of site and how much of it was occupied by the building(s), style of exterior architecture, and classroom size and arrangement.

6. If you were asked to serve on a planning committee for a new school, what special features would you strongly recommend, based on your own experience as a pupil, on your observations since then, and on your reading?

7. How is the "all-year school" supposed to help reduce outlays for new schoolhouses? (A school operated for four quarters per year, with each pupil attending three quarters.) What are the major problems associated with such a plan? Can you prepare a convincing discussion either for or against it? Try it.

8. School camps are generally viewed as making valuable contributions to the educational experience of boys and girls, usually fifth- or sixth-graders. If this is so, why do not more school systems have camps? Do some reading on the subject, and visit a camp if there is one within reach before you make up your mind.

9. In your opinion, is too much money spent for stadiums, gymnasiums, and auditoriums for the accommodation of spectators to the detriment of the educational program? Decide how you would answer this, and then defend your position.

10. Write for information on developments in schoolhouse design and construction in another country (or look it up in the library). Compare selected features and cost figures with those that seem representative of U.S. schools. (Countries in northern and western Europe, the U.S.S.R., and Mexico are probably the best ones for this topic.)

## SELECTED SUPPLEMENTARY READINGS AND FILMS

DE BERNARDIS, AMO, DOHERTY, VICTOR W., HUMMEL, ERRETT, and BRUBAKER, CHARLES WILLIAM. *Planning Schools for New Media.* Portland, Ore.: Portland State College, 1961. A guide for planning facilities for proper use of films, radio and television, electronic learning laboratories, intercommunication systems, reading accelerators, etc. Has a good bibliography.

DE CECCO, JOHN P. (ed.). *Educational Technology.* Readings in programmed instruction, by all major researchers. New York: McGraw-Hill Book Co., Inc., 1964.

ELAM, STANLEY E. (ed.). "Programed Instruction," *Phi Delta Kappan,* XLIV, No. 6 (March, 1963), 241–302. A special issue with sixteen articles by leaders in the field; not only descriptive but also coming to grips with both theoretical and practical problems.

FREEBERG, WILLIAM H. *Programs in Outdoor Education.* Minneapolis: Burgess Publishing Co., 1963. Points out ways to make all subjects more interesting by camping and various other types of outdoor education.

FRY, EDWARD B. *Teaching Machines and Programed Instruction: An Introduction.* New York: McGraw-Hill Book Co., Inc., 1963. An up-to-date comprehensive presentation of both theory and practical applications to a variety of learning tasks.

RICE, ARTHUR H. "Modern Education: Its Impact on Schoolhouse Design," *The Nation's Schools,* LXXI, No. 1 (January, 1963), 48–96. A forty-eight-page portfolio outlining, with many photographs and drawings, the evolution of modern schoolhouse design in response to changes in educational thought and practice.

SCHOOL BUILDING COMMISSION. *Planning America's School Buildings.* Washington, D.C.: American Association of School Administrators, 1960. The relationship of educational program to schoolhouse design underlies this comprehensive treatment. Separate chapters by experts are included on all aspects of planning. Intended as a guide for superintendents and board members, but probably interesting to students too.

TROW, WILLIAM CLARK. *Teacher and Technology: New Designs for Learning.* New York: Appleton-Century-Crofts, Inc., 1963. Written by a famed educational psychologist, this book shows how the new media can be used in conjunction with traditional methods to promote learning at various levels. The potentialities and limitations of new media are also discussed.

WITTICH, W. A., and SCHULLER, C. F. (eds.). *Audiovisual Materials: Their Nature and Use.* New York: Harper & Row, 1962. An up-to-date encyclopedic coverage of the subject by specialists.

## Films

*A U.S. Community and Its Citizens.* 20 minutes. Depicts life in a small town named Milford, Conn. The family's day begins with breakfast and getting off to school and to work. A class project in school is study of the community. The class group visits, observes, and makes reports on results of their study, and finally makes a motion picture to show the importance of the community and how people live and work together through its various agencies. New York: United World Films.

*Filmstrip of Architectural Exhibit.* Prepared from the annual display of about two hundred school building plans that is a feature of the national convention of the American Association of School Administrators. An explanatory text goes with the film. Washington, D.C.: American Association of School Administrators.

*Near Home.* 25 minutes. A lively film showing how a group of English school children use a field trip to study their community's history, industries, public utilities, government, geography, and other elements. They report their findings in an exhibit. Evanston, Ill.: Contemporary Films, Inc.

*New Tools for Learning.* 19 minutes. Shows how the film, along with a wide range of other materials, can bring richness and vitality to teaching. Effective methods of classroom use of films are demonstrated through scenes showing teachers and pupils at work in school situations. Wilmette, Ill.: Encyclopaedia Britannica Films, Inc.

*Teaching Machines and Programmed Learning.* 28 minutes. Presents B. F. Skinner explaining the theory of programed learning, Arthur Lumsdaine describing a variety of teaching machines and programed materials, and Robert Glaser discussing the implications of such machines and materials for education. Washington, D.C.: U.S. Office of Education.

# V

# THE EMERGING
# EDUCATIONAL
# PROFESSION

# 15

# PREPARING FOR AN
# EDUCATIONAL CAREER

Earlier chapters deal with the foundations of education, challenges to be met, educational program and services, and the organization and operation of the schools. From these episodes the reader should have some understanding of education in the United States and its counterpart in selected foreign nations. Perhaps he is ready now to consider the essentials of preparation for those who desire an educational career. This preparation can best be understood in the light of the job to be done and the manner in which American schooling is accomplished.

Since this book is intended primarily for prospective elementary and secondary school teachers, emphasis is placed chiefly upon initial preparation appropriate thereto. Some reference is made to other professional positions, and careful study of the latter is advisable as the individual moves ahead in his teaching preparation and contemplates the future. Many students will not know until they are teaching just what further professional advancement they will want to seek. Some reference is made also to preparation for careers at the college level. In a later chapter attention is given to advancement in the profession, graduate study, and related problems.

Teaching is considered to be a profession. One of the hallmarks of any profession is the nature of the educational preparation basic to successful service therein. Both breadth and depth are important. The status of the profession depends in no small degree upon this education and its evidence in the professional and general activities of the individual members.

A professional, in the broad sense of the term and without limitation to a single profession, has been characterized as follows:

Is a liberally educated person.
Possesses a body of specialized skills and knowledge related to and essential for the performance of his function.

Is able to make rational judgments and to take appropriate action within the scope of his activities, and is responsible for the consequences of his judgments and action.

Places primary emphasis upon his service to society rather than upon his personal gain.

Actively participates with his colleagues in developing and enforcing standards fundamental to continuous improvement of his profession and abides by those standards in his own practice.

Practices his profession on a full-time basis.

Is engaged in a continuing search for new knowledge and skill.[1]

The appropriateness of these attributes to the teaching profession is apparent. They are not all easily attainable, and there is argument sometimes as to what constitutes certain of them and how they are to be attained.

In this discussion attention is given to the following major categories of characteristics deemed essential in the successful professional teacher:

1. Desirable personal qualities
2. A liberal education
3. Knowledge of the subject
4. Professional competencies

These attributes are interrelated; and they are all of concern in any sound program of teacher education, both at the undergraduate and graduate level. No one alone nor any several together suffice; each and every one is basic to the effective teacher at whatever level he serves.


## QUALIFICATIONS FOR A CAREER IN EDUCATION

Many of the qualifications for success in one vocation or profession are equally important in other enterprises. This statement is particularly true with respect to personal attributes. In viewing the requisites for success, it should be remembered that both the contribution of the individual and his job satisfaction are dependent upon such traits.

The constellation of elements that comprise a successful and satisfied teacher cannot be analyzed with the definitiveness of chemical analysis. The dynamics of human relationship have yet to be defined with such precision. Many factors and forces are at work in the educative

---

[1] Margaret Lindsay, *New Horizons for the Teaching Profession* (Washington, D.C.: National Education Association, 1961), p. 6.

process involving the interaction of learners, teacher, and the elements of the experience itself. The art, as well as the science, of teaching becomes apparent in the behavior of the superior teacher at work.

Studies of teachers and teaching have been useful although often inconclusive in an objective sense. The findings point up a need for continued appraisal and for some new and imaginative approaches to evaluation. Hundreds of studies have been made of personal and other traits, usually with the hope of discovering definite and desirable patterns of behavior. Similarly, it has been attempted to ascertain the undesirable patterns. Thus there might be established on the one hand a list of characteristics that foster success and on the other a list of definite handicaps.

It seems safe to suggest that excellent teachers are not born nor can any amount of preparation transmute poor native ability and other well-intrenched disabilities into high-quality teaching. Much can be done with those whose personal attributes lend themselves to improvement and development. Both identification and recruitment are important, therefore, in bringing into teacher education those who have the potential to become fine teachers. More is said of this point later.

Lack of agreement on the specifics constituting excellent instruction handicaps the profession in determining prerequisites for entry into teaching. This condition also influences adversely the improvement of teacher education programs. As a result, many views held of qualifications are only tentative and require regular re-evaluation in the light of reason and additional evidence. At the same time it is important not to let teaching become a profession with low standards of admission. This latter tendency always exists, particularly when there is a shortage of teachers, a burgeoning school and college population, and public apathy or reluctance to meet increasing educational costs. Society will get no more than it deserves, and it deserves no more than it is able and willing to pay for.

## Desirable Personal Qualities

The personal qualities of an individual shade into professional qualities, and both are subject to environmental influence. The following categories of personal traits are important to those who contemplate teaching and should be noted by those who grant or withhold the opportunity to enter teacher education:

1. Scholastic aptitude and interest
2. Physical and mental health

3. Character and reason
4. Interest in and ability with people
5. Primary desire to be of service

It is recognized that these things are relative and that they tend to vary within an individual from time to time, as well as among individuals. They are also interrelated.

**Scholastic Aptitude and Interest.** Teaching is not properly a profession for weak students lacking in scholastic aptitude and interest. Aptitude and interest are treated together because of their dependency in terms of performance. It is suggested that the prospective teacher should be at least an average college student and preferably somewhat better by the time he has completed two years of college. Admittedly, this is a variable performance standard and perhaps not a sufficiently high one. At the same time, it should be recognized that teacher education is the most commonly found professional program in colleges and universities, and a reasonably high point of departure that will be generally accepted is essential to subsequent improvement as research directs the way.

Breadth of cultural and scholastic interest is also important. Though he may instruct in only one subject, the teacher should have broader interests that make him at home in a world of wide and varied concerns. He should be comfortable with ideas and able to work with them; indeed he should enjoy such activity. In his area of special interest, the prospective teacher's performance should normally exceed his overall grade point average, unless his general performance is excellent. A minimum average of C+ or B in this specialty is not uncommon among students in better teacher education institutions. The tendency for some professors to advise their weaker students into teaching should not be tolerated, and such students should not be misled by this improper counsel.

There is no implication that the teacher should not have a range of interests extending beyond the academic. Quite the contrary, such a range is desirable. The point is that the school is meant to be a scholarly place, alive with adventure and enthusiasm in teaching and learning. Such a condition depends a great deal upon the attitude of the teachers, especially in a world where anti-intellectualism is so apparent as it is today. "Teaching scholars" are essential if the work of the schools and colleges is to go forward.

Even in the so-called non-academic fields, it is important that the teacher view his discipline in a scholarly manner and perform adequately therein. A shop teacher who is a "hack" is a liability. A physical education teacher who has no regard for the basic sciences underlying his discipline belongs neither in the classroom nor on the playing field. In many ways all teachers share responsibility in contributing to the scholarly climate of school and college, for example, in communication and in the performance of their job.

A scholarly atmosphere does not mean a dull and dreary climate in which pupils are saddled with great loads of meaningless and repetitious work. It promotes, instead, a vital teaching-learning situation in which all learners are stretched, each being challenged to realize the full potential of which he is capable. Horizons are extended and expectations increased. Much high-quality work is done and is appropriately rewarded. Enthusiasm of teachers is matched by eagerness of pupils as they explore and discover, together and singly, the great scope and depth of human heritage—past, present, and future—with which education deals.

**Physical and Mental Health.** Teaching is a demanding profession. Those who serve well need sufficient vigor of mind and body and soul so that they can handle large numbers of children or youth during the day and do much school-related work at night. Week ends are not as free as some would have us believe, and summers are no longer all vacation. Emotional stability is of crucial importance to those who would influence favorably the lives of others through teaching.

Some persons who shy away from contact with people, especially of their own age, and who are insecure in the hurly-burly of modern living, see in teaching a haven or refuge from hard reality. This view is erroneous. The classroom is not an escape from reality, indeed if it is an escape at all it should be to reality. The climate of the classroom is definitely colored by the health of the teacher, and his outlook influences that of the learners.

Adults who seek to bolster themselves by dominating children and youth do the profession a disservice. All manner of cranks should be avoided. Normal and healthy children are under enough pressure and tension in modern living without the added burden of a maladjusted teacher in the classroom.

Perhaps the reader can recall good teachers who were a bit odd in common parlance or great teachers who were seriously unwell. There is no intent here to discredit these people nor to deduct from their contribution. However, it should be noted that such performance was accomplished in spite of these handicaps, the disabilities in some instances developing over the years of service. Persons whose mental and physical makeup are initially inadequate or discouraging in terms of their own future and that of the learners should seek employment elsewhere than in teaching.

**Character and Reason.** Much teaching is done by example; much learning by emulation. Good taste, honesty, dependability, morality, modesty, loyalty, optimism, resourcefulness, the use of reason, and related traits are important in the teacher. Children and youth seek ideals and values as well as ideas. Teachers should be the sort of people who can assist them in ways that foster self-development and self-realization within a socially acceptable framework.

At the same time, those who teach need not be either perfect or puritanical. Teachers are people and as such may err, as does most of mankind. But persons whose behavior flouts decency or whose lives are a mockery of the goals sought by the schools are not a good influence anywhere, especially in teaching.

Teachers should also feel and care, as well as know. Especially in their relations with others and in the performance of their civic, professional, and social obligations, should they care enough to respond to need and to do what seems right. Passivity and failure to act cripple the knowledgeable as well as the ignorant. Indeed, the latter may be excused where the former can rightfully claim no immunity. To care and to have courage to act are important elements of character for the teacher.

The importance of reason has been stressed throughout this book. It is related to both intelligence and character and is of fundamental importance in the teacher. If schools and colleges are to foster reasoning in learners they must have teachers who demonstrate as well as teach it. Reason is basic to proper individual and group behavior, as well as essential in the instructional process.

**Interest in and Ability with People.** One who would interest others in his ideas must first be interested in them and their ideas. In a real sense a teacher is a salesman who has a product to sell. He should like people, have confidence in them, and be able to work well with them. He is both assured and humble in this ability. Many times he will be competing with other persons and activities for the time, attention, and effort of the learner. Even in the classroom there are forces and factors that tend to free what appears to be a captive audience. Without external encouragement the learners' minds may be a million miles away. And there are times in the learning process when it is easy for the teacher to become discouraged but unwise to do so.

The teacher's interest in learners should extend beyond his wish to teach them. One who can be interested in others only for what he can get out of them, even in learning, is apt to be unhappy in teaching. Patience and hope go along with genuine interest, and these traits are especially useful in working with slower learners and those whose disinterest poses a challenge if not a threat.

Some people seem to have a knack for working with others. Possibly inherited in part and certainly learned in large measure, this trait is very significant in teaching. The teacher works not only with learners but also with teachers, administrators, supervisors, parents, and many others. His influence on learning is often dependent upon this ability as much as upon his knowledge of his subject. Those who do not see themselves as working well with others in teaching and in learning are not apt to find success or happiness in the classroom.

**Primary Desire To Be of Service.** Most people who pursue a vocation see in it an opportunity to render some type of service. For teachers this objective should be a primary motivation, and the accomplishment of service well done should yield sustaining satisfaction. The results of the teacher's efforts are not always easily observed. He sees no finished product in the same sense as one who builds with his hands. He needs to be capable of making an unrecognized contribution for which he often receives little or no thanks.

The monetary rewards of teaching have already been discussed. Few persons wisely enter the profession with the view of becoming wealthy. The service motive yields other abiding and deep satisfactions to those who possess it. The teacher should be such a person if he is to avoid the frustration and disillusionment that may otherwise develop.

These statements do not mean that those who enter teaching should be satisfied with unfair salaries and other conditions inimical to the profession. Indeed they should not. Adequate salaries do not militate against service-minded devotion to duty; they probably help. But prospective teachers should recognize that their satisfactions are to be found principally in other than monetary realms. One who does not feel that this achievement is probable for himself will likely find teaching a profession to avoid.

## Results of Trait Studies

One of the most exhaustive attempts ever made to identify traits related to success in teaching ranked the most significant ones in

terms of rural, elementary, and secondary school situations. Those
attributes with the highest composite rank were: [2]

| | |
|---|---|
| Good judgment | Enthusiasm |
| Self control | Magnetism |
| Considerateness | |

Other of these traits were as follows:

| | |
|---|---|
| Adaptability | Openmindedness |
| Dependability | Originality |
| Honesty | Promptness |
| Refinement | Scholarship |
| Forcefulness | Thrift |
| Cooperation | Breadth of interest |
| Fluency | Attractive personal |
| Health | appearance |
| Industry | Progressiveness |
| Leadership | as ambition |
| Neatness | |

Studies completed since this early one have yielded similar results.

One of the authors of this book conducted an unpublished study
of student ratings of college professors in the field of professional
education extending over a five-year period. More than 35,000 ratings of some 175 college teachers yielded the following complexes of
favorable responses:

1. Knows the subject, organizes it well, presents it interestingly,
   and evaluates fairly.
2. Is enthusiastic, stimulating, dynamic, and encouraging.
3. Understands students, involves them actively and thoughtfully
   in learning, evidences a genuine interest in individuals and their
   opinions, and takes time to help students, in class and out.
4. Has a good sense of humor, creates an encouraging classroom
   atmosphere characterized by permissiveness and motivation.
5. Offers good practical suggestions and illustrations, applies
   theory well, relates principles and practices.
6. Is himself an example of good teaching, practices what he
   preaches, sets the tone as a person of ideas and ideals.

The same student evaluations suggested the following as failings
of the college professors:

1. Course is poorly organized, lacks in substance and/or is repetitious, instructor talks off the cuff without adequate preparation,

[2] W. W. Charters and D. Waples, *The Commonwealth Teacher-Training Study*
(Chicago: University of Chicago Press, 1929), p. 18.

tells us what to do but does not do it himself, makes assignments that are not clear or are indefinite.

2. Poor evaluative practices: bad questions, unclear directions, poor criteria for grading, failure to hand back tests or to discuss them with students.

3. Unfruitful group discussion characterized by lack of organization and planning, usurpation of class time by individuals or by instructor for irrelevant discussion; instructor not really interested in course or in giving much of himself to it.

4. Sarcasm, caustic or destructive criticism, failure to understand students or appreciate their views.

These observations point up the interdependence of personal traits and knowledge and skills related to content and methodology. Most of them are appropriate to fields other than professional education and are applicable at any grade level from elementary through graduate school.

## A Liberal Education

Few people deny the importance of a liberal education, or as it is sometimes called, a general education. When the nature of such an education is discussed, however, there is apt to be disagreement. What is generally meant is a reasonable understanding and appreciation of our cultural heritage, past and present, and intelligent interaction with it in one's daily living. This interaction involves thinking of various types, communication in various media, discrimination among values, and the making of sound judgments.

In terms of schooling, exposure to the following fields of human experience is generally believed to be essential to a liberal education: language arts, humanities, sciences and social sciences including history. Occasionally, these broad fields are subdivided; for example, the science field may be broken into two areas—the biological and the physical. The field of physical education is also included sometimes. There is no reason why the practical arts cannot be liberalizing; but they are not generally included, while the fine arts are. The details of what should be included in these fields and how they should be organized and taught give rise to great argument, often long and fruitless.

**An Education To Liberalize and Free Men.** The intent of a liberal education is also an important consideration, particularly as relates to the teacher. In these days when the term liberal connotes political extremes of the left to many people, there is unfortunate danger of misunderstanding. The education referred to as liberal is that pertaining to a free man, one whose freedom and that of his fellow citizens rests upon his learning. It is a frame of mind that fosters the pursuit of truth and that promotes reason. The liberally educated person seeks opportunities for self-expression and self-fulfillment through liberty under law and extends the same rights and privileges to others. Such a person governs his own behavior, mindful that rights have responsibilities and that interdependency characterizes a democratic society seeking a better way of life for all its members.

Liberal Education in Perspective. It is important that liberal education be viewed in terms of the area of specialization and other courses that a student proposes to pursue. The lines between liberal education, specialized content education, and professional education are there chiefly for purposes of classification and convenience. Knowledge refuses the enclosure we sometimes impose upon it, and what is liberal or general to one person or in one situation may be special or professional in another. Consequently, the total educational pattern deserves consideration in discussing the liberal elements.

Usually, the general or liberal education spoken of is limited to that obtained at the college level. This limitation is unfortunate, for it fails to recognize that most of the earlier schooling provided is to further a liberal education. Much that is taught at the collegiate level is repetitious of what has been taught earlier. The importance of counseling and of articulation is apparent if the total impact is to be effective and economical. Attention to high school courses is important in planning liberal education at the college level. Opportunity to "test out" of required courses may serve to further the ends of liberal, special, and professional education.

A liberal education is of primary importance to the teacher regardless of his field of specialization. Because one proposes to work in the sciences, he is not therefore relieved of responsibility in the humanities and social sciences. Because he is to teach music does not mean that he can wisely profess ignorance in the language arts and the sciences. All teachers, at every level, should share a basic liberal education planned and executed with respect to their total program of studies.

## Knowledge of the Subject

A common complaint is that teachers take so many courses in professional education that they cannot or do not get enough knowledge of their subject field. Stated in another way, the critic is apt to say that educationists stress knowledge of *how* to teach and neglect knowledge of *what* to teach. If there is really any truth in these comments, it lies in individual points of view that are not discernible in the examination of many programs of teacher educa-

Practice teachers and cooperating teachers work together in many ways. (St. Paul, Minnesota, Public Schools.)

tion today. In his book on the education of American teachers, Dr. James B. Conant mentions the common misconception about courses in education and indicates the general refusal to accept the facts in the matter.[3]

**Knowing What To Teach Is Vital.** Knowledge of subject has been a concern of sound teacher education from the beginning. Many developments contributed to a rift between professors in subject areas and those in professional areas as specialization came about in collegiate

[3] James B. Conant, *The Education of American Teachers* (New York: McGraw-Hill Book Co., Inc., 1963), p. 45.

education. Something of the quarrel and of the consequences may be read in the first chapter of Conant's book, *The Education of American Teachers*. The need for specialization in education is apparent; and it is also imperative that those who prepare prospective teachers understand and appreciate each other, as well as work together.

**Patterns of Subject Preparation Vary.** The organization of programs pointed toward reasonable mastery of a subject for teaching purposes varies somewhat from one institution to another. The traditional major-minor plan is to be found widely in colleges and universities. Sometimes this plan is modified or altered for those preparing to teach as opposed to those who do not plan to teach. Generally, the purpose of this major-minor plan has been to give some depth in one subject plus less supporting depth in a cognate or related subject.

Because of the assignment and staffing patterns in many smaller schools and for other reasons too, different patterns of preparation have developed. Broad-fields majors, for example in the sciences or history and social sciences, have become common. These programs tend to give somewhat less depth in a single subject with more supportive distribution in related subjects within one or sometimes two fields.

When one examines the actual courses that students complete in given subjects and fields, he frequently finds great similarity regardless of the supposed plan pursued. Wise counseling by advisors and sensible election by students serve to give supportive breadth to the major-minor approach and to lend depth to the broader-fields approach. It should be remembered, too, that this discussion relates to preservice preparation culminating in a bachelor's degree. Such a four-year program prepares one only *to enter* teaching; subsequent graduate study with ample attention to subject content is essential to the career teacher.

There will be some overlapping of courses with respect to liberal education and knowledge of subject. The major in elementary education also adds professionalized content courses to this combination. These courses deal with content in a subject together with appropriate methodology of teaching, for example, arithmetic in the elementary school and science in the elementary school. The preparation of an elementary school teacher is particularly difficult in view of the broad range of subjects taught. More is said of this later.

**Knowing What To Teach Goes Beyond the Subject.** The impact of this discussion lies in convincing the reader that knowing *what* to teach is very important. Knowing *what* to teach bears heavily upon adequate preparation in the subjects that are to be taught; most people concede this point. One who has reasonable mastery of his subject matter can give the attention he should to the reaction of this content and the learners he teaches. If he is poorly prepared, his focus is apt to be divided and his instructional effectiveness reduced.

Not so generally recognized is the fact that knowing *what* to teach depends also upon other factors, as an illustration, the objectives sought, the background of the learners, and the teaching-learning materials available. Hence while the importance of knowing *what* to teach is clearly apparent, it should not be assumed that such knowledge alone is enough. There is more, much more, to teaching than knowing the subject.

## Professional Competencies

In addition to his desirable personal qualities, his liberal education, and his knowledge of the subject, the effective teacher is competent as a professional. It is in the practice of his profession that he makes his major contribution. These competencies enable him to do and to be what otherwise would not be possible—a teacher in the finest sense of the term. Without them he does not communicate his knowledge to others or help them to learn.

### Sociological Factors in Education.
It may be convenient to think of professional competencies in several categories, realizing first that these things are all interrelated. It is important that the teacher understand the social foundations of education and the place, purpose, organization, and operation of the school in the society. Related to this area is the place and value of his profession and his obligation thereto. It should not be difficult to see that some of this knowledge is important to the liberal education of all people as well as to the professional performance of the teacher.

### Psychological Factors in Education.
The nature of the learner and the educative process is of crucial importance to those who teach. How one learns, why he learns or does not learn, what promotes retention and use of learning, how students may be motivated, and many other important questions are usually dealt with in courses focusing on the psychological foundations of education. These foundations are also important for subsequent attention to methodology that explores the art and science of the teaching-learning process and the role of the teacher.

**Methodology and Experience in Teaching.** The more strictly applied and practical aspects of professional education deal with the development of learning experiences, the use of many and varied resources, and methodology appropriate to teaching and learning. Student teaching or an internship usually culminates this phase of the professional sequence. No other preservice experience gives the prospective teacher a more realistic grasp of himself as a teacher and the challenges to be faced. None is more basic to his subsequent success in the classroom.

**The Elementary Education Major.** The prospective elementary school teacher frequently has a major in the department of education, although many of the major courses may be taught in subject departments and not identified as education at all. Because he usually teaches most or all of the subjects his pupils study in a self-contained classroom situation, there is little that this elementary school teacher studies that does not add to his knowledge of what or how to teach. His major tends to be one of breadth rather than depth, and in that sense encompasses all the courses he takes.

At the same time, however, the prospective elementary teacher usually has opportunity and may be required to do some studying in a subject field. This may be a minor or a heavier concentration, depending upon the institution and the student. The trend seems to favor a strong liberal education plus increasing depth in a single subject or field, in addition to the professional sequence involving both specific content for the elementary school and appropriate professional competencies as discussed earlier.

## Qualifications for College Teaching

College teaching deserves qualifications of the same general type as those discussed for elementary and secondary school teachers. It does not always require or receive them, however, especially in terms of the professional competencies. A liberal education is recognized as essential at the collegiate level. In some instances liberal studies are pursued beyond the baccalaureate level by prospective college teachers. Generally, however, emphasis in graduate study is placed upon the subject or field of specialization.

**Less Stress on Professional Competencies.** Normally, the junior or community college instructor is required to have at least a master's degree with a major in his teaching specialty. Preparation beyond the master's degree is desirable, and many persons have it. Professional competencies are usually sought, although there may be no requirement to complete courses in professional education. This requirement varies from state to state and even among the institutions of a single state. Since many present-day junior college instructors have come from the ranks of high school teachers, more attention to professional competencies is apparent than in four-year colleges and universities. Perhaps this condition accounts in part for the greater importance attached to teaching in the junior institutions as compared with their senior members.

In four-year colleges and universities, growing stress is placed upon research, publication, and other creative endeavor exclusive of teaching. This stress calls for personal qualities strengthening one's scholarship and interest in scholarly endeavor. Depth beyond the master's degree in the teaching subject is usually required, and a doctorate is frequently specified. It seems to be assumed generally that those persons who have this graduate preparation will be competent teachers, and no work in professional education courses is usually called for. Instructional efficiency at the college and university level does not support this assumption, however, and an increasing number of departments are giving attention to ways of strengthening the instructional ability of their students who are preparing for collegiate teaching. Usually this effort is made within the department concerned and without seeking the help available in departments of education.

**Improved Teacher Education for the Prospective Professor.** As the quarrel between educators is settled, there may develop interdisciplinary cooperation in the preparation of college teachers. Possibly, too, ways other than the traditional Ph.D. degree program will be evolved for their preparation. There are good reasons to believe that the time-honored Ph.D. road is not the best nor the only way in which to move toward a collegiate teaching assignment. Some fields, usually in the professional rather than the academic realm, have already worked out other degrees. Imaginative leadership is essential at the collegiate level if we are to meet the diverse needs of the mounting hordes on the higher rungs of the educational ladder. And *teaching* must receive the recognition it deserves if instruction is not to deteriorate at the collegiate level.

## Qualifications for Other Professional Positions

In Chapter 1 career opportunities in education were divided into six categories, including teaching, administration and supervision, counseling and student personnel work, and other professional activities. Attention is now directed briefly to qualifications required for these non-teaching professional careers in education. For the most part these positions require at least a master's degree with appropriate specialization. In many cases teaching experience is prerequisite. Such experience prior to graduate study lends much meaning to the latter and is generally recommended. It is required by many collegiate institutions.

Personal qualities of the highest order are imperative to success in these various professional positions. The ability to work with people and to give leadership are paramount. The development of leadership in others and the delegation of authority to them are also important. Though requiring a high degree of specialization, a broad perspective supported by a liberal education is increasingly sought after. The qualities of generalist and specialist are blended in various ways according to the specific requirements of the type of position.

**Administration and Supervision.**  Some graduate study is usually required of departmental chairman and vice-principals, often a master's degree. The latter is a minimal requirement for principals and for supervisory leadership positions in schools of any but the smallest size. The doctorate is gradually becoming prerequisite for such positions in better schools, particularly for the superintendent and his close professional assistants in central office leadership roles.

Many coaches have become school administrators, even in elementary schools where they may not have had any prior experience. Gradually, there is developing a trend to seek administrators whose background of preparation lies in academic fields and whose graduate work includes preparation in such fields related to administration. Experience at the elementary and secondary levels respectively is increasingly required of those who would serve as administrators at these levels.

For elementary and secondary school principals, the master's degree with appropriate courses in administration is normally a minimum requirement. The same is true of school superintendents, with a strong movement developing toward a minimum of two years of professional study beyond the bachelor's degree. As the American Association of School Administrators takes the lead in pushing for higher professionalization among its members, it is likely that other groups of administrators will move in the same direction, although perhaps slowly.

Executives in state departments of education, teachers' organizations, and the U.S. Office of Education increasinglv hold a doctorate with specialization appropriate to their work. Collegiate administrators usually hold such dgerees and ordinarily have had college teaching experience, with the possible exception of junior college deans or presidents, many of whom move into college administration directly from high school principalships or school superintendencies. This pattern likely will change with increasing numbers of administrators coming from the ranks of junior college teachers. In recent years college presidents have been chosen outside the academic ranks also.

**Counseling and Student Personnel Services.** This area of endeavor is increasingly important at all levels of schooling, and there is growing opportunity for well-prepared persons to render much needed service. A warm, friendly personality and a deep interest and faith in people have long been recognized as essential to workers in this field. But these traits are not enough; and as the knowledge of what makes people as they are grows, the importance of specialized training increases. There is an unfortunate tendency for "do-gooders" and persons seeking their own adjustment to attempt entry into guidance and counseling. Appropriate screening is, therefore, very essential in this field.

For other than teacher-counselors performing a needed but limited guidance function, a master's degree has become the recommended if not the required minimum. Even the teacher-counselor needs some graduate preparation. Persons whose major role is in counseling and personnel services frequently have work beyond the master's degree, and the leaders in the field generally earn a doctor's degree. With the possible exception of school psychologists and social workers, most school counselors come into the field via classroom teaching. Such experience may be required for state certification as a counselor.

At the college level student personnel workers usually come from public school positions in the counseling field or move directly into their jobs following five or more years of college work, including appropriate specialization at the graduate level. Study in psychology, sociology, and education characterizes the typical background; although some college counselors and personnel workers emerge from the academic teaching ranks.

**Other Professional Specialists.** Librarians, audio-visual specialists, and other persons providing professional services in the schools normally come from the teaching ranks. At the college level this is less likely, especially as regards librarians. Graduate study is typically required at the master's level and beyond. Some technical workers in the audio-visual field are non-college graduates who have special training in the maintenance and repair of equipment. The service of these workers, while it is important, is not professional in the sense of the term as used here.

### Specialization and Professionalization

As the trend toward specialization continues in education, so also does the movement toward professionalization. Forces within the teaching profession and forces on the outside generally support these two parallel developments. At the same time, of course, counterforces serve to retard progress. As an illustration, when it becomes obvious that the type of service needed calls for more preparation than has been required, a new proposal for such training is often adopted only after considerable argument and delay. The new proposal usually has a "grandfather" clause exempting certain persons already holding positions in question from having to meet these new requirements.

The net result of this struggle in education is slowly increasing specialization and professionalization. Those who propose to do more than remain for a few years on the lower rungs of the ladder should realize that a return to college and graduate study will be necessary. In elementary and secondary schools various forms of in-service or on-the-job education are commonly carried on. Even at the college level there is growing concern for curriculum and instruction, such that professors are often involved in committee and related in-service activity. Sometimes they fuss about these matters, but the demands of the time are such that appraisal and improvement are in order.

The profession of teaching is on the move. With it society moves. Services rendered and rewards received are geared into this forward thrust. Only those who are willing to keep the step and keep the faith can find in the profession a contributing and satisfying place.

## THE ALL-INSTITUTION APPROACH TO TEACHER EDUCATION

Much that has been said supports a major thesis of this chapter: teacher education should be an all-institution responsibility and function shared by professors in the subject areas and in education. It is true that academicians in times past partially orphaned teacher education. Professors of education halfway adopted it. As a result the profession suffered as does a child caught between bickering parents whose accusations do more to injure him than to right the wrongful situation. There has been fault on both sides, and some critics have taken advantage of the situation in shaking public confidence far more than in stating truth or offering constructive direction.

Any approach to teacher education short of all-institutional dedication and effort will not provide the atmosphere and the education that are essential. Excellent teaching in liberal and subject-field courses contributes a great deal to professional competency. The same is true of instruction in education courses. A course in methods of teaching contributes much too, but only if it is well taught. Such a course will not completely overcome poor teaching to which prospective teachers may be subjected throughout college. In identifying and recruiting teachers, college professors can do much; and they should steer out of teaching the "weak sisters" that are sometimes "advised" into teaching. Effective selective admissions' programs should be institution-wide in development and administration.

The use of well-trained and properly experienced subject professors in the supervision of student teachers has much to recommend it. Joint appointments that link such professors with the department of education offer an added avenue to strong cooperation. The problems of fostering an adequate liberal education in the midst of sterilizing departmentalization can be overcome, if at all, only through interest and cooperation. The development of appropriate majors and minors, at both the undergraduate and graduate levels, requires an interest in teacher education across the institution at large.

To bring the public schools into proper partnership in teacher education also necessitates broad institutional interest and effort. Professors in subject areas have counterparts in the schools with whom they can and should relate. Field services of various types using these professors and those in education, together with public school and state department of education personnel, afford opportunities for service and relationships that pay off in better teaching and better teachers, at all levels.

The all-institution approach has value also in preparing prospective college and university professors. When it is finally realized that a large percentage of college graduates not usually thought of as teachers do actually go into teaching of one kind or another, the scope and importance of teacher education may be more widely recognized than is now the case. In too many institutions it does not get the support it should have.

In short, the principles and practices enunciated in the education of teachers can be effective only where the institution really believes in teacher education and acts upon that belief. Differences should be put aside where they exist, and common ground sought so that united effort can be put forth confidently in preparing teachers to meet a grave educational challenge at all levels.

# RECRUITMENT, ADMISSION, AND RETENTION IN TEACHER EDUCATION

The discussion of qualifications and related requirements supports a thesis stated earlier, namely, that not just anyone should be permitted to teach. Setting up essential roadblocks to screen out the undeserving is not enough, however; and it is often an unpopular position. Positive action to encourage promising young people to teach is also necessary. Once admitted to teacher education through a selective process, the individual may prove to be an unwise choice or he may be lured to other pastures. Recruitment, admission, and retention thus make up a series of related challenges of great importance to the teaching profession.

The good that excellent teachers do and the evil that inferior ones accomplish are reasons enough for selective admission and retention in teacher education. It should be noted also that almost every four-year college that opens its doors proposes to prepare teachers. The variation in the quality of programs is great. The ease with which colleges apparently can carry on programs and the general acceptance of their graduates tends to weaken the profession. Those who counsel and teach at the high school level have some responsibility in this regard, especially in terms of new prospects for the profession.

## Recruitment of Prospective Teachers

Any worthwhile program of recruitment takes into account the qualifications basic to success in the endeavor for which people are sought. Four major categories of such qualifications are discussed in the previous section of this chapter as follows: (1) desirable personal qualities, (2) a liberal education, (3) knowledge of the subject to be taught, and (4) professional competencies.

Evidence of certain of these qualifications, for example, personal traits, emerges earlier in individual development than it does for others. Certain of the attributes, such as subject specialization and professional competencies, develop later and possibly only after entry into teacher education. The kind of young people who show promise for teaching can likely succeed also in other professions. The demand for excellent personnel in all fields is great, and competition is often keen. Financial rewards and all that adequate remuneration brings within reach are greater in some fields than in education. Consequently, there is need to begin early in identifying the best prospects possible if teaching is to receive its fair share of the high-potential people. After all, so much depends upon the teacher that his profession is in many ways the most basic of all. Without it there would be no other professions.

**Identification and Recruitment in Elementary and Secondary Schools.** Personal qualities emerge early and are apparent by the time a child reaches the elementary school. While there is seldom reason to talk vocational choice to good prospects in the elementary grades, it is not too early for teachers to note those who learn readily and are helpful with other pupils. Qualities of leadership and empathy in learning activities are sometimes striking in children. Of course, many who play school at home and express a wish to become teachers will change their minds later. But intelligent fielding of the child's questions and care not to "run down" the teaching profession are helpful in beginning an effort to promote a stronger profession. The impressions formed of teaching in the early years often influence later choice of professions.

In the junior and senior high school, vocational concerns, at least of an exploratory nature, generally become apparent. Opportunity to assess one's personal attributes and to investigate the world of work are important to every youngster. In this endeavor alertness to good prospects for teaching is desirable. Work with youth groups affords experience useful to the individual and to those who may counsel him in tentative vocational decision making.

An organization for those interested in teaching, such as the Future Teachers of America, can, with proper sponsorship, do much to encourage good prospects to consider education as a career. Opportunities to study the profession, to delve into some of its supporting disciplines, such as psychology, and to assist with the teaching-learning process are worthwhile. For example, seniors who show promise and interest may serve as teachers' aides part-time in the elementary school or as laboratory or classroom assistants under teacher supervision. Properly handled, such arrangements facilitate learning as well

(St. Paul, Minnesota, Public Schools.)

(St. Paul, Minnesota, Public Schools.)

(Yonkers, New York, Public Schools.)

Children learn from many sources.

as assist in the identification and recruitment of good teaching prospects.

In various legitimate ways the teaching profession must do more than it has to recruit prospective educational workers of a high order. Colleges and universities are not exempted; teaching there is often poorer than in elementary and secondary schools. Such effort is less a campaign to sell teaching than it is a move to study young people and give them opportunities to look into teaching as a profession. Too often the interest of children and youth is brushed aside or the teacher's acts and words are discouraging, if not actually unprofessional. To neglect good prospects is bad enough; to drive them away is the height of folly.

At the high school level counseling services may do a great deal to assist youth in vocational and educational planning. Again, the profession of teaching should not be neglected. Pupils normally see more glamour and adventure in certain fields than in others. Unfortunately, teaching may not rate very high on the scale, especially if choices are made with only superficial knowledge. Cooperation with colleges and universities offering teacher education programs is important and can be very helpful in furthering appropriate vocational choice.

**Recruitment at the College Level.** In many four-year colleges and universities prospective teachers enroll as freshmen in schools or colleges of education. For the first two years, however, a very large percentage and possibly all of their courses are taken in arts and sciences. There is time, therefore, to work with students who are interested in teaching with the view of encouraging those who show promise and discouraging those who do not. In those institutions where entry into teacher education comes later, for example, at the beginning of the Junior year, a similar effort may be more difficult but is no less needed.

Professors should also be alert to the identification of good prospects who have not made teaching a choice, or perhaps have made no choice at all. This statement does not mean that an early vocational decision is necessarily wise nor that one should be forced. But for professors to disregard opportunity and deny any responsibility for helping students to study and make choices is most unwise. Again, the great need for good teachers at all levels, including the collegiate, should not be forgotten; and the professor's obligation to his own profession should not be denied. Perhaps most unwise of all is the counsel of professors that encourages the stronger to avoid teaching and the weaker to embrace it.

## Selective Admission to Teacher Education

Closely related to recruitment in both a positive and a negative sense is selective admissions. Gradually, it is being recognized that not everyone who seeks to teach should be allowed to do so. Teacher education programs do much to promote the selective function as they develop and administer criteria for admission.

At the present time success in student teaching and teaching seem to relate as closely to academic performance as to any other single criterion. It is realized that other factors are important, but their isolation and appraisal as predictors have not been well accomplished as yet. More study and research are called for, and many collegiate institutions are working at the problem, often in cooperation with public schools.

Attention to physical and mental health is also very important, and student health centers and counseling services can be of much assistance in this regard. Deans of students may also help in screening students as relates to disciplinary and related matters having a bearing on personality and character. The opinions of professors with whom students have studied and of advisors who know them may assist in providing a more complete picture of the individual than do written records alone. The latter are useful, of course.

Admission to teacher education is often by application only, and this procedure is preferred to more automatic acceptance. Application blanks provide data on the background of the student in relation to admission criteria and other matters of interest. Clues for further investigation may be sought, and the forms may call for data useful in researching the selective process. In the processing of applications, prior to committee action, the cooperation of the dean of student's office and the student health service may be very helpful as indicated earlier. Records of student performance are essential, and an interview may be required.

An all-institution committee on admission to teacher education is very useful. This approach affords representation to the various disciplines involved in the preparation of teachers. It serves generally to "tighten up" on admissions, especially as regards scholastic performance as a criterion. The participation of faculty members in this process provides opportunity for fruitful inquiry and discussion leading to better understanding and stronger programs of teacher education.

Persons admitted should understand the conditions of admission and retention in the teacher education program. Those denied admission should be told why they are not admissible and what, if anything, they can do to qualify later. Some who may be minimally admissible should be counseled to reconsider their vocational choice. In the absence of exact predictive criteria, much wisdom in judgment is called for; and committee decisions should not subsequently be changed without good cause.

## Selective Retention and Follow-Up

Admission to teacher education does not guarantee graduation or placement in a teaching position. Both of these developments are dependent upon the individual student. Only those whose performance after admission merits retention in the program should be allowed to remain and to complete the requirements. Just as some students who are initially denied admission may later gain it, so also will some who are admitted, early or late, fail to measure up. It is no favor to them or the profession to continue their program and put them in the classroom.

An increasing number of colleges and universities are keeping in touch with their graduates after they enter a teaching position. Many graduates in the past have used the placement services of their alma mater, but the follow-up proposed here relates to other matters. The performance of the graduate on the job is the real test of the teacher education program. The "feedback" that follow-up provides is basic in appraising various aspects of this program and in bringing about needed improvements. Teachers have responsibility to their institutions in this regard, although few meet it without institutional encouragement.

The cooperation between schools and colleges possible through follow-up and related endeavor has value for all concerned. Too often hypotheses upon which courses and programs are developed are faulty, or assumptions are in error. Improvements in the orientation and use of new teachers on the job are possible also, as well as changes in their preparatory programs. The follow-up offers a promising approach to three-way progress: the individual teacher, the employing school, and the preparatory institution. The profession and the public stand to gain everything and to lose nothing through such endeavor.

# CERTIFICATION AND ACCREDITATION

Professions do many things to safeguard their membership and to protect those whom their members serve. Certification and accreditation are two major and closely related processes of this type in teacher education and utilization. Each of these topics is subject to considerable controversy and pressure, and no teacher in the elementary or secondary school escapes their influence. Even college teachers are affected.

## Teacher Certification Programs

Each state has a certification or licensing program through which it controls the entry of persons into the teaching profession. This program is operated for the purpose of assuring the people that teachers employed in the schools meet some set of minimum standards. Teacher certification is thus a kind of protection of the public interest, a sort of warranty that teachers must be prepared for the profession they seek to enter.

Certification requirements reflect something of the value a state places upon education and is an index of public commitment to the support of education. High certification standards are generally associated with higher salaries and other conditions that relate to better service and higher professional status. The method of administration and application of certification requirements is also pertinent. When many exceptions are made, or there are easy means of exemption, the requirements become little more than guidelines that are disregarded whenever desirable or necessary. There are many teachers in classrooms today who do not meet the minimum standards, and these standards are often low.

Certification programs also serve to keep persons who would be harmful to or ineffective with children and youth out of the schools. The effectiveness of this function varies a great deal because of differences in state laws and the difficulty of determining in advance any but obvious cases of dangerous individuals. Loose administration of requirements exists also. In general, too, certification requirements are minimal and are set largely in terms of college credits and exposure to subjects studied. But it does serve as a second check on those who seek to teach.

**Degree and Credit Requirements.** In earlier days examinations were often used to license a teacher or to qualify him to teach, for example, in the schools of a given county. Frequently, these exams were very simple and not very valid or reliable. As state certification developed, a shift was made to requirements based on college hours completed, subjects studied, and degrees earned. In some states the requirements are more elaborate than in others. Often specified are some common minimal requirements, such as a bachelor's degree and a given number of credit hours in education courses, plus a prescribed number of credits in the single subject or subject fields that might be taught. Thus one person might be licensed to teach only in the elementary school and another to teach only English in the high school. Sometimes the term "endorsement" is used to identify the particular teaching assignments for which the individual qualifies.

For many years state departments of education have administered certification programs, frequently requiring only that an individual make application and forward a set of college transcripts for examination. If these transcripts indicate the meeting of prescribed requirements, the certificate is issued. Sometimes collegiate institutions themselves have been empowered to award teaching certificates.

**Institutional Recommendation and Reciprocity.** Today there is a well-established trend toward a system of certification that places growing responsibility upon teacher education institutions, but reserves for the state the right to issue the certificate. Reciprocity is also developing among states such that persons who qualify in one state will be qualified in other states. With differing certification requirements and more than a thousand teacher education institutions, the whole problem is complicated and has served to encourage the development of a national program of accreditation of teacher education.

Newer programs of state certification may or may not spell out specifics. The principal change from the past is a requirement that applicants for a teacher's certificate be recommended by the institution from which they graduated and that the teacher education program of that institution be approved or accredited. This type of certification places more responsibility upon the institution for certification than in the past and generally permits greater flexibility in teacher education programs than was once true.

At the present time, many states are somewhere between the older system of checking transcripts in terms of specified requirements and the newer one of approving teacher education programs and then relying largely or solely on institutional recommendation. It behooves students preparing to teach to check the requirements of each state in which they may wish to teach.[4] With change so characteristic of certification requirements in this era, inquiry of state departments of education for the latest information is recommended.

The General Nature of Certification Requirements. There is variation in the items that make up the certification requirements. A college degree, a specified number of hours of credit in the teaching field or subject, and a requirement in professional education courses are typical. Sometimes there is a requirement of a liberal education. If these specifications are not set forth by the certifying agency, they are usually established by the collegiate institution whose recommendation is basic to certification.

In most states, for example, a bachelor's degree is prescribed. The number of semester hours required in education courses ranges generally from thirty or more downward, with eighteen to twenty being fairly typical. Practice teaching credit is usually required also, generally to the extent of six to eight semester hours; although the range is greater. Certificates vary in type also; as an illustration, they may be provisional or temporary, standard, professional, or emergency. Certificates granted initially are usually good for a period of years, for example, five years; and for renewal, additional college work may be required. A graduate degree with appropriate specialization is generally required for professional or career-type certification and for special certificates in administration, counseling, and so forth.

## Regional and State Accreditation Programs

Teachers are also influenced by accreditation programs of several types serving several major purposes. State, regional, and national accreditation agencies bear upon the preparation and certification of teachers and on their utilization and working conditions in schools and colleges. Today there tends to be competition and duplication among the various accrediting associations; indeed, they are part of a growing power struggle among the agencies and forces that influence education.

Regional Accreditation. Beginning in the last decade of the nineteenth century, regional accrediting agencies today blanket the United States. These six agencies, of which the North Central Association of Colleges and Secondary Schools is the largest and most influential,

[4] Reference may be made to Elizabeth H. Woellner and M. Aurilla Wood, *Requirements for Certification* (Chicago: University of Chicago Press), published annually.

grew out of a mutual concern of high school principals and college professors for the education of the college-bound student. Their focus on the preparation and assignment of teachers, the educational facilities and program, and other matters related to the education of high school and college students displaced in hundreds of colleges the old emphasis on entrance examinations.

Graduates of regionally accredited high schools were admitted without entrance examinations to colleges and universities also accredited by the regional associations. This condition still obtains today, although the use of entrance examinations is increasing as competition for higher education becomes keener. Over the years many colleges have used placement tests as a basis for assigning students to courses and sections of courses in college; these tests should not be confused with admissions examinations. The latter determine entrance eligibility; the former are for the placement of students already admitted to college.

Although initially concerned at the secondary school level with only the academic program and the college preparatory student, regional accreditation gradually broadened its concerns to include all students and all aspects of the school. Indeed regional accreditation was one of the principal forces promoting the development of the comprehensive high school and the diversity of programs needed to challenge the entire spectrum of students. Beyond providing a minimum floor of requirements, the intent was and continues to be that of encouraging high-quality educational services.

Membership is by institutions in regional associations and is voluntary. However, the gradual acceptance of accreditation as a hallmark of quality makes it virtually essential in most places. The idea of voluntary accreditation and its practice have resulted in tremendous gains through cooperative endeavor. In time many of the policies, criteria, and procedures developed by these agencies became the focus of the standards of state accreditation programs operated by state departments of education. These latter accreditation programs may be voluntary or required.

**State Accreditation.** With the emergence of state departments of education, attention was also given to elementary schools that had not been given much, if any, consideration by the regional accrediting associations. This concern for the lower schools, which is obviously important, is resulting today in added attention by state accreditation to the total range—elementary, junior high, and senior high education. To a somewhat lesser degree, junior high school accreditation is being studied by regional agencies. The Southern Association also includes elementary schools.

**Accreditation Influence on the Teacher.** Prospective teachers are influenced specifically by regional and state accreditation in several ways. Most of them graduate from accredited high schools in which conditions are supported by accreditation requirements. The college or university they attend is probably accredited by a regional agency with its program that promotes improved higher education. Certification of the graduate is often predicated upon the accreditation of the collegiate institution he attends. This latter accreditation may include that of the National Council for the Accreditation of Teacher Education, about which more is said later.

When he enters upon a job, especially at the secondary school level, the teacher is further influenced by regional and state accreditation. His assignments must meet the minimum preparation standards prescribed. He may teach no more classes nor handle no more pupils than are called for. The provision of facilities and teaching-learning materials, desirable teacher-administrator-community relations, and many other aspects of personnel and school operation are covered by accreditation.

**Influences on Other Professional Workers.** Those who prepare for administrative, supervisory, counseling, and other professional careers will also find that accreditation requirements affect them and their job. Just as special certification often applies to these positions, so also do specific accreditation standards. Persons who assume administrative positions must be quite familiar with these standards as they are principally responsible for their application and adherence.

**Certification Plus Accreditation.** In a sense, certification guarantees that the teacher meets the prescribed standards to teach at a given level or in a given subject. Accreditation guarantees that he will be assigned only to a position in which he does meet prescribed standards. The need and value of close coordination between certification and accreditation is obvious, but it does not always exist. By and large, regional accreditation is moving slowly from a policing role focused on the maintenance of minimum standards to a leadership role focused on institutional self-appraisal and self-improvement. To a lesser degree, the same is true of state accreditation.

**National Accreditation of Teacher Education.** More recent on the scene is a national program of accreditation currently administered by the National Council for the Accreditation of Teacher Education. This is only one of the many professional accrediting bodies whose concern is focused upon some large single aspect of collegiate education. Schools of business, music, and law have rather similar agencies with which they work. These professional groups, including NCATE as the national accrediting agency for teacher education, serve as one way of improving an institution's programs and lend some prestige to these institutions.

The National Council for Accreditation of Teacher Education works with regional accrediting agencies that accredit *institutions,* and it accredits only *programs* of teacher education in these institutions. Attention is given to support, organization, staff, program of offerings and services, facilities, library, and other important considerations in determining the quality of a total teacher education program. The Council has been accused of inflexibility and overemphasis on requirements not supported by research, but seems to be weathering the difficult early years that all well-established and worthwhile accrediting programs have experienced.

## Institutional Autonomy and External Controls

There is no substitute for institutional autonomy characterized by a balance of freedom and responsibility in attempting, with courage and vision, to offer the finest teacher education possible. Certification and accreditation are, or should be, of much assistance in this effort; although they are not always helpful. Minimal requirements have a way of becoming desirable practicing standards, or even maximums, in the eyes of many people. They have been known to become ends rather than means, and once established they can add rigidity and diminish flexibility. Adherence to the Carnegie Unit with its slavish time-serving effect is a good example.

The problem is complicated by the ease with which poor programs of education at the collegiate level can generally be established, including teacher education. These programs, even within a framework of accreditation, tend to drive out the better programs. Hence, some reasonable compromise between internal autonomy and external control seems to be the most promising approach at the present moment.

# GRADUATE STUDY AND IN-SERVICE EDUCATION

With the professionalization of education, graduate study has become more important. The trend toward five years of collegiate study and/or a master's degree as desirable minimum preparation is well established, even in the face of a trying teacher shortage. At the same time, it is also recognized that much can be learned better on the job than in the college classroom. Individual schools and school systems find it both necessary and rewarding to develop strong in-service education programs.

Since this topic is discussed in detail in a later chapter, brief reference is all that is needed here. The major point is that one who seeks a professional career in education should not expect to realize fully this accomplishment with only a bachelor's degree. Nor should he imagine that he will graduate with such degree fully prepared to step into any school situation and move ahead without further study on the job. The bachelor's degree prepares the graduate, at best, only to begin to teach. His success and advancement will doubtless require both in-service education and graduate study.

## EDUCATIONAL COSTS AND TEACHER PLACEMENT

No sound professional education is cheap, either to the state or the individual. Those who expect to pursue a career in teaching should realize that they will have to put a sizable investment into their future, whether it be their own funds or money from other sources. Usually, before he has completed the bachelor's degree, the prospective teacher begins to seek a position in which to serve following graduation. Opportunities within the state and beyond its borders may be tempting to him, provided he knows about them.

### Costs of Teacher Education

This is a period of rising costs in higher education. Prospective college students should check the latest figures available directly from the institution in which they are interested. Some idea of costs in several hundred institutions may be obtained from various publications, for example, *The College Handbook*, of the College Entrance Examination Board. But changes in tuition and other costs soon render the figures assembled in such publications out of date. College catalogs and bulletins usually indicate that fees are subject to change.

There is variation in costs among collegiate institutions, even within the same state. Following are some approximate annual average figures for 1963–1964, which are probably lower than actual costs since then.

*State University in*
*the Midwest*

| | |
|---|---|
| Resident fees . . . . . . | $ 280 |
| Non-resident fees . . . . | 750 |
| Board and room . . . . | 825 |
| Books and supplies . . . . | 100 |
| Total for residents . . . | $1,205 |
| Total for non-residents . | 1,675 |

*State University in*
*the South*

| | |
|---|---|
| Resident tuition and fees . | $ 320 |
| Non-resident tuition and fees | 520 |
| Board and room . . . . | 510 |
| Books and supplies . . . | 100 |
| Total for residents . . . | $ 930 |
| Total for non-residents . | 1,130 |

*State University in*
*the Far West*

| | |
|---|---|
| Incidental and other fees, resident . . . . . . . | $ 145 |
| Tuition and fees, non-resident . . . . . . . | 645 |
| Board and room . . . . | 750 |
| Books and supplies . . . | 50 |
| Miscellaneous . . . . . | 125 |
| Total for residents . . . | $1,070 |
| Total for non-residents . | 1,570 |

*Private University in*
*North Central Area*

| | |
|---|---|
| Tuition and fees . . . . | $1,140 |
| Room and board . . . . | 845 |
| Books and supplies . . . | 125 |
| Total . . . . . . . | $2,110 |

These figures are meant only to be illustrative.

After the bachelor's degree, teachers who are making a career of education should plan to earn at least a master's degree. Again, costs vary. Teachers frequently attend summer school as a means of further education that does not interrupt their working during the school year. Added salary is usually paid for graduate degrees, and sometimes is paid for specified numbers of hours of credit earned beyond a given degree.

Many collegiate institutions have programs of financial assistance at both the undergraduate and graduate levels. Scholarships, fellowships, assistantships, other employment, and loans are available to those who qualify on a competitive basis. Through the National Defense Education Act, for example, selected students may be loaned as much as $1,000 a year to a maximum of $5,000 for the entire college career. Interest and repayment provisions are favorable. Special provisions apply to borrowers subsequently becoming teachers, entering the armed services, or continuing their education. Usually, there are more persons seeking aid than can be assisted; but many students are given assistance each year in each of the collegiate institutions they attend.

### Teacher Placement

Teachers seeking positions utilize a variety of means and services. Many school systems employ an application system and invite prospective teachers to apply. Some districts send personnel directors across the nation in search of qualified talent. Colleges and universities normally provide placement assistance, generally cooperating with schools seeking personnel. State and federal employment assistance is also available. Teachers' associations frequently afford help also, and there are numerous private placement agencies.

The Collegiate Placement Agency. The best and usually most economical and effective assistance is to be found in the placement services of the collegiate institution. Sometimes these services include initial placement, follow-up, and continued career assistance. Other institutions provide more modest help. These agencies keep in touch with the job market and the conditions of supply. Often they are familiar with working conditions and living conditions in specific schools and communities with which they have had experience over a period of years. Schools come to rely heavily upon the college placement agency as a primary source of well-qualified personnel, realizing that the preparatory institution stands directly behind and responsible for its graduates.

Usually, the prospective graduate goes to his institution's placement agency during the first semester of his senior year. A set of credentials is developed for him so that prospective employers may easily determine his background and qualifications. These credentials are sent to schools according to need and within the restrictions the prospective graduate may suggest as to locality, salary, and so forth. Arrangements are often made for interviews, many at the institution, some at the school. In various ways the placement agency seeks to bring prospective employers and employees together. Charges for such service are usually nominal.

Once they are placed in a position, many teachers let their registration with the placement agency lapse. They may be happy in their present position and seek only such advancement as is open within the school system or possible through personal contact. Others keep their credentials up to date or reactivate them occasionally as they seek advancement or a move. It is wise to check the manner in which the placement agency operates in terms of service available after initial placement.

## QUESTIONS, PROBLEMS, AND PROJECTS FOR FURTHER STUDY

1. After reflecting upon teachers you have had, prepare a list of the characteristics that made some of them effective and a list of attributes that

made some of them not so effective. Check yourself against these lists and those in this chapter.

2. Write out and analyze the reasons you have for considering teaching as a profession. In the light of this book, and especially this chapter, do you feel that your reasons are sound and sufficient?

3. Discuss the liberal education of a teacher in the context of the total education of a teacher. In terms of your proposed program of studies, where will your strengths and weaknesses in liberal education likely lie? What can you do to strengthen your own liberal education?

4. Projecting yourself ahead to a time when you may be a classroom teacher, what do you think you will need to know and be able to do to be an effective instructor? Is the total college program you are currently pursuing likely to give you these requisites?

5. How can you defend the statement that "only the best should be permitted to teach" at a time when there is a serious teacher shortage and a burgeoning school and college population?

6. Upon what grounds are courses in education justifiable for elementary and secondary school teachers? How would you justify such professional preparation for college teachers?

7. What do you see as the possible virtues and vices of certification and accreditation as they influence the preparation and assignment of teachers? What would you propose as fostering the former and eliminating the latter?

8. Look into teacher placement agencies in your collegiate institution and the state in which you want to teach, familiarizing yourself with such things as teacher supply and demand, placement services available, and costs.

## SELECTED SUPPLEMENTARY READINGS AND FILM

BEREDAY, GEORGE Z. N., and LAUWERYS, JOSEPH A. (eds.). *The Education and Training of Teachers.* The Yearbook of Education, 1963. New York: Harcourt, Brace & World, Inc., 1963. Prepared under the joint auspices of the Institute of Education at London University and Teachers College, Columbia University. A review of teacher education all over the world, including historical and theoretical studies.

CONANT, JAMES B. *The Education of American Teachers.* New York: McGraw-Hill Book Co., Inc., 1963. Chap. x presents a summary of the author's observations, but every prospective teacher should read carefully the entire book with its provocative questions and conclusions.

COTTRELL, DONALD P. (ed.). *Teacher Education for a Free People.* Oneonta, N.Y.: American Association of Colleges for Teacher Education, 1956. Chaps. iii and viii treat issues and problems in teacher education, college teaching, and teacher training practices.

HENDERSON, ALGO D. *Policies and Practices in Higher Education.* New York: Harper & Row, 1960. Chaps. x and xi deal with staffing at the college level and with the improvement of college teaching.

KINNEY, LUCIEN B. *Certification in Education.* Englewood Cliffs, N.J.:

Prentice-Hall, Inc., 1964. Presents a good discussion of the nature and development of certification, and of some new developments in the field.

LINDSEY, MARGARET (ed.). *New Horizons for the Teaching Profession.* Washington, D.C.: National Education Association, 1961. In chap. viii and ix the author discusses rising standards in the teaching profession and makes some observations for the decades ahead.

SCOTT, C. WINFIELD, HILL, CLYDE M., and BURNS, HOBART W. *The Great Debate: Our Schools in Crisis.* Englewood Cliffs, N.J.: Prentice-Hall, Inc., 1959. Chap. vii. Presents pros and cons about the justification of teacher training and certification practices.

STILES, LINDLEY J., BARR, A. S., DOUGLASS, HARL R., and MILLS, HUBERT H. *Teacher Education in the United States.* New York: The Ronald Press Co., 1960. Part III. This section of the book deals with the preservice education of teachers, certification, placement, and follow-up.

STINNETT, T. M., and HUGGETT, ALBERT J. *Professional Problems of Teachers.* 2d ed. New York: The Macmillan Co., 1963. Chaps. 3–4. Discusses the profession of teaching and the identification, selection, and retention of persons in teacher education.

WOODRING, PAUL, and SCANLON, JOHN. *American Education Today.* New York: McGraw-Hill Book Co., Inc., 1963. Part VI. Presents a series of articles on educating teachers and school administrators as edited from *The Saturday Review*'s education supplement.

## Film

*Preparation of Teachers.* 18 minutes. Deals with the education essential to teachers who are to help children become useful and responsible citizens. New York: United World Films.

# 16

# PROBLEMS OF THE
# TEACHING PROFESSION

Teaching is a highly personal occupation. As the reader may recall from the preceding chapter, the kind of men and women who enter teaching ought to measure up to more than ordinary standards in personal qualities, in general cultural and educational background, and in professional competence. As a highly respected superintendent of schools, Matthew W. Gaffney, once said, "You teach not what you know, but what you are." Once a person has become a teacher, he has further responsibilities to face up to and fulfill, if he means to acquit himself not just passably but with credit and honor. This chapter is concerned with major problems of career teachers, individually and as members of professional groups.

Not all of what we may regard as problems of the teaching profession can be dealt with in this book; however, those that seem to be of perennial interest are included. Others of recent origin but of rather heated contemporary interest are also discussed; whether they will be of more than transient significance must remain to be disclosed in the future. These are troublous times in the realm of human relations, and some of the most-debated topics related to teaching involve problems of human relations as much as they do professional standards and practices.

The subject matter of this chapter is discussed with special reference to teaching in public elementary and secondary schools. The authors believe, though, that many of the ideas and procedures mentioned and the questions raised implicitly or directly are applicable to non-public schools, to higher education, and in some degree to professional work other than teaching, such as administration, supervision, and research.

# IMPROVEMENT OF INDIVIDUAL COMPETENCE

Perhaps one of the most important areas of professional concern, and one about which the individual teacher can actually do something, is improvement of competence. For career teachers—for anyone who plans to work in education for, say, more than five years— a bachelor's degree is now generally regarded as an intermediate point, a way station, on the road to full competence. While it is possible in a few states to enter teaching with less than four years of college preparation, the general standard for initial certification is a bachelor's degree; and at least one more year is required in several states; while others require work beyond the bachelor's level for periodic certificate renewal.

## Self-Improvement an Individual Responsibility

It really does not matter too much to the truly professional motivated teacher what the law or the regulations are. He does not need to be told, he is a "self-starter." As standards of admission to teacher education continue to be stepped up by colleges and universities, more able and ambitious young people are entering teaching; and they know where their duty lies, as well as their advantage. No one can prescribe a uniform level of attainment, of course; the important thing is that people try to follow a course of continuous improvement in all the three main divisions of competence: personal qualities or traits, general culture, and mastery of the subject matter and professional techniques of his work.

Since some account must be taken of human frailty and the shortage of "self-starters," various devices are widely utilized to stimulate growth in service, the most frequent by far being salary increases and periodic renewal of certificates. Improvement in personal qualities is touched little or not at all, except indirectly, for example in recommendations for certificate renewal. General culture is formally provided for in many school systems by recognizing for "in-service credit" some academic study outside one's special field; travel in the United States and abroad, various kinds of summer work experience outside education, and so on. However, in these two areas the responsibility rests with the teacher himself; the authors know of no state or local requirements bearing on these two areas. On the mastery of content and techniques, the third area, state and local requirements are the usual thing; although they are far from uniform. Much

depends here, too, on a teacher's dedication, even though there may
be statutes and regulations. For example, by independent reading
and study, one may expand both his knowledge of subject matter
and of teaching "know-how." Keeping up with research findings in
one's field is one of the best (and most neglected) media of improvement.[1]

Whether or not one should earn a master's degree before beginning
to teach is a debatable question. There is a trend for prospective
senior high school teachers to remain in college or university for a
master's degree, a reaction to the vastly increased body of knowledge
in most fields, and also to the partial breakdown of strict departmentalization and the development of broad-field majors, as noted
in Chapter 15. Graduate schools used to recommend, on the basis
of observation mostly, that students teach two or three years before
returning for their master's degree. The students who taught first
seemed to get more benefit from graduate courses in their subject-
matter majors as well as from graduate professional courses. Undoubtedly, five-year programs of teacher education culminating in
master's degrees are going to be widely adopted in the next few years
by colleges and universities. More weight will then have to be given
to self-initiated improvement, and more care taken to weed out of
teaching those who think they can rest on their oars simply because
they have got a master's degree.

## THE TEACHER IN THE COMMUNITY

Teachers are brought into contact with home and community more
than workers in most other fields, through pupils, on various occasions when parents visit schools, and in school activities. The spirit
that prevails in school-community relations depends to a great extent
on the personal and professional behavior of teachers. In the old
days, but rarely found today, there were many restrictions on teachers'
personal freedom. Now these quaint rules have almost vanished, as

[1] As a start on this, an excellent and comprehensive series of pamphlets is
published by the National Education Association, prepared by experts and sponsored by the Department of Classroom Teachers and the American Educational
Research Association (NEA), under the general title, *What Research Says to the
Teacher*. Another good place to look is *The Handbook of Research on Teaching*,
a 1,218-page volume edited by N. L. Gage for the American Educational Research
Association, and published by Rand McNally and Co., Chicago, 1963. Excellent
bibliographies are in all these. Since research is going on in many fields and new
findings result, it is necessary to consult the journals in one's field and educational
research journals to keep up to date.

teachers have gradually won higher status and as they have become more fully participating members of community life.

## Wholesome Community Relations Essential for Good Schools

Schools have nothing to sell, in the commercial sense; their business is always good. But in order for them to receive both the moral and financial support of communities and states they serve, those who work in and administer schools and school systems are under a dual obligation: (1) to attempt to discover what communities need and want done that the schools can properly do; and (2) to inform the public systematically, comprehensively, and honestly about their schools' aims, achievements, and problems. The second of these two items, informing the public, is far the easier to do; but even so it is too much neglected or done in a sketchy way. The first, finding out what schools should and can do, is the source of much controversy because there are so many different views, and certainly no easy answers.

In any event, teachers have the leading role in fostering productive and cordial relations between schools and the public. Ideally, they must exhibit both in and out of school behavior of a professional type. Extremes of dress or manner are definitely liabilities. Relations with and treatment of pupils should be comparable to those between a physician and his patients: helpful and interested, dignified (not stuffy) but friendly and good-humored, poised and well balanced, confidential and inspiring of confidence. Out of school, teachers ought to reflect the best qualities of citizenship and support the attainment of American ideals. There is no need to "be in everything," but neither is it well to stay out of everything. Interesting in this connection is a quotation (far ahead of its time!) from the first issue of *The Hatchet,* a Kansas education journal that was published during 1877–1879:

Teachers when outside the school-room should be like all other good men and women. We do not like teacherish teachers and ministerish ministers who carry the cant of their professions into the store and railway car. Let a teacher do just what everybody else does, as far as it is right; go into society, drive a good horse, play all good games, laugh, teach in the Sunday school, and lead prayer-meeting if he wants to—in fact be a hearty member of society; but by all means avoid being known as a teacher by any outward mark, characteristic or sign, by any cut of the coat or tone of the voice.

A teacher in the school-room is all right—but a teacher out of the school-room is an insufferable bore.

## Desirable Personal and Professional Characteristics

Research on school-community relations shows that parents and other citizens favor most the same kinds of characteristics that pupils like in teachers. Knowledge of the subjects taught ranks high in these studies, on the professional side, followed closely by ability to control pupils or maintain "good discipline," and the use of good teaching methods. Most people still have a feeling that teachers should have a sense of dedication to their work, and some believe they should not be too much interested in such mundane things as salaries and working conditions. Dedication or "vocation" still ranks high; but the general public is aware that in our day it is not enough on which to marry, provide a home, and raise a family.

On the personal side, communities want teachers who possess integrity, who are somewhat above average in intelligence, have a friendly disposition, interest in the town and its affairs generally, not too narrowly confined to their own special interests. Although the former infringements on personal conduct and liberty have largely disappeared, as noted earlier, citizens still expect teachers to avoid the least worthy activities of the average man or woman. This is expected of others who hold positions of trust: officers of government, the clergy, and bankers, for example; not that all these do so conduct themselves, but high standards of personal and professional conduct are part of their code. Teachers do not have to be paragons, but parents want them to be the kind of men and women to whom they can send their children with confidence. Would any reader of this book, if he had children, want to send them to teachers who got drunk every week end, were sexually promiscuous, or used obscene and blasphemous language?

In Chapter 12 there are a few paragraphs on school-community relations that might well be reviewed at this moment, especially what is said about Parent-Teacher Associations. Since the PTA is a superior vehicle for the cultivation of close relations between schools and homes, it deserves the active and affirmative participation of every teacher, if not as a matter of high personal interest then as one of professional responsibility. Two other recommended activities are (1) visits to homes of pupils, when they can be arranged without parental embarrassment or antagonism; and (2) parent conferences at school in lieu of or in addition to periodic report cards. Teachers cannot carry out either of these activities, of course, without the cooperation of parents; and the ability to win that is part of a teacher's personal and professional equipment.

## ASSIGNMENT AND WORK LOAD

To most of the students who use this textbook, the first teaching position is a year or more in the future. Thus it may seem a bit premature to discuss assignment and work load, and in ensuing sections salaries, tenure, retirement, and fringe benefits. Nevertheless, so that prospective teachers may be aware of conditions that affect their intended careers, and that are the focus of much professional study and action and of state legislation, a short discussion of present practice and probable future developments is deemed to be appropriate. For those who will not become teachers, some exposure to working conditions in education may hopefully be beneficial to them in the future, in their capacities as citizens and taxpayers, parents of school children and friends of their teachers, and possibly as school board members or state legislators.

### Major Field of Study the Basis for Assignment

Happily, several forces have, in the last quarter-century, jointly had a salutary effect on teaching assignments. Formerly, it was not unusual for a beginning teacher to be given classes outside his major field of study, and extracurricular responsibilities unrelated to his college activities. This is a distinctly minor practice now; although many teachers are still assigned one class, infrequently two classes, in their minor fields.

Three influences have led to this improvement. Regional accrediting associations (Chapter 15) have increasingly stressed the importance of filling vacancies with teachers specifically prepared to handle the teaching assignments represented by the vacancies. Unfortunately, elementary schools are little touched over the country as a whole by accreditation procedures, so that elementary school positions are not infrequently filled by persons not adequately prepared. An acute shortage of elementary school teachers led in the decade following World War II to the employment of persons better prepared for secondary school teaching.

A second positive influence has been and is the continuing strengthening of certification requirements by the several states. In many states newly licensed teachers may be employed to teach only the subjects (or grades in elementary schools) for which approval is indicated on the certificate itself. (This is called an "endorsement.") The leading nationwide accrediting body for teacher-education institutions, the National Council for Accreditation of Teacher Education, has encouraged this constructive line of development by emphasizing institutional responsibility. This third kind of influence operating to improve teacher assignment gives much weight to individual college and university excellence. By periodic review of college programs of teacher education (normally every five years), with the advice that typically follows an inspection by visiting committees, institutions of higher education are encouraged or required to raise their standards of teacher education. Detailed statutes governing certification, specifying, for example, given numbers of credit hours to satisfy various requirements, are on the way out. Higher education institutions are under ever-stronger pressure to stand back of their graduates. This is a good thing, for it leads to stronger institutional undergraduate and graduate programs, and allows for diversity in conceptions of excellence in teacher education.

It is in order to point out one weakness or at least one unsolved problem in the foregoing developments: What constitutes adequate subject matter preparation of elementary or secondary school teaching, and adequate professional preparation, is not standardized. What would be considered a reasonably good subject matter major in some institutions is regarded as insufficient at others, and the same may be said of professional education. The North Central Association minimum standard of eighteen semester hours (twenty-seven quarter-hours) of college credit in a teaching *field* (e.g., science, social science, etc.) and five to ten semester hours (seven and a half to fifteen quarter-hours) in a specific *subject* (chemistry, history, etc.) is, in the authors' opinion, woefully low, way below an acceptable level of subject matter preparation. Yet there are small high schools that claim not to be able to employ faculties who can meet even these modest standards.

### The Work Load—Thirty Hours a Week?

A book for teachers was published in London in 1835 with the title, *The Teacher, or Moral Influences Employed in the Instruction and Government of the Young.* The author, Jacob Abbott, included this interesting admonition:

Every teacher who is commencing his work, should begin with the firm determination of devoting only six hours to the pursuit. Make as good a school, and accomplish as much for it, as you can in six hours, and let the rest go. When you come from your school room at night, leave all your perplexities and cares behind you. . . . Carry no school work home with you, and do not talk of your work. You will then get refreshment and rest.

Whether or not this is sound advice today, particularly on the six-hour day, is doubtful. Critics of schools and school taxes frequently charge that teachers work only thirty hours a week and for only thirty-six to thirty-eight (at the most forty) weeks a year for a total "work year," which is substantially shorter than the forty-hour week for fifty weeks taken as the norm. Abbott, quoted above, may have been one of the early sources of this critical view by opponents of popular education! However, one can see easily enough how the public might get the idea that teachers work only thirty hours a week. They report for duty usually about 8:30 A.M., and remain until 3:30 P.M., a period of seven hours, less an hour or so for lunch, leaving about six hours work time, five days a week, and for only thirty-six weeks. Why should they expect a "full year's pay" for little more than half a year's time? (Thirty hours per week times forty weeks would make only 1,200 hours, and only a small percentage of schools have that long a school year.) A considerable portion of most teachers' work is done outside the classroom, either at home or in connection with school activities of many kinds.

A survey of teachers' work week published in 1963 by the National Education Association gave detailed figures on average practice. Presented in the two graphs in Fig. 16-1, the data show that for elementary school teachers the average work week was forty-eight and a half hours, and for high school teachers about forty-six hours. These figures apply to the period of the school year, of course. In most schools and school systems, a conscientious effort is made to keep teaching load as nearly equal as possible. Elementary schools attempt to keep classes around thirty pupils. (Few places can reduce class size to twenty-five, which is preferred by a majority of teachers.) High schools attempt to take account of number and size of classes, sponsorship of those extracurricular activities for which extra pay is not scheduled, amount of paper work associated with certain courses, and the like. A simple and convenient method for measuring teaching load is available, and this or some similar instrument ought to be applied in every junior and senior high school once each year or each semester to see if teaching loads are pretty well equalized.[2]

## Ways of Reducing Teaching Load

One of the most common grievances of teachers is the numerous activities they are obliged to carry on that take time away from class-

[2] See Harl R. Douglass, *Modern Administration of Secondary Schools* (2d ed.; Boston: Ginn & Co., 1963), pp. 78–83.

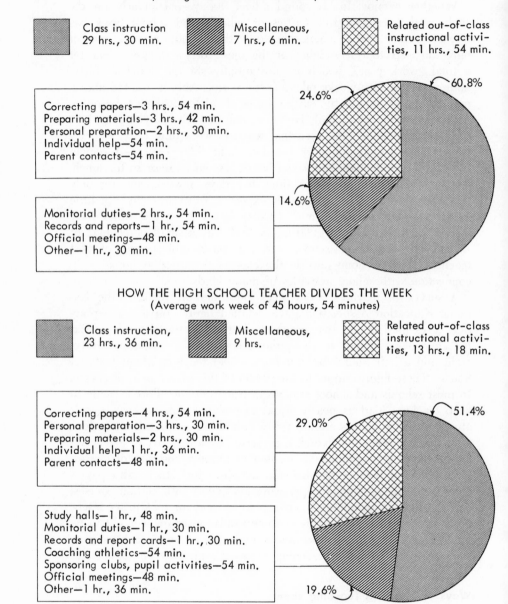

HOW THE ELEMENTARY SCHOOL TEACHER DIVIDES THE WEEK
(Average work week of 48 hours, 30 minutes)

Class instruction
29 hrs., 30 min.

Miscellaneous,
7 hrs., 6 min.

Related out-of-class
instructional activi-
ties, 11 hrs., 54 min.

Correcting papers—3 hrs., 54 min.
Preparing materials—3 hrs., 42 min.
Personal preparation—2 hrs., 30 min.
Individual help—54 min.
Parent contacts—54 min.

Monitorial duties—2 hrs., 54 min.
Records and reports—1 hr., 54 min.
Official meetings—48 min.
Other—1 hr., 30 min.

24.6%
60.8%
14.6%

HOW THE HIGH SCHOOL TEACHER DIVIDES THE WEEK
(Average work week of 45 hours, 54 minutes)

Class instruction,
23 hrs., 36 min.

Miscellaneous,
9 hrs.

Related out-of-class
instructional activi-
ties, 13 hrs., 18 min.

Correcting papers—4 hrs., 54 min.
Personal preparation—3 hrs., 30 min.
Preparing materials—2 hrs., 30 min.
Individual help—1 hr., 36 min.
Parent contacts—48 min.

Study halls—1 hr., 48 min.
Monitorial duties—1 hr., 30 min.
Records and report cards—1 hr., 30 min.
Coaching athletics—54 min.
Sponsoring clubs, pupil activities—54 min.
Official meetings—48 min.
Other—1 hr., 36 min.

29.0%
51.4%
19.6%

Fig. 16–1. How Teachers' Work Week Is Divided. These two charts
are based on information for 1960–1961 gathered by the Research Division
of the National Education Association and are here reproduced with permission of the NEA Research Division from *The American Public-School
Teacher, 1960–61*, Research Monograph 1963-M2, April, 1963.

room teaching. Quite a long list of such items can be compiled, including frequently items such as these (not an exhaustive list):

Collection of lunch money, milk money, etc.
Playground supervision at recess, before school, and during noon hour.
"Hall duty" before school, during lunch hour, and between classes.
Typing and duplicating tests and instructional materials.
Scoring standardized tests.
Cafeteria, lunchroom, and study hall supervision.
Helping little children take off and put on wraps.
Correcting spelling and arithmetic lessons, and themes in English and other classes.
"Taking attendance," making out reports of absence, tardiness, test scores, pupil achievement, etc.

All these activities do have something to do with the education of children, but of course they do not all require the professional touch of a trained teacher. Therefore, teachers in many school systems want school boards and administrators to employ subprofessionals or "paraprofessionals," as some writers say, at lower salaries than must be paid qualified teachers, to take over these "unproductive" activities. With this view the authors tend to sympathize, so long as teachers do not adopt too narrow a conception of what teaching is. Playground supervision is not unproductive if a teacher is deeply interested in knowing something more about pupils than their schoolroom faces. The lunchroom or cafeteria also possesses educational values. But insofar as highly routine activities are concerned, relief should be afforded and it is in better schools. Teachers' time and skills are too valuable to have them spent on typing and other kinds of work that can be done as well or better by persons on lower pay scales.

The employment of teacher aides and clerks for the numerous miscellaneous jobs that modern instructional programs call for is well established. Some schools of excellent repute employ paper-graders to help English teachers and others who have a lot of papers to read. Readers are carefully chosen from among women with college degrees and who are preferably former teachers or who have had some teacher training related to the field they will work in. Some undergo special intensive courses of preparation. It is important that such helpers work under the supervision of the teachers, and not go off on their own tangent; otherwise, teachers and aides may work at crosspurposes. How many teacher aides and clerks should be employed cannot be stated categorically. This depends a great deal on the character of the teaching staff, the scope of the school program, and the finances and traditions of the community. At the secondary level, help is needed mainly for typing and related work, clerical record-keeping, and paper-grading. At the elementary level, perhaps somewhat less clerical and typing help is needed, and more for playground, cafeteria, and other kinds of supervision. Another way to make instructional time more efficient is the provision of top-notch facilities in buildings and equipment, which has been discussed in Chapter 14.

One word of caution should be given on reduction of load or conserving teachers' time. Most of the remedies proposed by teachers and teachers' organizations seem to have the effect of separating teachers from pupils more and more, of reducing the number, kind, and extent of teacher-pupil contacts. Teaching used to be thought of as a sort of global activity, comprised of many and varied teacher-pupil relations. In an age of increasingly narrow specialization and of ever-higher educational goals, that approach must inevitably be untenable. Yet it is worth considering that we are losing a valuable quality associated with teaching boys and girls when teachers see less and less of them and in fewer and fewer different settings.

It must be granted that with higher expectations of teachers and pupils, the typically breathless daily schedule followed by many teachers, especially those in elementary schools, is not defensible. Probably the uneasiness expressed by the authors in the preceding paragraph is caused by a fear that too narrow and academic a meaning will be given to teaching, and teacher-pupil relationships will be too much reduced. In the next few years, however, it is probable that the U.S. school year will be fundamentally changed, to consist of 200 days of classroom and other school time (exclusive of holidays, teachers' conventions, and the like), with each day running from about 9 A.M. to 5 P.M. All academic and extracurricular work of pupils and teachers alike will be encompassed within these hours except for such extra time as either wishes to devote to school matters of their own volition. Under such a plan, only about 65 to 75 per cent of each teachers' time will be spent in direct pupil contact.

## TEACHERS' SALARIES, SALARY SCHEDULES, AND MERIT PAY

The subject of teachers' salaries is one of the most vexing problem areas of the profession. It cannot be properly considered except in a matrix of social, economic, political, and professional conditions, which means that there are no easy answers. Several important aspects are examined in the following pages; but underlying the whole is the authors' conviction that the American people are well able to employ and pay well as many teachers as are needed, as determined by the highest standards.

Indeed, the shortage of well-qualified teachers is a more serious problem than the availability of funds. Whatever else may be wanting, it is not financial ability. We as a people live at such a margin of luxury compared with any other people in the world that lack of money is entirely without foundation as an excuse for inadequate teachers' salaries. Getting the money needed for public education as well as for other essential public undertakings is difficult in a materialistic culture such as ours, and even more difficult for non-public endeavors that cannot use taxation to raise funds (Chapters 12 and 13). There are a number of other questions, however, that always confront those who are concerned about teachers' salaries. These along with prevailing practice and apparent trends are included here. It is well to remember, in a study of salaries, that it is impossible for anyone to state with certainty what is "right." What we may hope for is fairness and goodwill, and that teachers be paid enough so that they and their families have a reasonably good standard of living.

## Beginning, Maximum, and Average Salaries

Many surveys of public opinion made over a period of several decades show that a large majority of citizens think teachers' salaries should be increased. Opinions on how high they should be for beginning teachers, how high they should go, and what can be regarded as a decent average naturally changes with the times. In 1964, the typical salary for beginning teachers with a bachelor's degree was about $5,000 per year, and the maximum for experienced teachers with a master's degree (or fifth year of college work) was approximately $7,500. Average salary for all teachers was about $6,200. In some states many teachers received less, in others the figures were substantially higher. In the last few years salaries have been advancing by $200 to $350 per year, roughly 4 or 5 per cent annually. Many city and suburban districts pay only a little more than smaller school systems to beginning teachers, but in cities and suburbs the maximum tends to be several hundred dollars more per year than in smaller places. The highest schedule for teachers for the school year 1963–1964 (Culver City, California) provided for a minimum of $5,450 (bachelor's degree), and a maximum of $13,400 (doctor's degree), with $10,900 as the maximum for a person with a master's degree.

If one looks up teachers' salaries as reported by the U.S. Office of Education or numerous pamphlets and research reports of the National Education Association, there is reason for encouragement, tempered with a bit of patience. Table 16–1 illustrates the gains made over a period of years in actual dollars and in purchasing power and provides a comparison with average earnings of the total working population.

**TABLE 16–1**

Salaries and Purchasing Power of Teachers and All Workers
1931–1932 to 1959–1960

| School Year | Unadjusted Dollars | | Purchasing Power in Terms of 1959–1960 Dollars | |
|---|---|---|---|---|
| | Salary per Teacher | Average Earnings All Workers | Teachers | All Workers |
| 1931–1932 | $1,417 | $1,198 | $2,888 | $2,442 |
| 1935–1936 | 1,283 | 1,160 | 2,744 | 2,481 |
| 1939–1940 | 1,441 | 1,282 | 3,030 | 2,696 |
| 1943–1944 | 1,728 | 2,030 | 2,917 | 3,427 |
| 1947–1948 | 2,639 | 2,692 | 3,325 | 3,392 |
| 1951–1952 | 3,450 | 3,322 | 3,857 | 3,714 |
| 1955–1956 | 4,156 | 3,942 | 4,543 | 4,309 |
| 1959–1960 | 5,174 | 4,632 | 5,174 | 4,632 |

Adapted from *Digest of Educational Statistics—1963* (Washington, D.C.: U.S. Office of Education), Table 21.

Beginning salaries ought to be high enough to attract able and personable young men and women to teaching in preference to other fields. Actually, other fields offer $1,000 or more per year above what a neophyte teacher can expect. However, if one takes into account the difference in work years—fifty weeks versus thirty-six to forty— it is not so easy to decide who is the better paid. But teachers have to live all year, too; and that is why 60 per cent of the half-million men teachers engage in moonlighting, holding down one or more part-time jobs to supplement their salaries. In summer, 80 per cent get jobs. This is one of the serious problems of the teaching profession: the problem of full-year employment. A few school systems employ teachers for six to ten weeks in addition to the regular school year, as summer session teachers, as revisers of courses of study and curriculums, as recreation workers, and in other capacities. This does not really meet the need adequately.

Another solution sometimes offered by writers in the popular press is the so-called "all-year school," a plan whereby the school year is divided into four twelve-week quarters with each pupil normally in attendance three-quarters a year for a total of thirty-six weeks. One-fourth of the pupils are on vacation each quarter. Teachers would have the option of teaching either three or four quarters (thirty-six or forty-eight weeks) per year, and be paid accordingly. Besides the fact that teachers should not be compelled by economic or other pressure to work in the classroom forty-eight weeks a year, this plan has so many flaws that every school system that has tried it has given it up. Its main supposed advantage, besides making full-year employment possible, is the greater utilization of school buildings and equipment; but careful analyses have shown even this to be a dream and a delusion.

## Full Employment for Teachers

The authors are convinced that the nearest approach to full-year employment is the two-hundred-day school year mentioned previously or something very similar to it. This plan would add some twenty days a year for instruction, and yet incorporate several breaks at strategic times for the benefit of both pupils and teachers. The expansion of knowledge calls for more time in school; and with the rapid improvement of schoolhouse construction, year-round air conditioning will keep schools comfortable for study and play regardless of the weather. An example of how a teacher's work year might look for the school year 1965–1966 is given in this skeleton calendar.

*Fall Term.* Aug. 16–Oct. 29: Fifty-two school days exclusive of one day off for Labor Day (Sept. 6) and two days off for teachers' convention.
Oct. 30–Nov. 7: No school. (One week break.)
*Winter Term.* Nov. 8–Dec. 21, Jan. 3–Jan. 28: Forty-nine school days exclusive of two days off for Thanksgiving.
Dec. 22–Jan. 2: No school (Christmas and New Year Holiday).
Jan. 29–Feb. 6: No school. (One week break.)
*Spring Term.* Feb. 7–Apr. 15: Forty-nine school days exclusive of one day off for Washington's birthday.
Apr. 16–Apr. 24: No school. (One week break.)
*Summer Term.* Apr. 25–July 1: Fifty school days.
July 2–Aug. 14: No school. (Six weeks summer break.)

Such a calendar would, of course, vary somewhat from year to year, because of changes in dates of certain holidays. The dates of teachers' conventions are also different in the various states. It is fairly common practice for teachers to report a few days before the beginning of the school year and remain on duty a few days after the end, but these periods are part of full-time employment and in the proposed calendar would be additional to days of actual classroom teaching. Salaries would necessarily have to be increased presumably by something of the order of 11 or 12 per cent to compensate for additional time worked. Thus, as an example, a person earning $6,000 with a 12 per cent raise would be paid $7,200 for full-year employment.

From beginning salary to maximum, typically requires twelve to fifteen years, with annual increases of $200 to $300. There is great diversity of practice on this point. The authors believe that a beginning teacher just out of college should receive modest increases, perhaps $100 a year during the typical three-year probation period. If he is then placed on tenure, which ordinarily occurs at the beginning of the fourth year, an extra large salary increase should be given, somewhere between $500 and $1,000, and another one at the seventh year and perhaps at the tenth year. In between, smaller increments should be granted. If higher top salaries are widely adopted, and this seems definitely to be in the picture, the old rule of thumb that maximum and beginning salaries should be in the ratio of two to one is no longer adequate. The ratio should be about three to one, so that a young man or woman starting at $5,000 can look forward to $15,000 a year as a career teacher, providing he has high qualifications to go along with this high pay. The evaluation of teaching performance, discussed below, must be an integral part of high-level salary scales. Not every teacher should automatically be placed in the upper reaches of a salary schedule merely for sticking around. With materially higher maximums, the number of years required to proceed from beginning to maximum salary probably should be stretched out to between twenty and twenty-five. This would ordinarily mean that a person would, with advanced degrees, reach his peak pay between the ages of forty-five and fifty.

## Salary Schedules

At the beginning of this century, city school systems began to adopt systematic plans for paying teachers according to their experience and qualifications. In some cases elementary school teachers were paid several hundred dollars less than high school teachers; but this distinction gradually disappeared, leaving the other two bases in effect. Today, schedules based on years of college preparation or degrees and teaching experience—single-salary schedules—are practically universal except in very small districts. Merit pay plans have been adopted by some school boards as a supplement to single-salary schedules but not usually to supplant them.

There is very great diversity in salary schedules. Table 16–2 is an

**TABLE 16–2**

### A Single-Salary Schedule Based on Preparation and Experience

| Year of Service | Bachelor's Degree | Master's Degree | Master's Degree Plus One Year | Doctor's Degree |
|---|---|---|---|---|
| | | *Probation* | | |
| 1 | $4,800 | $5,125 | $5,250 | $5,475 |
| 2 | 4,950 | 5,175 | 5,400 | 5,625 |
| 3 | 5,100 | 5,325 | 5,550 | 5,775 |
| | | *Tenure* | | |
| 4 | 5,550 | 5,775 | 6,000 | 6,225 |
| 5 | 5,775 | 6,000 | 6,225 | 6,450 |
| 6 | 6,000 | 6,225 | 6,450 | 6,675 |
| 7 | 6,225 | 6,450 | 6,675 | 6,900 |
| 8 | 6,450 | 6,675 | 6,900 | 7,125 |
| 9 | 6,675 | 6,900 | 7,125 | 7,350 |
| 10 | 6,900 | 7,125 | 7,350 | 7,575 |
| 11 | 7,125 | 7,350 | 7,575 | 7,800 |
| 12 | 7,350 | 7,575 | 7,800 | 8,025 |
| 13 | 7,575 | 7,800 | 8,025 | 8,250 |
| 14 | | 8,025 | 8,250 | 8,475 |
| 15 | | | 8,475 | 8,700 |
| 16 | | | | 8,925 |
| 20 | | | | 9,075 |

example of one for 1963–1964 from a midwestern school system. All teachers, regardless of subject or grade taught, were paid according to this plan. Annual increments were provided in the schedule as long as a teacher stayed, after acquiring tenure the fourth year, until he reached his maximum. Not shown are numerous supplementary payments for coaching, directing, and supervising school activities, ranging from $50 for a one-act play to $500 for instrumental music direction and $400 for football coaching. Most school systems also have some allowance for teaching elsewhere, up to a maximum of between five and ten years.

In the last few years a plan called a ratio or index schedule has been adopted by some districts, including about 10 per cent of urban units. This plan gives a value of 1.00 to the beginning teacher's salary, and all other salaries are assigned a higher value with 1.00 as the base. The first three years are probationary. For example, a beginning salary of $5,000 would be given the value of 1.00. The plan might call for a 5 per cent increase each year, so that for the second year the ratio would be 1.05, the third year 1.10, etc. Once the index values for all the positions covered by the schedule are worked out, the relationships remain the same, even though the base salary, which is always given a value of 1.00, is changed. An example taken from a southwestern district, for the school year 1963–1964, shows this method (Table 16–3), of which there may be an infinite number of variations. (Extra pay for extra work is not shown.)

**TABLE 16–3**

An Index or Ratio Salary Schedule Based on Preparation and Experience

| Year of Service | Bachelor's Degree | | Master's Degree | | Master's Plus One Year | | Doctor's Degree | |
|---|---|---|---|---|---|---|---|---|
| | Ratio | Salary | Ratio | Salary | Ratio | Salary | Ratio | Salary |
| | | | *Probation* | | | | | |
| 1 | 1.00 | $5,000 | 1.07 | $5,350 | | | | |
| 2 | 1.045 | 5,225 | 1.12 | 5,600 | | | | |
| 3 | 1.09 | 5,450 | 1.17 | 5,850 | 1.24 | $6,200 | | |
| | | | *Tenure* | | | | | |
| 4 | 1.15 | 5,750 | 1.25 | 6,250 | 1.32 | 6,600 | 1.39 | $6,950 |
| 5 | 1.20 | 6,000 | 1.30 | 6,500 | 1.37 | 6,850 | 1.44 | 7,200 |
| 6 | 1.25 | 6,250 | 1.35 | 6,750 | 1.42 | 7,100 | 1.49 | 7,450 |
| 7 | 1.30 | 6,500 | 1.40 | 7,000 | 1.47 | 7,350 | 1.54 | 7,700 |
| 8 | 1.35 | 6,750 | 1.45 | 7,250 | 1.52 | 7,600 | 1.59 | 7,950 |
| 9 | 1.40 | 7,000 | 1.50 | 7,500 | 1.57 | 7,850 | 1.64 | 8,200 |
| 10 | 1.45 | 7,250 | 1.55 | 7,750 | 1.62 | 8,100 | 1.69 | 8,450 |
| 11 | 1.50 | 7,500 | 1.60 | 8,000 | 1.72 | 8,600 | 1.79 | 8,950 |
| 12 | | | 1.70 | 8,500 | 1.82 | 9,100 | 1.89 | 9,450 |
| 13 | | | | | 1.92 | 9,600 | 2.00 | 10,000 |
| 14 | | | | | | | 2.10 | 10,500 |

The ratio or index plan is probably a passing fancy. Its main weakness is that it relates all salaries to the same base, so that you get into questions like this: How many beginning teachers is a high school principal with ten years' experience worth? Different types of work should have different job specifications and different scales of pay, not necessarily related to each other.

## Merit Pay Plans: Paying for Superiority, Not Seniority

The single-salary schedule has done good service. It has virtually eliminated individual bargaining by school authorities and teachers, has helped elevate the salaries of elementary school teachers, and has made financial planning easier for both teachers and administrators of schools. However, the authors are convinced that there are two serious weaknesses in single-salary schedules now so widely used:

1. They tend to depress teachers' salaries generally because, whether we like it or not, they are geared to pay levels more acceptable to women than to men. For women, teaching is one of the best, probably the best, of the major occupations so far as financial rewards and working conditions are concerned; for men, teaching is only mediocre so far as remuneration is concerned. When the movement for single-salary schedules was at its height in the 1930's and 1940's, women comprised majorities as high as 85 to 90 per cent of the teaching force. In the last few years, larger numbers of men have entered teaching, and now constitute about 35 per cent of the total.

2. The single-salary schedule rewards all teachers alike, good, poor, and indifferent, by granting identical annual increments related to educational attainments and experience. Teachers with equivalent preparation, say a master's degree, and the same number of years of experience receive the same salary. Sometimes efforts are made for extra pay to certain persons thought to be more than ordinarily deserving by assigning them more or less nominal extra duties. Or overtime pay may be approved for ambitious and hard-working teachers, as in Los Angeles, where teachers who volunteer are paid about $8 per hour for each hour above the normal six one-hour periods per day.

There is yet a third consideration of equal if not more importance, which is nevertheless almost always overlooked: There is no way for teachers to advance in their profession (exclusive of salary gains) except by getting partly or wholly out of teaching! Men and women of more than average effectiveness in the classroom may be selected as department heads or supervisors in large secondary schools, or as leaders or "helping teachers" in certain grades of elementary schools, or as chairmen of teams for team teaching, or as principals of schools. In all cases, with rare exceptions, they get a reduced teaching load or are taken out of the classroom entirely, as with principals. Something is wrong with a system that rewards the best and the worst alike or, in recognition of superior service, removes the best to a different kind of work.

### Academic Ranks for Teachers

The adaptation of the system of ranks used in colleges and universities in many countries to the schools is a practical way to recognize and reward superior performance. In higher education in the United States, four ranks are usually established: instructor, assistant professor, associate professor, and professor. Other terms are used in other countries, but the principle is the same. For teachers in the schools similar categories could be recognized, such as probationary teacher, assistant instructor, instructor, and senior instructor, or the like. Periodic evaluations of performance would be made for promotion, and for each rank a higher range of salary would be established.

One of the strongest objections voiced by teachers and their organizations to the whole idea of evaluating or rating teaching service is their contention that no one is qualified to do it, and that it cannot be made sufficiently objective. The authors believe that principals should carry the major responsibility, on the grounds that they are the heads of their schools, close to the working front, and presumably prepared for this kind of work. They correspond fairly well to department heads in colleges and universities. Senior faculty members and perhaps others might well be called on for assistance in evaluation, as is done in many college departments. Criteria for promotion and periodic extra salary increases for exceptional merit would, of course, have to be carefully formulated by teachers and administrators working together over a period of two or three years. The criticism that evaluation cannot be made fully objective does not carry much weight, for in an enterprise embracing such a range and diversity of human relationships as teaching, complete objectivity is impossible to achieve. Fairness and judicious judgment are, however, attainable; and their exercise should be sufficient assurance of equitable treatment.

Often overlooked in discussion of merit plans is the fact that most school systems do now evaluate teachers during their first three years of service, with special attention in the third year, as a basis for recommending reappointment with tenure, or dismissal. It would seem only fair—and with this no one disagrees in principle—that superior performance should be recognized by promotion in status and by larger than average salary increases. If the principle is acceptable, then some practical way for it to be applied must follow. Several hundred school systems, most of them in the small city group of 10,000 to 50,000 population, have already adopted merit plans of one kind or another. This furnishes some evidence that merit pay plans can work.

## TENURE, RETIREMENT, AND FRINGE BENEFITS

Ever since the latter part of the 1930's, there has been a shortage of teachers; and it bids fair to continue for some time, although perhaps not quite so acute. The government in wartime and peacetime is a major competitor for college-educated personnel. Industry and business also offer more attractive beginning salaries in many cases to young college graduates and erode the number going into teaching. And so many employers now make various supplementary benefits available that school boards (and other public agencies) have been compelled to take steps to compete for and retain staff. In this section three kinds of provisions related to teacher welfare (other than salaries and work load discussed earlier) are briefly noted: (1) security of employment, usually referred to as tenure; (2) retirement provisions; and (3) fringe benefits.

### "Permanent" and "Continuing Contract" Tenure

The first tenure law was enacted in 1910, but only about three-fourths of all teachers are covered by either "permanent" or "continuing contract" tenure legislation. In general there is little argument about the desirability of job security for teachers, but there is a sharp difference of opinion on which type of tenure protection is the better.

Tenure is supported for a number of good reasons: (1) it helps a school system build a stable teaching corps; (2) it frees teachers from the bugbear of worrying about losing their jobs by whimsical or arbitrary and unjust actions of school boards; (3) it encourages able young men and women to enter and stay in teaching; and (4) it tends to foster a spirit of confidence in the staff. On the other hand, tenure laws may give undue protection to incompetents; that is why the evaluation of teachers' performance (usually in the third year) is so important, when reappointment constitutes virtually a lifetime position. A school board and its administrative officers must ask themselves, "Is this the kind of person we want to keep as a teacher in this community for possibly the next thirty or forty years?" Once a teacher acquires tenure, it may be more difficult for him to accept a position in a different school system, since he will have to go through another period of probation. Many school boards favor some kind of security for teachers but not so-called "permanent" tenure, as it is too hard to remove teachers judged to be incompetent. More favored is the "continuing contract" type of tenure, under which a teacher is automatically employed for the succeeding year unless he is notified of official board action to terminate his services at the end of the current year.  Usually, this notification date is in March or April.

## Teacher Retirement Programs

All the states have statewide retirement plans for public schools, but there is a wide range in their quality.  Experts on retirement have held until recently that retirement on one-half of one's final yearly salary was a satisfactory level, but only a few state teachers' retirement plans are that good.  Some are downright pitiful, providing for $1,200 or $1,500 a year in retirement benefits.  Social security benefits have been made available by Congress to public school employees, if the states enact legislation to participate in social security.  In about two-thirds of the states, teachers are covered by social security as well as by their state retirement plan.  Some large cities have their own retirement programs, which are similar to state plans.

No case needs to be made out for adequate retirement plans—the principle is too well established for argument.  But too much gestation has been shown in making retirement benefits more nearly adequate.  For example, the standard now recognized as most generally acceptable for professional people is an annual retirement income equal to two-thirds (not one-half) of one's final salary.  With better health care and medical service, retired people not only live longer, but they also lead much more active lives than in former generations.  Higher retirement income can be attained only through some or all such measures as these:  (1) higher contributions by employees and employers; (2) utilizing social security provisions as part of a total retirement program;  (3) requiring employees to complete a reasonably long period of active service (some plans now provide for full benefits after only twenty years);  (4) adopting more flexible rules to allow for full- or part-time employment beyond the normal or fixed retirement age;  (5) requiring that payments into retirement funds be held until released as benefits upon retiremnet (all but one state now permit a teacher who leaves teaching or leaves the state to withdraw his retirement contribution, with or without interest); and (6) working out a plan of interstate reciprocity so that teachers moving from one state to another do not suffer any impairment of their retirement plans.

While prospective teachers in college probably think of the subject of retirement as quite remote, it is nonetheless a most important factor in job satisfaction and security.  Its importance is attested by the fact that all states make provision for teacher retirement, and that in most states public school teachers have no option on joining but are required to be members of the plan.

## Fringe Benefits: A Fast-growing Aid in Competitive Recruitment

Even so recently as 1950, the term "fringe benefits" was scarcely ever heard in connection with employment in education; although it had become commonplace in business and industry. In higher education, too, certain fringe benefits were fairly widely recognized, such as sabbatical leave, travel allowances, and reduction of teaching load to make time available for research. Now, however, many school systems make a point, in recruiting and keeping teachers, of extending a variety of fringe benefits. Some help teachers financially by paying all or part of certain services, e.g., group life insurance premiums, tuition for college courses, and hospitalization insurance. Others help by making teachers' work more attractive or more secure, by providing for sabbatical leaves, sick leave, assistance in finding suitable housing (in small towns where housing is scarce, some districts own rental houses and apartments for teachers), and the like.

It is quite apparent that in the next decade fringe benefits in education will become both more liberal and more numerous. Industry and business may continue to lead, but their competitive advantage will be narrowed. The school boards that combine a reasonably broad spectrum of fringe benefits with other advantages such as a long summer vacation, first-rate facilities, and stimulating, creative working relationships will have little trouble in recruiting teachers. The items most frequently included in fringe benefits are listed in Column 1 below, and those beginning to assume importance in Column 2.

| Column 1 | Column 2 |
|---|---|
| Retirement plan | Liability insurance |
| Income protection (sick leave without loss of pay) | Health and accident insurance |
| | Housing services |
| Hospitalization insurance | Family allowances (for heads of households) |
| Financial assistance for academic study or travel, etc. | Tax-sheltered annuities |
| Group life insurance | Terminal or severance pay |
| Personal leave (other than for illness) | Credit union participation (office, staff and overhead) |
| Sabbatical leave | |

# PROFESSIONAL ORGANIZATIONS AND ETHICS

In our time, with its vast expansion of knowledge and its fantastically complex problems of human relations and communication, the pooling of effort by members of various professions and vocations has become essential to progress. The day of the lone wolf is largely a thing of the past; even innovations in the practice of a profession or trade are almost invariably the result of group activity, not of the activity of individual crusaders or reformers. Every occupation has its organizations: bankers, farmers, businessmen, barbers, morticians, truckers, physicians, and so on and on; and education has its share and maybe more.

## Values of Professional Associations in Education

Two purposes, not necessarily unique to the field, are of special importance in the rationale of teachers' associations. The first is to foster progress in educational service. A large measure of the advances made in our schools since about 1920 (when teachers' organizations began to flourish after half a century in the doldrums) is due to these voluntary groups. They have conducted extensive research, exposed to public consideration weaknesses discovered in educational service, proposed corrective measures, sponsored and lobbied for constructive school legislation—all directed toward the improvement of education. Problems of school attendance, teacher education, financial support, curricular reform, district reorganization, and numerous others have received attention in varying degrees in different states, but collectively on nothing short of a prodigious scale by local, state, and national organizations.

The second major purpose is to advance the status and well-being of the profession and its members. Under this head, fall endeavors to foster improvements in salaries, tenure, retirement, and working conditions. These matters are most successfully forwarded by group action to cultivate favorable public opinion and work for favorable legislation. In addition to these professional interests, numerous services are available to members that make their money go farther. Many kinds of insurance coverage are available at economical rates, tours for study or holiday purposes may be joined, housing at attractive rates for members who reach retirement age is rapidly expanding, and the like.

It is probably fair to observe that if professional associations place the greater emphasis on the first purpose, results are likely to help mightily in the attainment of the second. The more unselfish a profession is in its announced and actual objectives, the greater its stature and public support.

## State and National Organizations

In all states the state education association affiliated with the National Education Association of the United States enrolls a very large proportion of public school personnel—more than 90 per cent in most cases. The state associations direct much of their effort to procuring school legislation for the improvement of educational service generally and of teacher welfare and working conditions. They also publish journals along these same lines and offer a variety of services to their members.

There are also federations of teachers in about half the states affiliated with the American Federation of Teachers (AFL–CIO). Total membership is a small fraction of the NEA affiliated associations, between 5 and 10 per cent as a rule. At the state level, the teachers' unions engage in the same kinds of activities as the other associations but with even more emphasis on legislation concerning such teacher welfare measures as increased salaries and stronger tenure protection. Superintendents and principals are not admitted to membership in the union for fear of "administrative domination," although for the nation as a whole administrators constitute only about 5 per cent of the total number of educators.

At the national level, the National Education Association is by far the largest professional association of any kind in the country, and the largest in the world. With about 900,000 members in the parent organization or in thirty-three departments serving specialized interests, it carries on an immense and wide-ranging program from its impressive headquarters building in Washington, D.C. Hundreds of research, statistical, and other reports are prepared and published by the NEA, many of them revised annually. Its monthly *Journal* is probably the best general educational periodical available. The NEA dates its origin from a predecessor, the National Teachers' Association, set up in 1857 by ten state associations. Until about 1920 the membership grew very slowly, but since then it has flourished mightily.

The AFT began in 1916 as a protest against an ill-advised regulation of the Chicago board of education prohibiting teachers from joining labor unions. Such a preposterous rule naturally called for a strong rejoinder. The union's membership seems to fluctuate up and down as economic conditions and working relations of teachers get worse or better. While it formally abjures the strike as a weapon of collective bargaining for teachers, there have been strikes now and then engineered if not officially endorsed or sanctioned by the union, and even some sponsored by the union.

Other national organizations serve the special interests of certain other groups, for example, the National Catholic Education Association and associations for independent schools. Many persons working in non-public schools and in colleges and universities belong to the state and national organizations previously mentioned. In higher education the American Association of University Professors is an overall organization of close to one hundred thousand members, with nine hundred college and university chapters. There are also national, regional, and state organizations for every subject matter interest, e.g., the Modern Language Association, the American Political Science Association, and the American Association for the Advancement of Science.

Locally, there are thousands of associations, almost all affiliated through a state organization with one at the national level. The death rate of professional associations, like that of colleges, seems to be very low; a tendency to proliferate is most apparent. Perhaps there are too many teachers' organizations for the most effective action. Belonging to a fairly small number and taking active part in its program is a good stand for an individual to take. The authors would recommend that a teacher join one national organization, a state organization, and a local group. In addition, he might well enroll in a state and national association working in his field of special interest, such as social studies, foreign languages, health and physical education, elementary education, or art. The dues are modest, and (except for union members) few teachers pay all told as much as fifty dollars a year in professional dues.

### High Ethical Standards a Source of Professional Strength

One of the distinguishing characteristics of professions is their emphasis on observance of a code of ethics for the governance of practitioners. The members themselves adopt the code and undertake to secure unanimous compliance, with penalties for infractions. Professional codes represent higher ideals of service than mere legal licensing embraces, with respect to qualifications of members to practice, obligations to clientele, and standards of conduct. The degree to which a code is enforced by the profession itself, keeping its own house in order, so to speak, is important in generating and retaining public confidence and status, and in fostering self-respect of the members themselves.

The teaching profession in the United States has, through the NEA and affiliated state associations, adopted new and revised codes of ethics for several decades. In 1963 at its national representative assembly, the NEA approved a code consisting of a preamble, four statements of principle, and a number of specific applications under each principle. The four main parts relate to the student, the community, the profession, and professional practice. This is a good statement; few would quibble about its spirit or its contents. (For the text of this code see Appendix at the end of this book.) The weaknesses that critics usually focus on, and with considerable justification, may be summarized as follows.

1. Qualifications for entrance into the profession are too low, it is too easy to become a teacher, and there is no well-defined and generally agreed upon body of content and methodology for teacher education.

2. There is not enough professional control over the licensing procedure, in contrast to medicine, law, architecture, and other professions whose examining and licensing boards are made up wholly or almost so of practitioners. Authority for teacher certification is vested either in state legislatures or in boards composed mostly or entirely of non-educators.

3. Enforcement of compliance with teachers' codes of ethics has been weak; ejection from professional organizations for serious or repeated lapses is almost unheard of; teachers' organizations have defaulted, along with state certification authorities, on revocation of certificates for conduct violating professional standards.

Gradual improvement is nevertheless being made. Many colleges and universities in the last few years have embarked on programs designed to upgrade the preparation of students planning to become teachers, with the support and help of teachers' organizations. A nationwide movement is under way to raise standards of certification with the cooperation of legislatures, state education departments, higher education, and the teachers' associations. And on the third point stated above, a much stronger line of action is in the making, through the development of a plan to invoke "professional sanctions." From a definitive statement published by the NEA's National Commission on Professional Rights and Responsibilities, two paragraphs defining this term are quoted:

Sanctions, within the context of this statement, are defined as a means to prevent the violation of a right or a responsibility. A community should support its schools; school boards should discharge their functions with integrity and impartiality; administrators should use the procedures essential for the democratic administration of good schools; teachers should make every effort to provide the best possible learning experiences for students. Against those who fail to act by such standards, organizations of the education profession may impose sanctions.

As used by a professional education organization, sanctions mean censure, suspension or expulsion of a member; severance of relationship with an affiliated association or other agency; imposing of a deterrent against a board of education or other agency controlling the welfare of the schools; bringing into play forces that will enable the community to help the board or agency realize its responsibility; or the application of one or more steps in the withholding of services. Sanctions are used only to improve educational opportunities through the elimination of conditions detrimental to effective education. The most severe types of sanctions should be invoked only as a last resort where conditions are such that it is impossible for educators to give effective professional service.[3]

Perhaps the strongest influence for strengthening the professional spirit and stature of educators will be the self-policing or disciplining envisaged by the first clause of the second paragraph.

## ACADEMIC FREEDOM AND RESPONSIBILITY

Academic freedom is not only of the greatest importance to those engaged in teaching and learning, but it is also a concept grossly misunderstood only a bit less by educators than by the general public. Many citizens confuse freedom with license or irresponsibility. Teachers are likely to be well aware of their "rights," while ignoring the other side of the coin, professional obligations that must be assumed by those who claim those rights. Although academic freedom was not specifically referred to in the discussion of tenure, if the reader will turn back a few pages to that subject, he will see at once how implicitly the two are related.

### Freedom To Teach Not Carte Blanche

The meaning most frequently attached to academic freedom is the right of a teacher to teach what he knows and thinks with complete freedom, guided by his own integrity and without hindrance from any person or authority. A qualified teacher is expected to be able to gear his instruction to the maturity and achievement level of his pupils. Taken for granted also is his competence to select, organize, and present the subject matter of his field so that the growth and understanding of his pupils will be best furthered.

If a teacher wants to merit and enjoy such freedom, he must assume the obligation of attaining competence in his field and of keeping up to date as new content and concepts and reinterpretation of the old are infused. He ought to retain the student attitude, for no one knows everything there is to know in his teaching field. Along with this attitude, a teacher in fields where serious differences occur in the interpretation or weight given to certain facts and events should maintain

[3] National Commission on Professional Rights and Responsibilities, *Guidelines for Professional Sanction* (Washington, D.C.: National Education Association, November, 1963), p. 9.

a fair attitude. It is rarely possible to give "all sides" of any question; but the effort should be made to preserve a scholarly attitude and make a fair presentation, avoiding proselyting and propagandizing for one's personal preferences. Another obligation is to exercise self-restraint, not posing as an expert outside one's field of specialization. As a citizen, any teacher can say what he likes, and where he likes to say it, within the wide latitude the law allows. But teachers at all levels are in positions of more than ordinary influence, and an appreciation of their professional responsibility ought to warn them against making pronouncements in areas where they are amateurs.

### Freedom for Students To Learn

The pursuit of knowledge, truth, ideas, wherever it may lead, is a new experience for students when they first encounter it, for in everyday life they come up against many closed doors or taboos, in any society. The freedom to learn is one of the priceless attributes of an advanced culture, where the individual may study, speak, write, and question untrammeled by authoritarian controls that limit or deny such actions. The general rule in an enlightened society is that freedom may be exercised without limit so long as the freedom of others is not impaired or their well-being injured or endangered.

One reads and hears a great deal about creative teaching. A most significant meaning of this concept is the change that fine teachers work in their students—or in many of them—from being more or less passive (and bored) recipients of transmitted knowledge to being active searchers after the unknown, the unknown to them. The greatest reward for a teacher is seeing students investigate, question, criticize, dig, imagine, attempt the impossible. This is what freedom to learn means, and it is a part of the cherished heritage of academic freedom in our history.

If one stays with this long enough, he inevitably comes up against the problem of censorship. For centuries some people have taken it upon themselves to decide what their countrymen or fellow-religionists should be allowed to read, hear, or see. Many, many people "believe in" censorship beyond that provided for by laws commonly enacted against slander and libel, blasphemy, obscenity, pornography, and lewdness. In recent years it has become a rather popular pastime to advocate investigation and censorship of school textbooks and library books. Those who are most active in these matters are invariably self-appointed guardians of the morals, patriotism, or spiritual welfare of youth, not qualified by any special training or experience, and often using such tactics either to smear people they do not like for some reason or as a publicity seeking device for ulterior ends of their own. Some are, of course, well-meaning persons of highest motives; but in the authors' long experience these are only a small minority.

Everyone must settle for himself how he stands on censorship, freedom of speech, and similar matters. These concepts are not easy to live with. On censorship, which concerns us here most nearly, the difficulty is deciding whom one is willing to entrust with the authority to decide what one may and may not read, hear, and see. And then how much censorship; how far should it go? It is almost if not completely impossible to have a little censorship; once the wall of freedom is breached, the tide cannot be stopped.

In order not to be misunderstood, the writers state that not every book, film, play, or television program is fit for all children of all ages. Decisions on these matters are properly left to parents and teachers in their respective spheres, home and school. We must be ever on guard against self-appointed censors who take unto themselves these responsibilities. Our hope for elevation of taste and standards of decency must lie primarily with the institutions that play leading roles in the lives of children and youth: the home, the school, the church, and organizations dedicated to serving children and youth.

## QUESTIONS, PROBLEMS, AND PROJECTS FOR FURTHER STUDY

1. Make a list of six or eight American ideals that you rank highly important and that you believe the conduct of teachers should exemplify.

2. Formulate what in your opinion would constitute an ideal program for the preparation of teachers for (a) elementary grades (kindergarten through grade 6), (b) junior high school, and (c) senior high school. State grade or subject or both to be taught by the prospective teachers you have in mind, and any other appropriate conditions.

3. From educational journals of the last five years, summarize the major arguments in support of merit salary schedules and the main arguments against them.

4. Organize a committee (or several committees) of three students to interview (a) five to ten principals on their views about merit salary plans; (b) the chairmen of several local teachers' associations on the same subject.

5. Arrange for a debate by members of the class on the proposition: Resolved: That male teachers in the public schools should be paid more than female teachers.

6. Inquire of a state education association in your home state which fringe benefits for teachers have been most widely adopted in that state, and which three or four are being supported for adoption next. Report your findings, by arrangement with your instructor, being sure to define

carefully each kind of benefit. You may find it desirable to define the term "fringe benefit," too, in more detail than in this chapter.

7. Examine a recent year's file of a state teachers' association journal and write a review in two parts: (a) contents; (b) format and appearance. Consider what to include under each head. In conclusion, make recommendations for improvement of the journal.

As an alternative, do this for a national journal in the field of education, having due regard for the readers it is intended to serve.

8. Make a list of five real or fictitious examples of teachers' conduct (personal or professional) that you view as serious violations of profesional ethics. Then state, for each singly or for all as a group, how you think they should be dealt with by teachers' professional organizations.

9. Look up in several references the meaning of the term "profession" and summarize the main points. Then consider teaching in the light of these criteria and write your conclusions on the subject.

10. If your instructor agrees, arrange for a representative of the NEA-affiliated state education association and a representative of the state teachers' union to discuss in class the advantages of membership in their respective organizations.

## SELECTED SUPPLEMENTARY READINGS AND FILMS

CARR-SAUNDERS, A. M. and WILSON, P. A. "Professions." In *Encyclopedia of the Social Sciences,* Edwin R. A. Seligman (ed.-in-chief). New York: The Macmillan Co., 1933. Very helpful in understanding the earmarks of a profession. See also in same volume, C. F. TAEUSCH, "Professional Ethics."

CHANDLER, B. J. *Education and the Teacher.* New York: Dodd, Mead & Co., Inc., 1961. Chap. x includes a good discussion of national, state, and local teachers' organizations; professional obligations; and benefits. In chap. xiv the social, economic, and legal status of teachers is treated.

CROW, LESTER D., and CROW, ALICE (eds.). *Mental Hygiene for Teachers.* New York: The Macmillan Co., 1963. A collection of readings intended to give prospective and practicing teachers a realistic insight into problems of fostering mental health of their pupils as well as their own.

KLEINMAN, JACK H. *Fringe Benefits for Public School Personnel.* New York: Bureau of Publications, Teachers College, Columbia University, 1962. A comparative study of fringe benefit principles and practices in education, government, and private employment.

LIEBERMAN, MYRON. *Education as a Profession.* Englewood Cliffs, N.J.: Prentice-Hall, Inc., 1956. Calling for more autonomy for the teaching profession and less lay control by state boards and similar agencies, the author discusses many facets of professional work in education. A forceful and interesting book, but not always realistic in the views expressed.

NATIONAL CONGRESS OF PARENTS AND TEACHERS. *A Teacher's Guide to the PTA.* Chicago: The Congress, 1962. This eighty-page booklet emphasizes the common concern of parents and teachers for the welfare of children. Includes a clear-cut description of the organization, program, and operation of the PTA; what the teacher gives; and what he gains.

NELSON, JACK, and ROBERTS, GENE. *The Censors and the Schools.* Boston: Little, Brown & Co., 1963. Two journalists report on activities of pressure groups that attempt to influence the contents and selection of textbooks.

PETERSON, HOUSTON (ed.). *Great Teachers.* New Brunswick, N.J.: Rutgers University Press, 1946. (Published as a paperback in Vintage Books by Alfred A. Knopf, Inc. and Random House, Inc.) Twenty-two great teachers are recalled and "portrayed by those who studied under them." A unique, interesting, and inspiring book.

RESEARCH DIVISION OF THE NEA. *The American Public-School Teacher, 1960–61.* Research Monograph 1963-M2. Washington, D.C.: National Education Association, 1963. A scientific sample of classroom teachers was used as the basis of this interesting report on personal and professional characteristics.

ROBINSON, DONALD W. (ed.). *Teaching as a Man's Job.* Bloomington, Ind.: Phi Delta Kappa, 1963. An updating of an earlier publication of the same title.

STINNETT, T. M. *The Profession of Teaching.* Washington, D.C.: Center for Applied Research in Education, Inc., 1962. A brief treatise on the major problems of the teaching profession. A more extended and comprehensive book by Stinnett and Albert J. Huggett is *Professional Problems of Teaching.* 2d ed. New York: The Macmillan Co., 1963.

## Films

*Assignment: Tomorrow.* 32 minutes. Deals with the vital role of the teacher in our culture, his importance as a member of the community, and as a professional person. Also shows how a modern school helps develop in students the ability to think for themselves and of community needs. Washington, D.C.: National Education Association.

*Planning for Personal and Professional Growth.* 18 minutes. Case studies of four teachers and the types of adjustment they made to teaching. Emphasizes importance of planning for personal and professional growth, and illustrates why teaching is boring and frustrating for some but interesting and rewarding for others. New York: McGraw-Hill Book Co., Inc.

*Summer Harvest.* 29 minutes. Presents a closeup of a school system that decides it can no longer afford "do-nothing" vacations. Sam Levenson is the narrator. Washington, D.C.: National Education Association.

*The Big Classroom.* 30 minutes. Describes a tour sponsored by the National Education Association to show how teachers learn as they go, and how they bring back to their pupils knowledge of other lands and peoples. Cheyenne: Wyoming Education Association.

*The Teacher.* 13 minutes. Explains the role of a teacher in the community, her personal and professional life, her contribution to the furthering of education after extensive preparation and study. Wilmette, Ill.: Encyclopaedia Britannica Films, Inc.

# VI

# EPILOGUE:
# RECAPITULATION
# AND THE FUTURE

# 17

# IMPORTANT ISSUES AND TRENDS IN AMERICAN EDUCATION

Since the early 1950's, American education and American educators have been in a state of ferment, excitement, fear, enthusiasm, and confusion. In recent years, there has been an unusually great amount of uncertainty, misapprehension, and attempts at going off in all directions at once, bandwagon climbing, sitting still and not rocking the boat, and a type of "What are you doing in *your* school?" attitude.

In the middle 1950's, much attention was given to the sensational criticisms of men like Albert Lynd, former teacher turned New York businessman; Arthur Bestor, formerly professor of American history at the University of Illinois; Mortimer Smith of Chicago; and Paul Woodring, then professor of psychology at Western Washington Teachers College. They sharply and vigorously criticized the content and standards of the curriculum, condemning progressive education and life adjustment, about which no one of these particular critics seemed to have much knowledge, as clearly indicated by their own straw man definitions.

With the launching of Sputnik 1 in October, 1957, many educators and others became excited and emotional. A considerable number of these were mathematicians who had presumably acquired the discipline of thinking logically, and scientists who were supposed to have acquired the scientific method of thinking about problems. Among the critics were Rear Admiral Hyman Rickover, who, obviously ignorant of what was going on in the schools then, gave publicity to the "line" of criticism of Lynd, Bestor, and Smith, and a right wing organization, "Council on Basic Education." James E. Allen, Jr., Commissioner of Education for New York State, said that the rate of instructional innovations, good, bad, and questionable in the schools in New York State more than doubled within fifteen months after the launching of Sputnik 1.

Well-meaning friends of the schools, particularly parents and members of school boards, became excited in large numbers and made investigations of the conditions and curriculum and methods of teaching in their schools; although many of them started making conclusions before gathering any data. By 1960, it had become rather generally evident to the majority of people who were sincerely interested in the schools that they had been deceived and misled by the smear campaigns of superficial sensationalists. Nevertheless, they felt that school people should further review their whole program, including aims, objectives, philosophy, curriculum, and methods with a view to improving education to meet the changed times and the needs of the times.

## RECENT CHANGES IN AMERICAN LIFE WITH IMPLICATIONS FOR EDUCATION

There have been going on at a definitely accelerated pace important changes that have not only pointed up needs in American education, but have raised many questions and a considerable number of important issues. Among these changes and trends have been:

1. The critical changes that have taken place in the homes with mothers and wives holding jobs and parents having much less contact and fewer lines of communication with their children
2. The trend toward replacing traditional American idealism with economic materialism, as the interest in spiritual ideals seemed to wane among members of the churches
3. The shifts from simpler leisure pursuits involving home entertainment to commercialized entertainment of various kinds: automobile riding and viewing television
4. The great increase in juvenile delinquency, including doubling and tripling of serious offenses of certain types among teenagers in a fifteen-year period, as reported by the Federal Bureau of Investigation
5. The trend toward softer living and the development of an aversion to hard work and to physical exertion of any kind, including walking any distance
6. The greatly accelerated increase in population, which created such problems as straining the job market, increasing racial tensions, increasing unemployment, increasing new slums; problems of transportation, sewage disposal, and water supply; as well as problems in the detection and punishment of criminals
7. Accelerated developments in technology, including various kinds of machines calling for different types of vocational training and creating much unemployment

## The Knowledge Explosion

In the field of science and technology as well as in the fields of economics, sociology, political science, and business, there has been a greatly accelerated increase in the sum of human knowledge. There is much more to be learned, as the result of:

1. The increase in the influence of mass media of communication, particularly through the television, and also the very greatly increased number of readers of various types of journals and books
2. The increased importance of international relations throughout the world as the backward, small nations attempt to achieve effective democratic government and as the Communists and totalitarians take advantage of the confusion to infiltrate and mislead these peoples
3. The increased complexity of economic and government problems that have grown out of the population explosion, the increased power of very large corporations, the increased autocratic and undemocratic power of certain labor leaders, and greater complication of the problem of relationships between the schools and religion

## MAJOR FUNDAMENTAL ISSUES

### Education for All?

Supplanting the idea that education beyond the Three R's was for the abler children and those of upper economic status who could pay for it, there has developed in the present century rather widespread, almost universal belief that elementary education and junior high school education should be available to all, regardless of race, color, or economic conditions. In the past decade or two, there has been a belief that this should extend to include the senior high school. Furthermore, since 1960 there has developed on the part of many educators, parents, business and professional people the belief that junior college or community institute education, i.e., at least one or two years of education beyond graduation from high school, should be available to young people on the same basis as elementary education.

By 1970 we will have reached the point, although there will be differences among different districts and different sections of the country, when 85 to 98 per cent of young people will have finished six years of elementary school, 70 to 90 per cent will have graduated from high school, 45 to 60 per cent entering college and 25 to 35 per cent graduating, and 10 to 15 per cent doing at least one year of graduate work.

In planning schools on the basic assumption that twelve or fourteen years of education should be provided for all, there is, of course, the necessity of developing learning materials and learning activities and plans of organization and methods of teaching that are appropriate to the great variety of individual capacities for learning the present status and progress in fundamentals and vocabulary, and to future needs. This principle was given a strong boost in 1954 by the decision of the Supreme Court that it was contrary to fundamental rights and the Constitution of the United States to separate people in schools by reason of their race.

While desegregation has gone along quite slowly in all states where it existed, material progress has been made in about half of them and at least token and encouraging progress in all but the state of Mississippi. In the minds of the very great majority of intelligent and honest Americans, both in the North and in the South, this issue has been resolved. It is safe to predict that by 1980 or 1985, with the possible exception of Mississippi and Alabama, the majority of Negro boys and girls will be going to schools that are not segregated other than incidentally as the result of the nature of the neighborhoods in which they live; and even that deplorable condition will be on its way out of American life.

### Education of the "Whole" Child?

There has been a very vigorous and heated controversy between the "intellectuals" like Bestor, Lynd, Smith, Woodring, Rickover, and others that the schools exist for the training of the intellect with very little attention to be given to preparing youngsters for social adjustment, mental and physical health, the ordinary leisure pursuits, home-living, and parenthood and the rearing of children. While this also has been resolved in the minds of a very great majority of Americans who believe that while the home and the church have a prominent part to play in certain aspects of education of young people, the school also has an important part to play in these areas, and neither can do the job by itself but there should be strong efforts and cooperation put forth by the home, the church, and the school.

There is greatly increased knowledge about the nature and extent of mental ill health and personality disorders and about the importance of good mental health and superior personality. Added to this, is recognition of the fact that there has been a very material increase in the number and incidence of mental illnesses and personality disorders, resulting in enormous expense and sadness and grief to the individuals affected. There has also been a great increase in certain types of shocking and brutal crimes, such as the murder of parents, the murder of children, and murders growing out of sex insanity.

## To Serve the Individual or To Serve Society?

There has been considerable difference of opinion as to whether young people go to school to acquire growth and learning exclusively for the purposes of benefiting themselves. There has been a very large and recently increased and increasing number of educators and tax-payers who believe society has as important a stake as do the children in their education. Indeed, that was the major purpose and major claim made for the establishment and extension of public schools. This issue is becoming less controversial, as there has been a spread of understanding that both the individual on the one hand and the nation and community on the other should be benefited and that the interests of one should not be sacrificed in serving the interests of the

Teachers remember that learning is an active process. (Fairfax, Virginia, Public Schools.)

other.  Important are the benefits society receives from the better-edu-
cated citizens, more-effective workers, better wage earners and homemakers, and the consequent decreased juvenile delinquency and crime
and expense of relief.

## What Place for Guidance?

Guidance by specialists, thought by many who have very limited
knowledge of its possibilities, was for a long time thought to be hardly
worth the required time and expense.  They believe that classroom
teachers and others can give most of the guidance needed.  This belief
has given way to the recognition of the value demand of an increased
amount of guidance of young people in connection with such things
as military service, choice of vocation, preparation for vocation, choice
of a college, preparation for college, various types of social problems,
problems of emotional conflicts, and many others.  The belief for the
need for guidance along these lines has increased greatly in the last
few decades.  It is safe to predict that this issue is on its way to resolution and that at least for the rest of this century, though somewhat
spotty and different in different school systems, there will be a definite
increase in the number of guidance specialists and the quality of service that they give.

## Acceleration or Enrichment?

In the past a great many teachers and administrators have made
relatively feeble provision of materials and methods especially suited
to the bright and likewise to the dull learners.  Ignoring the results of
research by psychologists, they erroneously assumed that children of
the same age were also of the same level of social development.
They seemed to believe that it was undemocratic as well as unwise for
their social development to allow the bright students to go more
rapidly through school and the dull ones to go at a pace more likely
to insure mastery and confidence.

## Abuses of Tests and Testing

Old issues with respect to the uses of tests and testing programs have
become sharper as the result principally of the college admissions
squeeze and national programs.  The stampede toward testing has
been checked as it has become more widely known and recognized
that the use of test scores in predicting academic success, except for

the identification of the very bright person, provides a margin of error almost as great as if drawing students' names out of a hat had been used.

The effects of overemphasis upon test scores have been very unfortunate. Many teachers become coaches for examinations and abandon their philosophy of education and teaching for "untestable" objectives. There has been observed in a great many communities very unhealthy tensions and fears among junior and senior high school students resulting in tens of thousands of cases in the need of psychiatric treatment and in thousands of others in suicide, murder, or withdrawal from school.

The problem remains of resisting pressures from without and fear within—and of educating parents of the small significance that can be and will be in the future attached to test scores and, for that matter, to grades. Parents need to become aware of the very great part played by other factors in human happiness—in getting jobs and promotions, in being accepted and well liked, in being successful in marriage and with children—and to the less but important extent in prolonging their children's education and becoming creative. Important among such factors are participation in clubs and other extrasubject activities; the development of self-confidence; and the improvement of appearance, social graces and speech.

### How To Report to Parents

The traditional *report card* is becoming obsolete. Parents wish to have additional information about the growth and progress of their young, and an increasing number of teachers are providing it. There is a strong trend toward a dual marking system—one grade given objectively for growth and status in the subject, and another that is the teacher's estimate of the degree to which the student has achieved up to his potentialities; e.g., Harry Davis may in history or science get both a B— and D+, the B— indicating superior but not outstanding growth and the D+ indicating that he has not tried very hard.

Furthermore, teachers are supplying additional reports in notes, telephone conversations, home visits, and conferences at school during announced hours.

Formal reports are being given at greater intervals and more person-to-person reports in between. In an increasing number of schools, formal reports are given in the kindergarten grades only twice a year, if at all.

## How Valuable Are Extrasubject Activities?

Another issue that has for more than a half-century been one of the subjects of much emotional discussion has been the place of clubs, teams, and other extrasubject activities in the schools. There are educators who firmly believe that when properly managed with qualified sponsors, participation in extrasubject activities adds greatly to the desirable growth of young people; and they have the results of many research studies to support their position. It is clear that in spite of the pulling back in several hundred communities in which there were a great many parents interested in seeing that their youngsters were properly prepared for college and for a vocation, the place of extrasubject activities in the school program and in the school day has become more solidly established, and teachers are being trained, selected, and given extra pay in many instances for their working with groups of youngsters in various types of extrasubject activities.

## What Is the Place of Team-Teaching?

The employment of team-teaching in one form or another is one of the current trends that has raised several issues and that has divided the American education public into three groups: the enthusiastic proponents, the equally enthusiastic opponents, and the very great number who are sitting on the sidelines "waiting to see" or experimenting with it in the simple form. At the high school level, there is a growing belief that by the use of team-teaching there would be improvement of lectures and use of audio-visual aids for large groups and opportunity and more training in independent study, an end very much in itself worthwhile. Opponents of team-teaching call attention to the dangers involved in fragmentalizing the curriculum by dividing a subject up among several teachers, which is likely to result in a lack of coordination and interrelation; and they deplore the lessened opportunity to establish warm personal relationships between individual students and any one teacher.

At the elementary school level, the use of team-teaching in several forms has spread widely. Teachers are more than ever cooperating and planning together, particularly in the core curriculum and in the interchange of classes, so that the teacher may follow his or her specialty a little more and be relieved of a class in at least one field in which the teacher has inadequate background.

At the secondary school level, after a mushroom spread in the early 1960's, team-teaching is employed today only on a limited basis.

At the college level, several elements of team-teaching have been in use for many years; for example, at many large universities, several hundred students sit in on large group lectures in courses in psychology, history, physics, biology, and chemistry. They meet in smaller groups for discussion and "quiz," and there is much independent study on their own in the library and in the laboratory. This practice has been very common in the larger universities for at least a half-century.

### What Type of Grade Organization?

While it is quite clear that the 6–3–3 plan of organization will at least for many decades be the most common type enrolling the most students, there is still the issue as to whether that is the best organization and whether ninth-graders should be in junior high school and tenth-graders in senior high school.

As a result, there has developed in a few schools, and it is likely that the number will increase slowly over the years, one of the two following types of organization: There is the 8–2–2 plan, in which the ninth and tenth grades are in relatively smaller schools and the eleventh and twelfth grades are in a large parent school as is done in the Blue Island, Illinois, Community High Schools and in at least a score of other districts. There is also developing slowly the 5–3–2–2 plan, under the questionable assumptions that the departmentalized teaching should reach down into the six grade and that youngsters in grades 6, 7, and 8 are somewhat more homogeneous with respect to their physiological and social maturity than are the youngsters in grades 7, 8, and 9. These plans may be watched with considerable interest. In a few schools, there is experimentation with a 5–3–4 type of organization, in spite of the opposition of many parents to having ninth-graders in the same school as the more sophisticated twelfth-graders. In many four-year high schools, the students and faculty are organized into somewhat separate units—schools within a school.

There has been much discussion of "ungraded" schools. It is the plan of the ungraded school, as in the Melbourne, Florida, High School, to encourage students to move ahead in each subject field at their own rate. Few secondary schools have as yet adopted the plan, although a long and increasing number of elementary schools have an ungraded primary division instead of the first three grades.

### How Long the School Year and School Day?

In no important country in the world do the young people attend school so few days in the school year as in the United States. While the trend has been to lengthen the school year from 180 to at least 190 days, we are still behind other countries. Of forty-seven countries surveyed by UNESCO; only seven had school years of less than 180 days.[1] In the face of the facts that there is much less employment for young people in the summertime and there is much more education to be acquired, including knowledge to be learned, the idea of a longer school year is definitely spreading so that one may predict that before the end of the century (and much before then in the well-to-do districts), ten-month schools with more than 190 actual school days will be the rule in the United States.

The idea of an all-year school in which youngsters might go only any three quarters they wish does not conform to the desires of parents. Furthermore, it prevents the lengthening of the school year to nine and a half or ten months. The idea is rarely discussed and is only advocated by those for whom the major purpose of the all-year school is to reduce expenses for school buildings and teachers' salaries. Also, the idea of having youngsters attend school four quarters in the year so as to speed up their progress through school as a means of saving time and money for the students, their parents, and taxpayers has never been taken very seriously by any considerable number of educators.

## IMPORTANT CURRICULUM TRENDS

There are several trends that at the same time constitute issues in the curriculum of both the elementary and the secondary schools. More common among them are the following.

### Work Experience

There is a tendency to provide more work experience—paid work experience and non-paid work experience, vocational or civic, out of school and in the school. There is a growing feeling that work experience should be of a type that will give the youngsters the feeling that their learning activities are purposeful and that they are a part of real life.

### Audio-Visual Aids

A very pronounced trend, of course, is the trend toward greater use of audio-visual materials. The use of closed circuit television seems to have reached its peak, with relatively few schools using it because of

[1] "Keeping Abreast in Education," *Phi Delta Kappan*, XL, No. 1 (September, 1961), 36.

the facts that it is so expensive and that equally good audio-visual aids may be provided otherwise. There has been a very great increase in the use of tape recorders not only in language laboratories and the teaching of modern languages, but in the teaching in practically every grade and every subject in school. Also, there has been a definitely increased use in overhead projectors, opaque projectors, and of teacher-made audio-visual materials. In many schools, large collections of various types of visual and audio-visual aids and materials have been gathered; and in some, there has been installed a director of audio-visual education.

## Team-Teaching

Under the team-teaching plan, several teachers cooperate to teach one or more classes, each performing the duties for which he is especially well prepared, including very carefully prepared lectures to large groups of students. Also included is the provision for discussion and supplementary instruction in small groups and a very greatly increased amount of study outside the classroom. In secondary schools, the

Teachers know that learning is not confined to books. (Chicago Public Schools.)

trend has slowed down somewhat; but in elementary schools, it has increased materially.

## The Use of Teaching Machines

Just how teaching machines may best be used for different subjects, in various grades, and by students of greatly varying interests and learning abilities has not yet been determined; and the initial enthusiasm for the use of teaching machines has perceptibly decreased. Among other things, they seem to provide very poorly for the very bright and the less-able students; and they create chaotic situations with respect to where the students stand in their subjects at the end of each semester. There has been an increasing recognition of their limitations and an increasing amount of plans developed for their use in a modified way and on a scale of less importance than originally planned. The idea of having courses of study all laid out in advance by the planners of program materials is even more offensive to the better teachers than the idea of subservience to textbooks has been for several decades.

There is also the issue that the uses of programmed materials and teaching machines can never be developed so as to provide satisfactory human relationships between student and teacher and to provide an adequate method of adapting instruction to differences in ability to the learner.

## The New Mathematics

The new mathematics materials suggested by the national committees of mathematicians and teachers of mathematics will continue to be examined carefully by teachers and school administrators; although there are several real issues related to the matter of the grade-placement topics of the new and the changed materials: how far down into the elementary school the new vocabulary should be taught, and whether or not much of the material is appropriate for the student of average or less than average ability to learn mathematics.

## Foreign Language

The offering and teaching of foreign languages in the elementary schools is undergoing experimentation that will resolve some issues, such as whether or not it is worth the time and expense to study only two years of a foreign language and whether more than one year of credit should be given for less than three years of study, whether or not the teaching of foreign language in the elementary school is effective and worth the time and money unless it is taught by teachers especially well trained in the oral methods, and whether at least three clock hours a week can be devoted to class teaching. Unless the school day is definitely lengthened, there remains the question whether the values of teaching a foreign language in the elementary school are greater or as great as the values that accrue from spending the same amount of time in preparation and growth in such fundamentals as arithmetic, spelling, oral and written composition and instruction in the science, the social science, music, and art.

In many secondary schools, Russian has been added and Chinese in a small but increasing number. The offering of foreign languages in the seventh and eighth grades has increased. More students are enrolling for a third and a fourth year.

## Health and Physical Education

Many more elementary and secondary schools are providing superior instruction and training in health and physical education and strongly encouraging students to be involved each year that they are in school.

Developments along this line have been stimulated by (1) the poor showing on physical strength and skills tests by American boys and young men as compared to those of European countries; (2) the relatively large number of draftees in the army of the United States who were rejected by reason of inadequate physical conditions and developments; and (3) the obvious tendency of young people to avoid walking, physical work, and physical exercise.

As a logical consequence of stepping up requirements and enrollments in physical education, new content has been included in the offerings in that area, particularly for students whose participation is limited by physical conditions and defects as well as wider range of activities to meet the increased range of interests among boys and girls.

## Greater Interrelation of Subjects

There is disagreement as to how to bring about better interrelations between learning materials in different subject-matter fields. The core plan, the fusion plan, the correlated plan, the unified study plan, and the common learnings approach are each found in some schools and each has its proponents. There have been those who have held that, for at least a large part of the learning activities of students in school, the approach should be through the problems of life, particularly the problems that the young people feel that they need to deal with at the time. They have suggested employing materials and activities from any field or fields that may contribute to the solution of the problem or developing the students' effectiveness in the particular area, which also involves units of the extrasubject activities.

It seems that, for some time in the future, the prevailing approach will involve a compromise. Existing in many and in an increasing number of schools, particularly junior high schools, is the problem core approach, involving at least two subjects and employing broad-fields approach, adapting materials, and using methods of learning and teaching that will emphasize the applications and the use of materials for the type of psychological development that will enable the students better to participate and profit from various types of life activities.

### Religion and the Schools

The place of religion in the schools is not only a very controversial issue but a collection of issues toward the solution of which we are making progress. It is certain that the teaching of any type of religious material that can be construed as predisposing young people toward any particular denomination, or for that matter toward all sects of Christianity as a whole, is unconstitutional and is thought by the outstanding leaders both in the church and without to have no place in public schools. The furor about prayer in the schools was largely unwarranted. Without any question, prayers in the schools are not prohibited provided those prayers are to a supreme being rather than to a sectarian holy person such as Christ, Buddha, or Mohammed.

The controversy over this issue has resulted in accelerating the trend toward much more attention being given to the moral and spiritual values in the schools, which were being shoved into the background by the provincial intellectualists and the vocational and education for college preparation zealots.


## OTHER IMPORTANT CURRENT PROBLEMS

### Teachers' Load

In spite of the shortage of teachers in the past decade or so, there has been increasing recognition that quality education or any type of superior teaching can be done in at least 95 per cent of the schools only if the teachers' load is reduced. The real issue is how to finance load reduction. There is a definite trend to lighten loads in various ways, including the following:

1. Relieving the elementary school teacher of at least one class in the morning and one in the afternoon, such class to be taught by a specialist in some field in which the particular elementary school teacher is not best prepared; e.g., reading, physical education, art, music, or arithmetic.

2. Reducing the load in senior high school to no more than five classes daily or four classes a day plus homeroom or sponsorship of a club, and reducing the load in junior high school to five classes a day. With the extra pay being provided for teachers whose load exceeds this amount, there is less need for "moonlighting." Moonlighting means working at a second job requiring more than twelve or fifteen hours a week and is regarded as very unfortunate for the school.

Many administrators are administering the plan of extra pay for extra work in such a way as to increase the income of those teachers most in need of it, especially teachers who have families to support and who do no moonlighting.

## Teacher Rating and Financial Recognition of Merit

While some progress has been made toward developing valid procedures for rating the effectiveness of teachers, in inspiring and in directing the learning of students, much is left to be desired and not too much confidence may be placed in any type of rating. There has been a very definite issue for many years as to whether teachers of greatly different merit and success in teaching should be paid the same salary. In the 1950's, an increasing number of schools experimented with merit rating in various forms; and many have continued it although many dropped it or modified it very materially after a trial; and in many districts, the idea was dropped before being put into practice because of the opposition of teachers.

Along with the trend toward greater tenure security for teachers in their positions, there has been a growing criticism of schedules with annual increases for all or practically all teachers.

Beginning in the early 1960's, there has been much thought and discussion given to a plan that has been put into practice in only a few cities as yet that continues the present salary schedule plan but breaks up the number of years of increases into blocks of approximately four years so that every teacher who has served four years in a particular block, let us say one through four years of the probation period, or five through eight years beyond the probation period, will be very carefully considered in all of his or her activities of various kinds, reviewed, and evaluated as a means of determining whether or not the

teacher will be promoted into the next bracket—something like promotion from instructor to assistant professor, assistant professor to
associate professor, and from associate professor to full professor in
colleges and universities.

Under this plan, some teachers may remain in one salary bracket
of the normal four years for a fifth, sixth, or seventh, or even an eighth
or ninth, year. In many instances, the teacher who is not so promoted
will withdraw from the particular school system or maybe from the
teaching profession; as a number of people have observed, this might
be a good thing for everyone concerned.

**Housing and Equipment**

It seems rather certain that the issue of whether to continue with
the conventional or rectangular multiple story buildings in school
housing or to build circular or other non-rectangular shaped buildings
and other one-story types is on the way to being resolved in favor of
the latter. To be sure, some of the very odd types of buildings with
slanting roofs with considerable amounts of waste space or excessive
costs will continue only in districts with far more money than administrative leadership.

The tendency will continue to plan so that at least some of the rooms
may be decreased or increased in size, providing a few rooms for lectures to large classes and a considerable number of small rooms for
discussion work and committees. There will also without any question be found in an increasing number of new building plans a unit
for housing and storage of instructional materials of various kinds,
including audio-visual materials and equipment; but these materials
probably will not be in one unit with the library as has been envisaged
by many of the proponents of the instructional center idea. It is also
quite clear that the issue of whether or not the school buildings should
have swimming pools will soon be resolved so that for the larger
schools in the districts of average or better income and assessed valuation per child, there will be either indoor pools in the colder climates
or outdoor pools in the warmer climates. It is clear too that as elementary schools become larger, the new buildings will include multipurpose rooms that may be used as two or more of the following: gymnasiums, auditoriums, cafeterias, and libraries.

Wiring of school buildings for closed circuit television will no doubt
go on for some years to come, perhaps at a much slower pace as it has
been discovered that education television on the closed circuit plan
has proven to be much more expensive than imagined by most school

administrators and school boards. Tapes of television programs are being developed in large numbers, and machines for broadcasting them in classrooms are being produced at less than half the prices obtaining in 1960. By 1970, many schools will have available machines for making audio-visual tapes as well as machines for using them. The advantages of audio-visual tapes over commercial broadcasts and closed circuit programs are very great and rather obvious.

### School Finances

There has been since 1950 an almost incredible increase in the amount of money spent on education in the United States. Moving up from about four billion dollars in 1940, it had gone over twenty billion dollars in 1963, and will be more than thirty billion early in the 1970's, up from less than 4 per cent of the national income to more than 7 per cent. To be sure, much of this is for buildings; and there is a possibility that the outlays in this category will be reduced in coming years as the population explosion seems to be tapering off; but nevertheless there will be a definitely increased amount spent for increasing teachers' salaries, for increasing the number of teachers and specialized workers in the school, and for other means of increasing the quality of education.

The taxation on real estate has become so great that there is no question but that there will be a continued movement away from it, and that there will be an increased proportion of funds supplied by the state (up to 50 per cent) and an increase in the funds supplied by the federal government (up to 10 per cent) without control of the curriculum or the faculties of the schools by either the state or the federal government.

## ISSUES AND TRENDS PECULIAR TO THE ELEMENTARY SCHOOLS

### Curriculum Problems and Issues

**Grade Placement of Subject Matter.** There have been conflicting trends with respect to the grade location of much of the learning materials and activities in elementary schools. The trend back in the 1930's was to place some materials a little later in the curriculum, such as the more difficult and abstract things of arithmetic, believing that it is much better for young people to take these things in normal stride rather than to be pressured to learn as soon as possible. Since children were staying in school more and more years, there was no need of crowding them anyway.

Under the pressure and excitement generated by the Sputnik and the barbed criticisms of the intellectuals and ambitious parents, there has been a tendency to see how much earlier things might be taught. For example, it has been discovered that a bright child under favorable circumstances and under a capable teacher can learn some algebra in the fourth grade and that others may learn to read when they are four years of age. At first, the realization that this sort of thing could be done seemed to impress many people; but upon more mature and sober reflection and analysis, such questions and issues arose as, "Assuming these could be taught so early, what would be the advantage of so doing?" and "Assuming that things might be taught earlier under special circumstances to the abler students, what would happen to the average student who was in the classroom of the average teacher to say nothing of the less-able youngster in the classroom of the less-able teacher?" It has become obvious that the premature "bandwagon hopping" toward the pushing of learning materials down earlier in

Teachers use many devices and resources to promote learning. (Detroit Public Schools.)

the curriculum is not working well for any but the brighter children, and corrections have become necessary.

**Expanded Science Materials.** There is not much issue involved in the trend toward the teaching of more and more science in the elementary school other than whether or not elementary school teachers are prepared to teach science. With the definitely improved programs of education of elementary school teachers and the institutes for additional training of those whose preparation is inadequate and with the development of the practice of limited team-teaching, this problem is on its way to a rather satisfactory solution.

**A Countertrend in the Social Studies.** With the increased attention being given to science, arithmetic, and reading, there has been until recently less emphasis upon the teaching of the social studies. A countertrend has been observed in recent years; and while arguments will go on forever, particularly between the political conservatives and liberals, there is no real reason to doubt that the place of the social studies in the elementary school curriculum will be somewhat enhanced in the next few years. Economics in a simple form has been introduced in many schools.

### Instructional Procedures—Trends and Issues

Characteristic of recent trends and incidentally stimulating an issue and doubts in the minds of some is the tendency toward having groups of young people in elementary school participate in what may be well termed "group living in the classroom." The tendency to employ authoritarian methods with accompanying direct relations between the teacher and individual student has been giving way and will continue no doubt to do so. There is a pronounced trend in the direction of having students work together in cooperative groups with the guidance, direction, and encouragement of the teacher—not only entire class groups of twenty-five or thirty, but small subgroups of from three or four to six or eight.

### Guidance in the Elementary School

A very important problem and issue has to do with the place of guidance and counseling that is developing in the elementary schools fairly rapidly, and it seems clear that they will continue to do so for some years ahead.

This is particularly true in those districts, of which there seems to be many, from which there are at least a few children coming from what may be thought of as the underprivileged or "slum" areas where there are homes in which there is little culture, and few opportunities and materials for study, inspiration, or moral atmosphere, and also in districts where there seems to be a considerable number of emotionally disturbed boys and girls, which has been increasing alarmingly in recent years. Elementary school counselors should have training in home visitation. The counselor should play a more active part in attacking the problem of discovering why the underachiever is an underachiever and in how he can be motivated and also in identifying the potential dropouts, for the purpose of making a case study and advising teachers and administrators.

## The Ungraded School and the Promotion Rate

The idea of the ungraded school has made much progress in elementary education in recent years, particularly in the primary grades where the least-able youngsters and the most-able youngsters are identified and grouped separately from the majority who are mill run for the purpose of adapting appropriate learning materials and activities and the leadership of a teacher especially prepared or otherwise especially suitable for that responsibility.

Many parents deplore the prevailing practices of promoting practically all elementary school children every year. Results of many investigations show definitely that the child who repeats a grade learns little more the second year, but becomes discouraged, develops a dislike for school, and is forced to make a severe adjustment when withdrawn from his former classmates. Many schools are providing for dull and bright students to go more slowly or more rapidly. The solution of the problem seems to be pretty much agreed upon among educators: to have very few repeaters or grade "skippers," but some fast travelers who complete elementary education in five years and a rare one in four and some slow movers who take seven or even eight years. The dropouts come in very small numbers from the overaged slow goers, but in large numbers from the overaged repeaters.

## Education of Elementary School Teachers

Among important issues is one as to whether teachers in the elementary school should receive more or less preparation for the discharge of responsibilities and exploitation of opportunities to be of service to young people. The effects of misleading the public with reference to the matter of what proportion of the professional courses are courses in "methods" seem to be backfiring as the true situation becomes better and more widely known. There is a general feeling that school teachers need much practical preparation for their responsibilities in connection with the teaching of reading, the teaching of arithmetic, the teaching of music, and the teaching of other subjects as well as in connection with counseling and guidance and working with youngsters who in one way or another are problems if not actually emotionally disturbed young people.

An important issue of recent development has been that related to the relative desirability of having elementary school teachers in their preservice education take sufficient courses in one academic field to constitute a major. Opponents of this practice favor instead much more attention to the general education of teachers in a considerable number of fields, including science, English, history, the social studies, physical education, music, and art. It is quite likely that the five-year program toward which we are definitely moving nationally will provide the opportunities for settlement of many of these issues without denying the arguments of either side.

## Departmentalized Assignment of Elementary School Teachers

With respect to the teacher's load and assignment, there have developed several important trends and issues. There is a definite trend in lightening the teacher's load if by no other means than by relieving the teacher of one or two classes during the day. The issue with respect to departmentalization is much more definitely drawn. Those who seem to have experienced an obsession with advanced subject matter training would relieve the teacher of responsibility for teaching any subjects in which he has not had at least a minor in college if not a major, and this would of course mean departmentalization.

Any great degree of departmentalization is vigorously opposed by the great majority of teachers on the grounds that elementary school teachers need to have considerable background in a rather large number of fields, and also that departmentalization would tend to compartmentalize and isolate subjects and prevent the possibility of teachers bringing about closer correlation if not integration of two or more subjects.

# CURRENT TRENDS IN SECONDARY EDUCATION

## Current Curriculum Trends

High schools and their programs have been undergoing careful reevaluation and much transformation in the last decade, and this seems very likely to continue for some time to come. Most important among the trends are the following:

Science. In most schools, there have been very material changes in the curriculum, such as teaching in the elementary school much of the science taught in junior high school and making way for more new material—earth science and space science.

Modern Mathematics. There has been and still is a trend toward the introduction of the "modern" mathematics in mathematics classes for the average and especially for the abler students.

Foreign Languages. There are now increased offerings in foreign languages, including (1) earlier introduction and greater enrollments in third- and fourth-year classes, (2) the teaching of Chinese and Russian, (3) the offering of a first year of a modern language in grade 7, and (4) the offering of two or more sections at different levels for students having studied a modern language in the elementary school.

Health Education. There are improved provisions for training in health and body vigor and greatly increased enrollments.

English. In English, there have been the following noteworthy trends in the past few years: (1) more attention to oral and written English and language all the way through the secondary schools; (2) lightening the load of the English teacher or giving him assistance in the marking of papers; (3) more reading of the contemporary American authors such as Steinbeck, Hersey, and Drury, and less attention to those of only average pre-eminence.

Social Studies. The prominent trends in the social studies include (1) the giving of more time and attention to the peoples and their cultures in Asia, Africa, and Latin America; (2) requiring more work in history and the social studies—some schools now requiring it every year; (3) the offering of at least a semester, usually a year, of economics in the senior high school, and requiring at least a semester of work in it.

Home Economics. The trend in home economics has been in (1) less attention upon the preparation of foods, (2) less attention upon developing skills in the construction of clothing, (3) more attention to diet, (4) more attention to the financial aspects of the home, (5) more attention to child rearing, (6) more attention to the judging of home construction and planning of landscaping, (7) more attention to the aesthetic aspects of the home, and (8) more attention to the psychology of marital relations and problems of close living in small quarters.

**Arts and Crafts.** An outstanding trend in arts and crafts is the offering of a larger number of different types of arts and crafts so that the students in junior and senior high schools may have an opportunity to explore their interests and talents in a broader field. In many schools several teachers are employed who supplement each other so that as a team they can offer ten or twelve or more different types of arts and crafts in a suite of studios and shops.

**Vocational Training.** One of the outstandingly weak spots in the senior high school has been the limited provisions for education for employment. Usually, except in the field of diversified occupations, a secondary school offers vocational training in not more than five or six different kinds of positions; whereas their graduates who do not go on to college are likely to be employed in twenty to twenty-five occupations in the locality in rather large numbers.

As the result of very severe criticism by a national committee, educators in general, and the lay public, there is under way now in most schools plans for (1) providing vocational training for a larger number of positions, and (2) encouraging more students to enroll in courses of diversified occupations and in distributive education.

## The High School Program of the Future

Table 17–1 shows an example of what the high school program of the 1970's will be like if present trends continue.

A normal student program would involve courses with total number of periods in class 28 to 32 in grades 7, 8, and 9; 26 to 31 in grades 10, 11, and 12. In computing the total, work in agriculture, distributive education, and diversified occupations should count as twelve class periods. The most capable should be permitted to carry four or five hours more.

It may be added that there is a good but as yet feeble trend toward scheduling blocks of three periods daily in grades 7 and 8 for history, language arts, literature, and homeroom activities including group guidance. Provision is made in some schools for the ablest students to spend four periods a week in foreign language; while the others strengthen their abilities in reading, speech, and written composition.

# TABLE 17-1

## Secondary School Program

(for schools with seven class periods of forty-six to forty-eight minutes net)

### Number of Periods per Week

(Classes of bright students in academic subjects may well meet one less period a week, and classes of "slow" students one more period a week.)

| | Grade 7 | Grade 8 | Grade 9 | Grade 10 | Grade 11 | Grade 12 |
|---|---|---|---|---|---|---|
| Required: * | | | | | | |
| English † | 6 | 6 | 6 | 5 | 5 | 5 ** |
| History and Social Studies ‡ | 5 | 5 | 5 | 5 | 5 | 5 ** |
| Mathematics and Science (basic) § | 5 or 6 | 5 or 6 | 5 or 6 | 5 or 6 | 5 or 6 | 5 or 6 |
| Physical and Health Education | 3 | 3 | 3 | 3 | 3 | 3 |
| Electives: | | | | | | |
| Art ‖ | 4 | 4 | 4 | 4 | 4 | 4 |
| Music ‖ | 4 | 4 | 4 | 4 | 4 | 4 |
| Typing (personal) ‖ | | | | 4 | 4 | 4 |
| Shop or Crafts ‖ | 4 | 4 | 4 | 4 | 4 | 4 |
| Home Living ‖ | 4 | 4 | 4 | 4 | 4 | 4 |
| Foreign Language # | 4 | 4 | 4 | 5 | 5 | 5 ** |
| Foreign Language # | | | 5 | 5 | 5 | 5 ** |
| Vocational Courses (2 units credit each year): | | | | | | |
| Trades and Industries, Business, Home Economics | | | | | 12 | 12 |
| Distributive Education and Diversified Occupations (in school and out) | | | | | 18 | 18 |
| College Preparatory Mathematics (speed group) | | | 5 (algebra) | 5 (geometry) | 5 | 5 ** |

554

| College Preparatory Mathematics (regular group) | 5 | 5 | 5 | 5 |
| College Preparatory Science (including laboratory) | 6 | 6 | 6 | 6** |
| Speech ‖ | 3 | 3 | 3 | 3 |
| Psychology ‖ | 3 | 3 | 3 | 3 |
| Dramatics ‖ | 3 | 3 | 3 | 3 |
| Journalism ‖ | 3 | 3 | 3 | 3 |

NOTE: Three short periods of twenty-eight to thirty minutes should be scheduled between 11:30 and 1:00 for lunch, homerooms, clubs, and study. The school day will open at 8:00 A.M. or shortly thereafter and run until almost 4:00 P.M. with teachers on duty approximately four and one-half hours.

* Required for graduation from senior high school 13 units toward which 1 unit for algebra in the ninth grade and 2 units for three years of foreign language in grades 7, 8, and 9 may be counted, thus permitting industrious bright students either to graduate after five years in junior and senior high school, or to take several college-level courses in the senior year.

† English courses should include English literature, American literature, language and grammar, speech, written composition, reading, and listening.

‡ Courses in History and the Social Studies might well include a number of one-semester courses as well as Economics; Sociology; Types of Government; Anthropology; Geography; Japan, China, and Korea; India, Pakistan, and Afghanistan; South East Asia; Latin America; Russia and European Satellite Countries; Spain, Portugal, Italy, France, Germany, and Austria; southeast Europe, Turkey, Iran, and other Near East countries.

§ Mathematics and Science may be omitted by those taking both college preparatory mathematics and science in any year in senior high school. One semester each or three periods a week for each. Arithmetic and general mathematics in all six grades and general science in grades 7 through 11, biology and bacteriology in grade 12.

‖ One-half unit of credit each year above grade 8 toward graduation; a maximum credit of one unit in typing.

# Special sections for brightest students may well meet only four times a week, while sections for the least able students should meet at least one more period a week than those for average and near average ability. In schools employing modular schedules, the adaptation might well be in the form of shorter periods (e.g., thirty-five to forty minutes) for the sections of ablest students and longer periods (e.g., fifty-three to sixty minutes) for sections of least able students. One unit for foreign language in both grades 7 and 8.

** College-level courses should be offered to the ablest seniors in English, in science, in history, in some social science, and in mathematics—probably analytic geometry and calculus.

555

One period a week for all is given over to clubs or other student organizations.

**Separate Vocational and Academic High Schools.**  While the trend has been definitely for several decades in favor of the comprehensive secondary school, there has been a very aggressive vigorous minority ordering for separate schools for the abler youngsters and vocational schools for others.  A few schools of this type have been established, but it now begins to seem clear that this is not the answer since most students and most parents prefer that they go to a comprehensive high school rather than to be labeled as vocational or non-college going students.

### Ability Sectioning

A very outstanding trend in recent years has been the expansion and the improvement in appropriate educational materials and methods to the individuals who were not typical of the average boy or girl.  Ability sectioning is now carried on in a large majority of junior and senior high schools in the United States; and in the larger schools, there are four or five "tracks" in a number of fields and at least three in all the academic fields.  In the non-academic fields, more attention is being given to adapting the type of work assigned to the individual, watching for evidences of unusual creativity ability and encouraging it.

### Independent Study

Partly because of the greater emphasis upon going to college and because of the fact that about half of the young people entering universities and colleges "drop out" before entering the third year of higher education, a situation that will probably grow worse, there has been a very definite trend toward the provision of more practice and training in independent study.  This is also a major feature of the Trump Plan of team-teaching.  Study halls that have in many cases been supervised by non-certificated aides are being restored, and high school youngsters are being given more free periods in which to study at school.

### Class Schedules

With the increased emphasis upon independent study involving longer assignments, the permission for students to carry more subjects, and an increased degree of encouragement for high school students to belong to at least one club or organization, it has become impossible to schedule everything on the five-and-a-half to six-hour day exclusive of lunch periods that were so prevalent up to 1960. In its place, many have gone to an eight-hour day including lunch and other periods.[2]

## Length of Class Periods

There is a definite trend toward flexibility and variety in the length of class periods. It has become recognized that it is not desirable or necessary to schedule all classes for a uniform period length. There has developed what is called by many the "modular" type of schedule making that provides class periods of different lengths in specified units. In some schools, for example, some classes may meet for 60 to 65 minutes; others, 70 to 80 minutes, e.g., for science, art, physical education, slow student sections, and shorthand; and others for 90 to 100 minutes, for shop classes, typing, and home economics.

## Building Space Provisions

One of the most common features in building plans is the provision for flexibility so that some space may be employed as a large room seating one hundred to one hundred and fifty students and then broken up into smaller units of three to five rooms. Another new feature, much to be recommended, is the provision of teachers' offices. With the increase in the number of periods in the high school day from six to seven or eight, teachers have more free periods. Since it is not logical that they occupy the classroom as an office when not occupied by classes, in many schools offices are provided for teachers that usually include six to ten desks each to be used ordinarily by two teachers, with filing cabinets also provided. This enables more complete utilization of the school building and an opportunity for the teacher to prepare for classes and to examine the work handed in by students, and perhaps incidentally to relax their nerves a bit.

## Better Preparation of Teachers

Within the past few years, the standards of length of preservice preparation for elementary school teachers have moved up from

[2] A plan that would put high school students on an eight-hour day, instead of the present six hours, and give them an opportunity to complete the normal four years in two has been proposed for the New York City school system by a committee of present and former principals after a two-year study. *Phi Delta Kappan*, XLV, No. 3 (December, 1963), 158.

four to five years. This will have many effects, some of which are to
be desired. It will probably cut down on the number of young people
going into teaching, although that does not seem to be happening in
a large number of instances. Many teachers are going for a four-year
course and then picking up the fifth year in summer schools, and there
is much to be said for that plan since they then know what their problems are and what they would like to learn more about.

While the idea is still in the controversial category, there has been a
slight trend toward requiring students preparing to teach in elementary school to specialize somewhat in an academic field—in a
few institutions, a major being required.

### "Large Block" or Multiple Class Periods

In a great many schools, particularly junior high schools, two or
more periods are combined into what is called a "large block." While
the large block is used in a considerable number of schools, especially
junior high schools for the core plan of teaching, it is coming to be
used by far more schools as a place where English and the social
studies and group guidance are employed. In this latter case, three
periods a day are necessary, particularly if homerooms are to be included in this large block. In a few schools students who are superior
in English are encouraged to take a foreign language during four
periods a week of this block, while others bring their proficiency in
English up to a higher level. In a few schools, such as Shorewood,
Wisconsin, Junior High School, there is also a block period set aside
in which students study music, art, home economics, and shop work.
Not all students study in all these areas, and instruction in all these
areas does not run throughout the entire year and sometimes meets
only a few days a week.

### More and Better Counseling

Between 1953 and 1963, the number of counselors in the secondary
schools more than quadrupled and the number of social workers
tripled. By 1965, all but a very small percentage of counselors had at
least a year of graduate preparation for counseling. Many schools,
particularly in districts of above average financial status, provide one
full-time counselor for each three hundred students or major fractions
thereof.

## Emphasis upon the Fundamentals

More attention is being given to seeing that high school graduates are brought up to minimum standards in fundamentals of arithmetic, oral speech, and written expression.

Teachers in classes in various subjects are giving more attention to developing skills in these areas. A small but increasing number of schools are requiring seniors either to pass tests in skills in these areas or to take specially organized remedial courses in the area or areas in which they are deficient.

## Increased Emphasis upon General Education

In order that students may not have "blind spots" in their general education, more subjects and more units are being required for graduation. In an increasing number of schools, students are required to take above the sixth grade five or six years of English, five years of history and social studies, three or four years of science, and four years of mathematics. More students of average or better ability to learn will be encouraged to prepare for college admission while carrying a vocational curriculum of four or five units.

## Education for Jobs

The demand and trend is toward the development of more curricula that would prepare boys and girls for occupations for which they are not prepared in a considerable number of senior high schools today. There has been some development along this line, and it is quite clear that there will be much more in the years ahead.

# IMPORTANT ISSUES IN SECONDARY EDUCATION

There has been much change in the programs of junior and senior high schools, but there still are important issues upon which there is division of opinion. Among the more important issues are the following:

## Federal Influence upon the Curriculum

There is the very definite issue as to whether it is wise to have that degree of federal control that operates under the National Defense

Education Act in providing special funds for the improvement of training of teachers and other selected aspects of improvement of the curriculum and guidance.

## Preparation for College

A very important issue in the secondary school curriculum is an old one, namely, whether young people can be prepared well for college by having them take more work and do a better type of work in certain preferred fields such as mathematics, science, and foreign languages as compared with such things as the development of more precise vocabulary, development of skills in arithmetical computation, development of reading and study skills, good study habits, and the use of books in the library. There is also a very recently developed issue— whether provision should be made for students to follow a vocational curriculum in high school and at the same time take enough academic subjects to prepare for college.

## Extrasubject Activities

With increased tightness of the college admission squeeze and the consequent concern of parents, there has been a demand that less attention be given to extrasubject activities and more to quality work and excellence in the academic subjects. The results of research have been such that this group has not been given much encouragement, and the temporary trend of pushing clubs and other activities into after-school hours has been checked and reversed. With the lengthening of the school day and school year, the reversal will become more prominent. There is definite trend toward reverting to the old plan of having one period in the day set aside for clubs and homerooms and for the purpose of group guidance and discussion of current problems of adolescents and for weekly assemblies.

A problem of much importance and of greatly increased interest has developed in connection with the place and the regulation of interscholastic sports, especially in football and in basketball, which in many districts have recently become quite disruptive and have, especially in schools with night games, contributed to various types of socially unacceptable behavior as well as destruction of private or public property.

## Education of Teachers

As in the case of elementary school teachers, there has been a greatly increased interest in better preparation of secondary school teachers. There has been a very pronounced trend toward a five-year program that would permit better preparation in the major fields, better general education, and better professional technical training for the jobs to be done. The very large majority of secondary school teachers are employed in districts requiring a minimum of five years. The idea that each institution for higher education should be permitted to certificate its own teachers attracted much attention at first; but after careful consideration, the idea seemed to possess such definite limitations that it has not been put into practice widely.

### School Size

Enrollments in secondary schools have become so great, particularly in senior high schools, that many unfortunate effects have become noticeable and deplorable, including of course the lack of interpersonal relationships between the teachers and the students. The trend toward the construction of new high school buildings so as to permit division of the school into subdivisions usually referred to as "schools within a school" has been accompanied by such great degree of success that there is little doubt of the plan continuing to spread among schools of large enrollments.

## HIGHER EDUCATION

### Important Current Issues

The very great increase in enrollments in colleges and universities, including junior colleges, has created very great problems and raised some very important issues. Among the most important issues are the following:

1. Is every boy and girl entitled to the opportunity of having available at low cost two years of education beyond the high school?

2. Is the present trend toward increasing the costs of attending college, including the increase in tuition charged, definitely an unsocial and unwise measure from the point of view of the well-being of the nation and contrary to our ideals of democracy as opposed to that of an aristocracy that perpetuates itself as in England and in many other countries by providing higher education for the boys and girls of families of an upper economic and social strata?

3. Can provision be made for up to seven million or eight million

young men and women in college without decreasing the quality of their work?

4. Should there be colleges and universities of a variety of types and catering to and enrolling students of a variety of levels of ability to learn, especially in the academic field?

5. What shall we use for teachers? Should excellent teachers with only a master's degree be employed to teach undergraduate students, especially freshmen and sophomores, and be given opportunities for increases in salary and promotion without having published research and without having received a doctor's degree?

6. Should colleges be operated year round on something like the trimester or the quarter plan in order to utilize the limited faculty and limited buildings for a larger number of students by shortening the period that they must remain in college in order to complete the requirements for their degrees?

The solution of these problems and the resolving of these issues still lie ahead.


### Liberal vs. Vocational Education

A very important and live issue in higher education today is that of whether they have gone too far in the field of higher education in substituting vocational education for liberal or general education. The question is whether the university exists primarily for producing educated men and women or training people for vocations. While it is quite likely that the stepping up of the requirements in undergraduate college work in the fields of law and medicine and dentistry will tend to preserve the values of the general or liberal education, the same sort of development has not taken place in many other areas such as engineering, nursing, pharmacy, and agriculture. Indeed, in the case of the undergraduate academic programs of the prelaw and the premedic students, there has been a tendency to emphasize what is thought of as practical preparation for the vocational curriculum to come in the professional school.

The stepping up of years required for preparation for law and medicine has also very definitely stepped up the cost both to the students and his parents and to the institution providing such education. And there has developed the definite issue and problem as to whether the number of years might be reduced without impairing the quality of preparation of people in these professions.

## Scholarships and the Open Door

The increased amount of time necessary to be spent in colleges and universities in order to prepare for professions and the mounting cost has tended definitely to restrict the possibilities of going into these professions to a minority of high school graduates. This has been recognized as clearly not in the interests of the nation and its people. As a partial solution to the problem, there has been a very great increase in the number of scholarships to the abler and needy students. The problem, however, will not be solved until the number of scholarships has been at least quadrupled as compared to those available in 1964.

Because of the belief that the race problem will be solved only when the level of education is materially increased, scholarships for Negroes have in recent years been provided in much larger numbers.

## Intercollegiate Sports

Intercollegiate competition in the field of football and basketball has definitely moved into what may be an intensive stage that is very definitely approaching professionalism. The issue has been raised with increasing vigor and frequency whether or not the institutions of higher education legitimately should be in the field of public entertainment and amusement and in competition with various firms and people engaged in free enterprise public amusement and entertainment.

The question of the degree to which intercollegiate competition in sports tends to interfere with the application of college students to the study of their subjects has been raised for many years, but not very convincing evidence has been produced to make it clear that a great deal of damage is done in this area even though the football and basketball hero may cause the life and achievements of the university to seem much less important.

## Freedom To Learn and To Study

Another very important issue in the field of higher education is the degree to which instructors and professors in colleges and universities should be permitted to decide what should be taught to their students in their fields and whether the students may be permitted to decide what they want to learn—in other words, academic freedom of the faculty and the freedom to learn by the students. Ambitious politicians in many states, notably in Mississippi, Alabama, and California, have operated to encroach materially on these freedoms, though in the latter state their efforts have been discouraged in recent years by a large number of leaders and other educated people.

There is a definite question, issue, and problem as to the degree to which teaching in colleges and universities has been influenced, directly or indirectly, by the fact that institutions of higher education are largely dependent for their financial support upon gifts and bequests from individuals and corporations and upon appropriation from the state legislatures. This problem not only exists with respect to classroom teaching, but also with respect to what types and problems of research may be supported financially. This problem has grown to greater proportions in recent years and has become greatly challenging to clear thinkers, both in the profession of education and outside it.

While relatively few teachers, perhaps less than 1 per cent of all a year, lose their positions as the result of insisting upon exercising their right of academic freedom, a very large number are intimidated by fear and threats [3]—many fewer each year since the state and national education associations have begun to investigate cases and take positive stands.

## QUESTIONS, PROBLEMS, AND PROJECTS FOR FURTHER STUDY

1. To what extent do you think the schools should concern themselves primarily if not almost exclusively with developing the intellectual growth of young people and leave it to the church, home, and other agencies to develop health, social adjustment and responsibility, ideals, attitudes, emotions, etc.?

2. Be able to explain in class and answer criticisms of your idea of what kind of reporting should be done to parents.

3. What is your position with respect to extracurricular activities in the

---

[3] "Calvin Coolidge went fishing one week-end in a South Dakota stream. He returned a few days later to his duties in Washington, D.C., refreshed and smiling. Because of his genuine exuberance, he was approached by his secretary of state who asked him the extent of his 'luck' on the fishing trip. Without losing any of his enthusiasm, Coolidge told the secretary, 'There are forty-six thousand trout in that stream. I have never caught one, but I sure keep them all intimidated!'" From a letter received from Dr. Henry L. Bagley, Professor of Education, Grand Canyon College.

schools, and what do you think ought to be done to carry out your ideas on that point?

4. Make a list of the arguments pro and con of the various types of school organization such as the 6-3-3, the 8-4, the 4-4-4, the 8-2-2, and the 5-3-4; and be able to give and defend in class your preference for the type of organization.

5. Do you believe in a longer school day and a longer school year? If you do, how much longer and how should the additional time be used? If you are opposed, be able to give your reasons.

6. Be able in class to give your opinion of the following: (a) more work experience in the schools, (b) the core curriculum, (c) programmed materials and teaching machines.

7. What is your opinion of the place of religion in the schools, or do you feel that it has absolutely no place at all? Be able to defend your opinion in class.

8. What is your opinion of adjusting salaries according to the merit ratings of teachers? Be able to state your position clearly and defend it in class.

9. Which, if any, subject fields taught in the schools have been neglected in favor of other subjects?

10. What is your opinion of the very great increase in the amount of guidance service rendered in the schools? Do you believe there should be guidance programs and trained counselors in the elementary schools?

11. How far down in the grades do you think departmentalized assignment of teachers should go?

12. Be able to give in class and emphasize its strong points a plan for improving the preparation of high school graduates for academic success in college.

13. Be able to give in class your idea of what a really true liberal education is, and in what ways the programs of liberal arts colleges fall short in this respect.

## SELECTED SUPPLEMENTARY READINGS

BRIDGES, BERNICE, et al. "Voluntary Work Experience," The American Child, XL, No. 2, March, 1962.

BROWN, FRANK B. "The Non-Graded High School," The Bulletin of the National Association of Secondary School Principals, No. 283 (May, 1963), 64–72. The adaptation to the individual in the widely publicized Melbourne, Florida, High School.

CASS, JAMES. "Church, State, and School," in American Education Today. Paul Woodring and John Scanlon (eds.). New York: McGraw-Hill Book Co., Inc., 1963. Pp. 109–19.

CONANT, JAMES B. Slums and Suburbs. New York: McGraw-Hill Book Co., Inc., 1961. An eye-opener to a big problem that has stimulated new programs in many cities.

DIEDERICH, PAUL B. "Research Report: College-Educated Housewives as

Lay Readers," *The Bulletin of the National Association of Secondary-School Principals*, No. 282 (April, 1963), 201–11.

FOSTER, G. W. JR. "Turning Point for Desegregation?" In *American Education Today*. Paul Woodring and John Scanlon (eds.). New York: McGraw-Hill Book Co., Inc., 1963. Pp. 120–37.

GRUHN, WILLIAM T. "Developments in the Junior High School," *The Bulletin of the National Association of Secondary School Principals*, No. 271 (February, 1962), Part I, Chap. i, "Guidelines for Junior High School Education."

HAND, HAROLD C. "Myths Which Hoodwink the Public," *Educational Forum*, XXIII, No. 19 (November, 1958), 39. A prominent educator replies effectively to some of the criticisms being leveled at secondary education. Very interesting reading.

HARRIS, RAYMOND P. *American Education*. New York: Random House, Inc., 1962. Chaps. xi and xii.

HILLWAY, TYRUS. "The Future of American Education." In *Education in American Society*. Boston: Houghton Mifflin Co., 1961. Pp. 461–84.

ISRAEL, H. BOYD. "Will the College Maze Leave Us in a Daze?" *The Bulletin of the National Association of Secondary School Principals*, No. 277 (November, 1962), 11–19. Confusion created by college admissions procedures—critical and constructive.

MALLORY, DAVID. *New Approaches in Education*. Boston: National Council of Independent Schools, 1961. A study of experimentation programs in independent schools.

ORTON, DON A. "Issues Raised by Changes in Secondary Education," *The School Review*, LXIX, No. 1 (Spring, 1961), 1–11.

QUILLEN, I. JAMES. "The Curriculum and the Attacks on the Public Schools." In *Public Education in America*, George Z. F. Bereday and Luigi Volpicelli (eds.). New York: Harper & Row, 1958. Pp. 117–31.

THAYER, V. T. *The Role of the School in American Society*. New York: Dodd, Mead & Co., Inc., 1960. Chap. xvi. An excellent discussion of the merit and the lack of merit in some important criticism.

TRUMP, J. LLOYD. *Images of the Future*. Urbana, Ill.: Commission on the Experimental Study of the Utilization of the Staff in the Secondary School, 1959. 48 pp. A treatment of team-teaching by an eminent authority.

# Appendix

# THE CODE OF ETHICS OF THE EDUCATION PROFESSION

Adopted by the NEA Representative Assembly, Detroit, Michigan,
July, 1963 [1]

*Preamble*

We, professional educators of the United States of America, affirm our belief in the worth and dignity of man. We recognize the supreme importance of the pursuit of truth, the encouragement of scholarship, and the promotion of democratic citizenship. We regard as essential to these goals the protection of freedom to learn and to teach and the guarantee of equal educational opportunity for all. We affirm and accept our responsibility to practice our profession according to the highest ethical standards.

We acknowledge the magnitude of the profession we have chosen, and engage ourselves, individually and collectively, to judge our colleagues and to be judged by them in accordance with the applicable provisions of this code.

*Principle I—Commitment to the Student*

We measure success by the progress of each student toward achievement of his maximum potential. We therefore work to stimulate the spirit of inquiry, the acquisition of knowledge and understanding, and the thoughtful formulation of worthy goals. We recognize the importance of cooperative relationships with other community institutions, especially the home.

In fulfilling our obligations to the student, we—

1. Deal justly and considerately with each student.
2. Encourage the student to study varying points of view and respect his right to form his own judgment.
3. Withhold confidential information about a student or his home un-

[1] Reprinted with permission of the National Education Association, Washington, D.C.

less we deem that its release serves professional purposes, benefits
the student, or is required by law.

4. Make discreet use of available information about the student.
5. Conduct conferences with or concerning students in an appropriate place and manner.
6. Refrain from commenting unprofessionally about a student or his home.
7. Avoid exploiting our professional relationship with any student.
8. Tutor only in accordance with officially approved policies.
9. Inform appropriate individuals and agencies of the student's educational needs and assist in providing an understanding of his educational experiences.
10. Seek constantly to improve learning facilities and opportunities.

## Principle II—Commitment to the Community

We believe that patriotism in its highest form requires dedication to the principles of our democratic heritage. We share with all other citizens the responsibility for the development of sound public policy. As educators, we are particularly accountable for participating in the development of educational programs and policies and for interpreting them to the public. In fulfilling our obligations to the community, we—

1. Share the responsibility for improving the educational opportunities for all.
2. Recognize that each educational institution may have a person authorized to interpret its official policies.
3. Acknowledge the right and responsibility of the public to participate in the formulation of educational policy.
4. Evaluate through appropriate professional procedures conditions within a district or institution of learning, make known serious deficiencies, and take any action deemed necessary and proper.
5. Use educational facilities for intended purposes consistent with applicable policy, law, and regulation.
6. Assume full political and citizenship responsibilities, but refrain from exploiting the institutional privileges of our professional positions to promote political candidates or partisan activities.
7. Protect the educational program against undesirable infringement.

## Principle III—Commitment to the Profession

We believe that the quality of the services of the education profession directly influences the future of the nation and its citizens. We therefore exert every effort to raise educational standards, to improve our service, to promote a climate in which the exercise of professional judgment is encouraged, and to achieve conditions which attract persons worthy of the trust to careers in education. Aware of the value of united effort, we contribute actively to the support, planning, and programs of our professional organizations.

In fulfilling our obligations to the profession, we—

1. Recognize that a profession must accept responsibility for the conduct of its members and understand that our own conduct may be regarded as representative.
2. Participate and conduct ourselves in a responsible manner in the development and implementation of policies affecting education.
3. Cooperate in the selective recruitment of prospective teachers and in the orientation of student teachers, interns, and those colleagues new to their positions.
4. Accord just and equitable treatment to all members of the profession in the exercise of their professional rights and responsibilities, and support them when unjustly accused or mistreated.
5. Refrain from assigning professional duties to non-professional personnel when such assignment is not in the best interest of the student.
6. Provide, upon request, a statement of specific reason for administrative recommendations that lead to the denial of increments, significant changes in employment, or termination of employment.
7. Refrain from exerting undue influence based on the authority of our positions in the determination of professional decisions by colleagues.
8. Keep a trust under which confidential information is exchanged.
9. Make appropriate use of time granted for professional purposes.
10. Interpret and use the writings of others and the findings of educational research with intellectual honesty.
11. Maintain our integrity when dissenting by basing our public criticism of education on valid assumptions as established by careful evaluation of facts or hypotheses.
12. Represent honestly our professional qualifications and identify ourselves only with reputable educational institutions.
13. Respond accurately to requests for evaluations of colleagues seeking professional positions.
14. Provide applicants seeking information about a position with an honest description of the assignment, the conditions of work, and related matters.

## Principle IV—Commitment to Professional Employment Practices

We regard the employment agreement as a solemn pledge to be executed both in spirit and in fact in a manner consistent with the highest ideals of professional service. Sound professional personnel relationships with governing boards are built upon personal integrity, dignity, and mutual respect.

In fulfilling our obligations to professional employment practices, we—

1. Apply for or offer a position on the basis of professional and legal qualifications.
2. Apply for a specific position only when it is known to be vacant and refrain from such practices as underbidding or commenting adversely about other candidates.
3. Fill no vacancy except where the terms, conditions, policies, and practices permit the exercise of our professional judgment and skill, and where a climate conducive to professional service exists.
4. Adhere to the conditions of a contract or to the terms of an appointment until either has been terminated legally or by mutual consent.
5. Give prompt notice of any change in availability of service, in status of applications, or in change in position.
6. Conduct professional business through the recognized educational and professional channels.
7. Accept no gratuities or gifts of significance that might influence our judgment in the exercise of our professional duties.
8. Engage in no outside employment that will impair the effectiveness of our professional service and permit no commercial exploitation of our professional position.

# NAME INDEX

# SUBJECT INDEX